FROM
BEIRUT
TO
JERUSALEM

FROM
BEIRUT
TO
JERUSALEM

Thomas L. Friedman

FARRAR STRAUS GIROUX

New York

Farrar, Straus and Giroux
19 Union Square West, New York 10003

Grateful acknowledgment is made for permission to reprint the following previously published material:
Excerpt from *Waiting for Godot* by Samuel Beckett, copyright © 1954 by Grove Press Inc., renewed 1982 by Samuel Beckett.
Excerpts from the "PLAYBOY interview: Yasir Arafat," PLAYBOY magazine (September 1988), copyright © 1988 by PLAYBOY. Reprinted with permission. All rights reserved. Interview conducted by Morgan Strong.

Library of Congress Cataloging-in-Publication Data
Friedman, Thomas L.
    From Beirut to Jerusalem / Thomas L. Friedman.
        p. cm.
    Includes index.
    ISBN-13: 978-0-374-15895-8
    ISBN-10: 0-374-15895-9
    1. Friedman, Thomas L.—Travel—Middle East.   2. Arab-Israeli conflict—1973–1993.   3. Middle East—Politics and government—1979–.   4. Lebanon—History—Israeli intervention, 1982–1984.   5. Lebanon—Politics and government—1975–1990.   6. Israel—Politics and government—1967–1993.

DS119.7 .F736   1990b

                                                                    92148666

www.fsgbooks.com

13   15   17   19   21   22   20   18   16   14

For my parents,
Harold and Margaret Friedman

"Did you want to kill him, Buck?"

"Well, I bet I did."

"What did he do to you?"

"Him? He never done nothing to me."

"Well, then, what did you want to kill him for?"

"Why, nothing—only it's on account of the feud."

"What's a feud?"

"Why, where was you raised? Don't you know what a feud is?"

"Never heard of it before—tell me about it."

"Well," says Buck, "a feud is this way: A man has a quarrel with another man, and kills him; then that other man's brother kills *him*; then the other brothers, on both sides, goes for one another; then the *cousins* chip in—and by and by everybody's killed off, and there ain't no more feud. But it's kind of slow, and takes a long time."

"Has this one been going on long, Buck?"

"Well, I should *reckon*! It started thirty years ago, or som'ers along there. There was trouble 'bout something, and then a lawsuit to settle it; and the suit went agin one of the men, and so he up and shot the man that won the suit—which he would naturally do, of course. Anybody would."

"What was the trouble about, Buck?—land?"

"I reckon maybe—I don't know."

"Well, who done the shooting? Was it a Grangerford or a Shepherdson?"

"Laws, how do I know? It was so long ago."

"Don't anybody know?"

"Oh, yes, pa knows, I reckon, and some of the other old people; but they don't know now what the row was about in the first place."

—Mark Twain, *The Adventures of Huckleberry Finn*

Contents

A Middle East Chronology

1882   As a result of the persecution of Jews in Russia and Romania a year earlier, the first large-scale immigration of Jewish settlers to Palestine takes place.

1891   Arab notables in Jerusalem send a petition to the Ottoman government in Constantinople demanding the prohibition of Jewish immigration to Palestine and Jewish land purchases.

1896   Austrian journalist Theodor Herzl, the founder of modern Zionism, publishes his pamphlet *The Jewish State*, which argues that the "Jewish Problem" can be solved only by setting up a Jewish state in Palestine, or somewhere else, so that Jews can live freely without fear of persecution. A year later, Herzl organizes the first Zionist Congress in Basel, Switzerland, to promote immigration to Palestine.

1908   The first Palestinian Arabic newspapers appear: *Al-Quds*, in Jerusalem and *Al-Asma'i* in Jaffa.

1916   The Sykes–Picot Agreement is forged by Britain, France, and Russia, carving up the Ottoman Empire after its defeat in World War I. As part of the agreement, Britain wins effective control over the area of Palestine, and France over the area that is now Lebanon and Syria.

1917   The Balfour Declaration is issued by British Foreign Secretary Arthur J. Balfour, endorsing the idea of establishing a "national home" for the Jewish people in Palestine.

1920   France decrees the formation of the state of Greater Lebanon, knitting together Mt. Lebanon with the regions of Beirut, Tripoli, Sidon, Tyre, Akkar, and the Bekaa Valley.

1936–39   Inspired by other Arab nationalist movements, the Arabs of Palestine revolt in an attempt to halt the establishment of a Jewish homeland in Palestine. Both Jewish settlements and British army units come under attack.

1943   Lebanon's Christian and Muslim leaders agree on a "National Pact" for sharing power and balancing Lebanon's Western and Arab orientations, enabling their country to become a state independent of France.

1947   The United Nations votes to partition Palestine into two states, one for the Jews and one for the Palestinian Arabs, with Jerusalem to become an international enclave.

1948   Britain withdraws from Palestine. Instead of implementing the UN partition plan, the surrounding Arab states join with the local Palestinians to try to prevent the emergence of a Jewish state. Israel is established anyway; Jordan occupies the West Bank and Egypt the Gaza Strip.

1956   Israel, joining forces with Britain and France to attack Gamal Abdel Nasser's Egypt, occupies most of the Sinai Peninsula. Under pressure from both the United States and the Soviet Union, Israel later withdraws.

1958   The first Lebanese civil war erupts and some 15,000 American troops are sent to Beirut to help stabilize the situation.

1964   Arab heads of state led by Nasser establish the Palestine Liberation Organization (PLO) in Cairo.

1967   Israel launches a preemptive strike against Egypt, Syria, and Jordan as they are preparing for war against the Jewish state. The Six-Day War ends with Israel occupying the Sinai Peninsula, the Golan Heights, the Gaza Strip, and the West Bank.

1969   Yasir Arafat, leader of the al-Fatah guerrilla organization, is elected chairman of the executive committee of the PLO.

1970 King Hussein's army defeats Arafat's PLO guerrillas in a civil war for control of Jordan.

1973 Egypt and Syria launch a surprise attack against Israeli forces occupying the Sinai Peninsula and the Golan Heights.

1974 An Arab summit conference in Rabat, Morocco, affirms that the PLO is the "sole and legitimate representative" of the Palestinian people.

1975 Civil war breaks out again in Lebanon.

1977 Egyptian President Anwar Sadat goes to Jerusalem, addresses the Israeli parliament, and offers full peace in exchange for a total Israeli withdrawal from Sinai.

1979 Egypt and Israel sign their peace treaty.

1982—February The Syrian government massacres thousands of its own citizens while suppressing a Muslim rebellion launched from the town of Hama.

1982—June to September Israel invades Lebanon. Phalangist militia leader Bashir Gemayel is assassinated after his election as Lebanon's President. Phalangist militiamen massacre hundreds of Palestinians in the Sabra and Shatila refugee camps in Beirut, while the camps are surrounded by Israeli forces. U.S. Marines arrive in Beirut as part of a multinational peacekeeping force.

1983 The American embassy and U.S. Marine headquarters in Beirut are blown up by suicide car bombers.

1984—February The Lebanese government of President Amin Gemayel splinters after Shiite Muslims and Druse in West Beirut launch a revolt against the Lebanese army. President Reagan abandons hope of rebuilding Lebanon and orders Marines home.

1984—September Israel's Labor and Likud Parties join together in a national unity government after July elections end in a stalemate.

1985   Israel unilaterally withdraws its army from most of Lebanon.

1987—December   The Palestinian uprising, or *intifada*, begins in the West Bank and Gaza Strip.

1988—December   Arafat recognizes Israel's right to exist. U.S. Secretary of State George P. Shultz authorizes the opening of a dialogue with the PLO. Likud and Labor join together to form another national unity government in Israel after another stalemated election.

FROM
BEIRUT
TO
JERUSALEM

1

Prelude: From Minneapolis to Beirut

In June 1979, my wife, Ann, and I boarded a red-and-white Middle East Airlines 707 in Geneva for the four-hour flight to Beirut. It was the start of the nearly ten-year journey through the Middle East that is the subject of this book. It began, as it ended, with a bang.

When we got in line to walk through the metal detector at our boarding gate, we found ourselves standing behind three broad-shouldered, mustachioed Lebanese men. As each stepped through the metal detector, it would erupt with a buzz and a flashing red light, like a pinball machine about to tilt. The Swiss police immediately swooped in to inspect our fellow passengers, who turned out not to be hijackers bearing guns and knives, although they were carrying plenty of metal; they were an Armenian family of jewelers bringing bricks of gold back to Beirut. Each of the boys in the family had a specially fitted money belt containing six gold bars strapped around his stomach, and one of them also had a shoe box filled with the precious metal. They sat next to Ann and me in the back of the plane and spent part of the flight tossing the gold bricks back and forth for fun.

When our MEA plane finally touched down at Beirut International Airport, and I beheld the arrival terminal's broken windows, bullet scars, and roaming armed guards, my knees began to buckle from fear. I realized immediately that although I had spent years preparing for this moment—becoming a foreign correspondent in the Middle East—nothing had really prepared me for the road which lay ahead.

In Minneapolis, Minnesota, where I was born and raised, I had never sat next to people who tossed gold bricks to each other in the economy section on Northwest Airlines. My family was, I suppose, a rather typical middle-class American Jewish family. My father sold ball bearings and my mother was a homemaker and part-time bookkeeper. I was sent to Hebrew school five days a week as a young boy, but after I had my bar mitzvah at age thirteen, the synagogue interested me little; I was a three-day-a-year Jew—twice on the New Year (Rosh Hashanah) and once on the Day of Atonement (Yom Kippur). In 1968, my oldest sister, Shelley, spent her junior year abroad at Tel Aviv University; it was the year after Israel's dramatic victory in the Six-Day War— a time when Israel was very much the "in" place for young American Jews. Over the Christmas break of 1968 my parents took me to Israel to visit my sister.

That trip would change my life. I was only fifteen years old at the time and just waking up to the world. The flight to Jerusalem marked the first time I had traveled beyond the border of Wisconsin and the first time I had ridden on an airplane. I don't know if it was just the shock of the new, or a fascination waiting to be discovered, but something about Israel and the Middle East grabbed me in both heart and mind. I was totally taken with the place, its peoples and its conflicts. Since that moment, I have never really been interested in anything else. Indeed, from the first day I walked through the walled Old City of Jerusalem, inhaled its spices, and lost myself in the multicolored river of humanity that flowed through its maze of alleyways, I felt at home. Surely, in some previous incarnation, I must have been a bazaar merchant, a Frankish soldier perhaps, a pasha, or at least a medieval Jewish chronicler. It may have been my first trip abroad, but in 1968 I knew then and there that I was really more Middle East than Minnesota.

When I returned home, I began to read everything I could get my hands on about Israel. That same year, Israel's Jewish Agency sent a *shaliach*, a sort of roving ambassador and recruiter, to Minneapolis for the first time. I became one of his most active devotees—organizing everything from Israeli fairs to demonstrations. He arranged for me to spend all three summers of high school living on Kibbutz Hahotrim, an Israeli collective farm on the coast just south of Haifa. For my independent study project in my senior year of high school, in 1971, I did a slide show on how Israel won the Six-Day War. For my high-school psychology class, my friend Ken Greer and I did a slide show on kibbutz life, which ended with a stirring rendition of "Jerusalem of Gold" and a rapid-fire montage of strong-eyed, idealistic-looking Israelis of all ages. In fact, high school for me, I am now embarrassed to say, was one big celebration of Israel's victory in the Six-Day War. In the period of a year, I went from being a nebbish whose dream was to one day become a professional golfer to being an Israel expert-in-training.

I was insufferable. When the Syrians arrested thirteen Jews in Damascus, I wore a button for weeks that said *Free the Damascus 13*, which most of my high-school classmates thought referred to an underground offshoot of the Chicago 7. I recall my mother saying to me gently, "Is that really necessary?" when I put the button on one Sunday morning to wear to our country-club brunch. I became so knowledgeable about the military geography of the Middle East that when my high-school geography class had a teaching intern from the University of Minnesota for a month, he got so tired of my correcting him that he asked me to give the talk about the Golan Heights and the Sinai Peninsula while he sat at my desk. In 1968, the first story I wrote as a journalist for my high-school newspaper was about a lecture given at the University of Minnesota by a then-obscure Israeli general who had played an important role in the 1967 war. His name was Ariel Sharon.

During the summer that I spent in Israel after high-school graduation, I got to know some Israeli Arabs from Nazareth, and our chance encounter inspired me to buy an Arabic phrase book and to begin reading about the Arab world in general. From my first day in college, I started taking courses in Arabic language and literature. In 1972, my sophomore year, I spent two weeks in Cairo on my way to Jerusalem for a semester abroad at the Hebrew University. Cairo was crowded, filthy, exotic, impossible— and I loved it. I loved the pita bread one could buy hot out of the oven, I loved the easy way Egyptians smiled, I loved the mosques and minarets that gave Cairo's skyline its distinctive profile, and I even loved my caddy at the Gezira Sporting Club, who offered to sell me both golf balls and hashish, and was ready to bet any amount of money that I could not break 40 my first time around the course. (Had two racehorses not strolled across the ninth fairway in the middle of my drive, I might have won the bet.)

In the summer of 1974, between my junior and senior years of college, I returned to Egypt for a semester of Arabic-language courses at the American University in Cairo. When I came back to Brandeis, where I was studying for my B.A., I gave a slide lecture about Egypt. An Israeli graduate student in the audience heckled me the entire time asking, "What is a Jew doing going to Egypt?" and "How dare you like these people?" Worse, he got me extremely flustered and turned my talk into a catastrophe I would never forget. But I learned two important lessons from the encounter. First, when it comes to discussing the Middle East, people go temporarily insane, so if you are planning to talk to an audience of more than two, you'd better have mastered the subject. Second, a Jew who wants to make a career working in or studying about the Middle East will always be a lonely man: he will never be fully accepted or trusted by the Arabs, and he will never be fully accepted or trusted by the Jews.

After graduating from Brandeis in 1975, I decided to study with the masters of Middle Eastern Studies—the British. I enrolled at St. Antony's College, Oxford University, where I took a master's degree in the history and politics of the modern Middle East. St. Antony's was everything I had hoped for by way of formal education, but I learned as much in the dining room as in the classroom. As the center of Middle Eastern studies in England, St. Antony's attracted the very best students from the Arab world and Israel. Since there were only about 125 students in the college and we ate three meals a day together, we got to know each other

very well. At Brandeis, I was considered knowledgeable about
the Middle East, but among the St. Antony's crowd I was a
complete novice. I learned to be a good listener, though, and
there was plenty to listen to.

My years at St. Antony's coincided with the start of the Lebanese civil war. I shared a bathroom with an extremely bright
Lebanese Shiite, Mohammed Mattar, and a lunch table with Lebanese Christians and Palestinians; my closest friend at St. Antony's was an Iraqi Jew, Yosef Sassoon, whom I had met, along
with his wife, Taffy, in the laundry room. Watching them all
interact, argue, challenge each other at lectures, and snipe at one
another at mealtimes taught me how much more there was to the
Middle East than Arab versus Jew. A spectator of their feuds,
an outsider, I managed to stay on friendly terms with all of them,
as well as with the Israelis on campus.

While studying in England, I began my career in journalism.
One day in August 1976, I was walking down a street in London
and noticed a headline from the London *Evening Standard* which
read: CARTER TO JEWS: IF ELECTED I'LL FIRE DR. K. The article
was about how candidate Jimmy Carter was promising to dismiss
Secretary of State Henry Kissinger if elected President. How odd,
I thought to myself, that a presidential candidate could curry favor
among American Jews by promising to fire the first-ever Jewish
Secretary of State. I decided to write an Op Ed article explaining
this anomaly. My girlfriend and future wife, Ann Bucksbaum,
happened to be friendly with the editorial-page editor of the *Des
Moines Register*, Gilbert Cranberg. Ann brought him the article.
He liked it and printed it on August 23, 1976; thus did I find my
calling as a Middle East correspondent. Over the next two years,
I wrote more such articles, and upon graduation from St. Antony's
I had a small portfolio of Op Ed pieces to show for myself.

Shortly before graduating from Oxford in June 1978, I applied
for a job with the London bureau of United Press International.
I had decided that the academic ivory tower was not for me and
that if I was ever going to be able to hold my own on the Middle
East, I had to live there and experience the place firsthand. Fortunately, Leon Daniel, the UPI bureau chief in London, was ready
to take a chance on me—despite the fact that I had never so
much as covered a one-alarm fire—and gave me a job as a starting
reporter. I was so nervous my first week that I kept getting bloody

noses and eventually ended up in the hospital, much to the amusement of the grizzled and not always sober UPI veterans, who had
more than a few laughs about "the Oxford kid who thinks he can
be a journalist." My first news story was about the death by drug
overdose of Keith Moon, the drummer for the rock group The
Who. It was not exactly the kind of news I had hoped to be
covering, but my opportunity would come, much sooner than I
expected.

The Iranian revolution broke out soon after I joined UPI, and
the world oil situation became a major story. UPI had no oil
expert, so I jumped into the void. My only previous contacts with
oil were confined to salad dressing and whatever went under the
hood of my car. Fortunately, upstairs from UPI was the London
bureau of *The Petroleum Intelligence Weekly*, an oil newsletter,
and by hanging around their staff I picked up just enough basic
jargon to fake it. My big break, though, came in the spring of
1979, when UPI suddenly had an opening in its Beirut bureau.
The number-two correspondent there had decided Lebanon was
not for him, after being nicked in the ear by a bullet fired by a
man who was robbing a jewelry store. The job offer was accompanied by words to this effect: "Well, Tom, the guy before you
got hit with a little piece of bullet, but don't pay any attention to
that. We think you're the perfect guy for the job."

Nevertheless, with a lump in my throat and a knot in my gut,
I jumped at the opportunity. My friends and family all thought I
was insane. A Jew? In Beirut? I didn't really have a response for
them; I didn't really know what awaited me. All I knew was that
this was my moment of truth. I had been studying about the Arab
world and Israel for six years; if I didn't go now, I would never
go. So I went.

Lebanon was once known as the Switzerland of the Middle
East, a land of mountains, money, and many cultures, all of which
somehow miraculously managed to live together in harmony. At
least that was the picture-postcard view. It was not the Lebanon
that greeted Ann and me in June 1979. We came to a country
that had been in the grip of a civil war since 1975. Our first evening
at the Beirut Commodore Hotel I remember lying awake listening
to a shootout right down the street. It was the first time I had
ever heard a gun fired in my life.

Like most other foreign reporters in Lebanon, we found an

apartment in Muslim West Beirut, where the majority of government institutions and foreign embassies were located. Ann got a job working for a local merchant bank, and later for an Arab political research organization. These were the "Wild West Days of West Beirut." Although the civil war raged on, it was at a very low boil. Roads were open between East and West Beirut and much business and commerce was going on amid all the sniping and kidnapping.

After more than two years in Beirut with UPI, I was offered a job by *The New York Times* in 1981 and asked to come to Manhattan in order to learn the mysterious ways of that newspaper. After eleven months in New York, however, the *Times* editors decided to send me right back to Beirut, in April 1982, to be their correspondent in Lebanon.

When I returned to Beirut, I found the city abuzz with two different sets of rumors. One set involved an explosion of violence inside Syria, which had just happened, and the other an explosion of violence from Israel, which was expected to happen at any moment. The Syrian rumors, which most people found impossible to believe at first, alleged that the Syrian government had put down a rebellion launched from its fourth-largest city—Hama—and killed 20,000 of its own citizens there. The Israeli stories revolved around speculation that the Phalangist militia leader, Bashir Gemayel, had struck a deal with the Israeli government of Prime Minister Menachem Begin to mount a joint effort to drive the PLO and the Syrians out of Lebanon forever. Both rumors turned out to be true.

For the next twenty-six months, I reported on the Hama massacre, the Israeli invasion of Lebanon, the massacre of Palestinians in the Sabra and Shatila refugee camps, the evacuation of the PLO from Beirut, the arrival of the U.S. Marine peacekeeping force, the suicide bombing of the American Embassy in Beirut and the Marine headquarters, the departure of the Marines from Lebanon, and the ongoing fighting in the Lebanese civil war that accompanied all these momentous events.

Following these tumultuous years in Beirut, I was transferred by *The New York Times* to Jerusalem in June 1984, to be the newspaper's correspondent in Israel. My editor at the time, A. M. Rosenthal, thought it would be "interesting" to see how someone who had covered the Arab world for almost five years would look at Israeli society. Abe also wanted to dispense with an old unwritten rule at *The New York Times* of never allowing a Jew to report from Jerusalem. Abe thought he had broken that ban five years earlier when he sent my predecessor, David K. Shipler, until he boasted about it one day at a meeting with editors and was informed that Shipler was a Protestant; he just looked like a rabbi.

When the day came for me to transfer from Beirut to Jerusalem, I actually drove overland by way of several Arab and Jewish taxis. Altogether the trip took only six hours, but the driving time was no measure of the real distance or proximity between them. In some ways they were the same city with some of the same basic problems, and in other ways, they were worlds apart.

This book is about my journey between these two worlds, and how I understood the events and the people whom I met along the way. On one level, it is about a young man from Minnesota who goes to Beirut and confronts a world for which nothing in his life had ever prepared him. On a second level, it is about a student of Middle East politics who, upon graduation, actually goes out to the region and discovers that it bears little resemblance to the bloodless, logical, and antiseptic descriptions he found in most of his textbooks. On a third level, it is about a Jew who was raised on all the stories, all the folk songs, and all the myths about Israel, who goes to Jerusalem in the 1980s and discovers that it isn't the Jewish summer camp of his youth but, rather, an audacious and still unresolved experiment to get Jews to live together in one country in the midst of the Arab world. Lastly, it is a book about the people in Beirut and Jerusalem themselves, who, I discovered, were going through remarkably similar identity crises. Each was caught in a struggle between the new ideas, the new relationships, the new nations they were trying to build for the future, and the ancient memories, ancient passions, and ancient feuds that kept dragging them back into the past.

It is a strange, funny, sometimes violent, and always unpredictable road, this road from Beirut to Jerusalem, and in many ways, I have been traveling it all my adult life.

*   *   *

The events which I witnessed during my nearly decade-long journey through the Middle East cannot be understood without some historical perspective.

The roots of the Lebanese civil war, which is the backdrop for the first half of this book, can be traced back to the very foundation of Lebanon. The post–World War I modern republic of Lebanon was based on a merger between the country's two then-dominant religious communities, the Sunni Muslims and the Maronite Christians. The Maronites, an Eastern Christian Church founded in Syria around the fifth century by a monk named Maron, acknowledged the supremacy of the Pope and the Catholic Church in Rome, but also retained their own distinctive liturgy. They managed to survive for centuries in a sea of Muslims by entrenching themselves in the rugged terrain of Mt. Lebanon, and by regularly seeking help from, and forging alliances with, Christians in the West—from the Crusaders to modern France. By the late 1700s, their expanding population, openness to modernization, and high degree of communal organization made the Maronites the most powerful religious community on Mt. Lebanon. The second-largest religious community in the region were the Druse, a splinter sect of Islam whose exact religious beliefs are a communal secret. The Druse, too, had been drawn to Lebanon's mountaintops in order to practice their faith in solitude, without fear of conquering armies.

Following World War I and the collapse of the Turkish Ottoman Empire, which had controlled the Middle East for some four hundred years, the area that is now Syria and Lebanon fell to France. In 1920 the Maronite leadership managed to convince France to set up a Lebanese state which the Maronites and the other smaller Christian sects allied to them would dominate. But in order to make that state economically viable, the Maronites appealed to France to include in it not only their traditional Mt. Lebanon enclave—which was about 80 percent Christian and 20 percent Druse—but also the predominantly Sunni Muslim cities of the coast—Beirut, Tripoli, Sidon, and Tyre—as well as the Shiite Muslim regions of south Lebanon, the Akkar, and the Bekaa Valley. In this "Greater Lebanon," the Maronites and other Christian sects comprised only slightly more than 51 percent of the population, according to the 1932 census.

The Sunni and Shiite Muslims roped into this new state of "Greater Lebanon" were not consulted, and many of them deeply resented it, since they would have preferred to become part of Syria—with its Arab–Muslim majority and orientation.

The Muslims of the world have long been divided between Sunnis, who are the majority, and Shiites. In the seventh century, shortly after the death of Islam's founder, the prophet Muhammad, a dispute arose over who should be his successor as spiritual and political leader, known as caliph. One group, the majority, argued that Muhammad's successor should be appointed through the process of election and consensus by the elders of the community, as was the tradition of the desert. *Sunna* in Arabic means tradition, and those who held this view became known as the Sunnis.

A minority faction, however, argued that Muhammad's successors should come exclusively from his own family and their descendants. They insisted, therefore, that his first cousin and son-in-law—Ali—be appointed as leader of the community. Those who held this view became known in Arabic as the Shia, or "partisans," of Ali. The Shiites were clearly influenced by the notion of divine-right monarchy of pre-Islamic Persia (Iran). The Sunnis eventually defeated the supporters of Ali and installed their own chosen caliphs. Nevertheless, the Sunni–Shiite split has continued down through the ages of Islam, and a whole body of theological and even cultural differences developed, distinguishing Shiites from Sunnis. Summarizing these differences, Islam expert Edward Mortimer observed in his book *Faith & Power*: "Sunni Islam is the doctrine of power and achievement. Shi'ism is the doctrine of opposition. The starting point of Shi'ism is defeat: the defeat of Ali and his house. . . . Its primary appeal is therefore to the defeated and oppressed. That is why it has so often been the rallying cry for the underdogs in the Muslim world . . . especially for the poor and dispossessed."

Back in the 1930s and 1940s, the Sunnis of Lebanon, who were the second-largest religious community after the Maronites, tended to be the wealthiest, most urbanized, and best educated of the country's Muslims. The Shiites, who were the third-largest group, tended to live in the countryside and were less economically advanced and less well educated. Despite the initial reluctance of the Sunnis and Shiites to be drawn into the Maronites'

Greater Lebanon, their leaders eventually reached a political understanding with the Christians in 1943 that enabled the Lebanese republic to become independent of France. The Muslims agreed to abandon their demands for unity with Syria, while the Maronites agreed to sever their ties with France and accept the notion that Lebanon would be an "Arab" country. This unwritten agreement, known as the National Pact, also stipulated that the Lebanese President would always be a Maronite and that the parliament would always have a 6:5 ratio of Christians to Muslims—to ensure Christian predominance—while the Prime Minister would always be a Sunni Muslim and the Speaker of the Parliament always a Shiite—to ensure the country's Arab–Muslim character.

This understanding held up as long as the Maronites and other Christians made up roughly 50 percent of the population. But by the 1970s, rapid demographic growth among Lebanon's Muslims had turned Lebanon upside down. The Christians had shrunk to a little more than one-third of the population and the Muslims and Druse had grown to roughly two-thirds, with the Shiites becoming the largest single community in the country. When the Muslims demanded that political reforms be instituted to give them a greater share in power by strengthening the role of the Muslim Prime Minister, the Maronites resisted. They wanted Lebanon on its original terms or none at all. In order to support the status quo, the Maronites formed private armies. Most notable among them were the Phalangist militia, originally founded by Pierre Gemayel and later led by his son Bashir, and the Tigers militia founded by former Lebanese President Camille Chamoun and later led by his son Danny; the Lebanese Muslims and Druse established similar private armies to enforce their desire for change.

Around the same time that Lebanon's congenital Christian–Muslim tensions were heating up in the early 1970s, another major intercommunal conflict in the Middle East—that between Palestinian Arabs and Jews—was also coming to a boil. As it happened, I would be on hand when the two conflicts merged in Beirut.

The conflict between Jews and Palestinian Arabs began in the late nineteenth and the early twentieth century, when Jews from around the world began flocking back to their ancient biblical homeland in Palestine, driven by a modern Jewish nationalist ideology known as Zionism. The Zionists called for the ingathering of the Jews from around the world in Palestine and the creation there of a modern Jewish nation-state that would put the Jews on a par with all the other nations of the world. Most of the early Zionists either ignored the presence of the Arabs already living in Palestine or assumed they could either be bought off or would eventually submit to Jewish domination. Following World War I, Palestine fell under British control, in the same way that Lebanon had fallen to the French.

Out of the broad region known as Palestine, Britain carved two political entities in 1921. One entity consisted of the area of Palestine east of the Jordan River; it was named the "Emirate of Transjordan," and later simply "Jordan." There, the British installed in power Abdullah ibn Hussein, a Bedouin tribal chieftain educated in Istanbul, whose family hailed from what is now Saudi Arabia. Jordan's original population was about 300,000 people, half of whom were nomadic Bedouin and the other half "East Bankers," or Palestinian Arabs who resided on the East Bank of the Jordan.

In the western half of Palestine, between the Mediterranean Sea and the Jordan River, Palestinian Arabs and Zionist Jews wrestled for control under the British umbrella. As the Jewish–Palestinian conflict sharpened in the wake of a massive influx of European Jewish survivors of World War II, Britain announced its intention to withdraw from the western half of Palestine and wash its hands of the problem of who should rule there. London turned over to the United Nations responsibility for determining the fate of this disputed territory, and on November 29, 1947, the United Nations General Assembly voted 33 to 13 with 10 abstentions to partition western Palestine into two states—one for the Jews, which would consist of the Negev Desert, the coastal plain between Tel Aviv and Haifa, and parts of the northern Galilee, and the other for the Palestinian Arabs, which would consist primarily of the West Bank of the Jordan, the Gaza District, Jaffa, and the Arab sectors of the Galilee. Jerusalem, cherished by both Muslims and Jews as a holy city, was to become an international enclave under UN trusteeship.

The Zionists, then led by David Ben-Gurion, accepted this

partition plan, even though they had always dreamed of controlling all of western Palestine and Jerusalem. The Palestinian Arabs and the surrounding Arab states rejected the partition proposal. They felt that Palestine was all theirs, that the Jews were a foreign implant foisted upon them, and that they had the strength to drive them out. Just before the British completed their withdrawal on May 14, 1948, the Zionists declared their own state, and the next day the Palestinians, aided by the armies of Jordan, Egypt, Syria, Lebanon, Saudi Arabia, and Iraq, launched a war to prevent Jewish independence and to secure control of all of western Palestine.

In the course of that war, the Zionists not only managed to hold all the areas assigned to them by the United Nations but to seize part of the land designated for the Palestinian state as well. The other areas designated for the Palestinians by the United Nations were taken by Jordan and Egypt; Jordan annexed the West Bank, while Egypt assumed control of the Gaza District. Neither Arab state allowed the Palestinians to form their own independent government in these areas. In fact, Jordan's annexation of the West Bank dramatically altered its own ethnic makeup. The 450,000 Bedouins and East Bank Palestinians who had made up Jordan's population before the 1948 war were joined by 400,000 West Bank Palestinians and some 300,000 Palestinian refugees who had either fled or were driven out of areas which became Israel. In 1951, King Abdullah was assassinated by a disgruntled Palestinian in Jerusalem. He was soon succeeded by his grandson Hussein, who remains the King of Jordan to this day.

Following the 1948 fighting, Israel signed separate armistice agreements with Egypt, Lebanon, Jordan, and Syria. These agreements notwithstanding, the Arab states frequently allowed various Palestinian resistance groups to use their territory to launch raids against Israel, particularly from the Egyptian-occupied Gaza Strip. Eventually, in 1964, the Arab League, inspired by Egyptian President Gamal Abdel Nasser, organized the Palestinian resistance groups under one umbrella, which became known as the Palestine Liberation Organization. The PLO in those days was essentially a tool of the existing Arab regimes— intended to control the Palestinians as much as to support them.

In June 1967, Israel launched a preemptive strike against Egypt,

Syria, and Jordan, after Nasser had declared his intention to annihilate the Jewish state and forged military alliances with Syria and Jordan for that purpose, building up troop concentrations along his border with Israel and blockading shipping to the Israeli port of Eilat. The six-day war that followed Israel's surprise attack ended with the Israeli army occupying Egypt's Sinai Peninsula, Syria's Golan Heights, and Jordan's West Bank.

In the wake of this massive 1967 Arab defeat, a revolutionary mood swept through the Arab world. One immediate impact of that new mood was that radical independent underground Palestinian guerrilla organizations—known in Arabic as *fedayeen*—which had sprung up in the late 1950s and 1960s outside Arab government control, were able to take over the PLO apparatus from the Arab regimes. In 1969, an obscure Palestinian guerrilla by the name of Yasir Arafat, who headed the al-Fatah ("Victory" in Arabic) guerrilla group, was elected chairman of the PLO's executive committee. Then as now, the PLO was composed of a broad range of Palestinian guerrilla organizations representing many different political tendencies. Although Arafat carried the title Chairman of the Executive Committee, he would never wield complete and uncontested control over all the PLO factions.

The PLO guerrilla groups were granted significant economic aid by the Arab states in order to carry on the battle with Israel, while they watched from the sidelines. The PLO used this support and political backing to take control of Palestinian refugee camps in the weaker Arab countries, particularly Lebanon and Jordan, and to use those camps as bases of operation against targets in Israel and against Israeli targets abroad. In both Jordan and southern Lebanon, the Palestinian guerrillas assumed quasi-sovereign authority over certain regions bordering on Israel. Their raids on Israel brought about Israeli retaliations, which created tensions between the Palestinians and Lebanese and Palestinians and Jordanians.

Matters came to a head in Jordan in September 1970, when radical Palestinian guerrillas brought to Jordan three hijacked airliners and prevented the Jordanian army from getting near the planes or rescuing the passengers. Recognizing that he was on the verge of losing control over his whole kingdom, King Hussein decided to wipe out Arafat and his men once and for all by launching a full-scale offensive against the PLO-dominated Palestinian refugee camps and neighborhoods in the Jordanian capital, Amman. The PLO guerrillas responded by calling for Hussein's overthrow and vowing to wrest Jordan from his hands. In the end, King Hussein, who was supported by both Jordan's Bedouin-dominated army and many East Bank Palestinians who appreciated the order and prosperity the King had brought to their lives, prevailed. Arafat was forced to flee Amman disguised as an Arab woman.

But for Arafat this was not the end of the road by any means. He and the PLO immediately fell back on their other "state-within-a-state," which they had established in the Palestinian refugee districts of Beirut and south Lebanon. It was at this point that the Lebanese–Lebanese conflict became fully intertwined with the Israeli–Palestinian conflict. Arafat and his men, most of whom were Muslims, were welcomed by the Lebanese Muslims and Druse, who identified with their cause and, more important, thought they could use the PLO guerrillas to bring pressure on the Maronite Christians to share more power. The already serious strains between Lebanese Muslims and Lebanese Christians intensified in the early 1970s as the PLO increasingly used Lebanon as a launching pad for operations against Israel, and Israel responded by wreaking havoc on Lebanon. The Lebanese Christians demanded that the Lebanese army be deployed to break the PLO state-within-a-state the way King Hussein had in Jordan. The Christians wanted the PLO out not only because it was disrupting Lebanese life but because without the Palestinian guerrillas, the Lebanese Muslims would be unable to press their demands for more power. The Muslims, in turn, opposed any crackdown on the PLO, which, in effect, had become their biggest private militia.

As a result of this political deadlock, the Lebanese government and army became paralyzed—a situation that served Arafat's interests. Under the circumstances, the Christians felt impelled to turn to their own private armies—particularly the Phalangist and Tigers militias—to deal with the Palestinians. On April 13, 1975, unidentified gunmen riding in a speeding car opened fire on a church in the Christian East Beirut suburb of Ain Rammanah, killing four men, including two Phalangists. Late that same day, twenty-seven Palestinian civilians riding in a bus through East Beirut were ambushed and killed by Phalangists as revenge. The next morning, Palestinian guerrillas backed by Muslim militiamen fought pitched battles in the streets of Beirut with Christians from the Phalangist and Tigers militias. Eventually, Christian elements of the Lebanese army sided with their tribe, Muslims did the same, and Lebanon soon found itself in a civil war.

This Lebanese civil war proved to be a stalemate; neither side was able to impose its political will on the other. Besides the thousands of casualties it inflicted on Lebanese civilians, the war's main victims were the Lebanese government, which was stripped of all power, and Lebanese territory, which was informally partitioned. South Lebanon and the predominantly Muslim western half of Beirut became the power base of the PLO and various Lebanese Muslim militias, while the Christian eastern half of Beirut and the Christian enclave on Mt. Lebanon, to the north and east, became the turf of the Phalangists and their Christian allies. The rest of Lebanon—basically the northern port area of Tripoli and the Bekaa Valley—fell under Syrian control, after Syria dispatched its army to Lebanon in April 1976, ostensibly to try to end the civil war. The Syrians have remained ever since.

Between 1976 and 1979, Beirut limped along as a fractured city. The worst fighting of the war was over, and a measure of normality returned to the place, despite the sporadic flare-ups. One month the Syrians and Christians would fight against the Palestinians, another month the Syrians and Palestinians would fight against the Christians, and, in between, everyone would do business with everyone else. There were so many private armies running around the country, each being amply funded by one or another Arab regime, that dollars were plentiful and the Lebanese currency remained very stable amid the chaos.

It was in this bizarre city, caught between a Mercedes and a Kalashnikov, that my journey began.

BEIRUT

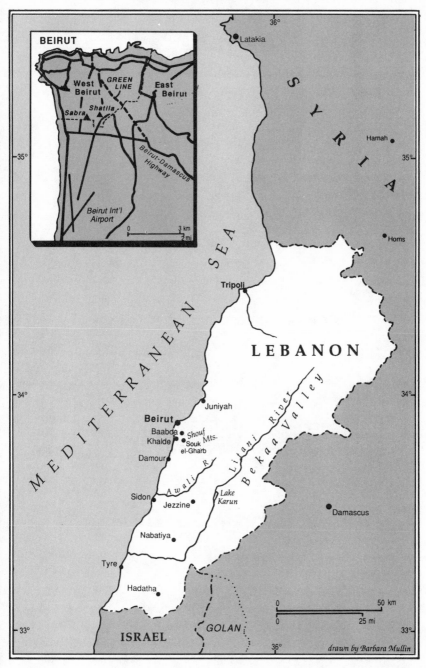

BEIRUT

West Beirut
GREEN LINE
East Beirut
Sabra
Shatila
Beirut-Damascus Highway
Beirut Int'l Airport
0 3 km
0 2 mi

36°
Latakia

S Y R I A

Hamah

35°

Homs

Tripoli

LEBANON

M E D I T E R R A N E A N   S E A

34°

Juniyah

Beirut
Baabda
Khalde
Shouf Mts.
Souk el-Gharb
Damour

Litani River
Bekaa Valley

Awali R.

Sidon
Jezzine
Lake Karun

Damascus

Nabatiya

Tyre

Hadatha

50 km
25 mi

33°

ISRAEL
GOLAN
36°

drawn by Barbara Mullin

2

Would You Like to Eat Now or Wait for the Cease-fire?

I once watched a man being kidnapped in Beirut. It took only a few seconds.

I was on my way to Beirut International Airport when my taxi became stalled in traffic. Suddenly I saw off to my right four men with pistols tucked into their belts who were dragging another man out his front door. A woman, probably his wife, was standing just inside the shadow of the door, clutching her bathrobe and weeping. The man was struggling and kicking with all his might, a look of sheer terror in his eyes. Somehow the scene reminded me of a group of football players carrying their coach off the field after a victory, but this was no celebration. Just for a second my eyes met those of the hapless victim, right before he was bundled into a waiting car. His eyes did not say "Help me"; all they spoke was fear. He knew I couldn't help him. This was Beirut.

Moments later the traffic jam broke and my taxi moved on to the airport. The Lebanese driver, who had kept his eyes frozen straight ahead the whole time, never said a word about the horror show which had unfolded in the corner of his eye. He talked instead about his family, politics, anything but what had happened alongside us. While he spoke, my mind remained locked on the kidnap victim. Who was he? What had he done? Maybe he was a bad guy and the others really good, or was it the other way around?

Beirut was always a city that provoked more questions than answers, both for those who lived there and for those who did not. The most frequent questions from my readers and friends back home all began with "How?"—How do people cope? How do people survive? How do people go on living in a city where violence has killed or injured 100,000 souls in fourteen years of civil strife?

What I always answered was that surviving Beirut required many things, but first and foremost, it required a wild imagination. Because in a few seconds on the way to the airport or to the corner grocery store you could find yourself watching something you not only hadn't seen before in your life but had never even imagined. The visitors who learned to respect the surprises that a place like Beirut could offer did well there; others, like the American Marines or the Israelis, who never really understood the shocks that could greet you around any Beirut street corner, paid heavily.

Amnon Shahak taught me that. Shahak, a brilliant Israeli major general who eventually rose to be Chief of Military Intelligence, commanded the Israeli division that was stationed in the Shouf Mountains, which overlook Beirut from the southeast, during the year following Israel's June 1982 invasion of Lebanon. Shortly before General Shahak assumed his post, the Druse and the Phalangist Christian militias became locked in a bitter, no-holds-barred fight for control of the Shouf—a fight they carried out with hatchets, bazookas, and tanks, uninhibited by the Israeli army surrounding both of them. General Shahak once told me about his first day in command in Lebanon—the day he discovered how much he did not know. Although he was a hard-bitten soldier who had seen many men die and had no doubt put away a few himself, Shahak admitted that he lacked the imagination Beirut and Lebanon required.

"The first night after I arrived," Shahak recalled, "I was in my room in Aley, in the Shouf, which we were using as our command post. At about 9:00 p.m. a group of Druse elders came to our headquarters and demanded to see me. They were very upset. They would not tell me what it was about, they just kept saying, 'Please, please, you must come with us.' I had just arrived. They seemed very angry, so I thought I had better go. When we got to the hospital, there was a crowd of about a hundred Druse men standing in front of the building. They were all shouting and waving their arms. They took me through the crowd to the front, and I found set before me on the steps three orange crates. One had human heads in it, another had torsos, and the other arms and legs. They said these were Druse sheiks whom the Christians had ambushed and then carved up. They looked to me like sheiks because all the heads had black beards.

"I was really shocked," Shahak continued. "I had never seen anything like this in all my years as a soldier. I decided that no matter what time it was, I was going to go down to the Phalangist headquarters in Beirut and get an explanation. So I got in a jeep and went down to Beirut. Fuad Abu Nader, one of the Phalangist commanders, was waiting for me with some of his men. He is a doctor by training. I demanded an explanation. Abu Nader listened and was very calm. When I got done describing everything, he said to me, 'Oh, I know this trick.' He said that there had been a fight that day between some of his men and some Druse, and that some Druse were killed trying to attack a Phalangist position in the Shouf, and the dead were left in the battlefield. He said the Druse took their dead away and then carved them up to make it look like the Maronites did it and then the Druse brought the chopped-up bodies to Aley to stir up their own people. I just shook my head. I realized at that moment that I was in the middle of a game I did not understand."

After spending nearly five years in Beirut, I eventually developed the imagination the city demanded. I came to think of Beirut as a huge abyss, the darkest corner of human behavior, an urban jungle where not even the law of the jungle applied. Experiencing such an abyss not only left scars but also new *muscles*. Life can no longer deal you many surprises or shocks after you've lived in Beirut. The experience leaves you wearing an emotional bullet-proof vest.

But like everyone else who lived there, I acquired mine the hard way.

It was June 8, 1982. The Israeli invasion of Lebanon had begun forty-eight hours earlier. Mohammed Kasrawi, the *New York Times* Beirut bureau driver and news assistant since 1953, and I had been down in south Lebanon covering the first exchanges of fire between Israeli and Syrian troops. That evening, when we returned to my apartment house, an ornate, high-ceilinged, six-story colonial building overlooking the Mediterranean, we got out of the car to find Nadia, my maid, looking down on us from the balcony in a state of total panic.

We had visitors.

Standing in the parking lot was an extended Palestinian family—father, mother, grandmother, with babies in everyone's arms and children of assorted ages at everyone's feet. Their eyes, too, were round with fear, like deer caught in my headlights. They were carrying bags of canned food and bulging suitcases with tongues of clothing licking out from all sides. What I remember most, though, was that the father was standing amid them all with a rocket-propelled grenade launcher on his shoulder. They looked to me like a weird Beirut version of Grant Wood's *American Gothic*. Like thousands of other Palestinian and Lebanese families, this extended clan had been driven out of the Palestinian refugee camps and neighborhoods on the southern edge of Beirut by merciless Israeli bombing and shelling and were desperately looking for empty apartments closer to the heart of West Beirut, where the fighting had yet to encroach. Other Palestinian refugee families had already broken into three empty apartments in our building, including the absent landlord's elegant penthouse, with its imported Italian marble floors and "Louis de Lebanon" overstuffed furniture. To get into the landlord's flat, the refugees had dynamited the two-inch-thick steel safe door he had installed to prevent precisely such an occurrence. This particular family in the parking lot had tried to get into my apartment, but Nadia had temporarily kept them at bay by saying I was a very important foreigner "with connections"—which in Beirut argot always meant connections to people who kill other people.

After Mohammed and I showed up, the family backed off. But this little encounter on the third day of the Israeli invasion led me to think that I would be much safer moving into the Commodore Hotel, where most of the foreign press corps was lodged; my wife, Ann, had not yet arrived in Beirut, as she was finishing up her job in New York. Mohammed, ever faithful to me and *The New York Times*, volunteered to put two of his thirteen children—his twenty-year-old daughter Azizza and seven-year-old daughter Hanan—into the apartment. If any more refugees tried to knock down the door, they would simply explain to them in perfect Palestinian colloquial accents that they, too, were refugees and were squatting in the apartment.

The plan worked until Friday evening, June 11. I finished writing my story that day for the *Times* and, as usual, sent it to my editors via the telex at the Reuters news agency in West Beirut. It was time to head back to the Commodore Hotel for the night. The stairwell in the Reuters building was totally dark, because the electricity had been out since the second day of thé war, and my colleague Bill Farrell and I were feeling our way down the stairs like two blind men, using the wall to guide us. Just as we rounded the turn onto the last flight of stairs, we were met by a human shadow, panting and breathless from racing up the lobby steps two at a time.

"Tom? Tom, is that you?" The familiar voice of the *Times*'s local Palestinian reporter, Ihsan Hijazi, issued from the shadowy figure.

"Yeah, Ihsan," I said nonchalantly. "It's me. It's me."

"Oh, thank God, you're alive," he said, gripping me by the shoulders, his face right up to mine. "Abdul just called. He heard it on the radio. Someone has blown up your house."

"Oh my God," I gasped. "Mohammed's children are in there. Mohammed just left to go see them."

We all scrambled down the stairs, tiptoed our way through the lobby packed with refugees living on mattresses and cooking with portable gas burners, and out the front door into Ihsan's old Dodge. Gas pedal to the floor, Ihsan sped through the empty streets to my apartment, which was located in the once-posh Manara (lighthouse) district of West Beirut. As we drove, I kept thinking to myself, This cannot be happening to me. I'm just a reporter, just a spectator. Why my apartment building? Sure, people kill reporters in Beirut, but I've been here only a few weeks.

When Bill, Ihsan, and I arrived at the apartment house, the first thing I saw was a piece of my blue metal window shutters that had been blown by the force of the explosion some seventy-five feet across the parking lot and was stuck deep into the side of a tree like a thrown hatchet. The apartment building itself had been blown in half. The part still standing was cut open, as though it were a life-size dollhouse, with jagged pieces of concrete dangling from every floor. Stainless-steel pots and pans still hung on the walls of someone's kitchen, unaffected by the blast. The pharmacist's wife who lived upstairs, a striking, tall, Lebanese blonde, was sandwiched with her son in her arms between two walls that had been blown together, forming a grotesque human fossil. Below, her dazed husband staggered around like a zombie looking for their other son. The half of the building that had been brought down by the explosion collapsed into a thirty-foot-high smoldering avalanche of concrete, steel reinforcement rods, books, clothing, and bodies that covered all the cars in the parking lot. I noticed my business cards peppered all over the pile. Red Cross volunteers were already picking through the tangled mound with crowbars, looking for survivors, while shouting with bullhorns into every crack to see if anyone was buried alive.

The second thing I saw was Mohammed. He was sitting on the back of a fire engine, weeping into his hands. Bill walked over and cradled Mohammed in his long arms, while he wailed in grief, "I am not a man of war. I never hurt anyone, I never hurt anyone."

In a sobbing voice Mohammed explained that a few hours earlier his wife, Nazira, age fifty, had come to the house to visit her two daughters and their only son, Ahmed, then eighteen, who had stopped by to say hello to his sisters. Ahmed left around 5:00 p.m., and minutes later, as Mohammed was on his way to the building, it was blown apart, with Nazira, Azizza, and Hanan all inside.

The pile of rubble proved to be too heavy for the rescue workers, and we had to wait until the next morning for a crane to arrive and lift the crushed concrete off the dead. On a clear blue Saturday morning Bill, Mohammed, and his surviving children sat under the tree with the piece of shutter stuck into it and waited as the crane went about its grisly task. First Nazira was uncovered, then Azizza, and finally little dimple-cheeked Hanan. They had obviously been in my office watching television when someone placed the explosive charge in the hallway, apparently not far from my door. We knew where they had been sitting because Hanan was found with her tiny fingers still gripping my black Texas Instruments digital watch, which she must have been playing with at my desk when the blast brought the walls down on them. The watch was still keeping time.

When they unearthed Hanan's body, Mohammed went to pieces. Only seven years old, she was Mohammed's favorite of his thirteen children. She had been born shortly after the Lebanese civil war began in April 1975 and had grown up in the anarchy of the ensuing years. She died never having known a day's peace.

We buried them the next morning in the Palestinian cemetery on the road to Beirut Airport. Their three bodies, covered only with white sheets and already beginning to decompose in the June heat, were laid out under a 130-mm cannon the PLO had hidden in the funeral chapel. A Muslim sheik with a red turban said a few prayers over the corpses in guttural Arabic that was innocent of compassion and empty of all grief. Then one by one, Nazira, Azizza, and little Hanan were gently fitted by Mohammed's sons-in-law into a single grave. They all had to be buried together; there wasn't room in the overflowing cemetery for three separate graves.

Who had done this? A few days later, the neighborhood police said that some of the Palestinian clans who had squatted in our building had apparently gotten into a fight over one of the apartments. Each family was associated with a different PLO faction, the police claimed. The clan that lost, they said, went to their PLO group and got someone to bring in some plastique explosives and blow up the whole building. Moments before they lit the fuse, they apparently warned their own kin, who scrambled out the doors. The rest were not so lucky. In all, nineteen people, including refugees, the Dutch banker and his huge Doberman in the apartment below me, and the beautiful blonde upstairs, whose name I never did know, died a Beirut death, which is the most absurd and scandalous death possible: death for no reason.

It was the ever-present prospect of dying a random, senseless death that made Beirut so frightening to me. Ever since the start of the Lebanese civil war, much of the fighting in Beirut has consisted of sniping or shelling from great distances; those doing the fighting often have no idea where their bullets or shells will land, and they care even less. When car bombs came into vogue in the late 1970s, life on the Beirut streets became even more terrifying, since you never knew whether the car you were about to walk past, lean on, or park behind was going to burst into a fireball from two hundred pounds of dynamite packed under its hood by some crazed militiaman.

One of the worst cases of Beirut death I ever witnessed, besides that in my own apartment house, occurred in August 1982, when Israeli jets bombed an eight-story building in West Beirut that was also packed with several hundred Palestinian refugees. The building fell into itself like a house of cards, burying everyone inside alive. Rumor had it that the PLO maintained a communications center in the basement, but I never found any proof of this. Shortly after I arrived on the scene, a woman who had lived in the building returned home only to find her whole family smothered in the rubble. She immediately tried to fling herself onto the ruins. A dramatic photograph was taken of her being held back by one arm, as she struggled to get free. Her other arm reached out toward her vanished family, while her face was twisted into a portrait of utter anguish. About an hour after that picture was taken, a small car bomb went off half a block away, across from the Ministry of Information, and this woman, who happened to be standing by the car, was killed instantly.

That was Beirut. No one was keeping score. No matter how you lived your life, whether you were decent or indecent, sinner or saint, it was all irrelevant. Men and women there could suffer wrenching tragedies once or twice or even three times, and then suffer some more. The evening Mohammed's family perished in my apartment we ran over to the local police station on nearby Bliss Street to see if, by some miracle, Mohammed's wife and children were among those who might have been taken out of the rubble alive to local hospitals. There was a lone policeman on duty. He was sitting at a bare metal desk watching television.

"Sorry," he said, between glances back and forth at the TV set, "no names." Nobody had bothered to even try to make a list, of either the survivors or the victims. No one was keeping score. Death had no echo in Beirut. No one's life seemed to leave any mark on the city or reverberate in its ear.

Hana Abu Salman, a young psychology researcher whom I got to know at the American University of Beirut, once did a project interviewing her classmates about their deepest anxieties. Among their greatest fears, she found, was this fear of dying in a city without echoes, where you knew that your tombstone could end up as someone's doorstep before the grass had even grown over your grave.

"In the United States if you die in a car accident, at least your name gets mentioned on television," Hana remarked. "Here they don't even mention your name anymore. They just say, 'Thirty people died.' Well, what thirty people? They don't even bother to give their names. At least say their names. I want to feel that I was something more than a body when I die."

As a news story, Beirut was always much more interesting for its psychology than for its politics. People always used to ask me if I wasn't terrified living in Beirut. There were moments, of course, but most of the time I was too intrigued observing people's behavior in this real-life Skinner Box to think about being frightened.

In his classic work *Leviathan*, the seventeenth-century English political philosopher Thomas Hobbes described what he called "the state of nature" that would exist if government and society completely broke down and the law of the jungle reigned. In such a condition, wrote Hobbes, "where every man is enemy to every man . . . there is no place for industry; because the fruit thereof is uncertain: and consequently no culture of the earth; no navigation, nor use of the commodities that may be imported by sea; no commodious building; no instruments of moving, and removing, such things as require much force; no knowledge of the face of the earth; no account of time; no arts; no letters; no society; and which is worst of all, continual fear, and danger of violent death; and the life of man, solitary, poor, nasty, brutish, and short."

Hobbes, who at the time of his writing was trying to defend the idea of absolute monarchy, believed that men escaped from

nastiness and brutishness—the state of nature—only by forming
societies wherein rulership was vested in a single authority with
absolute powers. Man, he argued, is moral only in a social context.
Therefore, a state, backed by force, was needed to socialize men,
to curb their savage instincts, and to prevent them from chaotic
behavior and the war of all against all.

I don't know if Beirut is a perfect Hobbesian state of nature,
but it is probably the closest thing to it that exists in the world
today. If so, Hobbes was right about life in such a world being
"nasty, brutish, and short," but he was quite wrong about it being
"poor" and "solitary." Indeed, if I learned any lesson from living
in Beirut it is that when authority breaks down and a society
collapses into a state of nature, men will do anything to avoid
being poor or solitary.

This instinctive desire to bring order and comfort to one's life
amid chaos is precisely what gave Beirut its distinctive and bizarre
flavor—a flavor best captured for me in a single sentence uttered
by a Lebanese socialite who had invited an American friend of
mine for dinner on Christmas Eve. The elegant holiday banquet
was held at her apartment near the Green Line, a swath of gutted
and burned-out buildings that formed the no-man's-land between
predominantly Muslim West Beirut and Christian East Beirut.
On this particular Christmas Eve in 1983, despite the holiday,
rival Christian and Muslim militiamen were trading artillery salvos
and machine-gun fire into the early evening, rocking the whole
neighborhood. The hostess put off serving dinner, hoping things
would settle down, but she could see that her friends were getting
hungry, not to mention nervous. Finally, in an overture you won't
find in Emily Post's book of etiquette, she turned to her guests
and asked, "Would you like to eat now or wait for the cease-
fire?"

Outsiders looking at Beirut only through newspaper photographs and 60-second television news clips might have thought
life in the city was one massacre after another, from sunrise to
sunset. It wasn't. In fact, the explosions of violence, while often
indiscriminate, were usually sporadic and unsustained—sometimes a few hours, maybe a few days, rarely more than a week.
The minute a cease-fire took effect in one neighborhood, the
storekeepers cranked up their steel shutters and life immediately
mushroomed back onto the streets, as people grabbed for any

crumb of normality they could—even if they knew it would last only an hour or a day. Beirutis always lived in this peculiar half-light between security and insecurity, war and truce, in which there were always enough periods of quiet to go about one's day but never enough to feel confident that it wouldn't be one's last.

Beirut was the par-5 first hole at the Beirut Golf and Country Club, where Ann and I were members in good standing. The golfers at the Beirut Club didn't call their first hole a "dangerous par-5" for nothing. Several members were hit by bullets in their backswings there, because the 460-yard hole ran perpendicular to a PLO firing range. The Beirut Country Club was the only golf course I ever played where I was actually relieved when my ball went into a sand bunker; it was the safest place on the course. When the Israeli army invaded Beirut in the summer of '82, a convoy of Israeli armored personnel carriers drove right up the first fairway. The members were not amused.

Beirut was also the announcement tacked to the bulletin board at the golf course during the summer of '82 which read: "Due to the circumstances, the club championship will be postponed."

Beirut was the slick advertisement in between the hairdresser ads and the wedding announcements of a popular English-language Beirut weekly, *Monday Morning*, offering shatter-resistant window coating "to protect yourself and the people around you from the danger of flying glass." The ad went on to warn: "Anytime, anyplace, an explosion can happen."

Beirut was the bridge in East Beirut with a sign at its foot which read: NO TANKS ALLOWED.

Beirut was the commercial that used to be aired on Lebanese television for Ray-O-Vac batteries. The commercial, which gave a whole new meaning to the term "long-life battery," featured a comely young woman being stopped in her car by a ragged-looking Lebanese militiaman who had set up a roadblock in the neighborhood—a common feature of Beirut life. The militiaman leers at the young woman and shines a flashlight in her face, while she flicks on the interior car light above her head. The militiaman then sings suggestively in Arabic, "What battery are you using?" When the young woman sings back, "Ray-O-Vac," the gunman smiles and lets her pass without any hassle.

Beirut was Goodies Supermarket—the gourmet food store that offered a cornucopia of foodstuffs ranging from quail eggs to *foie*

gras flown in daily from Paris. Amine Halwany, Goodies's un-
flappable and ever upbeat owner, used to tell me that his was the
ideal business for a city like Beirut, because he had products to
offer people under any and all conditions.

"In times of crisis," explained Amine, "everyone wants bread,
water, and canned food—things that are easy to prepare and won't
need much refrigeration. People go back to a very primitive style
of cooking. They also buy a lot of sweets and nuts during the
troubles—nervous food they can pop in their mouths while sitting
at home. But as soon as things calm down for a few days, the
high-class customers are back buying caviar and smoked salmon."

Actually, Beirut's wealthiest flocked to Goodies to buy all their
food. A gaggle of Mercedes-Benzes could always be found parked
outside. Legend has it that one day a disheveled young man
entered Goodies, walked up to the cash register with a rifle, and
demanded all the money. Within seconds three different women
drew pistols out of their Gucci handbags, pumped a flurry of
bullets into the thief, and then continued pushing their shopping
carts down the bountiful aisles.

Beirut was the Summerland Hotel, built along the coast just
west of the airport, which was opened in 1979 as the first resort
hotel designed for people who wanted to vacation inside a civil-
war zone—in style. The Summerland's innovations included the
installation of two 12,000-gallon fuel tanks to feed its two generators and satisfy all the hotel's energy needs for more than a
month, should the city's electricity be entirely cut off—which it
often was. The hotel also had a separate 3,400-gallon gasoline
tank for its own fleet of taxis and employee cars, thus ensuring
that both the staff and the hotel guests could move around the
city oblivious to the regular gasoline shortages. The Summerland
had an underground garage that doubled as a bomb shelter, its
own artesian wells and water purification system, its own fire
department, and a maintenance shop that could rebuild or repair
anything in the hotel. Instead of installing only the four large
refrigerators that a 151-room hotel would normally require, the
Summerland installed eighteen freezers, so that veal, beef, and
smoked salmon could be flown in from Paris and stored for an
entire summer season, when the hotel's pool and restaurant were
packed with Beirut's finest. Most important, the Summerland's
owners organized their own militia, which conducted the hotel's

"diplomatic relations" with the various other militias and gangs around West Beirut and protected the grounds.

When I asked Khaled Saab, the Summerland's cherubic general manager during my tenure in Beirut, about his well-armed team of bellhops, he demurred, "I wouldn't call [them] a militia, but let's just say if ten or fifteen armed men came here and wanted to cause trouble, we could handle them."

Because "the circumstances" in Beirut have kept foreign tourists away since 1975, the Summerland sold all the cabanas around its pool to Lebanese families and turned itself into an all-around amusement center, catering exclusively to locals. To this day, it remains open as a one-stop, totally secure fantasy village where for enough money any Lebanese can buy himself out of Beirut's nightmare for a few hours or days. The fantasy begins from the moment you pull off Beirut's pockmarked streets and cruise up to the Summerland's front door, where you are greeted by a doorman dressed in tails—with a revolver hidden in his back pocket.

Khaled Saab once summarized his regular clientele for me. "We had Lebanese tourists, foreign businessmen, politicians, and even a few hashish growers, arms merchants, pirates, and gamblers. While they were under our roof they all behaved like perfect gentlemen. We even had Gloria Gaynor come sing in 1980. She sang, 'I Will Survive.' It was really fantastic."

Indeed, the worse things got in Lebanon, the more the Lebanese seemed to refuse to accept a life of poverty. After the Israeli army invaded Lebanon and finally consolidated its grip over the southern half of the country, the first ship to arrive at the Lebanese port of Sidon when the Israelis allowed it to be reopened was loaded with videocassette recorders. Sidon was partially destroyed, people were desperately in need of cement, housing materials, and other staples, but what came steaming into the port first were VCRs from Japan—machines which enable people to enter a dream world and escape from reality. First things first.

Even when Beirut was at its most chaotic, the Lebanese figured out a way to profit from the vagaries of their own anarchy. They did this by speculating on their currency, the Lebanese pound. There were no exchange controls in Beirut, so Lebanese would constantly convert their pounds back and forth into dollars, trying to anticipate rises and falls in the two currencies. If, for instance, you converted your dollars to Lebanese pounds right before a prolonged period of quiet, you could take advantage of the Lebanese currency rising in value thanks to the economic stability; if you converted your pounds back into dollars a few hours before a car bomb exploded, you could make a windfall as the dollar soared and the Lebanese currency fell in anticipation of dislocations.

Today, the most frequently asked question in Beirut after a car bomb is not "Who did it?" or "How many people were killed?" It is "What did it do to the dollar rate?"

Why do people even bother learning to cope with such an environment?

To be sure, thousands of Beirutis haven't bothered; they simply emigrated. But many more have stayed. For some, Beirut is simply home and they cannot imagine living anywhere else, no matter how badly the quality of life in the city deteriorates. Others are captives of their assets. The homes or businesses they have spent lifetimes building are anchored in Beirut, and they simply cannot afford to start over somewhere else. Better, they say, to be rich and terrorized in Beirut than safe and poor in Paris. Still others cannot obtain visas to take up residence in other countries because the quotas for Lebanese have already been filled. So they learn to adapt, because they don't have any other choice.

I used to play golf in Beirut with a rosy-cheeked Englishman named George Beaver. George was a salesman for International Harvester in the Middle East and had lived in Beirut since the 1950s, because, as he would say, "of the absence of taxes, the availability of household help, and the low cost of whiskey." When it came time for George to retire, he chose to remain in Beirut. Although he was eighty-nine years old when I got to know him in 1979, he had played golf, usually by himself, almost every day since the Lebanese civil war began. He always walked the course with just three clubs in hand: a driver, a five-iron, and a putter. Sometimes he played the course backward, other days he played only the holes he liked, occasionally having to leave one out because the putting green was covered in shrapnel. Only the most intense bombardments in the summer of '82 kept him off the links. When I asked him why he kept playing, George just shrugged his shoulders and pronounced the motto of every Beirut survivor: "I know I am crazy to do it, but I would be even crazier if I didn't."

George, who died a natural death a few years ago, understood the secret of coping with the violence of Beirut—that it required something more complicated than just hiding in a basement shelter. It required a thousand little changes in one's daily habits and a thousand little mental games to avoid being overwhelmed by everything happening around you. Not all Beirutis were up to the challenge. Terry Prothro, who directed the Center for Behavioral Research at the American University of Beirut and was a longtime resident of the city, once suggested that what "we are experiencing in Lebanon is something that is unlike any stress problems psychiatrists or psychologists have had to deal with anywhere in the past. An earthquake, a Hiroshima, those are one-shot affairs. Even Northern Ireland can't really be compared to Beirut, because the central government there and all of its services always continued to operate and the level of Belfast's violence was far lower and more transient than here. The resilience of human beings is so great that they can always recover from sporadic violence. But Beirut is different. Beirut is fourteen straight years. No one ever thought about sustaining that kind of stress for years and years. I got some books out on disaster relief, but they had nothing to offer. There are no prescriptions about what to do about a Beirut."

So the Lebanese invented their own prescriptions, proving in the process that men and women can go on for years and years in what seem to be inhuman conditions by developing the right coping mechanisms.

The most popular means of coping I saw in Beirut was simply learning to play mind games—games that eased one's anxiety without actually removing any danger. For instance, Diala Ezzedine, a college student and Red Cross volunteer whom I met when she helped dig out the rubble of my own apartment, once told me that to calm herself during the worst bouts of violence she would make probability calculations in her head and try to convince herself that someone was actually keeping score.

"I [would] say to myself, 'There are 4 million people in Lebanon and so many in my family; what are the odds of anyone in my family getting killed?' " Diala explained, with great earnestness.

"I had a cousin who died recently. I was very sorry he died. But—and this may be a terrible thing to say—I also felt a kind of relief. Like, okay, that's all for our family now, we have made our contribution to the odds. It always reminds me of the joke about the man who carries a bomb with him whenever he goes on an airplane because the odds against there being two bombs on one plane are much higher."

Diala's mind games, though, went beyond calculating odds to calculating architecture. "I find that when I am in a building," she said, "I sometimes start to wonder, If a bomb were to go off right now, where is the best place for me to be standing? Should I be under the door frame? Or next to the stairs, or near a wall? I know there is nothing I can really do, but I can't stop myself from thinking about it, or making little adjustments."

Another popular coping game the Lebanese played was called "Conspiracy." During the entire time I was in Beirut I don't remember more than one or two cases where the perpetrators of a car bomb, an assassination, or a major killing were ever identified, caught, and punished. This always compounded the anxiety of living in Beirut, because not only was there constant random violence but you could never savor the peace of mind that comes from knowing that at least one of the killers was off the streets and safely behind bars. Beirut was all crime and no punishment. Often a car bomb would explode in East or West Beirut and no one would even claim credit for it, let alone be apprehended.

In an attempt to make the anxiety this produced more controllable, the Lebanese would simply invent explanations for the unnatural phenomena happening around them; they would impose an order on the chaos. Their explanations for why someone was killed or why a certain battle broke out were usually the most implausible, wild-eyed conspiracy theories one could imagine. These conspiracies, as the Lebanese painted them, featured either the Israelis, the Syrians, the Americans, the Soviets, or Henry Kissinger—anyone but the Lebanese—in the most elaborate plots to disrupt Lebanon's naturally tranquil state.

In 1983, Ann and I attended a dinner party at the home of Malcolm Kerr, then president of the American University of Beirut. During the course of the dinner conversation that evening, someone mentioned the unusual hailstorms that had pelted Beirut for the two previous nights. Everyone gave his own meteorological explanations for the inclement weather before Malcolm asked his Lebanese guests with tongue in cheek: "Do you think the Syrians did it?"

Sadly, Kerr, a charming, intelligent man, was himself assassinated a few months after that dinner—and though his killers were never caught, every Lebanese had a perfectly rational explanation for why the Christians, the Shiites, the Israelis, the Syrians, or the Palestinians had done him in.

Similar "rational" explanations were also employed to explain why the other guy got killed and you didn't. I rarely heard any Beiruti admit that the violence around him was totally capricious and that the only thing that kept him alive was callous fate— which was the truth. Instead, I would hear people say about a neighbor who got killed by an errant shell, "Well, you know, he lived on the wrong side of the street. It is much more exposed over there than on our side." Or they would say, "Well, you know, he lived next to a PLO neighborhood," or, "He shouldn't have gone out driving fifteen minutes after the cease-fire started; he should have waited twenty minutes—everyone knows that." In order to continue functioning, Beirutis always had to find some way to differentiate themselves from the victim and to insist that there was a logical explanation for why each person died, which, if noted, would save them from a similar fate. Without such rationalizations no one would have left his home.

Sometimes people even sought out these rationalizations in advance. Every time I went to the Bank of America in Beirut to withdraw money from my account, the two aged and overweight guards used to hop to their feet the second they spotted me stepping off the elevator. It wasn't out of respect; they just wanted to pump me for news. I was the foreign journalist and fount of all information. Surely I could predict the future. One day, Samir, the teller, confided in me as he counted out a stack of Lebanese pound notes that he had a problem: he and his wife were planning a vacation to Poland—of all places—from June 24, 1983, to July 8, 1983, and he had just a few questions: Would fighting break out before he left, after he left, or when he returned? Would it be worst in West Beirut, East Beirut, the Bekaa Valley, or the Shouf Mountains? Would it be heavy or light shelling? And then came the real reason for his question: Would it be okay to leave the children behind?

"I need to know," Samir whispered, "so I can go and come back without worrying about the children. You are supposed to be informed."

Maybe the most popular Beirut mind game of all, though, was learning how to view one's environment selectively. Richard Day, an incisive and sensitive American-trained psychologist who taught at the American University during the early 1980s, once studied the coping mechanisms of his students and discovered that those who survived the Israeli invasion of Beirut in the best physical and mental health were those who learned how to block out what was going on around them that was not under their own control and to focus instead only on their immediate environment and the things that they could control. This prevented them from suffering from "system overload." Day explained what he meant by viewing one's environment selectively: "I am on my way to play tennis, and an Israeli F-15 suddenly flies overhead. Can I do anything about it? No. Is he coming to bomb me? I don't think so. So I continue on and play tennis."

I learned to be quite good at this myself. Late one afternoon in the summer of 1982, I was typing a story at the Reuters bureau when the crackle of machine-gun fire erupted in the park across the street. Another American reporter in the bureau, who had just arrived in Beirut, ran to the window to see what all the commotion was. He became transfixed at the sight of a Lebanese militiaman firing a machine gun at someone off in the distance. Eventually this reporter peeled himself away from the window, rushed over to me, and said excitedly, "Did you see that? Did you see that guy? He was holding a gun like this right in his gut and shooting someone. Did you see that?"

I just looked up from my typewriter at this fellow and said, "Was he shooting at you? No. Was he shooting at me? No. So leave me alone, would you?"

Viewing Beirut selectively didn't mean being suicidal and simply walking obliviously through a firefight, but it did mean learning to isolate dangers in your mind and to take calculated risks in order to continue to be able to live a reasonably full life. Often you would be driving down a street and suddenly see all the cars in front of you screech to a halt and hurriedly turn around and go the other way; sometimes they would not even bother to turn around but would just go backward at 50 miles an hour. You would ask a pedestrian what was going on and someone would shout, "Snipers" or "Car bomb." In any other city people would probably go home, hide in their houses, and lock all the windows. In Beirut, they just drove two blocks out of their way and went around the trouble, as though the disturbance were nothing more lethal than the highway department doing roadwork.

My associate Ihsan Hijazi once told me, "When the civil war first started, if I heard there was fighting in the Bekaa Valley— fifty miles away—I would get the kids from school and bring them home. That was fourteen years ago. Today, if I hear fighting down the street, I ignore it. If I hear it outside my building, I move away from the windows into a safer room. I only start to worry now if the fighting is outside my own door—literally on my doorstep. Otherwise, it doesn't exist for me. I just ignore it, and turn up the volume on my television."

Beirutis talk about violence the way other people talk about the weather. When they ask, "How is it outside?" they are not referring to the chance of precipitation but, rather, to the security climate in the streets. Lebanese radio stations compete with each other for market share by trying to be the fastest and most accurate at warning drivers which roads are safe and which are not, the way local American radio stations do with traffic reports. You could literally hear a bulletin over Beirut radio saying: "The main crossing point between East and West Beirut was closed at 5:00 p.m. due to a gunfight between two taxi drivers. Drivers are urged to use alternative routes." Every Beirut driver knows the radio lexicon: a road described as *amina* is totally secured by army or police; a road described as *salika* is free of snipers or kidnappers, but not policed; *hatherah* means the road is passable, but with a roughly 30 percent chance of kidnapping or sniping; and finally, *ghair amina* means the road is unsafe at any speed.

Part of learning how to view one's environment selectively is learning to make oneself numb to some of the more grotesque scenes that are part of the texture of life in Beirut. Terry Prothro, the American University psychologist, used to say that in Beirut, at least, the ability to repress things was not necessarily pathological. It could actually be quite healthy and useful for survival.

I know it was for me. I covered more than a dozen car bombings in Beirut, and after a while I simply trained myself to stop seeing the gruesome aspects. I stopped noticing the stunned pedestrians with blood trickling down their cheeks who happened to be standing on the street when the lethal Mercedes—the favorite choice of Beirut car bombers—suddenly turned into a ball of flame. I stopped seeing the smoldering charred carcasses of the other automobiles engulfed in the blast or the chaos of the rescue workers as they scurried around on tiptoe among the shards of glass and twisted car parts to pry out the dead and wounded. Instead, after a while, I found myself focusing entirely on the incongruities: the juicy roast chickens that were blown all over the street from an adjacent restaurant but somehow still looked good enough to eat, or the smell of liquor from a shelf full of broken Johnnie Walker bottles. And eventually, after seeing enough car bombs, I started focusing on the leaves. When a car packed with one hundred sticks of dynamite explodes on a crowded street, the force of the blast knocks all the leaves off the trees and the road is left choking with them like an autumn lawn. My friends in the Lebanese Red Cross still tell the story of the man they found at a car bombing near the Ministry of Information whose chest was blown open. They knew he was still alive because, through the blood that filled his mouth, little air bubbles kept surfacing. The thing they remembered most, though, was that two leaves had come to rest gently on his face—one on each eye.

Not everyone can be so emotionally well defended in every situation, and that is when Beirut really starts to take its mental toll. When your blinders come loose or you start to actually think about the dangers around you that you cannot control, even the most insignificant daily routine can become filled with dread. I knew a longtime resident of Beirut, Lina Mikdadi, a Lebanese writer and the mother of two girls, who was hardened to virtually every danger the city had to offer—except car bombs.

"Snipers and shelling never bothered me," she would say. "But booby-trapped cars—that is what really scares me. If I am in a traffic jam, I get hysterical. I put my hand on the horn and I don't take it off until I get out. The children start screaming in the back seat because they don't understand why I am honking. I am afraid to tell them. I just want to get away from being trapped between all those cars."

Then, of course, there are the times when you are viewing your environment selectively, but you make the wrong selection. One night during an Israeli artillery bombardment of Beirut in the summer of 1982, Ihsan Hijazi and his daughter Yasmin, a medical student, were home in their fifth-floor apartment in West Beirut. Israeli gunners were raining shells down on their neighborhood, while overhead Israeli planes were crisscrossing the night sky, dropping glowing orange flares that hung over the Palestinian refugee camps like spotlights over a boxing ring. There was no electricity in the city, so Ihsan and Yasmin were lodged in the middle of their apartment, trying to avoid shrapnel and flying glass and using only a candle for light.

Suddenly they saw a mouse. The little gray rodent had crawled out from behind a loose baseboard and its two beady eyes were flashing right up at them.

"We forgot about everything going on around us," Ihsan recalled. "I can stand the bombing, but I cannot stand a mouse in the house. My daughter grabbed a flashlight and I found a big flyswatter, which was the only weapon we had in the apartment, and we chased that little mouse all over, even out onto the balcony. We didn't give a damn about the [Israeli] planes. Fear for us came from that little mouse."

While many Beirutis have become adept at viewing their environment selectively, some of them after fourteen years of civil war have also become too adept at it and tuned the world out altogether. This is dangerous, not just psychologically, but also physically, because it dulls a person's normal protective instincts as much as any drug. (Valium, though, is sold over the counter in Beirut, and the Lebanese are believed to be among the highest per capita users of the sedative in the world.) When I was working in Beirut for UPI and had to stay late many evenings at the office, I would often walk home alone at 11:00 p.m. I liked the eight-block hike for the exercise. One night I dragged Ann home from a movie at that hour. As we were walking down a sidewalk holding hands, a man jumped out of a first-floor window and landed right in front of us, like a cat. He was carrying a sack of something in one hand and a silver revolver in the other. We looked at him. He looked at us. We were all too dumbstruck to speak, so he just scampered away. Beirut was so dangerous usually even the criminals didn't care to be on the streets after dark. When I think back now on my habit of walking home late at night, I can't believe I actually did it.

Somehow it always reminds me of a story Terry Prothro told me when I asked him how much longer he could go on adjusting to the perversity of life in Beirut. He answered, "There is a test we used to do in class to see how easily living things can adapt. You put a frog in a pail of water and gradually turn up the heat. The frog just keeps adjusting to the new temperature, until it finally boils to death, because it is so used to adjusting that it doesn't think to jump out of the pail. I feel like that frog."

He wasn't alone. Dr. Amal Shamma, the spunky former head of the emergency ward at Beirut's Barbir Hospital and a woman for whom life no longer holds any surprises whatsoever, recalled being awakened once by a tremor rattling her bed. "We had an earthquake late at night that registered 5.5 on the Richter scale," said Dr. Shamma. "It shook my whole house. I woke up and said to myself, 'Oh, it's an earthquake,' and went right back to sleep. The next morning, I found out that everyone had gone down to the beaches [for safety]. Now, that scares me."

In coping with the violence of their city, Beirutis also seemed to disprove Hobbes's prediction that life in the "state of nature" would be "solitary." At those moments during the Israeli siege of West Beirut or in the depths of the Lebanese civil war, when Beirut society seemed to have disintegrated and when all formal law and order virtually disappeared, the first instinct of most Beirutis was not to go it alone, to rape their neighbor's wife or take the opportunity to rob the corner grocery store. Of course there were many incidents of thieving, bank robbing, and kidnapping for ransom, but they were not nearly as widespread as might have been expected under the free-for-all conditions that prevailed; stories of people being mugged on the streets or held up in their homes were relatively rare.

Rather, the behavior of Beirutis suggested that man's natural state is as a social animal who will do everything he can to seek out and create community and structures when the larger government or society disappears. Beirut was divided into a mosaic of neighborhoods, each tied together by interlocking bonds of family, friendship, and religion. When the larger, macro Beirut society and government splintered, people's first instinct was to draw together into micro-societies based on neighborhood, apartment house, religious, or family loyalties. These micro-societies provided some of the services, structure, and comfort that were normally offered by the government. They also helped to keep people alive, upright, and honest, sometimes even in spite of themselves.

Elizabeth Zaroubi, a young Christian woman who lived in West Beirut, said that during the summer of 1982 she discovered her family and neighbors as never before. "I live in the same building as my parents," she explained. "Before the war I used to see them for maybe five minutes a day. But during the fighting we would sit together for hours, prepare meals together, play cards, and chat with all the neighbors. If someone found strawberries or bread or cucumbers during the Israeli siege, he would buy enough for all the neighbors and everyone would come together. Before, we used to pass the neighbors on the street, but now we know all kinds of details about each other's private lives and children, and we ask about them. I discovered that I know the relatives of one of my neighbors. We have a common point now that we didn't have before. When you go through an experience with someone like that, you can't ignore them. You can't say anymore that you don't care about them."

Even in situations when people were confronted with strangers from outside their micro-society or neighborhood, their first instinct in dealing with them was often to try to establish some kind of personal link, a micro-micro-society, as it were. Terry Prothro discovered this one afternoon while trying to recover his collection of Persian carpets, which were stolen in the midst of civil strife back in 1976.

Terry and his Lebanese Druse wife and daughter had gone to the United States that year on a sabbatical. While they were gone they stored their valuable collection of Persian carpets in his mother-in-law's small apartment in the predominantly Druse Mseitbe neighborhood of West Beirut. Terry's mother-in-law was a well-known social activist in Beirut and involved in a variety of charities.

"The carpets were in her storeroom above the kitchen," Terry recalled. "While she was out one day, someone came in and stole

them all. After my mother-in-law came home and discovered what
had happened, my brother-in-law began asking around the neighborhood who was stealing carpets and he finally located the gang
that was responsible. He went to their warehouse and confronted
them. He was really angry and said to them, 'Do you know what
you did? You broke into the house of this lady who is a widow
and is the head of the Lebanese Children's Society.' The thieves
themselves were not Druse, but when they heard what my
brother-in-law had to say about my mother-in-law, they immediately apologized and said that they did not realize whose house
they had broken into. The gangleader told him, 'We were just
robbing, we didn't mean anything personal.' They took him back
in the warehouse and told him, 'Go ahead, choose your carpets
and take them home.' The room was full of stolen carpets, from
the floor to the ceiling. So my brother-in-law went through them
until he found all of ours. He didn't take one more or one less,
although I did tease him later why he didn't happen to recognize
a few extra Bukharas. As soon as the thieves recognized my
mother-in-law as part of some ongoing community network, they
were ready to treat her as a friend and not just as a target.''

Even when people found themselves in a solitary state in a
country in chaos, the instinct of most—though not all—was to try
to mobilize their energies to maintain as much structure and meaning as possible in their immediate lives. Instead of exploiting the
chaos, people fought it at every turn.

Myrna Mugrditchian was a delightfully articulate Armenian
dental student whom I also met for the first time when she came
to my apartment as a Red Cross volunteer to help in the rescue
effort. After that, we used to see each other regularly at post-
car-bomb scenes, and eventually we became friends. I once asked
her how she could have volunteered for such depressing work.
She told me it really was not out of altruism, but in order to keep
busy and maintain a purpose to her life. "I had a choice," explained Myrna. "I could sit home all day quarreling with my family
and going crazy, or I could get out on the street. The only way
to get out was to be either a helper or a fighter. I chose to be a
helper."

Elizabeth Zaroubi told me her elderly father went out every
morning in August 1982, at the height of the Israeli siege of Beirut,
and organized the children in his neighborhood to wash their

street with detergent. War or no war, he couldn't stand living in filth. He wasn't the only one. Gerald Butt, a BBC correspondent in West Beirut, happened to have an office that overlooked a communal artesian well, an important fixture in the summer of 1982 after the Israelis turned off all the water coming from the East Beirut–based water company. Each morning that summer, scores of West Beirutis would line up with their pails to get enough water to last them and their families the whole day.

"Every morning when I would get to work," said Butt, "I would look out and see people, mostly mothers and children, lined up with their cans and pails. I used to watch them from my window all the time. So one morning a man is in line. He gets to the front, fills his can with water, and then walks directly over to his taxi and splashes the whole can of water over his car. I just started to laugh. Here the Israelis were surrounding Beirut, there was a siege, and this taxi driver was washing his car."

In tilting against the windmills of chaos, many Beirutis actually discovered good things about themselves—and others—that they never could have learned except in a crucible like Beirut.

As Richard Day put it, "People discovered something about their inner strength when they were tested, like a metal that can only achieve its real hardness at the highest temperature."

Dr. Antranik Manoukian, the manager of Lebanon's only mental-health clinic, the Asfourieh Hospital for Mental and Nervous Disorders, told a symposium held in Beirut after the summer of 1982 that his patients who were caught in the middle of some of the worst Israeli shelling and bombing actually got better mentally and required less medication and treatment during the fighting than when it was over. This was largely due to the fact that the patients focused all their limited mental faculties on trying to survive the chaos and so actually became healthier. That could be said of most Lebanese to some degree or another, which is why the real mental-health crisis for Lebanon will come when the civil war ends and peace and quiet return. Only then, when people let down their guard and take stock of all they have lost, will they truly become crazy. Until then, many Lebanese won't simply survive, they may even thrive.

Anthony Asseily, the director of the J. Henry Schroder & Sons merchant bank branch in Beirut, said that after the start of the Israeli invasion in the summer of 1982 he closed his office and relocated to London, leaving behind thirty-two-year-old Munzer Najm—whose job had previously been to fetch coffee for the bank's employees and guests. Munzer's only instructions were to watch over the place as best he could. As far as Asseily knew, Munzer, the coffee boy, spoke only Arabic.

One day, during the height of the Israeli siege of West Beirut, Asseily was sitting in his office in London when suddenly his telex came alive. "It was Beirut on the line," he recalled. "My first reaction was to ask how the situation was. The answer came back: 'Not so good.' Then I said, 'Wait a minute, who is this on the line?' The answer came back: 'Munzer.' At first, I couldn't believe it. I thought maybe someone had a gun to his head and was telling him what to type. We had a [telex] conversation and eventually I found out that while he was sitting around the bank all that time with nothing to do, he had learned some English and taught himself how to operate the telex." Asseily remarked later that Munzer the coffee boy could just as easily have stolen the bank's telex and sold it on the street to the highest bidder as learned how to use it. There was no one to stop him: no police, no prisons, and no courts. But he didn't.

The real problem with the Lebanese today is that they have gotten too good at this adapting game—so good that their cure and their disease have become one and the same. The Lebanese individual traditionally derived his social identity and psychological support from his primordial affiliations—family, neighborhood, or religious community, but rarely from the nation as a whole. He was always a Druse, a Maronite, or a Sunni before he was a Lebanese; and he was always a member of the Arslan or Jumblat Druse clans before he was a Druse, or a member of the Gemayel or Franjieh Maronite clans before he was a Maronite. The civil war and the Israeli invasion only reinforced this trend, dividing Lebanese into tighter-knit micro-families, or village and religious communities, but pulling them farther apart as a nation.

But the very family, village, and religious bonds that provided the glue holding Beirutis together in micro-societies that could see them through hard times when the national government disappeared also helped to prevent a strong national government and national identity from ever fully emerging or lasting. When the city water supply collapsed, Beirutis dug their own wells; when the city electricity supply blacked out, they bought their own generators to power their homes; when the police disappeared, they affiliated themselves with private militias for protection. As the Lebanese sociologist Samir Khalaf summed it up: "Though the average Lebanese derives much . . . social support and psychological reinforcement from . . . local and communal allegiances, these forces are the same elements that . . . prompt him on occasion to violate and betray his society's normative standards. The Lebanese is being demoralized, in other words, by the very forces that are supposed to make him a more human and sociable being . . . The formation and deformation of Lebanon, so to speak, are rooted in the same forces."

I don't mean to suggest in any way that these ad hoc family, neighborhood, or religious communal associations are able to satisfactorily replace the Lebanese society that collapsed or that Beirutis find them preferable to a properly functioning government. They aren't really a cure for Lebanon's ills, just a palliative—Ace bandages on a body politic stricken with cancer. They make life in the Beirut jungle not quite as solitary, nasty, brutish, and short as might be expected—but it is still plenty frightening.

Beirut's enduring lesson for me was how thin is the veneer of civilization, how easily the ties that bind can unravel, how quickly a society that was known for generations as the Switzerland of the Middle East can break apart into a world of strangers. I have never looked at the world the same since I left Beirut. It was like catching a glimpse of the underside of a rock or the mess of wires and chips that are hidden inside a computer.

Steven Spielberg once made a movie called *Poltergeist*, which was about a lovely suburban house that, unbeknown to its inhabitants, has been built above a cemetery. The family who owns the house discovers what lurks beneath only when some of the dead spirits, angry at the fact that a house has been built on their graves, start rising up and haunting the place. Eventually the family hires an expert demonologist to purge their home of these angry spirits and she determines that a closet in an upstairs bedroom is the gateway through which the demons are entering and exiting. In the climactic scene, the expert, a tiny woman with her hair in a bun, delicately opens the closet door and out rushes a wild, screaming, fire-breathing monster, the embodiment of uncontrolled rage and violence, which bowls over everyone in its path.

Ever since I left Lebanon I have felt, no matter where I am, that I am living inside that house, never knowing when a door might fly open and suddenly I will be face to face again with the boiling abyss I glimpsed in Beirut. I go to baseball games or to the theater, and I look around at all the people seated so nicely and wonder to myself how easily all of this could turn into a Beirut. It has been my own private nightmare, but also a source of inner fortitude.

I realized that my first week in Jerusalem. When Ann and I finally moved from Beirut to Jerusalem in June 1984, we found ourselves going to a movie on our first Saturday night in the Israeli capital. Not knowing our way around the city, we hired a taxi to take us from the Sheraton Hotel to the Edison Theater. It turned out to be only a short ride, but the Israeli taxi driver tried to cheat us by not turning on his meter and then asking an exorbitant fare.

We told him we would give him 25 percent of that, and when he refused this offer and started screaming at us, we just put the money on the seat and walked away. The driver, his face flushed with anger, threw open his door, got out of the car, and began bellowing that he would do everything from beating us up to calling the police.

Ann and I looked at him and then looked at each other, and we both started to laugh.

"Do you know where we have come from?" I shouted at the driver in English, pointing a finger to my chest. "Do you know where we have been living? We've been living in Beirut, in goddamn Beirut. Do you know what that means?"

We had just come out of Hobbes's jungle and he was threatening us with the police!

We walked into the theater chuckling to ourselves, leaving him standing in the street spewing curses at us in Hebrew and Arabic. There was nothing that he could threaten us with that we hadn't already lived through.

We had been to Beirut.

3

Beirut: City of Versions

There is no truth in Beirut, only versions.

—*Bill Farrell*
Middle East correspondent
THE NEW YORK TIMES

In the winter of 1983, my friends David Zucchino of the *Philadelphia Inquirer* and Bill Barrett of the Dallas *Times Herald* hopped into a taxicab in West Beirut and rushed up to the Druse village of Hammana in the Shouf Mountains to track down some senior Druse officers who had just defected from the Lebanese army. At the time, their defection was a big story—a big story which my two colleagues wanted to get firsthand. When they arrived in their taxi at the outskirts of Hammana, David told me later, their driver just sped headlong into town, not noticing a dilapidated Druse checkpoint that they whizzed right through.

"The Druse went berserk," recalled David, "but our taxi driver just kept driving along, and we were saying to ourselves, 'Hey, this place looks interesting.' Then all of a sudden we see in the rearview mirror this car coming after us filled with all these guys with big beards flapping and guns poking out the windows. They cut us off. We pulled our car over and they all surrounded us, shouting and shaking their fists, yapping away in Arabic, and sticking their guns into the car. We thought, Oh shit, we are in deep trouble. We immediately began screaming '*Sahafi, sahafi*' [Arabic for journalist] and flashed our Druse press credentials."

The Druse militiamen examined the press cards, read them every which way, and then entered into a long discussion among themselves.

"I started to get real nervous—I mean, real nervous," said David. "I thought maybe they were discussing who gets the honor of putting a bullet through our heads first. Then suddenly the one with the biggest beard sticks his head back into the car and says, "Which one of you is from Dallas?"

Barrett said, "I am."

At that point the bearded militiaman, his eyes flashing fury, stuck his AK-47 rifle into the car, pointed it toward Barrett, and asked with a perfectly straight face: "Who shot J.R.?"

A second later the gunmen all erupted into howls of laughter and told the two reporters, "Welcome, welcome to our town."

It was from incidents such as this that I derived my first rule of Beirut reporting: If you can't take a joke, you shouldn't have come. A reporter must never lose his sense of humor in a place such as Beirut—not only because he will go crazy if he does, but, more important, because he will miss something essential about the Lebanese themselves. Even in their darkest moments, and maybe because of them, the Lebanese never forget how to laugh.

But being a reporter in Beirut, I quickly discovered, required something more than an appreciation of life's absurdities. Since I was sent to Beirut by UPI only eleven months after being hired, it was on the job there that I really learned how to be a journalist. In some ways, Beirut was the ideal place to practice journalism, in other ways the most frustrating, but in all ways it was un-forgettable.

What made reporting so difficult from Beirut was the fact that there was no center—not politically, not physically; since there was no functioning unified government, there was no authoritative body which reporters could use to check out news stories and no authoritative version of reality to either accept or refute; it was a city without "officials." After the civil war broke out in 1975, the center in Lebanon was carved up into a checkerboard of fiefdoms and private armies, each with its own version of reality, which it broadcast through its own radio station and its own spokesmen. The pure white light of Truth about any given news story in Lebanon was always refracted through this prism of factions and fiefdoms and then splashed on one's consciousness like a spectrum of light hitting a wall. As a reporter you had to learn to take a little ray of red from here and a little ray of blue from there and then paint in story form the picture that you thought most closely approximated reality. Rarely did you ever have the satisfaction of feeling that you really got to the bottom of something. It was like working in a dark cave with the aid of a single candle. Just when you thought you had spotted the white light of Truth, you would chase it, only to discover that it was someone else, also holding a candle, also looking for the light.

A few reporters found this news environment so bewildering that they began to try to impose an official-sounding order on it themselves. They created light where there was none. They didn't make up the news, but they came up with some rather interesting attributions for what they found. For instance, one wire service used to attribute information about fighting in Beirut to "a Beirut police spokesman who could not be identified according to government regulations." There was no Beirut police spokesman, and even if there was, there were no government regulations which would have inhibited him from giving his name. This same wire service occasionally used to write political stories attributed to "leftist sources." What is a leftist source in Beirut? I used to wonder. A person who is left-handed? Half of West Beirut's populace qualified as leftists. Quoting leftist sources in Beirut was about as meaningful as quoting "Jewish sources" in Israel, but reporters cited them to give their stories some authoritative quality in a city without officials.

Yet it was the very same chaos which made reporting from Beirut so stimulating. Being a reporter in Beirut was like being at a play in which the audience could, at any time, hop right up onto the stage and interview the actors as they were reciting their lines or acting out some dramatic scene. "Say, Hamlet, how do you feel about your stepfather?" There were no ushers to hold you back, no press pools or limits on access.

Because of this I got to witness encounters and to describe

scenes that would have been hidden away behind an official shroud in any normal country. On the second day of the Israeli invasion, my assistant Mohammed and I drove down to the Bekaa Valley in an attempt to confirm whether Syria and Israel had begun fighting each other. No one really knew for sure at that early stage in the war. As we got near Lake Karun in south Lebanon, we saw a line of six 130 mm cannon firing toward the Israeli border. Several men in ill-fitting business suits, wholly out of context on a battlefield, were standing under a nearby tree watching the guns fire. They all had the look of Syrian intelligence officers. We drove our car over to them and quietly asked, "Excuse us, are those Syrian guns firing?"

"Yes," they answered.

"And are those Israeli shells landing over there?" we asked, pointing to a hillside some 500 yards away.

"Yes," they nodded. We then ducked into our car and sped back to Beirut with our story before they had a chance to ask, "Who were those two guys?"

Unfortunately, when reporters were left to probe to the limits of their own bravery, it meant inevitably that some went too far. During Israel's 1978 incursion into south Lebanon, up to the Litani River, David Hirst of *The Manchester Guardian*, Ned Temko of *The Christian Science Monitor*, and Doug Roberts of the Voice of America rode down from Beirut to observe the fighting. They were told by Palestinian guerrillas in Sidon that the PLO had just driven the Israeli army out of the nearby village of Hadatha. The three reporters decided to check out the story and found that actually the Israeli army had driven the Palestinians out of Hadatha and then vacated it. When Israeli gunners saw the three journalists drive in, they thought they were returning guerrillas and fired rounds at them on and off for eight hours. The next day the three "surrendered" to a unit of Israeli soldiers sitting on a nearby hilltop and were taken back to Israel for their own safety. As soon as they crossed the border, an Israel Radio reporter walked up to David Hirst and asked him how it felt to be rescued by the Israeli army.

"After they stopped shooting at us," answered David, "it was fine."

Access, of course, was not totally unrestricted all the time. When going to visit any front, it was always wise, and often necessary, to obtain press credentials from the militia on whose side you would be viewing the action. The PLO, the Phalangists, the Druse, and the Shiite Amal militia all issued their own press credentials. Sometimes their spokesmen would travel around the front carrying the rubber stamp of their organization and an ink pad just in case you needed some credentials on the fly. Since reporters often traveled between different fronts on any given day, some of them kept their identity papers from the "leftist" militias in their left-hand pocket and from the "rightist" militias in their right-hand pocket, just to make sure they didn't get mixed up and present Phalangist identity papers at a PLO checkpoint, for example, which would have been considered bad manners, to say the least.

What passed for a press card in Beirut, though, would not exactly get you into the White House. Robin Wright, an intrepid American reporter working in Beirut on a book about radical Shiite groups, used to have to spend a great deal of time moving in and out of Shiite neighborhoods controlled by the radical Hizbullah, "Party of God," militia. For a woman, this could be a dangerous enterprise. So one day, Robin told me, she went up to a senior Hizbullah official and said, "Look, I'm an American. I am trying to write this book that will help us understand you people, but I am very nervous about driving around here without a press pass. Can't you do something for me?"

Hizbullah knew more about kidnapping journalists than accrediting them. "The guy really didn't know from press cards, yet he wanted to be accommodating," said Robin, "so he walked over to this wall full of these fearsome Hizbullah posters, with pictures of clenched fists and people holding up AK-47s. He pulled one of the posters loose, ripped off the bottom corner with the organization's emblem on it, and handed it to me. He said, Just show people this emblem and you won't have any problems. I said, Look, can't you date it or write your name on it or something? He just shrugged. But it worked! A few days later I was stopped at a Hizbullah checkpoint. I pulled out my poster fragment and they waved me right through, all smiles. Of all the press passes I brought back from Beirut, that is the one I have taken the best care of. You never know when it might come in handy."

* * *

I had my own particular identity problem. It could crop up at any time, and there was no ID card I could flash to solve it. One day, for instance, I myself was riding with David Zucchino in a taxi up the Beirut–Damascus highway to cover some fighting between Druse and Phalangists in the Shouf. Halfway up the mountains, we came to a hastily erected checkpoint at which teenage boys with pistols stuck into the belts of their tight-fitting Calvin Klein jeans were stopping cars and asking some people to get out and step over to the side of the road. We didn't know if they were Druse kidnapping Maronites or Maronites kidnapping Druse, but the poor Lebanese who were being taken from their cars seemed to know that they were dead, whoever the kidnappers were. Some of the hostages just sat along the roadside, their shoulders slumped and their heads hanging down on their chests in pathetic poses of resignation to their fate.

One of these teenaged thugs stuck his head into our taxi window and growled in Arabic, "What religion are you?"

I thought to myself, If I tell him the truth, that I am neither Christian nor Druse but Jewish, he'll never believe me. But if I don't tell him the truth, what do I tell him? I don't know if he is a Christian or a Druse. I don't know what he wants to hear.

We had a rather shrewd taxi driver, and when the militiaman demanded again, "What religion are you?" he answered gruffly, "They are journalists—that's it." Luckily for us, this was not their day for kidnapping journalists and they let us pass. I will never forget the look of envy which the hostages sitting along the road cast our way as we sped off.

Being the only full-time American Jewish reporter in West Beirut in the early 1980s was a tricky task at times, particularly during the height of the Israeli invasion. My policy was never to hide my religion from any friend or official who asked me about it straight out, but I did not go around introducing myself to strangers by saying, "Hi, I'm Tom Friedman and I'm Jewish." It wasn't that I was afraid someone was going to shoot me if they discovered I was Jewish, although in a place like Beirut one could never feel totally secure; I just didn't want my religion to be an issue that would get in the way of my reporting. I wanted people to judge me on what I wrote and not on who I was.

But there was never a moment in Beirut when I wasn't keenly aware of who I was. For the first few weeks after we arrived, I always felt as though there was a glowing neon sign over my head that was constantly flashing "Jew, Jew, this man Jew." I quickly discovered, though, that people assumed that if you were in Beirut you couldn't possibly be Jewish. After all, what Jew in his right mind would come to Beirut? Your name could have been Goldberg and most Lebanese still would have assumed you were a Gentile. I once went to apply for an Algerian visa, and when the embassy official filling in the form came to the blank marked *Religion*, he simply filled in the word *Christian* without even asking me. While Friedman is a recognizable Jewish name to Westerners, it is not so obvious to Arabic speakers unfamiliar with Western names.

Because I have dark Mediterranean features and a mustache, Lebanese were always asking me whether I was of Arab origin. "No," I would say, "I'm American. One hundred percent." But then they would ask, "What were you before that? What kind of name is Friedman?" I would always answer "Romanian," because my paternal grandparents emigrated to America from there, and somehow that would satisfy people and there would be no further questions. They would say, "Romanian," and nod their heads as if that explained everything.

Nevertheless, there was always a tension inside my gut, because I was constantly aware of the gap between who I was and who many people assumed I was. Whenever I was interviewing a militia leader or Arab statesman, my mind would start racing uncontrollably: What if this guy knew who I was? Would he care if he knew I was bar mitzvahed at the Adath Jeshurun Synagogue in Minneapolis in 1966? Would he be shocked to know that my oldest sister is a Lubavitcher Hasidic Jew with seven children living in Miami Beach?

In order to keep my mind vacant of such thoughts as much as possible, I became very adept at changing the subject of any conversation that seemed to be approaching the question of religion. I did not always succeed, however. Michel Khouri, the distinguished governor of Lebanon's Central Bank when I was in Beirut, invited Ann and me to a dinner party he was hosting at a seaside Beirut hotel one evening. I was seated next to the wife of the Minister of Public Works. As soon as we were introduced, she started in with the questions: "Friedman, Friedman, what kind of name is that?" She quickly found her way through the

maze of defenses I automatically threw up around the question
and established that I was Jewish. At that point I tried asking her
about the weather—really: "Nice weather we are having, eh?"

She answered me in a mischievous tone, and with a slight twin-
kle in her eye. "You're trying to change the subject?"

She didn't say it in a vicious way, but she wanted to talk about
me some more, to dwell on my identity a bit, maybe try it out
on the other people at the table—and I didn't. I had not been
subtle enough in diverting her questions and this had only piqued
her curiosity. We both started to laugh. I raised my arms in mock
surrender and told her with a broad smile that she had caught
me at my own game.

Then I changed the subject.

The truth is, I was usually much more concerned than I needed
to be. Lebanon was probably the best Arab country in which to
be an American Jewish reporter, because people there were quite
used to living with lots of different religious communities; it was
not like being a Jew in Qatar. Although virtually all Beirut's Jews
had emigrated by the time I arrived, they had been, in better
days, very much part of the fabric of life in the city. All my close
Lebanese friends knew I was Jewish, and it never made a dime's
bit of difference to any of them. In fact, they bent over backward
to make sure I felt at home. I was more relaxed as a Jew in their
presence than I was at times in my predominantly Gentile high
school back in Minneapolis, where anti-Semites in my class used
to throw pennies at us to see if we "cheap Jews" would pick them
up. (One of my earliest childhood memories from Minneapolis
is that of a Gentile boy in my grade-school class who had a lisp
calling another Gentile boy a "dirty Dew" when they got into a
fight.)

Even in the presence of people who did not know I was Jewish
I heard very little in the way of nasty anti-Semitic remarks in
Beirut. There was the usual canard about Jews being clever at
business or controlling America, which I occasionally heard from
former Lebanese Prime Minister Saeb Salam, but it never had a
hard edge to it. It was the kind of statement made more out of
awe than antipathy. Salam, a Sunni Muslim, knew very well I
was Jewish, because we often discussed it. I think he was always
proud of the fact that we were friends, and he and his family
always looked out for me. He did, though, enjoy shocking some

of his acquaintances with my identity. One day I was waiting to see Salam, while he was bawling out some wild-eyed Muslim sheik because his Friday mosque sermons were too hostile to the Lebanese army. As the little sheik with his red-and-white turban and thin beard was leaving Salam's office, Salam insisted on introducing him to me. He told the sheik that I was a reporter from *The New York Times*, that I had won a Pulitzer Prize, that I spoke Arabic, and, on top of it all, said Salam, "he is Jewish."

The words hung in the air for a second, before this poor little sheik's eyes bulged out. I thought his beard might fall off. He'd probably given a few Koran-thumping sermons about the Jews in his day, and I am sure I was the first one he had ever met in the flesh. After a limp handshake he scurried out the door.

Most of the PLO officials and guerrillas with whom I dealt regularly knew I was Jewish and simply did not care; they related to me as the *New York Times* correspondent, period, and always lived up to their claims to be "anti-Zionist" and not "anti-Jewish." On one occasion, however, my religion did become an issue with the PLO.

In early July 1982, in the middle of the Israeli siege of Beirut, Mohammed and I asked Mahmoud Labadi, who was then the personal spokesman of Yasir Arafat, for an interview with the PLO chairman. Labadi, I had heard, did not like Jews, and we had always had a very awkward relationship. I guess I was his nightmare during the summer of '82. Here was the PLO's biggest moment on the world stage and who has to be the reporter for the most important American newspaper but a Jew—not a self-hating Jew, not an anti-Zionist Jew, just a regular Jew. While I aimed to be rigorously objective, and he knew it, he also knew I was not one of the PLO groupies—those members of the press corps, mostly Europeans, who unquestioningly swallowed everything the PLO fed them.

A few days after I made the request for an interview with Arafat, Labadi took aside my assistant Mohammed (himself a Palestinian) and informed him that we would get an interview—but it would not be I who would get it. It would be "the tall one," as Labadi put, referring to my lanky colleague, Bill Farrell. Mohammed, on my instructions, explained to Labadi that I was the bureau chief and that the interview had to be done by me or not at all. After thinking about it overnight, Labadi relented. The

day of the interview arrived, and just as I was about to enter the
room with Arafat, Labadi pulled me aside by the elbow and said,
"I just want you to know that I have asked our office in New
York for a complete assessment of all your reporting on us."

"That's fine, Mahmoud," I said. "I've got nothing to hide."

The interview went well. It was published on the front page
and a week passed without my hearing anything from Labadi.
Then one day Bill Farrell was at Labadi's office getting his PLO
press credentials renewed, an always dangerous adventure, since
you never knew when the Israeli air force might arrive and ravage
the neighborhood. While Bill was having his papers stamped,
Labadi came in and threw a telex down in front of him. It was
from the PLO mission at the United Nations. The telex was an
assessment of my coverage, describing it as generally fair and
balanced, but noting obliquely that the "cousinly ways" of my
newspaper, an apparent reference to the *Times*'s original Jewish
ownership, sometimes made it less supportive of the PLO than
they would have liked. Labadi told Bill he wanted to talk to me
immediately. When Bill informed me of the encounter, the paranoia I had kept in check all summer ran riot and I lay awake in
my bed the whole night worrying that someone was going to burst
in and blow my brains all over the wall. Mohammed, my ever-
faithful and wise assistant, tried to calm me down by explaining
what was going on. "They are trying to squeeze you," he said,
twisting his hands together as though wringing out a piece of wet
cloth.

The next morning, Mohammed and I went to see Labadi. He
handed me the telex. I read it over and then read it aloud.

"Sounds okay to me, Mahmoud," I said, laying it down on my
lap.

"It's not good enough," Labadi said coolly.

Mohammed jumped in, saying that he had read every word I
had written that summer and it was all "very fair, very fair."
Labadi cut him off in mid-sentence, saying that Mohammed's
English was not good enough to understand the nuances of what
I wrote.

For a few seconds there was only silence in the room. I had
the telex resting on my knees and was staring at Labadi. Labadi
was staring at me, and Mohammed was staring off into space and

shifting nervously in his chair. I decided it was time to put all the cards on the table.

"Mahmoud," I said, "let's get everything out in the open. I'm Jewish and you know I'm Jewish. When my editors asked me how they could send a Jew to Beirut, I told them it was no problem. I told them that I had never encountered any difficulties with the PLO because of my religion. If the rules of the game have changed, then let me know and I'll go back to the Commodore and pack my bags."

"No, no," said Labadi, waving his hand. "That is not necessary. We have nothing against Jews. We just want you to do a little better in the future."

"Fine," I said. "I will try to be fair. I have been trying up to now."

After the meeting, Labadi took Mohammed aside and told him, "We know he's not bad. We just need more from him."

That was in early July of 1982, before the Sabra and Shatila massacre. I don't think Labadi and I said more than five words to each other the rest of the summer.

Despite the cordial way that I personally was treated, I never had any illusions that religion was not a basic element in the Palestinian–Israeli conflict. It couldn't help but be. This conflict involved not just two nations clashing over the same land, it also involved the clash of two religious communities, Muslims and Jews, with a long history of theological antagonisms behind them. Palestinians speaking among themselves almost never refer to the Israelis as Israelis, but always as "the Jews." It is not meant derogatorily. It is simply an honest expression of how they view Israelis—as Jews, as a religious community that has always lived under the control of Islam, not as a national community entitled to rule over Jerusalem and Muslim land. Yet as much as I tried to play the objective reporter and stay above the fray, something would always come along and kick me in the gut, to remind me how visceral and tribal this conflict really was—and that I was a member of one of the tribes.

In the fall of 1983, after a rebellion broke out against Arafat's leadership within the PLO, I decided to go up to Tripoli, in north

Lebanon, where the combined forces of Abu Musa and Syrian-sponsored Palestinian leader Ahmed Jebril had just routed Arafat from his last stronghold, the Badawi refugee camp. I shared a taxi to Tripoli with a visiting correspondent from *Time* magazine, Barry Hillenbrand, and we went straight to Badawi, where we found Jebril and his men occupying two four-story prefab apartment buildings, one of which had been used as Arafat's headquarters. We asked a few guerrillas standing guard outside whether we could interview Jebril. They told us to wait a minute while they went in and checked.

As we waited, two young Palestinian women, probably in their early twenties, gingerly approached the guards. I eavesdropped as the women explained that they lived on the ground floor of one of the buildings and had fled from the fighting two weeks earlier. They were now coming back to reclaim their apartments and check on their belongings. Could they go in? At first, the guerrillas growled "No," but when one of the women burst into tears, they relented and let them pass.

"Go in," one of the guerrillas instructed, "but don't take anything out."

The two women were inside for about two or three minutes before they flew out of the apartment house in a screaming rage, tearing at their clothes and wailing in grief. One of them went up to a guerrilla and started beating on his chest.

"Shame on you. Shame on you," she bellowed in Arabic. "You tell me not to remove anything—there is nothing left to remove. For ten years we worked—ten years. For what? For this? Everything is gone . . . You took it all!"

It was a heartbreaking scene, and I was on the verge of tears myself, before the other woman, her fists clenched in anger, started to scream at the guerrillas at the top of her lungs, "We are not Jews! We are not Jews! We are not Jews! Why did you do this to us?"

Necessity, as they say, is the mother of invention, and one of the most important journalistic inventions that necessarily developed in the chaos of Beirut was the local Lebanese "fixer." These were Lebanese or Palestinians who knew how to wend their way through the arabesque maze of Beirut and to pay the appropriate bribes to the appropriate people at the appropriate times—for the appropriate commissions.

I didn't employ a fixer, but would occasionally call upon Mohammed in times of need. Mohammed did everything from climbing up telephone poles to repair our phone lines when they were damaged in street fighting, to negotiating with the landlord of a neighboring building who threatened to cut our telex wire, which traversed his roof, if we did not pay him $7,000—in cash. One day during the summer of '82, when the Israeli siege of West Beirut was at its tightest, Mohammed spent an entire day walking around the city seeking to buy gasoline for our car—at $150 a tankful. Eventually he located a source of supply. That night, as we drove home in darkness from the Reuters bureau, we were stopped on Hamra Street by two Palestinian guerrillas standing by a jeep. One was holding a gun and the other was holding an empty water bottle and a long rubber hose. They asked, very politely, whether they could suck a few gallons of gas from our tank to get their jeep going; it was out of gas. Mohammed, having spent an entire day scrounging around for our gasoline, was not going to give it up so easily. Without blinking an eye, he began screaming that our tank was on empty, that we would be lucky to make it home, and if they did not believe him they could come over to his side of the car and look at the gas gauge themselves.

The gauge was resting comfortably on FULL. I couldn't believe what Mohammed was doing. I sat there stiff in my seat, with a stupid grin covering my face, praying to myself that one of the guerrillas would not call Mohammed's bluff; fortunately, they believed him. When we drove away, I told Mohammed in a quivering voice that if we ever got stopped again by guerrillas looking for gas he should give them however much they wanted—otherwise I would suck it out of the tank myself.

If there were a Beirut fixers' hall of fame, though, Abdul Wadud Hajjaj would occupy the central pedestal. In my day, Abdul was the fixer for both *Newsweek* and UPI Television News, and he was the most delightful and lovable operator I have ever known. His long career as a fixer finally came to an abrupt close in 1985, when *Newsweek* and UPITN sent to Beirut some bureaucratic-minded reporters who did not understand that in Wild West Beirut one does not hold to the accounting standards of Arthur Andersen.

Abdul used to keep a desk drawer full of blank receipts from every taxi company in Beirut, which many a reporter drew on to account for all kinds of misspent funds. I shudder to think how many champagne dinners and wild nights at the Casino du Liban were recorded on reporters' expense accounts under the bland cover of "Taxi ride from Beirut to Sidon." But when you needed something, Abdul could get it for you—whether it was a telephone, a driver's license, or an autographed picture of Yasir Arafat.

Among his many scams, Abdul was forever having the place of birth on his Lebanese passport changed according to which group, Palestinians or Lebanese, were the dominant force in West Beirut. To this day I still don't know if he was born in Lebanon or Palestine. Actually, it didn't matter. Abdul could talk his way into anywhere. On the wall of his office he had a display of pictures showing him posing with various famous and infamous people. One photograph featured Abdul shaking hands with Ted Kennedy, which was taken in the 1960s, when Kennedy paid a visit to the American University of Beirut campus and Abdul hosted him, I was told, as head of some Christian student society.

Abdul was a Muslim.

In return for his services, all Abdul asked of his friends was loyalty and an occasional story. Abdul hated to write, so when the *Newsweek* correspondent was out of town and he was asked to supply a story, we at UPI would pitch in and write a story for *Newsweek* under Abdul's name.

In Arab society it is considered impolite to show people the soles of your shoes. I used to love to come into Abdul's office, pull up a chair right in front of his desk, and then put my feet up onto the middle of his blotter so that he could see nothing but my soles. He would unleash a litany of vile Arabic curses on me and then we would both have a good belly laugh.

Not everyone, though, found Abdul as entertaining as I did. Among his detractors was Claude Salhani, then the chief photographer for UPI in Beirut and someone for whom Abdul often made life miserable with various tricks. Abdul loved to have just a little something on everyone; as a fixer, he never knew when it might come in handy. Claude was a Christian with family in East Beirut, and during the early years of the civil war Abdul would often tell him that PLO guerrillas had come looking for him but that he, Abdul, had told them that Claude was okay and not to harm him. Claude always longed for an appropriate revenge on Abdul, and one day he found a way to fix the fixer.

At the end of the summer of '82, after the PLO had departed and Israeli troops and the Lebanese army were fully in control of West Beirut, Abdul flew off on vacation. While Abdul was away, Claude went into his office, which was right across the hall from UPI, and removed the pictures Abdul kept on his wall. One picture showed Abdul arm in arm with Yasir Arafat, another showed him with George Habash, leader of the Popular Front for the Liberation of Palestine, and a third was a Polaroid head shot of himself.

"I spread the word that two plainclothesmen had come in and taken the pictures, after asking a few questions about Abdul," Claude later told me. "When Abdul called in one day from vacation, his secretary told him this story and he started shitting in his pants. As soon as he got back to Beirut, he came over to UPI and asked me who these plainclothesmen were. I told him that these men told me it was none of my business who they were and that they had guns, lots of guns—many, many guns. For weeks Abdul kept pumping me for more details."

All the time, Claude kept the pictures hidden away in his drawer. A few months later, Israel and Lebanon began negotiations over the Israeli withdrawal; the talks took place at a hotel in Khalde, just south of Beirut. One day while Claude was photographing the Khalde talks, he asked an Israeli official there to put some official-looking Hebrew stamps on the back of each of Abdul's pictures and to give him a cover letter on Government of Israel stationery, with only the words *Return to Owner* written on it. The Israeli official, when briefed on the ruse, happily complied. Claude then kept the whole package in his drawer for almost two years, until just before he was about to leave Beirut. The day he left, Claude gave the package to his replacement and asked him to arrange, once Claude was well out of town, to have one of the delivery boys in the building bring the package over to Abdul's office and hand it to him.

"The play went off perfectly," said Claude. "The delivery boy came in and told Abdul this package had been dropped off for him. They told me that he opened it up, saw the Israeli stamps all over his pictures, and went white as a sheet. He immediately panicked and called the Amal militia [which was then in charge of West Beirut]. He wanted to show them that he was really feared by the Israelis. To this day, Abdul never knew it was me, and he never knew what the Israelis might have had on him. It was such sweet revenge."

The home of all good Beirut fixers—not to mention all good Beirut reporters and crooked taxi drivers—was the Commodore Hotel. Every war has its hotel, and the Lebanese wars had the Commodore. The Commodore was an island of insanity in a sea of madness. It wasn't just the parrot in the bar, which did a perfect imitation of the whistle of an incoming shell, that made the place so weird; it wasn't just the front desk clerk, who would ask registering guests whether they wanted a room on the "shelling side" of the hotel, which faced East Beirut, or the peaceful side of the hotel, which faced the sea; it wasn't the way they "laundered" your hotel bills by putting all your bar charges down as "dry cleaning"; it wasn't even the sign in the lobby during the summer of '82 which read: "In case of shooting around the hotel, the management insists that neither television cameramen nor photographers attempt to take pictures. This endangers not only their lives but those of the guests and the staff. Those who are not prepared to cooperate may check out of this hotel." It was the whole insane atmosphere, an atmosphere that was neatly captured by the cartoonist Garry Trudeau in a series of *Doonesbury* strips he did about the Commodore during the summer of '82. My favorite shows his character, television newsman Roland Burton Hedley, Jr., calling down to the front desk from his Commodore room.

"Any messages for me?" Hedley asks the desk clerk.

"Let's see . . ." says the clerk. "Yes, a couple more death threats. Shall I put them in your box?"

"Yeah, look," says Hedley, "if they call again, tell them I only work for cable."

You did not stay in the Commodore for the quality of its rooms. The only thing that came with your room at the Commodore was a 16 percent service charge, and whatever you found in the blue-and-gold shag rugs. The lobby consisted of overstuffed couches, a bar, a would-be disco with a tin-sounding organ, and enough bimbos to stock a whorehouse. There was also a Chinese restaurant and an old dining room, where the service was always bad and the food even worse. When the Shiites took over West Beirut in 1984 and imposed a more fundamentalist regime, the Commodore management was forced to close the bar in the lobby and to open up what became known as the Ramadan Room on the seventh floor. (Ramadan is the Muslim holy month of fasting.) Hotel guests would knock on the Ramadan Room door with all the caution of entering a speakeasy during Prohibition. Yunis, the bartender, would peek out to make sure it wasn't some mullah come to break his bottles, and then let you in. Inside, guests would be sitting in the dark, sipping drinks on the couch, while Fuad, the hotel manager, would be shuffling back and forth uttering his favorite expression: "No problem, no problem."

If you got tired of visiting the battlefront, all you had to do was sit in the Commodore lobby and wait for the front to visit you. One quiet Saturday night in 1984, a large number of journalists were gathered around the bar, getting loose after a day in the field. Yunis was keeping the booze flowing, when suddenly shots rang out from the lobby. The journalists all ducked behind the bar while a band of Druse gunmen poured into the hotel from the front door and kitchen, chasing after a certain gentleman who was apparently cutting in on their drug business. They found him in the lobby and tried to drag him out, but he, knowing what was in store for him, wrapped his arms around the leg of a couch. In order to encourage him to let go, the Druse pistol-whipped him and then pumped some lead into his thigh. Just as this scene was unfolding, my friend David Zucchino happened to come out of the elevator.

"All you saw in the lobby was this poor guy holding on to the couch for dear life, while the gunmen were trying to drag him away; and over at the bar all these little eyes of journalists were peering out from behind the stools," Zucchino recalled. "At the front desk, two gunmen were beating the clerk, who was trying to call Amal for help. But what I remember most was that CBS correspondent Larry Pintak's Dalmatian, which he used to keep tied up to the AP machine in the lobby, got so excited by all the shooting that he broke his leash and started lapping up this guy's blood on the lobby floor. It was disgusting! The gunmen finally left and this guy let go of the couch, got up, and sat on a bar stool in shock. Fuad immediately showed up and pronounced, 'No problem, no problem.' "

Why did any sane journalist stay at the Commodore? To begin with, most deluxe hotels in West Beirut had been destroyed during the early years of the Lebanese civil war. But more important, the Commodore's owner, a Palestinian Christian by the name of Yousef Nazzal, who bought this fleabag in 1970 from a pair of Lebanese brothers who needed some fast cash to pay off their gambling debts before their arms were broken, was a genius at catering to journalists. He understood that there is only one thing journalists appreciate more than luxury and that is functioning communications equipment with which to file their stories or television spots. By paying enormous bribes, Yousef managed to maintain live international telex and telephone lines into his hotel, no matter how bad the combat became. In the summer of '82, he once paid someone to slip into the central post office, unplug Prime Minister Shafik al-Wazzan's telex, and plug the Commodore's in its place. Yousef never took politics or life too seriously. He loved to sit on the stiff blue couch in the lobby right around deadline time and listen to the hum of all the telexes going at once—at a rate of about $25 a minute. He would sneak up behind me and say, "Tom, my boy, some people make a living, other people make a killing."

The other important attribute of the Commodore was that it filled the void left by the defunct Lebanese Ministry of Information. For a "small consideration," also known as baksheesh, also known as a bribe, the Commodore would get you a visa at the airport, a work permit, a residence permit, a press card, a quickie divorce, or a marriage certificate. Hell, they would get you a bar mitzvah, if you wanted it. As long as you had money, you could buy anything at the Commodore. No money, see you later.

Pro-Israeli press critics used to complain that the Commodore was a "PLO hotel." There is no denying that many a Palestinian spokesman hung out there, but when the Israeli army invaded West Beirut, more than a few Israeli officers dined in the Commodore's restaurant and used it to contact reporters—the exact way the PLO had. The Commodore lived by the motto: The king is dead, long live the king. I would not be surprised if today a poster of Ayatollah Khomeini is hanging over the reception desk.

Every serious Beirut militia, whether Christian or Muslim, Palestinian or Lebanese, had a spokesman and a few assistants. The militia spokesmen were the real gatekeepers for Beirut reporters and we all knew it. If you wanted an interview with the big boss, you needed to stay on his spokesman's good side. Some of the spokesmen developed a reputation for honesty and integrity, and as a reporter you would be willing to give great weight to the information they passed on. Others were liars of the first order; you had to double- and triple-check anything they told you. They also were not above accepting a little baksheesh themselves, as in the case of one guerrilla spokesman who asked a group of reporters to buy him a refrigerator as a wedding present.

The most sought-after spokesman was the PLO's Mahmoud Labadi, whom I've described above. During the summer of '82, Labadi could often be found outside his office, sitting like a vacationing tourist in a lawn chair on the sidewalk of his deserted street filled with a sea of debris, broken windows, shrapnel, brass bullet cases, and dirt berms. Visiting journalists would pull up stools and get a briefing, after which they might check the latest additions to Labadi's sidewalk museum, which was made up of all the different kinds of bombs and shells the Israeli army had dropped on the PLO and West Beirut. It was a bizarre display of ordnance, which included several unexploded cluster bomblets (roughly the size of baseballs) that were kept inside a captured Israeli helmet. One afternoon the UPI bureau chief in Beirut, Vinnie Schodolski, a fine reporter with pretensions to being a juggler, showed up at Labadi's office to get his press credentials renewed. On his way in he picked up a couple of these cluster bomblets from the helmet, not knowing that they were still live, and began juggling them, walking at the same time into Labadi's office. Labadi happened to be sitting at his telex when Vinnie strolled in performing his act. Labadi looked up from the telex, saw Vinnie with the cluster bomblets in his hand and in the air, and became, in a rare instance, tongue-tied. Vinnie recalled later that Labadi's only word was "Yipes."

The PLO spokesman's office in Beirut has often been depicted by the Israelis as a slick Madison Avenue public-relations machine. It was anything but that. One tended to cover the PLO more in spite of Labadi's office than because of it. The PLO never had any conception of deadlines or the time differences between Beirut and New York. Arafat's idea of a press conference was to call in reporters late Saturday night, just in time to miss the Sunday paper's early deadline, so that whatever he said would not get printed until Monday morning. It was not for nothing that reporters in Beirut often felt the PLO's information office worked on the famous Arabic IBM principle: Will Arafat be here today? *Inshallah*,—God willing, they would say. And if not today, then when? *Bukra*,—tomorrow, they would answer. And if not tomorrow, well, *Maalesh*,—never mind. *Inshallah, Bukra, Maalesh*—IBM.

I rarely relied on the PLO spokesman's office for real news, but turned instead to the spokesmen for the smaller PLO factions such as Nayef Hawatmeh's Marxist Democratic Front for the Liberation of Palestine and George Habash's Popular Front. The DFLP and PFLP had many of the most interesting, best-educated, and intelligent people in the PLO working for them, some of them European-trained Marxists. Because they were part of the PLO, they were always well-informed about what was happening, but because their organizations were smaller and less bureaucratic, they were much more willing to share inside information. Indeed, one of my lasting memories of the summer of '82 was going to the Democratic Front office in West Beirut shortly after dusk on many nights to speak with their information chief, Jameel Hillal, who had a Ph.D. in political theory from the University of London. I usually found him sitting at his desk reading by a gas lamp and listening over and over again to a tape of Pachelbel's "Canon," with the sound of real cannon fire in the background. I became so addicted to this recording that at the end of the Israeli siege one of the first things I did was go into a music shop in London and buy a cassette for myself.

Naturally, no self-respecting reporter took just what the spokesmen said as God's truth. We were hardly under any illusions about the objectivity of their information. They were one source among many. Sometimes, of course, they tried to convey the image of knowing more than they did. Several times when I worked with UPI in Beirut, we had to contact the PLO office and get a reaction, or claim of responsibility, for some guerrilla raid against an Israeli target. We would call up the PLO office and ask, "Do you claim responsibility for the attack on the bus in Jerusalem?" Frequently, the voice would come back: "What attack? There was an attack? Let me check; call back in an hour." In an hour we would call back and be told that the "brave strugglers of the Muhammad Ali battalion" were responsible for such and such a raid. Occasionally, more than one group would claim responsibility for the same attack. Wire-service reporters in Beirut got so used to calling up the PLO for a reaction to this or that incident that when the actor John Wayne died, Ned Temko, then a reporter with UPI, could not resist calling up Labadi and seeking his response.

Just for the record, Labadi said that he did not like John Wayne and he did not like cowboy movies, and if he wanted to see cowboys in Beirut all he had to do was look out his window.

Gathering the news in Beirut was one thing—getting it all out was another. No discussion about the reality of Beirut reporting would be complete without mentioning a major reporting constraint journalists there faced: physical intimidation. Reporters, whether they are in Beirut or Washington, don't operate in a political vacuum. In order to do objective reporting a journalist has to negotiate with his environment. On the one hand, he has to develop access and intimacy with his subjects in order to gain real understanding of them, and on the other hand, he has to remain disinterested and distant enough from his subjects to make critical assessments of them. It is a delicate balancing act, but one that is essential to objective reporting. A reporter cannot possibly be fair and objective about a person or group if he doesn't truly understand them, but he also cannot be fair if he understands them alone. Intimacy without disinterest lapses into commitment to one side or another; disinterest without intimacy lapses into banality and misunderstanding. Maintaining this balance between intimacy and disinterest is a challenge for a reporter at any time, but trying to do it in a place such as Beirut was unusually difficult because you were living amid one side in a multisided conflict,

and that side, as well as all the others, was not above doing
physical harm to anyone who was too critical of them or too
understanding of their enemies.

There wasn't a single reporter in West Beirut who did not feel
intimidated, constrained, or worried at one time or another about
something he had learned, considered writing, or had written
involving the Syrians, the PLO, the Phalangists, or any of the
other forty-odd militias in Lebanon. Every reporter in Beirut was
fully aware that for $1.98 and ten Green Stamps anyone could
have you killed. Your newspaper would name a scholarship after
you, and that would be the end of it. Any reporter who tells you
he wasn't intimidated or affected by this environment is either
crazy or a liar. As my colleague John Kifner once wrote, reporters
in Beirut carried fear with them just like their notebooks and
pens.

The biggest threat in my mind was from the Syrians and the
extreme pro-Syrian Palestinian groups. The Syrians did not take
a joke well at all, and during a period in the late 1970s and early
1980s their agents in Beirut shot several Arab and Western journalists, including Salim al-Lawzi, the editor of the popular Arabic
weekly called *Events*, who, in March 1980, was abducted in Beirut
and found a short time later with a bullet in his head and his
writing hand mutilated from having been dipped in acid. The
situation got so bad that many Lebanese were afraid to even
mention the word "Syria" in public.

There was a joke that made the rounds during this period about
a Lebanese man who ran up to a policeman and said, "Officer,
Officer, a Swiss stole my Syrian watch."

The policeman gave him a quizzical look and said, "What do
you mean, a Swiss stole your Syrian watch? You mean a Syrian
stole your Swiss watch."

The Lebanese man looked at the policeman and smiled. "You
said it, Officer, not me."

The main PLO factions, the Phalangists, and the various Muslim militias were less direct, and much less touchy, than the Syrians, but no one had any illusions that they would tolerate much
seriously critical reporting. The biggest Sunni Muslim militia in
West Beirut was known as the Murabitoon. It was really more
of a street gang with a patina of Nasserite ideology than a political

party, but it took itself very seriously and had one of the most sophisticated public-relations offices in the heyday of the militia rule of West Beirut. The Murabitoon's efforts to cast their mafia-like leader, Ibrahim Koleilat, as a serious statesman were often richly comical, given the fact that he was little more than a thug. Nonetheless, Koleilat had a beautiful young woman working for him who handled his public relations. She came around to the UPI office one day in 1980, when I was still working for the wire service, and said to me, "Of course your Rome bureau will be covering Mr. Koleilat's upcoming visit to Italy," where he was scheduled to meet some low-ranking official on the Lebanon desk in the Italian Foreign Ministry.

"Why, ahhhh, of course our bureau in Rome will definitely be covering the visit," I stammered.

As soon as she left, I sent a message to our Rome bureau asking them to please write a dummy story about Koleilat's meanderings in Rome, unless they wanted me to end up in the Mediterranean sleeping with the fish. Sure enough, Koleilat's visit came, and the Rome bureau wrote up a story, only instead of putting it out on the general news wire read by all the newspapers, they sent it to us on a secondary message wire, read only by our bureau, since there was no way we could put such nonsense on the actual news wire. Koleilat's people did not know this, of course, and when they came around to the bureau to collect the story, as we knew they would, we presented them with an authentic-looking UPI news story just ripped off the wire. They immediately made photocopies of it and distributed them to every newspaper in West Beirut, while making each an offer they couldn't refuse to publish it. This dummy story about Koleilat appeared the next morning in almost every Beirut paper. The Murabitoon were happy, and we were off the hook. But the matter did not end there.

At Christmastime that year the young woman came back to our office carrying a very large round package wrapped in gold paper. She walked in the door, asked for me, and said, "Mr. Koleilat wants you to have this." The first thing I did was check to see if it was ticking. My Lebanese colleague David Zenian and I then went through a comic routine of "You open it . . . No, you open it . . . No, you open it." Finally, I pulled rank on him and he gingerly unwrapped the package, only to find a cut-glass

bowl filled with chocolates, courtesy of the Murabitoon. We were
so relieved that the thing did not blow up that we barely noticed
the chocolates were at least a year old.

My having said that Beirut was intimidating, though, does not
mean that reporters there were intimidated into total silence.
Certain press critics have taken the line that the West Beirut press
corps was intimidated by the Syrians and the PLO, hence the
reporters did not write the truth, hence the truth did not get out,
and hence Israel's image in the world was skewed.

The truth is that while most Beirut-based journalists were
keenly aware of the intimidating atmosphere at all times, their
reaction was not to simply fold up their typewriters on sensitive
subjects but, rather, to try to find another way, maybe indirect,
to get the news out. The reason the Syrians, or others, had to go
to the length of shooting reporters was precisely because all their
other levels of threats and intimidation failed to dissuade newsmen and women from writing negatively about them. I cannot
recall a single case in which reporters in Beirut knew about a
major news event and consciously covered it up because of intimidation—including for that matter the fact that journalists were
being harassed.

Reporters in Beirut found novel ways to negotiate the space
needed to learn and write the truth, while at the same time protecting ourselves. Sometimes we ran pieces without a byline, as
in the stories about how the Syrians were shooting journalists.
Sometimes to hide where we were we ran stories under a New
York or Cyprus dateline. Sometimes we quoted the local militia
radio stations on sensitive stories which we knew to be true ourselves but did not want to be the first to report. And many times
we simply wrote things that were critical of the PLO, Syrians, or
Phalangists and just hoped that they were not played back in the
Arabic press or seen by those who might take offense. Was it all
the news all the time? No. Was it an ideal situation? No. Was it
a cover-up? Also, no.

While I insist that the intimidating atmosphere of Beirut never
prevented a major breaking news story from being covered in
some way, there were, however, some slightly less immediate—
yet important—stories which were deliberately ignored out of
fear. Here I will be the first to say "*mea culpa.*" How many serious
stories were written from Beirut about the well-known corruption

in the PLO leadership, the misuse of funds, and the way in which the organization had become as much a corporation full of bureaucratic hacks as a guerrilla outfit? These traits were precisely the causes of the rebellion against Arafat after the summer of '82, but it would be hard to find any hint of them in Beirut reporting before the Israeli invasion. The truth is, the Western press coddled the PLO and never judged it with anywhere near the scrutiny that it judged Israeli, Phalangist, or American behavior. For any Beirut-based correspondent, the name of the game was keeping on good terms with the PLO, because without it you would not get the interview with Arafat you wanted when your foreign editor came to town. The overfocusing by reporters on the PLO and its perception of events also led them to ignore the Lebanese Shiites and their simmering wrath at the Palestinians for turning their villages in south Lebanon into battlefields.

As for the Arab critics, who never tire of complaining about how the Western media were just "Zionist agents," I have only two things to say. When my own editors took out the word "indiscriminate" from a story of mine about Israeli shelling of Beirut on August 4, 1982, I protested in writing with enough force to almost get me fired. At the time, my editors felt the word "indiscriminate" was "editorializing"; I felt that it was an exact description of the day's events, and that its omission was editorializing. I still feel that way. In the end, though, I wasn't fired, and in retrospect that was the only word ever changed for editorial reasons from any story I wrote out of Beirut. Moreover, during the summer of '82 when the Israelis were pummeling West Beirut, and the Palestinian cause was on the line, it should be noted that the first journalists to run out of town were the Arabs: the Kuwaiti, Saudi, Qatari, and other Arab journalists were nowhere to be found at the height of the Israeli siege. It was only the "Zionist Western media" that stuck around in West Beirut to tell the story, and it was the "Zionist" *New York Times* that ran a four-page reconstruction of the massacre at Sabra and Shatila—more extensive than any other newspaper in the world.

Some might ask why in the world anyone would put up with reporting from a place like Beirut, especially for almost five years. The truth is, I asked myself that question many times, especially when my colleagues began to be kidnapped. The first to be snatched, while walking to work, on March 7, 1984, was Jeremy Levín of Cable News Network, who lived in our apartment building just two floors above us. Levin had had a somewhat stormy relationship with the CNN bureau in Beirut, largely because he came in and tried to clean house and post work rules in what was a typical Beirut news bureau, where the local staff were all relatives and bookkeeping was "creative," to say the least. It was a bit like posting work rules in Sodom and Gomorrah, so when Levin was abducted in the spring of 1984 my first thought was that one of the Lebanese in his own bureau might have arranged a pair of cement boots for him. The day Levin disappeared, CNN sent a two-man film crew over to our apartment house to take one of those clichéd close-up shots of the mailbox with his name on it. I asked the film crew if their bureau had abducted him. They just laughed and laughed.

It later turned out that Levin had been kidnapped by Shiite extremists, and fortunately, he escaped after eleven months in captivity.

Levin's kidnapping, and the dozens that would follow, taught me a valuable lesson about journalism that one could learn only in a place like Beirut—to pay attention to the silence. In a city where there are so many spokesmen, so many militia radio stations, and so many people who want to come up and tell you their story, you can think after you have been there for a while that you know everyone, and everyone knows you. When ABC Television newsman Charles Glass was kidnapped on June 17, 1987, the first thing many of his friends said in defending the fact that he dared to continue working in Beirut was that "Charlie knew everybody." The truth was, Glass knew everybody who talked to journalists. But the people who kidnapped the Americans in Beirut, who blew up the American embassy and the Marine compound, who abducted the British hostage negotiator Terry Waite, didn't go around introducing themselves or drinking at the Backstreet Bar. They were the type who kidnapped or killed, and then, instead of running out to brag about it to journalists, savored it quietly at home over a Turkish coffee. They were the young men I passed on the street who did not speak my language or travel in my circles.

After the kidnappings began in Beirut, I acquired a healthy

respect for how little I had really penetrated the place. I gained an equally healthy respect for the notion that the real story is often found not in the noise but in the silence—and that is why it is so often missed. I now live by an adaptation of Groucho Marx's famous line that any club that would have me as a member I wouldn't want to join. My version is that any protagonist in the Middle East who is ready to talk to me cannot be worth talking to; he cannot be at the center of what is happening. It's the people who won't talk to me whom I really want to meet.

4

Hama Rules

An unceasing sound, like the creaking of a bullock cart, rises
from the river banks to permeate the narrow streets and pervade
the whole town—it is audible even as far away as the citadel.
This is the noise made by the waterwheels of Hama—a "cry"
almost, like the muezzin's call to prayer, harsh, plangent and
timeless.

> —From the chapter on the
> town of Hama in the 1977 guidebook
> SYRIA TODAY, by Jean Hureau

I found plenty of silence to contemplate in Hama, because by the
time I got there the waterwheels were broken. The muezzin's
voice was deathly still, and the only cries anyone heard permeating
the narrow streets came from the widows and orphans who had
survived the massacre.

Even when I arrived, some two months after the mass killings,
all the blood had not been washed away into the Orontes River,
which snaked through the town, forming a distinct signature that
once made Hama Syria's most beautiful city. Walking through
the nearly deserted streets, my notepad hidden in my back pocket
so no one would know I was a journalist, I was too shocked at
first to talk to anyone. I did not need to, though, since I found
whole neighborhoods of crushed apartment buildings bearing silent witness to the remarkable events that transpired here in the
first weeks of February 1982. The whole town looked as though
a tornado had swept back and forth over it for a week—but this
was not the work of Mother Nature.

To this day, no one knows for sure how many bodies were

buried under the sea of broken homes and layers of concrete, but Amnesty International, in its November 1983 report on Syria, said estimates ranged from 10,000 to 25,000 dead, mostly civilians; thousands more were left homeless. The Syrian regime of President Hafez al-Assad, which was responsible for carrying out the massacre, did little to dispute these figures or to tidy up Hama before reopening the main highway that ran through it from Damascus in May 1982. I am convinced that Assad wanted the Syrian people to see Hama raw, to listen closely to its silence and reflect on its pain.

That was how I was able to get in. I had arrived in Beirut a few weeks earlier to begin my tour there as the correspondent for *The New York Times*, and I had some time to explore. I wanted to know exactly what had happened in Hama. After all, it wasn't often that an Arab government destroyed one of its largest cities. Most textbooks on Middle East politics tend to ignore incidents such as Hama; they either dismiss them as aberrations or sanitize them in political-science jargon, saying, for instance, that "the system overloaded" or "there was a crisis of legitimacy." I wanted to try to understand whether Hama's destruction was an aberration, a one-time-only affair, or whether it could be traced to some more permanent features in the political landscape. I was to learn many useful lessons in Hama—lessons that would come in very handy in helping me navigate the road from Beirut to Jerusalem.

A city of about 180,000 inhabitants located 120 miles northwest of Damascus on the central Syrian plains, Hama has always been a Sunni Muslim town known for its piety. Many of its women kept their faces covered with veils, while many of its menfolk preferred the traditional *gandura* robe to Western suits and ties. Throughout modern Syrian history, Hama has been a hothouse for conservative Muslim fundamentalist organizations hostile to the secular central governments in Damascus. Not surprisingly, it became a constant source of irritation for Hafez Assad after he, as the Defense Minister, seized power in a coup d'état on November 16, 1970. Assad hailed from the village of Qardaha, near the Syrian seaport of Latakia, and he and his main allies were not Sunni Muslims but Alawites. The Alawites, a splinter sect of Islam with many secret and even Christian-like tenets, have lived for centuries in the isolated mountain villages of northern Lebanon and Syria. Alawites make up roughly 10–12 percent of the Syrian population of 11–12 million. However, owing to their tightly bound tribe-like solidarity, they have managed since the late 1960s to dominate the Syrian army and, through it, key power centers in the state and the ruling secular Baath Party. This has left Syria's Sunni Muslims, who make up about 70 percent of the country's population, in eclipse and frequently frustrated: the more religious elements among them viewed the Alawites as Muslim heretics or secular radicals, while the traditional Sunni landed aristocracy viewed them as mountain peasants totally unworthy of ruling Damascus.

Not long after Assad took power, the Muslim Brotherhood, a loosely knit underground coalition of Sunni Muslim fundamentalist guerrilla groups, which had existed on and off in Syria since the late 1930s, began working to topple the predominantly Alawite Assad regime through a ruthless campaign of assassinations and bombings. The Brotherhood drew its leadership from local Muslim clerics, or *ulama*, and its rank and file from the young urban poor and Sunni middle classes, who were either alienated from, or economically hurt by, the Westernization, secularization, and modernization of Syrian society being directed by Assad. By 1979–80, barely a week went by in Syria without a bomb going off outside a government institution or Soviet Aeroflot office, and brazen daylight shootings of Soviet advisers and Baath Party officials became almost routine; even President Assad's personal interpreter was abducted. Assad was usually referred to in Brotherhood literature as either "an enemy of Allah" or a "Maronite." The Assad regime countered with a state of emergency and selective assassinations and kidnappings of its own, particularly of prominent mosque preachers. It also distributed arms to Baath Party loyalists to help the regime liquidate the Muslim urban guerrillas. Civil war seemed to be inevitable.

The Brotherhood was aided at times by Muslim trade unions and other fraternal associations in Aleppo and Hama, who were estranged from the regime owing to its pervasive corruption, economic mismanagement, and abridgment of civil liberties. In early 1980, a coalition of clerics and trade unionists centered in Hama issued a manifesto demanding, among other things, that President

Assad honor the Human Rights Charter, abolish the state of emergency, and hold free elections. The petition was circulated through mosques and backed by a call for a general strike against the "infidel" government—in Syrian terms a declaration of war. This was not lost on the regime. Patrick Seale, in his authoritative biography of Assad,* with which the President himself cooperated, notes that at the Baath Party congress held in late 1979 and early 1980 President Assad's aggressive younger brother Rifaat called for an all-out war against the Muslim Brotherhood. (Rifaat commanded the Saraya al-Difa', the "Defense Companies"—an elite, heavily armed Praetorian guard, dominated by Alawites, whose sole responsibility was protecting the Assad regime from its domestic opponents.)

Stalin had sacrificed 10 million to preserve the Bolshevik revolution and Syria should be prepared to do likewise, Seale quoted Rifaat as telling the Baath gathering. Rifaat, Seale added, "pledged his readiness to fight 'a hundred wars, demolish a million strongholds, and sacrifice a million martyrs' " in order to defeat the Muslim Brothers. No, this was not a battle for the faint of heart. On June 26, 1980, Muslim Brotherhood assassins threw two hand grenades and loosed a burst of machine-gun fire at President Assad as he was waiting to welcome the visiting chief of state from Mali to the official visitors' palace in Damascus. Assad managed to escape with only a foot injury, thanks to the fact that his bodyguard smothered one of the grenades and he himself kicked the other away. His retribution was not long in coming, though. At 3:00 the next morning, June 27, some eighty members of Rifaat's Defense Companies were dispatched to Tadmur (Palmyra) Prison, which housed hundreds of Muslim Brothers arrested the previous year. According to Amnesty International, the soldiers "were divided into groups of 10 and, once inside the prison, were ordered to kill the prisoners in their cells and dormitories. Some 600 to 1,000 prisoners are reported to have been killed. . . . After the massacre, the bodies were removed and buried in a large common grave outside the prison."

Throughout the next year, surprise searches of Hama, Aleppo, and other Muslim Brotherhood strongholds became a weekly event. During these roundups, curbside executions were regularly

---

* *Asad: The Struggle for the Middle East* (University of California Press, 1988).

carried out against youths suspected of involvement with the Islamic underground. More than once Hamawis awoke to find a
sidewalk or a central square littered with bullet-riddled bodies.
Some more elderly Muslim clerics had half of their mustaches
shaved off, their beards burned, or were forced to dance in the
streets while wishing President Assad "long life," the Muslim
Brotherhood claimed. That was mild, though, compared to the
treatment meted out to those who had the misfortune to be sent
to government jails, where, as one arrested student from Aleppo
told Amnesty International, prisoners were introduced to "al-
'Abd al-Aswad,"—the Black Slave.

"Whenever a person is tortured," the student testified to Amnesty, "he is ordered to strip naked. Inside the room there is an
electric apparatus, a Russian tool for ripping out fingernails, pin-
cers and scissors for plucking flesh and an apparatus called the
Black Slave, on which they force the torture victim to sit. When
switched on, a very hot and sharp metal skewer enters the rear,
burning its way until it reaches the intestines, then returns only
to be reinserted."

The Muslim Brothers responded in kind. On November 29,
1981, Muslim guerrillas were accused by the Assad regime of
responsibility for the car bomb that exploded in the heart of
Damascus, killing 64 innocent bystanders and wounding 135. Two
months later, only a few weeks before the Hama massacre, Assad
discovered a Muslim Brotherhood–inspired plot in the air force
aimed at toppling his Alawite-led government. During their interrogation of the Syrian air-force officers implicated in the plot,
the Syrian intelligence agency, known as the Mukhabarat—the
mere mention of which sends a chill down the spine of every
Syrian—apparently obtained information linking the plotters to
the Muslim Brotherhood.

In February 1982, President Assad decided to end his Hama
problem once and for all. With his sad eyes and ironic grin, Assad
always looked to me like a man who had long ago been stripped
of any illusions about human nature. Since fully taking power in
1970, he has managed to rule Syria longer than any man in the
post–World War II era. He has done so by always playing by his
own rules. His own rules, I discovered, were Hama Rules.

*   *   *

Exact details of what happened in that February of 1982 are, to this day, incomplete. No reporters were allowed to enter Hama during the massacre. Most of the survivors were scattered or intimidated into silence; the Assad government refuses to talk about what transpired. What follows is a picture pieced together from five sources: Western diplomats in Damascus, my own visit to Hama, Amnesty International's report on the massacre, an analysis, based in part on Israeli intelligence, published by Israel Television's Arab affairs reporter Ehud Ya'ari (*Monitin* magazine, August 1985), and a book called *Hama: The Tragedy of Our Time*, published in 1984 in Cairo by the Egyptian Muslim Brotherhood publishing house, Dar al-I'tisam. This book—the cover of which features Hafez Assad with his hand dipped in blood and a smoldering city in the background—is the Brotherhood's own account in Arabic of what transpired. It is certainly the most detailed picture of the Hama massacre ever published, and, while obviously written from the Muslim Brothers' perspective, is quite sober.

According to Western diplomats in Damascus, President Assad entrusted overall responsibility for taming Hama to Rifaat, whose first move, according to Ya'ari, was to quietly infiltrate roughly 1,500 men from the Defense Companies into buildings in Hama, including a stadium, a school for activists from the Baath Party, and a cultural institute. At the same time, another 1,500 commandos attached to Colonel Ali Haydar's Special Forces erected a tent camp near a dam at the outskirts of Hama and dug out a landing pad for helicopters, which would be used later. Additional intelligence units and elements of the 47th Independent Armored Brigade, commanded by Alawite Colonel Nadim Abbas, with its T-62 tanks, were also stationed in and around the town.

Tuesday, February 2, 1:00 a.m., was set as the time for the "clean-up" of Hama to commence.

They say that it was a cold, drizzly winter night, the kind that you often find in Beirut or Jerusalem, where the combination of wind and rain leaves you chilled to the bone and wishing you never had stepped outside. The residents of Hama were shut inside their homes, most of which were warmed by oil-burning stoves or steam radiators. The operation began with some 500 soldiers from Rifaat's Defense Companies, along with a large contingent of Mukhabarat agents, surrounding the old Barudi neighborhood on the western bank of the Orontes River, where the most religious Hamawis lived in a beehive of narrow alleyways and arch-covered roads. The more modern eastern bank of the Orontes housed the main souk and government-built apartments for state employees, and had always been less troublesome.

As they entered the Barudi district, the Syrian officers apparently carried with them lists with the names and addresses of suspected hideouts and arms caches of the Muslim rebels. They did not get past the first name. According to Western diplomats in Damascus, the Muslim Brothers residing in Barudi had been tipped off that the regime was about to strike and had placed lookouts on several rooftops in the neighborhood. As the Syrian soldiers walked deeper and deeper into the web of alleyways, an alarm was sounded and the Muslim Brothers mowed them down with a fusillade of machine-gun fire, punctuated by shouts of "Allahu Akbar," God is greater [than the enemy]. Another group set up a barricade on the bridge leading from the western bank to the eastern bank of the Orontes to help cut off reinforcements. Defense Companies in the adjacent neighborhood were also attacked, and by dawn the Syrian troops were all forced to retreat, carrying their dead.

Word was quickly spread through the microphones atop mosque minarets that Barudi had held its ground and that Hama was being "liberated." The Assad regime had stumbled. The Muslim Brotherhood thought now was the moment to move in for the kill. The call for "Jihad"—Holy War against Assad and his Baath Party—echoed across Hama.

As dawn broke on February 2, thousands of additional government troops were rushed to Hama, and the 47th Armored Brigade was ordered to move from the outskirts into the city. Later the same morning, the Muslim Brotherhood commander, Sheik Adib al-Kaylani, called on his men to come up from the underground, to pull out their guns from under their beds and their secret hiding places, and to drive the "infidel" Assad regime from Hama and right out of power, according to the Brotherhood account. Al-Kaylani apparently hoped to spark a national rebellion. He told his men that it was better to die a martyr on the "altar of Islam" than await imprisonment, torture, and certain execution. For the first time since the conflict between the Muslim Brotherhood and the Assad regime began, there was to be a face-to-face battle in the light of day. Both sides understood that it was winner take all.

The Muslim Brotherhood, with the help of many secular neighborhood youths who had been alienated from the regime as a result of previous crackdowns on Hama, actually seized the initiative, attacking Defense Brigades positions around town and setting up their own roadblocks made of boulders and garbage. From the mosque microphones they blared the same message over and over: "Rise up and drive the unbelievers from Hama." Then they started their own little massacre. According to Western diplomats in Damascus, squads of Muslim Brothers ran through the city streets, ransacking the local armory and police stations, and then bursting into the homes of leading Baath Party officials. At least fifty local government and party functionaries were either machine-gunned in their beds and living rooms or stabbed to death by many hands. Mukhabarat agents who had the misfortune of driving through the wrong neighborhoods were dragged out of their cars or jeeps and murdered at roadside by roving bands of youths.

The army called in more reinforcements, particularly tanks, to burst through the rebel roadblocks and helicopters to alert soldiers from the air where the Muslim Brotherhood ambushes were being laid. Other units were ordered to cut all telephone and telegraph links between Hama and the rest of humanity, and then to secure the main roads bisecting the city, thereby isolating the Brotherhood cells in their respective neighborhoods.

The next morning, February 3, the government tanks tried to penetrate the winding streets and alleyways of the Brotherhood-held neighborhoods. Operating in the middle of a city and at very close quarters, the Syrian tanks initially were allowed to use only the heavy machine guns mounted on their turrets, but the Brotherhood strike teams proved quite effective in neutralizing them with a combination of rocket-propelled grenades and Molotov cocktails. That night Rifaat apparently decided that only overwhelming armored force would crush the rebellion. He called for the 21st Mechanized Brigade to join the battle for Hama. All the officers and soldiers in the 21st who were from Hama were transferred out, before the unit commander, Fouad Ismail, an Alawite, led the advance into the town along Said ibn al-A'as Street.

According to the Brotherhood, some twenty tanks started rumbling down the street on February 4, firing indiscriminately with their cannons at the barricades blocking the way and the homes overlooking the road. A multistory building went up in flames; the large mosque at the center of the street collapsed under the barrage. In a few hours, most of the buildings along the barricaded part of the street were destroyed. From then on, Rifaat's tactic shifted from trying to ferret out nests of Muslim Brotherhood men to simply bringing whole neighborhoods down on their heads and burying the Brotherhood and anyone else in the way. In addition to using tanks and attack helicopters for this purpose, the Syrian army units surrounding Hama engaged in direct artillery bombardments of the Barudi, Kaylani, Hadra, and Khamidia neighborhoods, where the Brotherhood was known to be at its strongest. The Brotherhood claims that it intercepted a radio transmission from Rifaat to one of his officers in which he allegedly decreed, "I don't want to see a single house not burning."

Judging from what I saw in the aftermath, Rifaat was not disappointed. Virtually every building in Hama was damaged in some way. Hama's most famous archaeological site, the 1,200-year-old Kaylani family palaces on the banks of the Orontes, were ravaged. Virtually every mosque had its minaret blown down, which wasn't surprising considering that the Muslim Brothers had used them as sniper's nests. Yet, despite these severe tactics, between February 7 and February 17, the Brotherhood succeeded in keeping control of many of the older neighborhoods on the western half of the river. With their commander, Sheik al-Kaylani, moving from position to position to encourage his fighters and to read with them from the Koran, the Brotherhood repeatedly repulsed Syrian commando teams which tried to penetrate their densely populated districts.

On the east bank, which the Muslim Brotherhood was forced to abandon, the Syrian army looted what was left of those homes in each neighborhood they "pacified," the Brotherhood said. Long convoys of trucks loaded down with furniture were reported to have been spotted driving away, and the Brotherhood claims to have killed a Syrian officer who was found with 3.5 million Syrian pounds on his body (then the equivalent of about $1 million). Entire families were apparently rousted out of their homes and gunned down on the streets, simply because a single member was listed by Syrian intelligence as being linked to the Brotherhood. Those civilians who could tried to escape through underground sewers or bribe their way through the ring of steel the Syrian army had thrown up around Hama, but few were successful.

On February 17, the Muslim Brotherhood's commander, Sheik al-Kaylani, was killed by a mortar blast, but it would take the army another ten days to finally snuff out the last pockets of resistance in the Barudi district. On February 22, the Syrian government broadcast a telegram of support addressed to President Assad from the Hama branch of the Baath Party. The message referred to Muslim Brotherhood fighters killing Baath Party officials and leaving their mutilated bodies in the streets. It added that security forces had taken fierce reprisals against the Brotherhood, "which stopped them breathing forever."

For the next several weeks, there was a settling of accounts between the Assad regime and Syria's fourth-largest city; many more people perished as a result. Most of the casualties in Hama apparently were registered during this phase. Syrian army engineers set about systematically dynamiting any buildings which remained standing in "Brotherhood" neighborhoods, with whoever was inside. Ancient Hama, the marketplace, craft quarters, and mosques, which provided the social fabric for the Muslim Brotherhood to flourish, were totally obliterated. As the army mopped up the city, many of those who had survived or had not fled were brought in for interrogation in makeshift detention camps set up by the Mukhabarat intelligence service. According to the Muslim Brotherhood, something called "Solomon's Chair," which was fitted with iron spikes, was offered to any prisoner who hesitated to talk. Others had their hands welded. The torture and interrogations, according to Ya'ari, were supervised by Colonel Mohammed Nassif, an aide to Rifaat.

Just to make sure that those people who lived in the Muslim Brotherhood districts would be dispersed and forced to find new housing and new jobs at the mercy of the government, Rifaat brought in bulldozers and crushed all those buildings and neighborhoods which had been shelled beyond repair. Then he brought in steamrollers to flatten the rubble like parking lots. According to both Amnesty International and the Muslim Brotherhood, groups of prisoners suspected of anti-government sentiments were taken from detention camps, machine-gunned en masse, and then dumped into pre-dug pits that were covered with earth and left unmarked. Amnesty also quoted allegations that cyanide gas containers were brought into the city, connected by rubber pipes to the entrances of buildings believed to house insurgents, and turned on, killing everyone inside. Virtually the entire Muslim religious leadership in Hama—from sheiks to teachers to mosque caretakers—who survived the battle for the city were liquidated afterward in one fashion or another; most anti-government union leaders suffered the same fate.

From the beginning of the operation on February 2, no reporters were allowed to even approach the city, and the Syrian government refused to give any detailed explanation as to what was happening there. In early March, after the campaign ended, the Syrian authorities gathered religious students from the villages around Hama and brought them in to sweep the streets, to wash off the blood, to gather up the bodies, and to leash the dogs that were taking over the bomb-ravaged neighborhoods, the Brotherhood said.

When I drove into Hama at the end of May, I found three areas of the city that had been totally flattened—each the size of four football fields and covered with the yellowish tint of crushed concrete.

My taxi driver and I rode across one such flattened neighborhood that sloped up from the still verdant bank of the Orontes. We stopped our car right in the middle. For a moment, I felt the same light-headed sensation I used to have as a boy when in winter we would drive our car out to the middle of a frozen lake in Minnesota to go ice fishing; it was that uneasy feeling of standing on top of something you know you shouldn't be on top of. I kicked the ground beneath my feet and uncovered a tennis shoe, a tattered book, and a shred of clothing; elsewhere pieces of wood or the tips of steel reinforcement rods protruded through the dusty surface. The whole neighborhood, with everything in it, had been plowed up like a cornfield in spring and then flattened. As my taxi driver and I rode off, we encountered a stoop-shouldered old man, in checkered headdress and green robe, who was shuffling along this field of death.

"Where are all the houses that once stood here?" we stopped and asked.

"You are driving on them," he said.

"But where are all the people who used to live here?" I said.

"You are probably driving on some of them, too," he mumbled, and then continued to shuffle away.

Yet even Hama Rules have a logic, and I spent much of the next few years trying to figure it out. I think the best way to understand what happened in Hama is to understand that politics in the Middle East is a combination of three different political traditions all operating at the same time.

The first and oldest of these traditions is tribe-like politics. I use the term "tribe-like" to refer to a pre-modern form of political interaction characterized by a harsh, survivalist quality and an adherence to certain intense primordial or kin-group forms of allegiance. Sometimes the tribe-like group that is in power in the Middle East, or is seeking power, is an actual tribe, sometimes it is a clan, members of a religious sect, a village group, a regional group; sometimes it is friends from a certain neighborhood, an army unit, and sometimes it is a combination of these groups. What all these associations have in common is the fact that their members are all bound together by a tribe-like spirit of solidarity, a total obligation to one another, and a mutual loyalty that takes precedence over allegiances to the wider national community or nation-state.

The best way to understand the influence of tribalism on political behavior in the modern Middle East is by looking at the phenomenon in its purest original form among the nomadic Bedouin of the desert. Life in the desert, observed Clinton Bailey, an Israeli expert on the Bedouin of the Sinai and Negev deserts, was always dominated by two overriding facts: first, in the desert, water and grazing resources were so limited that "everyone had to become a wolf and be prepared to survive at the expense of the other tribe. There just weren't enough wells or grass to satisfy everyone all the time. Often it came down to who was going to get the last blade of grass and you had to make sure it was you. This meant that every man was simultaneously hunter and prey."

Second, in the desert there was no outside mediator or government to enforce laws or to adjudicate disputes in a neutral way between tribes when they resorted to predatory behavior in order to survive. Your family, your clan, your tribe were out there searching for grazing space on their own. There was no police car patrolling the desert wadis and canyons, no 911 to call when you were in trouble, so you had to find ways to take care of yourself.

In such a lonely world, the only way to survive was by letting others know that if they violated you in any way, you would make them pay, and pay dearly. You sent that message first and foremost by banding together in alliances. These alliances began with the most basic blood association—the family—and then expanded to the clan, the tribe, and then to other tribes. Every Bedouin understood that because of the nature of his world, the bonds of kinship must be honored before all other obligations; anyone who did not behave in this way was totally dishonored. Hence the Bedouin Arabic proverb: "Me and my brother against our cousin. Me, my brother, and my cousin against the stranger." In Lebanon and Jordan, many rural tribes changed their names to plural forms in order to give the impression that they were larger than they were.

But even this was not enough protection. Sometimes you found yourself in the middle of the desert far away from your core kin group, and the temptation for others to violate you was great. Therefore, you had to make sure that if someone violated you in any way—even the smallest way—you would not only punish them but punish them in a manner that signaled to all the other families, clans, or tribes around that this is what happens to anyone who tampers with me. "Back off" was the credo. "I am my own defense force and I am good."

A tribe could earn this reputation either by using physical violence to badly hurt those who wronged them, or by using the Bedouin system of justice to get all the families, clans, or tribes in the area to impose a heavy fine on the offender. (This approach is by no means confined to desert tribesmen. The symbol of Scotland is the thistle, above the motto: "Nobody hurts me unharmed.") Either way, a family, clan, or tribe's first line of defense was always its known ability to go all the way in exacting a price from those who dared to tread on them.

To be sure, a tribe can make concessions to, or compromises with, their rivals, provided these concessions grow from proven strength or magnanimity in the wake of victory. Egyptian President Anwar Sadat could make his historic visit to Jerusalem in November 1977 only after he had led the Egyptian army across the Suez Canal in the 1973 war—that is, after he had proven to everyone around that he could exact a price on the Israelis and that in going to Jerusalem he was acting out of strength and not weakness. It was no accident that when Sadat returned to Cairo from his visit to Jerusalem and addressed the Egyptian parliament about his reasons for going, he kept referring to his people as *"Ya, Sha'ab October"*—Oh, you people of October—a reference to the Egyptians' victory over Israel in the early stages of the October 1973 war. Only such a victorious people can make compromises. In his speech Sadat used the reference eighteen times.

What you never do in the desert, though, is allow concessions to be arbitrarily imposed on you. If someone steals half your water, you can never say, "Well, this time I will let it go, but don't ever let me catch you doing it again," because in this world of lone wolves, anyone who becomes viewed as a sheep is in trouble—a point underscored by the Bedouin legend about the old man and his turkey. One day, according to this legend, an elderly Bedouin man discovered that by eating turkey he could restore his virility. So he bought himself a turkey and he kept it around the tent, and every day he watched it grow. He stuffed it with food, thinking, Wow, I am really going to be a bull. One day, though, the turkey was stolen. So the Bedouin called his sons together and said, "Boys, we are in great danger now— terrible danger. My turkey's been stolen." The boys laughed and said, "Father, what do you need a turkey for?" He said, "Never mind, never mind. It is not important why I need the turkey, all that is important is that it has been stolen, and we must get it back." But his sons ignored him and forgot about the turkey. A few weeks, later the old man's camel was stolen. His sons came to him and said, "Father, your camel's been stolen, what should we do?" And the old man said, "Find my turkey." A few weeks later, the old man's horse was stolen, and the sons came and said, "Father, your horse was stolen, what should we do?" He said, "Find my turkey." Finally, a few weeks later, someone raped his daughter. The father went to his sons and said, "It is all because of the turkey. When they saw that they could take my turkey, we lost everything."

Hama was Hafez Assad's turkey. Assad understood from the

start that at a certain basic level Hama was a tribe-like clash between his Alawite sect and the Sunni Muslim sect. He equally understood that if the Sunni Muslim Brotherhood was allowed to seize control of even one neighborhood in Hama, then the Alawites' blood would be in the water and all their other opponents in Syria would be feeding on them within days. That is why Assad did not just quell the rebellion. He did not just arrest the rebels. He took revenge—all the way—and with twentieth-century weapons, that revenge was devastating enough to be felt in the gut of every Syrian.

A Lebanese businessman who is a partner in several deals with Rifaat Assad once told a friend of mine about a conversation he had had with the Syrian general about the Hama rebellion.

"I guess you killed 7,000 people there," the businessman said to Rifaat.

Normally a politician would play down such a ghastly incident and say, "Oh no, we didn't kill 7,000. What are you talking about? That's only propaganda from our enemies. We killed only a few hundred troublemakers." But Rifaat knew what he was doing in Hama and, according to my friend, said to this Lebanese businessman, "What are you talking about, 7,000? No, no. We killed 38,000."

Rifaat was apparently proud of the figure, said the Lebanese businessman. If anything, he wanted to inflate it. He understood that in a tribe-like environment such as Syria the game is either do it or it will be done to you, so he did it and he wanted all his enemies and friends to know that he did it. Rifaat understood that in a world of lone wolves it is much safer—as Machiavelli himself taught—to be feared than to be loved. Men grant and withdraw their love according to their whims, but fear is a hand that rests on their shoulders in a way they can never shake.

Hama is hardly the only recent example of such a tribe-like response to a threat against an Arab regime. In March 1988, Iraqi President Saddam Hussein had some problems with Iraqi Kurdish tribesmen in the northeastern part of his country. For years the Kurds had been seeking independence with the help of Iran. Because Saddam was busy fighting a war with Iran when the Kurds began to militate for their own country again, the Iraqi President did not want to deploy a lot of troops to bring them under control. Instead, he simply sent a few planes to drop chemical warheads containing a mixture of mustard and cyanide gases on the northeastern Kurdish town of Halabja and some surrounding villages. According to reporters who visited Halabja in the aftermath, at least several hundred, and probably several thousand, men, women, and children were choked to death or had their lungs burned out by the yellow-and-white gas cloud that descended upon them without any warning. Even the cats died. The chemical attack was said to be one of the biggest uses of poison gas since the Germans virtually wiped out Ypres in 1917 with a similar killer toxic cloud.

The reason one can still find such tribe-like conflicts at work in the Middle East today is that most peoples in this part of the world, including Israeli Jews, have not fully broken from their primordial identities, even though they live in what appear on the surface to be modern nation-states. Their relatively new nation-states are still abstractions in many ways, for reasons which I will explain shortly. That is why Hafez al-Assad, even though he was the President of Syria, could order the killing of 20,000 of his own citizens. Because on some level Assad did not see the Sunni Muslim residents of Hama as part of his nation, or as fellow citizens. He saw them as members of an alien tribe—strangers in the desert—who were trying to take his turkey.

The second deeply rooted political tradition of the Middle East one could find at work in Hama is authoritarianism—the concentration of power in a single ruler or elite not bound by any constitutional framework.

The traditional authoritarian ruler in the Middle East assumed or inherited power based on the sword, to which his subjects were expected to submit obediently. The long tradition of authoritarianism in Middle East politics is related to the persistence of tribe-like affiliations. Because primordial, tribe-like loyalties governed men's identities and political attitudes so deeply, the peoples of the Middle East (as elsewhere in the world for many centuries) rarely created nation-states of their own through which they could rule themselves and be strong enough to withstand foreign invaders. The warring tribes, clans, sects, neighborhoods, cities, and hinterlands could not find a way to balance the intimacy and cohesion of their tribe-like groups with the demands of a nation-state that would be run by certain neutral rules and values to which everyone agreed. Most peoples in the area simply could not achieve the level of consensus needed for such a polity. Rare was the clan or sect that would voluntarily let itself be ruled by another, and rarer still was the town or village that would voluntarily submit to the hinterland or vice versa.

What happened, as a result, was that on some occasions a major Arab tribe or group of soldiers would, by sheer physical force, impose itself on the tribes and cities of another region—such as the Umayyads, who came out of the Arabian peninsula in the seventh century and imposed themselves on the Levant—while on other occasions non-Arab imperial invaders, such as the Persians, Mongols, or Ottoman Turks, did the same. In all these cases the form of rule imposed from above was authoritarian, similar in kind to that found in many other parts of the world. The ruler was often a stranger: someone to be feared, dreaded, avoided, submitted to, and, occasionally, rebelled against, but rarely adored; there was usually a tremendous gulf between the ruler and the society at large.

This authoritarianism, as it developed in the Middle East, came in two very distinct forms: one form I call gentle authoritarianism, the other brutal authoritarianism.

The most enduring example of the gentle authoritarian tradition was that of the Ottoman Turks, during the heyday of their rule over the Middle East, which lasted from the early 1500s until the beginning of World War I. The founders of the Ottoman dynasty imposed their authority on the Arab/Muslim world by force. However, as the Ottoman rulers became more legitimate in the eyes of their subjects, through piety, good deeds, and good government, their swords eventually moved into the background and were replaced by a type of rule by negotiation, which, generally speaking, gave the Ottoman authoritarian tradition in the Middle East a softer edge. The more popular support the Ottoman rulers garnered through the ages, the more they sought to sustain their authoritarianism without resort to force, but instead by building bridges to key sectors of the societies they ruled, by allowing others to share in the spoils and by never totally vanquishing their opponents, but instead always leaving them a way out so that they might one day be turned into friends. This approach earned the Ottoman sultans still more legitimacy, which reinforced their instinct for restraint and allowed them to operate in a way more consistent with the holy laws of Islam. (When I describe the Ottoman tradition as gentle authoritarianism, I am referring to its golden age and most idealized form. As the Ottoman Empire became more decentralized, and eventually went into decline, there were individual sultans or local Ottoman governors who could be as ruthless as any authoritarians.)

Even the most gentle Ottoman rulers always understood that occasionally a sharper edge had to be brandished in order to maintain order in regions fragmented by sects, tribes, clans, and neighborhoods, and they did not hesitate to do so. A colorful example of this can be found in the way in which the Ottomans controlled southern Palestine and the Negev Desert, which was inhabited by some particularly quarrelsome Bedouin tribes who were constantly at each other's throats. Legend has it that only in 1890 was a particular Ottoman governor, named Rustum Pasha, able to finally put an end to the tribal wars that had plagued the Negev throughout most of the nineteenth century. Rustum Pasha was known for his toughness and for his nickname, "Abu Jarida." The *jarida* is the stick of a palm frond, which Rustum Pasha regularly employed as a weapon with which to beat the Bedouin in order to keep them in line. The Bedouin of this era were relentless in their efforts to bribe officials like Rustum Pasha and divert them from his objective of bringing order. According to Palestinian historian Arif el-Arif, whenever a Bedouin chief tried to bribe Rustum Pasha he would bring him into his office and sit him down in a chair. Then the Ottoman governor would take out a red tarboosh. (The tarboosh, sometimes known as a fez, is a brimless, cone-shaped, flat-topped hat, usually made of felt, which was the favored headgear of gentlemen in the eastern Mediterranean, and the symbol of Ottoman rulers.) Rustum Pasha would set the tarboosh on a pedestal and then begin to have a conversation with it in Arabic in front of the Bedouin.

"O tarboosh," Rustum Pasha would say to the red hat. "What do you prefer? Money [*fulous*] or law and order [*namous*]?"

Then Rustum Pasha would pause for a moment, and in another voice he would answer for the tarboosh. "I want order," the hat would say. And with that answer Rustum Pasha would lift his *jarida* branch and whack the Bedouin sitting before him from head to toe.

Thus was order maintained among the tribes of the Negev.

Not every autocrat in the Middle East, however, enjoyed the legitimacy of the Ottoman sultans, which is why the history of the region is replete with examples of "brutal authoritarians"— rulers who did not simply rely on palm fronds to keep order. Many of these brutal autocrats were professional soldiers who never stayed in power long enough to win the support of those they governed, so they had to depend on totally despotic, arbitrary, and merciless forms of control that were in direct contravention of Islamic law. One of the first brutal authoritarians in Islamic history was the founder of the Abbasid dynasty in Baghdad, Abul-Abbas al-Saffah, who ruled Baghdad from A.D. 750 to 754. His name meant "Abul Abbas the Bloodletter"—a title which he proudly gave to himself, because he knew he enjoyed no consent from the Arab tribes he ruled and he wanted them to understand that he would show no restraint to those who might challenge him. The executioner was part of his royal court.

Precisely because so many brutal authoritarians rose up in the history of the Middle East, an entire body of Islamic political theory developed to justify even their style of rule—despite the fact that this style contravened all the precepts of Islamic political law, which demanded fair and consultative government. Middle Eastern societies were primarily merchant societies, which dreaded chaos and feared what might happen if control from above was eliminated and all their tribes and sects went at each other. Therefore, Islamic political thinkers gradually began to argue that obedience to even the cruelest, most illegitimate, non-Islamic despot, who at least kept some order, was preferable to the greater evil of a society left to the depredations of endless internal warfare. Or, as the ancient Arabic proverb put it: "Better sixty years of tyranny than one day of anarchy."

Islamic historian Bernard Lewis, in his book *The Political Language of Islam* (1988), observed that "in preaching this doctrine of submission, [Islamic] jurists and theologians made no pretense at either liking or respect for the oppressive government in question, nor did they make any attempt to conceal its oppressiveness. In a passage often quoted by modern scholars, Ibn Jama'a, a Syrian jurist of the late 13th and early 14th centuries, is quite explicit: 'At a time when there is no imam [a combination spiritual and political leader who rules by Islamic law] and an unqualified person seeks the imamate [spiritual and political leadership] and compels the people by force and by his armies . . . then obedience to him is obligatory, so as to maintain the unity of Moslems and preserve agreement among them.' This is still true, even if he is barbarous or vicious."

In the modern Middle East, the authoritarian tradition has survived in both its forms—the softer Ottoman approach and the more brutal, un-Islamic, Abul-Abbas-the-Bloodletter variety. In the most homogeneous Arab countries, such as Egypt and Tunisia, and in those countries where the rulers have won a high degree of consent from their people, such as in King Hussein's Jordan, King Hassan's Morocco, King Fahd's Saudi Arabia, and all the Gulf sheikdoms, the gentle Ottoman authoritarian tradition is very much in evidence today. To be sure, the sword is always there in these countries, but generally out of sight. These regimes have a good deal of legitimacy in the eyes of their people and hence they can afford to rule with a good deal of restraint: coopting opponents, even sharing a degree of power and allowing for some freedom of the press and expression. This accounts for the generally relaxed atmosphere one can find in these Arab states—provided one doesn't try to challenge the man in charge.

However, in those Arab countries where the societies are highly fragmented between different particularistic tribe-like sects, clans, and villages, and where the modern rulers have not been able to achieve much legitimacy—most notably Syria, Iraq, Lebanon, and North and South Yemen—the more brutal authoritarian tradition is in evidence. Restraint and magnanimity are luxuries of the self-confident, and the rulers of these countries are anything but secure on their thrones. It is no accident, I believe, that the two Arab countries that tell the most jokes about themselves, Egypt and Tunisia, are also the most homogeneous. The only joke I ever heard about Syrian President Assad was told by a Lebanese. It went like this: After a national "election" in Syria, an aide comes to President Assad and says, "Mr. President, you won the election with a 99.7 percent majority. That means only three-tenths of 1 percent of the people did not vote for you. What more could you ask for?" Assad replies, "Their names."

What makes the more brutal form of authoritarianism so dangerous today is that these insecure, nervous autocrats are not responding to threats against them with simple swords, let alone palm fronds, but with chemical weapons, modern armies, and devastating means of destruction that can reach beyond the royal court to far-flung regions.

Which brings us back to Hama. Hama was not just what happens when two tribe-like sects—the Alawites and the Sunnis—decide to have it out; it was also what happens when a modern Middle Eastern autocrat who does not enjoy full legitimacy among his people puts down a challenge to his authority by employing twentieth-century weapons without restraint. Hafez Assad was Abul-Abbas the Bloodletter, only with Soviet-built T-62 tanks and MiG jet fighters.

Assad and Saddam Hussein have survived longer than any other modern autocrats in Syria or Iraq—Assad has been in power since 1970, Saddam since 1968—not only because they have been brutal (many of their predecessors were just as brutal), but because they have been brutal and smart. They have no friends, only agents and enemies; they maintain overlapping intelligence agencies that spy on each other, the army, and the people, not just neighboring countries; they use everything that the twentieth century has to offer in the way of surveillance technology in order to extend the government's grip far and wide, so that no corner of the country is outside their control; they never waste time murdering those whom they hate—such as Jews or Communists—but only those who are dangerous, like those closest to them; and most important, they know not just when to go all the way against their opponents but when to stop before overreaching themselves. Men like Assad and Saddam are dangerous and long-lasting because they are extremists who know when to stop. They are a rare breed. Most extremists don't know when to stop, which is why they ultimately do themselves in by going too far for too long. But these men know how to insert the knife right through the heart of one opponent, and then invite all the others to dinner.

On July 16, 1979, Saddam Hussein, who had been the number-two man in Iraqi politics for eleven years, put all these lessons to good effect in order to shove aside his superior, the ailing President Ahmad Hasan al-Bakr, and have himself declared President. At the time of his takeover, Saddam was convinced that at least five of his closest friends and colleagues in the Iraqi leadership had some reservations about his succession. So, on the eve of his ascension, he had one of them arrested—Muhyi Abd al-

Husayn al-Mashhadi, the secretary-general of the Iraqi Baath Party. Al-Mashhadi was then apparently tortured into agreeing to make a confession that he was planning to topple Saddam with the help of some other members of the leadership.

Then, on July 22, with real theatrical flair, Saddam convened an extraordinary meeting of the Iraqi Baath Party Regional Congress in order to hear al-Mashhadi's confession—live. As al-Mashhadi would tell his story and mention the name of someone else in the leadership involved in the bogus plot, that person would have to stand, and then a guard would come along and drag him from the chamber. Al-Mashhadi just "happened" to mention as co-conspirators the four other members of Iraq's ruling Revolutionary Command Council—Mohammed Ayish, Mohammed Mahjub, Husayn al-Hamdani, and Ghanim Abd al-Jalil—who Saddam felt were not totally supportive of him. A videotape of the confessions was then distributed to Baath Party branches across Iraq, as well as to army units; a few bootleg copies even made their way to Kuwait and Beirut.

A Lebanese friend of mine saw the video and described it as follows: "This guy would be reciting his confession and he would come to a person and say, 'And then we went to see Mohammed to ask him to join the conspiracy.' And this Mohammed would be sitting in the room, and he would have to stand up. And you could see this guy crying, his knees shaking, and he could barely stay on his feet. And then this guy would say, 'But he refused to help us,' and then this Mohammed would slump back down into his chair, exhausted with relief, and they would move on to the next guy. I had nightmares about this video for months. In my nightmare I was accused and would have to stand up, only in my dream they would claim that I *did* cooperate with the conspiracy and the guards would come and drag me away."

On August 7, 1979, all five main conspirators, along with seventeen others, were found guilty and sentenced to death by "democratic executions." According to the book *Iraq Since 1958* (1988), an authoritative history by Marion Farouk-Sluglett and Peter Sluglett, the morning after the sentencing a firing squad consisting of Saddam Hussein himself and the remaining senior members of the Baath leadership executed the plotters, apparently with submachine guns. After the execution, no one questioned the "legitimacy" of Saddam's ascension, nor did anyone wonder why Saddam married his beautiful daughter Raghd to the commander of his personal bodyguards, Hussein Kamel.

"This episode was particularly remarkable," noted the Slugletts, "in view of the fact that many of those executed had been among Saddam Hussein's most intimate associates, particularly Hamdani, a close personal friend of long standing."

But tribalism and authoritarianism together still cannot fully explain Hama or Middle East politics today. There is a third tradition at work, a tradition imposed from abroad in the early twentieth century by the last group of imperial invaders of the region, the British, French, and Italians: the modern nation-state.

This was a very new concept for the Middle East, where there was a long tradition of authoritarian dynasties stretching from one end of the region to the other. In these sweeping dynasties, whether it was the Ottoman or Abbasid or any other, men did not identify themselves with, or hold patriotic loyalty to, their specific empire or country of residence. "Countries and nations existed; they had names, and evoked sentiments of a kind," noted Bernard Lewis. "But they were not seen as defining political identities or directing political allegiances" in the modern Western European sense. The empire and its dynastic ruler in the Middle East were distant, often alien, entities. Political identities tended to be drawn instead either from one's religious affiliation or one's local kin group—be it the tribe, clan, village, neighborhood, sect, region, or professional association.

In the wake of World War I, however, the British and French took out their imperial pens and carved up what remained of the Ottoman dynastic empire, and created an assortment of nation-states in the Middle East modeled along their own. The borders of these new states consisted of neat polygons—with right angles that were always in sharp contrast to the chaotic reality on the ground. In the Middle East, modern Syria, Lebanon, Iraq, Palestine, Jordan and the various Persian Gulf oil states all traced their shapes and origins back to this process; even most of their names were imposed by outsiders. In other words, many of the states in the Middle East today—Egypt being the most notable exception—were not willed into existence by their own people or developed organically out of a common historical memory or ethnic or linguistic bond; they also did not emerge out of a social contract between rulers and ruled. Rather, their shapes and structure were imposed from above by the imperial powers. These shapes had little or no precedent in either the medieval or the ancient world. Rather, boundaries were drawn almost entirely on the basis of the foreign policy, communications, and oil needs of the Western colonial powers that were to dominate these new countries—with scant attention paid to ethnic, tribal, linguistic, or religious continuities on the ground. As a result, these states were like lifeboats into which various ethnic and religious communities, each with their own memories and their own rules of the game, were thrown together and in effect told to row in unison, told to become a nation, told to root for the same soccer team and salute the same flag. Instead of the state growing out of the nation, the nation was expected to grow out of the state.

What happened in the twentieth century when these new nation-states were created was that in each one a particular tribe-like group either seized power or was ensconced in power by the British and French—and then tried to dominate all the others. In Lebanon, for example, it was the Maronites who emerged as dominant, in Saudi Arabia the Saud tribe. In today's Syria, the Alawites, and in today's Iraq, Saddam Hussein, along with other members of his home village of Tikrit, have scrambled to the top. In Jordan, King Hussein's grandfather Abdullah was left in charge by the British, and Hussein has managed to maintain the dynasty, as have many of his fellow monarchs and emirs in the Persian Gulf. What enabled these specific families or groups to initially dominate their societies and government bureaucracies was usually their tribe-like solidarity.

Not only were the boundaries of these new Arab states artificially imposed from above; so, too, were many of their political institutions. The British and French in conjunction with certain Westernized elites in each of these countries, imported all the accoutrements of Western liberal democracies—including parliaments, constitutions, national anthems, political parties, and cabinets. But the imperial powers left before these institutions could fully take root, and before these societies could really experience the political, economic, and social reforms that were necessary to give these institutions real meaning.

Nevertheless, despite the artificial origins of most Arab states,

it did not take long after their creation for certain vested interests
to take hold and make them concrete realities, not just agglom-
erations of disparate tribes, clans, villages, and religious sects with
only a flag in common. After a while, Syrian, Lebanese, Iraqi,
Yemeni, Jordanian, and Saudi nationalisms all became realities
to some extent. They still talked about pan-Islamism and pan-
Arabism, and tribes and clans, but everyone did learn to root for
his own country's soccer team to some extent. The Lebanese
historian Kemal Salibi put it succinctly when he observed: "As
men of political ambition began to compete for power and position
in the different countries, and as each of these countries came to
have its own ruling establishment and administrative bureaucracy,
the lines of demarcation separating them, hardly any of which
was a natural or historical frontier, began to harden."

Because of this, men like Hafez Assad and Saddam Hussein
cannot be viewed only as tribe-like chieftains or brutal authoritarians; they also have to be seen as the kind of men of ambition
to which Salibi referred: modernizing bureaucrats trying to solid-
ify and develop their relatively new nation-states. Both men have
to be given credit for engaging in initiatives for economic development that have greatly benefited their respective countries. This
has involved everything from building modern highways or low-
cost public housing in Syria to providing free education and medical care in Iraq. These practices won each of their regimes a
certain degree of legitimacy, which can be seen when one visits
some far-flung Syrian village in which the relatively stable Assad
government has built a new road, a medical clinic, a new school,
extended electricity, and connected telephone lines. It is quite
possible to find in such a village a Sunni Muslim villager who has
hung a picture of Alawite President Assad on his wall, not simply
because it will ingratiate him with the local party and intelligence
officials, but also because he sincerely feels that this man Assad
has behaved not just as an Alawite, and not just as a power-
hungry autocrat, but as his own President, with a national interest
in mind.

That is why, on a third level, the Hama massacre has to be
seen as the natural reaction of a modernizing politician in a relatively new nation-state trying to stave off retrogressive—in this
case, Islamic fundamentalist—elements aiming to undermine
everything he has achieved in the way of building Syria into a

twentieth-century secular republic. That is also why, if someone had been able to take an objective opinion poll in Syria after the Hama massacre, Assad's treatment of the rebellion probably would have won substantial approval, even among many Sunni Muslims. They might have said, "Better one month of Hama than fourteen years of civil war like Lebanon."

To reinforce these sorts of national feelings, Assad and Saddam have also consciously tried to shed their own tribe-like affiliations for more nationalist-oriented ones. The real name of Iraqi President Saddam Hussein, for example, is Saddam Hussein al-Tikriti. Tikrit was the home village of Saddam and of virtually all the key conspirators who took power with him in the 1968 Iraqi coup d'état. After Saddam and his clique were in power for several years, any Iraqi who was from anywhere near Tikrit added al-Tikriti to his name in order to draw closer to the regime. The preponderance of Tikritis in key positions in the Iraqi army, intelligence agencies, and ruling Baath Party prompted Hanna Batatu, a historian of Iraq, to observe once that "it would not be going too far to say that the Tikritis rule [Iraq] through the Baath Party, rather than the Baath Party through the Tikritis."

But in the mid-1970s, Saddam surprised everyone with a sudden about-face. Practically overnight, the Iraqi state-controlled media was ordered to drop al-Tikriti from the President's name and to refer to him solely as Saddam Hussein—Hussein is actually his middle name and also his father's first name—in order to downplay the tribal makeup of his regime and to emphasize its national pretensions. For years after this name change, however, Israel Radio's Arabic Service continued calling him "Saddam Hussein al-Tikriti," just to get on his nerves and remind the Iraqi people of the tribe-like character of their regime.

There is no question today that both the artificially imposed borders and governmental institutions of the relatively new Arab nation-states are beginning to take root. Over many generations the integrative nationalist ideologies and practices of men such as Assad or Saddam may win their regimes enough legitimacy and security for them to feel comfortable forging true social contracts with their people. Only then will these countries have real public spheres—neutral spaces where men can come as equal citizens, check their tribal memories at the door, and enter into a politics governed by mutually agreed-upon laws. Only then will the words "parliament," "constitution," and "political parties" have any real meaning for these countries and their peoples.

But that day is still a long way off, as the surviving members of South Yemeni President Ali Nasir Muhammad's last Cabinet can attest.

On the morning of January 13, 1986, Ali Nasir tried to give a whole new meaning to the expression "cabinet shake-up." My *New York Times* colleague John Kifner visited Yemen a few days later and described in detail what happened. Ali Nasir had called a meeting of his ruling fifteen-member "politburo" at his pastel-green headquarters near the Aden harbor for 10:00 a.m. As his ministers took their places around the Cabinet table waiting for Ali Nasir to arrive, one of the President's bodyguards started serving tea from a thermos, while another, named Hassan, went to the head of the table and opened the President's Samsonite attaché case. But instead of pulling out Ali Nasir's papers, as the guard usually did, he pulled out a Skorpion machine pistol and began raking Ali Antar, the Vice President, up and down his back with gunfire.

Moments later, other guards burst through the doors to finish off the rest of the ministers with AK-47 assault rifles. But this was no ordinary politburo. President Ali Nasir's Cabinet colleagues were also packing pistols, and they and their bodyguards began firing back. Kifner visited the politburo room a few days later, which he described as a grisly monument to all-out tribal politics, with blood still congealed on the wall-to-wall carpet and bullet holes peppered across the walls and chairs. Each of the ministers was associated with one or another tribe, so as soon as word spread about the shoot-out in the Cabinet room, the battle exploded on a grander scale in the streets of Aden. Before it was over, an estimated 5,000 people had been killed in less than a week of clashes between Yemeni tribes—some of them armed with heavy machine guns and artillery—who supported the President and those who opposed him; another 65,000 tribesmen were forced to flee to neighboring North Yemen. Kifner quoted Ali Salem al-Beedh, one of the three ministers to crawl out from under the Cabinet table alive, as saying, "Who would have thought a colleague could do such a thing? Why, only last June there was a resolution adopted by the politburo that anyone who resorted to violence in settling internal political disputes be considered a criminal and betrayer of the homeland."

I am sure al-Beedh had his tongue firmly in his cheek when he uttered those words. He knew better, of course, but unfortunately many Western observers of the Middle East do not. They don't appreciate the different traditions which make up the politics of this region. They assume that all the surface trappings of nation-statehood—the parliaments, the flags, and the democratic rhetoric—can fully explain the politics of these countries, and that tribalism and brutal authoritarianism are now either things of the past or aberrations from the norm; the lesson of Hama or Halabja or South Yemen is that they are not.

"The liberal tradition in the West tries to impute to the behavior of the native or the underdog an idealist position which is not really there," argues the Lebanese historian Kemal Salibi. "They want to think of the peoples of this region as 'noble savages,' as Jean-Jacques Rousseau put it. Instead of saying, what we have here is an outmoded form of thinking clashing with an attempt to construct modern nation states. . . . When it comes to thinking about Middle East politics, the American liberal mind is often chasing rainbows. They are living in a world of delusion."

The real genius of Hafez Assad and Saddam Hussein is their remarkable ability to move back and forth among all three political traditions of their region, effortlessly switching from tribal chief to brutal autocrat to modernizing President with the blink of an eye. They are always playing three-dimensional chess with the world, while Americans seem to know only how to play checkers—one plodding move at a time.

Their timing is what is most impressive. Assad and Saddam know just when to play the tribal chief or the brutal autocrat and level Hama or Halabja, and when to be the modernizing presidents and order their parliaments to rebuild these towns with low-cost government housing. (Assad rebuilt much of Hama after the massacre, including a new hospital, playgrounds, schools, apartments and even two mosques, but their use was tightly controlled to make certain that they could never again become breeding grounds for Muslim fundamentalists. According to Seale, the girl's Ping-Pong team from the Hama Sporting Club won the 1985 Syrian national championships.) One day Assad can be hosting former American President Jimmy Carter and playing the role of the Syrian President who only wants "peace" for his people and the whole Middle East, and the next day he can be meeting with Lebanese Druse tribal chief Walid Jumblat. Walid's father, Kemal, was assassinated, purportedly by Syrian agents, in Lebanon in 1977, when he dared to openly cross Assad. Walid was fond of telling friends about a particularly memorable meeting he later had with the Syrian President. Walid was ushered into Assad's huge office and at a distance he could see the President sitting behind his desk. From afar, Walid would say, Assad looked like a pea sitting on a cushion. As Walid approached, Assad greeted him warmly with the traditional Arabic salutation *"Ahlan wa sahlan, ahlan wa sahlan"*—my house is your house. The two men got to talking, and Assad in his roundabout manner intimated to Walid how he expected him to behave with regard to a certain situation developing in Lebanon. Walid evinced some reluctance. At one point, according to Walid, Assad looked at him lovingly and told him, with his thin smile, "You know, Walid, I look at you sitting there and you remind me exactly of your dear father. What a man he was. What a shame he is not with us. *Ahlan wa sahlan."*

Walid immediately understood that he was being made an offer he could not refuse. It is not for nothing that the Lebanese have a proverb: "He killed him and then marched in his funeral procession."

Whatever mode Assad and Saddam are in, though, I am certain that they never fool themselves about the underlying tribe-like and autocratic natures of their societies. They always understand the difference between the mirage and the oasis, between the world and the word, between what men say they are and what they really are. They always know that when push comes to shove, when the modern veneer of nation-statehood is stripped away, it all still comes down to Hama Rules: Rule or die. One man triumphs, the others weep. The rest is just commentary. I am convinced that there is only one man in Israel Hafez Assad ever feared and that is Ariel Sharon, because Assad knew that Sharon, too, was ready to play by Hama Rules. Assad knew Sharon well; he saw him every morning when he looked in the mirror.

A Lebanese Shiite friend of mine, Professor Fouad Ajami, an outstanding political scientist who grew up in Beirut, used to tell me about a man his father admired for his toughness. Fouad's father was a landlord in Beirut, as was this other man. Fouad's father would tell him that this other man was so tough he would not only eat the egg, "he would eat the egg and its shell. He never left anything for anyone else—not even the shell."

That was what Hama was all about and that is what politics in places like Syria, Lebanon, the Yemens, and Iraq are so often about—men grabbing for the egg *and* its shell, because without both they fear that they may well be dead.

5

The Teflon Guerrilla

PLAYBOY MAGAZINE: For years, people around the world have seen and heard you represent the PLO position on television. You're probably one of the most recognizable men in the world.

YASIR ARAFAT: You think so?

PLAYBOY: Your face and your Palestinian headdress are instantly recognizable. If someday people forget what Jimmy Carter or even Ronald Reagan looked like, they probably won't forget what you looked like.

YASIR ARAFAT [*smiling broadly*]: "Thank you. It's a good idea, no?

—Interview with Yasir Arafat in PLAYBOY *magazine, September 1988*

The true relationship between a leader and his people is often revealed through small, spontaneous gestures. Maybe that was why I was so intrigued watching Yasir Arafat marching down a Beirut street one day, his walking stick in hand, drawing children and mothers, grandparents and guerrillas, out of their apartments and into his wake like the Palestinian Pied Piper he most surely was. The scene was West Beirut in the early 1980s, minutes after Israeli planes had bombarded the Fakhani neighborhood, where the PLO maintained its political and military headquarters somewhere beneath the multistory apartment houses. One Israeli bomb had made a direct hit on a corner apartment block; it looked like a wedge of cake that had been smashed by a fist. Trapped inside were many civilians, including one old woman's four children. When Arafat walked up, this woman was hysterically trying to drag away the tons of concrete by herself to reach her missing kin. As soon as she spotted the PLO chairman, though, the woman stopped in her tracks. She climbed down off the rubble, ran up to Arafat, grabbed his pea-green army cap, threw it off his head, and began kissing his bald pate.

"I lost four of my family inside," the woman sobbed, "but I have nine more and they are all for you."

I reported about Yasir Arafat on and off for almost ten years. He is without a doubt one of the most unusual characters and unlikely statesmen ever to grace the world stage. He is, in many ways, the Ronald Reagan of Palestinian politics—an agent of change for his nation, a great actor who understands the soul of his people and how to play out their greatest fantasies, and, most of all, the ultimate Teflon guerrilla. Nothing stuck to Yasir Arafat—not bullets, not criticism, not any particular political position, and, most of all, not failure. No matter what mistakes he made, no matter how many military defeats he sustained, no matter how long he took to recover Palestine, his people forgave him and he remained atop the PLO. Something about this scraggily bearded man, living out of a suitcase, resonated in the heart of every Palestinian. *Al-Khityar*—"the Old Man," they called him affectionately—the Palestinian version of "the Gipper," and like Americans, the Palestinians were always ready to win one more for their "Gipper."

What was the source of this Teflon? It certainly wasn't Arafat's good looks or inviting smile. Only five feet four inches tall, with protruding eyes, a permanent three-day-old stubble, and a potbelly, Arafat was not what one would call a dashing figure or a man on horseback; in fact, in a television era, he was a walking, talking, Palestinian public-relations disaster. It also wasn't his military record. As a leader of men in battle, Arafat always had more in common with General George A. Custer than with General George S. Patton.

No, the secret of Arafat's political success and longevity can be understood only by locating him in the broad sweep of Palestinian history. Put simply: Arafat's great achievement was that he led the Palestinians out of the deserts of obscurity into the land of "prime time," and, at the same time, created an institutional framework to keep them there. To put it another way, Arafat did for the Palestinians what the Zionists did for the Jews: brought them from oblivion back into politics.

Long before Arafat came on the scene, there was a clearly defined Palestinian nation, but it was a nation to whom history had said no. At that very fluid moment between the end of World War I and the end of World War II, when all kinds of peoples were getting states of their own, the Palestinians missed the train, largely as a result of the failures of their own leaders and the conniving of their Arab brethren. After the 1948 Middle East war, when Israel was created, and Jordan and Egypt swallowed most of the land that the United Nations had designated for a Palestinian state, the Palestinians almost disappeared as a people. They were either subsumed into Israel as Israeli Arabs or melted into Jordan, Lebanon, Egypt, and Syria, as refugees. As Arafat himself liked to say, the Palestinians were being treated like "the American Red Indians," confined to their reservations—shafted by the Arabs, defeated by the Jews, and forgotten by the world. Arafat brought this people back from the dead, galvanized them into a coherent and internationally recognized national liberation movement, and transformed them in the eyes of the world from refugees in need of tents to a nation in need of sovereignty.

He did it by making the PLO into an organization unlike anything the Palestinians ever had before in their history, and endowing it with four unique attributes: independence, unity, relevance, and theatrics.

Yet for all his greatness at reviving the Palestinian cause and rallying the Palestinian nation, Arafat never delivered on his ultimate promise—turf, statehood, land. As I would discover in Beirut, and later in Jerusalem, the very skills and attributes that enabled Arafat to bring the Palestinians from obscurity to prime time would be the chains that would prevent him from bringing them from prime time to Palestine.

Many of the qualities Arafat conveyed to the PLO—its middle-class aspirations, its penchant for institution-building, its tendency for stagecraft as much as statecraft, its conspiratorial quality, its devotion to Palestine, and its deep need to play the Arab game on equal terms with all the other Arab states—were all traceable to Arafat's own youth and the political era in which he emerged.

Yasir Arafat was born in 1929 (either in Cairo or Gaza—he has told people both), one of seven children of a prosperous Palestinian merchant. His given name was Mohammed, but he quickly won the nickname Yasir, which means "easy." His mother died when he was four and his father sent him to live with his married uncle in Jerusalem, where he grew up inside the walls of the Old City. His house, in fact, was situated right next to the Western Wall of the Second Temple, revered by Jews as their holiest shrine. The Israelis, he liked to point out, demolished his home when they cleared away a piazza in front of the Western Wall after the 1967 war. After elementary school, he moved to Cairo and lived with his father, who had remarried. In his biography of Arafat, *Arafat: Terrorist or Peacemaker?* (1984) Alan Hart quotes Arafat's sister Inam as saying that her younger brother was obsessed with the Palestinian and Arab nationalist struggles virtually from the moment he emerged out of the womb.

"Yasir," she said, "was [always] gathering Arab kids of the district. He formed them into groups and made them march and drill. He carried a stick and used to beat those who did not obey his commands. He also liked making camps in the garden of our house. . . . Often I used to escort him [to school]. But he would slip away from the classroom. And often when I went to school to escort him home he was not there. The only time he seemed to be seriously interested in study was at home in the evenings with his friends. But he was acting. . . . When I entered the room Yasir and his friends would pretend to be doing their homework— but really they were discussing political and military matters."

Arafat eventually attended Cairo University and earned a degree in civil engineering, but during his spare time he was constantly active in Palestinian nationalist student organizations, fighting against the Zionists in the 1948 battles south of Jerusalem and in Gaza. In the wake of the 1948 defeat, though, Arafat admitted that even he thought the Palestinian movement was finished—that it had missed its moment. While all the other Arabs he had studied with in Cairo would get their turf, Arafat and his friends would have none.

"I was very discouraged . . . after we all became refugees," he revealed in an interview published in *Playboy* in September 1988. "During that period I was going to leave, leave the area entirely and continue my studies someplace else. . . . I was accepted into the University of Texas—I think it was the University of Texas, anyways, I didn't go."

Instead, Arafat went east. He found his way to Kuwait, worked for the Kuwaiti government for a year, and then started his own contracting company.

"I was well on my way to becoming a millionaire," Arafat said in the interview. "We built roads, highways, bridges. Large construction projects. . . . During that period . . . I had four cars. Nobody believes that, but I did. I had Chevrolets, and I had a Thunderbird and a Volkswagen. But I gave them all away when I left Kuwait to rejoin our struggle. All but one—the Volkswagen."

Indeed, Arafat and his Volkswagen became familiar features around the Arab newspaper offices in Beirut. In 1956, Arafat and a group of other middle-class Palestinians living in Kuwait decided to rededicate themselves to the liberation of Palestine and formed their own underground guerrilla organization called al-Fatah ("Victory"). Arafat was appointed spokesman for the group, prompting him to give up his contracting career in Kuwait and relocate to Beirut and Amman. He would often show up in the evenings at Arab newspapers in Beirut to plead with the editors to print "communiqués" about military actions against Israel undertaken by al-Fatah guerrillas. Most of the time he was given a cold shoulder and shown to the door. The struggle against Israel was, in the early 1960s, viewed as primarily, though not entirely, the responsibility of the Arab states. Few took seriously the idea of the Palestinians recovering Palestine on their own. The Arab heads of state founded the Palestine Liberation Organization in 1964 in order to control the Palestinians, and to use them for their own military and political purposes. Ahmed Shukery, the first chairman of the PLO, was a bombastic buffoon from an upper-class family who did what he was told.

No wonder Arafat and his colleagues were anxious to get their cause out of the hands of the Arab leaders, but not out of their pockets. They needed to assert independent Palestinian control over the Palestinian national movement, but without going so far as to lose the backing of the Arab world, without which an effective military and diplomatic struggle with Israel was impossible. Paradoxically, it would be Israel's victory in the 1967 war that would give Arafat and his colleagues their chance. Israel's devastating rout of the combined armies of Egypt, Jordan, and Syria in 1967 thoroughly discredited the entire Arab ruling class, including its Palestinian toadies, leaving an emotional vacuum and a leadership void. After the '67 defeat, the Arab world was hungry for a new face, a new hope, a new redeemer, and the Palestinian guerrillas emerged from the underground and stepped into all those roles. Thanks to several courageous confrontations with Israeli troops, Arafat's al-Fatah group achieved the greatest legitimacy among the emerging guerrilla organizations, and this enabled Arafat, in 1969, to wrest control of the PLO away from the discredited Arab states and to turn it into an umbrella organization covering all the Palestinian guerrilla groups, from the far right to the far left. It has never belonged to any Arab regime since, something which has always been a source of pride for Palestinians. The PLO under Yasir Arafat was the first truly independent Palestinian national movement.

Once he had the PLO in his hands, Arafat kept it independent, thanks first and foremost to his own natural political skills. Arafat was born with the cunning of a bazaar merchant, the now-you-see-it-now-you-don't hands of a magician, the balance of a Barnum & Bailey tightrope walker, and, most important, the skin of a chameleon, which took on whatever political colors were in season. This enabled him to tiptoe through the snake pit of inter-Arab politics, playing the Syrians off against the Jordanians, the Iraqis off against the Egyptians, and always maintaining for the PLO a tiny corner in which to operate freely.

Because Arafat gradually made himself synonymous with the Palestinian cause, and because the Palestinian cause became the most sacred cause in Arab politics, in Islamic politics, and even in Third World politics, Arafat was also able to turn himself into a kind of Arab Pope. One touch from his scepter could make the most vile Arab despot legitimate in Arab eyes. As Arafat himself told *Playboy*: "Maybe you don't know that in some circles, I am considered *more* than a freedom fighter. By some I am considered a symbol of resistance. It was only in some circles I was called a terrorist. . . . For your information, I am the permanent [chairman] of the Organization of the Islamic Conference chairmanship. The co-chairman changes every three years—but I am the permanent chairman. And I am the permanent vice-president of the

Nonaligned Countries movement. Just for your information."
Arafat's status as the keeper of the seals of Arab legitimacy
greatly enhanced his independence, because it meant that there
was always some Arab leader ready to throw him a life preserver
whenever he seemed to be drowning. Egypt's President Hosni
Mubarak, for instance, was always anxious to embrace Arafat in
order to ease Cairo's isolation after it had signed a peace treaty
with Israel. At a time when his popularity was at a low ebb in
the mid-1980s because of a seemingly endless war with Iran, Iraqi
President Saddam Hussein offered Arafat office space for headquarters in Baghdad. It never hurt an Arab leader to have his
picture taken with Arafat seated next to him on the couch.

No less important than the independence which Arafat won for
the PLO was the unity with which he endowed the organization.
Throughout their history the Palestinians had suffered from violent disunity. Palestinian Christians were often at odds with Palestinian Muslims, Palestinians from Hebron were at odds with
those of Jerusalem, pro-Jordanians were at odds with Palestinian
nationalists, and radical Palestinian factions were at odds with
more moderate ones. The Palestinians, as a result, spoke with
many and contradictory voices on the world stage.

Arafat managed to bring virtually all the Palestinian trends
together under the PLO umbrella and to keep them there. He
accomplished this through several skills. One was his personal
ability to be everything to all men in the Palestinian movement.
Arafat could sit in a room with representatives from eight different
PLO factions, listen while each one offered a different approach
to a given dilemma, and then go his own way—without making
anyone in the room feel that his views had been totally ignored,
or totally accepted; he was as easy to nail down as a lump of
mercury. In order to remain so fluid, however, Arafat often had
to talk out of both sides of his mouth. (This damaged his credibility, though, and would haunt him later in life when he wanted
to be taken seriously by the Israelis.)

Another unifying tactic adopted by Arafat was to keep the
PLO's ideology simple. He rejected calls by PLO Marxists, such
as George Habash, for a "class struggle" against the Arab
bourgeoisie, and he also rejected the idea of making the PLO an
extension of any particular Arab bloc. Arafat's line was, in effect,
"I will use the son of the Palestinian camp dweller for my army

and I will use the bank account of the Palestinian millionaire for my bureaucracy. My door will always be open to both."

The only firm ideological commitment Arafat stuck by for all the years that he was based in Jordan and Lebanon was the lowest common denominator in Palestinian politics—something which all Palestinians from the far left to the far right, from those living under Israeli occupation in the West Bank and Gaza Strip to those living as refugees spread out all across the Arab world could accept—the principle that Palestine was Arab land and that the right of the Jews to establish a state there must never be formally recognized. This position was embodied in the PLO Charter, written in Cairo in 1964. Beyond that red line, however, Arafat kept himself ideologically "loose" in order to bend with the wind and exploit whatever diplomatic opportunities were available. He was not a man who spent his time either reading or writing pamphlets.

It must be remembered that Arafat's primary base of support during his Beirut days came from those Palestinians living in the refugee camps of Lebanon, Jordan, and Syria. They formed the ranks of his guerrilla army and filled the positions of his bureaucracy. They were the very soil from which the PLO sprang. Most of these Palestinian refugees hailed from towns and villages that fell within the boundaries of pre-1967 Israel—places such as Haifa or Jaffa or the Galilee. They were not particularly interested in a West Bank–Gaza Palestinian state, because that is not where they were from. Gaza was as far from their homes as Beirut. Therefore, they were always more inclined to a maximalist Palestinian political position that held on to the dream that one day Israel would disappear and they would be able to return to their actual homes. It was their aspirations which Arafat reflected in the 1960s and 1970s; it was their dreams to which he catered. Many Palestinians living under Israeli occupation in the West Bank and Gaza would come to take a more realistic approach, since they had to contend with the reality of Israel every day, but during the 1960s and 1970s their influence on PLO positions was limited. The guerrillas were the dynamic element in Palestinian politics; they were the ones out fighting and dying, so the West Bankers and Gazans had to follow their lead.

Arafat's ability to keep the Palestinians unified was also a result of the fact that he was the first Palestinian leader in history able to meet a payroll over a long period of time. The paychecks weren't big, and sometimes they came late, but they came, and when they did they didn't bounce. Arafat was a genius at playing the good cop–bad cop routine with Arab leaders. He would fly into Saudi Arabia after some radical Marxist PLO faction had just hijacked an airliner or committed some outrage and say in effect to the Saudis, "Look, my friends, I am sitting on top of a volcano. If anything happens to me these people will really go out of control. Who knows what they might do. They are angry men, and angry men can do crazy things. So please, help me, support me, it is a small price for you to pay for peace of mind." Arafat then used this Arab conscience money to build a multibillion-dollar investment portfolio that could sustain more than $200 million a year in welfare payments, scholarships, newspapers, radio stations, health payments, educational programs, trade unions, diplomatic missions, weapons purchases, and salaries to bureaucrats and guerrillas in Beirut and around the Middle East—making as many as 60,000 Palestinian families directly dependent on Arafat and the PLO for their economic well-being.

The third attribute with which Arafat endowed the PLO was relevance. By unifying the Palestinian people under one banner, by creating an institutional framework to sustain that unity, Arafat assembled a critical mass behind the Palestinian cause that simply made it impossible to ignore, as it had been during the 1950s and 1960s. But it wasn't only the number of supporters Arafat could field that made him so relevant. The Arab states became an international financial force in the 1970s in the wake of the explosion of oil prices that followed the 1973 Middle East war. Arafat deftly exploited this newfound Arab clout to convince the United Nations and more than one hundred other countries around the world to accept PLO diplomats and to recognize the PLO as the sole legitimate representative of the Palestinian people. During the oil boom the Arab world could not be ignored, and that meant its favorite cause could not be ignored. It was no coincidence that Arafat was first invited to address the United Nations in 1974, just as oil prices were going through the roof. One cannot understand the rise of the PLO without connecting it to the rise of OPEC. Thanks to Arafat's strategy, the Palestinians' demand for self-determination was constantly represented on the world stage and in every conceivable international forum. This created a snowball of legitimacy for the PLO, which kept growing and growing year after year.

For those who were not disposed to listen, Arafat reinforced the PLO's relevance by engaging not only in guerrilla warfare with the Israeli army and civilians but also in terrorist operations outside the Middle East. Arafat learned a lesson from Kurdish rebel leader Mustafa Barzani. Barzani was once asked why the Kurdish national liberation movement, which he led, never got the world attention of some other national liberation movements, like the Palestinians. Barzani said it was simple: "Because we fought only on our own land and we killed only our own enemies." The PLO under Arafat did not make that mistake. They took their war to other people's countries; they killed non-combatants as well as people who had nothing to do with their conflict. They always fought on the world stage as much as in the Middle East, and they consistently reaped the benefits.

But these very attributes—independence, unity, relevance—which made Arafat and his PLO unique in Palestinian history were also a prescription for paralysis. Because Arafat's main constituency during the 1960s, 1970s and early 1980s was the Palestinian refugees living outside Israel, the West Bank, and the Gaza Strip, the only way he could maintain the PLO's unity was if he never formally acknowledged Israel's right to exist—otherwise his whole organization would fragment under him. Arafat was always a leader who reflected the consensus of his people; he did not shape it. He had seen what happened to Jordan's King Abdullah and Egypt's Anwar Sadat; he knew the fate of those who got out too far ahead of their nations.

This meant Arafat had a dilemma: as long as he would not recognize Israel in a clear and unambiguous manner he had no hope of recovering even an inch of Palestinian territory through negotiations. Israel simply would not consider any settlement with the Palestinians that did not include total acceptance of the Jewish state within at least its pre-1967 boundaries. At the same time, Arafat could not get an inch of land back by war, because he did not have the resources to tangle with Israel alone, and the Arab states, while ready to send him checks, were not ready to send him divisions. Arafat, in other words, was caught between a decision he could not make and a war he could not fight. Such were the cards that history had dealt him.

Arafat escaped from his dilemma, or at least made it tolerable, by investing the PLO and Palestinian politics with one last attribute—theatrics. Arafat plied the Palestinian people with hopes, slogans, fantasies in order to keep the Palestinian movement alive until that day when the Arabs might awaken to their cause enough to join them in a battle for Palestine, or when the West might awaken to their cause enough to force Israel to give them a piece of Palestine. Arafat the actor helped to keep a whole nation hoping that around the next corner, after the next summit conference, in the wake of the next war, a state was waiting for them—if they could just hold on a little longer and keep the faith.

He accomplished this by acting many roles, which simultaneously played on his own fantasies as well as those of his people. On some days, for instance, Arafat played the "Traveler." Arafat visited more countries each year than any statesman in the world, by far. For a Palestinian people, whose own freedom of movement was so restricted, who in many cases didn't even have passports to travel on, to have a leader who could travel anywhere, and didn't even need a passport, was their own dream come true. Even better, Arafat, when he arrived, was not told by a customs agent to go to a special room to be frisked or interviewed because he was a Palestinian. He got 21-gun salutes, he got motorcades, he got marching bands, he got red carpets, and he got Palestinian flags fluttering in the breeze. Arafat loved to arrive places, to inspect the honor guards, and to be treated as an Arab head of state equal to all the other boys on the block. Other days Arafat played the "General." He gave this Palestinian people who never really had military power, who for so long were disarmed, a leader with the title of commander in chief, who always wore a holstered Smith & Wesson pistol on his hip. Was it loaded? I don't know, but who cares. It was there. On other days, Arafat played the "Revolutionary." Arafat elevated the Palestinians from their sleepy village roots, merchant culture, and traditional conservative Arab homes and made them, overnight, "revolutionaries" who could eat with chopsticks at the table of Chairman Mao. On other days, Arafat played "Mr. Universe." He gave this Palestinian people, who for so many years were invisible to the world, who felt that the world constantly wanted to forget them, a leader whose face was as famous as, if not more than that of the American President.

On still other days, Arafat played the "Chairman"—busy, rushing, always shuffling papers, moving here and moving there, never letting his people believe that things were going nowhere, that some solution wasn't around the corner.

"Files! Files! Files!" Arafat once exclaimed in an interview with a reporter from *Vanity Fair* (February 1989) who was riding with him in his private jet. "These files never finish. Though I am not a chief of state, I must work twice as hard as one because I have to both administer a bureaucracy and run a revolution. . . . Do you see that carton over there? That is the not-so-secret fax, and do you see that aluminum suitcase? That is the very secret fax. I am very proud of our communications system. It costs a lot of money. The Sharp Corporation of Japan says the P.L.O. is its best customer, but every dollar is worth it. We can be in touch with any of our diplomatic missions anywhere in less than half an hour."

Finally, and most important, Arafat played the "Seer." He taught his people how to look at the world only through a crystal ball—his crystal ball. You see, the Palestinians' predicament, caught between Israel and the Arabs, was really an impossible one. It could not bear up to close scrutiny; it could never be examined under a microscope; it could never be subjected to a real empirical analysis—otherwise it would deliver heartbreak and resignation. It always had to be viewed through a crystal ball, where the difference between fantasy and reality would be blurred, distorted, and thrown out of proportion, where the scope for imaginative interpretations would be great, where defeats could be declared victories and total darkness transformed into glimmering lights at the end of the tunnel.

Life without illusions is unbearable, especially if you are a refugee, and Arafat gave the Palestinians all the illusions, and even some of the substance, which made their dispersion bearable. Arafat's approach, however, required a very special city— one that was open to illusions, tolerant of seers, free of laws, and fun enough to wait around in until Palestine was redeemed. After Arafat and his men tried to take over Amman, Jordan, in 1970, and were driven out by King Hussein, they fled to Beirut and found just the city they were looking for—or so they thought.

I will never forget the very first PLO press conference I attended in Beirut.

It was in June 1979 and Yasir Arafat and several other senior PLO figures were giving the briefing in a shabby apartment block in West Beirut. I don't recall a thing they said. What I do remember is that on my way in I noticed a big old black Cadillac Eldorado, one of those late-sixties models with big fins, parked outside. I asked another reporter who this Batmobile belonged to. He replied, "That revolutionary car belongs to Zuhair Mohsen." Mohsen was the leader of al-Saiqa, the pro-Syrian faction of the PLO. A bovine figure with silver hair and a diamond-dripping Syrian wife, Alia, Mohsen was an armchair revolutionary if there ever was one. He was known in Beirut as Mr. Carpet, because of all the Persian carpets he and his men had stolen during the Lebanese civil war. When the rigors of leading the revolution became too much for him, Mohsen would split to an apartment he kept on the famous La Croisette Promenade in Cannes, probably the most expensive stretch of real estate on the French Riviera.

In July 1979, Mohsen made one his frequent rest stops in Cannes, having overexerted himself leading the PLO delegation to an Organization of African Unity summit in Liberia. After a long night at the blackjack tables of the Palm Beach Casino, Mohsen walked back to his apartment in the luxurious Gray d'Albion building at one o'clock on the morning of July 25. Just as his wife opened the door to let him in, a young man, described as "Arab-looking," stepped out of the shadow with a .32-caliber pistol and blew part of Mohsen's brains all over the marble floor. I was in the PLO news agency office in Beirut the day after he died and Arafat's newsmen there put out a statement that was pure tongue-in-cheek, noting that this great revolutionary Palestinian "hero and martyr" was killed "on the way to the field of battle."

The cynicism of both Mohsen and his eulogizers disgusted me, but my encounter with this late-lamented guerrilla leader was an important lesson about Beirut. Beirut was a city built on myths. Every night there was one of the 1,001 Arabian Nights—seductive, theatrical, illusionary. The distinction between words and deeds was often lost in Beirut. It was a display culture, a city of amusement-park mirrors, which made short people look tall, fat people look thin, and insignificant people look important. Men loved to pose there—revolutionaries by day, merchants and gamblers by night. Life did not imitate art in Beirut; it was art. With a little money and a mimeograph machine, you could buy whatever identity you wanted in Beirut. Just by putting up one checkpoint manned by two teenage thugs on a busy highway in Beirut, you could turn yourself into a four-star general, a political party, a tax collector—hell, you could be a whole liberation movement if you wanted. The law of Lebanese politics was: I have a checkpoint, therefore I exist.

No one became more ensnared by Beirut's charms and chains than Yasir Arafat and his PLO. On the one hand, Beirut was a godsend for Arafat. He was able to use his manipulative skills to play off the Lebanese Muslims and Christians against each other, and carve out his own mini-state between them, thus enhancing his independence. The Fakhani, Sabra, and Shatila neighborhoods of West Beirut became Arafat's first quasi-sovereign territory—a tree house, where he could always run and hide from the pressures of the various Arab regimes. Beirut also enhanced Arafat's relevance, since it put the PLO in contact with a huge and generally uncritical international press corps, many of whose members identified with the PLO as underdogs and sixties-style revolutionaries. At the same time, Beirut provided Arafat and the PLO with a base for launching guerrilla raids directly into Israel and for recruiting and training operatives for spectacular hijackings or international terror attacks, such as the 1972 Munich Olympics massacre, which kept the Palestinian cause relevant and impossible to ignore. Finally, Beirut strengthened Arafat's ability to maintain PLO unity, since virtually all the PLO factions were headquartered in Lebanon (for the same reasons it attracted Arafat), and this enabled the PLO chairman to impose a certain limited degree of physical and economic domination over them by virtue of the fact that his own al-Fatah organization was the most powerful force on the ground.

But while Beirut enhanced Arafat's unique leadership attributes, it also tightened his political paralysis. Why? Because Beirut, city of illusions, made waiting for Godot fun. It made it easy for the PLO to continue avoiding the concessions for peace, which might have brought about a negotiated settlement with Israel, and to continue pretending that it was preparing for war with Israel, when in fact it was doing no such thing.

Beirut, and the mini-state Arafat created there, drained the PLO leadership, and to some extent the rank and file, of the impatience a normal national liberation movement would feel about achieving its avowed objectives, which, in the case of the PLO, was the recovery of all or part of Palestine. With its attractive nightlife, restaurants, and intellectual ferment, Beirut became for many PLO functionaries the *watan al-badeel*—the substitute homeland, as they called it, and one which in many ways was far more exciting than the boring Galilee villages in which their fathers were raised. Sitting in Beirut, it was very easy for the late Khalil al-Wazir, alias Abu Jihad, "Father of Struggle," then Arafat's top military deputy, to declare when asked why he wouldn't come to terms with Israel that "we will not be squeezed by time."

Why should they? The 1970s were a great era for Third World revolutionary politics, and the PLO joined in the jamboree. Their printing presses cranked out great manifestos and their silk-screen artists produced dramatic posters, with guns superimposed over maps of Palestine and Palestinian men and women in heroic poses. It was the Che Guevara era of West Beirut. George Habash went off to discuss the global revolution with the great Korean revolutionary Kim Il Sung; radical PLO guerrilla leader Nayef Hawatmeh talked about Lenin with Brezhnev, while Arafat held counsel with fellow revolutionaries from Castro to Mao. Palestinian intellectuals sat around Faisal's Restaurant in West Beirut arguing about the direction of their revolution and the evils of the Zionist enemy, all gulped down with some of the best hummus and arak in the Middle East. Ali Hassan Salameh, one of Arafat's senior intelligence operatives and a man with particular affection for silk shirts and tailored suits, married Georgina Rizk, the Maronite Lebanese beauty queen who once won the Miss Universe contest. She was enough to make any man's stay in Beirut tolerable. Ali Hassan's, however, was cut short by an Israeli hit team, who blew him up with a car bomb in downtown Beirut to avenge his role in the 1972 Munich Olympics massacre of Israeli athletes.

Arafat himself did not share in the corruption, but he tolerated it in his closest deputies. His longtime chief of intelligence, Atallah Mohammed Atallah, alias Abu Zaim, lived in an opulent apartment in West Beirut on Rue Beshir Kessar. Actually, he had one huge apartment, blanketed with mirrors, for himself, and two others for his twenty-two bodyguards—each of whom made about $300 a month. Abu Zaim had two wives, one in Jordan and the other a stunning Lebanese Maronite, who tooled around West Beirut in a red Mercedes. I got to hear a lot about Abu Zaim, because one of my best friends in Beirut knew his chief guard, who loved to regale him with stories of his boss's excesses. One of his favorite tales was about the night Abu Zaim was giving a party and called down to the chief guard on his intercom and ordered him to get a kilo of caviar from a well-known Beirut deli, the Mandarin.

The guard, a simple soldier, asked, "What is caviar?"

"Never mind," Abu Zaim told him. "Just go to the store and ask for it."

But this was 10:00 p.m., and when the guard got to the Mandarin it was closed. So he and his men woke up the neighbors, found out where the owner lived, and went to his apartment. When the guerrillas knocked at his door, the owner looked through the peephole, saw a bunch of armed men, and began begging for his life.

"We are from Abu Zaim," the guard reassured the owner. "He wants caviar."

When the owner heard this, he was so relieved that he threw on some clothes, went down to the shop, and gave the guard two kilos of caviar. The guard told my friend that he found this "caviar stuff" so offensive-smelling that he carried it back to Abu Zaim's apartment with his arms extended, the way one would carry a dead fish.

With such a city to run home to, no wonder Arafat passed up an excellent opportunity to make a clear-cut declaration about peace with Israel when the whole world was listening—when he was invited to address the United Nations on November 13, 1974.

Arafat's idea of a peace initiative was to point to the June 9, 1974, decision by the Palestine National Council, the PLO's parliament-in-exile, in which the PLO committed itself to establishing an "independent combatant national authority for the people over every part of Palestinian territory that is liberated." That was Arafat's way of hinting that he would accept a state in the West Bank and Gaza. Not surprisingly, the world, not to mention Israel, missed the point.

Five years later, Arafat would squander another excellent opportunity when Egyptian President Anwar Sadat negotiated the Camp David accords, which included a provision for Palestinian autonomy in the West Bank and Gaza that might have served as a springboard for the creation of a Palestinian state.

Even the PLO leaders in their franker moments admitted that since the early 1970s, when the PLO settled into Beirut, all it had done was tread water. Salah Khalaf, alias Abu Iyad, the number-two figure in the PLO's political hierarchy, once remarked in an interview with the Kuwaiti newspaper *Al-Anba* (September 7, 1988): "We have not taken a single step on the road to an independent Palestinian state since 1974."

In Beirut, the PLO not only enjoyed the hummus and the nightlife, but it also got to taste real power, and this, too, made it in less of a hurry to return to Palestine. The PLO had their boots on the necks of the Lebanese Muslims in West Beirut, and some of them loved it. These sons of Palestinian refugees, who had been kicked around by the Arabs and Palestinian upper classes all their lives, finally got to change roles, and they did it with all the relish and subtlety of a New York street gang emerging from the South Bronx to impose its rule on Park Avenue. Beginning in the early 1970s, the PLO became the dominant militia in West Beirut, partly just to protect its own civilians from the Phalangists and partly at the behest of the Lebanese Muslims to be their sword against the Christians in the civil war. The PLO eventually became so much a part of the Lebanese domestic conflict that Abu Iyad declared one day that the road to liberating Jerusalem "runs through Juniyah," the Phalangist militia-run port in East Beirut. In other words, before they could liberate Jerusalem they had to liberate Juniyah. Arafat became the effective mayor of West Beirut, and to his credit he kept it a relatively open and Westernized place. The same cannot be said for all his associates. When they were not busy fighting the Phalangists or the Israelis, PLO factions engaged in frequent street fights and turf battles with Lebanese Shiites and Sunnis in Beirut, Sidon, and south Lebanon—which was exactly what the PLO was embroiled in on the eve of the Israeli invasion in June 1982.

Lebanese political scientist Ghassan Salame had it right when he said, "The P.L.O. leaders were archetypical petit bourgeoisie. They were neither notables nor educated professionals, but rather school teachers, like Abu Iyad, or engineers, like Arafat. They were a frustrated class from families which had neither power nor wealth. So, just like any other Lebanese militia, the PLO became a machine for the social promotion and advancement of a certain class of people. Don't think for a minute that they didn't love giving orders to the sons of Palestinian notables. In Lebanon, the PLO became so obsessed with social promotion it stopped caring about Palestine."

The PLO had a bagpipe band in Beirut. I once heard it perform as part of an honor guard reception for Jesse Jackson when he came to visit Arafat in September 1979. The bagpipers were Palestinians who had defected from the British-trained Jordanian army, where they apparently acquired their musical knowledge from Scottish advisers. They were a slightly ragtag bunch, each with a different camouflage guerrilla uniform. Their performance for Jackson was a cacophony for both the eye and the ear.

As the PLO got spoiled in Beirut, it turned from an ascetic, authentic, and even courageous young guerrilla organization living primarily in the hardscrabble hills of south Lebanon and trying to lead an armed struggle against Israel, into a rich, overweight, corrupt quasi army and state, complete with bagpipe bands, silver Mercedes limousines, and brigades of deskbound revolutionaries whose paunches were as puffed out as their rhetoric. Instead of continuing to confront Israel in the only effective way possible—through painstaking, grassroots guerrilla warfare—the PLO drifted to two extremes which sapped its strength.

On the one hand, the more the Palestinians became part of the Lebanese game and display culture, where men loved to strut around in uniforms, the more they tried to develop into a conventional Arab army. They acquired old Soviet-made T-34 tanks and organized into brigades with officers and ranks and chauffeurs. Every other PLO official you met gave his rank as captain or colonel. The PLO's Korean War–vintage tanks and its army of colonels were great for posing in the Lebanese theater, and maybe even useful in a war with other Lebanese militias, but they proved useless in a conventional battle with the ultra-modern Israeli army.

On the other hand, some PLO factions went to the opposite extreme, eschewing any form of conventional warfare and concentrating instead on spectacular headline-grabbing terrorist attacks or airline hijackings inside and outside Israel, augmented by occasional guerrilla shelling of the Galilee. This terrorism was another form of theater. It was a means of winning attention in the television age, but it was no means for winning a war. There is no question that these spectacular operations put the Palestinian cause on the news agendas of Israel and the world at a time when the world would have been more than happy to go on ignoring the Palestinian issue. In this sense, I believe that terrorism, while morally repugnant, was functionally relevant for the PLO at its takeoff stage. The problem was that these spectacular terrorist operations became an end in themselves, instead of just a necessary phase or instrument in a larger struggle to achieve a political solution.

This media terrorism actually ended up hurting the PLO more than helping it, because the PLO leadership fell in love with their own press clippings. Headlines became a narcotic substitute for truly meaningful grassroots political or military actions and gave the PLO leaders a much exaggerated sense of their own strength. They mistook news reports for real power and theatrical gestures like hijackings for a real war with Israel. This helped them delude themselves into thinking that history was on their side, that they were getting stronger, and that this was no time for making concessions to Israel.

The cynicism and the theater of Beirut came together for me one afternoon in 1979, a day after someone tried to blow up Christian leader Camille Chamoun with a car bomb. The explosion was a split second late and missed him. The next day I went to Chamoun's apartment in East Beirut to interview him. I found his living room filled with get-well bouquets, many of which were affixed with the personal business cards of those who had sent them. As I waited for Chamoun to receive me, I discovered in a corner a huge floral wreath upon which was a white business card with the printed name: "Yasir Arafat." Arafat had sent Chamoun get-well flowers. These two men had sent so many young men to die in defense of their own personal power and status, and now they were sending bouquets. That was Beirut. Beirut was a theater and Arafat thought he could star in it forever.

Then one day an outsider stormed in, without even buying a ticket. He was a big man, a fat man, and he did not understand the logic of the play.

6

Inside the Kaleidoscope:
The Israeli Invasion of Lebanon

All your friends are false; all your enemies are real.

—Mexican proverb

Ariel Sharon never sent Yasir Arafat flowers.

Whatever one thinks of the former Israeli general and Defense Minister, Sharon did not play games with his enemies. He killed them. After a few years in Beirut, I came to understand a little why the Jews had a state and the Palestinians didn't. The European Jews who built Israel came out of a culture of sharp edges and right angles. They were cold, hard men who always understood the difference between success and failure, and between words and deeds. Because the Jews were always a nation apart, they developed their own autonomous institutions and had to rely on their own deep tribal sense of solidarity. This gave them a certain single-mindedness of purpose. They would never settle for a substitute homeland; life for them was not just another Mediterranean life cycle or fatalistic shrug.

The single-mindedness of the European Zionists also had a certain ruthless aspect to it. They emerged from ghettos in which they were never invited by the outside world to drink coffee. They were never part of a Middle Eastern kaleidoscope, like Lebanon, where today's enemy could be tomorrow's friend. For the Jews coming out of Europe, today's enemy was tomorrow's enemy. The world was divided into two: the Jews and the goyim, or Gentiles. The Arabs, for the Zionists, fell into two subsets of goyim—agents and enemies. Agents you ordered and enemies you killed.

The rhythm of life in the Arab world was always different. Men in Arab societies always tended to bend more; life there always moved in ambiguous semicircles, never right angles. The religious symbols of the West are the cross and the Jewish star—both of which are full of sharp, angled turns. The symbol of the Muslim East is the crescent moon—a wide, soft, ambiguous arc. In Arab society there was always some way to cushion failure with rhetoric and enable the worst of enemies to sit down and have coffee together, maybe even send each other bouquets.

My landlord in Beirut, Fast Eddy Ghanoum, was forever shouting at me from his balcony in his baritone voice: "Thomaaaaaas, come have coffee." I always thought of this invitation as a mating call, beckoning me into Eddy's diwan for some sort of Arabesque negotiating encounter. It always meant that Eddy wanted something from me: more rent, a new lease, a phony receipt for the tax man, in one case, an autographed picture of Ronald Reagan—but always something. And always, over coffee, we would work out some compromise.

When he was a young boy, my friend Fouad Ajami used to be sent out by his landlord father in Beirut to collect rent. "Before I would go," Fouad once told me, "my father would always say to me, 'Whatever you do, don't have coffee or tea with anyone. You are going to collect rent. If you have coffee or tea you won't come back with the rent.' Islamic society always threw a web over men that restrained them, but the European Zionists came out of a different culture and faith and they were not shackled by any webs. That was how they made a state. The Sephardim, the Arab Jews, never could have built Israel. They would have had coffee with the Palestinians instead."

Ariel Sharon epitomized the ruthless single-mindedness of the European Zionists. I will never forget a story he once told me about a secret visit he made to East Beirut in 1982, five months before Israel's June invasion.

"I wanted to see the Phalangists at home, to see how they looked there," Sharon recalled with a whimsical air. "The thing I remember most was coming into their harbor [Juniyah] at night. There were all these lights around. So I asked them, What are all these lights? They said, 'They are from our ships.' I said, What ships? They said, 'Our ships—we are trading. Ships are unloading here, and then the goods are being taken across to Saudi Arabia and the Gulf and all over.' They told me, 'Arik, war is war and business is business.' Then we drove all around Beirut. Bashir Gemayel drove me in his own car. We had a few guards, but we were driving around the city ourselves. I saw all these beautiful girls and everything that was going on there. They were in a war, but people were going about their business. Could we conduct our lives the same way? No. In Lebanon everything is a compromise. Compromises, compromises, all the time compromises. The question is, can we, the Jews, live here with a compromise, and I think the answer is no. When a country like Lebanon loses a war, the consequences of military defeat are a number of casualties, loss of prestige, and other things. With the Lebanese nothing ever comes to an end. Nothing is ever final there. Nothing. But with the Jews it can come to an end."

Then pausing for a moment to contemplate his own analysis, Sharon added tersely under his breath, "To a bitter end."

So Ariel Sharon never had coffee with anyone. He invaded Lebanon with a devastating singleness of purpose. But Lebanon, like any house of mirrors and illusions, is always easier to step into than it is to find a way out of. Arafat at least understood Beirut; he knew just what the city was and why he was there. Sharon, despite his secret visits, didn't have a clue about the place—the same was true of most Israelis—which was why, in the end, Sharon and his army would have to crash their way out almost the same way they crashed their way in.

I saw them come and I saw them go, and a strange group of invaders they were indeed. They arrived in Beirut like innocents abroad and they left three years later like angry tourists who had been mugged, cheated, and had all their luggage stolen with their traveler's checks inside.

*   *   *

Around 10:00 p.m. on June 13, 1982, the news first crackled over the Phalangist militia's radio station in a bulletin from East Beirut. We all huddled around the old German radio at the Reuters office and tried to imagine what our ears were telling us: The Israeli army had arrived at the gates of Beirut.

Today it is hard to remember how remarkable and shocking it was to us, and the world, that Israel was surrounding an Arab capital. One week after the invasion had begun, a column of Israeli tanks and armored personnel carriers were five miles from downtown Beirut, parked on a bluff near the Lebanese presidential palace in Baabda, with a deluxe view of all Beirut below. As a result, the main highway from Beirut to Damascus was effectively cut, and since all other roads leading into the city from the south had earlier been severed, Beirut was under siege.

The next morning, June 14, I rose early from my room at the Commodore Hotel and ventured across the Green Line dividing Muslim West Beirut, where I was living, from the Christian eastern half of the city; reporters and noncombatants could still move back and forth freely, if they didn't mind running a gauntlet of armies, militiamen, and freelance snipers. To be honest, I wanted to see for myself these Israelis, these fellow Jews, whom I suddenly found pitching tents at my doorstep and creating fear inside me as well as my Muslim neighbors. I came to Beirut thinking I would be virtually the only Jew there; suddenly I had company.

Their brown, dust-caked armored personnel carriers, about thirty in all, were parked in a perfectly straight row along the road leading into Baabda. Some Israeli soldiers with grizzled beards and tousled hair were lounging against the iron treads of their vehicles, either snoozing or eating breakfast from tin cans. Others were snapping pictures of Beirut from automatic cameras. I walked between the vehicles, notepad in hand, asking, "Does anyone here speak English?" I got mostly hostile stares, until one friendly boy sitting atop his APC shouted down at me, "Yeah, I do. Where are you from?"

"I'm from *The New York Times*," I said.

"The New York Times!" exclaimed the soldier in American-accented English. "Do you know Bill Farrell?"

Bill, who unfortunately has since died of cancer, was helping me cover the story in Lebanon. Several years earlier, though, he had been the *New York Times* bureau chief in Israel.

"Sure," I answered, "he's with me here in Beirut."

"Well," said the soldier, "he knows my folks from Jerusalem. Tell him when you see him that Rose Weinberg's son says hello."

Whenever I think of the Israelis invading Lebanon, I always think of Rose Weinberg's handsome, rosy-cheeked boy introducing himself on that sunny Beirut morning. He had the fresh face and warm innocent eyes of someone who belonged on a poster selling Jaffa oranges. Before the summer was over, though, Lebanon would erase both our smiles.

Today, nine out of ten Israelis will tell you that they opposed the Lebanon invasion from the start; this is sheer nonsense. The war did have a few outspoken opponents from the beginning, but the truth is that the myths, fears, and expectations that drove Defense Minister Sharon and Prime Minister Menachem Begin to launch the invasion were widely shared, and not just in the right-wing Likud Party but in the traditionally left-of-center Labor Party as well. The Labor Party probably never would have initiated a Lebanon invasion, but once the attack had begun, they jumped on the bandwagon and became willing accomplices in the early months. Labor's initial backing for the invasion was based on the same basic perception as the Likud's: that this war was only the latest round in Israel's long struggle for survival against its eternal enemy, the Palestinians, as represented by the PLO. The consensus view in Israel was that Arafat and his men had concentrated too much firepower in southern Lebanon, shelled northern Israel too many times over the years, and were gaining too much international legitimacy through their mini-state in West Beirut. Never mind that the number of Israeli casualties the PLO guerrillas in Lebanon actually inflicted were minuscule (one death in the twelve months before the invasion); never mind that the PLO was drifting aimlessly in Beirut, spending most of its time fighting with other Lebanese Muslim militias, especially the Shiites. The bogeyman Arafat had to be tamed before he grew any bigger. That is why none other than Yitzhak Rabin, the former Labor Party Prime Minister, stood with Ariel Sharon on the outskirts of West Beirut in the first month of the war and urged him to "tighten" his siege of the city and to cut off the water supply. That is why, around the same time, Hebrew University political theorist Shlomo Avineri, one of the Labor Party's leading ideologues, was understood to have lectured a gathering of reserve officers from the Israeli Army Education Corps that Israeli troops would be justified in entering the heart of Beirut to excise the PLO. Only when the war started to go sour, drag on, and become unpopular did the Labor leaders vociferously protest that they favored only a 25-mile-deep invasion—not a blitzkrieg all the way to Beirut—and that no one had told them about the war's "grand designs." Had those grand designs worked, however, Rabin and others would have cheered them along as well, because those designs, too, were based on myths and longings which ran as deep into the Labor Party as into the Likud. No war was ever launched or fought by one or two men, and the Israeli invasion of Lebanon was no exception. This wasn't just Begin's war and it wasn't just Sharon's war. It was Israel's war, and this is precisely what makes it worth reexamining.

The first weeks after the invasion began were heady days for the Israeli boys in Lebanon, days of discovery and, they thought, of making new friends. Every other Israeli soldier I met in Lebanon told me about his new Lebanese acquaintances "Pierre" and "Leila." More than a few Israeli officers enjoyed playing Lawrence of Lebanon, as they were put in charge of this or that occupied Lebanese village and treated like Lord-High-Everythings by natives bearing gifts who wanted to ingratiate themselves with Lebanon's newest occupiers. It seemed as though every Israeli soldier had brought his camera and was constantly taking pictures of the huge Lebanese hilltop mansions, the Swiss-chocolate-wrapper scenery, the Mediterranean fish restaurants in Juniyah port, and the buxom, Cleopatra-eyed Lebanese girls in designer bikinis that left little to the imagination. This was not the Sinai, filled with cross-eyed Bedouins and shoeless Egyptian soldiers. This was the world's biggest duty-free shop, and Israeli troops came back from the first weeks of the war loaded down with pastries, videos, cherries, and even some world-class Lebanese hashish. Many soldiers smuggled these goodies by stuffing them into the hollow armor plates covering their Merkava tanks. Who said war was hell?

Neri Horowitz, a young Israeli from Jerusalem who served as a paratrooper in Lebanon and had a keen eye for war's incongruities, once remarked that one of his first recollections of Beirut was not of a battle but of a shopping spree.

"My mother is crazy about Danish butter cookies and English tea," said Horowitz. "When I came home from Beirut for the first time I brought my mother tea and cookies and my sister a T-shirt with a Lebanese cedar tree painted on it. It was as if I had just been to Europe or something. I simply went into a supermarket in Baabda one day and went shopping. I actually took a shopping cart and pushed it down the aisles, alongside all these Lebanese housewives, with my Galilee rifle slung over my shoulder."

And then the American Jews came. The Hadassah women and the big donors to the United Jewish Appeal were bussed up to East Beirut and taken by the Israeli army on special tours of the front, where they got to pose in flak jackets atop mud-splattered tanks and peer through binoculars at real live artillery blasting real live "terrorists." The really big donors—$100,000 a year and above—got special intelligence briefings with topographical maps. There is nothing better for priming an American Jewish donor than giving him a ride with victorious Israeli troops. This wasn't like planting a tree or going to a kibbutz and watching some Israeli farmer milk thirty cows at a time. This was power, raw Jewish power, and the American Jews were made to feel part of it. Everywhere you went in Lebanon, Jews were getting their pictures taken. This was not a nation at war, it was a nation on tour. Admittedly, there were a few nasty street fights with pockets of Palestinian resistance around the south Lebanon port of Sidon that spoiled some pictures, but these would soon be "mopped up." The Israelis were always using terms like "mopping up"; Lebanon was just a dirty floor and they were there to clean it and restore its original shine.

Captain Teddy Lapkin, an intense and devoted young officer in the elite Golani Brigade that spearheaded the Israeli invasion, recalled the moment when his unit first crossed the Lebanon border. "We were by the village of Taibe, and you could see the Beaufort Castle [a mountaintop PLO stronghold in south Lebanon] perched on the hill, and you could see our planes, the Skyhawks, swooping in and dropping their bombs, and you could see the artillery fire impacting on the castle, and we just said to ourselves, 'Okay, let's do it.' I remember we passed one of the United Nations observation posts just across the border and this American captain walked out. We had so many tanks on the road, they were all congested in a traffic jam, so I started talking to this guy. Talk about hubris and arrogance. I said to him, 'We're going to finish this goddamn problem once and for all.' "

Two months later, recalled Lapkin, after his first tour in Lebanon was over and he had gained some inkling that this "goddamn problem" might not be so easy to finish, most Israelis still thought Lebanon was a nice place to visit, even if you didn't care to live there.

"I was hitching a ride up to Beirut with a reserve unit at the end of July," remembered Lapkin. "They were just going in for the first time. I think they belonged to the southern command and they were like a bunch of tourists. They were out with their cameras and shouting, 'Hey, stop the bus! We want to take a picture.' I was just freaking out. They reminded me of Israeli tourists on a bus going around London. I didn't say anything, but I remember thinking, What the hell do these people think they're doing? You see, there was a period until about September when it was fun to be in Lebanon. You would go up to Juniyah port and see the Christian enclave and take a jeep and just tell your officer, 'Hey, Yossi, I'm gonna take a jeep and go down to the restaurant, have some fish.' A lot of guys were carrying on with the Lebanese women in [the village of] Monte Verde above Beirut. A lot of the Lebanese women were gorgeous and their husbands were away working in Brazil. Guys were talking like, 'Hey, I'm gonna go skiing here when the snow comes.' It was the Indian summer of the Israeli invasion, like the last flash of summer before autumn would come and the roadside bombs would begin."

The attitude that Lebanon was a friendly place, where the Israelis might soon be able to come skiing in the winter, reflected the profound Israeli ignorance about the true nature of Lebanese society and the players there. Before the 1982 invasion, Israeli scholarship and intelligence on Lebanon was extremely scanty. Lebanon had never been an active enemy of Israel's, so few resources were devoted by the army or academic institutions to learning about it. Since few Lebanese Jews had settled in Israel, there was also a real shortage of people who knew the country and the subtleties of its politics firsthand. The few authentic Israeli experts on Lebanon tended to rely largely on newspaper clippings and radio broadcasts for raw material in making their assessments, and naturally these public media conveyed little of the richness and mendacity of Lebanese political life, which was like a gigantic Kabuki play, where everyone wore a mask, and where the politicians almost always did the opposite of what they said.

I once asked my friend Avraham Burg, who had served as an Israeli paratroop officer in south Lebanon, how well he had been prepared for the invasion; his answer really summed up what most Israelis, including government ministers and military officers, knew about their neighbor. "We knew that there were Christians in the south, but we didn't know anything about what was north of that belt," said Burg. "We knew it was some kind of complicated Middle East Belfast. Okay, so they had lots of tribes. It meant nothing. We didn't know about the differences between Sunnis and Shiites. And then, all of a sudden, we went in. It was like there was this window and we knew something was behind it, but we didn't know what. We went through it anyway. We discovered it was a kaleidoscope that keeps changing."

Indeed, instead of entering Lebanon with a real knowledge and understanding of the society and its actors, Israel simply burst in with tanks, artillery, and planes in one hand and a fistful of myths in the other—myths about the nature of Lebanon as a country, about the character of Israel's Lebanese Maronite Christian allies, about the Palestinians, and about Israel's own power to reshape the Middle East. It would take three months, but eventually these myths would undermine all that the Israeli military hardware achieved.

What the Israelis did not understand about Lebanon as a country was that the real Lebanon was two Lebanons—at least two. As I noted in the introduction, the real Lebanon was built on the merger between Maronites, representing the Christian sects, and the Sunnis, representing the various Muslim sects. It was a merger between equals. The reason most Israelis did not understand this simple fact was that their basic impressions of Lebanese society were formed not in 1982 but during the 1930s and 1940s, when contacts were first made between Zionist officials in Palestine and Maronite Christian representatives in Beirut. On the surface, the Maronites and the Jews thought they had much in common: some Maronites saw themselves as modern-day Phoenicians bringing all the Phoenician diaspora back to Lebanon, just as the Zionists were doing with the Jews; together they would restore the ancient Mediterranean civilization. Other Maronites and Jews saw themselves as kindred "beacons of Western civilization," bringing light to the hordes of Arab–Muslim unwashed still living in the Dark Ages. Through their contacts with the Lebanese Maronites (the Lebanese Muslims were not interested in the Jews, and vice versa) a view began to take hold among early Zionists that Lebanon was a Christian society in the same way that theirs would be a Jewish society. Sure, like Israel, Lebanon also had an Arab–Muslim "minority," said the Zionists, but it was basically a country dominated by Christian businessmen who would gladly recognize a Jewish state as soon as just one other Arab nation went first.

After the 1948 war, Lebanon, in line with all other Arab states, sealed its border with Israel and severed all links. As a result, I am convinced, the original romanticized Israeli views about Lebanon forged during the first contacts with the Maronites became fixed in the Israeli psyche. Between 1948 and 1982 if you asked any Israeli about Lebanon he would repeat the standard Israeli cliché: "We don't know which Arab country will be the first to make peace with us, but we know which will be the second—Lebanon."

I found that whenever I told Israeli soldiers in Lebanon that there were also Muslims there, it was like telling them that there were also Arabs in Israel. They would say, "Yes, yes. I know, but the Christians are the *real* Lebanese," just as they saw themselves as the *real* owners of Palestine. Who could blame them? Each Israeli soldier entering Lebanon was given a red-and-white pamphlet entitled *Lebanon*, published by the Israeli army education corps. The entire 14-page pamphlet, a condensed history of Lebanon, contained only two passing references to the Shiites, Lebanon's largest single religious community in the 1980s. As for the political objectives of the invasion, the pamphlet said: "The main goal of the Israelis in Lebanon is to secure the existence of the Christians and to make possible a political arrangement that will enable Lebanon to recover its sovereignty."

Had Israelis understood that the real Lebanon was two Lebanons, they would have understood that the only way to restore stability and sovereignty to the place was not by supporting only the Christians and driving out Yasir Arafat and his PLO guerrillas. The PLO's presence was only a symptom of Lebanon's ills; it exacerbated those ills, but it was not their cause. The real source of Lebanon's troubles was the fact that these two Lebanons—Christian and Muslim—frequently were at odds with each other, going back to the very foundation of their state, when they were literally thrown together. The PLO, the Syrians, and the Israelis were all at one time or another drawn into Lebanon by the Muslims and Christians, each of whom looked for outside help when they felt they might be vanquished by the other. The only time Lebanon was relatively peaceful and stable was when there was a balance of power between its Muslims and Christians—"no victor and no vanquished," as the Lebanese themselves liked to say—so that neither community felt the need to whistle up assistance from abroad.

Had the Israelis understood that the real Lebanon was two Lebanons, they also never would have entertained the notion that Lebanon could ever be the second Arab country to sign a peace treaty with the Jewish state. Lebanon made its living—a very good living at that—being the entrepôt between the West and the Arab world. Goods from the West were dropped off or manufactured in Beirut and then sent by plane or truck to Saudi Arabia, Kuwait, Syria, and as far away as Oman. Lebanese were educated in Western systems and then shipped off to run hotels and businesses in the Arab hinterland. In return, the Saudis, Kuwaitis, Syrians, and other Arabs used the Beirut banking system to handle their finances, its educational institutions to teach their children, and its mountains to relax in during the heat of the summer. With an economy so dependent on the Arab–Muslim world, Lebanon was destined to be the *last* Arab country to sign a peace treaty with Israel, because only after all the other Arab countries had reconciled themselves to the Jewish state could Lebanon afford to do so.

One myth begets another. Since Israelis mythologized the nature of Lebanon, they also mythologized Bashir Gemayel and his Maronite Phalangist militia, with which they teamed up to fight the PLO in the summer of 1982. Because Menachem Begin, Israel's Prime Minister from 1977 to 1983, saw Lebanon as basically a Christian country threatened by Muslims, he viewed the Maronites and other Lebanese Christian sects as similar to the Jews. Begin was forever asking aloud why the Christians of the world never spoke out when their co-religionists were being "slaughtered" in Lebanon by the Muslims. It was as though they were the Jews of Eastern Europe in the 1940s and Israel was going to save them. One of Begin's closest associates once told me, "You always have to remember that Begin grew up in a Catholic country, Poland, where he was persecuted by Catholics when he was a little boy. Begin absolutely loved the idea that he could now be in a position to save the Catholics of Lebanon. He was going to be their St. George, and he was going to do it all while snubbing his nose at the Catholics of Europe. It was his ultimate revenge. The Maronites also knew how to play Begin like a guitar. They were always reminding him of the story in the Bible about King Hiram of Tyre [a port in south Lebanon], who sent the cedars for Solomon's Temple. They all had that story down pat, and Begin loved to hear it."

Begin's mind was so clouded by his own mythology that he, along with most other Israelis, did not notice that these "Christians" they were going to save in Lebanon were not a group of hooded monks living in a besieged monastery but, rather, a corrupt, wealthy, venal collection of mafia-like dons, who favored gold chains, strong cologne, and Mercedeses with armor plating. They were Christians like the Godfather was a Christian. Motivated by a combination of fear and greed, these Christian warlords were determined to do anything necessary to hang on to the predominant governmental positions of power assigned to them by the 1943 national pact, despite the fact that in the intervening decades the Muslims had become the overwhelming majority in Lebanon.

The world did not speak out when these Christians were being killed, because frequently they were being done in not by Muslims but by each other, in wars for control over turf and the spoils that went with it. Only two years before the Israeli invasion, I was on hand to witness what became known as the "Day of the Long Knives." On July 7, 1980, Bashir Gemayel tried to wipe out his main Christian militia allies-cum-rivals in East Beirut, Danny Chamoun's Tigers. This was not a battle over dogma or sacred texts. It was about whose militia would control the illegal ports and patronage and insurance rackets in East Beirut. Gemayel's men launched a surprise attack against Chamoun's Tigers in their barracks and at the Safra Beach Club, where many of them were relaxing. Witnesses related that some of the Chamounists were shot in the head while Phalangist gunmen sat on top of them by poolside; others were cut down with machine guns, along with the innocent sunbathers who had the misfortune of being at the club that morning. Still others were thrown screaming out the windows of the Safra Hotel and shot in the air like ducks in a penny arcade. Gemayel was something of an expert in gangland murders. Back on June 13, 1978, he did the same to his other main Christian rival, Tony Franjieh, son of former Maronite President Suleiman Franjieh. Bashir Gemayel's hit team, led by a Maronite medical student, Samir Geagea, burst into Tony's bedroom in the northern village of Ehdene at 4:00 a.m. and riddled him and his wife, Vera, with machine-gun fire while they were sleeping; they did the same to the Franjiehs' three-month-old baby, Jehane, their maid, their chauffeur, and, for good measure, the family dog. Gemayel was quite at home with Hama Rules. As he once told Israel Television's Arab affairs correspondent, Ehud Ya'ari, when Ya'ari reproached Bashir for mistreating some Druse, "Ehud, this is not Norway here, and it is not Denmark."

Another reason the Israelis never saw who their Maronite allies really were was that the Israelis are terribly vulnerable to anyone who winks at them. This is understandable considering that Israelis have lived their entire history surrounded by a sea of hostile Arab faces. Naturally, they constantly long for a smiling face, some validation of their existence that will enable them to feel at home. One day from the back row of this hostile ring someone winked at them; his name was Bashir Gemayel. But Gemayel didn't just wink; he whispered the idea that the two of them could reshape Lebanon and forge a peace treaty. As a former Israeli Mossad secret service official described it: "The Maronites wined us and dined us. They gave us information about the PLO. Who would reject this? Only a fool. It was just a dose, but we got an overdose. It was like drugs. It was an addiction. You would come to Juniyah on secret visits and see beautiful girls in the harbor and Arab high society and get intelligence on the PLO on top of it. And then this camaraderie developed. Some of our people stayed behind to train some of theirs and became enchanted. It was an entree into the Arab world we had never had before with anyone—with a little taste of James Bond tossed in. Who could resist it?"

An Israeli friend told me of being at the Tel Aviv home of David Kimche in the late 1970s, at the time contacts were being intensified between Israel and the Maronite militias. Kimche, then a senior Mossad official, was one of the early architects of the alliance between Israel and the Gemayels. That particular evening he was hosting Danny Chamoun at his house and had invited several Israelis to join the discussions. As the evening at the Kimches' wore on, the wine began to flow and Chamoun got looser and looser. At one point Chamoun took my friend aside and told him in a wobbly voice, "Look, never forget something. You Israelis are instruments for us. If you don't help us, we will just turn to the Syrians."

My friend said, "I immediately went over to Kimche and told him what Chamoun had said. Kimche just dismissed it with a flick of his wrist. 'Don't pay any attention to him,' he said. 'He's drunk.' "

Chamoun may have been drunk, but his comments were sober and should have been heeded. But Kimche, and many of his colleagues in the Mossad, were not ready to listen. Whenever senior Phalangist officials used to talk about the Palestinians, they did so in the most blood-curdling terms, which prompted Israeli leaders to believe that the Phalangists hated the PLO even more than they did. What the Israeli leaders did not know was that the Phalangists often talked about the Lebanese Druse, Sunnis, and Shiites in equally deprecatory language. For the Phalangists, the summer of '82 was simply another round in the Lebanese civil war that had begun in 1975. Their prime objective was not to get the PLO out of Lebanon as an end in itself; their prime objective was to win, definitively, the Lebanese civil war, so they would not have to make any power-sharing concessions to the Lebanese Muslims. Like a good Lebanese tribe, the Maronites wanted the egg *and* its shell. The Israelis were the pigeons they thought would bring them both. And they knew just how to appeal to the Israelis: they would dangle the Palestinians in front of them, like worms before hungry birds.

An Israeli friend of mine who was a paratrooper in Lebanon told me of the day he realized he was being had. "Our battalion was based in the Shouf Mountains near Aley," he said. "One day a Phalangist officer came to our liaison officer in the Shouf and told him that he had some special intelligence: a house down the

road from us had four Palestinian terrorists from Saiqa [a pro-
Syrian PLO faction] inside. So we were ordered to go down and
destroy the house. We really put fire on it. I mean we used rockets,
everything. When we cleared the rubble we found four bodies.
They were all Druse. We felt really bad about it."

The Phalangists were always ready to fight to the last Israeli.
They hung back throughout the first three months of the war and
let the Israelis do all the dirty work inside the Palestinian camps.

"In August 1982, I was stationed with a unit on the roof of this
Christian guy's house in East Beirut, near Baabda, not far from
the Green Line," recalled Neri Horowitz, the Israeli paratrooper.
"Nearby we had a tank. We would keep an eye on Palestinians
trying to move from house to house with ammunition on the other
side of the Green Line, and if we saw any we would call in tank
fire onto the specific house. Well, this Christian guy who owned
the house we were on was always kissing us and coming up to
the roof to look through our binoculars whenever our tank fired.
Whenever we hit anything, he would cheer and jump up and
down. So one day the Palestinians figured out what we were doing
and they fired a shell at us. The guy's house got a little damaged.
He immediately ran up to the roof and screamed at us, 'Get out,
get out of here, go away.' "

Teddy Lapkin, the captain in the Golani Brigade, recalled how
at the end of the summer of '82 he was ordered to go with a unit
of Phalangists into the Muslim town of Mashghara, in the southern
Bekaa Valley, where the PLO and some local Muslims had stored
arms. "We took some prisoners. My men tied their hands behind
their backs and then the Phalangists just started beating the shit
out of them. I had to stop them myself, otherwise they would
have killed them. I put the prisoners all in a room and had one
of my people stand guard all the time to make sure the Phalangists
didn't kill them. The Phalangists were good for parades. Sarto-
rially they were well put out. They were well-armed hairdressers.
It was like a military fashion contest among them. If a guy had
a Kalashnikov with a sniperscope on it, they would all go, Oohh,
aahh, and if someone had a nifty knife, then he was hot shit.
They were paper soldiers: whooosh, you could just blow them
over. But they sure knew how to use us."

Whenever Israeli officers complained about the behavior of the
Phalangists, the word usually came down from on high to stifle

it. "Don't upset Bashir" was a popular phrase around the Israeli headquarters in Lebanon. As one Israeli intelligence officer explained it, "Once we were inside, we discovered a lot of things we didn't like, but it was too late then to turn back. We needed the Phalangists to lead us around, show us who was who. They were our only allies. But mostly we needed Bashir. The whole thing was built around him."

Not only did the Israelis enter Lebanon with a myth about their allies, the Phalangists, but also with one about their enemies, the Palestinians. Many Israelis had convinced themselves that there was no such thing as a legitimate Palestinian nation with a legitimate national claim to any part of Palestine. They saw the Palestinians instead as part of an undifferentiated Arab mass stretching from Morocco to Iraq and with no particular cultural, historical, or ethnic identity linked to the land of Palestine. This myth was one of the oldest and most enduring in Zionist history. In the early twentieth century, when the Zionist movement was just taking off, it may have been a necessary myth. To be able to convince Jews to pick up and leave their homes in Moscow, Johannesburg, New York, Mexico City, London, and Montreal and come to settle in Palestine, the Zionists had to look through the Arabs to some extent. If the Zionists had come to Jews around the world and said, "Look, we want you to come to Palestine, but you had better understand that there is another legitimate nation there, the Palestinians, who claim it as theirs and will fight you to the death," many Jews might never have come. So the Zionists had to believe, as the saying at the time went, that they were "a people without a land" coming to "a land without a people." Arafat wasn't the only political leader in the area who understood that at times the optimal way to achieve things— sometimes the only way—is by ignoring the facts and living instead by myths. Myths are precisely what give people the faith to undertake projects which rational calculation or common sense would reject.

Nevertheless, what distinguished Israel's founding father David Ben-Gurion from Yasir Arafat, and most other Israeli leaders as well, what gave him his lasting impact on Jewish history, was his keen understanding that while it was necessary to ignore some realities in order for a movement like Zionism to begin, at a certain point down the road it was also necessary to let reality in; the beginning myth will always destroy the desired end if it is not tempered with reality. Therefore, starting in the 1930s, Ben-Gurion accepted the notion of partitioning Palestine into two states—one for the Jews and one for the Palestinian Arabs—a program that was eventually adopted by the United Nations in 1947. Ben-Gurion felt that if the Jews were ever going to get their own state they needed international legitimacy and support, and the only way to get that was by compromise.

Ben-Gurion's archrival at the time, Menachem Begin, never accepted this accommodation with reality. He rejected the UN partition plan and consistently held out for Jewish sovereignty over all the ancient land of Israel, from the Mediterranean to the Jordan River and beyond, in line with the original Zionist program. After Begin's Likud Party defeated Labor for the first time in the 1977 elections and Begin became Prime Minister, he used his position to bring many Israelis around to his point of view. This was not all that difficult, since even many Labor Party supporters never really believed the Palestinians were a legitimate nation with whom they had to share the land. It was former Labor Party Prime Minister Golda Meir who said in a 1969 interview with *The Sunday Times* of London, when asked about the Palestinians, "They do not exist." Labor's support for partition in 1947 had been largely tactical; once they got the state, many laborites, too, preferred to think of the Palestinians as simply "Arab refugees" who should be resettled in the surrounding Arab states, with which Israel would eventually sign peace treaties. Even after Israel occupied the West Bank and Gaza Strip in 1967 and was again confronted with large numbers of Palestinians, most Israelis preferred either not to see them, or referred to them, as Begin did, as "Arabs of the land of Israel."

Because Begin fundamentally rejected the notion of a legitimate Palestinian nation, with a legitimate claim to Palestine, anything done politically or militarily on behalf of this "bogus" Palestinian nationalism was viewed by him as illegitimate and potentially criminal. But the PLO did not just pose a physical threat in Begin's eyes. It also posed a deeply troubling existential threat to the Zionist enterprise. The PLO officially embodied the Palestinian national claim to Palestine, which was the negation of the Zionist-Jewish claim to Palestine. Wherever the Israelis went, the PLO followed, holding up the deed to Palestine and telling whoever would listen that the land did not belong to the Jews. Whenever I talked to Sharon about the PLO, he would always refer to them as a "cloud" that hung over Israel's head. Then he would wave his hand above his head as though he were trying to sweep this cloud away.

In very simple terms, then, the "Palestine Problem" for Begin and Sharon, and a good many other Israelis, was not one of two equally legitimate national communities—Jews and Palestinians—seeking a national home in Palestine. The Palestine Problem was the problem of marauding Arab bands killing Jews, engaging in terrorism, and refusing to accept the Jewish people's God-given right to the land of Israel from the Mediterranean to the Jordan. The Arab organization that was most responsible for killing Israelis and spuriously claiming Jewish land as their own was this thing called the PLO. Therefore, the PLO was the Palestine Problem; if they could get rid of the PLO, thought Sharon and Begin, they would get rid of the Palestine Problem. Because with the PLO out of the way, they figured, the Palestinians in the West Bank and Gaza would stop demanding independence and accept some form of limited autonomy according to the Camp David accords. Israel would then be in a position to dominate all of Palestine, without having to share any land or real power with the "Arabs" living there, the same way the Maronites hoped to dominate all of Lebanon without having to share any real power with the Muslims.

The idea that Israel might finally be able once and for all to bring an end to the physical and existential challenge of the Palestinians was an intoxicating notion that touched the soul of the vast majority of Israelis, and this explains why so many of them were ready to join Begin and Sharon on their march to Beirut. Like all the other Middle Eastern tribes, the Israelis also knew how to reach for the egg and its shell.

In order to pull off the invasion, though, one more Israeli myth was necessary: the myth of power. Begin, who was born in 1913, spent the formative years of his youth in Poland in an era of rampant anti-Semitism, in a world in which Jews were spat upon. He lived for the chance to correct the indignities that he and his forefathers had suffered for centuries. Begin loved the idea of

Jewish power, Jewish generals, Jewish tanks, Jewish pride. They were his pornography. He needed a war to satisfy his deep longing for dignity and to cure all his traumas about Jewish impotence. Begin, I am convinced, needed a chance to lead 500,000 Jewish soldiers in a battle against Arafat, who for him was only the latest in a long line of anti-heroes who had risen up to slaughter the Jews. It was no surprise that at the height of the war, Begin declared, almost with enthusiasm, that in besieging Arafat he felt as though he were going after "Hitler in his bunker."

But what made Begin even more dangerous was that his fantasies about power were combined with a self-perception of being a victim. Someone who sees himself as a victim will almost never morally evaluate himself or put limits on his own actions. Why should he? He is the victim. At one point during the Lebanon war, a little Lebanese boy was injured, reportedly during an Israeli air strike, and President Reagan put a picture of his bandaged body on his desk. When Begin heard about this, he put on his desk a famous picture from World War II of a small Jewish child wearing a yellow armband with a Jewish star on it, raising his arms in surrender to some Nazis. Begin always reminded me of Bernhard Goetz, the white Manhattanite who shot four black youths he thought were about to mug him on the New York subway. Once you have been mugged enough times, as Goetz had, no one can tell you that you are not entitled to blow out the brains of some black kid for even thinking about mugging you. Begin, unfortunately, was a victim with more than a Saturday-night special; he was Bernhard Goetz with an F-15.

Yet for all his need for a war, Begin did not quite have the guts or the know-how to manipulate a whole country and a whole army to satisfy his quest. Ariel Sharon did. Sharon didn't share Begin's victim complex, but he had his own fantasies about power. Sharon knew how strong Israel was, and he believed, wrongly, that this military strength could, in an almost mechanical fashion, solve a whole knot of complex, deeply rooted political problems— that tiny Israel could drive the PLO out of Lebanon, install Bashir Gemayel as President, neutralize Syria and the Lebanese Muslims, get Lebanon to sign a peace treaty, and then force the Palestinians living in the West Bank and Gaza Strip to accept Israeli rule. Unlike Hafez Assad, Sharon did not know when to stop; he did not understand the limits of power in a fragmented, unpredictable place such as Lebanon. Assad was a brutal realist with a very limited agenda—survival. Sharon was a brutal realist with a strategic design, or, as Israeli political theorist Yaron Ezrahi liked to say, "Sharon was a realist at the tactical level and both a mythmaker and a man possessed by myths at the strategic level." That is precisely what made him so dangerous in Lebanon. He behaved with a decisiveness and unwavering sense of direction, as though he knew exactly where he was going strategically, when in reality he didn't have a clue about the world he was charging into. His strategic design in Lebanon was based entirely on self-delusions, which is why it eventually led Israel into a disaster. His was a classic example of false leadership.

But Ariel Sharon is a historical type which some people find very seductive, and one of them was Menachem Begin. Sharon understood that Begin needed a war, and Sharon, aided and encouraged by his Arab-hating Chief of Staff, Lieutenant General Rafael Eitan, had just the war for him—with maps and plans and even willing allies. Sharon understood, though, that the Israeli people would not accept his grand designs; they would not spill their blood to make Bashir Gemayel President. So Sharon called the Israeli invasion Operation Peace for Galilee, an operation designed to clear the PLO away from Israel's northern border. It was simple, modest, and logical—something all Israelis, Labor and Likud alike, would support. They would discover the full agenda later.

So the man-with-the-maps joined with the victim-in-search-of-dignity and together they led their country into Lebanon, promising that when it was all over there would be "forty years of peace."

The minute the Israeli army invaded Lebanon, Arafat's world of illusions started to crumble. The first to go was the notion that the PLO was still the vanguard of an Arab nationalist revival and the conscience of the Arab world. Arafat had repeated this notion so many times in speeches, he had clearly become convinced of it. What Arafat hadn't seemed to notice was that in the decade between 1973 and 1982 the Arab world had been broken, either by wealth or by the whip. The wealthier states had grown tired of the PLO's revolutionary rhetoric, its endless waffling, and its shakedown operations. At the same time, Ayatollah Khomeini's revolutionary takeover of Iran in 1979 posed a radical Islamic threat that the Arab oil states found far more frightening, both militarily and ideologically, than anything coming out of Israel.

Since the Arabs were unwilling to give the Palestinians enough resources or sacrifices to see them through to success, they compensated them instead with money and rhetoric. They adorned all the PLO's failures, whether in Amman or in Lebanon, with victory bouquets, and indulged them in all their revolutionary bravado, which the Palestinians, as a weak and victimized people, needed as compensation. The one thing the Arabs never did, though, was to take Arafat aside and tell him, "Look, my friend, the power realities are stacked against you. Your people got in the way of a bad storm called the Zionist movement. It could have happened to any of us, but it happened to you. If you really want to help your people, cut the best deal you can now with the Jews. Save whatever land you can and forget the rest." Instead, as Fouad Ajami put it, "the Arabs walked away from the Palestinian cause while swearing eternal fidelity to the Palestinians."

In the 1970s, Arafat used to boast that the Palestinian guerrillas would spread out around the Arab world like "fish in the sea," but thanks to Arab indifference in the summer of '82, they became fish in a barrel. Saudi Arabia's King Faisal fought the 1973 war with the oil weapon, but nine years later all that his successor King Fahd would lift to defend Beirut was his telephone to call President Reagan and plead with him to get the Israelis to turn the water back on to West Beirut. Given a choice between watching highlights about the Israeli invasion of Lebanon and the World Cup soccer matches that were being played during the summer of '82, most Arabs tuned in to the World Cup. This came as a bitter shock to many Palestinians. The PLO finally had its war and nobody came—nobody but Sharon.

This stone-cold reality was first brought home to Arafat not by the Arab leaders themselves but by their Lebanese surrogates— the Sunni Muslim bosses of West Beirut. The Sunnis of West Beirut had used the PLO as their club in the Lebanese civil war, and the PLO in turn had used them to be able to stay in town. But when the Israeli army began bombarding West Beirut, their bargain broke down. The cost of carrying the PLO became too great for the Lebanese Muslims to bear. So, after the Israeli army had been besieging West Beirut for almost a month, the Muslim leaders finally put the screws to Arafat to leave during a climactic confrontation on July 3, 1982.

The setting for this historic moment was a fitting one—the white three-story mansion of former Lebanese Prime Minister Saeb Salam, which had been built by his father in 1912, when he was a deputy in the Ottoman parliament. On that Saturday afternoon the eight leading Sunni Muslim figures of West Beirut gathered in Salam's marble-floored dining room to discuss how to persuade the PLO to leave encircled West Beirut. Arafat and his top political adviser, Hani al-Hassan, were invited to join the group at 12:30 p.m. Salam later described the scene for me.

When Arafat arrived wearing his tightly creased pea-green army uniform and cap, he and his aide were ushered into the dining room and seated around the long Chippendale table lighted by an antique chandelier. Salam, a crafty seventy-seven-year-old politician, opened the discussion by praising Arafat and reaffirming that his men had fought the good fight against impossible odds. "The PLO has covered itself in honor," said Salam, "and now it is time to leave with honor."

Arafat was seated to Salam's right. His cap was resting on the table. He listened to the various remarks of the Sunni bosses as to why he should quit Beirut, and he responded with counterarguments of his own. The dignity and honor of the PLO were at stake, he declared. This was a question of "saving face," and his men would never lose face before the Israelis. They would prefer to die fighting street to street, said Arafat, rather than walk out of West Beirut in disgrace. Seeing that his soft-spoken approach was not having its intended effect, Salam began to raise his voice. The military battle was obviously over, he shouted, and now was the time for the PLO to transform itself into a purely political organization—for its own sake and for the sake of the people living in West Beirut.

Clearly hurt and on the defensive, Arafat shot back, "Do you want to push us out? Is that it?"

"With all the sacrifices we have made for you and your cause," stammered Salam in a still louder voice, "you cannot say that about us. It is better for you, and for us, that you go—with your honor."

The discussion continued in this tone for four and a half hours, with others occasionally interjecting remarks to cool things down. At one point a crew from Lebanese Television arrived to take some posed footage of the meeting, but even as the cameras were rolling, the talks exploded into another shouting match between Arafat and the others. One of the Sunni leaders at the meeting had to use his influence with Lebanese Television to get the film destroyed before it could be shown on the nightly news. At 5:15 p.m. Arafat agreed to study what had been discussed and to put it before his colleagues in the PLO leadership. As it was Ramadan, the holy month when Muslims fast from dawn until dusk, Salam suggested that Arafat leave and return for the traditional evening *Iftar* meal.

Two hours later, Arafat and Hani al-Hassan returned and joined the Sunni notables and the Salam family around the dinner table. Everyone agreed that there should be no talk of politics during the meal of ground meat, cold yogurt, and eggplant. Arafat listened as the others exchanged anecdotes. He ate little except for the black olives set in the middle of the long table. After dinner Arafat, a devout Muslim, asked if he could be excused to perform the evening prayers alone. He went into Salam's den, faced south toward Mecca, and recited the ritual prayers on the white carpet in solitude. When he returned to the dining-room table, Arafat said he had something to deliver. He removed the ever-present notepad from his breast pocket and slipped out a folded piece of white PLO stationery. Putting on his black glasses, a distressed Arafat began to read from the document, written in his own scrawl under the letterhead of the PLO commander in chief. His voice full and resonant, Arafat read: "To our brother, [Lebanese] Prime Minister Shafik al-Wazzan. With reference to the discussions we have had, the Palestinian command has taken the following decision: The PLO does not wish to remain in Lebanon."

When he finished reading the crucial lines, Arafat handed the note to Salam, who immediately had it photocopied. Later that evening Salam had the note relayed to American special envoy Philip C. Habib.

But old myths die hard, and the bigger they are the harder they die. Three days after Arafat first signaled his willingness to leave West Beirut—a move which I always believed was a tactical stall on his part, designed to buy enough time for outside powers to rein in the Israelis and enable the PLO to remain in Beirut—I interviewed him at the PLO's press office on that shrapnel-littered street in the Fakhani neighborhood of West Beirut. He seemed buoyant of spirit, but the war was clearly taking its toll on him, which was registered in the red rims of his eyes and the way he nervously tapped his toe on the floor as he spoke. At one point I asked him if he was disappointed in the Arab response to the invasion. He looked me in the eye and asked rhetorically, "How long will the Arabs remain silent?"

The tone of Arafat's voice suggested he still believed the Arab world would jump into the war on his side, or do something meaningful to take the pressure off while the PLO fought for its life. After another month of Israeli bombing and shelling of West Beirut, though, he would have no such illusions; neither, for that matter, would any other Palestinians.

During the last weeks of August 1982, when it was clear to the PLO guerrillas that their sojourn in Beirut was finished, some anonymous person who called himself Ayoub began hanging card-board signs with Arabic messages on them on the shutters and door handles of shops just off West Beirut's main shopping street, Hamra. Each morning a new batch of signs would appear from the mysterious Ayoub, and Ihsan Hijazi and I would go out and read them before the shopkeepers tore them down. They were clearly the work of some frustrated Palestinian poet, and they expressed the bitterness of the whole Palestinian nation, a bit-terness that was not so much directed against the Israelis, who were their avowed enemies, but toward the Arabs, who were their avowed family—family who had failed to lift a finger mili-tarily to save the Palestinians in their dire hour of need.

"There are two kinds of Arabs today," read one sign. "The Arabs of fear and the Arabs of sheep. But we alone in West Beirut are making history—Ayoub."

"Today we are in shelters," read another sign, "but tomorrow the Arab leaders will be on shish-kebab skewers—Ayoub."

But the sign that intrigued me most, and seemed to be repeated most often, was the one that truly expressed the existential sense of abandonment which the Palestinians and the PLO felt that summer of '82. It read: "Tell your children what Israel has done. Tell your children what the Arabs have done. Tell your children what the world has done—Ayoub."

Ayoub is the Arabic name for Job, the biblical figure of endless, patient suffering.

The other myth the Israelis punctured was that the PLO was a real military force. The fact is, the Israeli invasion, for all that it was predicted, caught the PLO rather unprepared. While many of the Palestinian guerrillas fought bravely, the Israeli army cut through their lines and reached Beirut in less than a week with relatively little difficulty, except around the Palestinian camps in Sidon and in the Shouf Mountains, where Syrian tank units were posted. Had Israel not chosen for political reasons to avoid entering West Beirut in the second week of the war, the PLO, which was then in a state of confusion, might have been routed in a matter of days.

But for many of the Palestinians it didn't matter that they were being overrun on the field of battle. There was always a compensation—always a *badeel*. For some Palestinian guerrillas the compensation was just getting the chance to fight the war against the Jews that some of their fathers and grandfathers never fought in 1948. There were no Arab armies in the way this time; it was just the Jews and the Palestinians face to face. A few days after Israel had crushed all the PLO bases in south Lebanon, I met George Habash, the leader of the Popular Front for the Liberation of Palestine, in an underground bunker beneath an apartment building in West Beirut. This pediatrician-turned-guerrilla had been fighting the Israelis since 1948, when he was twenty-one, and was easily the most charismatic of all the Palestinian leaders. The air in the bunker was stale and musty and "Dr. George" sat erect behind a small table, surrounded by a knot of young guerrilla devotees. To him the fact that the battle in south Lebanon had been lost seemed totally insignificant. The most important thing was that there had been a battle at all. By marshaling their entire army to fight the Palestinians, the Israelis were in effect granting them the most profound form of recognition. His silver hair shining in the dim light, Habash punctuated all his comments by slamming his left arm down on the table, sending little puffs of dust into the air.

"I thank God," he shouted, oblivious to the irony of the great Arab Marxist invoking the Almighty. "I thank God," he continued, bringing his fist down onto the table, "that I lived to see the day that a Palestinian army fought an Israeli army. Now I can die. I don't need to see any more." Waving his arm around at his young acolytes, he added, "I feel sorry if anything happens to these young men, but now I can die, for we really fought them."

Habash didn't die, and neither did Arafat. Despite all their tough rhetoric, they agreed in the end to evacuate West Beirut. They said they were leaving to spare the city, but I don't think the Arab world or even many Palestinians bought it. They were leaving because they were surrounded, and were lucky to be getting out alive. The real tragedy is that all their theatrics and miscalculations had been staged on the backs of sincere Palestinians—guerrillas, refugees, and bureaucrats—men and women who had picked up and left Jordan, Syria, or other refuges to follow the PLO. They were entitled to a much better leadership than they ever got.

Arafat agreed to start evacuating his guerrillas from Beirut, beginning on August 21, 1982. I arrived at Beirut port early that day to wait for the international peacekeeping troops to land and escort the PLO out. The French peacekeepers were the first to hit the docks, and I accompanied some of them as they fanned out to take control of the main intersection on the road leading into the port from West Beirut, which they were supposed to take over from a unit of the Syrian-controlled Palestine Liberation Army. The PLA officer in charge had been out of touch with his commanders for weeks, however, and didn't have any orders that the French were coming. He demanded that the French officer sit down and write him a letter saying that the Palestinian officer had turned over his post "with dignity." The Frenchman borrowed a paper and pen from me and wrote out the letter in longhand. Then the Palestinian officer insisted that a formal turning-over ceremony be conducted. On one side, he lined up all his men, a ragtag lot who probably had not bathed for weeks, most of them wearing different helmets and pieces of uniforms. Facing them stood a unit of suntanned French Foreign Legionnaires, all of them wearing mirrored sunglasses and clean khaki uniforms, with their shirt-sleeves rolled up to reveal arms rippling with muscles.

They stood for a few minutes, each side barking out military commands, moving their guns from shoulder to shoulder. When the ceremony was complete, the Palestinian officer dismissed his men. They turned to run off, but one of them tripped and several others fell on top of him like Keystone Kops. But nobody laughed. Something about those guerrillas and the way they insisted on all the formalities after having held out for so many weeks bespoke a dignity which could not be tittered at. As I watched them I could not help but shake my head in awe at their commitment. They had guarded the approaches to West Beirut, armed with nothing heavier than rocket-propelled grenades, against an Israeli army deploying the most up-to-date weapons in the world; it was practically a suicide mission. They were nothing more than boys, but the look in their eyes said that, unlike their leaders, they would have fought to the end.

"Arafat muffed it," said *Manchester Guardian* reporter David Hirst, who had covered the PLO from its early days in Beirut. "The PLO was on the verge of its first real heroic moment. People were ready to go on. He blew it."

Maybe Arafat was wise to leave Beirut in order to fight another day, as he argued at the time. But the PLO was never quite the same after it quit Lebanon, and neither for that matter was the Arab world. Something in the Arab world died on August 30, 1982, the day Arafat himself boarded the Greek cruise liner *Atlantis* and sailed for Athens. (He refused to make any Arab country his first stop, so disgusted was he with the Arabs.)

Arafat's retreat marked the end of an era in Arab politics. After the fiasco of 1967, the PLO had emerged from the ashes like a phoenix that promised, and for a moment even seemed to deliver, a restoration of the lost dignity of the Arab nation. The guerrillas were going to lead a revolution that would sweep away the corrupt old regimes and make the Arabs again a force to be reckoned with. For the young, it was an age of political romance, and thanks to the OPEC oil revolution, there was plenty of money and Western sycophants around to feed the wildest expectations and illusions. But in the heat of the battle of Beirut the Arab nationalist dream, to which the PLO had anointed itself heir, crumbled into a heap of silk-screen heroes and empty slogans.

Lina Mikdadi, a half-Palestinian, half-Lebanese writer, was on hand August 30 when Arafat said goodbye to his Muslim allies at the home of Walid Jumblat. In her book *Surviving the Siege of Beirut* (1983), Mikdadi, who grew up in the heyday of the Che

Guevara–style Arab nationalist era of Beirut, with its student strikes, protest marches, and revolutionary poses, described the scene. "At Walid Jumblat's, the two men tried to maintain a brave front. 'I'm glad my father [assassinated Druse leader Kemal Jumblat] is not here to see this day,' Walid Jumblat said. . . . The show of bravado kept cracking; the wan smiles and niceties served to no avail. I felt a surge of anger and despair: Arafat might be going out alive, but we were defeated, utterly beaten. No, I refused to think that way: The Israelis didn't make it into the heart of West Beirut. Arafat stood up to leave, and I sobbed my heart out as the women threw rice in a last gesture of farewell. I cried for our lost Arab nationalism, the indifference of the Arab world, the thought of the Israelis at Beirut Airport."

Lebanese historian Kemal Salibi went down to Beirut port that day to watch Arafat actually walk up the gangplank. "What I remember most," said Salibi, "was Walid Jumblat. He was no great friend of Arafat's, but he accompanied him to the ship. When Arafat was about to leave, Walid took out a pistol and in the middle of this big crowd he fired it into the air as a salute. It was a very symbolic thing. It was not about the person Arafat, but about what the whole thing represented. West Beirut had become the last repository of the conscience of the Arab people. That was why in the last weeks of the summer many West Beirutis actually began to sympathize with the PLO. As much as they had wanted the guerrillas to be gone, they did not want to give the Israelis Arafat's head. It was as though West Beirutis recognized that in standing with the PLO against Israel they represented the last vestige of Arab dignity. It became a badge of pride to be in West Beirut in those last weeks of the summer. That was why I stayed. I wanted to be there. It was something you could touch, and this is what actually brought Walid to tears. To hell with the Arab world, he was saying, we are the only Arabs left. The only Arabs are the people of West Beirut."

Before he got on board, Arafat told his Lebanese friends with a certain unintended candor, "I am very proud because we had the honor of defending this part of Beirut. I am leaving this city, but my heart is here."

Some time after the PLO evacuation, I ran into Kemal Salibi in Amman, Jordan. Salibi was a true Arab nationalist, and a real lover of Beirut and all that it stood for. As we sat in an Italian

restaurant, I asked him to reflect back on that moment in August
1982 when Arafat left. What did it signify for Arafat, the PLO,
and the whole sixties generation of Arab politics? Instead of answering me straightaway, Salibi began reciting from memory a
poem, "Ozymandias," by Percy Bysshe Shelley. While a waiter
stood at tableside holding two bowls of soup, Salibi intoned:

I met a traveler from an antique land
Who said: "Two vast and trunkless legs of stone
Stand in the desert. Near them, on the sand,
Half sunk, a shattered visage lies, whose frown,
And wrinkled lip, and sneer of cold command,
Tell that its sculptor well those passions read
Which yet survive, stamped on these lifeless things,
The hand that mocked them, and the heart that fed:
And on the pedestal these words appear:
'My name is Ozymandias, King of Kings:
Look on my works, ye Mighty, and despair!'
Nothing beside remains. Round the decay
Of that colossal wreck, boundless and bare
The lone and level sands stretch far away."

Instead of turning West Beirut into his Stalingrad, as he vowed,
Arafat moved on to Tunis, where he relocated his headquarters
in the five-star Salwa Beach Hotel. I visited his men there shortly
after the evacuation. It was a strange scene: PLO officials lodged
in a 200-room hotel featuring an arboretum filled with strutting
peacocks in the lobby and waiters serving endless rounds of Arabic
coffee to retired guerrillas playing endless rounds of chess and
Ping-Pong. When people found out I had come from Beirut, all
they wanted to hear about was the only homeland many of them
really knew—West Beirut. The real Palestine was a dream: Lebanon was the concrete Palestine, where they had lived their lives,
gone to school, and controlled the streets. They pumped me for
information on friends and family and their favorite haunts. As
we sat in beach chairs, and the Mediterranean breeze danced
across the empty, pink-painted miniature golf course that guarded

the entrance to the hotel, there was a melancholy spirit in the air, a sense that something was over, that an opportunity had been lost.

"In Beirut, we were in exile," one of Arafat's senior aides remarked. "Here we are in exile from exile."

7

Poker, Beirut-Style

In the wake of the PLO's withdrawal from Beirut, Israel seemed to be on an unstoppable run of winning hands. Arafat and his men had been uprooted from their last independent base of operations and were dispersed around the Middle East in the grip of various Arab regimes, thereby eliminating them as a direct threat to Israel. At the same time, the Syrian air force and anti-aircraft units had been badly mauled in their confrontations with Israel and would take several years to rebuild. Syria's historic influence over Lebanese politics seemed to be in real danger of being broken. With some 14,000 PLO and Syrian fighting men having been evacuated from Beirut, the Lebanese Muslims were more or less disarmed and exposed to the dictates of the Phalangist militia and their Israeli backers. This made it possible for the Israelis and Phalangists to "persuade," through a combination of intimidation and bags of unmarked bills, enough Muslim members of the Lebanese parliament to elect Bashir Gemayel as the new President of the republic of Lebanon on August 23, 1982.

Bashir was the only candidate. During his six-year term, Begin and Sharon expected him to consolidate all the military gains the Israeli army had achieved during the first three months of the invasion, and thereby make it possible for Israel to withdraw from Lebanon without the country reverting to its old ways. Bashir was supposed to rebuild the Lebanese army so it could take over from the Israelis, keep the Syrians out of Beirut, prevent the PLO from ever taking root again in the Palestinian refugee camps, and, to top it all off, sign a peace treaty with the Jewish state. Begin and Sharon had bet everything on Bashir and now, it seemed, they were going to be able to cash in on his victory. The promised "forty years of peace" would soon be at hand.

But poker is a funny game. You can be winning all night long and then comes the final hand. You get cocky, so you bet the pot on four kings. It's virtually a sure winner, you tell yourself. Suddenly, the dealer smiles at you and says he wants another card. Right before your eyes he draws a card from the bottom of the deck and then lays his hand on the table: four aces.

All summer long Syria's President Hafez Assad had been losing his shirt in Lebanon. With Bashir's election, it looked as though Assad was going to have to resign himself permanently to an Israeli victory. But in Middle Eastern poker when the pot is at stake, the rules go out the window. The only rules become Hama Rules and Hama Rules are no rules at all. On the last hand of the summer, Assad topped the Israelis' four kings with an ace, which he pulled right off the bottom of the deck. The Israelis cried for the sheriff, and Assad just laughed.

"Around these parts," he told them, "I am the sheriff."

At 4:10 on the afternoon of September 14, 1982, Bashir Gemayel was meeting with a group of Phalangists at the party's Ashrafiye branch in East Beirut; Bashir came to the three-story apartment house every Tuesday afternoon at the same time. The purpose of this week's meeting was to discuss some details about how the Phalangist Party and militia would turn over power to Bashir's government and the Lebanese army that would be under his command.

What Bashir did not know, or had ignored, was the fact that living in this building were relatives of a twenty-six-year-old man named Habib Tanious Shartouni, who was a member of the pro-Damascus National Syrian Socialist Party, which espoused the idea of a merger between Syria, Lebanon, and Palestine, and was an active agent of Syrian intelligence. Shartouni had been assigned by his masters to observe Bashir's comings and goings in the building; since his sister lived inside, the Phalangist guards paid him scant attention. According to research by Jacques Reinich, a former senior officer of Israeli Military Intelligence who wrote his doctorate for Tel Aviv University on Bashir Gemayel, the Syrians decided to eliminate Bashir shortly after his election and before he was sworn in. Shartouni was ordered to come over to West Beirut by a senior NSSP official, Nabil al-'Alam, and was trained in operating an explosive device that fit into a suitcase and could be detonated by a remote-control button the size of an electronic garage door opener. On September 11, Shartouni, while ostensibly on a visit to his sister, moved the bomb into the apartment building where Bashir was to speak. On September 13, according to Reinich, Shartouni received a telephone call from a "Syrian intelligence officer" in Rome, who instructed him to assassinate Bashir the next afternoon. Shartouni placed his suitcase on his sister's living-room floor, which was directly above the room in which Bashir would be speaking. He then set the numbers on the bomb's digital readout to "51," which was the numerical code that primed the explosive to go off as soon as it received the proper radio signal.

Late the next afternoon Shartouni called his sister and told her to come over to his house immediately, saying that he had cut his hand; this was simply a ruse to get her out of the building. Shartouni himself climbed up to the roof of an adjacent apartment block and waited for Bashir and his caravan to arrive.

According to Reinich, Bashir began the meeting with a story about a statue that had been erected years ago of Lebanon's first President, Bishara al-Khouri. President al-Khouri's sons had complained at the time that the statue was not a very good likeness, but were told by those who erected it that they would "get used to it." "To all those who don't like the idea of me as President," Bashir told the Phalangist gathering, "I say, they will get used to it."

Moments later, Shartouni pressed the button on his remote-control device, emitting a radio signal that set off the bomb and shattered the apartment building, collapsing it into a cloud of dust and rubble. My colleague, *Washington Post* Middle East correspondent Jonathan Randal, said the only way they recognized Bashir's mangled corpse was from what remained of his prominent nose, the dimple on his chin, and his hexagonal wedding ring. Shartouni was arrested a short time later and confessed to the crime.

The Israelis immediately panicked, and for good reason. Bashir had been the keystone on which their entire invasion had been built. Having lost Bashir, Begin and Sharon decided they had better invade West Beirut and complete for themselves their immediate objective of wiping out the PLO as both a military and a political threat. The rest of their political objectives could be dealt with later. Ignoring an oral promise to the United States not to enter West Beirut after the PLO evacuated, Israeli troops fanned out across the western half of the capital in the early hours of September 15.

Two targets in particular seemed to interest Sharon's army. One was the PLO Research Center. There were no guns at the PLO Research Center, no ammunition, and no fighters. But there was evidently something more dangerous—books about Palestine, old records and land deeds belonging to Palestinian families, photographs about Arab life in Palestine, historical archives about the Arab community in Palestine, and, most important, maps— maps of pre-1948 Palestine with every Arab village on it before the state of Israel came into being and erased many of them. The Research Center was like an ark containing the Palestinians' heritage—some of their credentials as a nation. In a certain sense, that is what Sharon most wanted to take home from Beirut. You could read it in the graffiti the Israeli boys left behind on the Research Center walls: *Palestinian? What's that?* and *Palestinians, fuck you,* and *Arafat, I will hump your mother.* (The PLO later forced Israel to return the entire archive as part of a November 1983 prisoner exchange.)

The other target was the Sabra and Shatila Palestinian refugee camps, which had been two of the PLO's main bases of popular support since its arrival in Beirut in 1970. Sharon claimed he had intelligence that the PLO had left 2,000–3,000 guerrillas behind in these camps; I suspect this information was given to him by Phalangist intelligence. While the PLO undoubtedly left men behind, as much to protect their own civilians as to serve as cells for future organization, I am convinced that this figure was grossly exaggerated. In any event, the Israeli army would not enter Sabra and Shatila, only surround them. They had suffered too many losses trying to secure control of the Palestinian refugee camps around the south Lebanese port of Sidon earlier in the summer. It was time for their allies to do some work. So, on Thursday, September 16, 1982, two days after Bashir's death, the fateful Order Number 6 went out from the Israeli army general staff to Israeli troops in Beirut. It stated that the "refugee camps [Sabra and Shatila] are not to be entered. Searching and mopping up the camps will be done by the Phalangists and the Lebanese army."

I had gone on vacation after the PLO's withdrawal and was at New York's Kennedy Airport on my way to a few more days of relaxation in London when I heard myself being paged at the TWA terminal. It was my editors, with orders that came in a clipped staccato: "Bashir Gemayel has been assassinated. Go directly to Beirut. Do not pass Go. Do not collect $200." Beirut Airport was closed, so I had to fly to Damascus and take a taxi to Beirut. Normally this was a three-hour ride, but the Phalangists had blocked all the roads into Beirut from the east because of Bashir's funeral, so after a trans-Atlantic flight, I had to spend the night sleeping in my taxi driver's half-finished home in the Bekaa Valley. I literally didn't know where I was. All I remember was that there was so little light around I could see every star in the sky.

My driver and I rose early the next morning and headed for Beirut. It was Friday, September 17, 1982. Just as we got over the Mt. Lebanon ridge line and I could peer down into the city below, I saw someone fire a phosphorus shell, with its distinctive white smoke, into the area of town that I knew to be the Shatila camp. What could that be about, I wondered. When I finally reached the Commodore Hotel and met a few of my American press colleagues, they told me that they had heard a rumor that Phalangists were in Shatila. The camp was sealed off by the Israelis, though, so no one had been able to get inside. That night

at dinner, my friend from *Time* magazine, Roberto Suro, told me
he had managed to get to the edge of Shatila earlier in the day
and it had left him with an uneasy feeling. He had gone as far as
the Kuwaiti embassy traffic circle, which overlooked Shatila from
the west, and found a group of Phalangist militiamen relaxing,
being fed and provided for by a group of Israeli soldiers.

"There was this one Phalangist militiaman wearing aviator sunglasses who looked as though he might be in charge, so I decided
to try to talk to him," Roberto told me. "He was a tall, skinny
guy, and as we talked you could hear bursts of gunfire and explosions coming from the camps, but this guy didn't flinch. In
fact, he behaved as though it was perfectly normal. I asked him
what was going on inside and he just smiled. Not far away there
were these Israeli soldiers sitting on a tank. Even though there
was gunfire in the camp, they were just lounging around, reading
magazines and listening to Simon and Garfunkel on a ghetto
blaster. It was pretty clear to me that whatever was happening,
the Phalangists were going to be in charge of this area when it
was all over, so I asked this Phalangist officer what they were
going to do with Sabra and Shatila. I'll never forget what he said:
'We're going to turn it into a shopping center.' "

What none of us knew at the time was that a day earlier some
1,500 Phalangist militiamen had been trucked from East Beirut
to Beirut Airport, which they used as their staging ground. From
there, small units of Phalangists, roughly 150 men each, were sent
into Sabra and Shatila, which the Israeli army kept illuminated
through the night with flares. The Phalangists wanted to avenge
not only Bashir's death but also past tribal killings of their own
people by Palestinian guerrillas, such as the February 1976 massacre by Palestinians of Christian villagers in Damour, south of
Beirut. Sharon would give them their chance. From Thursday,
September 16, until Saturday morning, September 18, Phalangist
squads combed through the Sabra and Shatila neighborhoods,
liquidating whatever humanity came in their path.

Early Saturday, September 18, the Israelis "discovered" that
the Phalangists had been massacring Palestinians in the camp for
three days. The Israeli army command ordered the Phalangists
out of the camps, and then got as far away from the area as they
could so as not to be associated with the mass killings. That was

why when all of us showed up Saturday morning to check out the rumors, there was no one to stop us from going in and recording in detail everything that had happened.

The first person I saw in Shatila was a very old man with a neatly trimmed white beard and a wooden cane by his side. I would guess he must have been close to ninety. By the time I met him, he had been dead for hours. It was a clean job—a single bullet fired from close range that left only a tiny hole of dried blood in the center of his left temple. The killer probably looked him in the eyes, then pulled the trigger. He was sprawled on the ground near one of the western entrances to the camp, only a hint of what lay ahead in the death-scented alleyways. Farther inside, I saw a woman with her breast sliced open; a hastily dug grave of red dirt with an arm and a leg protruding from some poor soul almost demanding not to be forgotten; even horses were so riddled with bullets their bellies had burst. But mostly I saw groups of young men in their twenties and thirties who had been lined up against walls, tied by their hands and feet, and then mowed down gangland-style with fusillades of machine-gun fire. Where were the 2,000 PLO fighters supposed to have been left behind in the camps? If they ever existed, they certainly would not have died like this.

One old woman in a shabby brown dress, clearly out of her mind with grief, stood over a bloated body, waving a scarf in one hand and letters in another. She was shrieking over and over again in Arabic, "Yi, yi, are you my husband? My God, help me. All my sons are gone. My husband is gone. What am I going to do? Y'Allah. Oh, God, oh, God."

Across the street another mother emerged from the death scene in her house holding a faded color photograph of her son, Abu Fadi, and a wooden birdcage with a live yellow parakeet inside. While the bird danced and sang, the woman stumbled about and wailed, "Where is Abu Fadi? Who will bring me my loved one?"

No one knows exactly how many people were killed during the three-day massacre, and how many were trucked off by the Phalangists and killed elsewhere. The only independent official death toll was the one assembled by the International Committee of the Red Cross, whose staff buried 210 bodies—140 men, 38 women, and 32 children—in a mass grave several days after the massacre. Since most victims were buried by their relatives much earlier,

Red Cross officials told me they estimated that the total death toll was between 800 and 1,000.

Afterward, the Israeli soldiers would claim they did not know what was happening in the camps. They did not hear the screams and shouts of people being massacred. They did not see wanton murder of innocents through their telescopic binoculars. Had they seen, they would have stopped it immediately.

All of this is true. The Israeli soldiers did not see innocent civilians being massacred and they did not hear the screams of innocent children going to their graves. What they saw was a "terrorist infestation" being "mopped up" and "terrorist nurses" scurrying about and "terrorist teenagers" trying to defend them, and what they heard were "terrorist women" screaming. In the Israeli psyche you don't come to the rescue of "terrorists." There is no such thing as "terrorists" being massacred.

Many Israelis had so dehumanized the Palestinians in their own minds and had so intimately equated the words "Palestinian," "PLO," and "terrorists" on their radio and television for so long, actually referring to "terrorist tanks" and "terrorist hospitals," that they simply lost track of the distinction between Palestinian fighters and Palestinian civilians, combatants and noncombatants. The Kahan Commission, the Israeli government inquiry board that later investigated the events in Sabra and Shatila, uncovered repeated instances within the first hours of the massacre in which Israeli officers overheard Phalangists referring to the killing of Palestinian civilians. Some Israeli officers even conveyed this information to their superiors, but they did not respond. The most egregious case was when, two hours after the operation began on Thursday evening, the commander of the Israeli troops around Sabra and Shatila, Brigadier General Amos Yaron, was informed by an intelligence officer that a Phalangist militiaman within the camp had radioed the Phalangist officer responsible for liaison with Israeli troops and told him that he was holding forty-five Palestinians. He asked for orders on what to do with them. The liaison officer's reply was "Do the will of God." Even upon hearing such a report, Yaron did not halt the operation.

The Israelis had so demonized Sabra and Shatila as nests of Palestinian terrorism and nothing more that they didn't even know that probably one quarter of the Sabra and Shatila neighborhoods was inhabited by poor Lebanese Shiites who had come to Beirut from the countryside and bought the cinder-block homes of Palestinians who had managed to earn enough money to move from these shantytowns into the city. In fact, the street of the Shatila camp where the massacre began was populated largely by Lebanese Shiites. A picture in the *As-Safir* paper the day after the massacre was exposed captured the blind tribal rage of the Phalangists who tore through the camps. The picture, which occupied most of the top of the front page, consisted of a single hand. The fingers of this hand were locked around an identity card that could easily be read. The card belonged to Ilham Dahir Mikdaad, age thirty-two. She was a Shiite woman whose entire family, estimated to be forty individuals, was wiped out by the Phalangists. Her body was found lying on a main street in Shatila, with a row of bullets running across her breasts. It was clear what had happened: she must have been holding up her identity card to a Phalangist, trying to tell him that she was a Lebanese Muslim, not a Palestinian, when he emptied his bullet clip into her chest.

Sabra and Shatila was something of a personal crisis for me. The Israel I met on the outskirts of Beirut was not the heroic Israel I had been taught to identify with. It was an Israel that talked about "purity of arms" to itself, but in the real world had learned to play by Hama Rules, like everyone else in the neighborhood. The Israelis knew just what they were doing when they let the Phalangists into those camps. Again, as the Kahan Commission itself reported: during meetings held between Bashir Gemayel and Israeli Mossad secret agents, Israeli officials "heard things from [Bashir] that left no room for doubt that the intention of this Phalangist leader was to eliminate the Palestinian problem in Lebanon when he came to power—even if that meant resorting to aberrant methods against the Palestinians."

The Israelis at least held an investigation when they were involved in a massacre, which is more than the Syrians ever did. But for all their inquiring, what was the final outcome? Sharon, who was found by the Kahan Commission to bear "personal responsibility" for what happened in the camps, was forced to step down as Defense Minister and become a minister-without-portfolio instead, until the next Israeli government was formed, when he became Minister of Industry and Trade. Israel's Chief of Staff,

Rafael Eitan, who was also assigned blame for what took place in the camps, who had lied to dozens of world newsmen when asked if Israel had sent the Phalangists in, was allowed to finish his tour of duty with dignity and was then elected to the Israeli parliament. Brigadier General Yaron was told he could never get another field command, but was then promoted to major general and put in charge of the manpower division of the Israeli army, which handles all personnel matters. After fulfilling that job, in August 1986 he was handed one of the most coveted assignments—military attaché in Washington.

An investigation which results in such "punishments" is not an investigation that can be taken seriously. It was my introduction to a popular form of hypocrisy I would discover often on the road from Beirut to Jerusalem, what a Lebanese friend of mine liked to call "moral double bookkeeping." All the players in the Middle East do it. They keep one set of moral books, which proclaim how righteous they are, to show the outside world, and one set of moral books, which proclaim how ruthless they are, to show each other.

At the time, though, I didn't understand this kind of moral accounting. I took Sabra and Shatila seriously as a blot on Israel and the Jewish people. Afterward, I was boiling with anger—anger which I worked out by reporting with all the skill I could muster on exactly what happened in those camps. The resulting article—an almost hour-by-hour reconstruction of the massacre—was published across four full pages of *The New York Times* on September 26, 1982; it eventually won me a Pulitzer Prize for international reporting. I worked day and night on that story, barely sleeping between sessions at my typewriter. I was driven, I now realize, by two conflicting impulses. One part of me wanted to nail Begin and Sharon—to prove, beyond a shadow of a doubt, that their army had been involved in a massacre in Beirut in the hope that this would help get rid of them. I mistakenly thought at the time that they alone were the true culprits. Yet, another part of me was also looking for alibis—something that would prove Begin and Sharon innocent, something that would prove the Israelis couldn't have known what was happening. Although an "objective" journalist is not supposed to have such emotions, the truth is they made me a better reporter.

A week after the massacre, the Israelis granted me the only

interview given any Western journalist with Major General Amir Drori, the overall commander of Israeli troops in Lebanon. I was driven up to Aley, northeast of Beirut, to the Israeli headquarters at the summer palace of a Kuwaiti sheik. The interview was held at a long wooden conference table, with Drori seated at the head. Around the table sat all his staff, including Brigadier General Yaron, as well as my escort officer, Stuart Cohen, a gentle Israeli reservist from England whom I had taken a day earlier up to the roof of the Lebanese apartment building the Israelis had used as their headquarters outside Sabra and Shatila. I showed him through my own cheap binoculars—which were nowhere near as powerful as those used by Israeli troops—just how well one could see into certain open spaces in the camps, where the freshly turned dirt from mass graves used by the Phalangists to dump bodies was still clearly evident; Stuart was shocked. This was not the line that he had been fed from headquarters.

I must admit I was not professionally detached in this interview. I banged the table with my fist and shouted at Drori, "How could you do this? How could you not see? How could you not know?" But what I was really saying, in a very selfish way, was "How could you do this to *me*, you bastards? I always thought you were different. I always thought *we* were different. I'm the only Jew in West Beirut. What do I tell people now? What do I tell myself?"

Drori had no answers. I knew it. He knew it. It was clear his men either should have known what was happening, or did know and did nothing. As I drove back down to Beirut, I was literally sick to my stomach. I went back to the Commodore Hotel and called the *Times* foreign editor, Craig Whitney.

"Craig," I said, "the guy didn't have the answers. I really don't want to shovel this shit anymore. Let somebody else write the story."

"C'mon," said Craig softly, "you were there. You have to write it."

Of course I did, and I knew that, too. So the next morning I buried Amir Drori on the front page of *The New York Times*, and along with him every illusion I ever held about the Jewish state.

* * *

I saw Yasir Arafat in Amman, Jordan, a few weeks later, on October 9, 1982. The bodies from Sabra and Shatila were all buried, and Arafat had come to meet with King Hussein. It was his first visit to the Jordanian capital since the little King had ousted him in 1970. The first night Arafat was in town he addressed a rally in his honor at the PLO headquarters in Amman. He stood on the rostrum and with great fury and gesturing of arms told the thousands of Palestinians who had come out to greet him, "We lost 5,000 in Sabra and Shatila and we are ready to lose 50,000 before we liberate our homeland." Arafat always exaggerated the number of Palestinians killed in Sabra and Shatila. I felt that by exaggerating the number he only cheapened the lives of those who really did die, turning them into just another statistic to serve the PLO. The real figure was horrendous enough. But on that October evening in Amman, no one else seemed bothered by Arafat's arithmetic.

What I remembered most was that they just wanted to touch him. Arafat was like a rock star after a concert and the Palestinians there were grabbing at his clothes, trying to rub his beard or pat his checkered kaffiyeh as he ran a gauntlet of flying hands and arms. As he left the rostrum Arafat's guards had to drag him through a crush of people, and when he went by me all I saw was his head and smiling face being carried along on a sea of hands.

What was this all about? Arafat was supposed to be finished. What were these Palestinians touching? I think they were touching themselves in a way, making sure they were still there, still alive, still visible to the rest of the world. By all rights Yasir Arafat did muff it during the summer of '82, and in any other national liberation movement he would have been deposed as leader. But Arafat was saved by events. The abandonment of the Palestinians by the Arab world, the Phalangist massacre of Palestinians at Sabra and Shatila, coupled with Syrian President Assad's attempt a few months later to depose Arafat from the PLO leadership, intensified tenfold the bonding between Arafat and the Palestinian people at large.

For all his failings, Arafat's mere ability to survive against the forces that wanted to erase him, his ability to constantly bounce back, symbolized for Palestinians their own determination not to be forgotten and not to have their cause erased by the Arab and

Israeli forces that were so intent on doing so. The Palestinians
would not give these lions Arafat's head—as much as he might
have deserved it—because his head was their head.

After the summer of '82, Arafat became more than ever a
symbol, and maybe nothing more than a symbol, of the Palestinian
refusal to disappear. He was judged by Palestinians less for what
he produced than for what he represented. No one put it better
than a Palestinian coed at the West Bank's Bir Zeit University.
When I asked her why she stood by Arafat when he had brought
his people nothing but defeat, she said with tears in her eyes,
"Arafat is the stone we throw at the world."

Arafat's ability to turn himself into a symbol of Palestinian
survival, a human Palestinian flag, as it were, enabled him to
remain the leader of the PLO as if the summer of '82 had never
happened; a movement may trash its leaders, but it would never
trash its own flag. That became clear to me at the Algiers meeting
of the Palestine National Council, the PLO's parliament-in-exile,
which convened for the first time after the Lebanon invasion in
February 1983. To begin with, the meeting, instead of being a
serious critique of the PLO's behavior in Lebanon, was turned
into a festival of bombast about the "glorious PLO victory in
Beirut"—a victory, it followed, which did not necessitate any
change in the PLO leadership. An observer delegation from Hun-
gary presented Arafat with a bronze trophy, the Chinese brought
him a little red book, and a group of West Bankers delivered a
scarf knitted in the colors of the Palestinian flag.

When PLO moderate Issam Sartawi demanded to address the
PNC assembly, Arafat blocked him, so Sartawi resigned from the
organization in protest. As Sartawi was stomping out of the conference center he said to me, "It was outrageous that all the
secretaries general of the PLO organizations painted a picture of
Lebanon as a glowing victory. Lebanon was a disaster. I bow my
head to the courage of the people who fought there. But if Beirut
was such a great victory, then all we need is a series of such
victories and we will be holding our next national council meeting
in Fiji."

Sartawi added that the PLO had already accepted the Brezhnev
Middle East peace proposal that implicitly recognized the right
of Israel to live in peace; so, he asked, why not come out and
declare this recognition explicitly and derive all the political ben-

efits from it—American recognition and support from the Israeli peace camp to name two? Of course Begin was making it difficult for them by rejecting *a priori* any negotiations—ever—with the PLO, but that was all the more reason to put Israel on the spot. But such compromises with reality were not to be—and neither was Sartawi for much longer. On April 10, 1983, some two months after he walked out of the Algiers PNC, a Palestinian gunman walked up to Sartawi in the lobby of a hotel in the Portuguese coastal resort of Albufeira and pumped six bullets into his body at point-blank range. Sartawi had been attending the 16th Socialist International. In Damascus, the Palestinian radical Abu Nidal claimed credit for the assassination, saying Sartawi was "a cheap servant of the CIA, Mossad, and British Intelligence."

Instead of taking Sartawi's advice, the Algiers PNC adopted an approach which the Palestinians there dubbed *la'am*, a combination of the Arabic words for yes and no, which was a perfect depiction of PLO policy, then and for the coming years. *La'am* basically meant rejecting the Reagan Middle East peace plan and other initiatives that were then on the table, but not rejecting them so categorically that Arafat might run the risk of becoming totally irrelevant or leave an opening for King Hussein to supplant him as negotiator for the Palestinians.

I was naïve to have expected more than this. In the lobby of the Club des Pins conference center, where the Algiers PNC meeting was held, the PLO had set up a 50-foot-long photo display of huge, gruesome color photographs of men, women, and children who had been massacred at Sabra and Shatila. As I looked at these photographs, all I could think of was that what they should really have displayed was a series of blown-up color photographs of every Israeli settlement in the West Bank. But the PLO preferred to play the victim, because the victim never has to criticize himself. The PLO leaders also didn't really want to know what was happening in the West Bank, because really knowing would have required really doing something about it—"to be pressed by time," in Abu Jihad's words—and really doing something about it would have meant making either real concessions for peace or real preparations for war. Even after Beirut, Arafat was unable or unwilling to do either. He still behaved as though time were on his side, and in his view of history it was. In his view, the Zionists had no deep roots in Palestine; they were simply a post-Holocaust phenomenon foisted on the Middle East by the West and would one day wither away like other colonial implantations. In the interview he gave to *Playboy* in September 1988, Arafat was asked whether, when he began, he knew the struggle for Palestine would take this long.

"Yes," he answered. "We had a slogan from the beginning: 'It is not a picnic. It is a long hard struggle.' The Vietnamese took 35 years of continuous war. The Algerians, 150; the Rhodesians, about 100; the Saudis, 500. But from the beginning we believed that sooner or later, we would achieve our goals, because we are WITH the tide of history, while Israel is AGAINST it."

So, instead of presenting an accurate picture of Israel's reality and framing immediate political choices from it, Arafat did what he always did. He gave meaning to the suffering of the Palestinian refugees he represented by indulging them with hopes and slogans. To formally recognize Israel would be to say to the Palestinian refugees in Lebanon, Jordan, and Syria, whose homes were in Jaffa, Haifa, and the Galilee, that their forty years of suffering, and their dying in Beirut, were in vain. By refusing to do this, by holding out for the whole myth, Arafat was telling them that as long as they remained displaced, their suffering might eventually bring liberation. It is always easier to give significance to suffering than to compel people to face a reality that offers only two choices: bad and worse—either a tiny Palestinian state in part of the West Bank and Gaza, possibly independent, possibly federated with Jordan, or nothing at all.

Viewed from Arafat's time perspective, Beirut was a minor setback, a historical hiccup, but nothing which necessitated urgent decisions, let alone historical concessions. So while I was standing in the lobby of the Club des Pins looking at my watch and saying, "Why don't you people get your act together, accept Israel's right to exist, and save as much as you can for yourselves?" Arafat and his colleagues were looking at their watches and making their own calculations. Whereas on mine the dial was in minutes and hours, on theirs the dial seemed to be marked in decades and centuries.

Any lingering doubts I had about Arafat's inability to face this choice were erased in Amman in April 1983, when the PLO

chairman came to meet with King Hussein for a final round
of negotiations over the September 1, 1982, Reagan plan. The
Reagan peace initiative called for the creation of a self-governing
Palestinian entity in the West Bank and Gaza Strip, confederated
with Jordan. The plan gave no direct role to the PLO as long as
it formally refused to recognize Israel's right to exist. But it did
give the PLO an indirect role. It called for a Jordanian–Palestinian
delegation to be established to negotiate with Israel over the
return of the West Bank, and it was understood by everyone that
the Palestinians in the delegation would have to be approved and
directed by Arafat. Put bluntly, the Reagan plan was the best
opportunity for the Palestinians to recover their land and end the
Israeli occupation that had been laid on the table since Camp
David. More important, the American President was squarely
behind this proposal, which would have created a Palestinian
entity that could have developed into an independent state or
something very close to it. King Hussein formally sought from
Arafat either PLO acceptance of UN Resolution 242, which implicitly recognized Israel, or some kind of mandate for Jordan to
at least begin negotiations on the Reagan plan, which the Begin
government staunchly opposed. Had Arafat said yes, Begin would
have been in a bind. But instead, Arafat and the PLO leadership
said no to Hussein and no to Reagan. When several of my colleagues and I pressed Abu Jihad as to why, he shouted at us,
"What's in it for the PLO?" Not much up front—but there was
potentially plenty in it for the Palestinians, especially those in the
West Bank and Gaza.

Shortly before Arafat rejected the Reagan plan, he gave a news
conference in Amman at the PLO office there. It was a four-story
building and there were so many reporters crushed inside that we
were lined up on all four flights of stairs to get into the room.
While I was standing on the stairs sandwiched between shoving
cameramen, Yasir Abed Rabbo, the PLO's official spokesman
and a political hack of no small proportions, came down the stairs.
As he brushed by me and beheld the scores of reporters jostling
each other to get into the press conference, his eyes lit up. He
smiled a big smile, shook his head back and forth, and said,
"Great, great." Once again prime time would substitute for
Palestine.

Arafat apparently thought he could continue forever not making the real concessions for peace that would satisfy the Israeli moderate camp, or the real preparations for war that would have satisfied the Palestinian hard-liners. He talked "armed struggle" and dabbled with King Hussein, but he did not do either to the degree that would have made a difference. Beginning in the spring of 1983, however, the narrow fence Arafat was balancing upon after he left Beirut gradually began to be cut out from under him.

His troubles started with a mutiny in May 1983 from within his own al-Fatah wing of the PLO led by Colonel Saed Abu Musa, a longtime opponent of Arafat's. Abu Musa's revolt was in its origins an authentic protest movement, which began among al-Fatah guerrillas based in Lebanon's Bekaa Valley. The mutiny was touched off when Arafat named two of his cronies to senior command positions in the Bekaa and south Lebanon. One, Colonel Hajj Ismail, had been the PLO commander in south Lebanon, until he fled from his post in an ambulance on the second day of the war, leaving his men to fight undirected and taking the office safe with him. The other, known as Colonel Abu Hajem, had a long record of living high off the revolution. Anyone who was serious about confronting Israel would not have named such men to command posts. In an interview with the Arabic weekly *Al-Kifah al-Arabi*, Abu Musa, a widely respected guerrilla fighter, explained why he thought it was time for a change at the top of the PLO. "Arafat turned the Palestinian revolution into a bureaucracy so rotten that it is worse than the bureaucracy in any underdeveloped country. Naturally this institution was not capable of fighting. So when the war broke out, the leadership ran away, leaving the rank and file to pay the price."

Abu Musa also pointed out that the PLO was supposed to be a revolutionary movement, different from those Arab regimes where the leader gets to remain for life, no matter what he does. "Arafat did not inherit the PLO from his father," Abu Musa remarked on several occasions.

Abu Musa was a professional soldier who found that the PLO army he joined was much more corrupt than the Jordanian army he had left. But he had one problem: he was an honest man in a region that did not reward honesty. As soon as he declared his rebellion, the Syrians and Libyans rushed to embrace him with support, both ideological and on the ground. Arafat used this

Syrian and Libyan backing to completely discredit the rebels. I was on hand when the Syrian-backed Abu Musa fighters finally cornered Arafat's men in Tripoli, in northern Lebanon, in September 1983. Arafat, who had sailed in to lead his flock, summoned several of us reporters to a news conference in an olive grove outside Tripoli. First a group of his guerrillas arrived and formed a kind of honor guard, and then Arafat drove up in a green Mercedes. He got out of the car with his walking stick, marched through the honor guard in the middle of the olive grove, and gave a press conference under a tree. *Newsweek* had been promised an exclusive interview, and so Arafat took the magazine's correspondent, Jim Pringle, behind a tree all by himself. When we asked Arafat about Abu Musa, he said with a flick of his wrist, "Don't ask me about the puppets and the horses of Troy."

But how did Arafat explain this revolt? we asked. At that point Arafat removed a gold Cross pen he kept in his breast pocket, held it up in the air, and said, "This. Assad wants my pen. He wants the Palestinian decision, and I won't give it to him."

It was a brilliant move. Arafat—with Assad's unwitting help —turned a legitimate protest movement against his leadership into a Syrian plot against the Palestinian people. Naturally, when it became a choice between Arafat and the Syrians, all Palestinians sided with Arafat. Sure, they said, the PLO needs to be cleaned up and Arafat is a son-of-a-bitch, but he is our son-of-a-bitch and the only son-of-a-bitch we have who is really recognized and accepted around the world. Once again Arafat would survive, not because of what he had produced, but because of what he symbolized. This was the key to his Teflon, and the reason the Abu Musa revolt just wouldn't stick.

Arafat talked about making Tripoli his "Stalingrad," just as he had about Beirut, but when the ships came to take him and 4,000 guerrillas to safety—this time under French protection—Arafat again opted for life as a symbol rather than death as a martyr. My colleague Bill Barrett, then the Middle East correspondent for the Dallas *Times Herald*, interviewed Arafat shortly before his evacuation from the northern Lebanese port.

"I asked the chairman if he had ever heard of the Alamo," recalled Barrett. " 'Yes, yes,' he replied, 'that famous castle in Texas.' Then I asked if he saw any similarities between the Alamo and his current plight. 'Yes, indeed,' the chairman replied, and then he proceeded to talk about bravery and being surrounded by enemies and the importance of fighting for a cause and all that stuff. He was really warming to the topic. Then I asked the chairman if he was aware that almost everyone at the Alamo died. There was a pause—a very long pause. 'Come to think of it,' Arafat said, 'the Alamo really isn't that similar,' and then he went off to another topic."

When Arafat quit Tripoli, he lost his last rail of fence to sit on. He was now disconnected on a day-to-day basis from that body of Palestinians whom the PLO had both nurtured and developed out of—the Palestinian refugees living in Lebanon, Jordan, and Syria. Arafat would no longer lead them in any direct sense of the word, only through surrogates. He was also disconnected from his last direct point of contact with Israel. He could no longer hope to bring any significant military pressure on the Jewish state.

History, though, works in strange ways. Sharon thought that by going to Beirut and destroying Arafat he could impose permanent Israeli rule over the West Bank and Gaza. But what Sharon never understood, because he had so demonized the PLO, was that Beirut was theater and Arafat was ready to star in it for a long time. All Arafat really wanted was a little turf for himself and his people and a chair in the Arab councils of power; Beirut afforded him that. It wasn't Palestine, but it was tolerable. It had become the substitute homeland and had Sharon left well enough alone, the PLO might still be there today. But Sharon took the Lebanese theater seriously. By driving Arafat and his guerrillas out, he re-created their dilemma of homelessness and made them wandering men again. He left them no option but to invest virtually all their energy in diplomacy, as opposed to armed struggle, with the aim of recovering precisely the turf where Sharon had planned to impose his rule: the West Bank and the Gaza Strip. That was where the largest concentration of Palestinians resided, and where the direct confrontation with Israel would continue.

Arafat had to keep contact with the West Bankers, and make sure that King Hussein did not try to make a deal with them and the Israelis that might exclude the PLO. In order to constrain King Hussein and to keep a land bridge to the West Bank, Arafat reached an agreement with Jordan on a joint negotiating strategy on February 11, 1985. Even though this agreement was bitterly opposed by PLO hard-liners, such as George Habash, it really constituted just more *la'am*. For instance, while the February 11 accord affirmed the principle of trading land for peace, King Hussein was never able to pin Arafat down on the details—such as his accepting UN Resolution 242 or confederation with Jordan. Arafat gave Hussein just enough to keep him interested, but not enough to create a breakthrough with the Israelis. A year later, Hussein nullified the accord and threw the PLO out of Jordan, putting Arafat back into orbit. Yet, even with all the ground cut out from under him, Arafat, instead of falling flat on his face, floated in midair—drifting from New Delhi to Cairo and Prague to Geneva, held aloft by the Palestinian aspirations for national independence that he still represented.

In retrospect, one could say that from the moment Arafat quit Beirut in August 1982 he was like an actor in search of a role. He had lost his stage, much of his crew, and virtually all his supporting cast. He had always wanted to star as the Moses of his people, who would lead them back to the Promised Land, but the only role he was offered after Beirut was that of Noah, the great survivor.

Little did I know when I last saw him in Tripoli that five years later I would be on hand to watch him land a new part on a new stage. That part would be delivered to him by a different Palestinian cast from the one Arafat led in Lebanon. It would come from the West Bankers and Gazans under Israeli occupation, who would rise up against Israel one morning in December 1987 and find themselves in need of someone to speak their lines to the world. Arafat would be offered the starring role, but under one condition: he had to read the lines which the West Bankers and Gazans wrote, and those were different, much more difficult, lines than any he had been asked to speak in Beirut. But speak them he would, and they would pave the way for his comeback on the world stage. Humpty-Dumpty would be put back together again. But more about that later down the road.

Menachem Begin would also crack under the pressure of the Lebanon war, but he would not be put back together again.

From the day Israel invaded until the moment before Bashir Gemayel was assassinated, it didn't really matter what myths and illusions Begin or Sharon held about Lebanon, the Palestinians, or themselves. This was a conventional war, and Israel brought to the conventional battlefield such overwhelming superiority of force that she could and did literally steamroll over any mistakes or misperceptions on the way to her targets.

After Bashir was assassinated, however, the Israelis could no longer depend on his brute force replacing their brute force so that the Israeli army could withdraw. Israel would have to find its own way home, and in the process all her myths and misperceptions about Lebanon would come back to haunt her.

There were really only two ways for Israel to create a Lebanese government strong enough and stable enough to make sure that Lebanon would not return to the *status quo ante bellum*. One approach would have been to address the source of Lebanon's instability—the absence of a consensus between Christians and Muslims over how power should be divided. The only way to deal effectively with this problem would not be by helping the Phalangists definitively win the Lebanese civil war—because they could never hold their ground without Israeli support—but by encouraging the Phalangists to accept constitutional reforms that would involve sharing more power with the Muslims, while at the same time encouraging the Muslims to moderate their demands as much as possible. Only through such an approach might both communities feel that they had some stake in the emergence of a reasonably strong central government. To pull off such an arrangement would have been extremely difficult for even the wisest power. It would have required painstaking political maneuvering and a sophisticated use of carrots and sticks; it also would have required abandoning any notion of a formal Israel–Lebanon peace treaty—since Lebanon's fragile political consensus could not bear the strain of such an accord—and settling instead for quiet, de facto security arrangements.

The other approach was much simpler: Instead of treating the source of Lebanon's instability, the Israelis could treat its symptoms—the chronic lawlessness—by installing a strongman at the top of the Lebanese pyramid and relying on him to use an iron fist to stabilize Lebanon from above.

Since Begin and Sharon had no conception of how to play

Lebanese politics, no time to wait around Beirut, and no stomach for telling the Phalangists that they had to make political concessions to Lebanon's Muslims, they naturally opted for this latter approach, seeking out a new "man on horseback" to replace Bashir. They settled for a pale imitation—Bashir's older brother, sometime playboy, sometime businessman, all-time zero, Amin Gemayel. Amin, then forty years old, was elected President immediately after Bashir's death. He had all of Bashir's weaknesses and none of his strengths. In his younger days, Amin had been known around East Beirut as Mr. Two Percent, because he and his Phalangist loyalists seemed to have their fingers in every major business deal in East Beirut. He lacked Bashir's killer instinct, and always seemed to be much more concerned about the part in his perfectly coiffed hair than with serious affairs of state. His greatest accomplishment in life was being born the son of Pierre Gemayel, the founder of the Phalangist Party. Although previously known as a political "moderate," compared to his brother, as soon as Amin became President he evinced all of Bashir's contempt for the Lebanese Muslims—particularly Druse leader Walid Jumblat and Shiite Amal militia leader Nabih Berri. For reasons which I will explain in the next chapter, Amin ran roughshod over Lebanon's Shiites and Druse, driving them into the arms of the Syrians and turning up the ever-simmering Lebanese civil war to full blast. By the spring of 1983, the Israelis found themselves occupying a house on fire.

Begin was so obsessed with getting a peace treaty from Lebanon to justify the invasion that he barely seemed to notice the country was going up in flames. He had promised his people forty years of peace and he had to have a treaty to show for his troubles—not to mention 650 Israeli lives—and he used every available means to squeeze Amin for the document. Begin reminded me of a man determined to get a check from another man for an unpaid bill—even though everyone else knew the man had no money. The Lebanese, great wheeler-dealers that they were, were happy to provide the hot check. On May 17, 1983, Amin Gemayel's government signed a peace treaty with Israel, which included elaborate provisions for protecting Israel's northern border. Not one article of the treaty was ever enacted. The Syrians, through their Lebanese allies, put so much pressure on Amin he could not even consider implementing the document.

So, on the first anniversary of the Israeli invasion of Lebanon, Begin must have understood that he was really in trouble. Bashir Gemayel was actually dead and Amin Gemayel was politically dead. Israel had run out of strongmen. Its choices, too, were between bad and worse: bad was staying in Lebanon indefinitely to preserve the military gains of the war; worse was unilaterally withdrawing, without leaving any peace treaty or formal security arrangements behind. But the choice would no longer be Begin's. Like Arafat, Begin finally discovered that if you don't gradually let reality in to temper your mythologizing, it will sooner or later invade on its own. By the end of the summer of 1983, Begin was bowled over by such an invasion of reality, which came on the heels of the death of his beloved wife, Aliza, in November 1982. Together these two events drove him into a deep depression from which he has never emerged.

On August 30, 1983, the haggard and depressed sixty-nine-year-old Israeli Prime Minister convened his Cabinet for the last time. His remarks were brief: "I cannot go on any longer." Two weeks later he formally resigned, cleaned out his drawer, and locked himself in his Jerusalem apartment at 1 Zemach Street. Since then, he has rarely ventured outdoors. It remains one of the most remarkable cases in political history: a man totally engaged in his country's politics from even before its birth, his nation's greatest orator, who overnight became a man of silence. Israeli papers labeled him "the Prisoner of Zemach Street." It was not an inappropriate moniker, since for all intents and purposes Menachem Begin seemed to have tried himself, found himself guilty, and locked himself in jail.

Some say that it was the numbers that did it. The Israeli antiwar movement, led by the Peace Now organization, used to hold up a huge placard outside Begin's home that kept a running count of the Israeli boys who had died in Lebanon. Every day when he walked outside to go to work, Begin was confronted with those numbers. He wanted to be remembered as a man of peace, not war. But Begin was always a split personality: he had a manic side—in love with flags, medals, symbols, and determined to restore a dignity to the Jewish people that he was never able to enjoy in his youth—and he had a sober, punctilious, lawyerlike side, totally committed to the rule of law. The first side drove him to Beirut and the second side drove him home. The first side needed a war, a big war, a grand war, and the second side demanded justice when the true costs of that war were tallied. Faced with the real consequences of his own rhetoric, Begin went mute.

His was a lesson which more than a few Middle Eastern statesmen could well learn: whether you are an Arab or a Jew, you can't heal your grandfather's shame. The dead can never be redeemed—only the living can. He who is fixated on redeeming his father's memory will never see the opportunities of his own world.

When it became clear that the May 17 peace treaty was meaningless, Israel, in September 1983, began to unilaterally withdraw from Lebanon. The first step was for Israel to pull back from the Shouf Mountains overlooking Beirut and to hunker down along the Awali River in predominantly Shiite south Lebanon. There, the Israelis vowed, they would sit indefinitely in order to protect their northern border. If Lebanon would not provide them with a policeman, they would be their own. But this was easier said than done. The Lebanese Shiites had originally greeted the Israelis as liberators from the PLO guerrillas, who had turned the Shiite villages into a battleground and frequently helped themselves to any home, car, or product that struck their fancy. But when they realized that the Israelis were intent on staying in south Lebanon, the Shiites turned on them with a vengeance. Israel compounded the Shiite wrath, however, by using local Christian militiamen to help them control the region and by being highly insensitive to Shiite religious feelings, of which most Israeli troops were ignorant, since there are virtually no Shiite Muslims in Israel.

If there was any single incident that turned the Lebanese Shiites from potential Israeli allies to implacable foes, though, it was a little reported fracas which occurred on October 16, 1983, in the south Lebanon market town of Nabatiya. On that day, an estimated 50,000 to 60,000 Shiites were gathered in the center of Nabatiya, celebrating the most important holiday in their calendar, Ashura, which commemorates the martyrdom, in A.D. 680, of Hussein, the prophet Muhammad's grandson. Each year on Ashura, Shiites honor Hussein's death and struggle against unjust political authority, even going so far as to flagellate themselves to the point of drawing their own blood. In the middle of the Ashura services, an Israeli military convoy tried to drive through

Nabatiya, honking horns for people to get out of the way. It was the equivalent of someone turning on a ghetto blaster in a synagogue on Yom Kippur, the Jewish Day of Atonement.

The Shiites saw the Israeli intrusion as a crude violation of their most sacred moment, and they immediately began pelting the Israeli convoy with stones and bottles, even overturning some of the vehicles. The Israeli soldiers panicked and opened fire on the crowd, killing at least two persons and wounding fifteen others. Augustus Richard Norton, a former United Nations Truce Observer stationed in south Lebanon in the early 1980s, noted that while the Nabatiya incident was insignificant in the number of casualties involved, it crystallized all the resentment and anger that had been building in south Lebanon against the Israeli presence. Before the Ashura incident, attacks by Shiites against Israelis were sporadic and confined largely to tiny splinter factions. The mainstream Shiite community, which was represented by the Amal militia, remained on the sidelines. In the wake of the Nabatiya incident, Shiite clerics in south Lebanon warned that anyone who trucked with Israel would "burn in hell," and Amal began competing with other Shiite militias to see who could take the most Israeli casualties.*

The Shiites attacked the Israeli troops any way and anywhere they could—with hit-and-run ambushes, nail bombs, suicide cars, roadside bombs, exploding donkeys, Red Cross ambulances packed with TNT, and snipers. Syria and Iran were only too happy to provide advice and material aid. The Shiites displayed a relentlessness which the Israelis had never encountered from an Arab foe before: they weren't just ready to kill, they were ready to die; they didn't issue communiqués after each confrontation; they relished their successes in relative silence. South Lebanon became terrifying for Israeli soldiers, who grew to dread moving out of their base camps for fear that any object, rock, bush, or tree might explode next to them. By early 1984, the Israelis forgot about the Palestinian threat and began speaking of the "Israeli–Shiite conflict"; two years earlier, most Israelis hadn't even known what a Shiite was. In order to hold their ground in the face of mounting local opposition, the Israeli army had to impose Draconian security measures on south Lebanon: car searches, check-

* Augustus Richard Norton, *Amal and the Shia* (University of Texas Press, 1987).

points, travel restrictions, trade restrictions, which only angered the local Shiites even more.

Nobody saw that anger more clearly than Captain Teddy Lapkin, who, in 1984, found himself running the Israeli army checkpoint at Baader-el-Shouf, a mountain village along the Awali River. Teddy was a professional soldier, but having been raised in America, he knew a Vietnam when he saw one. When Israel pulled out of the Shouf and withdrew south to the Awali River, Baader-el-Shouf became the single crossing point for Lebanese wanting to move between south and north Lebanon—a bottleneck choked with frustrations. Lebanese had to wait as long as three days to pass through, and farmers often had to empty their entire vehicles of produce so that Israeli troops could search through the cucumbers and watermelons for hidden weapons. Twice, suicide car bombers drove their vehicles into the checkpoint and blew themselves up, taking a few Israeli soldiers and Lebanese with them each time.

"It was frustrating," Lapkin recalled. "I don't want to say that I didn't know what I was doing there—that sounds like Vietnam. I knew what I was doing there, I just had my doubts about the wisdom of the operation. It was dehumanizing in a way, because when you finally managed to kill a Shiite you would feel happy about it. Your first emotion was that finally you were able to hit back. There was this gut satisfaction. But then you would think about it and remind yourself that there were 150 more out there where that one came from. It was pointless, that's it—not frustrating, pointless. You were losing people and you would say to yourself, 'What am I going to say to their families?' It was a guerrilla war, and they won. There was no way we could win the hearts and minds of the population, so we were predestined to lose. Therefore, we should have cut our losses and gotten out, or allied ourselves with the Shiites from the beginning, instead of the Christians.

"I will never forget one day when we were up above the town of Jezzine. We knew it had been an infiltration route for people going south. So we decided to position an ambush there. We went to do a recon mission and tried to go up in jeeps from Jezzine to Arab Selim. It was a bad road and we couldn't get up, so the next day we came back with armored personnel carriers. Evidently we were seen the day before, and that night someone laid

a mine on the road. Our first armored personnel carrier stopped
just by chance a few meters in front of it. I was about to step on
it when one of our Bedouin trackers stopped me. The mine was
freshly laid, so we started tracking the guy who laid it. We tracked
him for seven hours. When we finally caught him, he was hiding
in this crevice of a rock and I saw the tips of his fingers. I fired
a couple of rounds in his direction, and instead of coming out
with his hands up, he tried to run, so I shot him. He was a Shiite,
and he was just saying—I don't know if it was Shiite fanaticism
or the Shiite version of the Hail Mary—but he kept just repeating,
'Allahu Akbar, Allahu Akbar' [God is greater than the enemy]
over and over and over. He had these worry beads, and he was
shot in the lung, and when your lung is shot you spit blood. So
he would say, *'Allahu Akbar—ppttuu'* and spit blood. We tried
to save him. We even gave him an infusion and called a chopper,
but he died on the way—DOA. Hey, he shouldn't have run. If
he hadn't run, I wouldn't have shot him. But he had a rifle in his
hand, so tough.

"I had no doubt at that late stage how dedicated they were to
getting us out of there. From our point of view it stopped being
a war for an objective; it became a war for revenge. It became
real personal: stay alive, get your revenge if you can, and stay
alive until they pull us out. We just never broke out of that vicious
cycle."

Mercifully, the July 1984 elections that followed a year after Begin's disappearance ended in a tie, and the Likud and Labor
Parties were forced to join together in a national unity government
led by Shimon Peres and Yitzhak Shamir. I say "mercifully,"
because without Begin I don't think the Likud on its own would
have found the moral courage to admit that Lebanon was a fiasco
and bring the troops home empty-handed. They needed Labor
to hold their hand, to give them political cover. As it was, even
in the national unity Cabinet, most Likud ministers voted against
withdrawing from Lebanon, arguing that northern Israel would
be exposed to constant rocket attacks. But they were defeated
by a narrow majority. In April 1985, the Israeli army completed
its unconditional pullout from Lebanon, save for a narrow secu-

rity belt it retained along the border to protect northern Israel. I had moved to Israel from Beirut by then, and I detected a certain wry sense of humor creeping into official Israeli discussions about Lebanon. It was the kind of humor men indulge in when they know they have been had. I recall visiting Itzhak Lior at the Israeli Foreign Ministry shortly after the Israeli withdrawal. Lior, who was in charge of the Middle East Department, had once been head of the Israeli liaison office in East Beirut. My visit happened to be at the time that Samir Geagea, the fanatical Maronite medical student, had seized control of the Phalangist militia and begun shelling the Muslims of the town of Sidon from nearby Christian villages for reasons which still are not clear to me. The shelling, which Geagea could not sustain or translate into any political gain, provoked the Muslim militias in the town to get together and not only drive Geagea and his men back but also overrun many of the Christian villages in the area—ousting from their homes Christians who had been living alongside Muslims peacefully for years.

"Tell me, Itzhak," I said, scratching my head, "why did Geagea do it? Why did he shell Sidon when it was certain to provoke a retaliation against all the Christians in the area?"

Lior thought for a moment, rubbed his goatee, took a puff on his pipe, and then said, as though the answer were perfectly obvious, "He did it because he had the ammunition."

No sooner were the Israelis gone than everything in Lebanon returned to abnormal. The civil war ebbed and flowed, the Palestinian guerrillas trickled back to south Lebanon and occasionally rocketed northern Israel, just as in the old days. For Israel, the final insult came in the winter of 1986, when it was reported in the Beirut papers that the Phalangists had started selling Lebanese passports and entry visas to the PLO so that some of Arafat's men could return to Lebanon and join the local Palestinians in fighting the Lebanese Shiites, whom the Phalangists had come to view as the greatest threat to their efforts to dominate Lebanon. "My enemy's enemy is my friend," says the Arab proverb. So Arafat and the Phalangists were once again friends. Such is life in a political kaleidoscope.

* * *

Just as the PLO and the Arab world were never the same after the summer of '82, so neither were Israel and the Jewish world. In "mopping up" Lebanon, Israel lost its luster. Esther Koenigsberg Bengigi, an American-born psychologist who immigrated to Israel in the late 1970s and married an Israeli paratrooper, once remarked to me that the Lebanon invasion actually changed her feelings toward Israel more than toward the Arabs. In this she was not alone, as a Jew or as an Israeli.

"It was always very important for me to feel that Israel was right, was smart, and that it always did things the right way, especially after having grown up during the whole Vietnam period in America and really feeling worked over by the government," said Bengigi. "I was taught that Israel wants peace more than others and just wants to be left alone. After Lebanon, everything wasn't so clear. I really felt anger."

Most Israelis, however, seemed to feel only numb. Lebanon became the war everybody wanted to forget. As Shlomo Gazit, a former chief of Israeli military intelligence, once said to me, "There would never be an Israeli Pentagon Papers for the Lebanon war. Too many people were guilty," he explained. Too many people and too much party politics were involved. "It is part of the rules of the game," said Gazit. "We should not embarrass each other to the very end. We cannot afford to go into a commission on Lebanon and hope to continue working together. We cannot allow ourselves to be demoralized completely. The cost is that the lessons may not be learned, but even if we have a commission, the lessons may not be learned."

Instead of really learning from the war together, Israelis explained it away—each according to his own politics—just enough to be able to forget about it.

One popular explanation within the Labor Party was that the war was all Begin and Sharon's fault. They were crazy. Begin was even proving it by locking himself in his house. Since these two had been put on the shelf, there was nothing more to worry about. A second explanation, popular among Likudniks, was that the Lebanon fiasco was all Labor's fault: they never allowed Sharon to fight the war with the iron fist he wanted. But this school always ignored the follow-up question: Even if Sharon had been able to use his iron fist to smash Lebanon from one end to the next, who would have taken over when that fist was withdrawn? But the most popular explanation of all, and the one that seems to have endured the longest, was that the reason the Lebanon invasion turned into a mess wasn't Israel's fault at all; it was Lebanon's fault. It didn't matter what Israeli policy was. In other words, instead of recognizing how specious were the Israeli preconceptions about Lebanon and how the Israeli presence there helped to make the situation even worse, Israelis held to their preconceptions and pronounced Lebanon insane—just another country where they hate the Jews. Whenever I heard this explanation from Israelis, I was always reminded of the cartoon by Pat Oliphant from the early days of the invasion, when the joke making the rounds in the Middle East was "Visit Israel before Israel visits you." The Oliphant cartoon showed an Israeli tank on the border of Tibet, with two soldiers looking across a great divide. On the other side were two little Tibetans firing slingshots at the onrushing Israeli soldiers. Underneath, the little duck says, "Imagine, anti-Semitism even out here."

This popular Israeli view of crazy Lebanon was perfectly, if unintentionally, enshrined in *Two Fingers from Sidon*, a movie the Israeli army made in 1985 to prepare troops for serving in Lebanon, though the army pulled out just after the filming was completed. The movie was shown to soldiers nevertheless and became so popular that the army eventually released it to the public. My favorite scene is when Gadi, a fresh-eyed young lieutenant just out of officers' school, arrives at a base somewhere in south Lebanon and asks another soldier to fill him in on the political situation in Lebanon. The soldier, Georgie, a jaded veteran of the Lebanon war, sits in a field kitchen peeling potatoes and explains what the war is all about.

"Look," says Georgie, "I'll tell you the truth. Seriously, I didn't know what was happening until yesterday. But yesterday, they brought in this expert on Arab affairs. He gave us a lecture on the present situation. Now I understand everything. It goes like this: The Christians hate the Druse, Shiites, Sunnis, and Palestinians. The Druse hate the Christians. No. Right. The Druse hate the Christians, Shiites, and the Syrians. The Shiites got screwed by them all for years, so they hate everyone. The Sunnis hate whomever their leader tells them to hate, and the Palestinians hate one another. Aside from that, they hate the others. Now, they all have a common denominator: they all hate us, the Israelis. They would like to blow us to pieces if they could, but they can't due to the Israeli army. Not all of the Israeli army—just the suckers, those who are in Lebanon."

8

Betty Crocker in Dante's Inferno

They Came in Peace

—*Inscription on the memorial
to the 241 Marines and other
servicemen killed in Beirut
in Camp Johnson,
Jacksonville, North Carolina*

Funny country, Lebanon. The minute one army packed up and rushed out, another one swaggered in and took its place. There always seemed to be someone knocking on the door to get in— and someone inside dying to get out. Unlike the PLO and the Israelis, though, the U.S. Marines came to Beirut as "peacekeepers"; they even had a list of ten rules governing when they could fire their weapons, to prove it.

Whenever I think back on the Marines' sojourn in Lebanon, which lasted from August 1982 until February 1984, I am reminded of a remarkable scene in Tadeusz Borowski's book about the Nazi concentration camps, *This Way for the Gas, Ladies and Gentlemen*. Borowski, a Polish poet and political prisoner of the Nazis, described how, at the end of World War II, a large group of Auschwitz inmates got hold of a Nazi SS guard and began to rip him apart, just as their concentration camp was being liberated by American GI's.

"At last they seized [the SS guard] inside the German barracks, just as he was about to climb over the window ledge," wrote Borowski. "In absolute silence they pulled him down to the floor and panting with hate dragged him into a dark alley. Here, closely surrounded by a silent mob, they began tearing at him with greedy hands. Suddenly from the camp gate a whispered warning was passed from one mouth to another. A company of [American] soldiers, their bodies leaning forward, their rifles on the ready, came running down the camp's main road, weaving between the clusters of men in stripes standing in the way. The crowd scattered and vanished inside the blocks."

But not without the Nazi guard. The prisoners dragged the German soldier inside their blockhouse, put him on a bunk, covered him with a blanket, and then sat on top of him—looking innocent and waiting for the American soldiers to show up.

"There was a stir at the door," wrote Borowski. "A young American officer with a tin helmet on his head entered the block and looked with curiosity at the bunks and the tables. He wore a freshly pressed uniform; his revolver was hanging down, strapped in an open holster that dangled against his thigh. . . . The men in the barracks fell silent. . . . 'Gentlemen,' said the officer with a friendly smile. . . . 'I know, of course, that after what you have gone through and after what you have seen, you must feel a deep hate for your tormentors. But we, the soldiers of America, and you, the people of Europe, have fought so that law should prevail over lawlessness. We must show our respect for the law. I assure you that the guilty will be punished, in this camp as well as in all the others.' . . . The men in the bunks broke into applause and shouts. In smiles and gestures they tried to convey their friendly approval of the young man from across the ocean. . . . The American . . . wished the prisoners a good rest and an early reunion with their dear ones. Accompanied by a friendly hum of voices, he left the block and proceeded to the next. Not until after he had visited all the blocks and returned with the soldiers to his headquarters did we pull our man off the bunk—where covered with blankets and half-smothered with the weight of our bodies he lay gagged, his face buried in the straw mattress—and dragged him on to the cement floor under the stove, where the entire bunk, grunting and growling with hatred, trampled him to death."

So it was with the Marines in Beirut—good, milk-faced boys who stepped into the middle of a passion-filled conflict, of whose history they were totally innocent and whose venom they could not even imagine. For a few months after the Marines arrived in Beirut the Lebanese natives sheathed their swords, lowered their voices, and sat on their hatreds, while these clean-cut men from a distant land spoke to them about the meaning of democracy, freedom, and patriotism. After a while, though, the speech got boring, and the wild earth beckoned. Unlike the concentration-camp victims of Borowski's tale, however, the Lebanese would not wait for the American lecture to end before returning to their feuding ways, so familiar, so instinctual.

So the Marines got an education they never bargained for, and like everyone else who went to Beirut, they got it the hard way.

In my observations of the Marines in Beirut, one of the things that always fascinated me was how concerned Americans were that our boys ate properly—a concern that at times reached mammoth proportions, as in the case of the melting burritos.

"We didn't know who they came from," said Lieutenant Colonel George T. Schmidt of the 24th Marine Amphibious Unit (MAU), the last Marine contingent to serve in Beirut, referring to a surprise airlift of Mexican food. "But the day we got [to Beirut] you can imagine the confusion. Right in the middle of that we get a phone call that there is a package at the airport for [us]. We get down there and it's about three thousand burritos. We didn't know who they came from—nothing about them. They were dry, [and] it was hot, so we sent a guy down to get them and [bring them] back, [but] in all the confusion they melted. Finally our doctor went down and stuck his thermometer in [them] and said, 'Hey, these things are gone.' So we dumped them. We [didn't tell] the press, because the press had made such a big deal about the [two thousand] hamburgers [someone sent from] Minneapolis. They were going to have a ball finding out that we trashed three thousand or five thousand burritos, or whatever it was. To this day I could not tell you where the burritos came from. There was some generous person in the United States that worried about the boys eating right.'"*

*The interview with Lieutenant Colonel Schmidt is drawn from the archives of the Marine Corps Oral History Program. The interview was conducted by Benis M. Frank, head of the Marines' Oral History Program, on March 17, 1983. I am indebted to Mr. Frank for allowing me to have access to this treasure trove of interviews he amassed.

The burritos were only the beginning. The Marine spokesman's office at their Beirut International Airport headquarters
became crammed to the ceiling with cardboard boxes stuffed with
chocolate-chip cookies, brownies, and homemade cakes, while
the walls were decorated with 50-foot-long letters signed by whole
schools or neighborhoods wishing the leathernecks godspeed in
their mission. I used to love visiting the Marine spokesmen just
for the opportunity to munch on their baked goods, although, I
have to admit, the practice always left me feeling strangely out
of sync with the wider Beirut environment, as though I were
nibbling Betty Crocker brownies in Dante's Inferno. I always half
expected one of these brownies to blow up in my hand. I had
been in Beirut too long. Not so the Marines. The way they inhaled
those goodies from Mom always symbolized for me the trusting
naïveté with which they walked through Lebanon's revolving
door.

If there is one sentiment that tied together everything the Marines did right in Lebanon and everything they did wrong, it was
naïve, innocent optimism. It showed itself right from the beginning in how the Marines got roped into the Lebanon operation
in the first place. One of the great ironies of the Marine mission
in Beirut was the fact that the man who first suggested sending
American troops to Lebanon was the man who would pass them
on the way out—PLO Chairman Yasir Arafat. During the negotiations over the PLO's withdrawal from Beirut in the summer
of 1982, Arafat, according to American diplomats, insisted that
American—along with French and Italian—troops be involved in
overseeing the departure of his men from Israeli-besieged West
Beirut. Arafat was no fool. He understood that an American
umbrella covering the PLO's withdrawal was the best insurance
against Israel breaking its promise not to invade West Beirut just
as the PLO was letting down its guard to leave.

So, to facilitate the PLO's withdrawal, President Reagan agreed
to dispatch an 800-man Marine contingent to Beirut harbor on
August 25, 1982. The American troops were scheduled to remain
for up to thirty days, according to the withdrawal agreement
worked out between American Special Envoy Philip C. Habib
and the PLO, through Lebanese intermediaries. However, because the evacuation of the 14,000 PLO and Syrian fighters was
successfully completed by the first week in September, and be-

cause Habib was determined to make sure that the Marines did not slip into any kind of open-ended mission in Beirut, the President ordered the leathernecks withdrawn on September 10, 1982—two weeks before the thirty-day limit. The French and Italians were quick to follow.

None of them had an inkling of how soon they would be back.

On September 14, only five days after he had reviewed a Marine honor guard, Lebanon's President-elect Bashir Gemayel was blown apart and Israel invaded West Beirut. The Sabra and Shatila massacre followed two days later. The pictures of butchered Palestinian bodies strewn about the filthy streets of Sabra and Shatila sent shock waves reverberating all the way to Washington. The message was loud and clear: Had the Americans not been in such a hurry to get the Marines out before the thirty-day deadline expired, the massacre never would have happened. The Reagan Administration felt compelled—as it should have—to return to Beirut out of an overwhelming sense of guilt. However, it could never admit that to the American people, who were not aware of the Administration's promises to Arafat that the Israelis would not enter West Beirut. As a senior member of the American embassy staff in Beirut at the time put it, "The Marines were sent back to Beirut because we felt guilty about what happened in the camps. We couldn't say that, of course. So at the time that we decided to send them back, Washington developed a rationale for their presence."

That rationale was formulated in the White House over the weekend between Saturday, September 18, when the massacre was exposed, and Monday, September 20, when America's new Lebanon policy was unveiled to the American people. President Reagan declared that the Marines were being sent back to Beirut "with the mission of enabling the Lebanese government to restore full sovereignty over its capital, the essential precondition for extending its control over the entire country." The Marines, said Reagan, were to act as a "presence" supporting the Lebanese central authority. The French and Italians agreed to return as well, but while they took up positions in the heart of West Beirut, the Marines, numbering 1,500, were stationed alongside Lebanese army units in the least populated area possible—Beirut International Airport and its environs. Their length of stay this time was left open-ended.

The impulse underlying this weekend whim was quintessentially American. It came out of something very deep in the American psyche: a can-do optimism, a conviction that every problem has a solution if people will just be reasonable.

At first, the American optimism seemed justified. The mere arrival of the Marines convinced many Beirutis that their then seven-year-old civil-war nightmare was about to come to an end and that the Lebanon of old would be reconstructed. After all, America, the greatest power in the world, had committed itself to rebuilding Lebanon's central government and army. Things had to get better. The Lebanese view of America was a view gleaned from movies and in the movies the cavalry was never late. As the Marines took up their positions in West Beirut, a contagion of optimism replaced fear in the streets: the main highway between East and West Beirut was reopened for the first time in years; bulldozers moved in to clear the Green Line as architects unfurled their plans to reconstruct the city center. Ghassan Tueni, the American-educated publisher of Beirut's leading newspaper, *An-Nahar*, boasted to me one afternoon after the Marines arrived that "the Che Guevara era of Lebanese politics is over. People have had their fling with radicalism. Beards and jeans are out now. Neckties are in."

The Marines found it easy to mingle freely among the Muslims and Palestinians of West Beirut and to chase Lebanese women, many of whom were only too happy to get caught. They spent their days making leisurely patrols and passing out bubble gum to the Lebanese kids they met along the streets. Not far from the Marines' airport compound was the densely populated Shiite southern suburb of Hay es Salaam, which, for some reason, was not on the maps issued to the American soldiers, so they dubbed it "Hooterville," as though it were some friendly American small town. A succession of Lebanese "Hey, Joes" used to come around the Marine compound selling everything from honey cakes to Arab headdresses, and they moved among the men as if they owned the place. So trusting of the Lebanese were the first Marines to arrive in Beirut that more than one hundred of them, including some officers, gave their uniforms to a mustachioed Lebanese male claiming to be a dry cleaner and promising prompt service. He hasn't been heard from since.

But it wasn't only the Lebanese who took the Marines to the

cleaners. In these heady days when the Marines were popular and relaxed, all kinds of American VIPs and performing artists flocked to Beirut to have their pictures taken with the American fighting men. But all this entertainment in the interest of the boys away from home was very costly, explained Lieutenant Colonel Schmidt: "As a matter of fact, we're still owed over $2,000 for having to foot the bill of these guys that would show up. You know, we had a country-Western group that showed up and they had no money—zero money. And a week or two later the cheerleaders from the Los Angeles Rams showed up. No money. So we had to pay the [cheerleaders'] bill to get them in the country and a little under-the-table fifty-buck fee [to Lebanese customs]. We had to pay their hotel bills, pay their chow bills, and they said, 'We'll send you the money right away.' Well, that was in December [1982] and it's now March [1983] and we have yet to see the first penny."*

The American officials who dispatched the Marines to Beirut seemed to believe not only that the Lebanese problem, like all problems, had a relatively easy solution, but that the solution could be understood in American terms. The Americans looked at Lebanon, saw that the country had a "President," a "parliament," and a "commander in chief" (sound familiar?) and said to themselves, in effect, "Look, they have all the right institutions. The only problem is that these institutions are too weak. So let's just rebuild the central government and army and they can be like us."

In other words, in order to make sense of Lebanon and to justify the American presence there, the Reagan Administration made Lebanon an extension of what it knew—and what it knew was American political culture, patriotism, and devotion to the concept of one nation under God. Therefore, when the young, Kennedyesque Lebanese President, Amin Gemayel, came to the Americans soon after they arrived and asked them to go beyond their symbolic "presence" role and assume primary responsibility for training and equipping the Lebanese army—which was under the direct authority of Gemayel and his Maronite commander in chief Ibrahim Tannous—so that it might one day reoccupy the whole of Lebanese territory, the Reagan Administration said yes.

*Marine Corps Oral History Collection. Interview conducted March 17, 1983.

This training process, which began in December 1982, created a
symbiosis between the Lebanese army and the Marines. The Lebanese army soldiers who graduated from the Marine–U.S. Army
training course were given khaki camouflage uniforms almost
identical to those worn by the Marines, making the two virtually
indistinguishable at checkpoints. At the same time, a team of
U.S. Army Special Forces advisers moved into offices in the Lebanese Ministry of Defense in Yarze, adjacent to the Christian
eastern half of Beirut, and they were frequently called on by the
Lebanese general staff for operational advice on troop movements
and other matters, which they innocently gave.

This military relationship would ultimately undermine the entire American mission in Lebanon. What the Americans did not
understand in December 1982 was that while they were making
Lebanon an extension of what they knew, the Lebanese were
doing the same thing in reverse. In order to handle the Americans,
to digest them, to make them fit into their tiny land, they made
the Marines an extension of what they knew and what they knew
was the feud. President Gemayel, instead of using the Marines
as a crutch to rebuild his country, began to use them as a club to
beat his Muslim opponents. Instead of using the strength he derived from his American backing to forge a political entente with
the Muslim and Druse leaders of West Beirut and make real
national unity possible—at a time when they had yet to side with
Syria and were open to compromises on moderate terms—he
began to behave with typical tribal logic, which says, When I am
weak, how can I compromise? When I am strong, why should I
compromise?

And Gemayel thought he was strong. His national security
adviser, Wadia Haddad, was so convinced of America's support
for the Lebanese President that he once boasted to Syria's Rifaat
al-Assad, "I have the United States in my pocket," according to
an Arab diplomat privy to the conversation. More than once
Amin's advisers warned his Muslim and Christian opponents,
"Toe the line. We are not alone."

Gemayel totally ignored feelers from Shiite Amal leader Nabih
Berri, whose support could easily have been won by a Lebanese
President ready to commit some resources to rebuilding the predominantly Shiite southern suburbs of West Beirut, which had
been savaged by the Israeli invasion. Instead, Gemayel's govern-

ment ordered that 20,000 Lebanese pounds (or the rough equivalent of $4,000) be set aside for rebuilding this neighborhood— enough maybe to repair a single three-bedroom apartment. Worse yet, one of the Gemayel government's first acts was to order the Lebanese army in West Beirut to bulldoze illegally built shanties that had encroached on roads in the southern suburbs. In other words, in the Beirut neighborhood most short of housing, he ordered houses demolished. As a young Shiite leader, Ali Hamadan, observed at the time, "Amin was interested only in dealing with us through the Ministry of Defense. The Ministry of Education, the Ministry of Public Works, the Ministry of Social Welfare, those he never wanted to send into our neighborhoods."

My friend Lebanese Shiite professor Fouad Ajami appeared on *Face the Nation* in October 1983 with the Marine commandant, General P. X. Kelley, and Amin Gemayel's ambassador in Washington, Abdullah Bouhabib. P. X. Kelley spoke earnestly about how he would follow the Lebanese army commander in chief Ibrahim Tannous "into battle anywhere," and Bouhabib waxed eloquent about how much America was needed to support Amin Gemayel's rebuilding of the Lebanese state, while Fouad, speaking for all the Lebanese Muslims who felt they were being abused by Gemayel's government, warned the Americans that they were getting involved in a family feud they did not understand. A few weeks later *Face the Nation* sent Fouad a transcript of the show and a glossy photograph of the three panelists in the studio with moderator Leslie Stahl. Shortly thereafter, Fouad told me, a friend of his visited Ambassador Bouhabib in his Washington embassy office and there he saw the same picture. Only there were just two people in the picture—P. X. Kelley and Ambassador Bouhabib. Fouad had been edited out, except for his elbow, which jutted in from the side like some loose end. Fouad's friend, who was also a Shiite, could not resist asking Bouhabib, "Abdullah, whose elbow is that?" This was a graphic depiction of how Amin Gemayel and the Maronites wanted to think of things: they and the Americans shaping Lebanon's future together— alone.

As for Druse leader Walid Jumblat, Gemayel tried to edit him out of Lebanon's future entirely, treating him as mountain peasant, unworthy of even being invited to the presidential palace. Worse, Amin stood by and watched, probably even encouraged, the Phalangist militia as it tried to settle an old score with the Druse over who would be rooster on Mt. Lebanon. The Druse in recent years dominated most of the Shouf district at the southern end of Mt. Lebanon, while the Maronites controlled the larger Kesuran region to the north and east of Beirut. The rough division of the mountain between these two communities—which had a long history of both antipathy and cooperation—served as the foundation for the larger power-sharing balance between all Lebanese Christians and Muslims.

After Israel invaded Lebanon, though, the Phalangist militia tried to take over the Shouf from the Druse with Israeli help. The Maronites claimed they were only trying to protect the Christian villagers in the Shouf, but these had been living quite peacefully with the Druse for years. The Druse, feeling their only real turf in Lebanon was being threatened, responded to the Phalangist infiltrations with a venomous force, and before long—only a month after Amin Gemayel had taken office in September 1982—a low-grade tribal war was under way between the Phalangists and Druse for control of the Shouf.

Gemayel even managed to alienate the conservative Sunni Muslims of West Beirut, who were actually quietly supporting his presidency. During the first year of his rule, some 1,000 Muslims and Palestinians disappeared in West Beirut; they were either swooped up by the army and imprisoned without trial or abducted by the Phalangists and suffered fates unknown. At first, many West Beirut Lebanese Muslims, starved as they were for law and order, welcomed the Christian-led Lebanese army when it came in and replaced the PLO. They were even ready to overlook some of its excesses, while they waited for a similar crackdown to take place in Christian East Beirut. But that crackdown never came, so West Beirut went into a slow burn and Muslims there began attacking the army. Gemayel responded by putting West Beirut under an 8:00 p.m. curfew. Across town in East Beirut, though, he turned a blind eye to the activities of his father's Phalangist Party and militia, with its illegal ports and private army, and refrained from even deploying the Lebanese army there, let alone imposing its authority. Muslim West Beirutis had to sit locked in their homes at night, listening to the Phalangist Radio carrying advertisements for the Jet Set disco in East Beirut, where customers were invited to dance "twenty-four hours a day."

Finally, Gemayel snubbed his nose at the Syrians and entered into direct negotiations with Jerusalem over a withdrawal of Israeli forces and a treaty governing security, trade, and tourism between the two countries.

If there were any in Lebanon's Muslim community whom Gemayel did not alienate, I didn't know of them. Gemayel's pigheadedness soon became America's liability.

"When we first arrived in Beirut, it was just great," Corpsman José Medina, who was with the first and last Marine contingents in Lebanon, told me one day. "People were always stopping you and giving you things. We really felt appreciated. The people saw us as their protectors from the Israelis. But eventually their anger began to rise, and for some reason they thought we were against them."

No wonder. As the Marines continued training and supporting Gemayel's Lebanese army, they increasingly came to be viewed by Beirut's Muslims as stooges of his regime. The first signs of trouble were felt by Marines on foot patrol, who, in the spring of 1983, six months after they had arrived, suddenly began reporting that Lebanese boys along the roads were throwing stones and taunting them with obscenities. In Beirut, no one throws stones for long. On March 16, 1983, five Marines were injured in a grenade attack in West Beirut. The Marines were not prepared for this. They had come to Beirut with a strict set of "Rules of Engagement" governing their use of force. Their ten rules included:

1. When on the post, mobile or foot patrol, keep loaded magazine in weapon, bolt closed, weapon on safe, no round in the chamber.

2. Do not chamber a round unless told to do so by a commissioned officer unless you must act in immediate self-defense where deadly force is authorized.

4. Call local forces to assist in self-defense effort. Notify headquarters.

7. If you receive effective hostile fire, direct your fire at the source. If possible, use friendly snipers.

A few weeks after the March 16 grenade attack, the Che Guevara era of Lebanese politics would make its comeback in full splendor and the Marines would be exposed for the first time to the local rules of engagement. It happened at 1:03 p.m. on April 18, 1983. At the time, I was sitting in the office of my new apartment, which was just around the corner from the one that had been blown up. I had my feet resting lazily on my desk and was listening to the BBC World Service. Three minutes into the news broadcast my transistor radio was knocked over by a tremendous blast that shook our building like a rattle. I ran down the stairs and out my front door and immediately spotted in the distance a gray mushroom cloud shooting up from near the seashore. Without thinking, I ran toward it. I ran and I ran, and as I got closer I started to say to myself, "No . . . Could it be?"

A suicide bomber had driven a Chevrolet pickup truck into the front door of the American embassy of Beirut, then detonated it into a massive fireball that ripped off the front of the building, killing more than sixty people inside. When I arrived, I stared open-mouthed at a man dangling by his feet from the jagged remains of the fourth floor, while the rooms below coughed smoke and flames like a dragon in distress.

In the best tribal tradition of Lebanon, some Muslim or pro-Syrian group had sent Amin Gemayel a smoke signal. The message was brief: Your American friends are not as invincible as you think. Beware.

A month after the embassy attack, the United States brokered the May 17, 1983, peace treaty between Gemayel's government and Israel, a lopsided—if impracticable—agreement favoring Israel that deepened Lebanese Muslim resentment all the more. Secretary of State George P. Shultz personally came out to the Middle East in April 1983 to put the finishing touches on this treaty by shuttling between Beirut and Jerusalem. Throughout the negotiations with Mr. Shultz, Lebanon's Muslim Prime Minister, Shafik al-Wazzan, the only top official in Gemayel's circle who lived in West Beirut, warned that the mood on the street there was increasingly against the kind of agreement with Israel that was being midwifed by the Americans. He kept urging Washington to curb the Israeli demands for formal security, trade, and diplomatic relations, and to settle instead for quiet de facto arrangements—for everyone's sake. On May 8, 1983, the last day of the Shultz shuttle, the Secretary met at the presidential palace in Baabda with a group of senior Lebanese officials to tie up the final details. When they were all done, everyone started shaking hands and slapping each other on the back in congratulation. Everyone except Wazzan. According to an official who was present, Wazzan looked directly at the American Secretary of State and declared, "I want you to know this is the saddest day of my life. This is not an honorable agreement. I don't believe America has done its best [in limiting Israel's demands]. I am a very unhappy man."

During the following summer and early fall, outgoing U.S. Ambassador Robert S. Dillon began to urge President Gemayel to make some conciliatory overtures to his domestic Muslim and Christian opponents, who were beginning to drift into Syria's pocket. Dillon understood that building the Lebanese army without also fostering national reconciliation was like building a house with bricks and no cement. Gemayel frostily dismissed his advice, and relations between the two men quickly deteriorated. When Dillon left Beirut for good in October, Gemayel refused to present him, as was Lebanese government custom, with the honorary Order of the Cedars. He left the task to his Foreign Minister Elie Salem in a calculated insult.

Whatever remained of American credibility in Lebanese Muslim eyes completely disappeared after Israel decided to withdraw its army from the Shouf Mountains and pull back to the Awali River in south Lebanon on September 4, 1983. The Israelis had spent a year sitting in the Shouf, overlooking Beirut, trying to pressure Amin into signing a peace treaty, but as soon as it became clear that he could not implement it, the Israelis decided to simply pull out of the Shouf and hunker down in south Lebanon, leaving the Marines to pick up the pieces in Beirut. The Israeli withdrawal from the Shouf left a vacuum which everyone rushed to fill. From one side came the Druse, led by their warlord Walid Jumblat, who saw the Israeli departure as his chance to roll back the Phalangist encroachments into his ancestral homeland. From the other came the Phalangists and Gemayel's Lebanese army, which saw the Israeli pullout as their opportunity to finally extend Christian and government control over this strategic turf. The Shiites, Sunnis, and Syrians backed the Druse. The Marines, who by then were totally intertwined with the Lebanese army, had no choice but to throw their weight behind Gemayel. The Reagan Administration policymakers apparently believed that they were supporting the right of a government to extend sovereignty over its national territory. Gemayel, in fact, was supporting the "right" of Christians to dominate Druse.

The specific event which turned the Marines from neutral peacekeepers into just another Lebanese faction was a battle for an obscure Shouf mountain village named Souk el-Gharb. Shortly after the battle for the Shouf began in September 1982, Lebanese army commander in chief Tannous began hinting to his American military advisers that he would like to see the Marines get more directly involved on the side of the Lebanese army, since the Syrians were actively supporting the Druse. The Americans consistently refused. However, at around 2:00 a.m. on September 19, 1983, Syrian- and Palestinian-backed Druse units launched a major artillery and ground assault on the strategic Lebanese army position at Souk el-Gharb, which controlled the ridge line overlooking Beirut. If the Druse and their allies took Souk el-Gharb, they would be able to shoot down directly on the presidential palace in Baabda, the Defense Ministry in Yarze, and Phalangist-controlled East Beirut. Some time between 7 a.m. and 8 a.m. on September 19, a group of senior U.S. Army trainers, as well as Brigadier General Carl Stiner, the military aide of the Special Middle East envoy, Robert McFarlane, were gathered in the operations room at the Lebanese Ministry of Defense. An agitated General Tannous came up to General Stiner and informed him that a "massive" offensive was taking shape against his army at Souk el-Gharb, that he didn't think his defenses could hold out another "thirty minutes" and that one of the three Lebanese army howitzer battalions providing support for Souk el-Gharb was out of ammunition. He needed American help immediately.

General Stiner passed all this on to McFarlane, who was staying at the nearby U.S. ambassador's residence and had been up all night due to the heavy shelling of the area. Without seeking any independent confirmation of Tannous's assessment, McFarlane ordered the Marine commander in Beirut, Colonel Timothy Geraghty, to have the navy ships under his authority fire in support of the Lebanese army. Colonel Geraghty strenuously opposed the order. He knew that it would make his soldiers party to what was now clearly an intra-Lebanese fight, and that the Lebanese Muslims would not retaliate against the navy's ships at sea but against the Marines on shore. But he was overruled by McFarlane and Stiner. Early on the morning of September 19, the guided missile cruisers *Virginia, John Rodgers*, and *Bowen* and the destroyer *Radford* fired 360 5-inch shells at the Druse–Syrian–Palestinian forces, to take the pressure off the beleaguered Lebanese troops. The next morning the Americans learned that only eight Lebanese army soldiers had been killed and twelve wounded in the whole previous day of fighting.

Had the Americans been had? No one will ever really know if it was deliberate, but as one senior American officer in Lebanon remarked to me later, it was "a nice opportunity for [Gemayel] to get what he wanted all along." What he had wanted was to make the Americans an extension of his feud, and that he did.

There was only one Marine sentry—Lance Corporal Eddie DiFranco—who got a glimpse of the suicide driver who slammed his yellow Mercedes-Benz truck filled with 12,000 pounds of dynamite into the Marines' four-story Beirut Battalion Landing Team (BLT) headquarters just after dawn on October 23, 1983. DiFranco could not remember the color of the suicide driver's hair, or the shape of his face. He could not remember whether he was fat or thin, dark-skinned or light. All he could remember was that as this Muslim kamikaze sped past him on his way to blowing up 241 American servicemen "he looked right at me . . . and smiled."

Sergeant of the Guard Stephen E. Russell never saw the smile, he only heard the roar. He was standing at his sandbag post at the main entrance of the headquarters, when his eye was suddenly drawn to a huge truck circling the parking lot. The driver had revved his engine to pick up speed before bursting through the fence around the complex and barreling straight for the front door. According to Marine Corps historian Benis M. Frank, Russell "wondered what the truck was doing inside the compound. Almost as quickly, he recognized that it was a threat. He ran from his guard shack across the lobby toward the rear entrance, yelling, 'Hit the deck! Hit the deck!' Glancing over his shoulder as he ran, he saw the truck smash through his guard shack. A second or two later the truck exploded, blowing him into the air and out the building."*

Colonel Geraghty was in his office around the corner, checking the morning news reports, when the explosion blew out all his windows. He ran outside only to find himself caught in a cloud.

"I ran around the corner to the back of my building, and, again, it was like a heavy fog and debris was coming down . . . and . . . then the fog cleared, and I turned around . . . the headquarters was gone. I can't explain to you my feelings. It was just unbelievable."†

For me too. It was 6:22 a.m. and I was sleeping ten miles away in the heart of West Beirut. Despite the distance, though, the explosion of the Marines' headquarters shook us out of our sleep. At first Ann and I thought it was an earthquake. There had been a tremor a few months earlier that had wiggled the house the same way. Ann and I did what we always did in such situations: we lay perfectly still in bed waiting to hear if there were sirens. No sirens meant that it was not an explosion, not an earthquake, but just one of a thousand sonic booms Israeli jets set off over Beirut. It took about a minute before the sirens began to wail from every direction. It was too early for me to track down my assistant, Mohammed, so Ann and I hopped into our Fiat and followed the first fire engine we came across. Careening through Beirut's empty streets, the fire truck eventually led us to the French paratroop barracks, a ten-story apartment block that had been completely blown apart by a suicide bomber, who had driven into the underground garage before detonating his car bomb. After I had interviewed people there for about an hour, someone mentioned that they had heard the Marines also "got a rocket," so several of us leisurely rode over to see the Marines, only to find them staggering about with bloodied uniforms, picking through what was the BLT building, where that afternoon there was supposed to have been an outdoor barbecue—American-style. Within hours of the blast, rescue teams using pneumatic drills and blowtorches had begun working furiously on the mound

---

*Benis M. Frank, *U.S. Marines in Lebanon, 1982–1984* (History and Museums Division, U.S. Marine Corps. 1987).
† Marine Corps Oral History Collection. Interview conducted May 28, 1983.

of broken concrete pillars, trying desperately to pry out the dead and wounded. Their efforts were hampered, though, by the fact that unidentified snipers kept firing on the relief workers.

Having come to Beirut to protect the Lebanese, the Marines now seemed to be the ones needing protection. As a Lebanese friend put it, "It's like diapers inside diapers."

Much of the discussion in the wake of the Marine headquarters bombing would focus on why the Marines did not have an extra barrier here and an extra guard post there to prevent such a suicide attack. The explanation is not a technical-security one but a political-cultural one. The Marines had come to Beirut with such good intentions that it took them a long time to realize (and some of them never did realize) that in being forced by their superiors in Washington to support Amin Gemayel they had become a party to the age-old Lebanese intercommunal war. Shortly after the BLT explosion, I wrote a piece for the *Times* in which I argued that the Marines had turned into just another Lebanese militia. The Marine spokesman in Beirut cut the article out and put it up on his bulletin board, where other Marines scribbled obscenities all over it, such as "Fuck You, Tom" and "Thanks, Asshole." Even once they recognized that they were embroiled in a tribal war, however, the Marines failed to take all the necessary precautions against something as unusual as a suicide car bomber, because such a threat was outside the boundaries of their conventional American training. Lance Corporal Manson Coleman, an enormous Marine with a warm smile and American small-town politeness, served as sentry in Beirut. He told me one day shortly after the Marine headquarters bombing, "We used to get reports all the time about different things terrorists were supposed to be planning against us. One day they said we should look out for dogs with TNT strapped to their bellies. For a few days we were shooting every dog around. Imagine, someone would stoop so low as to have dogs carrying TNT. Now, we have some ingenious ways of killing people, but we are restricted by the Geneva Conventions. Well, these people over here never had any conventions."

Colonel Geraghty, a taut, controlled man who always evinced an air of real decency, was no better prepared for Beirut's surprises than his men. But who could blame him? He was caught in the middle of two political cultures totally missing each other:

there was no course on Beirut at Camp Lejeune and there were
no rules of engagement among the Lebanese. When Colonel Geraghty was asked whether he ever anticipated a suicide attack, he
was categoric in his answer: "No, no. It was new, unprecedented.
We had received over 100 car-bomb threats—pickup trucks, ambulances, UN vehicles, myriad types. Those . . . things we had
taken appropriate countermeasures toward. But never the sheer
magnitude of the 5-ton dump truck going 50–60 miles an hour
with an explosive force from 12,000 to 16,000 pounds. [That] was
simply beyond the capability to offer any defense. When was the
last time you heard of a bomb that size?"

Colonel Geraghty then added, "There may have been a fanatic
driving that truck, but I promise you there was a cold, hard,
political, calculating mind behind the planning and execution of
it."*

Whether that mind was Syria's or Iran's or both together will
never be known for certain, but American intelligence officials
who have seen all the evidence are convinced today that one of
the two must have been involved. Which brings up the other
reason the Marines were caught unprepared: they were set up.
While the Marines were victims of their own innocence, they were
even more the victims of the ignorance and arrogance of the weak,
cynical, and in some cases venal Reagan Administration officials
who put them into such an impossible situation. Reagan, Shultz,
McFarlane, Defense Secretary Caspar Weinberger, and CIA Director William Casey will all have to answer to history for what
they did to the Marines. By blindly supporting Amin Gemayel,
by allowing Israel a virtually free hand to invade Lebanon with
American arms and by not curtailing Israel's demands for a peace
treaty with Beirut, the Reagan Administration had tipped the
scales in favor of one Lebanese tribe—the Maronites—and against
many others, primarily Muslims. Washington was helping to inflict
real pain on many people, and there would have to be a price to
pay for that. I will never forget that as I left my apartment house
on the morning of the Marine headquarters disaster, a group of
Lebanese were playing tennis on the clay court next door. The
explosion had probably shaken the ground from under their feet,
but it did not interrupt their set. It was as though they were saying,

*Marine Corps Oral History Collection. Interview conducted November 2, 1983.

"Look, America, you came here claiming to be an honest broker and now you've taken sides. When you take sides around here, this is what happens. So go bury your dead and leave us to our tennis."

The Reagan Administration also took far too long to understand that the United States, in having supported the Israeli invasion and the May 17 peace agreement between Israel and Lebanon, was undercutting Syria, which viewed Lebanon as part of its traditional sphere of influence, and that eventually there would be a price to pay for this as well. Finally, the Reagan team took far too long to understand that back in Teheran, Ayatollah Khomeini was still nursing a grudge against the Americans for having supported the Shah for all those years. Having driven them out of Iran, he wanted to carry on and drive them out of the region altogether.

All these aggrieved parties decided to fight the Americans in the only way they knew how, and that was not according to the Geneva Convention. I would never justify what they did, but I cannot say it was without logic. Colonel Geraghty was right: there were cold, calculating minds behind it.

America's arrogance was the arrogance of power. What the United States learned in Beirut, maybe even more than in Vietnam, was the degree to which the world has undergone a democratization of the means of destruction. For the first two hundred years of its history America lived in glorious isolation from the rest of the world. It was protected by two vast oceans, and its only serious foreign engagements after independence were the Mexican–American War and the Spanish–American War, which is to say no serious foreign engagements at all. There was no real need for Americans to learn the seamier dimensions of diplomacy, espionage, and covert operations in order to survive in the world. When the twentieth century arrived, America could no longer avoid being fully involved with the world in the First and Second World Wars; but by then, America was able to step into the world with such overwhelming power and weight that whatever she lacked in cunning and guile was easily compensated for in sheer military might. Who needed to be cunning when you had battleships like the *Iowa* and *New Jersey* that fired shells as big as Chevrolets? Where does a 1,000-pound gorilla sit? Answer: Wherever he wants.

That was true up until the Vietnam War, when American military and economic power began to decline relative to the rest of the world and the nature of warfare changed in a way that allowed an illiterate peasant with a shoulder-held Stinger missile to shoot down a $50 million fighter aircraft. Small powers, such as Syria and Iran, and even small militias, using highly unconventional methods, such as suicide car bombers, were able to neutralize American policy in Lebanon with just 12,000 pounds of dynamite and a stolen truck. Suddenly the United States found its power checked in a thousand different ways, but as the Marine encounter with Lebanon demonstrated, it had not yet generated a vision of the world, or of the exercise of power and diplomacy, that was as subtle, nuanced, and cunning as the world itself. The world had changed, and America was not ready when it did.

The American officials who dispatched the Marines, and the Marines themselves, were so enamored of their detailed maps and their night-vision equipment that they could not imagine that all their conventional force would not translate into military superiority in a place like Beirut. They were certain that weapons, like the *New Jersey* or fighter aircraft, used sparingly and in conjunction with verbal threats, would be enough to intimidate the local forces. They thought in such conventional terms they even extended to the Lebanese their concept of who the enemy was. One day the Marines reported spotting men on their perimeter wearing what they described as "Warsaw Pact uniforms." It was the Russkies all along! They did not realize that in Lebanon the color of a man's uniform was no more a tip-off to his real political allegiance than the color of his eyes. When I was interviewing Marines on the U.S.S. *Guam* helicopter carrier after their departure from Beirut, one earnest young man took me aside and asked in a whisper, so that his friends could not hear, whether it was true that "all Druse are Communists."

In the wake of the Marine bombing, the Italian ambassador to Lebanon, Franco Lucioli Ottieri, remarked to me, "You know how they say people are always fighting the last war? Well, you Americans have been preparing yourselves for the confrontation on the Eastern front. That's fine. The Eastern front with the Soviet Union is now secured. But you are deplorably unprepared for the war in the Third World. You are like a big elephant. If you are up against another elephant, you are fine. But if you are fighting a snake, you have real problems. Your whole mentality and puritanical nature hold you back. Lebanon was full of snakes."

A few months after the Marines arrived in Beirut, President Gemayel sent former Prime Minister Saeb Salam to Washington with a letter for President Reagan. The letter was meaningless; all that was important was the postman. Salam's chance to meet with Reagan was Amin's way of paying him off for supporting his presidency. A Sunni Muslim, educated at the American University of Beirut, Salam was the quintessential pro-American Third World politician. Like so many politicians born and raised in countries that had not managed their own affairs for years, even centuries, Salam was convinced that there was always somebody else in the world, some distant power, which had the ultimate word and the military might to impose it. When he was born, it was the Ottoman Turks; when he grew up, it was the British and French, and when he grew old, it was the Americans. People who have never really wielded power always have illusions about how much those who have power can really do. Whenever I would mention some problem that needed addressing in the Middle East, Salam would just shake his head back and forth and say, "America, America, America."

After Salam returned to Beirut from delivering his letter to Reagan—his visit was splashed on the front pages of all the Lebanese newspapers—I went to see him at his huge house in West Beirut. When he greeted me at the door, I found him dressed in a dapper gray suit adorned with a white carnation.

"Saeb!" I said, slightly startled. "Why are you wearing that carnation?"

"Because I met with Reagan," he answered, eyes twinkling, "and he told me that on Lebanon he has no reverse gear."

Eventually, though, Salam's carnation wilted and its petals fell; American policy went into reverse gear, after all, and a bitterly disappointed Saeb Salam probably never donned another carnation again. I learned a valuable lesson from this incident.

I have no doubt that when President Reagan told Saeb Salam that he had "no reverse gear" on Lebanon, he was simply mouthing one of those cute toss-off lines a head of state says to a visitor while escorting him to the door. Like the whole American decision to get involved in Lebanon, the statement was an afterthought. Reagan, I am sure, would never remember it. But Salam would never forget it. He went out and put on a carnation after hearing it—as though he had won the lottery. Many other Lebanese went further. In the months following the Marines' arrival, you could walk into virtually any Beirut home and find someone who would say, "I did this when I heard the Americans were coming." One of my closest Lebanese friends, a Muslim lecturer at the American University, went to the bank and changed his life savings of some $25,000 from U.S. dollars into Lebanese pounds. He was convinced the Lebanese currency would make an immediate comeback under the American umbrella. It was a bad calculation. At the time, the rate was about 4 Lebanese pounds to the dollar; today the rate is about 500 to the dollar.

I knew a young Lebanese couple, Nabil Yacoub and his wife, Vicky, who had been living in Abu Dhabi since the beginning of the Lebanese civil war. He had started his own electrical engineering business there, saved his money, and dreamed of one day returning home to Beirut when the war was over. After the Marines arrived, Nabil and Vicky decided the war was over. In the fall of 1982, the Yacoubs told me, they took all their savings out of the bank, spent $70,000 just to move their household and business from Abu Dhabi to Beirut, and then purchased a $150,000 three-bedroom apartment just off Hamra Street, where Nabil was going to open a consulting business that would specialize in reconstruction.

"I thought the Americans had it all planned out and nothing could go wrong," Nabil said to me, as we sat on the couch in the living room of his new apartment. "They kept talking about all their plans and commitments. We thought there would be a new order in Lebanon patroned by the United States."

But just when Nabil and Vicky finally got settled in Beirut in the summer of 1983, things began to unravel for Lebanon and the Marines. The Lebanese economy went soft and no one dared to invest in reconstruction. The last time I saw Nabil, he was unemployed. His final words to me, only half in jest, were: "I am preparing a lawsuit against Reagan for consequential damages, opportunities lost, and psychological harm. You Americans don't understand the confidence you inspire in people. You had a direct influence on our decisions."

Ghassan Salame, the Lebanese political scientist, who formerly taught at the American University, once pointed out to me how the daily White House and State Department briefings were played back in the Arabic press in Beirut. Those State Department briefings might each have been one hour long, and during that one hour maybe only one question was asked about Lebanon, to which the spokesmen gave some boilerplate answer about America standing by its commitments there. This statement would not merit even a passing mention in any American newspaper, but it would make front-page headlines back in Beirut. The State Department spokesman in 1983, Alan Romberg, would have won any name-recognition contest in Lebanon. "My students all thought that Reagan was talking about Lebanon every day," remarked Ghassan.

So, too, did President Gemayel. A senior American embassy official in Beirut during this period once told me that Gemayel "always made assumptions as to how far we would go in supporting him that were never consistent with what we told him. But the truth is, we were never clear enough with him. We never spelled out the limits as clearly as we should have. Also, all of those general statements by the President that we were with the Lebanese 'all the way' certainly contributed to Amin's misperceptions."

What is the lesson of all this? I think my friend Fouad Ajami captured it the best. "The Lebanese, like all Middle Easterners, are a people with a vivid imagination," remarked Fouad. "That is why a great power should never wink at anyone in the Middle East. Small winks speak big things there. You wink at Ariel Sharon and he goes all the way to Beirut. You wink at Amin Gemayel and he tries to invade the Shiite suburbs of Beirut. They all want America's license, its resources and its green lights. And they all want to implicate you in their schemes. They like you big, but they want to send you back small; they like you a virgin, but they want to send you back a whore."

The Druse–Maronite war for the Shouf intensified in early 1984, and as it did the Marines got to see the real Lebanon in all its tribal splendor. Eighteen months after they had landed in Beirut, armed with incomplete maps and "rules of engagement" and wearing naïve American optimism on their sleeves, the Marines finally understood that they had come to support the center in a country where there was no center—only factions. Once they realized this, there was nothing for them to do but dig in behind their sandbags, keep out of the Lebanese–Lebanese cross fire, and wait for Reagan to declare victory and bring them home. They stopped lobbing shells in support of the Lebanese army and simply tried to protect themselves, firing back twice at anyone who fired at them once. Forget the rule book, they said, let's just get even. The British, French and Italian "peacekeeping" troops adopted a similar approach. The Lebanese daily newspaper *As-Safir* began to refer to the multinational peacekeeping force as the "international militia." During these weeks of waiting for a graceful exit, it became a lot of fun talking to the Marines, because they stopped trying to see Lebanese politics as an extension of American politics and began to talk about it as just the opposite of American politics.

When I asked Marine Sergeant Jeffrey Roberts what he thought was happening in Lebanon, he explained, "To me it was a civil war, only it wasn't just the North against the South. It was North against South, East against West, Northeast against Southwest, Southeast against Northwest, and we were in the middle of it all. There were just too many different sides. If we picked one, we had four others against us."

Marine spokesman Captain Keith Oliver was even more succinct one afternoon as we walked around the Marine compound while the bass drumbeat of Lebanese militias pounding each other with artillery echoed in the distance. He said with a shake of his head, "You know, these people just aren't playin' with the same sheet of music."

In fact, they weren't playing with any music at all. The Marines' Beirut Airport headquarters was surrounded by areas of sand dunes and scrub where Lebanese boys used to like to hunt for pigeons each day. Even after the Marines were on alert, some Lebanese youths insisted on going out and hunting along the Marine perimeter. Eventually, a Marine officer was sent out to speak with them.

"Look," he explained to the Lebanese boys, "we are Marines. You don't hunt pigeons around Marines! Got it?"

But each day the Lebanese boys would come back with their old-style, muzzle-loaded bird guns and hunt for pigeons, constantly setting off alarm bells among the nervous leathernecks. The exasperated Marine sergeant who related this problem to me one afternoon at his checkpost growled under his breath, "You know what? You just gotta shoot these people. They don't understand anything else."

Having stepped into Beirut with a feeling that everything was possible and everything made sense, the Marines began to pack their bags with a feeling that in such a place nothing was possible and nothing made sense. The absurdity of their predicament eventually found its way into verse. The poem was written with a blue ballpoint pen on a 4-by-4 piece of lumber that served as a door frame for an Echo Company bunker on the perimeter of Beirut Airport. I met more than one Marine who had it memorized. It read:

> *They sent us to Beirut*
> *To be targets that could not shoot.*
> *Friends will die into an early grave,*
> *Was there any reason for what they gave?*

9

The End of Something

ESTRAGON: I can't go on like this.

VLADIMIR: That's what you think.

ESTRAGON: If we parted? That might be better for us.

VLADIMIR: We'll hang ourselves tomorrow. *(Pause.)* Unless Godot comes.

ESTRAGON: And if he comes?

VLADIMIR: We'll be saved.

—Samuel Beckett,
WAITING FOR GODOT

A man in a brown suit killed himself in the parking lot outside our front door one morning in November 1983, about a month after the Marine headquarters was blown up. Dave Zucchino's little girl Adrien was the first to spot him from their balcony, which was just below ours. Adrien was pointing at him through the balcony railings when her mother came along and noticed the corpse. Some of the other neighbors said afterward that the man in the brown suit had been wandering around our parking lot for a while, drinking from a can of poison marked with a skull and crossbones. In his other hand he was holding a plastic bag. As he keeled over and went into convulsions, the neighbors watched from afar. Eventually, someone called the police. When Beirut's finest arrived about forty minutes later, the man's eyeballs had rolled up into his head and his body was already cold. The police always preferred it that way: fewer witnesses to interview, less paperwork. When the police opened the plastic bag the man was carrying, they found it stuffed with hundreds and hundreds of

Lebanese pounds. After a brief discussion, they took the money and left the man. A little while later they returned with the coroner. He was supposed to take a picture of the corpse, but his camera kept jamming. Finally, one of the neighbors mercifully threw a pink sheet over the man in the brown suit, and a while later an ambulance carted him away.

Mike the barber, whose shop was around the corner and who dispensed free philosophy with his crewcuts, told me later that this was the third person to kill himself in my parking lot overlooking the sea. When I asked him why, he just shrugged and said, "They like the view."

This gruesome and absurd doorstep suicide symbolized for me the mood of Beirut at the end of 1983 and in early 1984—a mood of dashed hopes and utter desperation. The Marines had come to Beirut to project strength, presence, security, and calm, while the Lebanese resolved their differences and rebuilt their nation. But all these plans were made a mockery by the smiling suicidal driver who slammed his truck into the Marine compound and by the intercommunal war that began to rage out of control in the Shouf. After all the Lebanese had been through, after all the hopes they had pinned on America, it was devastating for them to discover that their fling with radicalism wasn't over, after all. The beards and jeans and the untamed tribal passions had not disappeared; they had only been in hibernation, waiting for the American season to pass.

No one had to tell the Lebanese that the American season was over; they could feel it in their bones. Around this time, I went to see my favorite political analyst in Beirut, Riyad Hijal, for a reading on the situation. Hijal never studied political science; in fact, he never studied much of anything. He sold window glass, and in Beirut he was the next best thing to a Gallup Poll. When his business was good, it meant that the Lebanese were optimistic, replacing their bomb-shattered windows with new ones. When his business was bad, it meant that no one had any confidence in the political situation and they were covering their broken windows with plastic wrap better suited for sandwiches—and a lot cheaper than glass. I found Hijal sitting amid stacks of unsold windows. The suicide attacks on the Americans were the turning point, he said. Business had gone downhill fast since then. Only a fool would invest in glass in Beirut now.

"We have not sold a window in weeks," Hijal moaned. "In fact, do you really want to know how bad it is? It is so bad that all the windows in my own apartment are shot out and I am not even replacing the glass. It's true. It's the fourth time my windows have been broken and this time we just put up plastic nylon instead. We're getting rockets every day. How can I put up glass anymore?"

How indeed? As the mushroom clouds from the Marine bombing and the Shouf fighting spread over Beirut in early 1984, I began to wonder whether the whole city wasn't finally going to suffer the same agonizing death as the man in the brown suit.

But why should anyone care about the death of the city?

Because Beirut was never just a city. It was an idea—an idea that meant something not only to the Lebanese but to the entire Arab world. While today just the word "Beirut" evokes images of hell on earth, for years Beirut represented—maybe dishonestly—something quite different, something almost gentle: the idea of coexistence and the spirit of tolerance, the idea that diverse religious communities—Shiites, Sunnis, Christians, and Druse—could live together, and even thrive, in one city and one country without having to abandon altogether their individual identities.

The spirit of Beirut is what was known as the Levantine spirit. The word "Levantine" derives from the Old French word *levant*, which literally meant "rising." The Levant, where the sun rose, was the geographical name given to all those countries bordering the eastern Mediterranean. The Levantine political idea, which grew naturally among the communities of the eastern Mediterranean, was an original way of dealing with diverse tribal, village, and sectarian identities, and it inspired the Beirutis and ultimately the Lebanese to believe that they could build a modern Arab republic, melding together seventeen different Christian, Muslim, and Druse sects. The Levantine idea posited the notion that if men cannot break with their tribal pasts, they can at least learn to check them at the door of the cities in which they live. That was Beirut at its best—a "plural society in which communities, still different on the level of inherited religious loyalties and family ties, co-existed within a common framework," in the words of my Oxford professor, the Lebanese historian Albert Hourani.

This Levantine spirit developed gradually in Beirut after the Industrial Revolution, as the burgeoning Lebanese silk trade and the invention of the steamboat combined to bring men and women of America and Western Europe in large numbers to the Levant. These settlers from the West were Catholic and Protestant missionaries, diplomats, and merchants, Jewish traders, travelers and physicians; and they brought with them Western commerce, manners, and ideas and, most of all, a certain genteel, open, tolerant attitude toward life and toward other cultures. Their mores and manners were gradually imitated by elite elements of the local native populations, who made a highly intelligent blend of these Western ideas with their own indigenous Arabic, Greek, and Turkish cultures, which had their own traditions of tolerance. "To be a Levantine," wrote Hourani, "is to live in two worlds or more at once, without belonging to either."

In Beirut, the embodiment of the Levantine idea was the city center. The Levantine spirit of coexistence was both produced in, and reproduced by, the covered markets and stone-arched alleyways, the red-roofed houses and craft workshops, the arabesque Ottoman fountains and bookstalls of old downtown Beirut, woven around Riyad el-Solh Square. In the Beirut city center seven thousand shops once stood shoulder to shoulder, with the Maronite cobbler next to the Druse butcher and the Greek Orthodox money changer next to the Sunni coffee seller and the Shiite grocer next to the Armenian jeweler. The Beirut city center was like a huge urban Mixmaster that took the various Lebanese communities from their mountains and villages and attempted to homogenize them into one cosmopolitan nation.

"When I was a little boy, I discovered Lebanese society there, the different accents and cultures and forms of dress," remarked Salim Nasr, a Lebanese sociologist. "It was where the country met the rest of the world and the different components of the country met each other."

With the destruction of the Ottoman Empire after World War I, the Levantine idea was gradually choked to death in Smyrna, Basra, Salonika, Alexandria, and Aleppo, by Greek, Turkish, and Arab nationalists who had no patience for, or interest in, heterogeneous cultures and the spirit of tolerance of a bygone era. But in Beirut the idea lived on—primarily among the elite Christian and Muslim classes. These Lebanese Christians and

216   B E I R U T

Muslims intermarried, interacted, became business partners, and produced new ideas together, and they were the ones who really made Beirut a cosmopolitan Manhattan of the Arab world—a refuge for the politically radical and a springboard for the Arab avant-garde. Effete Arab politicians ousted by coups d'état came there to write their memoirs, and aspiring Arab artists and poets came there to make it on the Arab Broadway.

Beirut was the ideal hothouse for this Levantine spirit to survive, because the near-perfect balance of power between Muslim and Christian sects made it impossible for any one group or nationalist ideology to impose itself and smother the diverse mix of cultures necessary for a Levantine society. Moreover, there was a powerful economic base for the Levantine idea in Beirut. Because it was a city which had no real natural resources other than the cunning of its multilingual inhabitants and their ability to make money serving as a bridge between Europe and the Arab world, Beirutis had to learn to come together peacefully in the city center and to cooperate with one another in order to play the profitable role of middlemen between the Arab East and the Christian West. That role was further enhanced by Beirut's banking secrecy, casinos, and wild, salacious nightlife, which made it an attractive oasis for an Arab world that had yet to discover London and Marbella. Every region of the globe needs one city where the rules don't apply, where sin is the norm, and where money can buy anything or anyone. Asia had Hong Kong, Europe had Monaco, and the Middle East had Beirut.

The first round of the Lebanese civil war that broke out in April 1975 and lasted until the end of 1978 wounded Beirut, but not mortally. These early years of the Lebanese civil war primarily involved Lebanese Maronite Phalangists in East Beirut versus Palestinians and later Syrians in West Beirut, supported by a few small Lebanese Muslim militias. The extent of actual Lebanese-versus-Lebanese fighting was relatively limited. Nevertheless, the street fighting that did occur in these years was extensive enough to break the Beirut Mixmaster in half. The main confrontation line, the so-called Green Line, that separated the combatants in East Beirut from the combatants in West Beirut ran right through the Beirut city center, turning it into a ghost town of gutted buildings. The symbol of Beirut's unity became the symbol of its disunity. Despite this separation, though, national institutions, government ministries, the Central Bank, the national airlines, and even the American University of Beirut continued to function to some degree, and the multicultural flavor of Beirut continued to live on in pockets on both the eastern and western sides of the Green Line. During periods of calm, many Lebanese Christians crossed from East Beirut to work in West Beirut and many Lebanese Muslims felt free to do the same in the other direction. The country was partitioned more physically than psychologically, and many Lebanese sincerely believed that their state would one day be put back together more or less as it had been—as soon as all the "outside agitators" were removed.

The definitive dismemberment of both Beirut and Lebanon came in early 1984, and it wasn't "outside agitators" wielding the butcher knife; the Lebanese themselves would carve up their own country and their own flag with their own hands.

The event which set this national suicide in motion was the culmination of the war for control of the Shouf. The Phalangist offensive against the Druse in the Shouf was a naked power play, and the longer it went on, the more it brought out the Druse's deep-seated tribal feelings of solidarity and self-preservation. The Druse–Maronite fighting became a war without prisoners or restraints. During the Shouf fighting, I once came across a Druse militiaman who was wearing the distinctive pea-green uniform of a Phalangist militiaman, whom the Druse had just killed that morning. He had made off with the Phalangist's khakis and polished black high-top Gucci boots like an Indian with a scalp. When I asked this Druse how he had come by those duds, he smiled the thin smile of a cat that had just swallowed a parakeet.

Indeed, the only kind of military battle the two sides seemed to know was the massacre. They not only attacked each other's villages, they torched them black as coal before they left. A senior Israeli officer in the area once told me about his attempts to negotiate prisoner exchanges between the Druse and the Phalangists when they took each other's civilians hostage.

"One day the Druse kidnapped a bunch of Christians, so the Phalangists went out and kidnapped eighty Druse. We immediately tried to mediate," said the Israeli officer. "Dr. Samir Geagea, the Christian commander in the Shouf, was in my office and he had a list of the eighty Druse his men had kidnapped. While we were negotiating the telephone rang. It was a call from one

of Geagea's men saying that the Druse had killed fourteen of
their Christian hostages. Geagea just shook his head and said, 'If
they killed fourteen, I have to kill at least twenty of theirs.' Then,
right in front of me, I mean right in front of me, he took out a
pencil and started crossing off names on his list of Druse prisoners.
These were the ones to be killed. There was no emotion. He was
like a businessman doing some accounting.''

The war in the Shouf unleashed a virus of intercommunal tension that floated down from the mountain to infect first Beirut
and then the rest of Lebanon. As the battle for the Shouf intensified in early 1984, Gemayel's Christian-led Lebanese army attacked Shiites in West Beirut to prevent them from aiding the
Druse in the mountains; the Shiites in turn attacked Christians
wherever they could find them, and then took control from the
Lebanese army of as many Beirut neighborhoods as they could.
When the Sunni Muslims saw the Druse and Shiites swallowing
all the turf in West Beirut, they sent their militiamen into the
streets to preserve a corner of their own, leading to shoot-outs
with the Shiites and Druse. Before anyone knew it, Beirut was
in the grip of a war of all against all. Suddenly the outsiders—
the Israelis, the Syrians, and the Palestinians—were on the sidelines, and it was just Lebanese going at Lebanese. Every Lebanese
became aware of himself and his neighbors. Everyone knew that
no matter what his political views, he could be killed just for the
religion on his identity card, so safety meant drawing even closer
to one's own sect or seeking shelter in one's own religious canton.

Nadine Camel-Toueg, a young Christian Lebanese journalist
who was living in West Beirut at the time, summed up the mood
of the city as the Shouf war reached fever pitch. "Every community had to go to its own corner," she said. "You could not
be a Muslim pro-Christian or a Christian pro-Shiite anymore.
There was no room for subtleties. I was working as part of a team
of Muslim and Christian journalists in West Beirut, and most of
us frankly were pro-Arab, pro-Palestinian. But when the Shouf
war came, all of a sudden everyone revealed his true colors, as
though they had been at the bottom of people all along and were
just covered up. We had a Christian guy who was against the
Phalangists, but all of a sudden he was with them. And all of a
sudden another guy started being a Shiite. Who are you? A Shiite?
Then join your clan. Who are you? A Christian? Then join your

clan. There was no place to stand anymore. The Lebanese government couldn't even hold a Cabinet meeting, because there was no neutral space where everyone could agree to meet."

The fighting in the Shouf and Beirut climaxed on February 6, 1984, when all the pent-up anger in West Beirut against Amin Gemayel finally came to a head. The day before, all the Muslim members of Gemayel's Cabinet quit under pressure from their supporters, after a week in which the Lebanese army, having been prevented by Shiite and Druse militiamen from moving reinforcements to West Beirut, began indiscriminately shelling apartment houses in the Shiite neighborhoods. On the evening of February 5, Amin Gemayel belatedly reached out to his Muslim and Christian opponents and called for reconciliation talks and the formation of a national unity Cabinet representing all political factions. It was too little too late. What I remember most about Gemayel's televised peace overture was that it was scheduled for the time slot immediately after the weekly showing of *Dallas*, which was as popular in Beirut as it was in America. Because Gemayel's speech kept being delayed, Lebanese Television kept showing the same *Dallas* segment over and over again for four hours. I was waiting for the speech at the Reuters news bureau, and after we had seen *Dallas* for the fourth time, one of the Reuters Lebanese reporters opined that it was the best possible preparation for Gemayel's remarks: "It is very appropriate that *Dallas* is being shown now. It is just like the Lebanese problem. Everyone is against everyone else, and it all keeps going around and around in circles without anyone ever winning or anything being accomplished."

How right he was. The next morning, in a last desperate attempt to assert his authority, Gemayel's Lebanese army ordered an immediate curfew in West Beirut; anyone on the streets an hour later would be shot on sight. The Druse and Amal militias ignored the curfew and met the army in the streets for one final shootout. There was a real panic as people raced to get home from their offices. I saw cars speeding backward, crashing into each other, mothers scooping up their children from sidewalks, and people cramming into supermarkets and grabbing armfuls of anything they could eat. I ran to get Ann from the newspaper office where she was. I just took her by the arm, announced, "This is the real thing," and pulled her out the door, while her colleagues

watched dumbstruck. We managed to get to the Commodore
Hotel just before the fighting, which began in the suburbs with a
distant rumble, hit the center of the city with the roar of a tidal
wave. I wrote my story that night hiding in my bathroom at the
Commodore, with my mattress propped against me for extra protection from flying glass.

That night we slept with some two hundred other people in the
hotel's basement disco, not knowing that outside in the streets
Druse, Shiite, and Sunni soldiers were deserting the Lebanese
army in droves and joining their respective militias to drive the
remnants of Gemayel's army out of West Beirut for good: their
answer to his peace overture. In the Shouf, the Druse finished
off the Phalangists once and for all, often dragging their bodies
behind cars for good measure. Without the Israelis and the Lebanese army to protect them, the Phalangists proved to be the tin
soldiers everyone believed they were. The Lebanese government
and army the Marines had come to rebuild were reduced to a
shambles; the "center" they came to buttress was no more. Even
President Reagan could figure that out, and he lost little time in
ordering the leathernecks home.

On February 26, 1984, the day the Marines completed their
pullout from Lebanon, chief operations officer Lieutenant Colonel Ernest Van Huss and his commander, Colonel Pat Faulkner,
decided that they would have a formal ceremony to turn their
Beirut Airport complex of bunkers and gun positions back over
to whatever was left of the Lebanese army. The Marines and the
Lebanese army had shared a joint command post at Beirut Airport. On the wall there the Marines' American flag was hanging
crossed with a Lebanese flag. Being Marines, they didn't just
want to take the flag down; they wanted to have an official ceremony to strike their colors. The Marine commanders had
planned to take the flag back to America and present it to the
widow of the last Marine to die in Lebanon.

As Lieutenant Colonel Van Huss said later, "We had no intention of leaving our flag there to be abused or ignored or whatever. That to us represented U.S. authority and we had no
intention of leaving the Stars and Stripes there to become a souvenir for some unauthorized representative of the government of
Lebanon."

The problem was that the Lebanese army commanders could

not get to the airport, because they had been thrown out of West Beirut. So at 8:15 a.m. a Muslim Lebanese army captain who happened to be hanging around the airport and a few other stragglers were rounded up to attend the ceremony. The Marines told me they did not know who half of them were or whether they were loyal to the government or some Muslim militia chieftain. To ensure that some official Lebanese was on hand, though, the Marines had Colonel Fahim Qortabawi, the Lebanese army officer responsible for liaison with the Americans, flown in from East Beirut by helicopter.

Colonel Faulkner delivered a few brief remarks thanking the Lebanese for their cooperation, and then he requested that he and his men be allowed to "strike our colors," which were hanging on a flagstick on the wall, crossed with a red, white, and green Lebanese flag. The Marine officers reached up, carefully took the Stars and Stripes off the flagstick, and began to fold it with great dignity into a precise triangle, according to United States military regulations.

"We did it all with the dignity the U.S. flag deserves," Colonel Van Huss told me proudly. "The Lebanese army officers were watching us very carefully, and well, I guess they were a bit overwhelmed by what we were doing."

Just as the American officers finished folding their flag, Colonel Qortabawi reached up, grabbed the Lebanese flag from the wall, folded it in no apparent pattern, and handed it to Colonel Faulkner. "Please," he said. "You might as well take our flag, too."

Looking chagrined, Colonel Qortabawi, who was a Maronite, then turned to Colonel Van Huss and said. "You are leaving?"

"Yes, we are really leaving," answered the Marine officer. "Our eastern positions have already been vacated. We're in fallback positions now . . . and we're in the final throes of the embarkation. Yes, Colonel Qortabawi, we are really leaving."

Qortabawi, with downcast eyes, then got to the point. "I have no way home," he told his Marine hosts. "To go home I have to go through Muslim checkpoints. [Maybe] you can get me to the Ministry of Defense by helo ride?"

"Yes, we can do that," Van Huss recalled telling the hapless Lebanese army officer. "So Colonel Qortabawi left with us. We gave him a helo ride to the Ministry of Defense. He linked back up to [the Lebanese army command] and it was all very final and over."

Many Lebanese were either too young to remember or too poor to have ever tasted the cosmopolitan life of the Beirut city center, so they never mourned its passing. But for those members of the Christian and Muslim bourgeoisie who really exploited the beautiful side of Beirut, life will never be quite the same again without it. True, they had never paid much attention to the Shiite, Palestinian, and even Christian underclasses upon whose backs Beirut's *joie de vivre* rested, and they believed in the fantasy of Lebanese democracy much more than they ever should have, but they were my friends and I happened to be a witness when their world was murdered.

Long after the civil war began, many of these true Beirutis kept the addresses of their offices in the ravaged city center on their stationery as symbols of solidarity with the past and hope for the future. As the years went by, some of them emigrated, unable to tolerate a Beirut in which Christians and Muslims were being forced to live in separate, isolated ghettos. But many of them stayed, and today they form a whole new class of Beirut refugees. They are existential refugees, homeless souls, internal exiles. They are still sitting in their old apartments with bucolic paintings of the Lebanese countryside decorating the walls, in their favorite chairs and with their favorite slippers—but they are no longer at home and never will be again. They did not leave Beirut, Beirut left them.

My favorite member of this breed was Nabil Tabbara, an architect and professor of architecture at the American University, and a man quick with a smile that always set his whole face aglow. Like many of his generation, Tabbara, whose uncle was Saeb Salam, grew up being taken by his father on trips through the Beirut city center. The smell of the bazaar there, its spices and breads, its colors and sounds, and, most of all, the warmth of people mixing together, would always be part of his identity and his sense of Beirut as home. At the height of the civil war in 1976, it appeared that the graceful stone archways and marketplaces of the old city center were going to be destroyed forever. To keep a personal archive for himself of the Beirut he cherished, Tabbara took a leave from his architectural job and decided in the middle of the civil war that he would try to sketch and photograph what remained of the city center before it vanished.

"I didn't know what would be left of the old Beirut," Tabbara explained when I asked him what motivated this personal adventure, "and I always remembered the people of Warsaw who broke into their municipal archives after the Nazis invaded and hid all the plans and drawings of the Warsaw city center, which they used to rebuild it later."

Armed only with his Nikon camera, pencil, and sketchpads, Tabbara spent a month obtaining passes from all the different Muslim and Christian militias fighting along the Green Line, in order to freely enter the battle zone. Then he headed off to capture the last remnants of his youth.

"I would go down to the Phoenicia Hotel every morning, park my car, and then walk to the Green Line," he recalled. "At first the gunmen would say, 'Look at this fool sitting on the rubble sketching with the rockets and bullets going by.' They thought I was absolutely crazy. But after a while they really got into what I was doing. Some days they would lay down a barrage of machine-gun fire to cover me, so I could run across a dangerous street, or they would break into a building so I could get a particular view from the roof."

After three months of work, Tabbara took all his sketches and photographs, as well as the street signs of famous avenues which he made off with when he could, and put them away for safe-keeping. In late 1976, the civil war died down, and many even thought that the government would soon rebuild the city center almost as it was. It didn't happen, but for eight years Tabbara's sketches, pictures, and street signs sat in a drawer. After the Israeli invasion, as I noted, the Lebanese government actually began to rebuild the city center, and once again it seemed as if the Green Line was going to be erased. But then came the Shouf war, and it was a hope that was erased for good.

Shortly after the Lebanese army collapsed in February 1984, I came to see Tabbara at his West Beirut apartment across from the Sanaiyeh Gardens. We sat in his living room and ate a tableful of Lebanese salads prepared by his maid and talked about his past finally going up in flames a few miles down the road.

"I felt like I was contemplating something very near to me that

was dying," moaned Tabbara. "These were the roots of my generation, and I felt that I was losing my roots for good."

Under such circumstances men do funny things. In order to
hold on to a fragment of his past, Tabbara painted. He took out
the eight-year-old sketches and photographs from the bottom of
his drawer and, using them as his guide, painted a series of wa-
tercolors of the streets and shops of the old Beirut city center as
he remembered them. Even though some of the paintings showed
crumbled buildings, they were brightly colored and exuded pal-
pable warmth and serenity.

"They express my own joy," said Tabbara, slowly unveiling
one picture after the other, "because the atmosphere was the
most important thing in my recollection. The variety of one shop
next to the other brought a sense of life and togetherness. Now
people just belong to their sectarian neighborhoods. Do you call
this belonging? This is ghettoism."

At one point during the conversation, Tabbara's young daughters scampered into the room. They had no idea, he sighed, what
these paintings were about or what they could possibly mean to
him. They called them "Daddy's crazy hobby." His friends,
though, the people Tabbara grew up with, all wanted to buy a
picture, any picture, and some offered to pay any price. There
was a certain desperation in their appeals—grownups begging for
a crumb of memory. So it is with men who know that no matter
where they go and no matter how long they live they will never
feel at home again.

Lebanese were forever asking me whether I had visited Beirut
before the civil war began.

"No," I would say, "I never had the pleasure." Then they
would get a faraway look, and a mist of reminiscence would fog
their eyes, and they would wax eloquent about how "life was so
beautiful then—Lebanon really was the Switzerland of the Middle
East." It certainly looked that way on the postcards: snowcapped
mountains towering over Beirut, a bank on every corner, and a
parliament with all the trappings of a European-style democracy.
But how could a city go from being a vision of heaven to a vision
of hell practically overnight? Because it was too good to be true,
because Beirut in its heyday was a city with a false bottom.

My first glimpse of Beirut's real bottom came at the Commodore Hotel bar on February 7, 1984—the day after the Druse and Shiite Amal militias had seized control of West Beirut from the Lebanese army. Groups of Shiite militiamen belonging to the radical new pro-Iranian organization, Hizbullah, "Party of God," had gone on a rampage that morning, ransacking heathen bars and whorehouses just off West Beirut's Hamra Street. Some they set ablaze, others they smashed apart with crowbars.

I was enjoying a "quiet" lunch in the Commodore restaurant that day when I heard a ruckus coming from the lobby. I turned around and saw a tall, heavyset Shiite militiaman with a black beard, a wild look in his eyes, and an M-16 in his hands, heading for the bar. It was clear he wasn't going for a drink. Anticipating such a visit, Yunis, the bartender, had hidden all the liquor bottles under the counter and had replaced them with cans of Pepsi-Cola and Perrier, which he had carefully stacked into a tall, rather absurd-looking pyramid. The militiaman wasn't fooled. He stalked behind the bar, shoved Yunis aside, and began smashing every liquor bottle and glass with his rifle butt. He didn't miss a single one. When he was done, he stalked out of the lobby, leaving behind a small lake of liquor on the floor and a stunned crowd of journalists frozen to their chairs.

The scene was terrifying on many levels. The relentless manner in which that gunman smashed bottle after bottle with the butt of his rifle left me with the uneasy feeling that he could easily have done the same to any human heads which might have stood in his way. He had Truth with a capital T, he was from the Party of God, and nothing could stop him. But what was no less unsettling to me, and I think many members of the Commodore staff who watched this scene with lips grimly pursed and arms folded across their chests, was that this man was our neighbor. He was not an invader from Syria or Israel. He was a Lebanese, probably a Beiruti. He had been living for years in the same city with us, maybe even in the same neighborhood, and we really never knew he was there—our fault not his. It was as though with his rifle butt he not only smashed the Commodore bar but also right through Beirut's false bottom. Suddenly what remained of the genteel Levantine spirit of Nabil Tabbara's drawings was torn aside, only to reveal a pool of tribal wrath that had been building in intensity for decades beneath the surface among all those Beirutis who were never really part of the Beirut game, or, if they were part of it, played it with a mask on.

This turbulent pool was made up largely of Lebanese Shiites. The Shiites of Lebanon were the country's perpetual underclass, a rural people who for centuries seemed to silently accept their role as Lebanon's beasts of burden. But the Palestinian–Israeli fighting in south Lebanon in the seventies and eighties drove thousands of these Shiites from their native villages in the south to shantytowns on the outskirts of Beirut, where their neighborhoods were aptly dubbed the "Belt of Misery." They lived at the gates of Beirut, but the city never really admitted them—not socially, not politically, and not economically. By the early 1980s, the Shiites of Lebanon were the largest single religious community in the country, making up close to half the total population, but they were represented in the government by corrupt feudal lords and were looked down on by the Sunni aristocracy as much as by the Maronites.

By 1984 the Shiites of Lebanon were tired of waiting for the city's gates to open. The Israeli invasion and the Shouf war had shown them how weak the Lebanese state was and the Iranian Islamic revolution had shown them the power which Shiites could exert in the world. Emboldened by the distant whistle of a pied piper named Khomeini, the Shiites of Lebanon decided that their days of violation and silence were over. It was time for a cleansing, time for a people who had always been denied to claim Beirut for themselves. And so they did. West Beirut has been dominated by the Shiites ever since.

The Shiite who broke up the Commodore bar, though, was not only taking revenge on the symbol of something he had been denied but also on the symbol of something he probably never really comprehended. What Nabil Tabbara and his friends did not understand was that the Levantine spirit which infused them— the most modern, secularized, urbanized classes in Lebanese society—had not penetrated many of their other countrymen—not just the Shiites from villages in south Lebanon, but all of those Lebanese Muslims and Christians living in the hinterlands, beyond the city limits, where the spirit of their ancestors continued to rule the day. They called themselves Beirutis or Lebanese, but these identities were just uniforms that many of them wore to work in the city center. These people mimicked the genteel Levantine language when they walked the streets of Beirut, but at home they spoke a different vernacular. At moments of inter-communal tension, such as the Shouf war, they were always ready to answer the call of the tribe. For them Lebanon was never the Switzerland of the Middle East. It was always the Tower of Babel.

The day the Marines left Beirut, I went down to Green Beach, their landing zone, to watch the last Marine contingent ride out to their mother ships in amphibious armored personnel carriers. The Marines had worked out a deal ahead of time with the Shiite Amal militia in which Amal promised to protect the Marine perimeter as they pulled out from their base at Beirut Airport, in return for the Marines letting Amal take over their abandoned bunkers, gun positions, and the Green Beach docks. When I arrived at Green Beach, I noticed an Amal militiaman at the gate reporting to his commanders on the Marines' progress via walkie-talkie. A second after the last Marine amphibious vehicle stuck its nose into the Mediterranean whitecaps and headed out to sea, this Amal militiaman shouted into his radio that the Marines were gone. A second after that, a jeep with a machine gun mounted on the back came careening into Green Beach. A wild-eyed Shiite youth, his curly locks flying in the sea breeze, was holding fast to the machine gun for dear life. After the jeep sank to a halt in the white sand, all the reporters present ran over to the vehicle and stuck their microphones into the face of the driver. What did the inheritors of the earth have to say for themselves? Specifically, I asked the driver, what was his reaction to the Marines' departure.

He was just a boy. He looked at me quizzically, then squinted his eyes, scrunched up his nose, and said with a grin, "I don't speak English."

After the Marines evacuated Beirut, the Lebanese knew that there would be no one from the outside to save them and no more "outside agitators" to blame for their troubles. Nothing was more depressing for Beirutis. It was one thing to suffer and have it be front-page news in *The New York Times*; it was another to suffer and be a two-paragraph item on page 28C, next to a story about a bus falling off a bridge in Calcutta. Samia, the secretary to the publisher of the *An-Nahar* newspaper, said to me shortly after the Marines pulled up stakes, "You know how when you listen to the news and the story about the Iran–Iraq war comes on and that's when you turn the radio off? That's how the world is treating the Lebanese. There is only one thing worse than being shelled, and that is being shelled and turning on the BBC the next morning and not hearing it reported on the news."

But it wasn't Samia and her friends I felt most sorry for. They had lived a myth and paid the price. Their children were different. They only knew the price. I would periodically get a group of Beirut high-school and college students together to talk about their lives. Shortly before I left Beirut, I convened such a discussion group at the American University. As we got started, I asked each one of the students to give his or her name and age. Before anyone could respond, though, one girl, Rima Koleilat, a twenty-five-year-old sociology graduate student, whispered softly to herself, "We are all one hundred years old."

It must have seemed that way to the lost generation of Lebanese youth—those kids who were nine and ten when the civil war began. They were just really waking up to the world, starting to read newspapers, understand a little politics, and dream of what they wanted to be when the civil war descended in 1975 and destroyed their adolescence before they knew it was gone. One day they were kids, the next day they were adults. Chronological age meant nothing in Beirut. "Normal" for Lebanese youths meant studying for finals with the rock radio channel turned up louder than the shelling. "Normal" for them meant virtually never going out at night. "Normal" for them meant having at least three close friends and one relative who had died a violent death. Few of them could distinguish between Chuck Berry and Little Richard, or early Beatles and late Beatles, but by their fifteenth birthdays practically all of them could distinguish between a Katyusha rocket and a 155-mm mortar just by listening to the sound of the incoming whistle. While their parents knew a different life and would never really feel at home again without it, their kids had never known anything else and would never really feel whole because of it.

Over dinner one evening, Nada Sehnaoui, an aspiring young Lebanese filmmaker, captured the essence of that emptiness for me when she turned a conversation about her parents into a fairy tale of whimsy about herself. "Most of us feel we've just missed it," said Sehnaoui in a flat, emotionless voice. "My mother had a wonderful time in the fifties and sixties. She's always saying, 'Oh, you don't know what you missed.' I guess we were just born in the wrong place at the wrong time. I would have liked to have been Italian, I think. Or maybe Egyptian. No, Italy would have been lovely. Anywhere, really. Anywhere but this place, this time."

This lost generation of Lebanese not only missed out on their adolescence; they also missed out on having a country. For them, most of Lebanon was a foreign country—just a picture on an old calendar in the attic or a faded postcard in the drawer—nothing they ever experienced, smelled, or touched. The Syrian and Israeli occupations, coupled with the partition of Lebanon into sectarian cantons, had made some parts of the country off limits to virtually every Lebanese religious community. Hassan Tannir, a Muslim student at Beirut University College, whom I met when he was a Red Cross volunteer, remarked that were he not a rescue worker he never would have had any idea what Christian East Beirut or its chic port, Juniyah, looked like.

"My younger brother," said Tannir, "is always asking me what is behind the Green Line, what Juniyah looks like, what the autostrada to the north looks like. He doesn't know. He doesn't know our house in the mountains. He has never climbed a tree in his life."

Indeed, the youngest children, those under the age of ten who didn't even have a distant memory of more normal times, were the most scarred of all. It is frightening to imagine what sort of adults they will make. For instance, a thunderstorm will probably never be the same again for Ramsi Khalaf, who was two years old when I left Beirut in 1984. When shelling in his neighborhood used to get very heavy, Ramsi's parents, Samir and Rosanne, used to calm his nerves by telling him that the flashes and booms rocking their apartment were only a thunderstorm. After a while, though, Ramsi began to realize that something was amiss. When the shelling became very intense one evening, he looked up at his father and asked, "Daddy, is it raining without water again?" Sofia Saadeh, a Lebanese academic, told me she came home from school one afternoon and found her ten-year-old son and four-year-old son were playing "Beirut" in the apartment. They had set up cardboard checkpoints between all the rooms and insisted that their mother show them her identity card before they would allow her to pass from room to room.

How did the lost generation get lost in the first place? I was up in the Shouf one day in February 1984, shortly after the Druse had completed their takeover of the region from the Phalangists, and I had a conversation with a father there which made it all clear. The man was a fifty-four-year-old Druse merchant named Nabih. He was standing outside his shop in the village of Qabr Chamoun with his fifteen-year-old son, Ramsi. The shop had been ravaged by weeks of Phalangist artillery and machine-gun barrages. All the windows had been blown out and parts of the ceiling were dangling ganglia of wires and steel rods. Nabih described for me in great detail what he called the "savagery" of the Phalangists and the devastation they had wrought in trying to take over the town. Then he proudly rested a hand on the shoulder of his son and said, "See this boy? He was in the fight, too."

Ramsi then picked up the story, with an aloof air and a matter-of-fact tone: "I was in school, but I quit and came here because they were killing our people. If we don't fight they will kill us all."

Nabih beamed with pride at his son's answer. Fathers in Lebanon do that. A few weeks later I repeated the story over lunch to Richard Day, the American University psychologist. I was asking Richard what kind of psychological revolution would be required to bring peace to Lebanon. Richard, part of whose job was to counsel Lebanese students whose minds had been warped by the war, just threw the question right back in my face. "When will there be peace in Lebanon?" he asked in a voice larded with cynicism. "When the Lebanese start to love their children more than they hate each other."

Having been left by the world to sort out their own feuds, Lebanon's Muslim and Christian warlords convened a peace conference in Lausanne, Switzerland, under Syrian sponsorship, in March 1984. Because there was no neutral space left at home where they could all agree to meet, they had to go to an entirely different country. The various factions, along with President Gemayel, gathered together at the elegant Beau Rivage Hotel, on the banks of Lake Geneva. Lebanese militia leaders, trailing bodyguards in ill-fitting suits with huge bulges in their jackets, waited in line to pass through the metal detector in the hotel lobby behind wealthy European dowagers trailing diamond-collared poodles. The Swiss had surrounded the hotel with barbed wire and sandbags crowned by machine-gun nests and had covered the windows of the conference hall with 20-foot-high steel plates. I could never figure out if all this armor was intended to keep intruders out or the Lebanese in.

The surreal atmosphere was compounded by the fact that *Vogue* magazine had months earlier scheduled a fashion shoot at the Beau Rivage, and by chance it coincided with the Lebanese conference. The enterprising *Vogue* photographer knew a good thing when he saw one and got two Swiss soldiers guarding the lobby to handcuff one of his models, who was dressed in the latest Paris designer fashions. While the Lebanese warlords argued inside the conference hall, outside the Swiss guards dragged a stunning red-head through the lobby as she "struggled" to escape their grasp. As the *Vogue* photographer frantically snapped pictures, all the time coaxing the model with "Great, great, wonderful, look at me, look at the camera," the news photographers started taking pictures of the two of them. In the background, a crowd of print reporters shouted with delight at the two Swiss soldiers, "Hit her again, hit her again."

It was easily the highpoint of the conference, which got off to a bad start when Druse warlord Walid Jumblat insisted on placing a Druse flag, as opposed to a Lebanese flag, in front of his seat. Things went downhill from there. Walid spent most of his time in his suite giving an interview to *Playboy*. Every time a negotiating session began he would announce to his bodyguards, "Okay, it's showtime, let's go." After nine days of fruitless negotiations, interrupted only by banquets of smoked salmon and lobster bisque, the peace conference collapsed as the pigheaded Lebanese politicians refused to make any compromises with one another. Back in Beirut, the newspapers openly mocked the militia chieftains by showing pictures of them stuffing their faces with Chateaubriand next to pictures of Lebanese children mutilated in the latest street fighting.

Following the fiasco at Lausanne, everyone rushed back to Beirut for what would turn out to be yet another phase of the Lebanese civil war. The defeat of the Lebanese army by the

Shiites and Druse and the failed Lausanne conference forced
Amin Gemayel to recognize that he could not rule Lebanon by
himself. So, under pressure from the Syrians, he invited the other
militia leaders to join him in the Cabinet, headed by Rashid
Karami, which was formed on April 30, 1984. Shiite Amal militia
leader Nabih Berri became Minister of Justice and Hydroelec-
tricity; Walid Jumblat became Minister of Transport, Tourism,
and Public Works; Maronite chieftain Camille Chamoun became
Minister of Finance and Housing; Phalangist militia founder
Pierre Gemayel became Minister of Posts and Health; and Shiite
leader Adel Osseiran was named Minister of Defense, a perfect
post for a man who was seriously ill with Parkinson's Disease.
Now every militia not only had a piece of the country's turf, it
had a piece of the army and a piece of the government to boot.
The wolves were finally in charge of the henhouse. For the time
being, there was nothing left to fight for between them.

Yet the fighting along the Green Line between East and West
Beirut went on—only sporadically at times, but it went on. At
first no one, including myself, could understand why. When I
asked my neighbor Dr. Munir Shamma'a, a physician at the
American University of Beirut Hospital, he just threw up his
hands and said, "This is not a war, this is an earthquake. You
can't learn anything from an earthquake. When you have an
earthquake, people just die. That's what it's like here. There are
no obvious reasons for the fighting anymore. It just happens.
Come rain or shine, sea or mountains; it just happens, like an
earthquake."

My assistant Ihsan Hijazi described what it felt like to be on
vacation abroad and to come back home to a city caught in the
grip of such a war: "You feel as if you are coming into a room
where you know that inside everyone is fighting with everyone
else and no one knows why. At the door of this room you have
Syrians and Israelis each passing out weapons to all the people
going inside, saying, 'Here, take this, it's sharper, it kills better.'
Once you are inside, you start fighting like everyone else. The
only way to survive in this room is to find a corner and put your
back up against the wall."

Around this time, I was walking to Ihsan's office after a day of
heavy mortar exchanges between East and West Beirut had
wrought havoc with his neighborhood. The curb was lined with

cars that had been set ablaze by shellfire. The owner of one of the burned-out cars must have come out after the barrage and found that his automobile had been turned into a twisted, charred wreck, unfit even for a junkyard. On the mangled carcass of his car he scribbled out an Arabic note and hung it from a jagged piece of glass where his front windshield once stood. It read:

> *What have we done to deserve this?*
> *We are human beings.*
> *Somebody please help us end this war.*

But, as always, there was a logic to this earthquake. The logic was that Lebanon no longer was caught in the grip of a single civil war. It was caught in the grip of three simultaneous civil wars, which no one could keep straight—including the combatants.

The first and largest of these wars was the one that began in 1975 and culminated in the Shouf in 1984: the civil war over who should control the Lebanese government, which was fought out between the Christian and Muslim militias. It was this confrontation which had broken Beirut and Lebanon in half. The second civil war began in the late 1970s within the two halves of the country. It involved Muslims fighting against Muslims and Christians fighting Christians to decide which Muslims and which Christians would control their respective halves of Lebanon. In this second civil war one could find Druse fighting Shiites for control of a particular West Beirut street on Monday, and Shiites fighting Sunnis for control of a neighboring street on Tuesday. Across the Green Line in East Beirut the same sort of confrontation was going on between the Christian Phalangist militia and the Christian-led Lebanese army, as well as a host of smaller Christian factions.

The third civil war was a silent civil war, the one that always intrigued me the most. It began in the early 1980s and engendered as many passions as the first two, for it pitted all the Christian and Muslim militiamen who benefited from Lebanon's chaos on one side and all the Lebanese civilians who suffered from that chaos on the other.

During the first decade of Lebanon's civil war, the various Christian and Muslim militias became not only private armies

representing the interests of different religious communities but
also vehicles for the social and economic advancement of members of the Lebanese underclasses. The longer the civil war continued, the more the members of this underclass were able to
take over Lebanese society from the traditional aristocracy, cap-
italists, and industrialists. Small-time crooks like Muslim militia
leader Ibrahim Koleilat, frustrated middle-class lawyers like Shiite
militia leader Nabih Berri, government schoolteachers like Shiite
extremist Hussein Musawi, and medical students like Phalangist
boss Samir Geagea (who became known as "Dr. Samir" only
after his appointment as a Phalangist militia chief retroactively
made him a medical school graduate) became big men around
town overnight. The civil war provided them with a route to the
top that would otherwise not have been available to them. Suddenly one didn't need a degree in business administration, economics, or even good family connections to "make it." One didn't
need to speak French or have graduated from the American University of Beirut. One didn't need to be efficient or inefficient,
an importer or an exporter. All that mattered was that one was
connected to a militia.

This class of nouveau thieves, militia merchants, and gangsters
hiding machine guns under political manifestos formed what my
Lebanese banker friend Elias Saba liked to describe as "the war
society," and although they were constantly fighting each other,
the Christian and Muslim members of this war society understood
intuitively that for all their political differences they shared a
common interest in making sure the Lebanese government, army,
and police never came back to life. Members of the war society
even had their own "official" car—the Mercedes sedan, usually
silver in color and always bristling with so many radio-phone
antennae that it looked as though it needed a haircut.

The militia merchants—through their illegal private ports and
highway checkpoints—made money by using their military power
to control the sources of distribution for any number of goods
and services, from hashish to state-subsidized gasoline. Saba explained how the system worked on a micro-scale: "My bank has
a small branch in my home village of Kura, in north Lebanon.
The local branch of the National Syrian Socialist Party is the
dominant militia in the area. They came to me one day and
demanded the right to approve whom I would appoint as the bank

manager. Then they asked how many employees I would have. I said fifteen. They said, 'Fine, we will appoint five of them.' Then they added that they would also expect a monthly 'insurance' payment to make sure that nothing unpleasant happened to the bank. It is the same story with gasoline. Gasoline is sold by the state at what is supposed to be a controlled price. It comes from terminals in East Beirut. As soon as the trucks come into West Beirut, they are met by militiamen. The militiamen will buy the whole truck, for, say, one million pounds. The driver sells it to them and gives the government its share. Then the militiamen take the gasoline around town and sell it for triple the government price."

I knew of a contractor in East Beirut who wanted to build a multistory luxury apartment house near the sea, but the Lebanese government would give him approval for only four stories. He paid one million pounds to the Phalangist militia and they got him permission to build a fifth story. A short while later President Amin Gemayel's father, Pierre, died, and Amin decided he wanted to build a statue to him in his home village of Bikfaya. The contractor paid a man from Bikfaya one million more pounds toward the statue of Amin's father and then got permission to build a sixth story. Given the number of militia merchants in East Beirut, he probably could have gotten permission to build a sky-scraper if he had had the money.

Show me someone involved in the distribution of goods and services in Lebanon today and I will show you a militiaman, the brother of a militiaman, the cousin of a militiaman, or the friend of a militiaman.

Parallel to the development of a war society in Lebanon, though, came the development of a peace society, which united both Christian and Muslim noncombatants. What happened was that the takeover by the militias of the Lebanese Cabinet and economy brought Lebanon, for the first time, to the brink of collapse. The Lebanese pound went from about 5 to the dollar when I left Beirut to 500 to the dollar just three years later. The economy became a sniper no one could escape, whether he was a Christian or a Muslim, a resident of East Beirut or of West Beirut.

The yearning for the return of a government that could prevent total economic ruin cut right across Christian and Muslim lines. So, too, did the visceral hatred for the war society. This mood was best captured in the spring of 1984, when the *Beirut Daily Star* sent a photographer and reporter into the streets of the city to ask random pedestrians, "What would you do if you were running the country?" Four of the eight people quoted said that they would murder all the country's politicians. Amal Tawil, a student, age thirty, put it most explicitly, saying, "If I were President I would execute all political leaders without exception and throw their bodies into the sea."

It was such attitudes that formed the glue that held Lebanon's peace society intact, and emboldened them to dare to challenge the war society in an open confrontation. It was an uneven battle from the start, however, because the peace society was armed only with outrage and moral suasion in a country where even a peace movement needs a militia to protect it.

I happened to be on hand when the peace society declared war in the balmy spring of 1984. As the ritualistic fighting along the Green Line continued for no apparent reason, the civilians, those anonymous people who had nothing to do with politics or militias, the real people behind Beirut's sterile casualty figures, finally screamed, "Enough." The ducks in the shooting gallery said they simply would not take it any longer. If the Marines could not save them, and their own politicians could not save them, then they would try to save themselves. They called their revolt a "peace movement." It was really a right-to-life movement for Lebanese adults, the first of many.

It all started in the living room of a twenty-nine-year-old kindergarten teacher in West Beirut named Iman Khalife, on the afternoon of April 10, 1984—three days before the ninth anniversary of the original civil war. "I was sitting at home evaluating some Arabic children's books for the library," Khalife told me during an interview in her office. "There was terrible shelling outside. I had this yellow pad in my hand, and I said, 'I want to write something for all the silent people sitting in their homes.' "

Khalife then wrote a kind of stream-of-consciousness poem suggesting a peace march. She read it to a journalist friend, who told her that if she would get fifty signatures on it, he would distribute it to all the local newspapers. Within a few days most

Beirut papers ran the Arabic poem on their front pages. It began like this:

Nine years have elapsed of this war,
and we have been watching all the solutions disappear,
resigned in our shelters . . . eating . . . drinking . . . sleeping.
Has not the time come to ask ourselves, Where to?
Until when?
Are we going to allow the tenth year to do us in?
Are we afraid? What is left to be afraid of?
Let us all go out and give our voices to the other silent voices
so they become a resounding scream.
Let us walk out of our silence and scream in one voice,
No to the war. No to the tenth year.

Drawing on a network of friends in East and West Beirut, Khalife, who always refused to tell me her own religion, set May 6, 1984, for her peace march. Organizing committees were formed on both sides of town to spread the word. They even had posters and little stickers made that said YES TO LIFE, NO TO WAR. Iman's plan was for people in East Beirut and West Beirut to meet on the Green Line at the Beirut National Museum crossing point, the only road open at the time, and then to engage in some sort of spontaneous embrace.

"Maybe if we get really excited," she said with a mischievous gleam in her eyes, "we will tear down all the barricades. People told me, 'We will die if we march.' I said, 'Okay, let's die. Every day when we go to work or out to buy things we are risking our lives. So why not risk them while at least saying something?' " When I asked her if she had sought permission to march from the police or the militias, she snapped, "Do you think people need a permit to revolt?"

No, but they do need guns. Even before May 6 rolled around, rival militiamen from all over West Beirut joined hands in ripping down the YES TO LIFE, NO TO WAR posters, which they knew were directed at them. Then, on the night of May 5, the militiamen in East and West Beirut, as if by agreement, began pounding each other with mortars and artillery across the Green Line, in one of the worst bouts of shelling since the civil war began.

Twenty-two people living near the Green Line were killed and another 132 wounded in only a few hours—all to snuff out a peace march. Khalife and her friends decided that they had to call off the demonstration lest the militiamen slaughter even more civilians. The shelling stopped minutes after the cancellation of the march was announced on the radio. When Nawaf Salam, an American University lecturer and one of the organizers, called to tell me the news, he added wryly, "One of our main aims was achieved. As soon as we called off the march, all of the militias stopped fighting and Beirut enjoyed one of its quietest nights in months."

Khalife was so bitter she would not even talk to me. "People know how I feel," she said, and hung up the phone. The next morning Salam and six other organizers decided they had to do something, so they drove down to the Green Line near the museum crossing. I tagged along for the ride. First, they removed the 6-foot-high white marble plaque—engraved in Arabic with the words YES TO LIFE, NO TO WAR—which they had planted on a mound of dirt and had planned to unveil that morning. The scene was like a funeral. While one of the women in the group wept into a tissue, Salam and Dr. Najib Abu Haidar lifted the marble slab and put it very gently in the trunk of a car, as though it were a victim who had just been gunned down in the cross fire. Before leaving, they observed a few moments of silence, for their plaque and for themselves and for Beirut, and then read a statement into the wind. It said: "The Sixth of May committee has decided to remove the marble plaque today as a protest against the circumstances that led to the cancellation of this march."

Just as they finished reading, two sloppily dressed Lebanese army soldiers, who apparently had not heard that the march was called off, came trudging up the empty, shell-scarred street, carrying above their heads a placard with a pink carnation taped to the front. Written in English with a black pen, the sign said: PIECE NOW.

Shortly before I left Beirut in June 1984, I decided that I wanted to see what remained of the Beirut National Museum, which was located right on the Green Line. The aged director, Emir Maurice Chehab, was only too happy to give me a tour I shall never forget.

Soon after the Lebanese civil war began, and the museum was engulfed in cross fire, the most precious pieces were spirited away and hidden, but the big statues, bas-reliefs, and stelae in the main halls were impossible to move. So Chehab had wooden frames built around each piece and then filled those frames with poured concrete, leaving each priceless object encased in a foot of protective cement that would repel any bullet or shell. When the war ended they could be chiseled out. This made for a rather unusual display, because when you entered the Gallery of Ramses on the ground floor, what you saw were huge square pillars of cement reaching up from the floor to various heights. But Chehab, who had been the director of the museum for ages and knew every piece by heart, gave me a tour anyway. He would point to a 15-foot-high, 5-foot-wide block of cement and say, "Now, here we have a spectacular Egyptian statue found at Byblos." Then he would walk a few paces and point to another identical block of cement and say in a voice brimming with enthusiasm, "And here is one of the best preserved stelae of early Phoenician writing." For emphasis he would pat the pillar of cement. After about an hour of this I started to believe I could actually see the objects he was describing.

Whenever I think of Lebanon today, I am reminded of that tour. I still feel that there is a core of the original Levantine spirit left in the place, if only it could be chiseled out from under the layers of scar tissue built up over so many years of civil war.

In September 1988, Amin Gemayel's term as President expired, but the Muslim and Christian parliamentarians were unable to agree on a successor. A Maronite Lebanese army general, Michel Aoun, was appointed by Gemayel as a caretaker chief of state until elections could be held. The Muslims, however, refused to recognize Aoun's authority and have appointed the Prime Minister, Selim al-Hoss, as their acting chief executive. As of this writing, there is a Lebanese government in West Beirut and a Lebanese government in East Beirut. Despite this split, those radical Christian or Muslim groups which are calling for formal partition have found little support. Each side has insisted on keeping up the façade of Lebanese statehood and legality and maintaining the option of reunification. Even today, the ideal political future for most Lebanese still seems to be a new, reformed version of the old unified Lebanon.

Even the vast majority of Shiites in Lebanon just want to be Maronites—not religiously, but socially, politically, education- ally, and materially. Now that they have inherited Lebanon's ruins, most Shiites seem to long for some of its old content. Now that they have earned an equitable slice of the pie, they want there to be a pan again.

Nadine Camel-Toueg, the young Christian journalist from West Beirut, told me in 1987 that for years her apartment building had had a Christian doorman named George, but during the Shouf fighting George had fled to East Beirut and was replaced by Hassan, a devout Shiite from a village in south Lebanon. One morning while Nadine was sitting in her living room, Hassan the Shiite concierge came up and knocked on her door.

"He was standing there holding a piece of paper," recalled Nadine. "He said to me, 'Could you please fill out this application for me.' I said, 'Yeah, sure.' So I read it and it was an application for a very posh school—the Collège Protestant. He tells me his daughter is living in the Ivory Coast and there are no good French schools there, so with the money she is making she wants to put her kids in a good French school in Beirut. Then he tells me, 'You know, if we were living in south Lebanon there is great French school there—even better than all these in Beirut—they don't even allow the kids to speak Arabic during recreation.' The guy is a Shiite, he has 'There is no God but Allah' written in Arabic all over his door, but he wants to send his kids to a French school where they don't allow them to speak Arabic. That tells you something."

What has been happening in Lebanon since 1975 is not just a tribal civil war, argued Lebanese historian Kemal Salibi. "You can also call it a competition to acquire civilization. What the Shiites were saying to the Christians and the other Muslims is 'We want to be like you. We may be doing it in a clumsy way, because we don't know how to express ourselves, but we want to be part of the game.' My family are Christians. In 1866 they were goatherders in the mountains. They had feuds and were constantly killing each other and fighting other tribes. Then they came to Beirut and after three generations they stopped being like this. We thought the same of the Sunnis—that they were boors, but now they are bourgeois . . . so who can say what the future will bring?"

Shortly before finishing this book, I had a reunion in London with my closest Lebanese friend, a quintessential Lebanese optimist, Nawaf Salam. Salam, a Sunni Muslim academic and a member of the elite Salam clan which once ruled West Beirut before the rise of the Shiites, explained to me the facts of life back in West Beirut, which he staunchly refused to leave, let alone give up on.

"All the myths are gone now," said Salam, "but maybe that is the beginning of wisdom. That is what keeps people like me going. We now know that the democracy we had was not a democracy at all but a sectarian balance of power. Liberty was not real liberty, but a kind of organized anarchy, and the diversity of press was largely a cacophony of voices subsidized by the Arab world. But even with everything having fallen apart a certain open society still exists. A united Lebanon is still the first choice of the Maronites, not a separate state, and a united Lebanon is still the first choice of the Shiites, not an Islamic republic. With no water, no electricity, and no police, we still enjoy a certain quality of life that you cannot find in any other country in the Arab world. There are still more books published today in Beirut than anywhere else in the Arab world. There is still more of a free press today in Beirut than anywhere else in the Arab world. Even today I will take the American University of Beirut over Amman University. I will take *An-Nahar* newspaper over [the Syrian daily] *Al-Baath*. Even with everything destroyed, the idea of Beirut is still there. The challenge now is to rebuild it on real foundations, not phony ones."

It is said that some men are born to times they cannot change. As I listened to Salam across the dinner table, I wondered if that would be his fate: a good man born in a bad neighborhood, an optimistic soul born to a bad time he simply could not change. But the more I listened to his enthusiasm and optimism, the more I thought I had better hold off on writing Lebanon's obituary.

Just after I saw Salam in London, I came across an Associated Press article in the *Jerusalem Post* about life in Beirut in the late 1980s. The article explained that since the Syrian army had returned to West Beirut in 1987 to help provide some law and order for the Muslim half of town, the Shiite fundamentalist gunmen were being driven underground and a small measure of the good life was being restored. New bars and restaurants were opening on the ruins of the old.

"To be sure," the article said, "car bombs still explode in busy thoroughfares . . . killing or wounding passersby in Lebanon's eternal cycle of violence. Few days pass without shell blasts and gunfire jolting both sides of Beirut, as rival militias shoot it out. . . . Telephones work haphazardly and letters from abroad can take months to be delivered. . . . Yet newspapers are filled with advertisements for stylish clothes, Parisian perfumes, and night-club floor shows. Billboards for sexy lingerie line the Hamra and Mazraa thoroughfares."

As I read that article, it suddenly hit me that hope in Lebanon is not a flower, it's a weed. Give it just the slightest ray of sunshine, and the tiniest drop of water, and it will shoot right up and multiply between the cracks in Beirut's rubble. The Lebanon of old is gone now; it cannot be rebuilt as it was, any more than an egg can be sewn back together. But can there be nothing like it again? Here, I am more hopeful. Some essence of the old Lebanon still remains beneath the rubble and ruins. Who knows? One day it may yet reappear in a new form. That is why I insist that I saw the end of something, but maybe not everything—not as long as people like Nawaf Salam are around, not as long as a peace society continues to exist beneath the war society to push up the weeds.

10

Time to Go

On a rainy night in April 1984 I decided that it was time for me to leave Beirut. Ann had been evacuated by Marine helicopter, along with several hundred other Americans, during the Shiite uprising in February, so I was staying in our cavernous apartment by myself. The Druse had set up an old 50-caliber-machine-gun nest adjacent to our building in order to scare off any Phalangist or Israeli ships that cruised too close to shore. There is nothing that gets the adrenaline flowing faster than being woken in the dead of night by a burst of 50-caliber-machine-gun fire, which always sounded to me like a whole army of crazed militiamen storming my apartment. I had perfected a move whereby the second I heard the gun go off I could roll out of bed and right under it with two turns of my body.

In any event, on that April evening a terrible thunderstorm was beating down on Beirut. I somehow managed to get to sleep between thunderclaps but was jarred awake at about 2:00 a.m. when several explosions shook the apartment and rattled the win-

dows. Half asleep, I couldn't tell whether it was thunder or shelling. I listened carefully for a moment and then detected the
whistle of incoming mortars. Our whole West Beirut neighborhood was being shelled from East Beirut.

My first instinct was to jump out of bed and run into the bathroom in the middle of the apartment, because it was the only
room that did not have any windows. There I sat on the toilet,
my head in my hands, waiting for the shelling to stop, while
listening through the pipes as the women in the apartment below
me, who were also hiding in their bathroom, wailed, "God save
me, I just can't take it anymore." As the shelling intensified, my
news instincts came alive and I crawled on my hands and knees
from the bathroom into my office and dialed the telephone number of the *Times* foreign desk in New York. Before anyone answered, though, I put the phone down.

You idiot, I thought to myself, this kind of shelling has been
going on every night since the civil war started. Nine years! To-
night it just happens to be your house, but it's not news. If it
were anywhere else in town, you would have put the pillow over
your own head and gone back to sleep.

So I crawled back into the bathroom, sat back down on the
toilet, and waited for the cease-fire. All I could think was: This
is really crazy. I am the *New York Times* correspondent in Beirut.
I am being shelled, and it's not news. It's time to leave.

It would be a few more months before I would actually depart,
but as the day approached, I began having second thoughts. I
was drawn to the Beirut story like a moth to a candle. Some of
my colleagues had come to Beirut and could not leave because
they had become hooked on their own adrenaline and on the daily
bang-bang that gets you on the front page or the evening news.
I was not immune to that myself, but there was always something
more for me. When I think back on Beirut now, I barely remember the close calls or the adrenaline highs. Instead, I always come
back to certain moments—all those remarkable human encounters I got to witness that taught me more about people and what
they are made of than the previous twenty-five years of my life.
I got to see with my own eyes the boundaries of men's compassion
alongside their unfathomable brutality, their ingenuity alongside
astounding folly, their insanity alongside their infinite ability to
endure.

Of course, for the Lebanese who starred in the moments of my memory, there was no thrill, only the numbing routine of survival, punctuated by an occasional moment of levity. I never forgot that my moments were usually their nightmares. Gerald Butt, the BBC correspondent in Beirut, told me a story that happened toward the end of the summer of '82 that really brought this home to me. A group of Lebanese doctors and nurses had decided to organize a protest march across the Green Line from West Beirut to East Beirut, in order to draw world attention to the Israeli siege, which had caused a shortage of medical supplies in West Beirut. The march took place at the Galerie Sama'an crossing point between East and West, a barren mile-long stretch of road flanked by half-destroyed apartment buildings purged of all life except snipers.

"At the time, I really didn't think about it being dangerous," Butt later recalled. "I just thought, Well, here's a story that I should be covering, so I joined the march. There were about twenty doctors and nurses and someone at the front carried a Red Cross flag. When we got about halfway across the Green Line, I looked around and saw that there was no cover anywhere. We were in the middle of the Green Line! There was shelling nearby, snipers all around, and I was walking with these doctors. I just said to myself, 'What am I doing here?' And then I turned to look back and I saw a Lebanese man just a few meters behind us, and he was leading a white horse. A white horse! It looked like a racehorse. He must have heard that there was going to be a march across the Green Line and he wanted to use us for cover to get his horse out of West Beirut. He probably couldn't feed it because of the shortage of food and water. It was so surreal. These doctors, and the Red Cross flag and the shelling, and this man tagging along with his white racehorse."

It is for such moments that a reporter is drawn to Beirut, and stays there long after good sense tells him he should leave. The front-page stories, the six-column headlines over my byline, all were a great thrill at the time. But they don't last; only the moments do.

I learned this lesson, like every other one in Beirut, the hard way. I had had an understanding with my editors that I would stay in Beirut during the summer of '82 until the day the PLO finally was evacuated. Then I was planning to go on vacation to settle my frayed nerves. My editors understood that it was personally very important for me to be in Beirut until the climax. Having witnessed the invasion from the very beginning, I wanted to see how the story would end and be able to write the last chapter of the PLO in Beirut for *The New York Times*.

As I noted earlier, the first day of the PLO's departure, August 21, 1982, I had gone down to the port early to watch the French peacekeeping troops land. A few hours later, trucks of PLO fighters began to arrive. Everyone seemed to be wearing new uniforms; I don't know where they got them. There were some tearful farewells, but mostly V-for-victory signs, and so much firing of bullets into the air in celebration that the ground at my feet became carpeted in brass shell cases. We watched as truck after truck entered the harbor and the guerrillas piled onto the Cypriot ferries for their trip to Tunis. In a few hours it was all over.

I stayed behind afterward just to savor this scene, which marked the end of an era. I fell into conversation with some young Palestinians who had bade farewell to their brothers and became so absorbed in our discussion that when I finally said goodbye to them I discovered the street was empty, save for two other people, Arthur Blessit and his son Joshua. Arthur Blessit was known as the Sunset Boulevard Preacher; he had walked to West Beirut from Israel to pray for peace, dragging a 13-foot-long wooden cross with a wheel on the bottom. His young son Joshua carried a similar, smaller cross on his shoulder. Arthur, to put it bluntly, was one of the many lunatics that the Beirut war attracted. He and Joshua had also come to see the PLO off that day. As I was leaving the port, Arthur picked up his huge cross, set it gently on his shoulder, and said to his son, "Well, Joshua, I guess we saw the peace we came for. It's time to go home."

For me, too. It was about 4:00 p.m. by then, and I immediately went to the Reuters office to write the story for which I had waited three long and difficult months. I wrote and wrote with the energy of a reporter who knows that his article will form a small part of an important historical record. And then my reporter's nightmare came to life.

Just as I finished typing out my story, all the communications lines between West Beirut and the rest of the world went dead. Dead—even the Commodore's communications. The telephone. The telex, everything. Kaput. Finished. There I was, with the final chapter of the summer of '82 all typed and no way to send it to New York. The generator at the Beirut Post, Telegraph, and Telex office had burned out, and there was no one who would venture down to the Green Line on a Saturday afternoon to fix it. It was the first and only time Beirut was completely cut off from the outside world that whole summer. The blackout lasted twenty-four hours. The telex operators at Reuters punched my whole story into telex tape and I sat up all night by the Commodore telex, just in case the lines suddenly came alive and I could feed my story to the *Times*. They never did. *The New York Times* used an Associated Press story filed earlier in the day, before the communications had crashed. I was left with a souvenir, my farewell to the PLO and the Sunset Boulevard Preacher, which no one will ever read. I still have that story in a shoe box, but, more important, I have the moment, which I will always cherish more than any yellowed newspaper clipping.

Having said all this, I know there is some attraction Beirut held for me that I can't explain, not even to myself. It is a sort of irrational pull that I think many newsmen feel once or twice in their careers, and it prompts them to do something normal people would consider utterly crazy, like covering Beirut and enjoying it. Whenever I tried to explain it to friends, I was always reminded of the story Woody Allen tells at the end of the movie *Annie Hall*.

A man goes to his doctor and says, "Doctor, Doctor, I have a terrible problem. My brother thinks he's a chicken."

The doctor says, "That's crazy. Your brother's not a chicken. Just tell him that."

And the man says, "I can't, I need the eggs."

That went for a lot of us who covered Beirut. Plenty of times it just didn't make sense to be there, but we kept coming back because we needed the eggs.

JERUSALEM

34°   35°   Tyre   36°

SYRIA

33°   *GOLAN*   33°

MEDITERRANEAN

Haifa   *Lake Tiberias*

SEA

Netanya   Tulkarm

Tira   Nablus   Balata

WEST BANK

Jordan River

Tel Aviv

Beit Yam   Deir Nizam

32°   Ramallah   Ofra   *Amman*   32°

Beth El

Kalandia

al-Ram

Jerusalem   Bethlehem

Beit Sahur

Ashkelon   Gush Etzion

Kiryat Arba

Hebron   *Dead Sea*

GAZA

Khan Yunis

Rafah

ISRAEL

31°   31°

JORDAN

SINAI

EGYPT   –·–· Boundary of Former Palestine Mandate

– – – Armistice Line, 1949

30°   30°

0   20   30 km
0   10   20   30 mi

34°   Eilat   36°   *drawn by Barbara Mullin*

11

Crosswinds

And mine hand shall be upon the prophets that see vanity, and
that divine lies: they shall not be in the assembly of my people,
neither shall they be written in the writing of the house of Israel,
neither shall they enter into the land of Israel . . . Because, even
because they have seduced my people, saying, Peace; and there
was no peace; and one built up a wall, and, lo, others daubed
it with untempered mortar: Say unto them which daub it with
untempered mortar, that it shall fall: there shall be an overflowing shower; and ye, O great hailstones, shall fall; and a stormy
wind shall rend it. Lo, when the wall is fallen, shall it not be
said unto you, Where is the mortar wherewith ye should have
daubed it?

Ezekiel 13:9–12

The existence of neighbors is the only guarantee a nation has
against perpetual civil war.

—Paul Valéry

On the morning of June 1, 1984, I drove from Beirut to Jerusalem.
The taxi came early and Mohammed and I said our goodbyes in
my sandy parking lot overlooking the Mediterranean, while Eddy
the landlord watched us from his balcony. I cried more than I
had ever cried since I arrived in Beirut. I cried for all that Mohammed and I had been through together, and for all that he
would still have to endure living in the ruins of this broken city
after I was gone.

The Beirut taxi driver took me as far south as the Israeli army
lines, along the Awali River, where I had to get out with my
suitcases and golf clubs and drag them through the Israeli checkpoint and down a mile-long stretch of road to link up with another
Lebanese taxi that would take me to Rosh Hanikra, on the Israel–
Lebanon border. The Christian and Shiite militiamen who
stopped me at their checkpoints on the roads of south Lebanon
were endlessly fascinated by my golf clubs. They assumed that

any long steel shaft with a malletlike head on one end had to be a weapon.

The golf clubs also held me up at the Israel–Lebanon border station because the girl soldiers there *knew* what they were but simply refused to believe that anyone could be arriving from Hobbes's jungle carrying a set of Wilson Staffs on his shoulder. They tried to twist the head off my pitching wedge to see if I was smuggling bullets or contraband inside. Then they pulled all the golf balls out of the bottom pocket of my bag and placed them on a table. Naturally, it took only seconds for the golf balls to spill onto the floor and start bouncing around the customs hall, where the soldier girls and I scurried about trying to chase them down before they rolled back into Lebanon.

After collecting my gear, I hired a taxi for the drive to Jerusalem. As I watched the Israeli farm fields go by and my mind danced with memories of Beirut, I noticed a road sign I will never forget. It was located on the highway between Haifa and Tel Aviv, and it said in Hebrew something like BEWARE OF CROSSWINDS.

Imagine, I thought to myself as we sped past the sign, I am leaving a country where people are dying like flies and coming to a place where they warn you about the wind! Now, that's a real country.

I quickly discovered, though, that I didn't know which winds they were talking about—that this sign was not a meteorological warning but a political diagnosis. I quickly discovered that Israel and Lebanon, Jerusalem and Beirut, had much more in common than I ever could have dreamed.

The similarity between Israel and Lebanon is rooted in the fact that since the late 1960s both nations have been forced to answer anew the most fundamental question: What kind of state do we want to have—with what boundaries, what system of power sharing, and what values? For Lebanon, as I saw, it was internal demographic and social changes which forced these basic questions to be reopened; for Israel, I would find, it was the fortunes of war that did it. Either way, both the Lebanese people and the Israeli people have failed to resolve their differences on these fundamental questions, and have each become politically paralyzed as a result.

Only the style of their paralysis differs. Whereas in Lebanon the government became paralyzed because the various Lebanese political factions insisted on facing up to their differences, and literally fighting them out in the street, in Israel the government became paralyzed because the different political parties agreed not to face up to their differences, but rather to fudge them and find ways to reach pragmatic compromises that would maintain the status quo. Whereas in Lebanon the Cabinet was ineffectual because it represented no one, in Israel the Cabinet was ineffectual because it represented everyone. In Lebanon they called the paralysis "anarchy" and in Israel they called it "national unity," but the net effect was the same: political gridlock.

To fully appreciate the reasons for Israel's paralysis one must go all the way back to the birth of the nation. The Zionist Jews who founded Israel had three basic objectives in mind when they thought about the kind of state they wanted to build, Israeli political scientist Areyh Naor liked to tell me: They wanted to create a Jewish state, a democratic state, and a state that would be located in the historical homeland of the Jewish people—the land of Israel—which technically included all of Palestine from the Mediterranean Sea to the Jordan River, and even some areas beyond, in what is today Jordan. In November 1947, when the United Nations offered the Jews roughly half this area for their own state, while promising the other half to the Palestinian Arabs, the Zionist leaders were forced to answer that fundamental question: What kind of nation do we want to be? David Ben-Gurion, then the leader of the Zionist movement in Palestine, and a true statesman, did not shrink from clearly laying out the choice before the Jewish people and then building a constituency among them for the option he believed was most correct. Ben-Gurion essentially said in effect to his nation: "In this world we can only have two out of three of our objectives. We are being offered a chance for a Jewish state and a democratic state, but in only part of the land of Israel. We could hold out for all the land of Israel, but if we did that we might lose everything. If we have to compromise on our objectives, let it be on obtaining all the land of Israel. We will settle now for half a loaf, and dream about the rest later."

So between 1948 and 1967 Zionism lived, and even flourished, with two and a half of its goals satisfied. Israel was a Jewish state with a massive Jewish majority, it was a democratic state, and it was a state located in part of the land of Israel—but not all of it.

Then came June 1967. Israel, in the course of the Six-Day War, occupied the West Bank and Gaza Strip, extending, in the process, Jewish control over virtually all the historical land of Israel originally sought by Zionism. From that moment on, Israelis again faced the monumental question: What kind of nation do we want to be? Once again, it could only have two out of three of its objectives. One choice was to keep all the land of Israel, including the West Bank and Gaza Strip, and to remain a Jewish state, but this could be done only by curtailing Israeli democracy. The only way Israel could permanently control the Palestinian inhabitants of the West Bank and Gaza Strip would be by physically suppressing them and ensuring that they were never given political rights.

The second option for Israel was to annex the West Bank and Gaza and remain a democracy, but this could be done only by giving up the Jewish character of the state, because if the 1 million-plus Palestinian Arabs then residing in the occupied territories were allowed to vote, along with the 500,000 Israeli Arabs, by early in the twenty-first century they would outnumber the Jews, if the same birth and emigration trends continued.

The third option was for Israel to remain a Jewish and democratic state, but this could be done only by either getting rid of large areas of the West Bank and Gaza or by getting rid of large numbers of West Bankers and Gazans, in order to guarantee a Jewish majority well into the twenty-first century. Since the world would never tolerate a forced transfer by Israel of Palestinians from the occupied territories, this option really came down to relinquishing territory.

So, on the seventh day of the Six-Day War, amid the jubilation and flag waving, a huge question once again hung over the Israelis: Who were they? A nation of Jews living in all the land of Israel, but not democratic? A democratic nation in all the land of Israel, but not Jewish? Or a Jewish and democratic nation, but not in all the land of Israel?

Instead of definitively choosing among these three options, Israel's two major political parties—Labor and Likud—spent the years 1967 to 1987 avoiding a choice—not in theory, but in practice; not on paper, but in day-to-day reality. I arrived in Jerusalem expecting to find crosswinds, as the sign said, but instead I found no winds of change at all.

My arrival in Jerusalem coincided with the July 1984 national election campaign, a campaign that will always be associated in my mind with Israelis on surfboards. Neither the Labor Party nor the Likud Party focused its television campaign commercials on the key existential issue facing the state of Israel—what to do with the West Bank and Gaza Strip. Instead, each party aired pop commercials, with lots of beaming faces and Pepsi-generation Israelis cavorting about and testifying in singsong voices how wonderful life was in a Likud-led Israel or how much better it would be in a Labor-led Israel. What I enjoyed most about these campaign commercials was that both parties featured brief film clips of Israelis surfing on Waikiki-size waves off the Tel Aviv coastline—as though surfing were a popular sport in Israel and surfing movies were the key to reaching a crucial uncommitted constituency of beach denizens. I realized only later that the surfing shots were an unintended metaphor for the way Israel's two major parties were being swept along by events and trying to glide over the painful choices lurking just beneath the waves.

The 1984 election campaign naturally required me to interview the senior Israeli politicians. My first encounter was with Labor Party opposition leader Shimon Peres. We met in the Labor offices on the Tel Aviv seafront, and he smoked nervously from the beginning of our conversation until the end. What struck me most about Peres was that when I asked him about his position on the West Bank and Gaza he began to choose his words very carefully, as though tiptoeing through a minefield. Despite several attempts on my part to get him to be more specific, he refused to use the words "territorial compromise." That is, he refused to be quoted as saying his party would exchange land for peace, because, his aides told me later, he feared that this would frighten off potential right-wing voters. When I pressed him on what Labor would do differently from the Likud regarding the West Bank and Gaza, Peres said that Labor would "stop putting settlements in the densely populated Arab areas," which did not exactly impress me as a strong alternative to the status quo. What struck me even more, though, was that Peres referred to the West Bank by the

biblical terms preferred by the Likud—"Judea and Samaria." To
name something is to own it, and it seemed to me that using the
names applied to the West Bank by Israel's religious-nationalist
right wing was hardly the way to go about convincing a majority
of Israelis to give it up.

A few weeks later, I went to interview Likud Party Prime
Minister Yitzhak Shamir. His remarks in general were far from
memorable, but I will never forget that when I asked Shamir
whether he still stood by the 1967 UN Security Council Resolution
242, which calls on Israel to withdraw from territories occupied
in the 1967 war in exchange for implicit Arab recognition of
Israel's right to live within "secure and recognized boundaries,"
he said to me, "We don't accept that formula anymore." Israel,
he said, must keep building West Bank settlements everywhere,
"without any pause."

Hmmm, I thought to myself. I hadn't realized Israel had drifted
that far to the right. Here I had come from Beirut, where for
years reporters had played this exhausting game with Arafat,
trying to get him to say that the PLO accepted Resolution 242,
only to be told by Israel's Prime Minister that he didn't accept
this formula either, but for different reasons.

Several months after the 1984 election was over and, rather
appropriately, produced a tie between Labor and Likud, forcing
them to join together in a national unity government, I was at a
dinner party at the elegant Jerusalem home of Gita Sherover, a
prominent Israeli philanthropist. It was a Saturday night and Defense Minister Yitzhak Rabin, of the Labor Party, was at the
dinner. At one point the telephone rang and the maid came in
and announced that there was an urgent call for Mr. Rabin. He
left the room for several minutes to take the call, and then slipped
back into his seat at the dinner table. Gita could not resist asking
him what the call was about.

"It was Weizman," grumbled Rabin, referring to the former
Likud Defense Minister Ezer Weizman. "He wanted me to allow
the Qawasmeh family to bring [Fahd] Qawasmeh's body back to
Hebron to be buried. Weizman feels guilty for expelling him."

Fahd Qawasmeh was the former mayor of the West Bank town
of Hebron whom Weizman had expelled in May 1980, after the
killing of a Jewish settler in Hebron. Qawasmeh was assassinated
in Amman on December 29, 1984, by what were believed to be

Syrian agents. He was apparently targeted because of his moderate approach to Palestinian–Israeli negotiations. The day after his murder, his family asked Weizman to appeal to Rabin to at least allow him to be buried in his own hometown.

"So what did you tell him?" Gita asked Rabin.

"I told him no—I don't want any demonstrations," Rabin said, with a flick of his wrist.

This answer was followed by a few moments of uncomfortable silence around the dinner table as everyone contemplated the chill in Rabin's voice. I was not the only guest who was stunned by his absence of compassion for a dead man whose family wanted nothing more than to have him laid to rest in the soil of his forefathers, something I felt any Jew, and certainly one from the Labor Party, should have understood.

Gita, reading everyone's mind, finally pierced the quiet by saying softly into her soup, "What would have been so bad if you had let him be buried here?"

After encounters like these, I began to ask myself what the difference was between Labor and Likud, between Rabin and Shamir, between Shamir and Peres, or between Peres and Rabin? They all called the West Bank "Judea and Samaria"; they all believed that Israel's military occupation was benign, "the most enlightened in history"; and they all seemed prepared to set their ideological differences aside and maintain the status quo forever.

Why?

Maybe the most important reason Israeli leaders tended to avoid answering the question about what to do with the West Bank and Gaza was that for years they had Arab neighbors who did not pose the question in a clear-cut manner that might have forced Israelis to answer it. The Arabs never gave Israelis the feeling that they could leave these territories and still maintain their security, hence most Israelis were ready to stay at any price; the Arabs never really encouraged Israelis to come up with any alternative to the status quo. In August–September 1967, three months after the war, the Arab states convened a summit conference in Khartoum, Sudan, where they resolved not to recognize Israel, not to negotiate with Israel, and not to make peace with Israel—a policy they and the PLO would maintain for many years.

Only Egypt dared to break away from this approach in 1978 and offer Israel a proposition which it could not avoid: Are you ready to exchange all the occupied Sinai Desert in return for full peace? When the question was put that way, Israel answered yes. But, until only recently, this was the exception.

I was out shopping in downtown Jerusalem one drizzly afternoon in the winter of 1987, and as I hurried back to my office with my coat hood tied tightly over my head, I noticed a small circle of people, maybe twenty in all, gathered in Zion Square. In the middle of the crowd stood two young Israeli men, one of whom was carrying a sign that read in English: END THE OCCU-PATION. STOP ISRAELI BRUTALITY NOW. Both young men were arguing jaw to jaw with Israeli members of the crowd. The rain was soaking the whole group, but no one seemed to notice. There was real anger in the air, veins bulging out of people's necks and spit flying from points being made a little too forcefully. I could pick up only snippets of the arguments, but they were the familiar litany: "The Arabs want to kill us," "You are so naïve," "Fascist." While this little throng conducted their sidewalk debate, many other Israelis and even a few Arabs walked by without taking any notice, let alone joining in. As I broke away from the crowd, I thought to myself that there was something emblematic about the scene—something about Israelis debating with themselves in the rain which evoked in my mind larger images of the state of the Israeli–Palestinian dialogue before 1988.

But while this scene may explain to some degree why Israeli politics became paralyzed over the question of what to do with the occupied territories, it is by no means the whole story. The truth is that as much as Israelis expected and even hoped that the Arabs would come forward and negotiate land for peace in June 1967, few Israelis were really in a hurry to give the West Bank and Gaza back, and Israel did not exactly go out of its way to encourage Palestinians, or the PLO, to pop the question.

The reason is that both the Labor Party and the Herut Party, which forms the backbone of today's right-wing Likud bloc, fell in love with these territories. After all, the Old City of Jerusalem, Jericho, Hebron, Nablus, and all the other West Bank towns were the real heartland of historical Jewish consciousness and the stage where the drama of the Bible was actually played out—not the coastal plain of Tel Aviv and Haifa. They were the core of the land of Israel the Zionist founding fathers came to reclaim, and the mere mention of their names touched something deep in the Israeli soul, both among Likudniks and Laborites. Indeed, the Labor Party felt the metaphysical connection with the whole land of Israel just as much as their right-wing opponents—if not more. The very core of the Labor Zionist program was the ethos of redeeming and settling all the land—something most American Jews have never understood.

The differences between Ben-Gurion and Begin were more over tactics than ends. Hiking around Israel with the Bible as a map had been a weekly exercise of Labor youth movements since the very beginning of Zionism. When Ben-Gurion first accepted the notion of partition, as far back as 1937, he did it with the greatest of regret. In a speech on August 7, 1937, to the 20th Zionist Congress in Zurich, Ben-Gurion declared: "I say from the point of view of realizing Zionism it is better to have immediately a Jewish state, even if it would only be in a part of the western land of Israel [Palestine west of the river Jordan]. I prefer this to a continuation of the British Mandate . . . in the whole of the western land of Israel. But before clarifying my reasoning, I have to make a remark about principle. If we were offered a Jewish state in the western land of Israel in return for our relinquishing our historical right over the whole land of Israel, then I would postpone the state. No Jew has the right to relinquish the right of the Jewish people over the whole land of Israel. It is beyond the powers of any Jewish body. It is even beyond the power of the whole of the Jewish people living today to give up any part of the land of Israel."

That is why for Ben-Gurion's political heirs, the Labor Party generals who actually conducted the 1967 war—Moshe Dayan, Yitzhak Rabin, Mordechai Gur, Uzi Narkiss, David Elazar—coming back to Jerusalem and the West Bank was not like meeting a strange woman for the first time. Far from it. It was like being reunited with an old flame, and as soon as they were back in each other's arms, many deeply repressed desires came to the surface. No wonder the Israeli mood in the wake of the '67 war was best summed up by Labor Minister of Defense Moshe Dayan's famous remark about negotiating with King Hussein: If he wants to talk, "he knows my telephone number." Otherwise, Israel was happy to stay put.

It was the Labor Party Prime Ministers from 1967 to 1977—
Levi Eshkol, Golda Meir, and Yitzhak Rabin, with a boost from
their ministers Shimon Peres and Yigal Allon—who laid the foundations of Jewish settlement in the West Bank, not the Likud.
At first, the Labor leaders argued that only settlements necessary
for security reasons, such as those along the Jordan River valley
or around Jerusalem, would be allowed. But once Labor agreed
to annex the Old City of Jerusalem and the Temple Mount immediately after the war, fusing modern Israel with the very core
of its biblical past, it set a precedent for other biblically inspired
settlements throughout the West Bank. It was only a matter of
time before these settlements would mushroom everywhere.

The time arrived on April 4, 1968, when on the eve of Passover
a group of Orthodox Jewish families, led by Rabbis Moshe Lev-
inger and Eliezer Waldman, went with their children to Hebron,
where they rented the small Arab-owned Park Hotel for the holiday. They had told Israeli officials they would be in the hotel for
the week of Passover only, but had an option to stay longer. The
visitors took over the hotel, made its kitchen kosher, and then,
when the holiday was over, vowed not to let anyone evict them
from the town where the Jewish patriarchs Abraham, Isaac, and
Jacob were buried, and where Abraham, the Father of the Nation,
had purchased, for 400 shekels of silver, his first piece of land in
Palestine (Canaan). As Rabbi Waldman later remarked, "We
took out an option for a lifetime."

None other than Labor Party minister Yigal Allon, a kibbutznik, was among the first Israeli officials to visit the Jewish settlers
and lend support, telling them, "There have always been Jews in
Hebron, the cradle of the nation, until they were violently uprooted. . . . It is inconceivable that Jews be prohibited from
settling in this ancient town of the patriarchs."

Eventually the Labor-led government, torn by mixed emotions,
caved in to the settlers, allowing them to stay in a military camp
in Hebron and later to build a Jewish settlement there called
Kiryat Arba. When I asked Rabbi Waldman why he and his
colleagues found it so easy to sway the Labor-led government to
their position, he answered with two words: "Jewish roots."

Sitting in his apartment in Kiryat Arba, Waldman explained,
"We were coming back to our roots. Moshe Dayan and Yigal
Allon were competing with each other over who would be our

patron. We had had contacts with [the Labor Party Prime Minister] Eshkol for months before we came to Hebron. He never said no, don't go. He just said wait, wait. Finally one day Yigal Allon said to us, 'If you don't create the fact, nothing will come of it. Don't wait for the government okay—just go out and do it.' Allon would come to us after every Cabinet meeting and tell us what was going on. I will tell you another thing. When Allon came out with the Allon Plan [which called for returning half of the West Bank to Arab control] we were surprised and hurt. We came to him and he, Yigal Allon—Yigal Allon!—said to us, 'Jews have to be smart. No Arab will ever accept this plan.' That was all he said. That was Yigal Allon.''

To some extent Allon and his Labor Party colleagues were swept away by the sheer intensity and ideological devotion of the Jewish settlers, who probably reminded the tired Labor leaders of their own youth when they, too, danced the hora around the campfire and when they really believed in something with zeal. If there is one thing I have learned in the Middle East, it is that the so-called extremists or religious zealots, whether in Jewish or Muslim society, are not as extreme as we might think. The reason they are both tolerated and successful is that they are almost always acting on the basis of widely shared feelings or yearnings. As Israeli political scientist Ehud Sprinzak rightly put it, these so-called extremists are usually just the tip of an iceberg that is connected in a deep and fundamental way to the bases of their respective societies.

The West Bank Jewish settlers were no exception. As Israel became a more modern, materialistic, sterile, Americanized society after 1967, many Israelis identified in their hearts with those men climbing the rocky hills of the West Bank, rifles in hand and barbed wire at their feet, keeping watch for the Arabs gathering in the distance. The settlers worked out the increasingly bourgeois Israeli's repressed yearnings to once again be a pioneer. Because the Labor Party leaders got caught up in the intensity of what the settlers were doing, and because they had no real ideological vision strong enough to stand up against them, they never really stopped and examined the long-term consequences and never noticed that the passion of so many of the settlers was a subsidized passion—a passion that began by living in tents and caravan homes but would insist on swimming pools, paved roads, army protection, tax breaks, and ranch-style suburban homes before they were through.

Nevertheless, a pattern was begun in Hebron that would be repeated all over the West Bank during the next decade: Jewish settlers would go out and create facts, the government would respond halfheartedly, with some of the Labor ministers openly supporting the settlers, the government would reach some ambiguous compromise allowing them to stay, and then another group of settlers would go out and create another fact.

It wasn't only the tug of historical memories that encouraged Israel's Labor leaders not to face up squarely to the dilemmas imposed by the Israeli occupation of the West Bank and Gaza. It was also the fact that they got drunk on their own power. One of the strengths of Labor Zionism had always been its strong pragmatic outlook, its philosophy that a new reality can be built only by careful planning and then constructing things brick by brick, acre after acre. It was precisely this relentless, anthill approach to politics and military planning which enabled the Jews to build a state and smash three Arab armies simultaneously in the Six-Day War.

But, as the Israeli philosopher David Hartman has argued, while Labor won the 1967 war thanks to this outlook, it lost the interpretation of the war by forgetting it. Israel's victory was so sweeping, and so much in contrast with the mood in the country on the eve of the war, when people were actually digging graves to get ready for what many thought would be another Holocaust, that many Israelis could not believe it was done only with their own hands. The result, said Hartman, was that "Israelis began to tell stories, all of which seemed to go something like this: 'There we were in the middle of the Sinai Desert, facing 5,000 Egyptian soldiers. We were only six men and one tank. But we fired off a few rounds in the air, said a few prayers, made a lot of noise, and suddenly, as if by miracle, all the Egyptians started to run away.' No one talked about the crack troops, the years of careful preparation, the endless hours of practice bombing. The 1967 war was an Auschwitz waiting to happen. That it didn't happen, Israelis decided, was all just a miracle."

This sudden passing from vulnerability to omnipotence produced an "intoxication," according to Abba Eban, who was Israel's Foreign Minister at the time. The 1967 victory, he explained, while it was a "military salvation, with enormous political gains . . . was a total psychological failure, because the victory was interpreted providentially and messianically. Once it became a messianic thing, the government and the parliament were no longer sovereign. . . . We lost sight of the fact that the Arab regimes, while defeated, were still intact. Our victory was not total. All of our statements, though, were in the imperative: 'We shall, we will, we demand.' "

The party leaders and generals, particularly Rabin, Dayan, and Allon, these once austere pioneers, became world-renowned figures. They were toasted in the best salons in America and Europe. The kibbutz boys were suddenly riding in limousines. The world fell in love with Dayan's eye patch. Caught up in the drunkenness of the moment, Labor lost touch with reality. They offered no vision of where the nation should be going, let alone a realistic guide to getting there. When they wanted to know what to do, they took a poll, and the polls told them that many Israelis loved their new real estate. In the deepest sense, no one was governing. The spirit of grandiosity was so pervasive that Rabin, the chief of staff in the 1967 war, declared in August 1973 that Israeli Prime Minister Golda Meir "has better boundaries than King David and King Solomon."

This festival of grandiosity was punctured by reality only two months after Rabin's boast, when Egypt and Syria simultaneously attacked Israel on the Yom Kippur holiday in October 1973. Israel's defense line on the Suez Canal fell to the Egyptians in ninety minutes, as Israeli soldiers were caught totally by surprise. Practically overnight Israeli society went from a manic high to a depressive low. Four years later the Labor Party would be thrown out of power for the first time since the state was founded. It was somehow fitting that Labor, already tainted by several financial scandals, would finally fall after it was discovered that Leah Rabin, whose husband, Yitzhak, was then Prime Minister, had been maintaining an illegal bank account in Washington.

Labor was replaced by Menachem Begin's Likud Party, which in effect rode to power promising to restore the post-1967 grandeur and glory of Israel, which had been lost in the 1973 war. Begin and his Likud Party also loved the miracle stories, and it got hooked on them in a slightly different way, thanks to the Gush Emunim (Bloc of the Faithful) messianic Jewish settler movement, which really took off in the ideological doldrums that followed the '73 defeat.

Gush Emunim explained that the victory in 1967 was actually the work of the hand of God, reuniting the two halves of the land of Israel. Israel's reunification, Gush rabbis argued, was the necessary first stage for the redemption of the Jewish people and ultimately universal redemption. Hence to give up the land of Israel would be to reject the mandate of God and turn one's back on the redemptive revolution.

The Likud found two aspects of this Gush Emunim philosophy enchanting. First was its all-or-nothing outlook—the notion that if you did not have the whole thing you had nothing. For the Likud nationalists, if the Jews did not have the whole land of Israel, including the West Bank, then they simply were not fully home. And for the Gush Emunim messianists, if the Jews did not have the whole land of Israel, then there simply could be no redemption. Neither outlook allowed for a territorial compromise of even an inch. But, equally important, Gush ideology provided the Likud with an interpretation of history that enabled it to believe that it could have it all. Gush's version of the miracle story, that the 1967 victory was God's work, pushed Israeli politics further into the messianic realm, a realm in which strength did not grow out of one's perception of reality but out of one's belief. Gush rabbis said that as long as Israelis believed in the redemptive mission of the Jewish people returning to their homeland, they could hold whatever they wanted and ignore whatever anyone else wanted. Once settling the West Bank became part of a messianic process, no rational logic was needed to sustain it. So when a group of Hebrew University professors challenged Begin one day on how he would deal with the growing reality of 1.7 million Arabs in the occupied territories, he simply answered them by saying, "I don't understand you. Back in the early 1920s, when we were only 100,000 and they were a million, you did not lose hope then. So if you didn't lose hope when the odds were 1 to 10 in their favor, why give up now when we are the majority?"

In other words, why worry about consequences? If our cause could overcome objective reality once in our history, went the argument, then it can do it always, as long as we keep the faith.

The minute you lose faith in the full myth, the minute you make even the smallest compromise with reality, everything is lost. This philosophy became so entrenched in the extreme right that it began to be taken to absurd lengths to justify virtually any policy that did not seem grounded in reality. Israel can't withdraw from Lebanon, a Jewish settlement leader told me in 1984, because the minute it loses faith in the army's ability to hold on to territory, no matter what the cost and how useless, it will be on a slippery slope to giving up the West Bank. The same people argued in 1987 that Israel had to go on building the multi-billion-dollar Lavi fighter jet well after it was clear that this would bankrupt the country, because the moment Israelis stopped believing that they couldn't do the impossible, then they would lose the strength to do the possible.

Every year on the Halloween-like Purim holiday the state-run Voice of Israel Radio does a spoof on the news. On Purim 1988, Voice of Israel began the day by announcing that Israel's most popular basketball team, Maccabi Tel Aviv, had been sold to a wealthy American Jew who was going to move the players to New York and rename them the Brooklyn Sabras. The news report was so realistic, including interviews with players about how happy they were to be relocating in America, that several Israeli politicians began calling for action to keep the team in Israel. My favorite reaction was that of Yuval Neeman, of the ultra-nationalist Tehiya Party, who, not knowing the radio was pulling everyone's leg, actually declared in an interview broadcast nationwide that if "today we lose Maccabi Tel Aviv, tomorrow it will be Judea and Samaria."

As long as the Labor Party was in power, it could at least keep the settlement movement limited to the sparsely populated Jordan Valley and those isolated locations "forced" on it by the ideological settlers. But after Labor was ousted by Begin's Likud bloc, all Begin had to do was take Labor's precedent of applying the Zionist ethos to the West Bank and play it out to its logical conclusion. Today there are more than 140,000 Israeli Jews living in East Jerusalem and 130 West Bank and Gaza cities and settlements, three-quarters of which were built after 1977. Not only did Likud and its right-wing allies extend Labor's logic, they actually ran off with its pioneering symbols. In the 1984 elections, the pro-settlement Tehiya Party used as its campaign poster a picture of the late Yakov Shabtai in an Iwo Jima–like pose, hoisting an Israeli flag. The picture had been taken in 1949, when Shabtai was attending a Labor Party youth camp, and it became the symbol of the young pioneer. A talented writer, Shabtai grew up to be an ardent supporter of the Israeli peace movement, so ardent in fact that he refused to ever set foot in the West Bank. But because his picture epitomized nationalist pride and the youthful vigor of settlement, Tehiya adopted it. Shabtai's widow had to engage a lawyer and threaten a lawsuit against Tehiya to force them to quit using her husband as its symbol.

Although Begin talked a hard line, the fact is, he, like the Labor leaders, also had to relinquish part of his ideology for a more pragmatic approach. Begin's nationalist ideology called for annexing the West Bank, but after he came to power in 1977, he discovered that he could not carry out his program because of American pressures, domestic pressures, and regional constraints. More important, in order to obtain the peace treaty with Egypt, Begin had to agree to the 1978 Camp David accords, which recognized the "legitimate rights of the Palestinian people" and affirmed that the Palestinians would be allowed to establish a self-governing authority in the West Bank and Gaza Strip for a transitional period, after which the final status of these territories would be negotiated.

Since he could not annex the West Bank, but had no intention of giving it back or even allowing the Palestinians the real autonomy promised them under Camp David, Begin simply continued Labor's functional pragmatic approach of leaving the final status of the West Bank formally open, while building a whole new reality on the ground: more roads connecting the territories to Israel, more land expropriations, more Jewish settlements. Both Labor and Likud found this pragmatic policy a convenient way to avoid having to face the existential and moral questions posed by the occupation. Labor officials could point to the *de jure* legal status of the West Bank and tell themselves that all options were still open, while at the same time enjoying cheap shopping on weekends in the West Bank marketplaces, low-cost housing in the new West Bank suburbs of Tel Aviv and Jerusalem, the security provided by all this extra land, and the psychic pleasures of walking the hills where Joshua once trod. At the same time,

Likud officials could point to the *de facto* situation in the occupied territories and tell themselves that all options were being closed and that this land was effectively being annexed. But by not annexing it formally, they could have all the Jewish settlements they wanted without ever having to pay a real political price, either domestically or internationally. They could always tell the world that everything was just "temporary," until there was a final settlement; then they would add under their breath, "That would make it all permanent."

By the early 1980s, in other words, it was clear that the functional differences between most of Labor and Likud over the West Bank were quite insignificant. The only difference between them was in rhetoric. I once covered a Peace Now rally in Hebron, in which Jewish peace activists held a demonstration hand in hand with a group of dovish Palestinian intellectuals. A group of militant Jewish settlers tried to scuttle the rally by holding a sitdown strike. When I arrived on the scene, I found a dozen Peace Now buses all backed up on the highway into Hebron and a group of twenty army soldiers surrounding about twenty settlers, who were sitting in the middle of the road singing *"Am Yisrael Chai"*— "The Nation of Israel Lives," a popular nationalistic song. But what I remember most was that a girl soldier, who could not have been more than eighteen years old, was standing guard over the settlers along with her male colleagues. She had a rifle slung over her shoulder that might have been longer than she was. As the settlers clapped and sang their songs with great vigor, I watched this soldier girl, who was supposed to be helping break up the demonstration, mouth the verses of each song to herself. The way her lips moved silently up and down with the lyrics perfectly captured the difference between Labor and Likud. Likud wanted to sing at the top of its lungs that the West Bank was theirs, while Labor was ready to just quietly mouth the words.

Those in Labor and Likud who refused to accept this charade and demanded that their respective party leaders face up to the ideological positions stated in their party platforms were simply forced out. Labor did not want to face the reality that Israel's occupation of the West Bank was perverting the secular, socialist, and humanistic ethics at the core of Labor's ideology, any more than Likud wanted to admit that it would be impossible ever to annex "Judea and Samaria." So after Begin signed the peace

treaty with Egypt in 1979, the true annexationists in Likud broke
away and formed their own party—Tehiya, led by former Likudniks Geula Cohen and Yuval Neeman—while those members
of the Labor Party who were truly committed to its stated princi-
ples of secularity, liberalism, and territorial compromise were
either dropped from the parliament, like Abba Eban, or split off,
like Shulamith Aloni, Yossi Sarid, and Amnon Rubinstein, and
formed parties such as the Democratic Movement for Change
(DASH) or the Citizen's Rights Party (RATZ), which demanded
real humanistic politics and real withdrawal. As David Hartman
put it, "All of Israel's moral prophets were farmed out by the major parties to these small factions, where they became insignificant
voices in the wilderness and were easily ignored by Labor and
Likud, who each traded in their ideological myths for functional
pragmatism." (That was why Labor and Likud eventually found it
possible, even easy, to form a national unity government together:
In many respects, they have much more in common with each
other than with the small radical parties on their extremes.)

Outsiders watching a debate in the Israeli parliament, the
Knesset, would marvel over what a healthy democracy Israel
had, when they saw all these politicians arguing with each other.
But in fact all that was going on was that two minority fringes,
one on the right and the other on the left, were shouting at each
other across a massive, inert, Likud–Labor functional pragmatic
alliance in the middle. It was a chorus of monologues in which
everyone was speaking and no one was listening. In America,
advertising is the most hysterical and competitive between products that are virtually the same, such as dog food or breakfast
cereal. The same applied to Labor and Likud. They each pointed
to their written platforms and said, "Look how different we are
from them," but in daily life they were each selling the same
Puppy Chow.

The unspoken pragmatic understanding between Labor and Likud
was temporarily disrupted by the Lebanon war. Although Likud
Defense Minister Sharon presented the war as being about "peace
for Galilee," it had little to do with that part of Israel. In going
to Beirut, Sharon was actually trying to solve the existential dilemma posed to Israeli society by the 1.7 million Palestinians in

the West Bank and Gaza. He hoped that by destroying the Palestinians' representative, the PLO, he could force those in the West Bank and Gaza to abandon their demands for an independent state and accept whatever limited autonomy Israel offered them, thereby making it possible for Israel to retain the West Bank forever without feeling guilty that it was depriving Palestinians of their right to self-determination.

"Look," Sharon hoped to tell the world, "our Palestinians are ruling themselves. We can be Jewish, democratic, and still keep all the land of Israel, including the West Bank and Gaza. Who said you could have only two out of three?"

The Lebanon invasion, therefore, reopened the fundamental divisions in Israel over the questions: What kind of society is Israel to become? What kind of values does it stand for? Is it going to be a Jewish South Africa, permanently ruling Palestinians in West Bank homelands, is it going to be a Jewish Prussia, trying to bully all of its neighbors, or is it going to be a state with borders that will be based solely on considerations of what will preserve a secure, democratic, and Jewish society at peace with its neighbors?

In suddenly putting all these questions on the table again, the Lebanon war also revealed yet another reason why Labor and Likud could not answer them in a decisive way. It was that they each understood that if forced to confront the real and passionate ideological differences in their country on these questions, they could end up like the Lebanese: arguing first in the parliament and then in the streets. To put it bluntly, asking an Israeli leader to really face the question "What is Israel?" is like inviting him to a civil war.

That point was made clear to every Israeli on February 10, 1983, when Emil Grunzweig, a thirty-three-year-old Peace Now activist, was killed by a grenade thrown at him by a fanatical Begin supporter during a demonstration in Jerusalem against the Lebanon war. The *Jerusalem Post* reported that when the Peace Now demonstrators wounded by the grenade blast were taken to Shaarei Zedek hospital, some Likud supporters shouted insults at them as they were brought into the emergency ward.

"It is a pity they didn't blow them all up," the *Post* quoted one man as yelling.

Several years later, Avraham Burg, a young religious Labor Party member, who was slightly injured in the attack, told me he thought Grunzweig's murder was a major turning point for Israeli politics. It brought both sides back from the brink and encouraged Labor and Likud to shrink from addressing the existential question right when it began to seem inescapable.

"People saw what happened to Grunzweig and said, 'Oh-oh, this is too much,' " said Burg. "They got a glimpse into the real depth of the divisions between us and they decided to back away. It was too frightening."

Indeed, after Lebanon and after Grunzweig, Israelis wanted unity, not truth; they wanted quiet, not a painful debate about existential dilemmas. Israeli politicians were only too happy to oblige, which was why when I arrived during the July 1984 election campaign both Labor and Likud were focusing their campaign commercials on surfers, and promising, if elected, to form a national unity government. Maybe it is no accident that an increasingly popular new definition of a consensus comes from an Israeli statesman, Abba Eban. A consensus, said Eban, means that "everyone agrees to say collectively what no one believes individually."

Without Israelis realizing it, their country became almost as leaderless as Lebanon. Under the national unity government formed in September 1984, both major parties agreed to go back to postponing all the tough questions, and to deal only with consensus issues such as healing the economy. It was like postponing all real politics, because what is politics if not the making of hard choices, and what is leadership if not the framing of concrete choices for the public and then urging one over another? Peres, Rabin, and Shamir were too frightened to try to lead Israelis away from the status quo, too frightened to present them with a mirror of reality in the West Bank and then frame immediate choices out of it.

Instead, Israeli leaders fell into two categories: moderates with no guts and heroes with lost causes. Shamir declared that Israel must remain in Judea and Samaria for "eternity" and promised that "something would happen" in the future to free the Jewish state from the fact that the Palestinians could outnumber the Jews by the early twenty-first century: Russia would set free its Jews;

there would be a pogrom in America; something would happen. Peres, by contrast, declared that Israel must and could do something about the West Bank and Gaza, but he promised that the way out could be painless. Israel would not have to deal with the PLO or any Palestinian demands for independence. Rather, it would convince Jordan to take back part of the West Bank in return for full peace, but only after a long, long transition period. Peres and Shamir, in other words, not only failed to lead, they actually made the Israeli public dumb: they got them to believe in the unbelievable, to hope for the hopeless, to feel weak where they were strong and strong where they were weak, and to feel that the winds of time were at their backs when in fact they were blowing in their faces.

David Ben-Gurion had always understood that his first constituency was the facts and that his second constituency was his people, whose subjective will had to be shaped to the facts. Shamir and Peres saw things in just the opposite way. They thought their first constituency was the subjective will of the people, which they measured religiously with polls, and that reality should be adjusted to the mood of the week. These were not incompetents, Peres, Rabin, and Shamir. They were all technocrats of substance, with real accomplishments. They helped to build a nation from scratch. Most of them were recruited as deputies and army officers by Israel's visionary founding fathers precisely for their administrative skills and their bland, unchallenging political personalities. They always saw their tasks as that of implementing the visions of others, not positing visions themselves. All three would have made good governors for Rhode Island or Delaware, but Rhode Island and Delaware are not faced with monumental existential questions and terrible moral dilemmas.

By the late 1980s there seemed to be a symbiotic paralysis between Israel's leaders and the nation they led. The major political and security issues facing the country appeared to both of them to be too awesome, too frightening, and too intractable. Leaders and led both seemed to feel that no one could really make a difference, so the Israeli politicians just went through the motions of leadership, always reacting to events, never taking the initiative, while the Israeli public went into emotional hibernation.

"Do me a favor, let's not talk about 'the Situation,' " became a

common refrain among Israelis. When the state-owned Israel Radio and Television networks went on strike for almost two months
in the fall of 1987, most Israelis loved it. For once they didn't have
to listen to politicians screaming at each other and saying nothing.
The public knew they were not missing anything because they
knew that the politicians had long ago stopped being able to produce anything that could possibly be defined as real news. Israeli
politics had become like a daytime soap opera—the Jewish equivalent of *As the World Turns*. You could go away for two months
and tune back in and find that you hadn't missed a thing.

Confronted by daily newspaper headlines shouting, NO EXIT
from the Arab–Israeli conflict, Israeli artists, too, increasingly
dropped political themes and sought refuge in the abstract, anti-
intellectual, postmodernist trend, in which the object was to say
nothing, or at least nothing clear. This, after a decade characterized by sharp-tongued antiwar and protest art, some of the
best of which was produced by Moshe Gershuni, a balding middle-
aged painter who at the height of the Lebanon war was doing
canvases dominated by blood-red smears and the theme of the
sacrifice of Isaac, with Israeli eighteen-year-olds starring as Isaac.

Gershuni told me that several months after the Lebanon war
began, at the peak of the daily death toll announcements, he
decided on the spur of the moment to abandon the sacrifice of
Isaac theme and started to paint only flowers, mostly cyclamens
and anemones. When I asked him why, Gershuni said he asked
himself the same question. "I asked myself, 'What are you doing?
Are you crazy?' [But then] I realized that if I didn't stop being
involved, I would ruin myself. It was time to take care of myself
and stop carrying all the burdens of Jewish history. So I stopped
reading newspapers and I stopped listening to the radio, and I
am not a political animal anymore."

So it was with many Israelis. Shortly after speaking with Gershuni—in mid-1987—I went to see Israeli filmmaker Amnon Rubinstein and he told me an identical trend was apparent in Israeli
cinema. "People don't want to know and don't want to hear,"
said Rubinstein. "We feel we are stuck in an impossible situation,
and nobody has any solutions. It is like we are in a dark tunnel,
and when we look around the only light we see is the train that
is coming at us."

*   *   *

Veteran Israeli religious politician Yosef Burg used to tell a joke about two Israelis discussing philosophy. One says to the other, "Are you an optimist or a pessimist?" and the other answers, "I'm an optimist, of course. I am certain that today will be better than tomorrow."

Every Israeli I knew used to laugh at that joke, because they knew they were laughing at themselves. The Israeli political system is not only paralyzed today by a lack of leadership and clarity from the top, and not only by the fact that Israel's enemies, the Palestinians, were for so long unable to pose existential questions from their side; it is also paralyzed by a deep fatalism seeping up from the basement of Jewish history below.

The Zionist revolution was meant to liberate Jews from the age-old ghetto mentality of the weak, helpless victim. It set out to prove that Jews were not doomed to be objects, but that they could be subjects—that this people whose reality and destiny were always defined for them by external forces could become a community of choice, with the power to construct their own political history. It sought to accomplish this by creating a Jewish citizen, a Jewish government, a Jewish army, a Jewish Cabinet, a Jewish President, and by reviving the Hebrew language. The tragedy and the irony of the Zionist revolution is that although it created all these instruments and institutions from the ashes of the Holocaust, it failed to eradicate the collective self-image of the Jew as victim. Although they can now speak their own language and walk with their heads held high, many Israelis today still feel as though they are victims of circumstance and living on borrowed time as much as any Jewish ghetto dwellers in history. They have not really broken out of the prison of their past.

That is why despite the fact that Israel has one of the most powerful and advanced armies and air forces in the world, the country's leadership finds it almost impossible to imagine bold ways in which they could unilaterally use their overwhelming power to shape positive new options for themselves, particularly regarding the West Bank and Gaza. They still see themselves as a people who react to history, rather than shape it. Israeli leaders are always waiting for the phone call from the Arabs; few of them know how to dial themselves. Even the Camp David accords had to be initiated by Sadat; Begin never would have done it. If I were to draw a caricature of Israel today, it would be of a lifeguard at the beach. The lifeguard would be bulging with muscles from his head to his toes, but whenever someone pushed him into the pool, all he would do would be to tread water.

"It is all very strange," Abba Eban once remarked. "When we were really weak and vulnerable and objectively exposed to the prospects of destruction, we were more relaxed and buoyant and self-confident. Now, when talk of destroying Israel by the PLO is really ludicrous, there is a sense of vulnerability and tension. The reality of our power doesn't seem to enter into people's minds at all. The vision of Israel—embattled and in danger—and the use of such words as 'liquidation,' 'extermination,' and 'destruction'—these have all become part of the national vocabulary, and from our national vocabulary they have taken root among our friends in America as well. You'd think that we were a kind of disarmed Costa Rica and that the PLO was Napoleon Bonaparte, Alexander the Great, and Attila the Hun all wrapped into one. Israeli rhetoric is no longer based on contemporary realities but on Jewish memories, and that is a failure of leadership."

One of the most important works of Israeli Middle Eastern studies in the 1970s was a book by former chief of military intelligence Yehoshafat Harkabi entitled *Arab Strategies & Israel's Response*. I always loved that title. The Arabs have strategies; the Israelis only have responses. It is like all those Middle East maps that the Israeli Foreign Ministry propaganda department used to put out, showing a tiny Israel surrounded by Arab countries, and in each of these Arab countries there were little cannons and tanks all pointed toward Israel. The maps never showed any Israeli cannons pointing toward the Arabs.

Wherever you go in Israel today you can feel the past lapping up against society, whispering like a late-afternoon tide that the destiny of Israelis, like all Jews, is to be the victim. Remembrance Day, Yom Hazikaron, which commemorates those who fell in Israel's wars and comes every year one day before Israeli Independence Day, was when I would feel it most. On that day at 12:00 noon a siren is sounded across the land—from Metulla in the north to Eilat in the south—and every Israeli Jew stops in his tracks. The first year I was in Israel I was driving down a highway with photographer Micha Bar-Am when the siren blasted. Suddenly, without explaining anything to me, Micha veered over to the shoulder, screeched to a halt, threw open his door, and stood at attention by the side of our car. Every other driver on the highway did the same. It was a remarkable and eerie sight, as though everyone's mind had suddenly been taken over by some signal from outer space, and I, still sitting in my seat, was the only one not affected. The following year I saw the same scene repeated in the heart of Jerusalem: cars halted at all angles in the middle of intersections, people frozen on the sidewalks, at lunch counters, in classrooms, at gravesides, all locked at attention in order to remember. They remembered the dead from '48, '56, '67, '73, '82 and every battle in between. The siren wailed and they just stood there, while the past, silent and invisible, wrapped them in its web.

"So many Israelis walking the streets today feel that it was just by accident that they were not in Auschwitz, or Bergen-Belsen, or on the Suez Canal the day the Egyptians burst through in 1973," explained David Hartman. "When they look at scenes of the Holocaust, they say to themselves, 'There but for the grace of God go I.' They go to the funerals for their buddies from all the wars and they ask themselves, 'Why am I not dead?' So there is a sense that pervades this place that your presence here is not something that is organic and nurtured by the environment. You are not rooted. You are here against everyone's will. You can never really relax. The leaders here don't wake up in the morning, stretch their imagination, and say to themselves, 'I have all this strength at my disposal, what multiple options should I explore today?' They just want to get through the day, get through the week, get through the month. That is about as far as their minds can stretch. Imagine celebrating Independence Day the day after Remembrance Day. One day you are watching crying widows and orphans from all the wars, and then the next day, the very next day, you are told to go out and celebrate. Hey, happy Independence Day! Nobody knows what to do. So they go out and bop each other over the head with silly plastic hammers. How can you feel normal and gay after all this? It is a celebration out of nowhere. Every year you are celebrating at the edge of a volcano. Every day you are dancing on tombstones."

Sometimes literally. I was at a party once at the Bonanza Bar in Tel Aviv when Israeli rock star Yehuda Eder introduced me to another Israeli rock star, Danny Sanderson.

"Tom, meet Danny Sanderson," Eder said with a yank of his thumb. "He and I played the '73 war together."

I couldn't help but laugh. It was so natural. It wasn't "We played the Monterey Jazz Festival together." It wasn't "We played Woodstock together." It was "We played the '73 war together." Where else in the world would one rock star introduce another in such a way? Israeli musicians are assigned to special units to provide entertainment for the troops during wartime, and for many, like Danny and Yehuda, these concerts are the stepping-stones to stardom, not to mention some of the most intense moments they remember, musically and emotionally.

Israeli novelist David Grossman once recounted for me the most memorable moment of his wedding: "My Aunt Itka came, and she is a survivor of Auschwitz with a number tattooed on her arm. When she arrived at the wedding, she was wearing a bandage over her number. I asked her why she had on a bandage. Had she hurt herself? No, she said, she put it on because she did not want to take away from the joy of the moment by having people see her number. You see, that bandage is Israel. All of Israel is living on that bandage and everyone knows that underneath it is an abyss, a holocaust, that you can fall into at any moment."

This feeling that many Israelis have of living on borrowed time accounts for some of the more unpleasant aspects of daily life in Israel—everything from the way drivers honk at each other if the car in front of them does not move within a nanosecond of the traffic light turning green, to the way so many people cut corners in their business and personal dealings. There's no sense worrying about politesse or whether or not a customer will come back tomorrow if you don't really believe in tomorrow.

I once bought a tape recorder–radio in Jerusalem that came with a one-year warranty. After about nine months the radio broke, and I brought it back to the shop for replacement. The shopowner knew me well, as we had done a lot of business together. I put the radio and the warranty on the counter and said to the owner, "I need a replacement." He checked that the radio was dead, read over the warranty, and then just shook his head. "Mr. Thomas," he said, "if the radio had broken after one month, or maybe three months, okay, we would have replaced it. But nine months? I'm sorry."

"No, no, you don't understand," I said. "This radio has a warranty of one year. One year means one year. It is not optional. It is not at your discretion."

He just shook his head again. He did not understand one year. His mind could not see that far, no matter what the Japanese manufacturer had told him. By then I had been in Israel too long to try to fight this mentality. In the end, we worked out a complicated Middle Eastern barter deal, which involved me giving him the broken radio and several hundred shekels and getting a brand-new, bigger radio in return.

It, too, came with a one-year warranty.

And so does Israel. Israel is a country with a one-year warranty—that no one is sure will be honored.

If Israel wasn't founded on the basis of such a fatalistic outlook, then how did it take over?

The motto of Theodor Herzl, the Austrian journalist considered to be the founding father of Zionism, embodied the spirit of choice and initiative he hoped to instill in the Jewish people. "If you will it," said Herzl, "then it is no dream."

The first Jewish kibbutz collective farm built by the Zionist pioneers in 1909, Degania, was a monument to that motto. In the early years of the state of Israel it was common for native-born Israelis to feel contempt for the Jews who died in the Holocaust, and even for some of those who survived, because they were viewed as sheep who simply went off to slaughter, while the Zionists were men of bold initiative, who went out and fought the British and the Arabs and built a Jewish state.

Ruth Firer, a researcher at the Hebrew University School of Education and a specialist in the teaching of the Holocaust in Israeli high schools, recalled the spirit of those early days. Firer was born in Siberia, where her Polish parents were exiled by the Russians during World War II. Thanks to this exile, her immediate family survived the Holocaust, but all her parents' relatives were wiped out. In 1949, her father brought the family to Israel.

"When I was a student here in the 1950s, the Holocaust was a family secret—a shame," Firer explained one afternoon over coffee in her Jerusalem apartment. "In those days, we barely learned about the Holocaust in school. The feeling, the whole atmosphere, was that the future must triumph over the past. All of us, parents and kids, tried to cover up what had happened. When we taught the Holocaust then, we taught the heroism of the Warsaw Ghetto—that was it."

Unfortunately, a succession of traumatic events conspired to reawaken in every Israeli's soul the spirit of the Holocaust and everything it represented in Jewish history. In the process, Israel's motto changed from Herzl's "If you will it, then it is no dream" to *"Kacha, Ma Laasot?"*—which means "That is how things are, what can we do?" In other words, the future is fixed: a permanent struggle for survival against a hostile world.

The change began, I believe, with the trial of Nazi war criminal Adolf Otto Eichmann in 1961, which brought both the Holocaust and the survivors out of the Israeli closet. Older people were forced to reexamine their feelings, and the new generation of Israelis, who intently followed the gripping testimony of the survivors, developed an interest in this previously unmentionable chapter in the family album.

"For the first time in public the stories of the survivors came out and were legitimized," said Firer. "Every day people heard in the court and read in the papers the stories of the survivors. They were no longer seen as sheep led to slaughter. It turned out that many of them resisted, many of them were heroes—heroes we Israelis could understand. Theirs was a fight to survive and we could honor it."

After the Eichmann trial, Holocaust survivors were invited to speak in high schools, and for the first time the subject of the Holocaust was included in the Israeli twelfth-grade high-school curriculum. But it wasn't until five years later, in May 1967, that every Israeli got a whiff of the Holocaust in his or her own nostrils. It is easy to forget today that in the month before the June 1967 war, when Egyptian President Gamal Abdel Nasser began beating his war drums, established a joint military command with Jordan, and threatened to wipe Israel off the face of the earth, many Israelis became convinced that their borrowed time was up. May 1967 was one of the most important months in Israel's history. It was the month when for the first time the widening awareness of the Holocaust among Israelis would begin to merge with their immediate predicament.

One can get a sense of the impending doom that was triggered in Israel in May 1967 by just glancing through the headlines in the *Jerusalem Post* from the eve of the war. For example, on May 25, 1967: SHELTERS INSPECTED. RELIGIOUS AFFAIRS MINISTER RECITES PSALMS IN THE KNESSET. 3,000 LEAVE [the country]. WAREHOUSES OPEN ALL NIGHT FOLLOWING RUSH ON SHOPS. TORAH SCROLLS TO FIELD SYNAGOGUES. RABBINATE CALLS FOR SPECIAL PRAYERS TODAY. This item went on to say: "The Chief Rabbinic Council yesterday called for special prayers to be recited in the country's synagogues at 4:30 p.m. today. The services are to begin with Psalms 20, 35, 38, to be followed by the Avinu Malkainu [a prayer extolling God's greatness and compassion], and the penitential prayers said during the Ten Days of Penitence between Rosh Hashanah and Yom Kippur." The next day's *Jerusalem Post*, on May 26, reported that a "middle-aged self-styled inventor yesterday offered the army three of his patents: a cosmic death ray, an engineless airplane, and an instant water desalinization machine. This was one of a multitude of offers flowing into the Defense Ministry."

"No one in this country will ever forget that month before the Six-Day War," remarked Firer. "All the Arab countries around us were making military pacts in order to destroy us. We were filling sandbags outside our houses and stockpiling food. From all sides people really feared that we were going to be slaughtered. That moment was the strongest empathy I felt with the Holocaust. We suddenly realized that it is not only 'If you will it, then it is no dream.' We had this feeling of being caught in circumstances beyond our control, just like the people in the Holocaust. It made people think it can happen again—even here. Maybe the Third Temple will just be a short experience and Jewish history will repeat itself."

She paused for a second and then added, "Now all of us are carrying the past on our shoulders, and it is quite a heavy burden."

Although the victory in 1967 temporarily lightened that load, the 1973 war, in which Egypt and Syria engaged in a simultaneous surprise attack on Yom Kippur, brought it back in an even heavier form. Since then it has stayed. Virtually every Israeli carries it

now. Whoever didn't have it when he came, whoever didn't inherit it when he was born, has it now. Israeli leaders such as
Golda Meir, Menachem Begin, and Yitzhak Shamir, instead of
fighting against the "Holocausting" of the Israeli psyche, actually
encouraged it, turning the Palestinians into the new Nazis and
Israel into a modern-day Warsaw Ghetto aligned against the
world. Begin, more than any other figure, reintroduced into public
rhetoric the language of the Israeli as the inheritor of the traditional Jewish role of victim, whose fate, like that of all Jews in
history, is to dwell alone.

Today—unfortunately—the teaching of the Holocaust is an essential element of Israeli high-school education and in the Israeli
army officers' course. No one goes to Kibbutz Degania anymore.
Most Israeli youngsters I met had no idea what it represented.
Degania is not viewed as the gateway to Israel. Instead, that role
has been taken over by Yad Vashem, the massive hilltop memorial
in Jerusalem honoring the 6 million Jews killed in the Holocaust.
Where is the one place the Israeli government takes all official
visitors? Yad Vashem. Today, all Israeli youngsters are not only
taken on field trips to Yad Vashem but also go by the hundreds
on field trips to Poland, where they visit firsthand the death camps
of Auschwitz, Majdanek, and Treblinka. The subliminal message
is that these camps are what the state of Israel is all about.

One day I came across a story in the *Davar* newspaper about
how a typical Israeli seventeen-year-old preparing to enter the
army was affected by a day-long Yad Vashem seminar on the
Holocaust. It read:

> Avi Levy, a twelfth-grade student in the computer elec-
> tronics program of the ORT school in Holon, did not think
> of building his future in Israel. Though he is a native of
> Israel, life here did not seem a bed of roses. Tourist adver-
> tisements about America and Europe appealed to him, and
> he decided he would leave Israel. He had the chance to leave
> before his military service. However, because "people died
> so that I could live here, I am willing to serve and contribute
> for those who will come after me," he said. The lecture by
> Avigdor Efron, head of the Holocaust Education Depart-
> ment of Yad Vashem for the Tel Aviv area, and other things
> he heard during the day-long seminar . . . convinced Avi to

change his mind. Of course, even before this, he knew what had happened in the Holocaust. He had studied about the 6 million, the extermination camps, and the gas, but he never digested these things. Photographs he saw at Yad Vashem were not absorbed by his consciousness. "I felt a bit alienated and I did not see myself as part of them," he said, "but during the lecture I felt that they were actually me. Suddenly, I saw myself at the extermination camp. I felt that this could happen to me if I left Israel." Today he says, "I am not leaving Israel. This is my home—real, exclusive and concrete." He emphasized the last word.

It was no shock to me that when I left Israel in the summer of '88 one of the leading pop albums was a recording of songs, many on Holocaust themes, by musician Yehuda Poliker and poet Ya'acov Gilad—both Israeli-born children of Holocaust survivors. The album was called *Ashes and Dust*, and one of the most popular tracks was entitled "The Little Station Treblinka." It told the story of a ride on the death train to the camp at Treblinka, where an estimated 750,000 Jews were exterminated in the gas chambers. One of the verses in particular stuck in my mind. It went:

> *Sometimes the journey takes*
> *five hours and forty-five minutes.*
> *And sometimes the journey lasts*
> *your whole life until your death.*

Israel today is becoming Yad Vashem with an air force. The past has caught up with the Zionist revolution and now may be in the process of overtaking it. The Holocaust is well on its way to becoming the defining feature of Israeli society. Even Sephardic and Oriental Jews who came to Israel from Muslim countries and who never experienced the Holocaust now treat it as part of their personal family memories. "The Holocaust is no longer a trauma that affected certain families in Israel," said Sidra Ezrahi, an Israeli expert on Holocaust literature. "It has become a collective pathology affecting the entire nation."

This explains in part why Israelis have always been ready to

tolerate almost any hardship from their government with barely
a peep of protest. Whether it is outrageously high taxes or having
to do an extra thirty days of reserve duty each year, Israelis just
seem to swallow it. Sidra's husband, Yaron, himself a native-born
Israeli, explained why: "As long as there are no gas chambers,
and no genocide of Jews taking place, I'm afraid everything else
seems tolerable to many people."

Fortunately, the "Yad Vasheming" of Israel is not quite complete. Not all Israelis have reverted to a pre-Zionist sense of their
own strength. With proper and healthy leadership, the trend may
still be reversible. I was convinced of that after a visit I made to
Hatzerim air force base. While I was there I had the opportunity
to interview the Israeli air force pilot who commanded the Israeli
F-16 bomber squadron that in 1981 destroyed the Iraqi nuclear
reactor in Baghdad; he is now in charge of the training of all
Israeli pilots at the air force flight school. Colonel Z—I promised
not to use his name—was born and raised on a kibbutz near Haifa.
He has the handsome features, intelligent eyes, and erect bearing
of a pilot who has just walked out of a recruiting poster. Like so
many senior officers in the Israeli army, he had no doubt about
Israel's real strength and power to shape its own future; he had
not yet been totally infected by the apocalyptic rhetoric of the
politicians.

I began our discussion by telling him that I had heard from a
friend that the Israeli air force had sponsored a "Holocaust quiz"
to see which pilots knew the most about the massacre of the 6
million.

"It was terrible," said Colonel Z. "I went to the head of the
air force, [Major General] Avihu Binun, and I pleaded with him,
'Don't allow this. It is terrible.' They actually asked questions
like 'How many Jews were killed in Treblinka? How many were
killed in Buchenwald?' They wanted to make sure people knew
the numbers. One question was about how many Jews were put
in a concentration camp that was set up in Libya, and one boy
answered 500,000, when the real answer was 500. But you see,
you just build it all up into something that is so big that you lose
all perspective and then you can't grasp what it means when five
or six Jews are killed. If you take a club and beat a child with it
constantly when he is three years old, when he is eighteen he is
still going to be afraid. Our basic outlook is that of a beaten child.

This is the basic orientation of Israel today. Look, I am named after my grandfather from Romania, who was killed by the Nazis. I grew up on stories of Jews being beaten, so even I have the complex to some degree. Rationally I know I should not, but I can't escape it."

If you could make a speech to the whole nation, knowing what you do about the power of the Israeli air force, what would you tell people? I asked the colonel.

"I would tell them that we have the strength to compromise, that a strong confident nation can make concessions with dignity," he answered without hesitation. "If people only knew what I know, they would be much less afraid of making concessions. If we see ourselves always as weak victims, we can't see our own strength and that we have options. Because of that, we have lost many opportunities. I am trying to teach my son that, but it is not easy."

No, I suppose it is not. A country that sees itself living on the lip of the volcano, or inside the eerie hallways of Yad Vashem, doesn't plan for the future and doesn't think about bold initiatives. It only holds on for dear life.

Shortly after Yitzhak Shamir became Prime Minister in October 1986, I went to see him with A. M. Rosenthal, then the executive editor of *The New York Times*. Shamir, whose entire family was wiped out in the Holocaust, exemplifies those Israeli leaders whose vision of tomorrow is yesterday.

As the interview drew to a close in the Prime Minister's office, Abe asked Shamir one of those cosmic questions reporters always ask heads of state. "Mr. Shamir," said Abe, waving his hand over an imaginary horizon, "two years from now, when your term of office is up, what would you like people to say about you?"

Shamir leaned forward, clasped his hands together, looked Abe in the eye, and said, "I want them to say that I kept things quiet."

12

Whose Country Is This, Anyway?

Riding a bus down King George Street in Jerusalem recently, I hadn't particularly noticed the young woman in the back of the bus who sat down next to the Haredi [ultra-Orthodox] Jew since he, in his black hat, black coat, and long beard, and she, in her sandals, skirt, and sleeveless top, were part of a typical scene that included soldiers on leave, a babushka-capped grandmother, five-year-olds with knapsacks, and an occasional American-looking rabbi late for an appointment. It was only after the young woman quietly asked the Haredi to please close the window that I lifted my eyes out of the newspaper and watched him turn to her rather matter-of-factly with the words "Would you please lengthen your sleeves?"

"Mister," the woman said, her voice rising to match her indignation, "the open window is bothering me!"

The Haredi seemed nonplused.

"Madame, the bare arms are bothering me," he responded.

Her face was now grim and determined as she slowly extracted every single syllable from her mouth and planted them into every ear on the bus: "Are they my arms or your arms?"

—*Rabbi Shlomo Riskin*
in the JERUSALEM POST,
May 20, 1988

Back in the 1930s in Tel Aviv's Mughrabi Square there used to be a big clock with no glass covering the face. Legend has it that one day Mayor Meir Dizengoff ordered that the clock be removed. When residents of the area asked him why, Mayor Dizengoff explained that it was because every Jew who walked by the clock reset it according to his own watch.

I heard that story shortly after I arrived in Jerusalem, but I understood how true it still was only after living in the country for a while. Israelis, I discovered, cannot decide what their nation should stand for not only politically, for all the reasons I outlined in the previous chapter, but also spiritually.

Indeed, the most amazing thing about the world's only Jewish state is that it managed to be built, and hold together, despite the fact that there are deep and fundamental disagreements among its citizens as to what exactly a Jew is and what kind of Jewish life a Jewish state should represent. I used to meet many Jews from America and Western Europe who told me that they had come to Israel to "find" themselves as Jews. I always told them that Israel was probably the most confusing place in the world to do so. It is the place to lose yourself as a Jew, because if you don't know who you are before you arrive, you can get totally lost in the maze of options that present themselves as soon as you plant your feet on the land.

Like most American Jews, I was raised on a Judaism without land—the same Judaism Jews have practiced since they were expelled from Palestine by the Romans two thousand years ago. This is a Judaism that revolves around the synagogue, around the holidays, and around communal get-togethers. Spiritually speaking, Jews in the Diaspora are differentiated from one another only by how they relate to ritual observance, that is, whether they practice Judaism in the Orthodox, Conservative, or Reform manner—Orthodox being the most observant and Reform the least.

Not so in Israel. Jews in Israel are not differentiated by synagogue affiliations as much as by how they relate to the land of Israel and to the state. The Jewish people's reconnection with their land and their building of a modern state there have opened up a whole new set of options for defining oneself as a Jew—some of which were totally unknown in the Diaspora.

Those myriad options can be broken down into four broad schools of thought. The first and largest is made up of secular and nonobservant Israelis, men like Shimon Peres and Yitzhak Shamir—those who really built the new state of Israel. The secular Zionists came to Israel in part as a rebellion against their grandfathers and the Orthodox synagogue–oriented ghetto Judaism practiced in Eastern Europe. For the secular Zionists, being back in the land of Israel, erecting a modern society and army, and observing Jewish holidays as national holidays all became a substitute for religious observance and faith. In Israel, they said, the sky is Jewish, basketball is Jewish, the state is Jewish, and the airport is Jewish, so who needs to go to synagogue? For them, coming to the land of Israel and becoming "normal" meant giving up religious ritual as the defining feature of their Jewish identity. Science, technology, and turning the desert green were their new Torah.

These secular Israelis, who make up roughly 50 percent of Israel's Jewish population and send their children to state-run secular schools, were convinced that they were the wave of the future and that tradition-bound Jews were a passing episode in Jewish history. They were ready to allow any Jew in the world who wanted to live in their new state to become a citizen immediately, because they were certain that within one generation of being reconnected with the land those ultra-Orthodox Jews who were living in self-imposed ghettos either in Europe or Jerusalem would throw off their black hats and coats and join the Zionist revolution. After all, why would Jews want to re-create a medieval Polish ghetto inside a modern Jewish state, these secular Zionists asked themselves. More than one secular Israeli told me that when he was a young boy his father took him to Mea Shearim, the ultra-Orthodox neighborhood of Jerusalem, and told him something like this: "Look at these people while you can. They are relics from the past, dinosaurs from the basement of history. Behold them now, because in another generation they will be gone."

The second major school consists of religious Zionists. These are traditional or modern Orthodox Jews, who fully support the secular Zionist state but insist that it is not a substitute for the synagogue. They see the state and the synagogue and a way of life according to the precepts of the Torah as all being compatible. They believe that the creation of Israel is a religious event, and that Judaism, when reinterpreted for the twentieth century, can flourish in a modern Jewish state. Religious Zionists, who make up roughly 30 percent of the Jewish population, serve in the army, celebrate Israel's Independence Day as a new religious holiday, and send their children to state-run religious educational institutions.

The third school is also made up of religious Zionists, but of a more messianic bent. These messianic Zionists, who make up about 5 percent of the Jewish population, form the backbone of the Gush Emunim Jewish settler movement in the West Bank. For them the rebirth of the Jewish state is not simply a religious event; it is the first stage in a process that will culminate with the coming of the Messiah. The state, in their view, is a necessary instrument for bringing the Messiah, and Israel's politics, defense and foreign policies should all be devoted to that end. That means, in particular, settling every inch of the land of Israel.

Finally, there are the ultra-Orthodox, non-Zionist Jews, known in Hebrew as Haredim, "those filled with the awe of God." They constitute about 15 percent of the Jewish population. The Haredim, although they are highly observant, do not see in the reborn state of Israel an event of major religious significance. They believe that a Jewish state will be worth celebrating religiously only after the Messiah comes and the rule of Jewish law is total. In the meantime, they are content to live in the land of Israel, no matter who is in charge—the secular Zionists or the British—because they feel closer to God there, because they can fulfill more of the Jewish commandments there, and in order to be on hand when the Messiah arrives.

The Haredim believe that since the beginning of the Diaspora two thousand years ago, the pinnacle of Jewish life and learning was that which was achieved by the great eighteenth, nineteenth, and twentieth century yeshivas and rabbinic dynasties in the Jewish towns and ghettos of Eastern Europe, which were largely isolated from the Gentile world surrounding them. They have tried to re-create that life in Israel. That is why their menfolk still dress in the dark coats and fur hats worn by eighteenth-century Eastern European gentlemen. They even name many of their yeshivas in Israel after the towns in Eastern Europe from which they came. They also prefer to speak Yiddish, the language of Eastern European Jews, not Hebrew, and most of them neither send their sons and daughters to do army service nor celebrate Israel's Independence Day. They have been ready to serve in the Israeli parliament purely for the purposes of advancing their own campaign to make Israeli society more religious and in order to obtain state funds to support their own private educational network of yeshivas.

Forty years ago, when the secular Israeli fathers were taking their sons down to Mea Shearim to show them the Haredim before they supposedly disappeared, what they didn't know was that the Haredim were taking *their* sons over to the secular neighborhoods of Jerusalem and telling them: "Behold these empty secular Jews! In another generation they will realize that the Jews' return to their land is not a political act but a spiritual one—and one which demands a spiritual response. Forty years from now, they will all be like us."

In fact, each of the four main schools in the great Israeli identity debate was so convinced that the others would wither away that as a group they were never willing, or able, to sit down and hammer out a consensus about the meaning of the state of Israel and the land of Israel for the Israeli people. As a result, the different visions grew side by side. Israel became more secular and more Orthodox, more mundane and more messianic, all at the same time. Far from having built a "new Jewish identity," or a "new Jew," Israel seems to have brought out of the basement of Jewish history every Jewish spiritual option from the past three thousand years; the country has become a living museum of Jewish history. That is why Israel today has more Lithuanian-style Haredi yeshivas under its roof than the Jews ever had back in Lithuania, at the same time as it has the only Jewish gay bar and the only Jewish surfing shop.

Nothing better dramatized the radically different Jewish trends that have grown in the Israeli hothouse in the last forty years than the November 1988 national election campaign, which involved twenty-seven different parties competing for 120 Knesset seats. During the runoff, the Lubavitcher rebbe, Menachem Mendel Schneerson, who resides in Brooklyn, threw his backing behind the ultra-Orthodox Agudat Yisrael Party. The rebbe indicated his support with a series of full-page advertisements in Israeli newspapers inviting voters to fill out a coupon swearing that they had voted for Agudat and to send it to him. In return, the rebbe promised to make a blessing in the voter's name—a blessing that the voter should have "health, a long life, happiness, and success in all endeavors." Meanwhile, one of the rebbe's main rivals, former chief Sephardic rabbi Ovadia Yosef, took out a television advertisement promising blessings and "many sons" for anyone who voted for his Shas Party. Part of Rabbi Yosef's advertisement, however, was censored by the election board—the part in which he warned, "Whoever does not vote Shas—will be punished by the Holy One blessed be He." Not to be outdone, Agudat Yisrael printed postcards with the picture of a dead Moroccan Jewish holy man, the Baba Sali, an Israeli equivalent of Father Divine, revered for his powers of healing and prophecy. On the back of the postcards was printed: "There is no doubt that from the heavens Baba Sali is blessing all those who support and vote for Agudat Yisrael." Two other ultra-Orthodox sects vowed not to eat fruit until after the elections in order to bring bad luck on their rival party, Degel Hatorah, whose symbol was a fruit tree. From the other side of the political spectrum, the secular, liberal Shinui (Change) Party published a full-page advertisement showing the not particularly appealing head of an ultra-Orthodox Jew, with long sidelocks, above the headline: HE IS FREE FROM ARMY SERVICE AND HARASSING YOU AT THE SAME TIME.

Watching these campaign advertisements, I began to understand what an Israeli friend of mine meant when he said, "It is a lot easier to pray for the ingathering of the exiles than it is to live with them."

I also began to understand why it is literally exhausting at times to be an Israeli Jew. One afternoon in June 1988, I sat in the Ramat Aviv home of Israeli historian Ya'acov Shavit, trying to figure out just what time it was in Israel. While a light breeze fanned us through the open door and his seventeen-year-old daughter, Noga, prepared lunch in the kitchen, Shavit discussed the strains of living in a country where all the clocks still had open faces.

"I must tell you," he confided, "I just came back from two years in Germany. It was paradise. It was Germany, but it was paradise. No news. No one waiting for the Messiah. It was so relaxing. Here, you live in a very dynamic state. You are always involved in everything. Always listening to the news. You can't escape the utopian aspirations of the left or the messianic expectations of the right. You can never relax. People are always arguing about your identity. People are always asking you to decide. Are you a Jew? Well, what kind of Jew? Are you a Zionist? Well, what kind of Zionist? You turn on the television and people are arguing about the borders, about the boundaries between religion and state—nothing is ever settled here. You just can't relax."

At that point Noga stuck her head out of the kitchen, where she had been quietly peeling potatoes, and shouted across the room to her father, "Dad, that's the fun of the place."

"Yes, fun," mused Shavit, rolling his eyeballs upward with the look of a man who could do with a little less fun.

"Anyways, Dad," added Noga, just to nail down the point, "don't you know they commit suicide in Switzerland more than anywhere else in the world?"

Israel need never worry about suicidal boredom.

In order to get a better understanding of the four main visions competing for Israel's Jewish soul, I asked four Israeli acquaintances of mine—all of them once Americans, all of them drawn to Israel for totally different Jewish reasons—Just whose country is this, anyway?

If the Rimon School of Jazz and Contemporary Music in Tel Aviv—Israel's first and only university for rock 'n' roll—had a school crest, the motto running across the middle would say in fancy Hebrew characters: "Jews just wanna have fun."

The Rimon School is the physical embodiment of a vision of Israel shared by many secular Westernized Israelis, which is to be free of all religious obligations and to be normal the way Frenchmen are normal—blessedly normal, boringly normal, go-to-the-beach-and-pop-open-a-beer-every-weekend kind of normal. What those who share this vision enjoy most about Israel is the warmth and familylike security of living in a Jewish community, but they want the warmth of the ghetto without its isolation, without its constant *Sturm und Drang*, and, most of all, without its rabbis. They want the Rimon School.

The Rimon campus looks like an army base gone to seed—low-slung barracks with peeling white paint and a lawn that has needed cutting for months; it was once a school for the mentally handicapped. Some ultra-Orthodox Israelis think it still is. The classroom for rehearsing rock music consists of an underground concrete-and-steel bomb shelter that is known around campus as the "heavy-metal department." There, on the day of my visit, I found a pickup band shaking the two-foot-thick walls, belting out "Johnny B. Goode" and a few strains of an old Israeli favorite, "Me and My Surfboard," which is said to be the first Hebrew surfing song since Moses crossed the Red Sea with the Children of Israel singing in his wake. The pickup band was pure rock 'n' roll Zionism: the dark-eyed lead singer wearing an oversized sweatshirt and red high-top sneakers had immigrated from Tunisia; the saxophonist's family had come from Argentina; the lead guitarist had immigrated from Long Island; and the electric organist traced his family roots to Poland. The Rimon School is where the spirit of Elvis Presley meets the vision of Theodor Herzl.

Started in 1984 by four Israeli jazz and rock stars intent on providing a serious program for Israeli youth interested in studying contemporary music, Rimon offers classes in music composition, voice, jazz guitar, rock, and arranging, to name but a few. By 1988, it had 25 faculty and 135 students and had already graduated the first class from its three-year program. It was also being subsidized in part by the Israeli Ministry of Education. Who said Israel has lost its soul? People just don't know where to find it. Yuval Nadav Haimovitz, a voice student and a member of the school's traveling *a cappella* group, told me he was convinced that the Rimon School represented the essence of what Zionism was supposed to be about.

"I think Herzl would have been very pleased," said Haimovitz, with real conviction. "I think that he wanted this to be a country like any other country. If we can have such a school, then Israel has become just what Herzl had in mind."

It's certainly what Ze'ev Chafets had in mind. It was Ze'ev who first told me about the Rimon School. If Theodor Herzl and Janis Joplin had had a child together, it would have been Ze'ev; he even looks like a cross between the two. A native of Detroit, Chafets has that dockyard philosopher's sense of what makes the ordinary man tick and the finely tuned ear of a frustrated rock star who knows what makes men dance. I first got to know Ze'ev back in the early 1980s, when he headed the Government Press Office for Prime Minister Menachem Begin; today he makes his living writing books. Over some Goldstar beers at his favorite local, the Bonanza Bar off Tel Aviv's Dizengoff Street, Chafets, now in his early forties, puffed a fat cigar and talked about his own Israel, the one for Jews who just wanna have fun.

"I came in 1967," said Chafets. "I was at the University of Michigan. On one level, I came to be a student, and to learn Hebrew. I was thinking of becoming a rabbi, you know, all that stuff. On the American level, it was the sixties and everybody was going someplace. Some of my friends dropped out, some of my friends went to Canada, some went to the Peace Corps, and some went out to the desert and smoked dope all of their lives.

I traveled like everybody else, and happened to land here. That was the *Easy Rider* side of it."

While that explains how Chafets got to Israel, what held him was something more intangible, he said, something actually tribal. It is the same feeling that prompts American Jews to applaud when their El Al plane lands safely in Tel Aviv. They applaud for the crazy notion of a Jewish airplane landing on a Jewish landing strip at a Jewish airport. Who ever heard of such a thing before 1948? That is the glue that binds many Israelis to the land—not Bible, and not religion, but the poetry of a Jewish airport.

"What really holds this place together at bottom," explained Chafets, as other customers in the bar shouted their greetings to him, not all of which were fit to print, "is not democracy. It's not Zionism. It's not any ideology or any system. It is that tribal Jewish sense of solidarity. For two thousand years, all these people have been crying and pleading and begging God to give them a country. I wanted to see it, but when I came here I found out that Israel resonated for me. I quickly realized I felt at home here, even though these people were not like people I had grown up with. When the Moroccans first came to Israel, there was this thing that Moroccans always used to walk in the road. And people would ask why. Didn't they have sidewalks in Morocco? No. The reason was that this was *their* country. There's no plantation owner around. Now they can walk in the fucking street if they want to. I had a little bit of that feeling myself. Israel is how Jews behave when they are off the plantation—when there are no Gentiles around watching over them. All the things here that Americans complain about I liked. I liked the bad manners. I liked the directness, I liked the excitement, the adrenaline. I felt comfortable with these people. I never really articulated it, but on some unconscious level I got off the airplane and thought to myself, This is the place. I belong here."

So what do you do for fun?

"I have great fun; for example, getting together with some of the top musicians in Israel and playing rock 'n' roll, and playing for big parties from time to time. Why? Because it's something that in America I could never do. Before Yom Kippur every year, Shaul the bartender and I and a few other people go sit on Dizengoff Street and we drink beer and eat hummus, and as people come by—if we know them and, as we get progressively drunker,

even if we don't know them—we stop them and say, 'If I did
something wrong to offend you this year, I apologize. Please
forgive me.' It's great fun and people smile and laugh and say,
'Yeah, me too, brother. Forgive me, too,' and they just walk
along. I like getting up on Saturday mornings and hanging out
on the beach with some friends at this shack owned by a Tunisian
woman. You feel the Mediterranean part of this country. The
slow pace, the sensuousness of the women, the warmth, the
colors. Israel is the only country where the Puerto Rican girls are
all Jewish. Fun was watching the Israeli basketball team beat the
Russians in 1977. Not just because it was great, but because it
was us against them. On one level it was Tal Brody [the Israeli
team star player] and all these guys beating the Russian team,
which is from a big country, remember, and on another level it
was my grandfather beating them. It was our retroactive victory
over the Cossacks. And we all understood it that way. Nobody
had to say it. It would have sounded corny to say it to each other,
but we understood it that way."

One of the things I always liked about Chafets, one of the
reasons he is typical of a certain, very popular strain of Israelis,
is that he always has a sense of humor about Israel. He always
appreciates that most Israelis are not heroes, let alone holy men,
nor do they even want to be, but people just struggling to get
through the month, eke out a little happiness, make love—not
always with their spouses—and visit America at least once every
three years. The extent of their ideology is their recognition that
they are doing all this in a Jewish state, serving in the army and
saluting the flag.

"Now, you could say, Well, if you wanted to have fun so much,
why didn't you move to California?" Chafets continued, anticipating my question. "Why live in Israel? I wanted to have fun
and I also wanted to live in a Jewish country—to participate in
that. It is fair to say that my goal as a Zionist was to live in a
Jewish state, and it wasn't ever to live in a particular kind of
Jewish state. It is enough for me to be in a country that is owned
and operated by my family. And if my family decides it wants to
be in the fur business instead of the drug business, that's fine.
That is why it never really made a critical difference to me what
government there is here. You often hear people saying, If Sharon
is going to be Prime Minister, I am leaving. My feeling is that

under no circumstances am I leaving, any more than anyone would leave a country where he belongs. I think it was in *The French Connection* when Popeye Doyle was talking to this French cop and the French cop was bragging about Marseilles and Popeye says, 'I'd rather be the lid on a garbage can in New York than the mayor of Marseilles.' Not to be offensive about other countries, but I'd rather be the lid on a garbage can here than live anywhere else.

"Having grown up in America I was very much aware of the gap—in what I think is a good country—between rhetoric and performance, between ideology and reality. So I didn't think this country had to become perfect in order to be enjoyable. It's like the guy who says, 'I can't live with a woman unless she's perfect,' and another guy who is more easygoing and says, 'You know, maybe she's a little fat and maybe she's a little stupid, but you know, what the heck, I love her.' That's kind of how I feel about Israel. Twenty years ago, when I first came, people here still had this sort of grandiose image of the country, but that was too austere, too demanding to last for long for most people. What you see now is a loosening of the bonds of discipline and ideology. It's like a woman taking off her girdle after the party is over. People sacrificed for a long time, they want to have some fun. One of the great lessons to me about Israel is that Jews are real people. We're not stereotypes, we're not creations of Bernard Malamud.

"This is what we are," pronounced Chafets, cocking his thumb toward the now packed bar. "How many times have you seen a bar with only Jews in it?"

But how can living in a Jewish state resonate so deeply for you, while at the same time you are totally nonobservant as a Jew? I asked. You seem to agree with those who say that because the sky in Israel is Jewish, once there you don't have to observe at all anymore.

"Well, there's something to that. One of the great things about Israel for me is that it allows me not to be Jewish, not to be observant," answered Chafets. "It is like the difference between someone who has to pay his rent every month and someone who buys the house. This is mine now. I don't have to go on being religiously Jewish to distinguish myself from the Gentiles. When I'm here, I don't have to think, Is the woman I meet Jewish? I don't care if she's Jewish, because if I met her here, and she's able to speak Hebrew and live in this society, she's Jewish enough for me. I don't have to worry about eating Jewish food to demonstrate culinary solidarity. I don't need a delicatessen to show that I am Jewish. And for the same reason, I don't need a synagogue. The whole country's my synagogue. The part of the synagogue I always liked was the social hall, and the kitchen—you know, not the sanctuary. And so being here is a relief. I can be myself and Jewish but without having to think about it all the time. If you want to be a Jewish guy in America, you really have to agree to play by the American Jewish rules—which means that you have to be a nice boy. Israel is the only country where you can be Jewish but you don't have to be domesticated. If you don't want to be an ophthalmologist and you don't want to be a lawyer and you still want to be Jewish—this is the place to do it."

Just don't try to have a newspaper stand in the wrong neighborhood.

Shimon Tsimhe used to have the hottest-selling Hebrew newsstand in B'nei B'rak—before the bombing. Now he scratches out a bare living selling falafel sandwiches.

B'nei B'rak is an ultra-Orthodox suburb of Tel Aviv, populated solely by Haredim. It is only twenty minutes' drive from the Bonanza Bar—twenty minutes and about two hundred years, that is, since Jewish life in B'nei B'rak today has much more in common with Jewish life in eighteenth-century Lithuania than anything happening in north Tel Aviv. If they had wanted to film the movie *Hester Street* here, they would not have needed to bring in many props or costumes.

My first visit to B'nei B'rak was prompted by a small item in the *Jerusalem Post* about Tsimhe. A tiny band of B'nei B'rak's Haredim decided to purify their neighborhood of all newsstands selling non-religious, pro-Zionist Israeli newspapers. The religious community in Israel has its own newspapers, which not only concentrate on news important to them—such as which rabbi is taking over which yeshiva or advertisements by matrimonial matchmakers—but also print only the most puritanical advertisements and take a rather dim view of news about the secular state.

Tsimhe learned that the hard way. "I used to sell lots of newspapers—lots," he told me one afternoon, while plopping mashed chick-pea balls into a deep-fat fryer and nervously looking back and forth to make certain none of the black-coated ultra-Orthodox men waiting for the bus were eavesdropping on our conversation. "I was the biggest in the whole area, not just B'nei B'rak. Every Friday I would sell five hundred copies of *Yediot Achronot* and *Ma'ariv*. I made 15 percent on each one."

"But then the threats started," said Tsimhe, a rail-thin man with a black yarmulke resting uneasily on his head. Then there was a bomb—just a small one. Someone placed it right up against the kiosk. It didn't totally destroy the newsstand but was powerful enough to send debris and shrapnel flying across the street, breaking the window of the tailor's shop. The tailor was not amused. Tsimhe was terrified. On the back of Tsimhe's kiosk, into which a group of Haredim also locked him one day to help persuade him that it would be best not to sell Israeli dailies like *Yediot* and *Ma'ariv*, someone bluntly scrawled in spray paint: STOP OFFERING NEWSPAPERS.

Didn't you complain to the municipality? I asked him incredulously.

"They said it would be better if I didn't sell newspapers anymore," said Tsimhe. "They said it would be better if I sold falafels." (The municipality is also run by Haredim.)

Then, putting on a smile like a Halloween mask, Tsimhe turned back to serve one of his ultra-Orthodox customers with an abruptness that said to me, "Please go away. I have had enough troubles."

As I walked down the main street of B'nei B'rak, distancing myself from Tsimhe's stand, I decided to conduct a little sidewalk experiment. I stopped a modern-looking Orthodox man who was carrying a briefcase and wearing the knitted yarmulke of the kind preferred by religious Jews who are also Zionists.

"Excuse me," I asked in a loud voice, "do you know where I can get a copy of *Ma'ariv* around here?"

The man's eyes flashed wide, as though I had inquired where I might find a prostitute for the evening. He kept walking, but motioned me closer with a nod of his head so that he could speak to me in a whisper.

"Don't you know what is happening in B'nei B'rak?" he hissed. "It is terror, ultra-Orthodox terror."

Then, still without breaking stride, he used his eyes to direct my attention down toward the thin manila folder he was carrying in his briefcase. He opened the top of the folder just a sliver, like some pusher offering me a whiff of cocaine. The opening revealed a copy of *Yediot*, Israel's biggest-selling newspaper, sandwiched into the folder. He smiled a sly grin and then quickly strode away, swallowed by a stream of black hats and coats.

I found this whole affair troubling for what it said about the rising power of the extremist elements within the Haredi community, and I used it as the basis for a long story in the *Times* about the struggle within Israel between Haredim and secular Jews. Shortly after I wrote this article, I was flooded with hate mail from ultra-Orthodox Jews in America and Israel who felt that I had maligned their community, only a small portion of whom, they said, were of the type who turned Tsimhe from a newspaper salesman into a falafel maker overnight. I responded by asking why, if the majority of ultra-Orthodox Jews in Israel were so moderate, more of them—any of them—didn't rush to defend Tsimhe's right to sell Israeli newspapers. I got no answer. One of the complainants, though, wouldn't let go. He was polite, even engaging, but relentless in his determination to educate me on the merits of the Haredi community.

I was not Rabbi Nota Schiller's first project. Schiller is the director of Jerusalem's Ohr Somayach yeshiva, an ultra-Orthodox institution which specializes in bringing Jews who have drifted away from Judaism back to Torah learning. Some have accused him of running a factory for brainwashing Jews, but Schiller vehemently denies this charge, although not without adding, tongue in cheek, that some Jews could use having their brains washed. Ohr Somayach is probably the most liberal face of Haredi Judaism in Israel; its moderation and openness to dialogue do not typify the Haredi community. Nevertheless, when Schiller invited me to spend a day at his yeshiva in order to prove to me that the Haredim had a vision for Israel that was as dynamic, compelling, and noncoercive as any Zionist one, I decided to take him up on it.

I quickly discovered that the Brooklyn-born rabbi, with a bachelor's degree in English literature and psychology from Johns Hopkins, brought a certain endearing Madison Avenue quality to selling Orthodox Judaism. We began our talk at his yeshiva—

which was founded in 1972 and is situated in a modern apartment
block in Jerusalem's French Hill neighborhood—with Schiller explaining why his community was being slandered.

"The Jews never would have made it here to these shores,"
began Schiller, who first came to Israel himself in 1961 as a twenty-
four-year-old student, "if it were not for the learning that went
on in the yeshivas of Eastern Europe and for the fact that the
grandfathers of the secular Zionists who founded this country
lived the way I do. The Israelis are still here as Jews only because
of the Orthodox life-style their grandfathers led. It is as though
their grandfathers deposited money in the bank, and now this
generation is writing checks on it. So secular Jews have a debt to
that life-style. Therefore, when we are presented as retrogressive,
primitive madmen, it is simply not true. We are just saying, Let
us live the way we want to live. I am not asking you to live like
me, but I am asking you to appreciate that there is a certain sanity
and consistency rooted in Jewish history in my position and that
you have a debt to that position, and that debt may allow me to
ask you to make certain compromises that we can negotiate together. There is in the code of Jewish law a case in which the
rabbis were asked what happens if two ships are coming through
a narrow strait at the same time from opposite directions. One
ship is laden with cargo and the other is empty. Who has to give
way? One of Israel's first great rabbis, Reb Avram Yeshayau
Krelitz, used this case when arguing with Ben-Gurion for greater
sensitivity to the needs of the Haredi community. Krelitz told
Ben-Gurion that the rabbis decided that the empty ship must give
way to the one laden with cargo. He then went on to tell Ben-
Gurion: 'Look, we are carrying a few thousand years of cargo
with us; you are still an empty ship. You have to give way
for us.' "

When I observed that the Haredim did not show much sensitivity to Tsimhe's way of life, Schiller retorted that this was because they had had so many years of being abused by the secular
community.

"The secular Israeli community looks at Haredim in one of
three ways," explained Schiller. "The ultra-secularists say that
the Haredim should be asked to leave—they are an anachronism,
an embarrassment, and are frustrating the growth of the country.

We should amputate this sick limb. Another group sees us as their Fiddlers on the Roof. These are the secular Israelis, who are sentimentally attached to the ghetto image of the Jew. America has its Disneyland theme park, so Israel has its theme park in Mea Shearim. They view it as charming and interesting, and it can bring in a few tourist bucks for the country, and it reminds them of their grandfathers—but let's not take it too seriously. Then there is a third response: just as there was the concept of the Shabbos goy—the Gentile who came into the synagogue and put out the lights on the Sabbath for the Jews—so there is the concept of the Shabbos Jew. Secular Israelis want someone to keep Shabbos for them—us—so that their grandchildren, who are nonobservant, will be exposed to enough real Jewishness in order to maintain even their secular Jewish identities."

Okay, I conceded, maybe you are right—without Orthodox Judaism keeping the Jewish people and its traditions alive for all these centuries, Judaism would never have survived. But what I am wondering is whether with Orthodox Judaism alone the Jewish people will be able to survive the next fifty years. None of your women and virtually none of your men serves in the Israeli army; virtually none of your yeshivas recognizes Israeli Independence Day as a holiday on which it should be closed for celebration; and maybe most important, you totally reject the validity of the Reform and Conservative streams of Judaism, without which thousands upon thousands of Jews would have drifted away from Judaism altogether in the twentieth century—since they are repelled by your interpretations and life-style. So what makes you such a bargain anyway? I asked. And furthermore, what is that picture of a baseball player doing by your desk?

"That is Cal Abrams, who was the first Jewish baseball player for the Brooklyn Dodgers," explained Schiller, taking last things first. "He played left field in the 1950s. I was a teenager in Brooklyn then. The Dodgers always had a problem in left field. After he was called up, for the first half of the season he hit .477. It was clear to me and my friends that Cal Abrams was going to be the Messiah. That was the only way to explain how a Jew could hit .477. He was a lefty and he hit only to left field, so the opposing teams would put this super shift on for him. Well, midway into the season he went into a slump and could not buy a base hit. So what did we decide? We decided that the Messiah will come only when the generation is ready. Cal Abrams was supposed to be the Messiah, but the generation did not deserve him. We were not ready."

Fine, but what does that have to do with Israel? I asked.

"Hopefully, the state of Israel will not turn out to be a Cal Abrams," said Schiller, rubbing his salt-and-pepper beard. "But if it does, it won't be the end of the Jewish people. I am going to do everything I can to make sure the state makes it—but my Judaism won't hinge on that."

Now we're getting somewhere, I said. Why isn't the secular Zionist state of Israel essential for you?

"We want a Jewish state, run by Jewish law," said Schiller. "The secular Zionists want a state for Jews. That is the difference. I want a Jewish state, but I am ready to live and argue with all the secular Labor Zionists of the world today, because by keeping the discussion going with them, I am convinced that their children or grandchildren, disciples or fellow travelers, will one day pitch up at Ohr Somayach, or somewhere like it. They will eventually enter into the fold of Torah Jews. Jews can survive and have survived for two thousand years without Israel and without a Temple. If we have our druthers, we want Israel, we want the Temple, and we want the preferred boundaries. But there is only one thing we cannot survive without and that is Torah. We survived all of these years as a people, thanks to Torah. Had we depended on the land and the land alone, we would have disappeared the way other cultures disappeared."

Yet surely there is some special significance for you as a Jew in the fact that the state does exist here? The land, at least, has special meaning for you?

"Of course," said Schiller. "When the Jewish people stood before God at Mount Sinai, they were commissioned to fulfill their genius as a nation in this land. The Jews are not just a collection of individuals, they are a nation, and every nation must have its ball park, its field. It is as if this is Yankee Stadium for the Jewish people, and we are the Yankees. You just can't play without a ball park. You can't play all your games on the road and hope to be a successful team—otherwise you never get to bat last. You cannot have the ideal fulfillment of Torah without living in this land. There are certain *mitzvot* [commandments]—ob-

serving the sabbatical year,* for instance—which can be performed only here in the land of Israel. But the advantage of being
here is not just that you can fulfill more commandments. There
is a total Jewish experience here that cannot be found elsewhere.
The Jew who is living abroad is a weekend Jew. He can take a
time-out whenever he wants. Here there are no time-outs. The
clock is running because you are always on the court. To throw
garbage on the streets of Jerusalem is a spiritual transgression,
not just a municipal violation."

Well, if the land is that important, then why have 20,000 Haredi
men arranged for draft deferments excusing them from army service? Don't you feel you have a responsibility to protect this land
with your life?

"Anyone within our community who does not recognize the
importance of what the secular Israeli is doing to protect us is an
ingrate," answered Schiller. "But anyone who doesn't recognize
the contribution of yeshiva boys is ignorant. I think it is legitimate
to postpone serving in the army as long as someone is productive
and learning in a yeshiva, because I think there are too few people
who are aware and learned enough to fight the enemy of assimilation. Our survival in the next generation will depend on that,
too. It is not like our young men are going to the beach each day
instead of serving in the army. The rigid intellectual discipline
and life-style of a yeshiva boy is not a casual conscientious ob-
jection. It is not like going to Canada. There are much easier
ways to get out of the army."

If the land of Israel has spiritual value for you, I asked, why
is it that many prominent ultra-Orthodox rabbis in Israel are doves
when it comes to giving back the West Bank and the Gaza
Strip—in contrast to the Zionist Orthodox Jews represented by
the Gush Emunim Jewish settler movement, who believe that
occupying all the land of Israel is the necessary first stage for
Jewish and universal redemption?

"A Torah society always comes before a specific territory,"
answered Schiller, explaining where his Haredim part company
with many religious Zionists. "It is only through a return to

*The Torah commands that a sabbatical year be observed every seven years in Israel,
during which time all agriculture should be suspended and the land be allowed to lie
fallow.

Torah—not a specific place—that there can be a redemptive process. Redemption comes when we earn the privilege, not because we sit in a certain location. Being in Israel is part of earning that privilege, but there is no urgency today to institute the ideal biblical boundaries. That will happen at a time when it is supposed to happen, and I don't have to precipitate the process at the cost of Jewish lives. We need the courage of humility, and Gush Emunim lack that. If I can secure the continuity of this state by giving back some land to the Arabs, then it is my responsibility to do so. Some people are fighting for the land and some people are fighting to ensure that the land is worth protecting."

But for which Jews? The Haredi community is at the forefront of the fight to delegitimize Reform and Conservative Judaism, just because they offer a less stringent interpretation of Torah. How can you be for the survival of the Jewish people and against Jewish pluralism?

"I have no problem awarding a Reform or Conservative Jew a certain status as a person and a Jew," answered Schiller. "If that is pluralism, then I am a pluralist. But what I reject of pluralism is the idea that we are all equally right. We are not. There was a revelation at Sinai. A message and a code for interpreting that message were passed down through the generations. The boundaries of interpretation were delimited from the start. Within those boundaries, there is an opportunity for discussion. But not outside those boundaries, and that is where Reform and Conservative Judaism has gone. It is as if you have a baseball team and someone comes along and says, Why don't we do some football exercises? Well, we're not playing football, we're playing baseball. If someone starts to pluralize that way, he loses the point of the whole activity. In baseball you can throw curveballs, fastballs, and strikes, but not forward passes. That's a different game. But Reform and Conservative are calling it all the same game, and it is not. My argument is not with the Reform Jew. That he is Jewish I acknowledge. My argument is with Reform Judaism."

Before leaving, I took up Schiller's offer to sit in on one of his yeshiva's Torah-study sessions. It turned out to be highly revealing, although not for the Torah portion. There were about twenty young men in the class, all of them between the ages of nineteen and thirty-nine. They all seemed to be either Americans or Western Europeans. At least half of them were wearing

LaCoste sport shirts with crocodiles on the breast, which left me wondering whether I hadn't walked into a fraternity meeting. Their appearance reminded me in every way of the kids with whom I'd first come to Israel twenty years ago to live on a kibbutz for a summer and play pioneer. But this was no kibbutz, and no one here was interested in picking tomatoes, as I had been.

"What are you doing here?" I asked them all point-blank. "You're not supposed to be in a yeshiva. That's not why Americans come here. Where've you been? You're supposed to be on kibbutzim, draining swamps, dreaming about being an Israeli fighter pilot, chasing girls down on the beach. What is this?"

The answer came as if from one man: "Mr. Friedman, that was your generation—not ours."

Suddenly all those statistics published by the Ministry of Absorption indicating that immigration to Israel by secular American Jews interested in the pioneering Zionist dream was slowing to a trickle were staring me in the face. Maybe Schiller was right— there are not that many more Ze'ev Chafetses out there, into rock 'n' roll Zionism. As long as everyone was devoted to building the country, said one of Schiller's recruits, there was enough excitement around for the secular to drain the swamps and for the Orthodox to do their thing—and plenty of Jewish immigrants for both. But when it came time for an end, he said, it turned out that the secular had no end and the Orthodox did. They had something to offer once the swamps ran dry, and that is why practically the only Jews coming to Israel these days from America and Western Europe are ultra-Orthodox or their recruits.

Ya'acov Asher Sinclair, a thirty-eight-year-old Englishman who decided to take a break from his cosmopolitan life in London to investigate religious life in Israel, put it to me straight. "Unless you have some other agenda going on, to come here and be a hero, well . . . I don't think it's got that romantic image anymore," said Sinclair, with no hint of regret. "What were the figures last year? Some 8,000 Jews came and 24,000 left. Who are the ones leaving? They are the people who grew up with the secular side of Zionism, which has proven vacuous, unfulfilling, and nonsustainable. There was a certain kind of romanticism to their attachment to Israel, and now they are undiscovering Israel for the same reason. It is not romantic enough for them anymore. It was transitory. It was an infatuation. What is lasting, attractive, and compelling is the Torah. I came here several times for visits, but only when I became religious did I really want to be here, because I felt it was the only place I could really learn at the level I wanted. I'm not here to fly an airplane, I'm not here to be a doctor, I'm not here to work the land, I'm not here to feel taller or freer, and I am not here to go to the beach or get a tan. I am here to learn exclusively about Judaism. I am here to learn Torah only. If Torah were better in the States or South Africa or Madagascar, that is where I would be. But it's better here."

It sounds seductive when you are inside the yeshiva walls, and block out three-quarters of Israel and 90 percent of the Jewish people, who are totally alienated by this religious vision. As I walked the Tel Aviv beachfront a few days later, though, I wondered to myself, How can Schiller's vision ever flourish in the long run, when what it tells Israelis is that they will survive as Jews only to the extent that they imitate their grandfathers. How long can he tell dignified and self-confident Israelis, who built a whole state from scratch, that they are surviving as Jews because of the investment of eighteenth-century rabbis? How long can he tell Israeli high-school students that they must put their bodies on the line so that yeshiva students can study in peace? I can't resist calling Schiller a few days later and asking whether he really isn't fighting a lost battle. As always, he is ready with an answer and a story.

"I studied in a yeshiva in New York under Reb Isaac Hutner," said Schiller. "He came on a visit to Israel once and went to Kibbutz Yad Mordechai. At one point during his discussion with the kibbutz elders he told them, 'Ben-Gurion thought that time was in his favor because as the country becomes more materialistic it cannot help but drift away from its shtetl origins and become less sentimental about the attachment to the old-time religion. Therefore, Ben-Gurion avoided a direct confrontation with the religious and instead chipped away at them wherever he could. He figured they would fall into his lap eventually. Ben-Gurion was wrong. We can trace the peaks and valleys in Jewish history, and always just when it looks as if our way of life is going to evaporate, there is somehow a resurgence and the thing comes to life again. You people here on Kibbutz Yad Mordechai, I can tell you one thing: your children will either end up in Los Angeles or in Ohr Somayach. They won't be in Yad Mordechai. Or your grandchildren, for sure.'

"I can't help but feel that there is a deep truth ringing in those words," said Schiller, with the firmness of a man who feels the wind at his back. "And as each day and hour goes by, it is ringing more and more true."

But not every Jew in Israel is ready to wait for that day when the Messiah will come forth out of the blue riding a donkey, to usher in a complete Torah society. Some devised a plan to bring him sooner.

It was a simple plan, really. The small group of West Bank Jewish settlers would steal explosives from an Israeli army camp on the Golan Heights, place their homemade bombs at the base of the Dome of the Rock—the third-holiest shrine of Islam—and then blow the blue-and-gold mosque to smithereens. The Dome of the Rock is situated on Jerusalem's Temple Mount, the site of the first and second Jewish Temples, and the Israeli plotters were convinced that the Messiah would come only once this Muslim "desecration" was cleared from the very throne of God on earth, the focal point of Jewish national sovereignty. This was their way of dusting off the throne and making it more inviting for the Messiah. Or, as Yehuda Etzion, the messianic settler behind the plan, told his colleagues, "This act will be an incomparably appropriate opening move in pursuing our cause. We must view ourselves as messengers who bring the kingdom [of God's] good tidings."*

Fortunately for Israel, and the world, this plot to prod the Messiah was never realized, but not for want of trying. The explosives were already prepared when the Israeli police uncovered the cabal and, in June 1984, brought charges against twenty-seven men alleged to have been part of a Jewish terrorist underground based in the West Bank. The crimes for which these Jewish terrorists were later convicted included not only the plot against the Dome of the Rock but also the 1983 murder of three Palestinian

*Haggai Segal, *Dear Brothers: The West Bank Jewish Underground* (Beit-Shamai Publications, Inc., 1988).

students at Hebron's Islamic College, in revenge for the killing of a yeshiva student in the same town, the maiming of two Palestinian West Bank mayors, Bassam Shaka and Karim Khalef, and an attempt to sabotage Arab buses in Jerusalem.

I was not in Israel when the Jewish terrorists committed their crimes, but I was on hand in the Jerusalem District Court on July 10, 1985, when most of them were sentenced to varying prison terms, from life to a few months—almost all of which have since been reduced by Israel's President Chaim Herzog. As I watched these young Jewish terrorists in their yarmulkes and long beards walking around the courtroom, I could not help but be struck by their self-confidence and self-righteousness. The way they strutted about, chatting with their wives, chomping on green apples, and almost literally turning up their noses at the judge, was galling. I had seen the same arrogance among members of Hizbullah, the Party of God, in Beirut. These were simply the Jewish version. While they were being sentenced by the judge, I kept wondering to myself, What dark corner of Jewish history did these people crawl out of? Are we really members of the same religious community? Nobody told me about Jews like this when I was preparing for my bar mitzvah back in Minneapolis.

In order to figure out where they came from, I paid a visit to Rabbi Eliezer Waldman, one of the founding fathers of the West Bank settler movement, and a man to whom some of the terrorists had turned for spiritual guidance. Although Rabbi Waldman was not involved in the Jewish terrorists' plots, he was steeped in the religious vision which stirred them. As noted earlier, Rabbi Waldman was among the *Mayflower* families of West Bank Jewish settlement—the group that rented out Hebron's Arab-owned Park Hotel for the week of Passover 1968 and really opened the West Bank and Gaza for settlement based not on security rationales but in order to fulfill biblical visions. Born in Israel but raised in America from the age of three, Waldman now resides in Kiryat Arba, in Hebron, where he splits his time between running a yeshiva and working for the ultra-nationalist Tehiya Party, which is dedicated to annexing the West Bank. Now fifty-one, Rabbi Waldman has the beard of Santa Claus, the feather-light voice of a dove, and the delicate hands of a violinist—all in stark contrast to the seemingly untamed messianic visions dancing in his head. What struck me most about his book-lined apartment in Kiryat Arba was how badly the paint in the hallway had peeled and how tall the trees were in the front yard. Those trees thick with the rings of twenty winters and those paint fragments dusting his doorstep seemed to mock the Israeli—and international—debate about whether or not Jews should settle the West Bank. Waldman has been here a long time already. His walls say so. His trees say so. His Bible says he is going to be here much longer.

I began our discussion by asking Rabbi Waldman why, when he came back to Israel from America at the age of nineteen, he did not go to a regular ultra-Orthodox yeshiva, of the kind Rabbi Schiller attended, but chose instead to go to the Mercaz ha-Rav yeshiva, which was founded in 1924 by Abraham Isaac Kook, a mystical rabbi who believed that the return of the Jews to the land of Israel marked the beginning of a process of Jewish, and ultimately universal, redemption—salvation from a life of sin, and the introduction of a reign of perfect peace and justice. After Israel occupied the West Bank in the 1967 war, the teachings of Rabbi Kook, and his son Rabbi Zevi Judah Kook, were adopted as spiritual and political guidelines by the Gush Emunim Jewish settler movement.

"When I came to Mercaz ha-Rav in 1956, there were only thirty-five boys," recalled Waldman. "It was located in an old house near the center of Jerusalem, near Zion Square. I went there because I knew that its ideology was the direction I wanted. It was the only yeshiva that understood that the phenomenon of Jews being awakened to come back to Israel, to establish settlements and build the land, was all part of the godly decision to begin the process of redemption."

What do you mean by redemption? I thought that was a Christian notion, I asked.

"The Christians took the redemptive idea from us," explained Rabbi Waldman. "Our sources say it means the Jewish people coming back to their land, renewing their life as a Jewish people and independent nation, and living according to Jewish values. Only in that way can they continue toward the achievement of their goals of spiritual and moral perfection and be what they were ordained to be—a light unto the nations that will show the way to spiritual and moral perfection for the whole world."

So what you are saying is that returning to the land of Israel implies certain Jewish obligations?

"That is correct," said the rabbi. "The prophets said that only when we are an independent nation and responsible for ourselves will we arouse respect from the nations of the world. Anyone who has read the Bible knows and understands that for the well-being of the peoples of the world the Jewish people must return to their land and their glory and their spiritual values. The Jewish religion is the only one that obligates both the individual and the nation to live up to certain spiritual and moral ideals in everyday life. It is not just a matter of going to a place of prayer one day a week. True Jewish holiness means expressing spiritual values in the everyday life of the individual and in the everyday life of the nation. Therefore, a spiritual people which is disconnected from the everyday life of a nation will not be a light to other nations. Some Jews—the secular Zionists—came back to Israel and declared that Torah and the commandments were there just to keep the Jews together in exile, and that now that we have returned to our land we don't need these tools of exile any longer. I tell them it is just the opposite. Only when we have returned to the land can we fully play the role which God assigned us.

"In exile we lived as individual Jews. We could express our spiritual values only in personal life, in family life and synagogue life—but the key to our role in world history is expressing those values in public life! That requires us to be living on our land as a nation. A suppressed people can perform all the commandments of the Torah, but a suppressed people cannot project a spiritual life. For hundreds of years we lived in exile with our spiritual morals. Were we respected for our spiritual morals? We were not. We were trodden upon. And you know what they say: 'The wisdom of the downtrodden is belittled.' It's just like a teacher before a class—if you can shout at him, he is not going to be respected. It is like that with nations, too. The return to the land is necessary as a base for Jews being a light unto the nations and projecting their values for all the peoples of the world.

"This is mentioned to Abraham, when God first told him, 'Go, leave your father's house and go to the land which I will show you.' God doesn't finish his first words to Abraham without adding, 'All the families of the world will be blessed by you.' And how will all the families of the world be blessed by you? By you reaching a certain stage of completion. You cannot bless others until you reach such a stage. That doesn't mean that all the non-

Jews will convert, but that the general values, the belief in one God, spiritual values, and values between man and his fellow man, and goodness and kindness—those general values will be exemplified by the Jews and this will bring about redemption."

And when will the Messiah come?

"The Messiah will come as the final stage of this redemption," said Waldman. "The only way for us to hasten the coming of the Messiah is by proving ourselves worthy of him by redeeming ourselves as much as possible. What we are doing here in redeeming the land of Israel is hastening the coming of the Messiah."

How is it that Rabbi Kook understood all of this while the rest of the ultra-Orthodox Haredi community did not? Most ultra-Orthodox Jews rejected Zionism, and even today feel ambivalent about the state of Israel, which they see as a secular enterprise.

"I believe it is because they have not delved deeply into the subject according to the sources of redemption in the Torah and among the teachings of our sages," said Rabbi Waldman, as if stating the obvious. "It was a great mistake for them not to understand what was happening. They should have understood. Why did they not understand the greatness of the hour? Because this matter of redemption, this deep subject, was not learned from the sources by the multitudes of Orthodox Jews."

How could so many Orthodox rabbis be so wrong for so long? I asked.

"For many centuries Orthodox Jews when studying the Talmud and the law books did not study laws pertaining to life in the land of Israel because they were not here," said Rabbi Waldman. "They studied laws pertaining to life in exile. All those laws pertaining to Israel were not studied by them because it was a farfetched matter. For this reason they did not study the subject of redemption and the relationship between religious Jews and nonreligious Jews. You know what they called a nonobservant Jew in exile? They would call him a goy. A goy! They looked at Zionism and said, 'If we join this movement we may become nonreligious.' They said this cannot be a godly made effort if it is led by secular Jews. The Haredim believe that redemption comes only when the process is complete—when all the Jews have repented and the leadership has become observant. They say that as long as we are not at that stage we are nowhere. There is no redemption. They believe that this is a godly land, but until the Messiah comes and men have achieved spiritual perfection, the secular state of Israel in the land of Israel has no real religious significance. That is why they don't celebrate Independence Day. But Independence Day was always something special at Mercaz ha-Rav yeshiva. We were practically the only ones in the yeshiva world who celebrated it. We see redemption as a process. Even though it is incomplete, one must recognize the value of each stage in the process. The secular Jewish state built primarily by secular Jews is one stage in that process. Israel's liberation of Jerusalem and Judea and Samaria in 1967 is another stage. They are all steps on the way—great steps on the way to redemption. We see Zionism as a godly phenomenon and Theodor Herzl as a godly *shaliach* [envoy], a messenger sent by God to arouse the Jewish people. God knew that if He sent an Orthodox Jew to arouse the Jewish people, all the secular Jews would ignore him. So he chose Herzl, a nonobservant journalist. Zionism was like a lifeboat. First you get all the Jews to hang on, and after we get them all on, all involved, then we will teach them and explain to them about Torah and redemption. That was God's idea."

But even if all that is true, I say, why can't you redeem the Jewish people within the pre-1967 boundaries of Israel? Why do you need all the land of Israel?

"It is a commandment of God to the Jewish people that we settle all the land of Israel," said Rabbi Waldman, somewhat indignantly. "That means that as long as we don't have all the land, we are not going to be complete spiritually and total redemption will not be possible. Judea and Samaria are the heart of the land of Israel, so they must be settled in order for the Jewish people to be redeemed. You need a base and that is our base. Remember, our sages always described this *mitzvah* of settling the land of Israel differently from other *mitzvot*. They put it in a central position. The *mitzvah* of settling the land of Israel, they said, is weighed against all the other *mitzvot*. This is said about only seven *mitzvot*. Why? Because a majority of the 613 commandments can be performed only in an independent land of Israel, by an independent Jewish nation. Only a minority of the *mitzvot* can be performed outside Israel—the *mitzvot* related to family life, private life, individual life, and certain rituals. But a lot of *mitzvot* are concerned with national life—with the Temple, with the land, with the sabbatical year. They are the national *mitzvot*. We cannot be a complete Torah society without them. We did not invent the value of the land of Israel. It is in all the sources. Our sages tell us that godly inspiration is to be felt only in the land of Israel. Prophecy is possible only in the land of Israel. It means that to reach the highest spiritual levels you can do it only here."

You mean to tell me that you, Rabbi, felt incomplete as a Jew before the 1967 war?

"Yes," answered Rabbi Waldman. "Before 1967 my friends and I figured that we had sort of missed the boat with regard to our contribution to the renewal of Jewish national life. During the 1948 war of liberation, I was ten. But when the Six-Day War came, we had a feeling: Now's our chance. God has given us the privilege to participate in this great phenomenon. Because we saw the results of the Six-Day War as something more godly, and an even greater step forward, than the war of liberation. Why? Because what we had after the war of liberation was not the heart of Israel. We had the outposts of Israel. Our parents and grandparents and previous generations, when they dreamed about the land of Israel, what did they dream about? Tel Aviv? Haifa? The coastal plain with its sand dunes? No! They dreamed about Judea and Samaria, Jerusalem, Hebron, Shechem [Nablus], Jericho, the Jordan River. This is where the Jewish people grew up. Since 1967, I feel that I have come home. If there is any meaning to coming home in Israel it's being in Hebron—not Tel Aviv. Hebron is where it all started. This was the first capital of the united Israel and this is where the patriarchs Abraham, Isaac, and Jacob are buried. We didn't make a territorial compromise in 1948 to give up half the land of Israel. We had no choice. We didn't have anything. They offered us part, and even then it was painful to accept just part, but okay, we said, we'll take a part and then see what happens afterward. We saw the Six-Day War as God opening the gates of the heart of Israel before us, and therefore we felt that He was telling us our obligation is to settle and to build. To turn our backs on that is to turn our backs on the whole redemptive process."

Are you sure that God would not prefer that you give some of the land back in return for peace with the Palestinians?

"Why did it take forty years for the Jews to get from Egypt to

Israel?" said Rabbi Waldman, always ready to answer a question with a question. "Moses sent spies to see what was the best way to get into Israel. [Almost all] the spies came back and said, There are giants in the land and we will not be able to overcome them in war, and they described the land as a land 'that devours its inhabitants'—meaning it was difficult to get the fruits out. These spies frightened the Jewish people not to continue on to Israel. When that happened we find in the Bible the most extreme expressions of rebuke by God. He says, 'For how long will my people provoke me in disbelief after everything I have done for them? I took you out of Egypt, you received the Torah, you are receiving bread from heaven and you still disbelieve me.' So God said, 'You don't want Israel, you won't get it. Your carcasses will fall in the desert and remain there. Only the next generation, your children, will understand and believe,' and that is why the Israelites were in the desert for forty years, and only their children came into Israel. After two thousand years of exile, a Holocaust, a war against 50 million Arabs, I believe that God has done for us at least as much as He did for the generation coming out of Egypt. If we could hear God's words today, wouldn't He say the same thing to us as He said to them? Can you imagine us going back to God and saying, 'Okay, you gave us all of Israel, thanks a lot. We really appreciate it. But you can take part back. There are too many difficulties involved. I don't want problems. I want an easy life.' What would God say? Tell me, what would He say?"

The last stop on my journey of spiritual discovery in Israel began at the bar mitzvah of my gentle Israeli cousin Giora. The ceremony was held at a small synagogue in the coastal city of Ashkelon, not far from the secular, Labor Party-supported collective farm where he was born and raised. Following the bar mitzvah, my aunt and uncle invited the immediate family to lunch at a nearby restaurant known for its hearty country-style fare. When the waitress came by to take our orders, I was anxious to see what the bar mitzvah boy would choose on this special occasion. A sirloin steak? Fried chicken heaped with french fries? Maybe a pizza with all the toppings? Giora would have none of these. He knew what he wanted, and when the waitress turned his way he did not hesitate over the menu.

"I want white steak," he declared, using the Hebrew euphemism for pork chops.

I couldn't help but chuckle. We hadn't been out of the synagogue more than fifteen minutes before the bar mitzvah boy was sinking his teeth into pig meat, strictly forbidden by Jewish dietary law. I wasn't offended. I don't keep kosher myself. I was simply struck by the irony of the moment. I thought about the meaning of Giora's pork chops for several days. They seemed to contain a larger message, and in order to decipher what it was, I consulted my own rabbi, David Hartman, founder and director of the Shalom Hartman Institute for Advanced Judaic Studies, whom I have quoted elsewhere in this book.

It is a short drive from the Ohr Somayach yeshiva to the Shalom Hartman Institute, but don't look for a shuttle bus to take you. David Hartman and Nota Schiller actually attended the same yeshiva high school in Brooklyn, Chaim Berlin. Hartman was a basketball legend in his day, and Schiller often used to watch him play. Today basketball may be all that the two of them have left in common. Although they are both Brooklyn-born, American-trained Orthodox rabbis—Hartman studied for ten years with Rabbi Joseph B. Soloveitchik, Yeshiva University's renowned Talmudist—they were attracted to Israel by radically different Jewish visions of what the place was, and should be, about. Hartman is viewed by Israel's Orthodox establishment as a dangerous radical—far more dangerous than any Reform or Conservative rabbi—because he comes out of the very heart of the Orthodox yeshiva tradition. He was a prominent Orthodox rabbi in Montreal from 1960 to 1971, during which time he also obtained a doctorate in philosophy from McGill University. He emigrated to Israel with his family in 1971 and opened a center for advanced Jewish studies, which aimed to produce a new cadre of Jewish thinkers and educators who would integrate the best of Western thought with the classical Jewish talmudic tradition. The institute attempts to discover innovative ways for Judaism to renew itself and to establish foundations for pluralism within the Jewish community and sources of tolerance among Judaism, Christianity, and Islam. The institute's motto, in effect, is: Not only must Jews physically leave the ghetto, but their whole intellectual and spiritual heritage must leave it as well.

I often discussed anomalies I came across in Israel with Hartman, so it was natural for me to go to him to make sense of Giora's pork chops. In answering my question, he laid out the vision which he, a religious Zionist, felt Israel should represent. It is a vision shared by many of those who came to Israel because they were observant Jews, but at the same time wanted to play an equal part in the secular Zionist state—without claiming to be redeeming the world.

I began our discussion by observing that Israelis were constantly telling me that in two more generations all American Jews were going to assimilate and disappear, so they had better move to Israel to save themselves as Jews. But, I wondered aloud, if emigrating to Israel means eating pork chops after bar mitzvahs, how will immigration deter assimilation?

"Let me answer your question with a question: Can you assimilate speaking Hebrew? The answer is yes," said Hartman. "In America, most Jews want to be Jewish at least three days of the year—two days on Rosh Hashanah, one on Yom Kippur; many Israelis don't even want that. The secular Zionists who founded this country were rebelling against their grandfathers and the whole universe of Eastern European ghetto Judaism. They wanted to make building the nation, serving the state, flying an Israeli flag, joining the army, and speaking Hebrew substitutes for any conventional spiritual identification. This was their Judaism. A bar mitzvah for them was not a religious affair but an expression of national affiliation—like some tribal headdress you put on—but it is an expression devoid of any Jewish religious content or significance.

"Have you ever been to a wedding at a kibbutz? Like all Israeli weddings they are officiated over by the state Orthodox rabbinate. The state sends a rabbi, and he says all the prayers and fills out all the forms, and through the whole ceremony all the guests just stand around and talk to each other, or joke or eat from the smorgasbord. There is no sense of sacredness, no sense that this is a moment for spiritual reflection. The rabbi might as well be a justice of the peace, for all the Jewish content he provides. There is a spiritual emptiness, an alienation from the Jewish tradition. If the actual Jewish content of the average Israeli's personal life were transplanted to Los Angeles, or anywhere else in the Diaspora, it would never sustain the Jewish people. What your pork-chop story shows is that no matter how we would like to project ourselves to the outside world, no matter how spiritually central we would like to feel we are for the future of Judaism, this is how most Israelis, who are nonobservant, really live. This is how many Israelis really relate to Judaism: I will go into the army. I will serve. I will make heroic sacrifices in battle. But that's it.

"The Labor Zionists built a country with a Judaic void in its heart," Hartman continued. "Ben-Gurion thought that having a Weizmann Institute of Science would sustain the excitement of the pioneer era. I have enormous respect for the creative achievements of those who built this state. The kibbutz is a marvelous experiment in social justice and communal living. The growth of Hebrew literature and culture is a profound revolution. The transformation of the Jew from student to soldier and farmer cannot be underestimated. But I deeply believe that the Jewish people cannot be sustained by literature and science alone. You can't build a Jewish state on the basis of national pride alone. The Jewish soul requires spiritual nourishment. Any political leader in Israel who thinks he will capture the imagination of the Jewish people by promising to make Israel the Silicon Valley of the Middle East is gravely mistaken. People need significance in their personal lives. They need to feel that their families and lives are built around a Judaism that can live with the modern world."

What you are saying, I remarked to Hartman, is that the secular Zionists built a nationalism without reclaiming Judaism. They simply abandoned religion to the Haredim. A friend of mine once told me about an Israeli woman she knew who lived on Kibbutz Yodfata, near Eilat, at the southern tip of the Negev Desert. After the Six-Day War, the kibbutznik took her seven-year-old daughter to Jerusalem to see the Western Wall. It was her daughter's first trip to Jerusalem. While they were standing near the wall, they were naturally surrounded by Haredim dressed in their long black coats and fur hats. This Israeli woman's daughter tugged at her mother's sleeve and exclaimed, "Look, Mom, there's a Jew." It was the first time she had ever seen a Haredi, and for her that was a real Jew.

"I'm not surprised," answered Hartman. "Ben-Gurion and the Labor Zionists thought they could build a state and turn over the question of Judaism to the last remnants of their grandfathers— to the Haredim and the Orthodox rabbinical establishment, which had the narrowest, most retrogressive Eastern European view of religion. It was like building a house and leaving a little room in the basement for Grandpa, where he can read and walk his dog and be quiet. Then one day, forty years later, Grandpa comes up from the basement, resurrected. It turns out he has not been walking his dog but has been busy having children, and he starts telling you that he wants to set the rules for the house. He wants to take over the kitchen and the bedroom and, above all, tell you how you are to use your leisure time. Because the Labor Zionists themselves had not bothered to build an interpretation of Judaism that could live with the modern world, they had no alternative spiritual vision to offer Israelis."

So Gush Emunim and the Haredim are right that draining the swamps is not enough, that carrying an Israeli passport is not enough. Many Israelis are hungry for some spiritual content. Isn't that what they are giving them?

"I may agree with some of their diagnosis about the spiritual emptiness here, but not with their prescriptions for what to do about it," said Hartman. "Gush Emunim say there is an emptiness here, so let's take a messianic trip into the future. The Haredim say there is an emptiness here, so let's not worry about the state and the national framework, let's go back to a passion we once had when we were all living like Fiddlers on the Roof in the ghettos of Eastern Europe—nice and isolated from the goyim. One offers a politics of fantasy and the other offers a politics of regression.

"What I say is, I am not living in the future, and I don't want to live in the past. I want to offer Israelis a present—a now—that gives relevance to daily life."

But how? Is there really an interpretation of Orthodox Judaism that can appeal to the many nonobservant Israelis, without losing the traditional, truly observant Jew?

"Let's start at the beginning," said Hartman. "First of all, I am a religious Zionist. What does that mean? It means I have made my commitment to live and interpret my Judaism in a state in which many Jews do not share my religious ideology. I have chosen to build my spiritual life together with Jews who totally disagree with me as to the meaning of God and what the Jewish people should be. It is not that I accept the secular person's position as equally valid to my own, but I have accepted the

permanence of our differences. I don't look at them as potential
converts waiting to be brought back to their heritage. I see them
as dignified people who have a different perception of what it
means to be a Jew. Therefore, I believe religious pluralism must
be a permanent value for Israeli society—because spiritual diversity will be forever part of the political landscape here. Furthermore, because I have chosen to place my existence within a
collective framework called the state of Israel, I have an obligation
to that framework. I have no right to say that secular women
have to serve in the army and my daughters, who are observant,
don't have to. Because what I have said is that you and I share
together in the flourishing of this political entity. I cannot live
parasitically off you. To be a religious Zionist is to share in all
aspects of this enterprise."

But how can you ask Orthodox Jews to be so tolerant of secular
Jews? Or vice versa? The Haredim say that there is only one
legitimate way of life and that is theirs.

"What I say to them is that there is a level of mutual commitment that is more important than our differences," said Hartman.
"There is a sense of my being part of a Jewish nation that comes
before my having received the Torah. My point—Soloveitchik's
point—is that we share a common Egypt. We were all together
as Jews in Egypt before Moses led us out into the desert to receive
the Torah at Mount Sinai. The Jews in Egypt were pagans. They
were not a religious community, but the sojourn in Egypt is still
an essential part of our history and memory because it was there
we became a nation. We shared a common yearning for political
freedom, we shared a common sense of suffering, we shared a
common sense of peoplehood, we shared a common political
fate—before we discussed the content of our religious community.
Never forget, Egypt precedes Sinai. Passover precedes Shavuot
[the anniversary of the giving of the Torah by God to Moses at
Mount Sinai]. The Haredim often forget this. For them the world
begins and ends with Sinai—and their own interpretation of Sinai.
It defines everything for them. When they ask, Who is my
brother? the answer is, The one who shares my covenant and
form of observance. They know Jewish law says that a nonobservant Jew is still a Jew, but they don't know how to relate to
him, because they have no concept of the Jewish people without
Sinai. My view is that first you have to become a people before

you can come to Sinai. No one would have made it to Sinai alone."
Fine, but how does this relate to Israel today?

"It means I am ready to accept that despite the diversity of religious views here, we are a nation," answered Hartman. "Now, who are the players in this nation? Who's on this team? Everyone who lined up with me in Egypt, everyone who lined up with me in Auschwitz, everyone who says, I want Jewish history to continue, no matter how vague his or her commitment or how different an interpretation he gives to that history. That's my team. I'm playing on that Jewish team. Okay, next. Now, how are we going to play the game? What are the rules going to be? That's Sinai. Sinai is where we established the rules."

But from what I have seen of Orthodox Judaism in Israel, the official interpretation of the rules doesn't mix too well with the modern world. How does your interpretation of what happened at Sinai differ from that of the Haredim or Gush Emunim?

"Let me begin by saying I believe we are still battling about what we heard at Sinai," Hartman responded. "Sinai symbolizes for me that the Jewish people have to ask content questions. Shared destiny and shared suffering and shared oppression without a content are not enough to sustain a community. That is what the secular Zionists did not understand. The secular Jews who founded the state of Israel cared only about the experience in Egypt that made us a nation, and they ignored the content offered at Sinai. For me Judaism should be a way of life not just for the individual, but should offer some deeper value guidelines for politics, economics, and social policy, and in all the issues that surface in the collective life of a nation. What does that mean? It means I have to interpret my tradition in a way which can flourish in a political sovereign state. Now what kind of state do I want? I want a political sovereign state that respects freedom of conscience. How do I know that? Does Judaism say that? Some Orthodox rabbis here say democracy is not a Jewish value. I say I don't care if Judaism says democracy is a value. This is a new political value that I have acquired. Liberty is an important political value. Autonomy and personal conscience, too, are important values which America has taught me. I see the work of our institute as trying to find ways in which classical Orthodox Judaism can absorb these new very important political values into itself without destroying itself.

"In our institute we have Christians coming to study, some of the best New Testament scholars in the world, some of the best political philosophers in the world," Hartman added. "We read each other's texts together. Why? Because I haven't got it all. I have left the ghetto. In the ghetto, I had it all, because I didn't see anything else and I didn't read anything else. When the Jews finally left the ghetto, some of them thought the goyim had it all, so they gave up their Jewish identity. My view is: Wait, I've got a home. I have an identity. I have roots. I have a family. I have a history. I have a Torah. I don't deny any of that. I love it, but my history, my family, my roots, and my Torah are not the only show in town. My Sinai is not a closed book. My Torah lives in dialogue with the world. I learn from Aristotle. I learn from Kant. I say all the wisdom of the world was not found in Sinai. Sinai is my point of departure, but I don't remain there. From Sinai I learn from the world and I absorb the world into Sinai. That is the difference between modern religious Zionists and the Haredim. They say, 'Everything is in the Torah. I have nothing to learn from the world. I live in the world, but I don't value the world. It has nothing to offer me. I don't have to rethink my position on Torah because of what Kant wrote or Kierkegaard or Freud. What do the goyim have to teach me? They are goyim.' That is not how I see it. For me Israel, and Judaism, should be the foundation from which Jews can absorb the best values of the world and learn from them—without losing their particularity. We can't afford to give the keys of our tradition to people who repudiate modernity. Otherwise the ghetto will take over Israel. You can never forget the past living in Israel. It haunts you from the ground, from every street corner. That is why if you don't reclaim your past, if you don't reinterpret it in a way that makes it compatible with the modern world, it will claim your future."

You mentioned Egypt and you mentioned Sinai, but after Sinai there was the Promised Land—Israel. What do you see as the significance of the land?

"The significance of the land is that it allows you to see Judaism as a way of life. Coming back to the land of Israel is a way of saying that Judaism was never meant to be just a synagogue-based framework, centered around prayer and the holidays, which is what some Haredim seem to feel. Judaism was to be a total way of life that could provide answers for how to deal with hospital strikes and with the exercise of power. In other words, for me, you come back to the land in order to implement Sinai. I came back to the land not to rebuild the synagogue Judaism of European ghettos. I came back to the land to get back to the beginning—Judaism as a total way of life, not just ritual."

So you see the land as a corrective to the Haredim and their obsession with ritual. But what about Gush Emunim and their mystical interpretation of the role of the land in redeeming the Jewish people and the world?

"The land, in my view, is also a corrective to Gush Emunim," said Hartman. "The land says that Judaism is not about salvation and redemption of the soul, which is central to Christianity. It is not a religion trying to get you to heaven. The land says that the crucial place you have to be is on earth. You have to build community. You have to build a reality. You have to build a national existence in the present. That is why even when we did not live in the land, the land was an important symbol. We kept on saying, 'Next year in Jerusalem,' because that was the definition of Judaism. Judaism was never supposed to turn into some sort of faith of salvation. It was always meant to be a way of life for a people. It was always a stepping-stone to today, not to another world. This is what Gush Emunim fails to understand. For them the land is a stepping-stone to redemption and a messianic kingdom, which will be run according to Torah. I say to Gush Emunim that I have no blueprint as to how the Lord is going to redeem Israel or the world. The significance of Israel is not that it is going to lead to the messianic triumph of the Jewish people in history. That is a grandiose mythology which I reject. It overblows the whole role of Israel and the Jewish people for world history.

"For me, the land, the stones, are not what will create the redemptive quality for this society," said Hartman. "The important thing is what kind of human love and what kind of daily life I live. Gush Emunim believe that if they redeem the land then God will redeem the people. My view is that you have to redeem the people, period. Where the redemption of the people will lead I don't know, but it can't be bad. I believe tomorrow will be better than today if today I treat my barber and my grocer and my taxi driver better, not because I sit on a hill in Hebron. I believe tomorrow will be better than today if I expand ethics, expand morality, expand coexistence among people of diverse

cultures, expand the quality of life—but not by expanding boundaries. I can't bring the Messiah by abusing 2 million Palestinian
Arabs today. I can't say that what I am doing now is going to
bring universal redemption. That is what Stalin said, so he killed
20 million people. All people who think they are redeeming the
world don't see the evil that they are doing every day. If your
eyes are on eternity you can be blind to the person sitting next
to you.

"Remember," concluded Hartman, "the holiness of the people
precedes the holiness of the land. There is no mystical significance
to land. There is only a significance to what human beings do.
Holiness in Judaism does not come from stones or books. It comes
from you and me and how we live here and now."

13

The Fault Line

The first thing one notices after walking across the Lebanon border into Israel is how straight everything looks. In contrast to the chaotic farm fields of Lebanon, the Israeli banana groves are planted in perfectly parallel rows, and the kibbutz family houses are built in symmetrical patterns that smoothly and gently carry the eye along. The roads are straight and the white lines down the middle all seem freshly painted. Indeed, the whole vista exudes a sense of planning and order. Even Israel's coastline looks straighter than Lebanon's.

For a while after I arrived there, Israel's straight lines fooled me. It took my eyes several months to penetrate the forest of right angles and to discover the jagged and volcanic fault line that lurked just beneath the surface of Israeli society. Whereas Lebanon was built on many different fault lines, separating the seventeen different Christian and Muslim sects that make up the country, Israel and the occupied West Bank and Gaza Strip are built over just one, which separates Israeli Jews and Palestinian

Arabs. In Lebanon, the government was constantly being shaken by tremors which exploded along its sectarian fault lines. Eventually, a tremor came along in 1975 that was powerful enough to open them all at once and send the whole country crashing into an abyss.

In Israel, the government was much stronger and more cohesive. For twenty years, from June 1967 to December 1987, the Israeli government was able to absorb all the shock waves and tremors that built up along the fault line dividing Palestinians and Jews—so much so that many Israelis, and even some Palestinians, forgot that it was even there. But living in Beirut had made me very sensitive to geological disturbances; like any earthquake survivor, I never stopped feeling them.

Whenever I told Israelis that their country reminded me of Lebanon much more than they might have thought, they bristled with indignation. "What are you talking about," a prominent Hadassah Hospital neurologist sputtered at me when I made such a comparison at a Jerusalem dinner party. "Civil war in Jerusalem? Gaza is like Beirut? You have spent too much time in Lebanon."

Indeed I had.

On Friday, November 6, 1987, the *Jerusalem Post* ran the following item about the Palestinian owner of the Dallas restaurant in East Jerusalem, one of the city's more popular purveyors of Arabic food:

"If Mohammed Hussein has his way, observant Jews may soon be able to grab a bite in [Arab] East Jerusalem. Last month Hussein applied to the local religious council to receive a kashrut certificate for his restaurant Dallas . . . in the heart of the city's main Arab shopping district. According to Hussein, there is a great demand for a kosher restaurant in East Jerusalem. 'Jews come here all the time and ask if we have a certificate,' he said. Hussein believes that the restaurant—a stone's throw from Salah e-Din Street, the courts, and the Justice Ministry—will attract a kashrut-observing clientele. A religious Muslim, Hussein understands the burden of dietary restrictions: 'I look at this as a chance to help people observe their religion.' "

Mohammed Hussein's plans to make his Arabic restaurant kosher were not the mad antics of an isolated Palestinian quisling trying to curry favor with his occupiers. To the contrary, they were emblematic of the extent to which Israelis and Palestinians from the occupied West Bank and Gaza Strip were inexorably melding together into a single binational society during the twenty years that followed the 1967 war.

From their side, the Israelis integrated the West Bank and Gaza Strip into their own systems of municipal government, zoning, town planning, road signs, and transportation. When you drove from pre-1967 Israel into the West Bank, there was no WELCOME TO THE WEST BANK sign to tell you where you were, and there was no change in the road or physical scenery. The two regions blended together in a way that was seamless, which explains why Israelis who grew up after 1967 often don't have a clue where the border runs and would be hard-pressed to draw the outlines of the West Bank on a map. By the late 1980s some 70,000 Israelis had moved into towns and settlements in the West Bank (not including East Jerusalem). Most of them were not gun-toting religious zealots in search of the Messiah but Israeli yuppies in search of a house with a yard and armed with nothing more dangerous than briefcases stuffed with the commuting schedules to Tel Aviv and Jerusalem. Indeed, roughly 85 percent of the Jewish settlers living in the occupied territories today reside in ten urban centers within a 30-minute commute of Tel Aviv or Jerusalem. Maybe that was why few Israelis seemed to take notice when a Hebrew version of Monopoly was issued in which players could buy houses and hotels in the West Bank towns of Hebron, Bethlehem, and Nablus as easily as in Haifa and Tel Aviv.

Shopping for bargains in Arab villages and markets on Saturday became a weekly routine for many Israelis. In fact, I knew a very senior Israeli military intelligence officer who told me that every Sunday, after giving a top-secret briefing to the Israeli Cabinet on the week's intelligence developments, he would drive directly from the Prime Minister's office to his favorite Arabic restaurant in the West Bank town of Bethlehem to sate his appetite for grilled lamb and Arabic salads.

But while all the world seemed to be focusing on how Israel was sinking roots into the occupied West Bank and Gaza Strip, few paid attention to how much the Palestinians living in these areas were sinking their own roots—voluntarily and unconsciously—into Israeli society. No one observed this process of Palestinian integration with more insight and honesty than Palestinian philosopher Sari Nusseibeh, who teaches at the West Bank's Bir Zeit University. The son of a prominent Palestinian politician, Anwar Nusseibeh, Sari, now in his late thirties, was born and raised in Jerusalem in the days before 1967, when it was under Jordanian control, and he watched every step of the way as his Palestinian compatriots slowly became "Israelified."

"It all began with an Egged bus," said Sari, referring to the Israeli national bus cooperative. "After the 1967 war, Palestinians would not get near an Egged bus. It looked like a terrifying monster from outer space, transporting aliens from one foreign place to another. Some people said we should never ride the Israeli buses because it would be recognizing the Israeli occupation. But slowly, Palestinians started using the Egged buses; they figured out where they were going and where they were coming from. The Israeli system is the Egged bus, and we have learned to use it."

The Palestinians felt they had no choice: either they learned to ride the Egged buses and did business with the Israelis on Israeli terms or they resisted and didn't eat. Israel controlled all the means for importing raw materials and exporting finished products and would not allow them to develop their own industrial infrastructure that might compete with the Israeli economy or serve as the basis for an independent state. The Israelis did, however, encourage Palestinians to work as laborers in Israel, to trade with the Israeli economy, and to export their surplus agriculture to Jordan. In this way, Israel hoped that the Palestinians would prosper as individuals but remain impoverished as a community. The Palestinians chose to play the game by Israel's rules, while all the time denouncing the Israeli occupation. It was their version of moral double bookkeeping and it enabled them to survive, and in some cases thrive, without feeling they had abandoned their claims to independence.

Observed Nusseibeh: "If you look at our workers and trade over the past twenty years, you'd have to say that the salient feature was how we integrated and assimilated into Israel. We were, in a word, coopted, and our whole economic well-being and existence became parasitic on our being coopted. Whatever form of Palestinian activity you saw, it required some kind of assent from the Israeli authorities and we, ourselves, went out and got it. Although as individuals we talked about Palestinian independence and uniqueness, as a community we behaved just the opposite."

Indeed, by the late 1980s roughly 120,000 Palestinians living in the West Bank and the Gaza Strip would wake up each morning and drink their Israeli-made Tnuva milk and Israeli Elite coffee, slip on their Israeli-made jeans, tuck their Israeli-issued identity cards in their back pockets, hop into a pickup truck belonging to an Israeli contractor, factory owner, or shopkeeper, and spend their day working in an Israeli town and speaking Hebrew. Later on, these same Palestinian workers would pay their income taxes to the Israeli government, maybe bribe an Israeli official for a building permit, read their Israeli-censored Arabic newspaper, and then drive to the airport with their Israeli-issued licenses to fly abroad on their Israeli-issued travel documents. While the parents were abroad, their children would use Israeli Tambour paint to spray anti-Israeli graffiti on the walls outside their homes. After sunset, some Palestinians, bought and paid for by the Israeli Shin Bet domestic intelligence agency, would inform on their neighbors. The next morning they would rise again at dawn to build with their own backs every Israeli settlement in the West Bank and Gaza Strip. In some cases, Palestinians even worked on settlements that were built on their own confiscated land.

In the Old City of Jerusalem, in Bethlehem and in Jericho, Palestinian merchants would sell yarmulkes, menorahs, "I Love Israel" T-shirts and other Jewish items—most of them made by Palestinian labor—right alongside kaffiyehs and Korans and other traditional Arabic souvenirs. A Palestinian-owned pasta factory in the village of Beit Sahur, a tahini factory in Nablus, and an RC Cola factory in Ramallah were among the dozens of Palestinian food manufacturers which arranged to receive kosher certification from rabbis hired from adjacent Jewish settlements; it was their only way of gaining access to the lucrative Israeli market. By 1987, some 800 West Bank and Gaza Palestinians who had worked officially in Israel for more than ten years, and then turned sixty-five, were receiving old-age pensions from the Jewish state they did not recognize.

I was once visiting Rabbi Jonathan Blass and his wife, Shifra, two Jewish settlers who live with their children in the West Bank

Jewish settlement of Neve Tzuf, about twenty miles north of Jerusalem. In the course of interviewing them about life on their settlement, they mentioned with pride the fact that their fourteen-year-old son, Shlomo, had gone into business with the son of the muezzin of the neighboring Palestinian Arab village of Deir Nizam. (The muezzin is the Muslim cleric who traditionally calls other Muslims to prayer five times daily from atop the mosque's minaret.)

And what did they do together?

"They make yarmulkes," said Mrs. Blass. "Well, not exactly. The muezzin's son has a group of women working for him in the village and they knit the yarmulkes. Shlomo, our son, gets them the orders and sells them. Many of the yarmulkes worn by Gush Emunim settlers were sewn by the women of Deir Nizam. They just exported a shipment of five hundred to a group of observant Jews in South Africa. The muezzin's son gets the patterns to sew on them from a book that we gave him that was put out by B'nai Akiva [the religious Zionist youth movement]. He knows the colors and the styles that the different groups of Jews like to wear. He makes a beautiful one with the skyline of Jerusalem sewn on it. He does Hebrew letters, too—whatever you want."

The Palestinians did such a brisk commerce under the ever-vigilant eye of the Israeli tax collectors that Israel started to make a profit from occupying them. A study done by the West Bank Data Base Project, an independent research organization focused on the occupied territories and headed by former Jerusalem Deputy Mayor Meron Benvenisti, concluded that "the occupied territories never constituted a fiscal burden on the Israeli treasury. On the contrary, the Palestinian population contributed large sums to the Israeli public consumption." According to Benvenisti's study, the Israeli government raised tax revenues from West Bankers and Gazans through two means. One was by local income, property, and value-added taxes collected in the occupied territories. These funds were used to support the Israeli military administration and its capital expenditures on roads, hospitals, and municipal infrastructure in the West Bank and Gaza. The other was through value-added taxes on goods purchased by Palestinians while in Israel, as well as excise taxes, import duties, and payroll deductions. Any West Banker or Gazan who worked officially in Israel had about 20 percent of his salary withheld to cover National Insurance payments. But since most of the insurance benefits were applicable only to Israelis, the Palestinian contributions were transferred directly to the state treasury. Some of these funds went to make up the deficit between the cost of the Israeli occupation and the amount of taxes collected locally from Palestinians. What was left over—roughly $500 million during the first twenty years of the occupation, according to Benvenisti—was used by Israel for its own development.

At the same time, the Palestinians—as a community—were so well behaved under the Israeli occupation that between 1967 and 1987 Israel had to deploy only about 1,200 soldiers a day, along with a few hundred Israeli Druse Border Police and a few hundred Shin Bet agents, to control all 1.7 million Palestinian inhabitants of the West Bank and Gaza Strip. Israel maintained its occupation so cheaply and efficiently by using a network of contact points to which they got the Palestinians to voluntarily submit, hence little brute force or manpower was required to keep them in line.

"For 95 percent of these contact points to be effective in controlling the Palestinians they required our consent and cooperation," said Nusseibeh. "For example, you were sent an order telling you to come to the military governor's office in Beth El, and you knew that they were going to arrest you, yet you came anyway, on your own, instead of just ignoring the order and forcing the Israelis to send a whole army unit to your village to get you. You were told you needed a building permit to add a wing to your house. Instead of just building the wing and ignoring the Israelis, most people went down and waited in line for a permit, without anyone holding a gun to their heads. The same was true with press censorship. Even the most radical Palestinian papers went to the Israeli censor every day. We were once sent an order to close Bir Zeit University. We read about it in the newspaper, and instead of everyone turning out at the university and challenging the Israelis to throw them out, we all just sat home. The symbol of the Palestinian acquiescence to the Israeli occupation was our willingness to hold [Israeli-issued] identity cards. The Israeli ID was the cornerstone of the occupation. It told the Israelis where you were from and who your family was and where they could find you. The Israelis set things up so that we could not travel, drive, trade, import, or go to a hospital without presenting our ID card, and we cooperated. I would say that only 5 percent of the Israeli occupation involved brute force—Israeli troops physically forcing Palestinians to comply with some order or regulation. Ninety-five percent of the time we did it ourselves."

While the Palestinians in the West Bank and Gaza constantly complained about the symptoms of the Israeli occupation—the land confiscations, the arbitrary arrests, the house demolitions, and the curfews—as a community they did very little to undermine the system of occupation. There would be an occasional strike or demonstration by lawyers or students—those highly politicized elements of the society—and an occasional casualty from a confrontation with Israeli troops, but rarely anything sustained or widespread. Mass civil disobedience that would have shaken the system of occupation was constantly discussed in the PLO literature that was distributed throughout the occupied territories in the 1970s and '80s, but it was virtually never implemented. When in 1980 the military government issued Order 854, which would have put all the university curricula and teaching under the authority of the Israeli army, the Palestinian universities and students banded together and rejected it; eventually the Israelis backed down. That was real communal resistance, but it was the exception, not the rule.

Why didn't the Palestinians get themselves organized, resist more as a community, and disengage from the Israeli system? To begin with, they had no stable independent economic base to fall back on and they were not willing to endure the economic and personal hardships that mass civil disobedience on the scale required to really bring pressure on Israel would have entailed. Second, Israel used its military power and its Shin Bet domestic intelligence service to disrupt any Palestinian attempts at mass organization and to arrest any Palestinian who remotely behaved like a local leader; Israel would tolerate Palestinian spokesmen, but any spokesman who got more than three people to follow him was eventually arrested, expelled, or harassed into submission. Third, with the PLO guerrilla leadership in Beirut, and later Tunis, claiming to have responsibility for confronting Israel and making all political decisions, it became very convenient for the Palestinians in the West Bank and Gaza Strip to accommodate

themselves to the Israeli system, even profit from it, while declaring that liberation was the PLO's responsibility. Whenever I
would ask West Bankers when their liberation would start to
become their own responsibility, they never really had a convincing answer.

Fourth, as in Lebanon, Palestinian society was riven with ethnic, clan, sectarian, and regional divisions, which always made
concerted popular action difficult to organize. Palestinian Christians suspected Palestinian Muslims, Muslim fundamentalists suspected Communists, pro-Jordanians suspected pro-PLOniks,
Hebronites suspected Jerusalemites, the members of one extended family in a village refused to cooperate with those of
another. These rivalries also explain why the Shin Bet never had
any problem recruiting what they called "Shtinkers"—Palestinian
informers who kept them abreast of who was saying what to
whom in every village and refugee camp in the West Bank and
Gaza Strip.

Finally, the Palestinians in the West Bank and Gaza had so
convinced themselves that the Israeli occupation was being carried
out by brute force—and not by their consent and cooperation—
that they did not believe they had within themselves the power
to challenge the Israeli system. Clinton Bailey, the Tel Aviv University Bedouin expert, once told me of a conversation he had
had with a Palestinian merchant he knew in the Old City of
Jerusalem that vividly underscored this self-imposed Palestinian
impotence.

"I had gone to the Old City to buy a present, and I went to a
shop on David Street," said Bailey. "It is owned by a Palestinian
merchant in his thirties, a very gregarious and charismatic fellow
who was always dressed in modern jeans and always flirted with
the girls who went by. So he invited me to have tea with him,
and as we sat down I asked him what was happening in his life.
He said, 'Well, I am a Hajji now.' " (A Hajji is the honorific title
bestowed on any Muslim who goes on the pilgrimage to Mecca,
which is known in Arabic as the Hajj.)

"So I asked him, 'When did you go?' and he said, 'Just this
last summer [1987].' So I said, 'You must have been there when
the big clash took place between the Saudis and the Iranian
pilgrims.' "

(In August 1987, Saudi troops shot and killed some 400 Iranian pilgrims after the Iranians, according to the Saudis, began to riot while making the pilgrimage to Mecca. The Iranians, however, said the Saudi attack was unprovoked.)

The Palestinian shopkeeper answered, "Yes, I was there. I saw the whole thing. My hostel was right on the corner in Mecca where the clash happened."

Bailey then asked him who was telling the truth about what happened, the Saudis or the Iranians. The shopkeeper, according to Bailey, answered with a real air of contempt: "The Iranians, of course. Don't talk to me about the Arabs. The Arabs are shit. We would sell our own mothers. The Saudis ambushed the Iranians without warning. They shot and killed a lot of people, and many others were wounded. But I tell you, none of the Iranians cried. I went down to the street to help people and I wanted to help this Iranian woman who was wounded and to move her out of the sun. She said, 'No no, take your hands off me. It is *haram* [forbidden] for a man to touch a woman.' I told her she would die, and she just said, 'Take your hands off me.' I saw this Saudi policeman come up to this old man and ask him, 'Are you an Iranian or a Turk?' And this man knew that if he said Iranian the policeman would beat him, but he said it anyway. The policeman beat him all over until he bled—but he didn't cry.

"Every story he told me ended with the same line—'but they didn't cry,' " recalled Bailey. "He was in awe of their courage, because I think it was in such contrast to that of his own people. The Shiites in Lebanon, the Afghans, everybody else was out there ready to pay a price for their freedom, but not them, not the West Bankers."

Instead of organizing real and significant communal resistance on their own, some of the most articulate Palestinian leaders and community spokesmen in the West Bank and Gaza became professional complainers, ready to be interviewed at any hour of the day on American television about their suffering under the "brutal" Israelis.

Jonathan Broder, a colleague of mine, was an Associated Press reporter in January 1970, when former British Foreign Secretary George Brown visited Israel and the West Bank as a guest of Israeli statesman Yigal Allon. As part of his visit, Brown went to Nablus and was received there by the mayor, Hamdi Qana'an, who came from the one of the wealthiest merchant families in the West Bank—a fact attested to by his huge stomach.

"Before their talks began," Broder told me, "Brown and Hamdi sat side by side on this ornate couch for a photo opportunity. But Hamdi couldn't wait to launch into the Palestinian 'lament.' So while we were all standing around them, Hamdi started to say to Brown, 'You know, the Israelis, they are breaking our bones, they are stealing our land, they are beating our children, they are taking the food from our mouths.' With that last line Brown couldn't take it anymore. So he looked over at Hamdi, whacked his big fat belly with the back of his hand, and said in this heavy British accent, 'You don't seem to be doing too badly for yourself, old chap.' At which point we were all ushered out of the room."

A reserve [Israeli] army unit stationed in Ramallah spent several days chasing down and shooting at kites decorated with the colors of the PLO flag. The "dangerous" kites were caught by the soldiers, taken away from the children, and burned.

—from Israel's *Ha'aretz* newspaper,
August 25, 1985

One of the most popular fads among West Bank Palestinian youths in the early 1980s was to wear T-shirts emblazoned with the words *I Love Palestine* over an olive tree. They would usually wear them, though, under their regular shirts, so the Israeli soldiers couldn't see them. If Israeli soldiers caught Palestinians dressed in such attire, they were under orders to strip them and then arrest them. I always wondered what the charge would be. Inflammatory underwear? Seditious skivvies? This Israeli crackdown on T-shirt terrorism only served to produce some imaginative alternative tactics by the Palestinians. One favorite ploy was to lasso the tops of small supple trees, tie a red, white, green, and black Palestinian flag to the treetop, and then let the tree spring back up, leaving it for Israeli soldiers to figure out how to get the flag down. Usually the Israelis just took an ax and chopped down the whole tree. In recent years it was hard to find a laundry line in the West Bank or Gaza Strip that did not have some item of clothing hanging on it in the colors of the Palestinian flag, and few Palestinian youths did not own at least one scarf, key chain, necklace, or bracelet in the shape or colors of Palestine that was made in a secret underground factory.

This was no idle West Bank fad that would fade away after a season, to be replaced by mini-skirts and pet rocks. Rather, it was an expression of a process of Palestinian nation-building and identity-building, which took place as a direct result of the Israeli occupation which began in 1967. Men are as often defined by their enemies as by themselves and this was particularly true of the Palestinians in the West Bank and Gaza.

How so? It must be remembered that after 1948 Palestine was broken up into three different pieces—one chunk had been taken over by the Jews, another chunk in the Gaza Strip had been seized by the Egyptians, and a third chunk, the West Bank, had been carried off by the Jordanians. Palestine as a geographical entity was done for, which was one reason the whole Palestine question went into remission between 1948 and 1967. After all, an evicted people might be able to get its land back from one nation, but not from three. Paradoxically, Israel's occupation of the West Bank and Gaza in 1967 put Palestine back together again as a geographical entity and put the Palestinians from the West Bank, Gaza, and Israel back together again as a single community. As a result, the whole Palestine issue came back to life: once again the exact same communities—Jews and Palestinian Arabs—were fighting over the exact same territory—British Mandatory Palestine—that their forefathers had fought over twenty years earlier. The only difference was that the British were not around anymore to oversee things; the Jews were now in charge.

At the same time that Israel's victory in 1967 enabled the Palestine issue to be reborn, it also created the conditions for a rebirth of Palestinian identity as well. The process began with the young generation of Palestinians who came of age after the 1967 war and spread upward to their parents. The older generation of Palestinians grew up between 1948 and 1967 when the West Bank was under Jordanian rule and the Gaza Strip was under Egyptian rule. Because Egyptian and Jordanian cultures were in many ways similar to that of the Palestinian Arabs, the older generation did not feel compelled to constantly assert their uniquely Palestinian identities—not politically and not culturally. In fact, many members of the older generation of West Bankers and Gazans actually became "Jordanized" or "Egyptianized" between 1948 and 1967. Since Jordan granted Palestinians citizenship (Egypt did not) many Palestinians of this pre-1967 generation came to look upon the Bedouin King Hussein as their leader more than any Palestinian.

But the Palestinian youths from the West Bank and Gaza Strip who were born under Israeli occupation had their identities shaped in an entirely different atmosphere. They never had the chance to inherit the world of their fathers. Jordan was not around when they came of age in the West Bank, or Egypt in the Gaza Strip. Israel had supplanted both and had brought with it its own unique blend of Western and Hebrew culture, which was not an option for Palestinians growing up in the occupied territories in the way Egyptian or Jordanian culture had been an option for their parents. To the contrary, these youths despised the Israelis and wanted to emphasize how different they were from them. Since Jordanian or Egyptian identities were no longer available, it was natural for Palestinians to fall back on their own roots and to emphasize more than ever before their uniquely Palestinian political and cultural heritage.

It would not be an exaggeration to say that it took the pressure of a truly foreign, non-Arab community like Israel to provoke Palestinians in the West Bank and Gaza into fully asserting their own distinctive identities. Munir Fasheh, the dean of students at Bir Zeit University, who grew up in the West Bank when it was under Jordanian control and continued to live there after it fell to Israel, once remarked to me that "between 1947 and 1967 whenever anyone asked me what I was, I always hesitated. Legally I was Jordanian, but emotionally I was Palestinian. Now there is no kid on the West Bank under the age of twenty-five who has ever experienced anything other than being a Palestinian. When you consider that 60 percent of the West Bank population is under the age of twenty, it means that for three-quarters of them Jordan is something that doesn't exist."

At the same time, it took a Western-style democracy such as Israel to allow Palestinians the liberty to establish ostensibly non-political trade unions, universities, newspapers, theater groups, and other cultural associations—with a level of free expression that while not equal to that of Israelis was far greater than anything Palestinians had ever enjoyed in Jordan or Egypt. Yasir Arafat's picture and name probably appeared in the Israeli-censored Palestinian Arabic press in East Jerusalem more frequently than it ever did in Amman. These Palestinian cultural institutions became the vessel and rudimentary framework for their national aspirations.

As I noted earlier in my Beirut journey, the 1967 war also created the conditions for those Palestinian refugees living outside the area of Palestine—in Lebanon, Jordan, and Syria—to be transformed from poor forlorn refugees into a political force. In the wake of the '67 defeat, the Arab regimes for the first time allowed the Palestinian refugees to take control of their own destiny after having monopolized the Palestinian cause and made it an exclusively pan-Arab issue between the years 1948 and 1967. Having been vanquished by Israel, the Arab regimes needed some time to regroup, and while they did, they gave the Palestinians and the PLO free rein to carry on the war with Israel. It was this opening, this emancipation, which Arafat and his PLO exploited to the fullest.

In short, the biggest victors of the 1967 war turned out to be the Palestinians, both the refugees outside and the West Bankers and Gazans inside. But while these two different Palestinian communities shared the same objectives, they developed along very different, parallel tracks. Instead of being shaped by Israel, the PLO and its followers in Beirut were highly influenced by inter-Arab politics, Lebanon, and the whole late 1960s revolutionary mood. Arafat and the PLO came on the scene at the same time as students in Paris were manning the barricades and the Vietcong were challenging the American superpower.

The West Bankers and Gazans, however, were shaped by a very different history and in a very different furnace. To begin with, because they were confronted with Israeli culture, which they could not and did not want to be a part of, they became more and more Palestinian in their minds and in their communal institutions. But because Israel absorbed the West Bank and the Gaza Strip, and because many Palestinians living there physically assimilated into the Israeli system for economic reasons, they became less and less Palestinian in their bodies. This put them into an identity bind. From the head upward they swore allegiance to Yasir Arafat, and from the shoulders downward they paid allegiance to the Prime Minister of Israel. The T-shirts Palestinians from the West Bank and Gaza wore under their sweaters, the Palestinian calendars they put on their desks, and the key chains they hid in their pockets were not meant for the Israelis; they were meant for themselves. They were their own identity cards, issued by themselves to themselves—the tangible proof that they really were Palestinians, as their minds declared, and not Israelis, as their bodies seemed to suggest.

I first detected this identity bind listening to Palestinians living in the occupied territories talk about how they no longer felt at home in their own houses and their own villages—even though they were feeling more and more Palestinian in their heads. Sometimes, Palestinians would say, it was just the little things that made them feel not at home—like dialing a number somewhere in Israel or the West Bank and getting a recording in Hebrew, which they could not understand. Sometimes it was the road signs, with Hebrew and English letters spelling out place names, sandwiching the smaller Arabic in between. In Ramallah, an exclusively Arab town north of Jerusalem, for example, the local Israeli police station sign spells out "Police" in Hebrew and English, but not in Arabic—as if police protection were not something meant for Palestinians. Sometimes it was the little indignities. A Palestinian teenager in the Kalandia refugee camp outside Jerusalem told me how one hot summer day the residents of his camp were on a political strike. That afternoon, he said, an Israeli soldier stopped him, took away his watch and his bicycle, and told him he would not get either of them back until he got a shopkeeper to open and give the soldier and his unit some ice cream. And sometimes it was the big things: the insecurity of never knowing when your land might be confiscated—Israel has seized or restricted use of more than 50 percent of the land in the West Bank and 30 percent of the Gaza Strip since 1967—or not knowing when your son might be arrested in a security sweep after a bombing, or when your father might be slapped before your eyes for saying the wrong thing to an Israeli soldier at a checkpoint.

I was once interviewing an Israeli infantry soldier, Moshe Shukun, about his work in the Gaza Strip. He said the strangest missions he had to go on were always those that involved arresting Palestinians in their beds at night—which is standard Israeli procedure, since that is when they have the best chance of finding someone home.

"When we go into homes, we surprise people at night," Shukun explained to me. "Sometimes you burst in at delicate times. One time we came in on this couple in Gaza and it was either just before or just after—ah well, you know. And this Palestinian woman was wearing a very see-through nightgown. I mean it was something that did not leave anything to the imagination, and this lady was beautiful. And there we were—four guys with machine guns pointed at her husband. He got out of bed and asked us if he could go out back to take a piss. So we said okay, and then the four of us just stood there watching over this girl with our guns pointed at her. I have to tell you, they had to practically drag us out of there."

Listening to this story, I could not help but wonder how terrifying, not to mention humiliating, it must have been for that Palestinian man and woman—guilty or not—to have had their most private sanctum and moment violated in such a way.

Not surprisingly, for many young West Bank Palestinians "home" has become the most frightening place in the world. Mohammed Ishteyyeh, a short, curly-haired, Bir Zeit University political-science graduate in his early thirties, came from a village near Nablus and had been arrested at home three times for political agitation. Home is not where his heart is any longer.

"I don't feel at home when I am at home," Ishteyyeh told me. "Actually, my family's home is the most dangerous place for me, because that is the address where the Israelis will come to find me. When the Israelis came to arrest me in 1979, it was at night and the dogs in the village started barking. Ever since then, I hate that sound. When I am at home and the dogs bark at night, I spend hours sitting in front of the window watching who is coming. I wish the daylight could be for twenty-four hours. I don't feel comfortable sleeping in my own bed. I always sleep better out of the country. It is really sad for my mother. When I am home she is afraid. But when I am not home, she wants me there."

Johar Assi, a twenty-five-year-old Palestinian from a village near Ramallah, whom I met while interviewing Palestinian inmates at Israel's Dahariya prison near Hebron, took me by surprise when I asked him whether he was anxious to get out and return home.

"How can I feel at home?" he growled, "when I have five uncles in Jordan who are not allowed to travel here. When I am in my village I am afraid to go for a walk outside the village because I might run into an Israeli soldier who will ask me for my ID card and want to know where I work and then tell me to come to the military headquarters tomorrow so they can try to talk me into being a collaborator. If I go for a walk in the village and someone sees Johar talking quietly to Mohammed, there will always be some informer around who will tell the Israelis, and a week later I will get called in by the army and they will say, 'Why were you and Mohammed whispering to each other last week?' So I just keep to myself and to my house and talk a lot to my father."

But Israelis didn't only make it so Palestinians didn't feel at home in the West Bank and Gaza; they made it so that at times the Palestinians didn't feel at home in their own skin—even when they were far away from Israel. As I noted earlier, the PLO, in order to grab the attention of the world when it emerged in the late 1960s, engaged in some spectacular acts of terrorism and airplane hijacking. This gave the Israelis an opportunity to brand the entire Palestinian national movement and cause as a criminal "terrorist" phenomenon. Eventually, the two words "Palestinian" and "terrorist" became fused together in the minds of people the world over. Although 99 percent of the Palestinian people have never been involved in terrorist activity, this label—"terrorist"—became a heavy cross they all had to bear wherever they traveled.

Its weight was felt the minute the immigration officer, the customs inspector, the airline official, or the hotel clerk looked at their travel document: the black ink said only *Palestinian* under nationality, but the invisible ink said *terrorist*. The reading of it was often followed by a suspicious stare and then the words "Could you please step over here." I came to appreciate how upsetting this could be when a Palestinian friend, Jameel Hamad, a prominent West Bank journalist from Bethlehem, told me of the bitter end to a journey he had made to the United States.

"I was in Frankfurt Airport, coming home from New York,"

said Hamad, who, with his neatly trimmed mustache, glasses, and salt-and-pepper hair, looks more like a grocer without his apron than a potential hijacker. "I was in transit to Tel Aviv. After I went through security in New York, they checked my bags all the way through to Tel Aviv. When I went up to the Lufthansa gate in Frankfurt to get on the flight to Tel Aviv, they asked for my ticket and passport. I was traveling on an Israeli Laissez Passer [a special travel document Israel issues for Palestinian refugees]. The man at the gate said to me, 'You are flying to Tel Aviv?' I said, 'Yes.' So he said, 'Where are you coming from?' I said, 'New York.' Then he said, 'Where are your bags?' I said, 'I already checked them through in New York.' He said, 'Please stand over here.' They let all the passengers get on the airplane. Then they took me outside to the runway. They took all the luggage off the plane, and I was asked to identify my bags. All the passengers were sitting on the plane watching me out the window. It took about an hour for them to get all the bags off and for me to find mine. Then they took me to a room and told me to take all my clothes off—everything. They checked my groin area even—everything. Then they finally let me on the plane. The people had been waiting inside for ninety minutes, so they were really angry with me. I said to the people seated around me, 'Ladies and gentlemen, I am very sorry. I wasn't in the bar, I wasn't getting drunk; my problem was very simple: I am a Palestinian.' "

How did you feel at that moment? I asked.

"I have never felt like such a stranger, like such an outsider before," Hamad said through clenched teeth. "I was just not part of the symphony. I was mad at everyone, the whole world. At that moment, if I had had a bomb, I would have dropped it on the world."

I was invited for lunch one afternoon at the Islamic University of Gaza, an austere complex of low-slung buildings in the heart of the Israeli-occupied Gaza Strip, but the setting proved far more interesting than the meal. The only decorations on the peeling walls of the university consisted of a few framed Koranic verses, written in a flowing Arabesque script. But in the student cafeteria, on the north wall, hung a huge photograph, maybe fifteen feet

high by twenty feet long, of what appeared to be Waikiki Beach
in Hawaii, replete with palm trees, white sand, a clear blue sky,
and a calm azure ocean.

"What is that doing there?" I asked my Palestinian hosts.

"We wanted to make some kind of compensation for students,"
explained Dean of Students Atif Radwan. "They are surrounded
by miserable scenes all day long. It is important that when they
eat they see something beautiful."

Murals of Waikiki or Swiss mountain panoramas can be found
almost as frequently as Koranic verses in Palestinian homes in
the West Bank. These calendar scenes always struck me as substitute windows on the world for Palestinians; since the Israeli
world enveloping them only left them feeling like strangers in
their own land, they imported their own panoramas—with land-
scapes empty of Jews, unthreatening, soothing, and, most important, mute. For the Israeli shadow that followed Palestinians
wherever they went was a shadow with a voice, and the voice
kept whispering in every Palestinian's ear, "It's not yours. Palestine is not yours. It's ours."

Try as they might, though, most Palestinians could not shut out
that whispering Israeli shadow for long. Sooner or later it came
in through the door or in a window or over the phone. This
produced a Palestinian rage, which built in intensity with each
year of the Israeli occupation. It was enraging to Palestinians that
just at the moment when their Palestinian identities were crys-
tallizing and being recognized as never before on the world stage,
they could not fully express them politically or culturally. That
Palestinian rage formed like pockets of geothermal steam beneath
the crust of Israeli society.

In Jerusalem, you could see that steam rising each day around
5:30 a.m. in what became known as the human "meat market."
Just as the sun would curl up over the mountains of Moab to the
east, Palestinian workers would begin their morning ritual. Some
of them, still bleary-eyed from having left their West Bank villages
as early as 4:00 a.m., would line up on the sidewalk leading out
from the Damascus Gate of the Old City, clutching their lunch
bags in one hand and warming their lungs with cheap cigarettes
in the other. There they would stand for hours in front of the Ali
Baba Hotel, forming a human labor pool, waiting for Israeli build-
ers and other employers to drive by, look them over, and pluck

out the lucky ones for a day's work. One morning I got up and joined them.

An Israeli contractor in a green Volvo was the first to cruise up. His car drew a dozen Palestinian workers off the sidewalk, each elbowing the other for the chance to cram his head into the open front windows. The contractor got nervous. He did not like being surrounded.

"How much? How much?" the workers shouted at the Israeli.

"Twenty-five shekels [$14.50] for the day," he answered in Arabic, holding a walkie-talkie in one hand.

"What is the work?" the men asked.

"Asphalting," said the contractor.

For twenty-five shekels there were few takers. Most of the men had come by bus or taxi from Hebron, which cost them around $5.00 round-trip, so they just shook their heads silently and walked away; but a few young ones hopped into the back seat. The contractor sped off. Then a mini-van approached, the driver slowed down, the workers swarmed toward his vehicle, but the driver suddenly bolted away. As he peeled off, one of the Palestinians spit at the van.

How do you decide who gets the work when it is offered? I asked Mohammed, a forty-year-old father of ten from Yatta, a village near Hebron. "We just attack the car," he explained. "Whoever gets there first wins. It is like fifty dogs chasing a bone. I would work in Hebron for half the price, but there is no work there."

I asked a group of teenage boys milling around whether any of them had helped to build Jewish settlements in the West Bank.

"You don't go to your own funeral," said one, explaining why he would never do such a thing. But most of his friends silently nodded their heads yes.

"Don't you think we know we are helping them build their state?" said Muhammad Nawaf, a twenty-four-year-old Bethlehem University student, who was quick to show me the bit of finger he lost on the job in Israel.

"I helped build Efrat," he added matter-of-factly, referring to the Jewish settlement near Bethlehem. "It is a real humiliation. Neither side is happy with you, and you know you are doing something against your own people, but you need the food."

Someone in the back shouted, "Let Arafat do something for us and we would not need to work for the Jews."

The discussion was cut short by another car driving up, offering work for the day, and, as always, while their mouths spoke of their own dignity and pain, their bodies responded otherwise. The car drew them all away from me like metal filings to a magnet.

It is not easy to have one's soul be the rope in a tug-of-war between body and mind. It can be excruciatingly painful. Abu Laila taught me that. A twenty-one-year-old Palestinian with a black mop of hair whom I got to know in the Kalandia refugee camp north of Jerusalem, Abu Laila had been in and out of Israeli jails since he was first arrested at age fourteen for membership in a pro-Arafat youth group. Abu Laila, "Father of Night," was his nom de guerre; he never told me his real name. After Abu Laila left school in 1982, whenever he wasn't in an Israeli prison, he found himself looking for work in Israeli towns. His double life epitomized for me the Palestinian men of his generation—militant Palestinian activist by night, Israeli coolie by day.

"I got my first job in Israel in 1982 right after the Israelis invaded Lebanon," Abu Laila told me one night as I sat around a living room in Kalandia with him and some friends. "It was in the Mahne Yehuda market in Jerusalem. I would carry vegetables around. The only reason I got the job was that the Israelis had all gone into the army. I knew I was working in the place of soldiers who were killing my brothers in Beirut, but I had no choice. What could I do? I needed the money. Some days we would be driving around in trucks picking up vegetables and the radio would be on in Hebrew and they would be saying the Israeli army entered here and entered there and entered and entered and entered, and all the time I would feel smaller and smaller and smaller."

The West Bank and Gaza Palestinians were never the most brutalized Arabs in the Middle East—the Israeli occupation was mild compared to some other regimes in the area. They were, however, the most humiliated.

Around noon on December 18, 1986, in the predominantly Christian West Bank town of Ramallah, a sixteen-year-old Palestinian schoolboy walked innocently toward an Israeli soldier patrolling the busy Manara traffic circle in the center of the city.

The Israeli soldier was in full battle dress, armed with a Galili assault rifle, several grenades, and a knife. The Palestinian teen-ager was carrying a blue school bag, the kind normally used to transport books. As the youth approached the Israeli soldier, he reached into his school bag, pulled out an ax, shouted something about Palestine, and began hacking away at the soldier.

"I felt someone hitting me repeatedly from behind," the sol-dier, Ariel Hausler, told reporters later. "When I turned around he hit me again, and the ax grazed my forehead. It was a miracle that I wasn't more seriously hurt."

Bleeding from his head, Hausler managed to grab the youth while another soldier wrestled him to the ground. A few days later some Israeli reporters asked the Israeli army spokesman whom the young Palestinian worked for—that is, which PLO faction enlisted him to carry out this brazen daylight attack. The spokesman said that the interrogation of the boy revealed some-thing slightly disturbing from an Israeli point of view: no one had paid him to do it. He was acting on his own initiative. He ap-parently just got up that morning and decided he wanted to plant a hatchet in the head of an Israeli soldier—so he did.

The incident intrigued me, and I tried to get an interview with the boy, but was turned down. Somehow I felt there was a larger message in his act—that while as a community the Palestinians, particularly the adults who had a great deal to lose economically, had allowed themselves to be coopted by the Israeli system, some individuals and small groups were spontaneously resisting Israel, even as they continued to integrate with it. This individual resis-tance, which began immediately after the occupation started, was carried out mostly by the young, who had little stake in the system. To the contrary, many of them had gone to high school, technical colleges, or universities, but the only jobs the Israeli system of-fered them when they graduated were sweeping floors, waiting on tables, or laying bricks.

In early 1987, I got a group of Palestinian students together at the West Bank's Bir Zeit University to talk about the rage building up beneath the surface of Israeli–Palestinian society—a rage that seemed to be exploding to the surface in small bursts with in-creasing frequency. The students spoke passionately about the frustrations of their generation, which looked into the future un-der Israeli occupation and saw only dead ends—politically, culturally, and in terms of their own careers. An eighteen-year-old dark-eyed coed named Meral, speaking with clenched fists and a voice seemingly on the verge of tears, captured the mood when she said, "I think that our generation of Palestinians has reached a point psychologically where we want any means of getting back at the Jews. You just get the feeling that the Jews want to aggravate us. Palestinian violence now is something that just happens. It's not planned. It just occurs."

Meron Benvenisti's West Bank Data Base Project actually charted this mounting Palestinian rage, like a geologist taking the earth's temperature. Each year Benvenisti counted the number of acts of violence against Israelis involving firearms and perpetrated by organized PLO cells, compared to what he characterized as more spontaneous incidents of stone-throwing, fire-bombing, or knifing. Between 1977 and 1984, he found, there was an average of eleven spontaneous acts of anti-Israeli violence for every one planned from outside. In 1985, there were sixteen spontaneous acts for every one planned abroad, and by 1986 the ratio had ballooned to 18:1.

"This widening ratio," explained Benvenisti in 1986, "indicates a new phase in Palestinian resistance and the intercommunal strife. Violence is now largely carried out in broad daylight by individuals and groups who spontaneously express their feelings, undeterred by the consequences of their actions."

Dr. Eyad el-Sarraj, the only Palestinian psychiatrist for Gaza's entire population of 700,000, didn't need any figures to convince him that a volcanic rage was building within the soul of his community. When I interviewed him in Gaza in the summer of 1987, Dr. el-Sarraj told me of a visit he had just had that left him trembling about what the future might hold.

"I had a teenage boy come into my clinic," recalled the Palestinian psychiatrist. "He said to me in a whisper, 'Doctor, I have a secret.' I thought, Okay, another paranoid—that is how they usually introduce themselves. He then said, 'I just want to kill one Israeli. I have decided that the solution to the problem is that we must each kill just one Israeli.' He said that he heard that I had 'influence' and maybe I could get him a bomb. I explained to him that I had no such influence. Then I thought, I'd better examine this kid. I was certain that he was psychotic.

"So I examined him for an hour," said Dr. el-Sarraj. "He was perfectly normal."

So was Yehuda Ben-Tov.
Shortly after an Israeli civilian was shot and killed by an un-identified Palestinian while shopping in the Gaza marketplace in 1987, the seventeen-year-old Ben-Tov, who hailed from the victim's hometown of Ashkelon, was interviewed by the *Jerusalem Post* and asked how Israel should deal with its Gaza problems.

"What they ought to do," said Ben-Tov, "is bring in the air force to level it—all of it. Like that tornado [which just swept through] Texas."

Yehuda Ben-Tov was not alone in holding such feelings. Just as a rage began to simmer and bubble to the surface among Palestinians vis-à-vis the Israelis, who never let them feel at home, a similar rage grew inside Israelis vis-à-vis Palestinians, who never let them relax and enjoy their country.

The 1967 war was the turning point here as well. For some Israelis, the 1967 war expanded their sense of home spatially, thanks to the addition of the West Bank and Gaza Strip. Israelis, who felt as though they had been living in a tiny room for twenty years, could finally stretch their legs, put their cars into fifth gear, and really let out their breath. For the first time they enjoyed a feeling of space, of a back yard with a lawn and garden. For other Israelis, the occupation of the West Bank, Jerusalem, and Gaza deepened their sense of home spiritually. Coming back to Hebron, the Old City of Jerusalem, Nablus, and Jericho was, as we've seen, the real return to Zion for many spiritually minded Israelis; up to 1967 they felt as though they had only been living on the doorstep, peering into the house through the front window. "For me to live in Judea and Samaria is to return home in the deepest sense," Jewish settler leader Israel Harel told me one day at his West Bank home in Ofra. "The attachment to the land is almost erotic."

Sometimes on the Passover holiday when you walked through the Jewish markets in Jerusalem you could smell matzo baking. On Friday evenings in Jerusalem a siren sounds across the city to herald the coming of the Sabbath. On Sabbath mornings there are often so few cars on the road in Jerusalem that residents returning from synagogue, often still draped in their prayer shawls, walk down the middle of the streets. Where have Jews ever felt so much at home?

Yet, there was a catch. These very territories—these additional rooms—that expanded and deepened the Israelis' sense of being at home came with a population which constantly made the Israelis feel unable to relax. The new rooms contained 1.7 million Palestinians whose own national identity and claim to ownership of the house was sharpened by their contact with the Israelis.

What bad luck! Just at the moment when Israelis were really beginning to believe they had ended their exile, that they had more power than any Jewish collective in history, they found themselves constantly reminded by the Palestinians that they could not take their shoes off.

While the Palestinian challenge to Israelis—both political and military—had existed from 1948 to 1967 as well, in those days it was primarily viewed as an external threat. The Palestinians were seen by Israelis as part of a general Arab horde challenging their existence, and the Palestinians' own unique identity was submerged to some extent in that pan-Arab coalition. But once the Palestinians in the West Bank and Gaza fell under Israeli authority, they were no longer an external threat that Israel could just build a fence against or unleash its air force on; they were no longer an enemy that lived behind a clearly delineated borderline, with barbed wire and guard towers, which, if you avoided it, meant you could go through the day without giving security much of a thought. Instead, they became an internal threat that made the lives of every Israeli uncomfortable wherever they went in their own country.

This internal threat was accompanied, as was noted, by the rise of the PLO after 1967 as an international representative of the Palestinian people and as a guerrilla force based in Beirut. With the PLO working from the outside and the West Bankers and Gazans from the inside, the Palestinians as a whole were able to shadow the Israelis as never before. Whether it was at home or abroad, at the United Nations or at women's conferences in Nairobi, around every corner Israelis bumped into their Palestinian shadow, which by word and deed was always whispering: "It's not your home. Palestine is not yours. It's ours."

This constant challenge, like a continual poke in the ribs, really got to Israelis. Palestinians planted bombs in Israeli supermarkets, on their airplanes, under the seats of their buses, and even in an old refrigerator in the heart of Jerusalem. They hijacked their airplanes, murdered their Olympic team, and shot up their embassies. None of this threatened Israel's national existence in the way Egypt or Syria could. But in some ways it was worse. It destroyed the Israelis' sense of belonging, of feeling fully at home, just when they most wanted to feel at home, and it introduced a frightening unpredictability to their daily lives. It was like living in a beautiful mansion on a beautiful plot of land that was constantly being burglarized. Every time an Israeli walked on the street, went to a movie, got on a bus, or stepped inside a supermarket, his eyes were on the lookout for unattended packages and objects. When *The New York Times* has empty space on a page it will often run a tiny filler advertisement for the Fresh Air Fund, a New York charity that sends inner-city youth to summer camps. When the *Jerusalem Post* has empty space, it runs a filler ad that reads: "Suspicion saves! Beware of suspicious objects!"

Dalia Dromi, the spokeswoman for the Israeli Nature Preservation Society, was born and raised in Netanya, a coastal town just north of Tel Aviv. Before the 1967 war Netanya was considered, strategically speaking, one of the most dangerous spots in Israel, because it was situated at the narrowest point in the bottleneck between Tel Aviv and Haifa—only nine miles from the nearest Jordanian West Bank military outpost in the town of Tulkarm. After the 1967 war, though, Dalia discovered that her whole sense of home had changed in a way she never would have predicted.

"In Netanya before the '67 war, if you put your car in fifth gear you could find yourself across the border," explained Dromi. "Yet, in a funny way, in those days I never felt the border. What I mean is that Israel was a narrow country then, but I never felt personally threatened. You knew where the border was, you knew that there was an army there protecting you from the enemy on the other side, and you just went about your life. Now I feel threatened all the time. I don't know where the border is or where the enemy is coming from. Before 1967, I would go to the beach by myself all the time; now I would never go by myself. If I go to the beach, I never sit with a crowd where someone might put

JERUSALEM

a bomb. Before 1967, I never remember being afraid. Since 1967, I am always afraid. Israel was very small before 1967, but it is only now that I feel I am in a small country. Whenever anyone talks to me about 'strategic borders,' I laugh. Today the border is everywhere. It is in the village of Wadi Ara when I drive past and get a stone from a Palestinian, and it is on the road to Haifa when I pass [the Israeli Arab village] Jisr a-Zarqa and I get a stone. You see now the border is really in my own bed. It goes home with me at night and gets up with me in the morning. Before, when Israel was nine miles wide, I felt as though it was my country alone. Yes, there were Arabs living here, but they were not thought of as Palestinians who threatened you personally. They were thought of as Israeli Arabs, citizens of the state. I felt free to go everywhere without feeling threatened. Fear came to me only after 1967."

If I had to reduce Israeli life to a single picture, it would be a photograph taken by Israeli freelance photographer Toby Greenwald. It is the only picture of Israel I brought home to remind me of the place. It shows a beautiful old almond tree, its limbs stretched wide, standing on the banks of the Sea of Galilee. The tree is alone, framed by the placid blue waters of the Galilee. By all rights it should be a picture of total serenity, except that in the shade of the tree, next to its base, is a steel drum set into the ground. On top of the drum is written in Hebrew: SECURITY HOLE. This is where police dump unexploded bombs; such drums are all over Israel.

I had a neighbor in Jerusalem, a young Israeli college student who loved to play Led Zeppelin and other heavy-metal music full blast at 2:00 a.m. on Friday nights. The noise from his speakers would literally jolt me out of bed sometimes. I would lie awake, seething with anger. There I was in my own house, in my own bed, and I could not relax. On more than one occasion I fantasized that I had a bazooka and I was firing it straight into the guy's apartment, blowing his stereo and speakers to sawdust, leaving behind only a glorious silence. I think many Israelis, without admitting it aloud, developed similar fantasies about the Palestinians, who never let them relax in their own beds and always ruined their pretty pictures. When the racist Israeli rabbi Meir Kahane used to call for transferring all Palestinians in the West Bank and Gaza to Jordan, he would always conclude his proposal by looking his Israeli audiences in the eye and declaring, "Remember, I say what you think." There is a little bit of Kahane in every Israeli.

Ruth Firer, the Israeli high-school teacher whose Polish parents managed to survive the Holocaust and bring her to Israel from Siberia as an infant, has soft, welcoming eyes, but when the subject of Palestinian violence against Jews is raised, her face hardens into granite, her eyes turn a remorseless steel gray, and her liberal politics go out the window.

"These days," she said to me at a time when the number of Palestinian attacks on Israelis was again on the rise, "I have stopped going to the Old City because of all the stabbings of Jews there. On Shabbat it used to be the place we went to shop and look around. Going there was like going to Disneyland—you passed from the modern world to the exotic Oriental world. Now, to be closed by fear in your own home is horrible, shameful. We came here to this land so as not to be frightened. At the end of the war, my father was offered the chance to go to America, but he said no, he wouldn't be able to feel at home there. He didn't want to start all over again being a Jew in a Gentile country. His whole family was killed by the Nazis. So he came here and made this his home. Now the Palestinians are trying to take from us the feeling of being home and we won't let them. They cannot take from me my basic right to feel at home here. I am ready to share with them, but if they want Tel Aviv and Haifa, too, then they will have to fight me and my two sons. We are not going to live through Masada again—no more."

Making this whole situation all the more upsetting for Israelis is the fact that they have one of the most sophisticated air forces in the world, an army that could mobilize close to 1 million men and women, and hundreds of modern tanks.

"I am frustrated," Israel Harel, the Jewish settlement leader, remarked to me one day. "I am frustrated that I have all this might and yet I am unable to use it to protect my property. When I served on the Suez Canal in the 1973 war, I was not afraid in the immediate sense. I fought to be in the first wave of people who would cross. I felt a kind of abstract fear. But let me tell you something. A few years ago I was driving from Petach Tiqvah to Elkanah [a West Bank Jewish settlement] and I had to pass through Kfar Kassem [a Palestinian town]. As I was driving, I suddenly saw a roadblock ahead of me and tens of Palestinian children blocking the way. I could not go around them and they all started to throw stones at my car. My only option was to put the car in reverse. I started backing up and I found dozens more closing in behind me. I felt like a trapped mouse. I thought that after all the wars I had fought, this was going to be my end. The only thing I could think to do was take out my gun and start shooting, but I didn't, because I knew if I killed one or two I would still be killed. So I just hit the gas pedal and went into reverse really fast. I hit a few of them lightly but I got away. Here I am, Israel Harel; I was with the first Israeli paratroop unit that entered Jerusalem in 1967. I was with the first units that crossed the Suez Canal in 1973. I know the power we have, and I was the one who was frightened—by children!"

In order to feel at home despite the constant Palestinian challenge, Israelis adopted several different approaches. One school, led by left-wing peace activists, argued that home was, and could only be, the place where one's own people were in a majority and where one could live a free and democratic Jewish life, without the feeling of suppressing another people. Therefore, home was pre-1967 Israel—without the West Bank and Gaza, which, they argued, should be returned to Arab control. Many members of this school intentionally avoided crossing the Green Line into the occupied territories in order to feel at home in their pre-1967 houses. They somehow felt that if they didn't see Nablus and the hate in the eyes of the Palestinian youths there, they could still feel at home in Tel Aviv. As Janet Aviad, an Israeli sociologist and one of the leaders of the Israeli peace movement observed, "No doubt the biblical areas of the West Bank speak to me very deeply. But despite that, I have erected a boundary in my own head, and I never go there. I don't want to be associated with a colonization process. I only cross the Green Line for demonstrations. I struggle all the time to re-erect the Green Line, but to my dismay I look at all the maps today and it is not there."

Around the twentieth anniversary of the 1967 war, a group of peace activists went out on weekends with cans of green paint, brushes, and maps of pre-1967 Israel and actually painted a green line on the streets of Israeli towns and across fields, to remind themselves and others just where home was.

But while Israeli leftists can never feel at home as long as Israel retains the occupied territories, those on the right, led by the messianic Jewish settlers, declare that they could never feel at home if Israel gives them away. The Jewish settlers argue that home is not necessarily where you are in the majority, but where history or the Bible or your very soul tells you you are home. In order for the settlers to feel at home in a place like Elon Moreh, the Jewish settlement overlooking Nablus, a West Bank town with 100,000 Arab inhabitants, they simply pretended that the Palestinians were not there. On a visit to Elon Moreh once, I asked some residents there what they saw when they drove past Nablus and the surrounding Arab villages to get to their homes.

"I feel I am driving through the pages of the Bible," answered Elchanan Oppenheim, the head of the education department at Elon Moreh. "When I see the Arab women harvesting their crops, I see Ruth the Moabite in the fields of grain. I live in the Bible. I look above all these immediate things."

The silent majority of Israelis in the middle simply learned to live with the situation, because it was usually quite livable. Most of them rarely visited the occupied territories. Whenever I came back from Gaza or Nablus, Israelis would always quiz me as though I were Mark Twain describing some distant land. "Is it really like that?" people would say. At most, they shopped at some West Bank marketplace on Saturdays, went to Bethlehem occasionally for Arabic food, had their cars repaired in the low-cost Palestinian-owned garages, hired cheap Palestinian labor to build additions to their houses, or used the roads through the West Bank as shortcuts on the drive from Jerusalem to the Galilee. They saw the Palestinians, but they did not view them as members of another legitimate national community inhabiting the same space; they saw them either as Arab terrorists, who should be shot or jailed, or, more often, as objects—waiters, carpenters, maids, and cooks—who could be ordered around. When Ann and I moved to Jerusalem from Beirut, we looked at an apartment next to the King David Hotel that had a very small living room. When we asked the Israeli real-estate agent whether we could knock down a wall to make the living room larger, she answered without hesitation, "Sure, no problem. Just get an Arab and knock down the wall." It wasn't get a hammer. It wasn't get a workman. It was get an Arab.

* * *

Raja Shehadah just wanted to cry. It was August 1985 and the Israeli government had just revived the practice of administrative detention, a security measure inherited by Israel from the British Mandate, which allows the government to arrest and hold any suspected troublemaker (read: Palestinian) for up to six months without bringing any charge against him or her. At the time, the only requirement for putting someone into administrative detention was that the person be brought before a military judge within ninety-six hours. The judge had to review the evidence the security forces had gathered against the detainee and either confirm, reduce, or cancel the detention order. The week the practice of administrative detention was revived, Shehadah, one of the leading Palestinian lawyers in the West Bank, found that two of his colleagues had been arrested under this statute and he went to an Israeli military court to plead on their behalf.

"The first group of fifteen administrative detainees had just been arrested, and among them were two field-workers from Law in the Service of Man," said Shehadah, referring to a legal protection organization which he helped found in the West Bank. "I came to Jeneid Prison [near Nablus] to make appeals on their behalf. I was ushered into a room and found myself with eight other lawyers. We were all looking at each other wondering what the procedure was. After a short while, a rather wolfish-looking man came in carrying a big cardboard box filled with papers, which he hugged to his chest. In my stupidity I thought he was another lawyer who had really prepared well. It made me feel guilty. All I was carrying was a copy of Military Order 378, which described all the procedures for dealing in the military courts with people accused of security offenses. We all sat around waiting for the judge."

Finally the Israeli army judge showed up. In the West Bank and Gaza all Palestinian security offenses are dealt with through the Israeli military courts, which have their own judges and prosecutors.

"The judge sat down," recalled Shehadah, "leaned back in his chair, and announced, 'Who would like to speak?'

"I said, 'What should I speak about? Where are the charges? Where is the evidence?'

"He said, 'It is a free place—speak about whatever you want.'
"So first one lawyer stood up, then another, and another, and
they each spoke about their clients," Shehadah recalled. "There
was no reaction from the judge, no court reporter taking anything
down. We were just little children he wanted to please by letting
us speak to our heart's content. I was sitting in front of the wolfish-
looking man, who had placed his box of papers under his chair.
One of the Israeli lawyers really thought he had a good case. He
argued that his client was being arrested because he had refused
to become a collaborator. At that point, the wolfish man got up,
walked over, and said something to the military prosecutor. I
finally realized that this man was from the Shin Bet [whose secret
agents were responsible for gathering the evidence against suspected Palestinian activists]. So we all spoke to our heart's content, and then the judge asked us to please leave the room. After
a while, we were called back. All the prisoners were there. The
judge said that there was no point in dealing with each case
separately, so he ordered the fifteen prisoners to stand and then
he announced, 'I confirm the administrative detention order for
all of you.' "

As with every case in which the Israeli army accuses a Palestinian of security offenses, the lawyers were not allowed to see
the evidence against their clients because it was gathered covertly—through informers and wiretaps—by the Shin Bet, and
divulging any of it to the accused or his lawyer might expose the
secret means by which it was gathered; at least that was what the
Shin Bet argued. This made mounting a defense rather difficult—
if not absurd—and made a mockery of the principle of due
process.

"I was sad and insulted," Shehadah told me after the incident.
"I walked out with tears in my eyes. My clients had to cheer me
up. They said, 'Don't worry, six months in prison isn't that long.
It will be over soon.' I just walked out thinking, What am I doing
here?"

Deep down, Raja Shehadah knew what he was doing there,
and it had little to do with justice or with him. The Shin Bet and
the military courts became the tools through which the Israeli
public took out its rage against the Palestinians for all the rocks
they threw, all the bombs they left under bus seats, all the terrorist
attacks they mounted against Israeli targets abroad, and all the

speeches they made at the United Nations. The Palestinians, on their side, threw stones, and the Israelis, on the other, threw the book at them.

Dealing with the Palestinians through the Shin Bet and the military courts had two advantages for Israelis. First, it was practically invisible—to Israelis and to the world. The Shin Bet operated like an unseen hand, arresting Palestinians at night, recruiting informers, tapping phones, beating the living daylights out of Palestinians behind the closed doors of interrogation rooms, and, it was widely rumored, even arranging for certain particularly troublesome Palestinians to "accidentally" blow themselves up while supposedly assembling bombs meant for Israelis. This meant the Palestinians were kept in line without any Israelis having to trouble themselves as to how. It was like having an occupation with no hands. Better yet, it was all "legal"—in Israeli terms. The military courts provided a legal veneer that enabled the Israelis to get their revenge on the Palestinians while still feeling clean and civilized. The Israeli security forces rarely did anything "illegal" in dealing with the Palestinians in the occupied territories. Every act of repression, no matter how arbitrary, was usually in line with some paragraph in the Israeli military code. When it wasn't, the code was changed to accommodate it. It was, as Meron Benvenisti used to say, "rule by law, not rule of law."

Why did Israelis insist on this pretense of law? Because without the mask of the law, the conflict between them and the Palestinians would just be a messy tribal feud, and that would not be consistent with how the Israelis see themselves and how they want the West to see them. So, instead, there are the military courts, with their judges and lawyers and benches and legalese. A Palestinian's lawyer, such as Raja Shehadah, would come to the military judge and tell him a sad story about his client, a true story, maybe a Jewish story even, and the Israeli judge might say, "Look, I'd love to hear it. I really do feel sorry for your client." But then he would recite forty-nine paragraphs of the legal code which the Palestinian had violated according to secret evidence gathered by the Shin Bet which no one could see.

"I'm sorry, it's nothing personal, my hands are tied," the judge would tell the accused with his eyes. "It's the law and I've got to live by the law . . . Ten years in jail . . . Next case."

I actually began to think of the Shin Bet and Israeli military courts as two huge buildings erected right on the Israeli–Palestinian fault line. By their sheer weight and strength these two buildings were able to absorb all the tremors and steam building up beneath the surface of Israeli society and to keep the fault line from cracking open. Israelis could walk down the street, point at these two buildings, and feel good about themselves and their society. Everything looked normal—from the outside. But what Israelis didn't see, and didn't want to see, was that as the Palestinian tremors were becoming more frequent and intense, the foundations of these two buildings were beginning to warp. Eventually, something snapped and cracks began to appear on the outside of these structures for all the world to see.

The first major crack occurred on the night between April 12 and 13, 1984, when four eighteen-year-old Palestinians from the Gaza Strip hijacked an Israeli Egged bus as it was heading south from Tel Aviv to Ashkelon. Israeli antiterrorist units eventually shot out the bus's tires, forcing it to a halt. After a siege that lasted throughout the night, specially trained Israeli troops stormed the bus at dawn, killing two of the hijackers immediately, as well as a young girl soldier who had failed to keep her head down. The two other Palestinian hijackers, cousins by the name of Majdi and Subhi Abu-Jumaa, were dragged off the bus alive. Avraham Shalom, then head of the Shin Bet and the man in charge of the rescue operation, ordered five of his agents on the scene, along with six soldiers and policemen, to beat the two hijackers to death, which they did with a combination of fists, rifle butts, and stones, crushing their two skulls. It was apparently an instinctive tribal reaction on Shalom's part—one which his men clearly understood and carried out with relish. They all knew that Israel has no capital punishment and that if revenge was not exacted on the spot those two Palestinians might be released in a few years in a prisoner exchange and come back to haunt them. So an eye was taken for an eye and a tooth for a tooth, and when it was all over the Israeli army spokesman was told to tell the world that these two Palestinian hijackers "died on the way to the hospital."

But there was a problem. A new Israeli tabloid newspaper, *Hadashot*, had taken pictures of one of the handcuffed hijackers being escorted from the bus very much alive, and insisted on investigating how he happened to die on the way to the hospital. (Another Israeli newspaper, *Ma'ariv*, also had photographs but chose not to report the story.) The matter was kept under wraps by the Israeli censor until my predecessor as *Times* bureau chief, David K. Shipler, defied censorship and exposed the existence of the photographs. A series of government investigations followed, and in the face of each one Avraham Shalom and three of his aides organized a careful cover-up, directing all the blame onto Brigadier General Yitzhak Mordechai, then the chief infantry and paratroop officer, who had been involved in the initial interrogation of the hijackers to find out if they had booby-trapped the bus. In the fall of 1985, the truth was first exposed when the deputy head of the Shin Bet, Reuven Hazak, and two colleagues informed Prime Minister Peres that while General Mordechai had roughed up the two Palestinians in his interrogation, he had turned them over to the Shin Bet very much alive and that Avraham Shalom was responsible for the murder and cover-up. The senior Shin Bet officials were apparently motivated to speak to Peres, not out of any disquiet over what had happened to the Palestinians, but because of the systematic lying of their superior. Peres for his part did nothing with the information—except stand aside while Avraham Shalom had Hazak and his two associates fired for informing on him.

However, Attorney General Yitzhak Zamir—a true defender of the rule of law, of which there are still many in Israel—got wind of the story and insisted on following the matter up with a police inquiry in May 1986. The whole affair exploded into the headlines a month later, when Shamir, Peres, Rabin, along with most of the Cabinet, decided to get rid of Zamir and replace him with a more pliable Attorney General ready to brush the case under the carpet. A deal was soon struck in which Shalom resigned as Shin Bet chief and in return President Chaim Herzog, on June 26, 1986, gave blanket pardons to him and three aides who had assisted him in the cover-up. The three aides were allowed to keep their jobs, including a Shin Bet lawyer who had fabricated evidence. President Herzog told me a week later that his mail from the Israeli public ran nine to one in favor of the pardons.

As these and other cracks appeared in the Shin Bet's edifice, the government appointed a commission to look into the practices of the domestic intelligence service with regard to its handling and interrogation of Palestinian security prisoners. The commission was headed by a former Supreme Court Justice, Moshe Landau, and in January 1987 it issued its report. The standard practice for convicting Palestinians from the West Bank and Gaza Strip who were alleged to have been involved in violence or political action against the state of Israel was not by arresting them and bringing them to trial. There were simply too many, and if each one was granted a trial, the limited Israeli military court system would become totally swamped. More importantly, a Palestinian suspected of involvement in a particular political or violent crime usually would be arrested by the Shin Bet on the basis of covertly gathered evidence which might not be admissible in court or which the Shin Bet would not want to reveal in court to a Palestinian defense attorney. The Shin Bet overcame this problem by getting the vast majority of those accused of security crimes to confess—thereby obviating any need for trials, the gathering of admissible evidence, or appeals. The accused would be brought to court, affirm that he had signed the confession, and then be sentenced. What could be more convenient?

One might ask why the Palestinians were so willing to confess. This was explained for the first time publicly by the Landau Commission. After a Palestinian suspect was apprehended, a Shin Bet agent would take him into a room and tell him that he could either confess to the crime or face an interrogation. Many confessed. Those who chose interrogation were subjected to what the Landau Commission called "physical pressure"—i.e., torture—until they agreed to confess. Once they agreed, an Israeli policeman was brought into the room to take down the confession in Hebrew that would be presented in court. When the Palestinian's day in court arrived, the Israeli military judge would ask him if he had confessed of his own free will. Many would say no, that they were tortured with a black bag tied over their heads, and could not even read the Hebrew confession statement. The policeman who took the confession would then be summoned to the courtroom and he would testify that he saw no torture or intimidation whatsoever. He would say the accused simply confessed voluntarily right before his eyes, and then signed the statement.

In 1971, however, in the face of repeated allegations that Palestinian prisoners were being tortured before the police were brought in to take their confessions, the military courts decided to begin summoning the Shin Bet agents involved in each case to hear from them.

As the Landau Commission put it: "Now [in 1971] for the first time the [Shin Bet] interrogators faced a serious dilemma: On the witness stand they had to answer questions under oath concerning the extraction of the confession. The law of course obliged them like all witnesses in court to tell the whole truth and only the truth. . . . [But] truthful testimony would have forced [them] to reveal what was happening in the interrogation facilities, including the methods of interrogation, and, as a result, to render these methods ineffectual in the future, when they became known to the enemy. We are speaking of many and varied methods, including means of pressure used against those interrogated."

So what did the Shin Bet do? "From the start," the Landau Commission found, "the interrogators chose to hide . . . their use of physical pressure" and "lied to courts." For seventeen years, every time a Palestinian claimed to have been tortured or intimidated into confessing, the Shin Bet told the courts the accused had made up the story. In virtually every case the Israeli military courts accepted the word of the Shin Bet agent over that of the Palestinian—no matter how many black-and-blue marks he showed the judge. The Landau Commission described the Shin Bet practices as "ideological criminality," since, it said, they were born out of a desire to confront Palestinian terrorism. The commission went on to say that it did not recommend that criminal procedures be taken against any of the Shin Bet officials involved because "they were just carrying out orders." It added that "the political, judicial and military authorities did not know of the Shin Bet's practice of perjury and therefore are not to be held responsible for it" either. Then, as always happens when Israel finds that in fighting the Palestinians the law has become an obstacle, the Landau Commission recommended that the law be changed. It recommended an undisclosed series of "guidelines for . . . limited . . . psychological and physical pressures," that is to say, torture and intimidation, and these were accepted by the Cabinet and the parliament without debate.

But it wasn't only the Shin Bet which was engaged in moral double bookkeeping. When Jewish settlers took revenge on Palestinians by themselves, the system was remarkably understanding. Of the numerous examples of this, one of the most egregious took place in October 1987, when Nissan Ish-Goyev, an Israeli West Bank settler, was driving a garbage truck in the Nablus area. On his way to the Balata refugee camp, he came upon a group of Palestinian youths who were throwing stones at passing cars. Two Israeli policemen who witnessed the confrontation testified that the stones thrown at Ish-Goyev "were nothing serious." Nevertheless, they said, the Israeli settler got out of his truck and shot two bursts from his Uzi submachine gun at the group, "from the hip, at a straight angle," killing thirteen-year-old Hashem Lutfi Ib-Maslem, who was standing more than 100 yards away. The Israeli policemen on the scene immediately confiscated Ish-Goyev's gun and booked him.

When the case went to trial, the prosecuting attorney, Moshe Shiloh, called for a ten- to twelve-year sentence in order to deter other settlers from taking the law into their own hands. Tel Aviv District Court Judge Uri Strosman, who tried the case, saw things otherwise.

At one point during the trial, prosecutor Shiloh said, "From the moment the accused discerned the stone-throwing, he simply should have left the place." Judge Strosman then interjected, "At one time they educated us differently, you know, Mr. Shiloh."

After hearing all the arguments, Judge Strosman handed down his decision on February 22, 1988, saying: "Now, as I am coming to determine the judgment, and in giving my opinion on the circumstances in which the accused found himself, and, to my sorrow, these circumstances were caused by [Palestinian] children and youths who, instead of being, in these mad days, under the supervision of their parents and educators, are engaged in throwing stones to the point of danger and bringing out the police, I do not think that the accused should be punished with the full severity of the law for the killing. Accordingly, I sentence the accused to six months' imprisonment, which he will carry out in public service."

The Israeli Supreme Court later overturned Strosman's ruling and sentenced Ish-Goyev to three years in jail.

The Supreme Court's actions underscored the fact that the Israeli system of military justice and occupation law wasn't entirely a sham, by any means. Most of the Palestinians convicted by the Shin Bet were guilty of planning or carrying out violent acts against Israeli civilians, even if the evidence against them was incomplete, inadmissible, or obtained through intimidation. Moreover, the mere fact that Israel maintained a legal code and system of courts in dealing with the West Bank and Gaza Strip created a restraining legal culture that had a certain effect on the Israeli military authorities. But the longer the occupation went on, the less restraint the legal system seemed to exercise.

Frankly, I never found the Israeli legal abuses particularly surprising. The Israelis were fighting a war with another community living right next door—a community that itself was not playing by any rules. It was the Israelis' pretense I found tiresome—their self-delusions that somehow they were always behaving in purely legal and morally upright ways, while their enemies, the Palestinians, were simply vile terrorists beyond the pale of civilization. The truth was, each side understood that they were in a war for communal survival. One side had knives and pistols; the other had secret agents and courts. While each constantly cried out to the world how evil the other was, when they looked one another in the eye—whether in the interrogator's room or before inserting a knife in a back alley—they said something different: I will do whatever I have to to survive. Have no doubt about it.

And so, for twenty years, the play went on: Palestinians talking to the world about resistance, even resisting individually, but resigning themselves as a community to the Israeli system; Israelis talking to the world about their "enlightened" occupation, and then doing anything they had to, behind closed doors, to keep the Palestinians quiet.

This relationship turned Israelis and Palestinians into intimate neighbors and bitter enemies at the same time. On any given day, one could find the Israeli army arresting all Palestinian males ages eighteen and over in one West Bank village, while in the next village an Israeli contractor would be hiring all Palestinian males eighteen and over to build a new Jewish town. As for the Palestinian, on the same day he could be installing the bus stop at a new Jewish settlement in the West Bank in the morning and in the evening leaving a parcel bomb under the seat of that same bus stop in order to kill or maim any Jew who sat there. Meron Benvenisti termed this crazy conflict a "twilight war"—a half-war half-peace kind of existence in which there were no trenches, no front lines, no barbed wire separating the two sides, and no accepted distinctions between civilians and soldiers, enemies and neighbors. It was a war, as Benvenisti liked to say, "between two peoples who shared the same sewers."

But then Benvenisti should have known. He lived in a sprawling old stone house in one of the few mixed neighborhoods of Arabs and Jews in Jerusalem. A few years ago, one of his Palestinian neighbors planted a bomb in the front garden of a Jewish home a couple of doors down from Benvenisti's. It wasn't a big bomb, just a small plastic bag filled with a little dynamite and a crude detonator—maybe enough to blow apart a small person.

The police soon arrested Zuhair Qawasmeh, the eldest son of Benvenisti's next-door neighbor, who confessed to planting the bomb. He was sentenced to eighteen years in jail, but was released after only four years as a result of a prisoner exchange between Israel and Palestinian guerrillas in Lebanon. Shortly after gaining his freedom, Zuhair Qawasmeh got married and, like a good neighbor, invited Benvenisti to his wedding. He invited him in Hebrew, which he had learned during his stay in prison.

"So there I was at the wedding," Benvenisti remarked to me one day, "and I am asking myself, Who is he? My enemy or my neighbor? He is my neighbor, but he is a man who could have killed my children. In America you can have a neighbor who is also your enemy, but not in this sense. He is my mortal enemy. He is a soldier. He is fighting for his own people against my people, like in war—but he is my neighbor."

Precisely because this twilight war involved two entire communities, two peoples, two tribes, two nations, fighting each other without a frontline, neither one really made any distinction between civilians and soldiers. Each side viewed the members of the other community as the potential enemy, and hence as potential soldiers in the enemy army. Relations between Israelis and Palestinians became so thoroughly politicized that after a while there was no such thing as a crime between them, and there was no such thing as an accident between them—there were only acts of war.

There was also no such thing as death between them; there was only martyrdom. Ofra Moses, a thirty-five-year-old mother of three, lived in the West Bank settlement of Alfei Menashe, fifteen minutes from the suburbs of Tel Aviv. On April 11, 1987, she was riding with her family to buy matzo for Passover when a Palestinian hiding in an orange grove threw a fire bomb through the window of her Ford Escort and burned her alive. Mrs. Moses thought she was an innocent civilian, but many Palestinians saw her, by her very existence as a West Bank settler, as an occupier, a perpetrator of violence, a soldier, and therefore a legitimate target. The most moderate West Bank Palestinian lawyer I know said to me with great indignation, "I heard on the Israel Arabic radio that the mayor of the Arab village next to Alfei Menashe went to the settlement to express his people's sorrow at Mrs. Moses's death. They weren't sorry. She was a settler, the root of all evil, and they expect us to believe that people are sorry she was killed? I'm not sorry one bit."

Two days after Mrs. Moses died, Musa Hanafi, a twenty-three-year-old Palestinian from Rafah, in the Gaza Strip, was shot and killed by Israeli troops during a Palestinian nationalist demonstration at the West Bank's Bir Zeit University. Mr. Hanafi may have thought he was at Berkeley in 1968, taking part in a campus protest, with a little harmless stone-throwing and tire-burning, but that is not how the Israeli soldiers receiving the stones viewed him.

Lieutenant Colonel Yehuda Meir, the Nablus area commander, was not in Bir Zeit that day, but he has faced many similar demonstrations. I asked him what his men saw when they looked through their gunsights at the Palestinian student demonstrators.

"They see soldiers without uniforms or ammunition," said the Israeli officer. "But if [the Palestinian demonstrators] had ammunition they would use it. This is not Berkeley. They are not protesting for books or tuition. These students are motivated to do what they do by a nationalist cause."

The lack of distinction between civilians and soldiers carried right through to the graveyard. Normally, civilians who are killed in a war get a civilian burial. But not in this twilight war. In Israel and the occupied territories, civilians who died in any way remotely connected to the conflict were buried as martyrs and war heroes, and each community used these deaths to reaffirm the rightness of its cause and to justify revenge against the other. Palestinian and Israeli funerals were so similar it was uncanny. Each side stood over its coffins and drew out the old familiar slogans like pistols from a holster.

At Mrs. Moses's funeral, Minister of Transportation Chaim Corfu delivered the eulogy. And what did he say of this woman who was killed buying matzo? "Just as the soldiers who fell yesterday [in Lebanon] were killed defending the security of the Galilee, so you, Ofra, fell in the defense of the security of Jerusalem," declared Corfu. "You, Ofra, you are our soldier."

Within a week of her burial, Mrs. Moses had a monument erected to her on the spot where she was immolated.

As for Hanafi, his funeral was more problematic. Israelis understand the power of the memorial, so when Palestinian students are killed, the army usually impounds the body, conducts an autopsy, and then compels the relatives to bury the corpse at midnight, with only immediate family present. (A month before Hanafi's death, Awad Taqtouq, a money changer from Nablus, was "accidentally" killed by Israeli soldiers. That evening 500 of his friends and family hid in the Nablus cemetery after dark, taking Israeli soldiers totally by surprise when they showed up with the corpse at midnight for a quick burial.) Hanafi's friends went further. They brought a car to Ramallah hospital and slipped his body out the back door before the Israeli troops got to it. His friends then kept the body packed in ice at a house in the West Bank. Finally, a few days later, they got hold of a car with Israeli license plates and used it to take Hanafi's corpse back to his home in the Gaza Strip, undetected by Israeli troops. The family quickly put out the word that Musa was back, and 5,000 people turned up to watch his body, draped in a Palestinian flag, lowered into its grave.

"It was kind of a political festival," said Mohammed Ishteyyeh, who attended the funeral. "People praised Hanafi as a 'bridge to liberation.' It was a real push for new sacrifice. You could feel the anger in the young boys there. I was watching them. They had lost the smile of childhood. Everybody was ready to die."

The next day Israeli troops were reported to have dug up Hanafi's body and brought it to Tel Aviv for an autopsy. Two days later it was returned and buried again—at midnight.

It seemed as though this situation would continue forever, with Israelis and Palestinians living their strange twilight existence: not exactly war, not exactly quiet; never really friends, but not always enemies; always longing for peace, but never really sacrificing to achieve it.

Most Israelis certainly thought it would last. In June 1987, on the twentieth anniversary of the Israeli occupation, the Civil Administration—the Israeli euphemism for the military administration which runs the West Bank and Gaza Strip—published a glossy booklet, with colored photographs on very expensive paper, entitled *20 Years of Civil Administration*. Its cover showed a golden wheat field with a West Bank Arab village off in the distance. At first glance, I thought the booklet was an annual report for an international commodities firm. It included page after page of all the good things the Israelis were doing for the Palestinian natives, from improved public services and hospitals to the installation of modern telephones. In the introduction, Shlomo Goren, who holds the title Coordinator of Government Operations in Judea, Samaria, and the Gaza District, a rather nice name for a former senior intelligence officer who runs the occupied territories from his bureau in the Ministry of Defense, concluded by saying, "All the achievements of the past twenty years could not have come about without the devoted work of the staff, both civilian and military, of the Civil Administration. To them we extend our deepest gratitude. I am sure that the population of the areas join me in thanking them."

One aspect of the arrogance of power is that it presumes knowledge. Goren was an Israeli "expert" on the Palestinians, but he did not have a hint what was brewing in their souls on the twentieth anniversary of the Israeli occupation.

Paradoxically, though, neither did many Palestinians. On a warm afternoon in July 1987 I sat on the patio underneath the pomegranate tree of Sari Nusseibeh's parents' house and asked him where the Palestinians were headed. How much longer could they lead their twilight existence? The Nusseibeh family home is situated right on what used to be the Green Line dividing Israeli-controlled West Jerusalem and Jordanian-controlled East Jerusalem. A Jordanian army pillbox could still be seen jutting through the twenty-year-old brush and foliage that had grown over it since June 1967. It was an apt metaphor for our discussion about Palestinians being absorbed by Israel yet remaining in their minds distinct and separate. Unlike Goren, Sari was certain that a radical change was in the wind, but he didn't know what.

"The only thing that is missing is the consciousness, the self-awareness of what we have been doing," said Sari of the Palestinian assimilation into Israel. "While our Palestinian bodies are now immersed in the Israeli system, our heads are still above water. Our bodies integrate with it, while our consciousness rejects it. But when consciousness and reality are so far apart, sooner or later either reality will be made to fit the consciousness, or the consciousness made to fit the reality."

Either the Palestinians will stop paying taxes, stop talking about joining the Jerusalem city council, stop building Jewish settlements, and stop riding the Egged buses, as their heads tell them they should do, said Sari, or their national strategy will be made to fit their assimilation. That is, they will stop trying to wage a twilight war against Israel and demand instead to be made citizens of the Israeli state—with rights equal to the Jews'. Sari thought it was going to be the latter. He told me he had the feeling that the Palestinians were going to wake up one morning soon, realize that they have been in bed with the Israeli system for twenty years, and demand a marriage certificate. And when they did, predicted Sari, the real moment of truth for Israel would arrive.

Sari was wrong. The Palestinians did wake up and find themselves in bed with the Israeli system—but instead of a marriage they demanded a divorce.

14

The Earthquake

Students of Gaza, teach us some of
what you know, for we have forgotten.
Teach us to become men, for our men
have turned into soft clay.
Crazy people of Gaza, a thousand halloos.
You freed us from the rotten age of political logic
and taught us to be crazy, too.

> —"The Angry Ones," by
> Syrian-born poet Nizar Kibani.
> Published in THE NEW YORK TIMES,
> February 14, 1988

The Israeli National Tourist Bureau canceled an advertisement
it was running in Dutch newspapers that said Tel Aviv and Jerusalem were only a "stone's throw" apart.

> —News item in USA TODAY,
> February 18, 1988

It had been a bad week for Yasir Arafat, and neither of us knew
when I sat down to interview him that it was about to get much
worse. The kings and presidents of the Arab world had just completed a summit conference in Amman, Jordan, in the second
week of November 1987. But for the first time since the Arab
League was founded in 1945, the main item on the summit's
agenda was not the Palestine question. Instead, it was how to
deal with the relentless threat to the Arab world from Ayatollah
Khomeini's revolutionary Iran.

Arafat was relegated to such secondary status that his longtime
rival for Palestinian leadership, Jordan's King Hussein, felt free
to snub the PLO chairman and not even bother to greet him at
the airport. Hours after his arrival, while Arafat was still simmering over this slight, an acquaintance of mine, a woman journalist from the Beirut office of Agence France-Presse, went to

Arafat's suite at the Amman Palace Hotel to interview him. Arafat greeted her warmly and told her to wait in his living room for fifteen minutes while he paid a courtesy call on the Emir of Qatar. While Arafat was gone, the AFP reporter went into an adjacent suite to interview PLO spokesman Yasir Abed Rabbo, an old friend of hers from Beirut. When Arafat returned, he asked where the reporter was and was informed by an aide that she was in Abed Rabbo's suite.

"Well, if that's who she wants to talk to, then that's who she can talk to," Arafat fumed, then stomped into his room, slammed the door behind him, and refused to speak to the woman. She was distraught and Abed Rabbo was insulted—so much so that he stormed into Arafat's suite bellowing, "What? Am I nothing? No one can talk to me?" The two men then had a shouting match about each other's relative importance in front of everyone in the room.

I arrived for my interview two days later, only two hours after the summit had closed. Arafat had woken from an afternoon nap just as King Hussein was holding a televised press conference. When Arafat strode into the living room of his suite, his guards all scrambled to attention.

"What is he talking about?" Arafat asked about King Hussein.

"You," said one of his aides.

King Hussein, in fact, was telling reporters that "hopefully" the PLO would be invited to an international Middle East peace conference, but not necessarily as an independent negotiating party. It might be represented as part of a joint Jordanian–Palestinian delegation. This was yet another dig at Arafat, since one of the few concessions the PLO chairman had wrung from the summit was affirmation that the PLO would be represented at any peace talks on an independent and "equal footing" with all other participants. No sooner was the ink on the final communiqué dry than King Hussein was declaring otherwise. After listening to the King's remarks, Arafat walked into the dining room and took a seat at the head of a long, polished table.

"What did you think about King Hussein's statement?" I asked.

"There is nothing to worry about," Arafat said with a dismissive wave of his hand. "It is all spelled out very clearly in the final communiqué. That is all that counts," he said, "the final com-

muniqué—not what King Hussein says in any press conference."
Then, just to underscore the point, Arafat asked me, "Do you
have a copy of the communiqué?"

"Yes, right here," I answered, handing him the English version
I had been given by the Jordanians on my way to Arafat's hotel.

Pointing with his finger to the resolutions about the PLO—
which came after those about Iran—Arafat put on his eyeglasses
and began to read from my copy. When he got to the sentence
about the convening of an international conference, he began to
read aloud. "Here it says, 'under the sponsorship of the United
Nations and with the participation of all parties concerned, including the Palestine Liberation Organization . . . Including the
Palestine Liberation Organization' . . ."

Arafat kept repeating the line, as if something he expected to
follow it wasn't there. Then he brought the text up to his eyes
and said in a voice quivering with fury, "No, there is something
missing."

While twisting a chain of worry beads in one hand and tapping
on the communiqué with the other, Arafat went into a boil right
in front of me. "This is a scandal," he stammered in Arabic. "You
have a big story. You have a scoop."

Arafat had just discovered that the English translation of the
summit's final communiqué, which the Jordanians had distributed
to the world press, omitted the standard reference to the PLO as
the "sole and legitimate representative of the Palestinian people."
This was apparently King Hussein's way of sending Arafat home
with the same sort of slap in the face with which he had received
him.

Shifting back and forth in his chair with irritation, Arafat kept
repeating, "This is bluffing, this is bluffing . . . Where did you
get this?"

"I got it from the Jordanians," I answered, slightly dumbstruck
at the scene I was watching unfold before my eyes.

"Yes, the Jordanians," Arafat hissed in a voice larded with
suspicion. "You cannot take from them. You have to take from
the Arab League. You have a big scoop . . . It is a scandal. This
is a scandal."

At that point, Arafat lifted a pen from his breast pocket, took
my copy of the communiqué, and carefully wrote in his own
longhand the words "the sole and legitimate representative of the

Palestinian people" after the reference to the PLO. At least one reporter would have a correct text! I kept it as a souvenir.

I never did get my interview, however. Arafat became so distraught over the missing language that he could talk of virtually nothing else. In retrospect, this was not surprising. Ever since Arafat had been driven from Beirut by the Israelis in 1982, he and the Palestinian cause which he symbolized had been drifting aimlessly. With his headquarters in the backwater of Tunis, his guerrilla army spread out to the four corners of the Arab world, and the Jordanians and Israelis keeping him away from the West Bank, Arafat seemed to be in danger of becoming irrelevant, and the petulance he demonstrated in Amman suggested that he knew it. When the substance of power vanishes for a leader, all the symbols, the trappings, and the insults take on mammoth proportions—because that is all there is.

Maybe the most telling sign of how low Arafat had fallen was the assassination in London of the famous Palestinian newspaper cartoonist Naji al-Ali. Al-Ali was shot in the face on July 22, 1987, outside the Chelsea offices of the Kuwaiti newspaper *Al-Qabas*. His killer was never found, but Scotland Yard reportedly suspected that the assassin was dispatched either by Arafat or by PLO officials very close to him. Al-Ali had regularly lampooned Arafat as an armchair revolutionary who always flew first class and a leader who had surrounded himself by a venal and corrupt clique. One of his last cartoons was of a woman alleged to have been a girlfriend of Arafat's, who was supposedly giving her cronies jobs on the PLO-funded general secretariat of the Palestinian Writers and Journalists Association. Al-Ali, himself a Palestinian refugee, had been thrown out of Kuwait in 1985—reportedly at Arafat's insistence. Arafat had always prided himself on the image that he had no Palestinian blood on his hands; he never liquidated his rivals but, rather, coopted or outmaneuvered them. That he might have become obsessed with the drawings of a cartoonist to the point of having him murdered indicates just how small Arafat's world had become. But then, when the emperor has no clothes, the barbs and arrows of even a cartoonist sting as much as any bullets.

I was almost embarrassed watching Arafat stomp around his Amman suite that afternoon, showing every PLO and Arab League official who walked in my copy of the communiqué with the missing language. But there was one thing Arafat said that stayed in my mind. Another reporter in the room asked Arafat if he thought the Jordanians were effectively eroding his position as leader of the Palestinians. At that point, a smile crossed the PLO chairman's face. "Just ask the people in the West Bank and Gaza," he said confidently. "They will tell you."

Arafat had no idea how right he was. He had no idea that the Palestinians under Israeli occupation—who constitute a little under half of the 4 to 5 million Palestinians in the world—were about to revive his political career and give him back the leadership role and the army he had been searching for from the day he walked up the gangway in Beirut harbor. As always, it wasn't great decisions or actions on Arafat's part that would resurrect him. Instead, it was his role as a symbol, and some unexpected emotional chemistry within the soul of the Palestinian community under Israeli occupation, that would bring him back to political life. The way the Palestinian issue was shunted aside by King Hussein and the other Arab leaders in Amman, the way Ronald Reagan and Mikhail Gorbachev ignored it a few weeks later at their summit meeting in Washington, the way Israeli leaders were boasting that no one cared about the PLO any longer, were taken as direct insults by many West Bankers and Gazans. After all, Arafat and the PLO were the symbols of their national aspirations, their only symbols on the world stage; if they were being marginalized by the Arabs and the Great Powers, this meant that all Palestinian aspirations were being marginalized—possibly for good. This fear would combine with twenty years of steadily mounting rage against Israel to leave the Palestinians in the West Bank and Gaza Strip feeling that the Arabs, the Jews, and the world had humiliated them just one too many times. As with an individual who suffers too many slights, there comes a moment when he gets so angry he says to himself, "The next person who lays a finger on me is really gonna get it."

Who would have thought that a careless Israeli truck driver would be that person?

On December 6, 1987, a forty-five-year-old Israeli Jew, Shlomo Sakle, a merchant from the northern Negev town of Beit Yam, went to the Gaza marketplace to do some shopping. The prices were always lower there and the selection of merchandise rich and varied. While Sakle was standing inside a shop browsing through some women's clothing, an unidentified Palestinian slipped in behind him and stuck a knife into the back of his neck. Blood splattered onto the floor as Sakle staggered toward the door. His attacker beat him to the exit, though, and was quickly swallowed up in the maze of shops and alleyways that make up the Gaza souk. As soon as the nearby shopkeepers spotted Sakle awash in his own blood, they rolled down their steel shutters and disappeared into the afternoon sun before the Israeli soldiers could question them. Sorry, they would say after Sakle died, we saw nothing.

Two days later, at around 4:00 p.m. on December 8, 1987, an Israeli trucker driving a large semi trailer on the main road out of Gaza carelessly turned his vehicle into a lane of oncoming traffic. That traffic consisted entirely of Palestinian workers packed inside station wagons and tenders, returning to Gaza from their day jobs inside Israel. Four Palestinians were killed and seven others wounded in the accident. All the casualties hailed from Jabaliya, Gaza's largest Palestinian refugee camp. Israeli police rushed to the scene and held the driver for questioning.

Rumors immediately spread through the Jabaliya camp and the adjacent Shifa Palestinian hospital that the Israeli truck driver had intentionally swerved his vehicle into the onrushing traffic to avenge the murder of Sakle. Some said he was Sakle's brother; others said he was a cousin. Either way, everyone knew that when it came to Jews and Palestinians there were no accidents, only acts of war.

Shortly after 8:00 a.m. the next day, December 9, 1987, Palestinian youths in Jabaliya pelted a group of Israeli reserve soldiers making their morning rounds through the refugee camp in an open safari truck. The Israeli officer in charge ordered his soldiers to dismount, and he personally led them against the Palestinian youths, who evaporated like a mirage. As the Israeli soldiers scurried about the camp trying to find the stone-throwers, they left only one sentry behind to guard their truck. When they returned, they found their vehicle surrounded by a group of angry Palestinians, one of whom was trying to wrestle the rifle from the lone sentry's hands. Out of nowhere, someone threw two flaming bottles at the truck, and then the thickening crowd began to close in on the soldiers. Did they want to kill them? Probably not. Similar confrontations had happened hundreds of times in the past. But the crowd was furious, and they apparently wanted the soldiers to taste some of that fury. The Israeli officer in charge panicked and opened fire, putting two bullets through the heart of Hatem Abu Sisi, a seventeen-year-old Gazan, who went to his grave unaware that his death would spark a full-scale Palestinian uprising that would become known in Arabic as the *intifada*. Later that day the army tried to take Abu Sisi's body for an autopsy and the usual midnight burial. They would not succeed. Thousands, some say as many as 30,000, Palestinians from Gaza gathered in Jabaliya camp around the Shifa hospital, took Abu Sisi's body from the morgue, and held their own mass funeral procession, which quickly turned into a riot. The Israeli reserve soldiers who were sitting at their checkposts inside the camp found themselves overwhelmed. The angry crowd, armed with bottles, rakes, stones, and tree limbs, devoured the army's tear-gas grenades and rubber bullets, which seemed only to nourish their rage. Israeli soldiers said they heard shouts of *"Itbach al-yahud"*—murder the Jews.

The next day, Thursday, December 10, 1987, the nearby town of Khan Yunis joined in the demonstrations, then the Balata and Kalandia refugee camps in the West Bank, then small Palestinian villages and city neighborhoods: there were more confrontations with Israeli troops, more casualties, and more burning tires smudging the skies of the West Bank and Gaza for days on end. Before anyone knew it, virtually all the Palestinians under Israeli occupation were engaged in a spontaneous primal scream that would be heard around the world.

What exactly were they saying?

"I'm going to fuck your mother, I'm going to fuck your sister," the Palestinian teenager shouted at the Israeli soldier in Hebrew, pointing his finger at the same time to make sure that the soldier knew it was his mother and his sister who were going to get fucked.

"Curse your mother's cunt that brought you into this world," the Israeli soldier shouted back at the Palestinian in Arabic, using a familiar vulgarity.

"I am ten years old and I will fuck you, you maniac fucker," another Palestinian youth shouted back in Hebrew, as he stood 100 yards away.

"Fuck you," blurted the Israeli soldier, his fingers wrapped tightly around his riot stick, which already had a few dents in it. "Curse your sister's cunt," he added.

"If you are a real man, you will put down your gun and come here and fight," screamed another Palestinian youth, gripping a stone in his hand. Then, as if to deliver the ultimate insult, the Palestinian added in Hebrew, "Your father is an Arab."

I watched this encounter in the middle of the Jabaliya refugee camp during the third week of the Palestinian uprising. Jabaliya is a wretched place—a warren of open sewers, corrugated-tin-roofed houses, and dusty unpaved streets, all sandwiched together in the heart of the Gaza Strip. On this particular day, I had gone out with an Israeli army patrol to get a feel for the street. There were no television cameras around. No one knew I was a reporter, so I got to see the real, unedited confrontation taking place between eighteen-year-old Israelis and eighteen-year-old Palestinians, and it was repeated 1,001 times across the West Bank and Gaza Strip for months after.

What the Palestinians had to say during these early clashes with Israeli soldiers wasn't really political, and it certainly wasn't diplomatic. It wasn't "242" or "338," and it wasn't "Let's give peace a chance." It was an expression of basic, elemental rage—rage at the Israelis who never allowed them to feel at home, rage at the Arabs who were ready to sell them out, and rage at a world that wanted to forget them. As East Jerusalem Palestinian merchant Eid Kawasmi put it when asked by *Moment* magazine about the origins of the *intifada*: "First of all Palestinians have been angry a lot. Their anger makes this uprising. It is an uprising of anger more than having a purpose. At the beginning, it had no purpose or aims. It started just like that."

Abu Laila, one of the leaders of the uprising in the Kalandia refugee camp, north of Jerusalem, told me one night in an almost dreamlike voice of the raw hurt he was expressing by taking stone in hand against the Israelis. "When I throw a stone, I feel there is a movie going on in my head. And it is showing all the pain, all the time that I spent in prison, all the times the Israelis asked me for my identity card, all the insults Israeli soldiers said to me. I see all the times the soldiers beat me, and beat my parents. That is what I feel when I throw a stone."

Brigadier General Ya'acov "Mendy" Orr, the Israeli division commander in the Gaza Strip, said he first realized just how deep and pervasive was the anger that had burst spontaneously from inside Palestinians like a volcanic eruption when he went on patrol through the Jabaliya camp in the early days of the *intifada.* "I was walking down a street and I saw this little boy—I think he was a boy—he wasn't much more than one year old," General Orr said. "He had just learned to walk. He had a stone in his hand. He could barely hold on to it, but he was walking around with a stone to throw at someone. I looked at him and he looked at me, and I smiled and he dropped the stone. I think it was probably too heavy for him. I'm telling you, he had just learned to walk. I went home and he went home. I thought about it later, and I thought, For that little kid, anger is a part of his life, a part of growing up—as much as talking or eating. He still didn't know exactly against whom he was angry; he was too young for that. He will know after a while. But for now, he knew he was supposed to be angry. He knew he was supposed to throw a stone at someone."

General Orr then paused for a moment and added for a third time, while shaking his head, "He had just learned to walk."

But as the uprising continued and widened, the Palestinians began to realize that they were also trying to say some very specific things with their rocks. It was almost as though once their raw anger burst the psychological dam inside them, the West Bankers and Gazans discovered a whole range of feelings and ideas which they had been developing for years, and, which, through the *intifada,* would finally be given tangible expression. What began as an irrational primal scream of rage on their part gradually developed into something very rational and sophisticated: a complete liberation strategy that was in many ways unique in the history of the Palestinian struggle.

The reason it was unique was that many of the feelings which the West Bankers and Gazans expressed, and many of the strategies they eventually developed, were forged—and could only have been forged—by Palestinians who had been living under Israeli occupation for twenty years. The *intifada* was, in every sense of the word, "made in Israel." Those Palestinians living in refugee camps in Jordan, Lebanon, and Syria, those PLO officials following the *intifada* through FAX machines in Tunis, will never fully understand what happened to their compatriots in the West Bank and Gaza Strip in the winter of 1987–88. They can admire what they did and they can identify with what they did, but they can never fully understand why they did it the way they did it; you had to have been there for the previous twenty years.

To begin with, I believe the most important feeling the West Bankers and Gazans wanted to convey to the Israelis—after they got their raw anger out of the way—was: "I am not part of you." They wanted to tell Israelis with their stones: "I may have worked in your fields and factories for twenty years; I may have spoken Hebrew, carried your identity cards, and sold your yarmulkes. But I am telling you here and now that I am not part of you, and I have no intention of becoming part of you."

One cannot understand the *intifada* unless one appreciates how deeply the Palestinians of the West Bank and Gaza had integrated with, and been coopted by, Israel. I was always struck by the fact that it was the Palestinians who named their uprising an *intifada*. They did not call it a *thawra*—the standard Arabic word for a revolt. This was odd, because for years one of the most popular Palestinian chants among the PLO guerrillas in Beirut was *"Thawra, thawra, hat al-nasr"*—Revolution, revolution, until victory. The standard Hans Wehr *Dictionary of Modern Written Arabic* translates *intifada* as a "tremor, a shudder or a shiver." But to understand the real reason this word was chosen over *thawra*, one needs to go back to its root. Almost all Arabic words are based on a three-letter root, which, in the case of *intifada*, consists of the Arabic letters *nun, fa', dad*, or *nafada*. *Nafada* means "to shake, to shake off, shake out, dust off, to shake off one's laziness, to have reached the end of, be finished with, to rid oneself of something, to refuse to have anything to do with something, to break with someone."

The West Bankers and Gazans used this term instead of "revolt" because they, unlike their compatriots in Lebanon, did not see themselves, first and foremost, as overthrowing Israel as much as purifying themselves of "Israeliness"—getting Israeli habits, language, controls, and products out of their systems. I was always struck by the fact that one of the first things the underground leadership of the *intifada* did was to order a commercial strike— either full days or partial days, depending on the situation. But they never issued any demands. Initially, I couldn't understand this. I would drive past all the shuttered stores in East Jerusalem and ask myself, Who goes on strike without issuing demands? It is like saying, I am going to hold my breath until you turn blue. But then I realized that the strike was not meant to bring pressure *on* Israel, it was meant to disconnect the Palestinians *from* Israel.

Indeed, throwing stones at Israeli soldiers, erecting stone barricades at the entrances of their villages, and going on commercial strikes was the Palestinians' way of reasserting some psychological distance between ruler and ruled, and of re-creating the conditions of hostility between the two communities, after years of sleeping together. Palestinian storekeepers literally told Israeli soldiers, "Our leadership will decide when to open and close from now on, not you." Before, the Israelis had always defined the terms of the relationship. Suddenly the Palestinians said they were going to define their own terms. It was their way of recovering their bodies, which had been sucked into the Israeli system.

That is why I always think of the *intifada* as an earthquake— an eruption of twenty years' worth of pent-up geothermal steam— raw Palestinian rage—that opened the Palestinian–Israeli fault line and created a physical chasm between the two communities. But it didn't open a chasm wide enough to totally disconnect the two communities. That would take time and much effort, because Israelis and Palestinians were simply too intertwined.

Early in the uprising, Dr. Andre Kerem, an Israeli heart specialist working at Jerusalem's Bikur Holim Hospital, found himself performing a heart catheterization on a thirty-four-year-old Palestinian contractor from Hebron. It was a delicate operation, done only with a local anesthetic. While the Palestinian was laid out on a surgical table and Dr. Kerem was going about his work, one of the Israeli nurses, who was supposed to assist him, burst into the hospital room, shrieking at the top of her lungs, "They burned our car! They burned our car! The Arabs burned our car."

"She said she had just received a phone call from her husband that some Palestinians had fire-bombed their car," recalled Dr.

Kerem. "She lived in an area of Jerusalem near an Arab neighborhood.

"She was absolutely hysterical," added the Israeli doctor. "She said she had to go home immediately and would not be able to assist us. People don't behave like that in the operating room. I told her to shut up and to get out immediately. All this time, the Palestinian patient, who had this nice big beard, was lying on his back looking up at me. He could see that I had a very angry look on my face. I was mad at the nurse, but he didn't know that, so he became frightened. When I looked back down at him, the first thing he said to me—in Hebrew—was: 'I wasn't there. I wasn't there.' He was afraid I was going to blame him for this nurse's burned car and take it out on him. I said to him, 'I know you weren't there! You were right here!' "

According to a Palestinian journalist I knew, Leaflet Number 10, one of a series of instruction sheets issued by the secret underground leadership of the *intifada*, the Unified Command, was photocopied by a Palestinian activist at the Israeli Ministry of Interior office on Jerusalem's Nablus Road. The young man walked into the building with a bagful of Israeli money and the illegal leaflet. He made 100 copies and then stepped out onto Nablus Road and began distributing them to Palestinians walking by. The copy machine is subsidized by the Israeli government.

Most of the cloth for the thousands of green, red, black, and white Palestinian flags that were hung up on telephone lines across the West Bank and Gaza Strip came from Israeli manufacturers. "Where do you think we get all the material for our flags?" a youth in Kalandia asked me. "We just go into the store and say to them, 'Give me the four colors,' and they know just what we want."

The mere fact that both Palestinians and Israeli soldiers spoke a common language—Hebrew—and were of the same generation at times made for certain unusual interactions.

"One day we were throwing stones at soldiers all morning and they were charging at us. We were going back and forth," said Abu Laila from Kalandia. "Finally we sent one of ours up to one of theirs and said, 'You go eat and we'll go eat and we'll all come back later.' They agreed. So we all went home."

No wonder Musa al-Kam, a Palestinian lawyer in his early

thirties whom I met in Israel's Dahariya prison, near Hebron, did not hesitate when I asked him what was the most important thing the *intifada* had accomplished.

"First of all, it was to show the Israeli public that we are not Israelis," said al-Kam, who had been arrested shortly after the uprising began, for alleged Palestinian nationalist agitation. "If it did not happen today, we would be just like Israelis—only without our land and without our Palestinian identities. In twenty more years Palestinians would be without personalities. We would be Israelis in our thoughts."

In pulling their bodies out from under the Israeli system, which was a painful process, many Palestinians were also performing a form of penitence. They were punishing themselves for having allowed themselves to be bought off and coopted by the Israelis for twenty years. One day in June 1988 as I was driving through the West Bank with Palestinian journalist Daoud Kuttab, we decided to stop for a drink at a roadside stand north of Ramallah, directly across the street from the Israeli West Bank military jail and Civil Administration headquarters at Beth El. The restaurant was owned by a Palestinian, Samir Ibrahim Khalil, age thirty-five, a refugee from the Jerusalem area. Samir explained to us that he had opened the restaurant five years earlier to cater primarily to Israeli soldiers working at Beth El. He even gave his restaurant a Hebrew name: Mifgash Beth El—Samir, which roughly translated would be Samir's Beth El Meeting Place. The menu was in Hebrew and Arabic, and the radio was set on the Voice of Peace, an Israeli station. Samir would speak and joke with the Israeli soldiers in their native tongue.

After the *intifada* began, though, Samir said he got religion. When we stopped in, it was just before noon and Samir was about to close for the day, because the Unified Command had ordered through leaflets that all commercial shops operate only on half time. It was the Palestinians' way of establishing their own time zone, distinct from Israel's. Two Israeli soldiers, their assault rifles lying on the table, were chomping away on hummus-filled pita sandwiches and sipping RC Colas when Samir came out to pull down his shutters.

"Why are you closing?" one of the Israeli soldiers shouted at

Samir. "Are you afraid? You think the *shabiba* [Palestinian youth] will shoot you if you don't close?"

"No," said Samir, continuing to lock his shutters. "I am closing out of conviction."

The Israeli soldier grunted and went back to his sandwich.

As the soldiers got up to leave, I engaged Samir in a conversation about how the *intifada* had affected him. He was eager to talk. I had the feeling we were in a confessional. "I used to sell Hebrew newspapers and cigarettes here," explained Samir. "It was strange. I felt as if I was in my own country, among my own people, yet the Israeli soldiers who came here felt as if they were in Tel Aviv. But after the *intifada* began, I stopped selling Israeli products. No more.

"Everything you see here is old," he insisted, showing me the sell-by date on a box of Israeli chocolates, "and I am not ordering any new stock. That is it. Now we are selling Palestinian cakes and cookies. See, right here; they even come in the colors of the PLO flag. I am paying a price for my pride and freedom, and I am happy to pay it. I am looking forward to the day when I run out of money. I am looking forward to the day when I cannot afford to buy lunch. It means I have exchanged the money for other things which make me happier. Before, I had reached a situation where I felt closer to Israelis than I did to Arabs. I was talking to them in Hebrew, eating together with them, and some of us became friends. For twenty years we saw stone-throwing, but before, when I saw people throwing stones, I would tell them to stop it. I never thought it would accomplish anything. I felt the same when the *intifada* began, but then I could see that this was something special, so I started throwing stones myself. Since then the population has become like one. Before, the people were jealous of me because I made so much money, but now they worry about my business because I am open only a few hours. Before, we Palestinians felt that our national identity was over and it was every man for himself. I get Israeli-made Coca-Cola and Palestinian-made RC Cola for the same price, but now I charge one and a half shekels for the Coke and half a shekel for the RC Cola to help my own people."

I then asked Samir who drew the three handwritten stylized Hebrew signs hanging over his kiosk. He confessed that he had drawn them himself. He had picked up the expressions from a

movie. They were in many ways the real yardsticks of how far
this man had strayed from his own Arab tradition and culture.
One Hebrew sign said: "Your mother doesn't work here, so please
clean up your own mess." The second said: "Eat here and leave
your wife home." The third said: "Eat and fuck, because you are
going to die tomorrow."

"Every day I look at those signs and say to myself I want to
take them down." Samir sighed.

He stared at them for a moment and then with three quick
snatches ripped them off the ceiling right before my eyes. He
angrily tore each one to shreds and then stuffed the scraps in the
garbage pail.

The Palestinians, however, didn't just want to tell the Israelis,
"We are not you." They also wanted to tell the Israelis and
themselves who *they* were. The fact that the uprising spread so
spontaneously from the refugee camps of Gaza to the opulent
Palestinian villas outside Ramallah, and from the most remote
hilltop villages to the Westernized cities, and from young to old,
was the Palestinians' way of demonstrating to the Israelis and
themselves what the Israelis had always denied and what they
themselves had begun to wonder about: that they were a nation.
When the uprising began, it was hard to tell who was more surprised by its spontaneous nature—the Israelis or the Palestinians.

One of the most impressive photographs from the *intifada* appeared on the front page of the *Jerusalem Post* of March 7, 1988.
It showed a middle-aged Palestinian Christian woman wearing a
stylish tight black dress with a slit up the leg. She had just walked
out of Sunday church services in the village of Beit Sahur, near
Bethlehem, and had taken off her high-heeled shoes, which she
was holding daintily in one hand. In the other hand she was
heaving a rock at an Israeli soldier. Next to her were three boys,
one of whom was firing a slingshot. I am sure that for twenty
years that woman went to church services every Sunday and then
went home, had lunch, and cursed the Israelis in private. But
with the *intifada* something snapped. She suddenly crossed a line,
picked up a stone, and, in effect, told the Israelis: "You don't
know me. You thought you knew me. You thought you were
'experts' on the Arabs. But you only knew my body, as it waited

on your tables and swept your floors. You never knew my mind. This is who I really am, and this is how I want you to think of me from now on."

The very reason that Israelis, particularly right-wingers, insisted at first that the uprising was not spontaneous, that it had been ordered by a small group of agitators, was that if all these Palestinians were spontaneously rising together, if they were all feeling the same thing at the same time, then they had to be a community with a shared past and a shared destiny; people with nothing in common don't rise up in unison. Since most Israelis viewed the West Bankers and Gazans as a disparate and amorphous collection of Arab individuals—either waiters and carpenters who could be ordered around like objects or terrorist criminals who could be ignored or killed without a second thought—their appearance as a nation came as quite a shock.

I don't believe it was a coincidence that after the *intifada* became a mass movement, many Israeli newspapers began for the first time to print some of the names of Palestinians killed by Israeli soldiers. Before then, they were just faceless, nameless objects. "Three Palestinians were killed in Nablus today" was usually all one would find in the Israeli press. But once the Palestinians proved to the Israelis that they were a community, that they were subjects trying to take charge of their own lives, the Israelis bestowed upon them an almost unconscious recognition by printing their names more frequently. Suddenly the gardener had a name, suddenly his dead son had a name, suddenly the whole community living on the same land with the Israelis had a name—Palestinians. This also explains why several Israelis remarked to me after the *intifada* began that they felt as though they were living in a new country, because a reality that had always been invisible suddenly became visible. The whole human landscape looked different.

No less so for Palestinians. Only through the *intifada* did the West Bankers and Gazans really emerge as a nation in the fullest sense. Every nationalist movement has a defining moment—a moment of real bonding—when all differences are suspended, and this was theirs. The *intifada*, in effect, marked the culmination of the process of transforming the West Bankers and Gazans from Jordanized and Egyptianized Palestinians into a Palestinian people—period. In many ways, it was Israel, through its repressive and humiliating treatment, which managed to give the Palestinians a common experience of bitterness to reinforce their historical and cultural ties and cement them together; whatever differences they had with each other, they eventually discovered, paled in comparison with the differences they had as a community with the Israelis.

For so many years thousands of Palestinians in the West Bank and Gaza had talked about being one people, but they hadn't behaved like it. That changed with the *intifada*. All PLO factions began working together within a unified command leadership. Muslim fundamentalists set aside their differences with secularists and Christians, and in virtually every village collaborators were either punished, or stood up, apologized to their neighbors, and vowed never to work for the Israelis again. In fact, the thing Palestinians kept talking about over and over again in the first few months of their uprising was not their "victories" over the Israelis but their own newfound sense of solidarity. Said Musa al-Kam, the imprisoned Palestinian lawyer, "In some towns or villages I had friends who went out and got arrested when all their other friends did. They just wanted to be with their friends; otherwise in the eyes of the society they would not be good."

The unity and courage Palestinians demonstrated in challenging fully armed Israeli soldiers with stones gave the West Bankers and Gazans a sense of dignity and self-worth that they had never previously enjoyed. It also gave them a new weight in PLO decision-making. In the old days, it was Arafat and the guerrillas in Beirut who gave the orders and the West Bankers and Gazans who were largely on the receiving end. After Arafat was driven from Beirut, though, the balance of power gradually began to shift in favor of the Palestinians under Israeli occupation, and that shift was made even more pronounced as a result of the *intifada*. The West Bankers and Gazans were no longer sitting on their hands by their radios listening to news of what Arafat and his guerrillas were doing in Amman or Beirut or Baghdad. Now it was Arafat and his guerrillas listening to the radio reports about them. "We're suffering the casualties," West Bankers could and did tell the PLO, "and you're flying first class."

Moreover, the West Bankers and Gazans were no longer whining about this or that Israeli arrest or house demolition; they were going out and literally daring the Israelis to arrest them, or shoot them, by the hundreds. They were no longer waiting for others to save them; rather, they were taking responsibility for saving themselves—not as individuals, but as a community. The fact that in the early stage of the uprising masses of Palestinians took to the streets meant that Israel could no longer control these 1.7 million people with a few hundred border policemen and Shin Bet agents. It required whole battalions of the Israeli army—thousands of men around the clock—and this led to thousands of public confrontations. In the first year of the uprising, the army arrested nearly 20,000 Palestinians, killed more than 300, and injured between 3,500 and 20,000, depending on whose figures one trusts. (During the same period only 11 Israeli soldiers and civilians died at the hands of Palestinians, while some 1,100 were injured.)

I once met a strapping, muscle-bound, twenty-year-old Palestinian man in the Kalandia refugee camp by the name of Jameel. With his physique, he would have been an elite commando in any Palestinian army. But when I asked him whether he was trying to hurt Israelis when he threw a stone, he answered in a way that made me realize how much the stone was really meant for him— meant to liberate him from his own sense of impotence and humiliation.

"A woman is being raped," said Jameel, "and while she is being raped she uses her nails to scratch the body of the rapist. Is that violence? We have been raped for years, but instead of our brothers helping us, they stood around and watched."

And now that you have taken your destiny into your own hands?

"The wounds of the rape are starting to heal," he said. "The woman is combing her hair and looking in the mirror again."

When the uprising began, Palestinians threw stones at the Israelis, not because they had all suddenly read the teachings of Mahatma Gandhi and become nonviolent, not because they didn't want to hurt the Israelis, but because when their anger suddenly exploded, stones and clubs and kitchen knives were all that most of them found available and operationally expedient.

The Palestinians under occupation knew their enemy well. Un-

384　　　　JERUSALEM

like the PLO bureaucrats in Beirut and Tunis, they knew the real dimensions of Israel's strength and weaknesses. They knew that in contrast to the Syrians or the Algerians or the Jordanians, the Israelis would not simply move in tanks and mow down hundreds of protestors with machine-gun fire, or level whole villages or towns, to quell the rebellion. The Israelis could be ruthless, the Palestinians under occupation knew, but not that ruthless. They might have played by Hama Rules in Beirut, but not in their own back yard surrounded by television cameras. Yes, the Palestinians labeled them Goliaths, but they knew in their heart of hearts that the Israelis were, as Benvenisti liked to say, "Goliaths with David's guilty conscience."

The Palestinians understood that, as long as they used stones, the Jews would respond with largely—though by no means exclusively—proportional measures: sporadic gunfire, imprisonment, tear gas, plastic bullets, and even a machine they invented to throw pebbles at a very high speed. Palestinians knew that although these Israeli countermeasures were sometimes lethal, they would never be sufficient to snuff out the rebellion; one or two casualties a day would not be enough to dissuade people from taking to the streets. Whenever I probed Palestinian youths as to why they threw stones, they did not respond by quoting Martin Luther King, Jr. They simply said, "Because we don't want to face Israeli tanks." With good reason. Prime Minister Shamir was once asked what would happen to the Palestinians if they began to use firearms widely in their *intifada*. He answered tersely, "There will not be even a memory of them left."

Every Palestinian in the West Bank and Gaza was aware of the relative restraint under which Israeli troops operated. Daoud Kuttab, the Palestinian journalist, interviewed a fourteen-year-old Palestinian boy from the village of Burka on the West Bank, who told him that he was out throwing stones during a demonstration one day when he was arrested by Israeli soldiers. They put him in handcuffs, and as they were leading him away, he told Daoud, one of the Israeli soldiers wound up to give him a belt. The boy said he told the soldier in Arabic, "No, no, [Defense Minister Yitzhak] Rabin said that you are not allowed to hit me after I am already in handcuffs." The soldiers started to laugh. "What— you know Rabin and Shamir?" the boy quoted one of the soldiers as saying to him. In the end, the soldiers were so amused and amazed by the youth's pluck, and in particular his ability to throw Rabin's orders back in their face, that they opened his handcuffs and let him go.

The fact that the West Bankers and Gazans had adopted stones for operational reasons was immediately encouraged and exploited by Yasir Arafat and the PLO leaders outside for diplomatic and propaganda reasons. Arafat was no fool, and he also watched television, lots of television. He could see that the nightly broadcasts of heavily armed Israeli troops opening fire on Palestinians armed only with stones had the potential to erase the mark of Cain—the label "terrorist"—which the Israelis had managed to slap onto the forehead of the whole Palestinian national movement. The West Bankers and Gazans, by daring to challenge the Israelis the way David challenged Goliath, actually rehabilitated Arafat and gave him a respectability on the world stage which he had never before experienced. No one loved to rub this point in more than Arafat himself—the man whom the Israelis had turned into the global symbol of the terrorist. As Arafat said in his interview with *Playboy* (September 1988), shortly after the uprising began, and repeated in virtually every interview after: "Everyone has now discovered who is the REAL terrorist organization: It is the Israeli military junta who are killing women and children, smashing their bones, killing pregnant women. You just have to look at television to see this. So now it is clear and obvious who the real terrorists are."

But as the uprising developed, the use of stones became symbolic of an entirely new strategy of Palestinian resistance—a strategy which, again, could only have been developed by the West Bankers and Gazans who had lived under Israel. What the Palestinians under occupation were saying by using primarily stones instead of firearms was that the most powerful weapon against the Israelis was not terrorism or guerrilla warfare, which the PLO had practiced futilely for twenty years. Israel was simply too strong to be moved by such tactics, and only an immature liberation movement would think otherwise.

The most powerful weapon, they proclaimed, was massive nonlethal civil disobedience. That is what the stones symbolized. They symbolized not working in Israel, refusing to cooperate with the Israeli military government in the occupied territories, no longer buying Israeli products, going on strike half the business hours of each day, choking the Israeli prisons with detainees, and generally making the Palestinians as a community indigestible for Israel. In that sense, the use of stones was simultaneously a critique of the PLO's tactics and a discovery by West Bankers and Gazans that they had had within themselves the power to challenge the Israelis all along. They simply had never tapped it. No wonder one of the most popular Arabic chants during the uprising was "Don't fear, don't fear, the stone has become a Kalashnikov."

"The Palestinians came to understand through the uprising what made the Israeli occupation work—it was themselves and their own cooperation with the whole Israeli system," said Sari Nusseibeh. "The most important achievement of the *intifada* was to show Palestinians where their chains were and how they could remove them."

At the same time, though, the stone also contained a political message meant for the Israelis. The Palestinians in the West Bank and Gaza, generally speaking, had always had a slightly different political agenda than those Palestinians living in the refugee camps of Jordan, Syria, and Lebanon, who had been Arafat's main constituency when he was in Beirut. Because most of the refugees living in Jordan, Syria, and Lebanon were from those parts of Israel that fell within the pre-1967 boundaries—from places like Haifa, Jaffa, or the Galilee—the only way they would ever feel truly at home again was if Israel disappeared entirely and they were allowed to return to their original villages and original houses and original land. The West Bank and Gaza were as foreign to them as the southern suburbs of Beirut. Their problem, in short, was the Israeli in their house.

This was not true for many of the 1.7 million Palestinians in the West Bank and Gaza Strip. To be sure, more than one-third of them were also refugees from pre-1967 Israel living in camps, but even as refugees they were at least residing in homes within Palestine. The majority, though, were Palestinians whose families have lived in towns and villages of the West Bank, and to a lesser extent the Gaza Strip, for generations—long before the Israelis arrived in 1967. Their immediate problem was Israel's occupation, not its existence. Their problem was not an Israeli family living in their house but an Israeli soldier stationed on their roof. If Israel's occupation of the West Bank and Gaza ended, and Israeli soldiers got off their roofs and returned to pre-1967 Israel, many

West Bankers and Gazans could feel at home again in the fullest sense. Therefore, they were, as a community, much more willing to accept a two-state solution—any solution—that would get Israel back into its pre-1967 boundaries and leave them with their own Palestinian state in the West Bank and Gaza. It wasn't that they had come to recognize the right of the Jewish people to a homeland, or that they had abandoned all dreams of recovering Haifa and Jaffa; they simply recognized that Israel was too powerful to be eradicated and that they could solve their own immediate problems by coming to terms with her. That, I believe, is what many Palestinians in the West Bank and Gaza were trying to signal by throwing stones—to tell the Israelis that they were not out to murder them but were ready to live next door to them, if they would only vacate the territories and allow a Palestinian state to emerge there. In fact, from the moment the uprising began, most West Bankers and Gazans were telling Israelis privately—and in a garbled way publicly—that this was what the *intifada* was all about.

But the West Bankers and Gazans were afraid to speak this message aloud to the Israelis, because they knew that they did not have the authority to sign away half of Palestine—only the PLO did—and because they also knew that within the refugee camps of the West Bank and the Gaza Strip, not to mention in Lebanon, Syria, and Jordan, were many Palestinians who still dreamed of and insisted on returning to their original homes in pre-1967 Israel, Palestinians who would kill to defend that right.

The day I went to Dahariya prison to talk to Palestinians arrested in the *intifada*, I began by interviewing the warden, Lieutenant Colonel David Zamir. The first thing I asked him was to recommend the most interesting prisoners with whom I could speak.

"I have something like 1,200 prisoners in this prison," said Zamir. "Out of those 1,200, 1,199 say they are innocent. They are innocent. They didn't do a thing. They were home sleeping or taking a shower or playing *sheshbesh* [backgammon] when for some reason, they say, Israeli soldiers came and arrested them. They had nothing to do with stones or anything. Everybody is innocent. Except one guy. I have one guy here who says he's guilty and proud of it."

Naturally, I asked to interview him.

A few minutes later I was introduced to Mazen Khair Ahmed Radwan, fifteen years old, from the Kalandia refugee camp. He told me that for the past year he had been working in an Israeli juice factory in Atarot—filling and packing bottles of juice.

"I am the oldest son and the only one who can bring money for the family," he told me, "but I felt that by working I was helping the Israeli economy. It made me hate the Israelis more. They kill people in the streets and come in houses with tear gas. The last time I worked they told me they had no money to pay me."

So what exactly did you do that landed you here? I asked.

"I threw a stone at some Jews," said Mazen.

Why?

"Because I didn't have a grenade. If I had had a grenade I would have thrown that. The stone and the grenade are the same thing for me."

What is the *intifada* about for you?

"We want our land back."

Which land?

"The land the Jews took in 1948."

Through their *intifada* the West Bankers and Gazans put the whole Palestinian national movement on a new track. They implemented a new method of resistance—massive, relatively non-lethal civil disobedience—and a new message—clear-cut, unambiguous acceptance of a two-state solution. No more yes-no business. What they needed, however, was a Palestinian leader with enough international standing to take their message to the world and with enough credibility to be able to say to Mazen Khair Ahmed Radwan and all the other refugees living in camps in Jordan, Syria, and Lebanon what the West Bankers and Gazans were saying to Israelis privately: We must formally accept Israel if we are ever going to get anything.

Enter Yasir Arafat. Arafat, as I noted earlier, had been casting about for a role to play ever since Beirut. The uprising gave him that role; if he hadn't existed, the West Bankers and Gazans would have had to invent him. But when they put out their casting call, the West Bankers and Gazans made it clear to Arafat that they were now the dynamic element within Palestinian politics—

not the refugees or PLO bureaucrats on the outside—and that Arafat would have to speak the lines which they dictated. That meant Arafat would have to say the "I-word"—Israel. He would have to publicly recognize the Jewish state.

For a variety of reasons, Arafat was more than ready to grab the deal which the West Bankers and Gazans in effect offered him. To begin with, Arafat had to have known perfectly well how little he and the PLO leadership were responsible for the *intifada* in its origins; it clearly took them by surprise as much as everyone else. The biggest revolt by Palestinians since the 1930s had begun without PLO direction. Arafat also could not have escaped noticing the fact that his picture was little in evidence when the Palestinians in the occupied territories first took to the streets. They were almost as angry at the PLO for abandoning them as they were at the rest of the world. If Arafat had not fallen in line with the political direction laid down by the West Bankers and Gazans, he would have risked losing his position as leader and symbol of the Palestinian national movement, and he would have opened the door for an alternative authentic leadership to emerge from the occupied territories—the same way he and his cohorts emerged in 1967 and ousted their effete elders. But the time was also right for Arafat to recognize Israel. He and his colleagues had been on the road too long; they wanted to cash in their chips and get at least something for their efforts before the bank closed entirely. Moreover, the Arab world had mellowed since 1967. While the Arab consensus was not ready to embrace Israel, it was increasingly ready to tolerate recognition of its existence. Finally, most of the Palestinian refugees, particularly those exposed to daily threats in the Lebanese jungle, were ready to consider any pragmatic solution that might get them a state of their own to reside in—even if they were not able to go back to their original homes *immediately*. Pronouncing the "I-word" was a small price to pay for such an opportunity, and Arafat, wordsmith that he always was, would do it without saying explicitly to the refugees in Lebanon, Jordan, Syria, and elsewhere that they wouldn't ever be going home, after all; he would keep some shred of dream alive for them. But more about that a little further down the road.

* * *

It was an ambush of sorts. The orange Opel 1900 was cruising along the highway into the Gaza Strip about two hundred yards ahead of our car, when a Palestinian boy sauntered into the middle of the road. The Opel's driver slowed down to avoid hitting the boy and, as soon as he did, other Palestinian youths hiding in the brush by the side of the road jumped up and pelted the car with stones, totally knocking out its front windshield. The Israeli driver, a stout little fellow wearing blue jeans, white tennis shoes, and a ski vest, was hopping mad. His anger was not just political— Jew versus Arab; it wasn't just that the stone could have killed him or the flying glass blinded him; and it wasn't just that he felt this was *his* road and no one had a right to assault him on it. It was that some son of a bitch had just broken his windshield, his $250 windshield, and he wanted him dead.

When we pulled up behind his car, we found him in the process of locking and loading an M-16 rifle he had in the trunk, and heading off to hunt down the Palestinian youths, who had evaporated into the adjacent village. But as the man stalked from his Opel up the dirt path on which the Palestinians had fled, he was suddenly confronted with a scene that forced him to freeze in his tracks. Down the path trudged three Palestinian women dressed in long black robes and beating two dozen sheep with canes. It was the most biblical scene one could imagine, the shepherdesses and their flock walking past mud huts framed in palm trees and cactus plants. It easily could have been 1888, or 1288, or 1088 B.C. Nothing much had really changed since the days of Isaac and Ishmael—not the stones and certainly not the passion; only the Opel and the fancy rifle were new. Israeli soldiers on the scene eventually talked the man out of going into the village. We left him sweeping shards of glass off his front seat and muttering to himself, as a young Palestinian woman riding a donkey-driven cart rolled by—no doubt quietly savoring the scene behind her blank stare.

This encounter, which took place early in the *intifada*, popped into my mind months later when Aluph Hareven, a prominent Israeli social analyst who specializes in educating for Arab–Jewish coexistence, told me about a conversation his daughter had had with an Israeli taxi driver. His daughter had been discussing with the driver how Israel should respond to the uprising and the driver told her, "You know what we should do? We should take our clubs and hit them over the head, and hit them and hit them and hit them, until they finally stop hating us."

The Palestinian *intifada* set off an equally intense explosion of rage on the Israeli side of the fault line. Unlike the Palestinian explosion, however, the Israeli outburst never acquired a name, but it was there nonetheless. You could see it in the X-rays of the hundreds of Palestinians who had their arms or legs or ribs broken by Israeli soldiers; you could see it in the Palestinian shops, whose doors and windows were kicked in by Israeli soldiers when the owners refused to open during the hours set by the Israeli authorities, and you could count it in the number of Palestinians killed by Israeli soldiers, who were supposed to be shooting at their legs.

The anger that went into the Israeli clubs and bullets was, like that of the Palestinians, fed by several different sources. On one level, many Israelis felt like the homeowner who wakes up one morning and discovers his live-in maid standing in the master bedroom, playing the stereo at full blast, and announcing to the boss that she is not just a faceless object that can be ordered around but that she is an equal—with an equal claim to his house.

It was enraging for Israelis to have these "niggers"—which was exactly how many Israelis viewed the Palestinians—these people whom they had given "good jobs," medical care, and all the other benefits that Israelis claimed went into their "enlightened occupation"—suddenly getting uppity and saying that they would not accept their second-class status any longer. More than a few Israelis wanted these "thankless" Palestinian maids and waiters to be put back in their proper places.

Yet there was something else behind the Israeli rage. By repudiating the Israeli system, by openly mocking Israeli authority, by making it unsafe for Israelis to travel on some of their own roads, the Palestinians were depriving the Israelis of their sense of being at home. What the Israeli club said to the Palestinian was just what the taxi driver in Aluph Hareven's story indicated: "You bastards. How many times do I have to beat you, how many of your bones do I have to break, how many of you do I have to kill, before you recognize that I am here and entitled to relax in my own house?"

There is nothing more frustrating than feeling that you are strong but that you cannot use your strength in a way that will enable you to take your shoes off. Ze'ev Posner, a cameraman for Cable News Network (CNN), told me about a scene he witnessed in the West Bank village of Halhul in February 1988 that drove this point home. An Israeli general arrived in the village, along with a contingent of officers, to observe the Israeli troops there quelling a Palestinian riot. "All of a sudden," said Posner, "one of these Palestinian kids with his head wrapped in a kaffiyeh decided that he was going to be real brave and stepped forward with a slingshot and fired a stone right at the general, but it missed. The general really got mad. He decided he was going to deal with this himself, so he started chasing after the kids. And he is a general, right, so he has this big belly and everything. The kids knew the village and they ran into all these side alleys. I was following with my camera. All of a sudden this general finds himself in a dead end, facing a row of shouting and cursing kids about 15 meters away. They were all screaming at him, 'Palestine, Palestine.' And once he was close enough to get a good look at them, he could see that they weren't even teenagers; they were just a bunch of twelve-year-olds. He didn't know what to do. So he just started waving his Motorola walkie-talkie at them and shouting, 'Go home! Go home! What are you doing here? Go home!' It was all he could do."

Finally, there was also real fear behind the Israeli clubs.

The fear came from the fact that the Palestinians threw stones and bottles to announce to Israelis that they were there, that they wanted to be treated as subjects not objects, but for almost a year they failed to accompany those stones and bottles with a clear message explaining to Israelis exactly what their objectives were. From the Israeli point of view, the maid announced that she was moving out of the basement, but without stating explicitly how much of the house she would be satisfied with. Sure, privately many Palestinian individuals in the West Bank and Gaza said they just wanted an end to the Israeli occupation, but they never said it publicly as a community. That is why although there was an asymmetry in firepower in the clashes between Israeli soldiers and Palestinian youths—Israelis had vastly superior weapons compared to the Palestinians—there was not an asymmetry in the stakes. Israelis felt just as deeply as Palestinians that their communal survival was at stake in what was happening in the streets.

True, many Israeli soldiers were deeply troubled by having to go out and beat Palestinians with clubs, or chase women and children. There was no heroism in such a war and they felt none; Israelis who served in the West Bank and Gaza never told war stories. But 99 percent of them served without question, because if they didn't do it, where would the stone-throwers stop? No one was quite sure they wouldn't follow the Jews right back to Tel Aviv. An Israeli army spokesman who escorted me on many interviews I conducted with Israeli soldiers during the *intifada* always used to say to me of duty in the West Bank, "We hate it, but we do it."

"I did reserve duty in Gaza several times before the uprising, but in those days we just sat around in cafés and drank coffee," Menachem Lorberbaum, an Israeli soldier in his mid-twenties, told me after completing twenty-two days of service in Nablus shortly after the *intifada* began. "In the old days, the Border Police ran the occupation. We didn't need to get that involved. This time in Nablus I went forty-eight hours without sleep. We were on the go constantly. I had to chase Palestinians into their homes after they threw stones. They all run into the shower. Really. They run home, tear off their clothes, and get in the shower. You burst in and find the one you're looking for and he's sopping wet. He says, 'Hey, I wasn't throwing stones, I was here taking a shower.' It is disgusting to have to meet people on such a level. It wasn't that I felt I shouldn't do it. I knew I had to do it, but it was simply disgusting. I always knew there was an occupation in the abstract, but I never really thought about the Palestinians. They washed the streets and cleaned up the garbage. Now you can't ignore the fact that you are an occupier of another people. You have to arrest people and put blindfolds on them and then ride through the middle of Nablus with them in the back of your jeep and everyone in town staring at you. You feel like an occupier.

"I want to come home and tell everyone I meet how bad it is," added Lorberbaum, as we stood on the stairs of the school at which he taught. "But look at that lady over there pushing her baby carriage, what does she care? What does she want to know? All she knows is that people are rioting and someone has to stop them."

In the long run, nothing will pressure the Israeli Cabinet into making territorial concessions to the Palestinians more than pressure from Israeli soldiers disgusted with serving in the territories. But as long as the Palestinians are even the slightest bit ambiguous about where their stone-throwing stops and where the Jewish state begins, that pressure from the army will always be diluted—no matter how morally disturbing the occupation becomes. In November 1988, for example, twenty-one Israeli officer trainees were driving past the Kalandia refugee camp when some youths pelted their bus with stones. The twenty-one officer candidates, the future leadership of the Israeli army specially selected from the rank and file, ordered the driver to stop; they piled out of the bus and went on a rampage through Kalandia—smashing windows, overturning cars, and breaking in doors. In their defense, the officers said they were just following orders. When an Israeli newspaper quoted an unidentified senior military official as saying the officers would be disqualified from their course, the Israeli public responded with such a howl of protest that Defense Minister Rabin was forced to write letters to the parents of each of the officer candidates, promising that all twenty-one would be able to join a future officers' program.

The Palestinian rage that exploded in December 1987 not only opened up the fault line that ran through the West Bank and Gaza Strip but also the one through pre-1967 Israel as well. It took nearly two weeks to hit, but on December 21, the fissure shot right across the Green Line when Israel's 700,000-member Israeli Arab community mounted a general strike in solidarity with their compatriots' uprising in the West Bank and Gaza. The strike was called Peace Day, although it was anything but peaceful. From Jaffa to Haifa to Nazareth, Israeli Arab youths took to the streets, waving PLO flags, throwing stones at Jewish cars, and rhythmically shouting such Arabic slogans as *"In baladna, yahud kalabna"*—"This is our country and the Jews are our dogs."

Many Israelis professed to be shocked by the reaction of the Israeli Arabs. They had no right to be. For twenty years certain Israeli leaders and Jewish settlers had been insisting that the 1967 boundary between Israel and the West Bank and Gaza did not exist anymore, and that it was all one grand land of Israel. But if there is no 1967 border for the Jews, why should there be one for the Palestinian Arabs?

My friend Laura Blumenfeld wasn't shocked by Peace Day—
just a little disappointed. I met Laura one day while washing my
car. She said she had heard I lived across the street and wanted
to talk to me. She had been working in an Israeli Arab village,
Tira, northeast of Tel Aviv, for nine months, and had gathered
many stories. Her tales of Tira were captivating. I gradually realized that Laura was like a woman who was standing on her
porch with her Instamatic camera when the earthquake hit. As
the ground opened between Israelis and Palestinians, she captured it frame by frame, and this was how it looked from the
epicenter.

A twenty-four-year-old American Harvard University graduate, Laura had come to Israel to work for Arab–Jewish coexistence as part of a program called Interns for Peace. Interns sent
teams of Jews and Arabs into Israeli Arab and Jewish towns to
organize dialogues between Arab and Jewish youngsters and,
ideally, build long-term personal relationships that might one day
seal the fault line for good. Educated in a yeshiva in New York
and speaking fluent Hebrew and some Arabic, Laura was assigned
to Tira, in September 1987, three months before the *intifada*. As
a going-away present when she left New York, her brother had
given her the cover of a *New York Times Magazine* article I had
written on the Israeli–Palestinian conflict called "My Neighbor,
My Enemy." The color cover photograph showed an Arab woman
and her child tilling a field, while off in the distance a group of
Jews were marching with a flag. In the middle of this picture
Laura's brother had drawn a little stick figure labeled *Laura*, and
out of her mouth he drew a bubble with a voice saying, "Let's
all be friends."

Although she had spent a great deal of time in her youth in
Israel, and like many liberal American Jews had grown intrigued
with the native Arab community, it was actually an encounter
that her father had had with an unknown Arab that drove Laura
to Interns for Peace.

"An Arab shot my father," she explained to me in an even
voice during our first meeting. "My father was visiting Israel as
a tourist," she continued. "He was walking back to his hotel on
Friday night after visiting the Kotel [the Western Wall]. He was
walking down David Street, just as the Arab shopkeepers were
closing their stores. From Butchers' Alley someone fired a shot

and my father fell. He felt his head and he was bleeding. He started to shout, 'Help me, help me,' but all the shopkeepers just turned away and went into their shops. He managed to drag himself to the police station and they took him to Hadassah [hospital]. The bullet had grazed his skull. What was so strange about it was that on that very same night, March 7, 1986, I, as the president of the Harvard–Radcliffe Zionist League, was hosting a dinner at the Harvard Hillel for the Harvard–Radcliffe Arab Students' Society. Right before dinner I get this call, and the first thing my father says is, 'Laura, I'm okay, no matter what you hear on television, I'm okay.' So he tells me what happened, and thirty minutes later I'm sitting across the table from Palestinian students chatting away. This person who shot my father was faceless and in the dark, and I wanted to meet him. It was very important for me to look him in the eye and say to him, 'Look, jerk, my dad wants a Palestinian state alongside Israel and his daughter was meeting with Palestinians at the Harvard Hillel the night you shot him.' "

Like her fellow interns, Laura had started out believing that with enough education and contact Arabs and Jews could overcome their differences. "The elementary school in Tira where I worked faced the West Bank," she explained. "One time during one of these meetings between Arab and Jewish schoolchildren, I was looking past the parents and the kids and out the door and I saw the hills of the West Bank, and I thought to myself, Stupid dirt. It is just dirt. Stupid hills. I could never understand this idea of fighting over dirt. I had this idea that nothing is more dear than the soul of a human being, and I think that they are crazy fighting over land and 'liberating' territories. What did they liberate? Grass? It was a very American reaction. So I got up to shut the door and the door wouldn't shut. It kept swinging open. I wanted to shield my kids from the dirt. They were sitting there singing some nauseatingly adorable song and I kept trying to shut the door, but the handle was broken and it kept swinging open. The hills were laughing at me. I just couldn't close them out."

Nevertheless, during her early months in Tira, Laura thought she was making enough headway that she might not have to shut the world out. One day, she asked her class of Arab fifth-grade boys in Tira to put together collages using pictures and headlines from *The New York Times*. She later showed them to me, stopping at the one which had caused her the most pain. One of the Arab boys had pasted together a picture of Israeli troops putting down a Druse demonstration in the Golan Heights, a picture of Shimon Peres, and a picture of Nazi war criminal John Ivan Demjanjuk, who was convicted by an Israeli court of murdering Jews at the Treblinka death camp. Under the picture of the Druse, the boy wrote: "The doing of the Jewish in the Golan." Under Peres's picture, he wrote: "I feel angry with Peres because he talks something he cannot do it." And next to Demjanjuk he wrote: "I feel too bad from Demjanjuk."

"So I said to him," recalled Laura, "why do you feel bad for Demjanjuk? He said, 'Because I think he is innocent.'

"So I said, 'Do you know that he is accused of killing many Jews?' And he said, 'Well'—and this is one of my most sensitive students—'even if he killed Jews, that would be a good thing.'

"It really hit me right here," said Laura, pounding her chest. "I remember feeling hot, scared, and sad all at the same time. I also felt despair. I said to him, 'Do you know that I'm Jewish?' I had been working with him for months, and he was a really nice kid. He turned completely red. And he said, 'Oh, I'm sorry. I didn't realize that there could be Jews like you.' And he took this collage out of my hands, ripped off the picture of Demjanjuk, and scribbled out what he had written with a blue crayon. The next day he showed up at my house with this huge crate of strawberries and said, 'I want to give these to you. I am sorry. You really taught me something.' That at least made me feel that I was accomplishing something, breaking down at least some stereotypes and getting people to know each other as human beings."

The first stage of Laura's work in Tira involved her in preparing the Arab fifth-graders for meeting the Jewish fifth-graders from the adjacent Israeli town of Kfar Saba.

Said Laura, "I asked them one day, 'How many here have ever seen a Jew?' They all stood up. Then I asked, 'How many have ever spoken to a Jew?' They all sat down. 'So where did you see a Jew?' Well, one said he saw this soldier on television, and another said he saw an army patrol come through Tira."

Nevertheless, kids being kids, the first get-together between the fifth-graders from Kfar Saba and the fifth-graders from Tira proved to be a smashing success, with many friendships formed, including one between Said of Tira and Eitan of Kfar Saba, two of Laura's favorites. Said was so eager to show Eitan around and demonstrate his rudimentary knowledge of Hebrew that he pointed out everything in sight, including: "This is a donkey, this is a house, this is a cemetery." The boys ate at Said's home, visited a mosque together, and heard a lecture about the meaning of the pilgrimage to Mecca. A relationship was born.

"When the *intifada* happened a few weeks later, it had no impact at first on our programs," said Laura. "It was as if we were in our own little world and I was keeping the door to the outside shut. I thought I could keep it that way. Then Peace Day came along. That day I was visiting Said's mother, and he comes running in and says, 'Guess what, Laura, I was on the road throwing rocks at Jewish cars.' He had been the most enthusiastic kid during the meetings with Jews. It was one of those moments that I realized no matter how much you clear away you always have a bedrock. At that moment I felt so sad. I felt frustrated, and I even felt a little bit frightened. His mother didn't say anything. I felt as if things were suddenly changing. Then we started to see Arabic graffiti on the walls in Tira: *We are all together; We support our Palestinian brothers until the land is liberated; The hand of our enemy will be cut off.* That night, I locked my door for the first time. A few days later, I was in a taxi from Kfar Saba to Tira and the driver had the PLO radio station on. At one point they took a break from the nationalist songs and gave a weather report. The broadcaster said there would be unusually strong winds in Palestine today and a mother in the taxi looked at her little girl and said, 'Allah is blowing the poison gas back on the Jewish soldiers.' "

The shift in mood on the Jewish side came just as quickly.

"About a week later I was in the teachers' lounge at the school in Kfar Saba," said Laura. "Eitan's mother walked in and literally grabbed me by the collar and said, 'Look, I have a son. From the night he turns eighteen to the morning he wakes up at fifty-five life for me is going to be one sleepless nightmare [because he would have to be in the army and then do annual reserve duty]. I am not ready to lose sleep yet. What are you dragging my kid to Tira for? He is ten years old.' Then Eitan's teacher joined in: 'Who are you? You are an American, naïve. You come here, preach democracy, and tell us what to do, and then go home and sit on your cozy leather couch and watch us on television and say, Tsk tsk, how inhumane. You are only doing this so you won't feel embarrassed at your company's cocktail parties.' They were really angry. I tried to explain that the Israeli Arabs wanted to continue with the contacts and that they would be alienated all the more if the Jews rejected them now. So the teacher said, 'Of course they want to continue! Don't you know they are a double-dealing people. Here we went and raised their standard of living, and you know what our thanks will be. We will all end up living in Manhattan!' Then this other teacher jumps in and says, 'My son is beating Arab children in Gaza. How can I bring my students to meet Arab children in Tira? I want to freeze all activity.' "

At that point, recalled Laura, the school principal joined the argument. "Did I hear someone talk about freezing the meetings?" said the principal. "Do you know where I come from? I come from Poland. I lived in a ghetto. I couldn't travel. I lost two of my friends fighting the Arabs of Tira in 1948. I lost them so that Jews could have a place to feel free and safe, and if you don't get on the bus tomorrow to Tira, then we're all going back to the ghetto, and I will be damned if we're going back to the ghetto."

The next Arab–Jewish meeting did go ahead, but only twenty out of the forty Jewish kids attended. The Arab kids were hurt, said Laura. It wasn't a political thing. They were offended personally. Where is my friend from Kfar Saba? they asked her. Why is he afraid to come to my house? What does he think I am? A week later it was time for a return visit by the Arab kids to Kfar Saba, and this time some of the Jewish parents kept their kids home from school, including Eitan's mother.

"Said was crushed," said Laura. "To him it was purely a personal thing. He said, 'That's it. I don't want any more meetings. No more.' "

The next week Laura was back at the Jewish school in Kfar Saba. "I explained to the kids what happened," she said. "I told them that for now there would be no more meetings because of the parents, but that we could still be pen pals. I suggested that for now they write letters to the kids in Tira. In the middle of my talk to the class, this alarm goes off—*rrrrrrrrrrrr*—and this teacher bursts in and says, 'We are having a civil-defense drill, pretend that the Arabs are attacking.' So the classroom was drained. All the kids went down to the bomb shelter, and I sat

on this low cement wall shivering in my Interns for Peace T-shirt."
So where does it all leave you now? I asked.

"It leaves me feeling that blood is thicker than water—literally," said Laura. "Here is Tira, here is Tulkarm [a West Bank Arab town] and here is Ra'anana [an Israeli Jewish town]," she explained, splaying out three fingers from one hand. "What we now have is the Arabs in Tira donating their blood to the Arabs in Tulkarm so that the Arabs in Tulkarm can throw stones at the Jews in Ra'anana. And Laura is in the middle saying, 'Let's be friends.'

"Before, when I asked the Jewish kids, What is the difference between the people who live in Tira and the people who live in Tulkarm? they would say, 'Well, the ones in Tira are like Jewish Muslims and the others are real Arabs.' I would patiently explain to them that there are West Bank Arabs and there are Israeli Arabs and why they are different. But ever since Peace Day I cannot say that anymore. The Israeli Arabs themselves are schizophrenic. First the Israeli side dominated them; now the Palestinian side is taking over.

"Every weekend I come home from Tira to Jerusalem to relax," Laura continued. "So I go in last week and put on the television, and you know what series has been playing on television here all year? *North and South*, the one about the American Civil War. I don't know whose idea that was. I would just turn the television off and shut myself into my room and put on my Vivaldi. I had some Reese's Pieces I had brought back with me from America—a whole supply. I would take some of them out and just lose myself in my Reese's Pieces.

"They are enemies. They really are enemies and I cannot deny that anymore," concluded Laura of the Palestinians and Israelis. "In all relationships we pretend that things are wonderful and we get along, and then you hit a certain level where there is just conflict and you can't get beyond it. I really think that my work is really ignoring reality, but sometimes that's the only way you can live and be happy."

When the fault line cracked open, anyone who tried to straddle it was pulled apart like a wishbone. Ask Naomi Shapiro, an American Jewish woman in her mid-twenties, who had also worked as an Intern for Peace in Tira for two years. Like many American Jews who came to Israel and got involved in working for Arab–Jewish coexistence, Naomi found that she always lived sort of a double life. She sympathized with the Palestinians of Tira, but never to the point of giving up her own Jewishness or identification with Israel; she identified with Israel and Zionism, but never so blindly that she could not also understand the Palestinians' quest for their own state. That balancing act worked fine until the *intifada* opened the fault line wide enough that Naomi had to jump to one side or the other. Her moment of truth came quite unexpectedly one day while she was trying to buy a piece of cake at the cafeteria in the Central Bus Station of Jerusalem.

"It was several months after the *intifada* had started," Shapiro told me, "and I was wearing a button that said END THE OCCUPATION, written in Hebrew, English, and Arabic. I went up to the counter to order, and there was this Palestinian waiter there. I had seen him before. He must spend his whole day serving Jews and being polite to them. As he took the piece of cake I wanted out of the glass case and was about to hand it to me, I caught him staring at my shirt. I suddenly remembered that I was wearing this button. We had been speaking in Hebrew, but he immediately switched to English and said, 'Where did you get that button?'

"I told him I got it from a friend," recalled Shapiro. "So he said, 'Do you have another?' I said no. So then he started to plead with me. I mean he really started to beg. He said, 'Please, please, let me have that button. I want that button. I need to have that button.' "

Seeing that he was obviously desperate, Shapiro took off the button and handed it to him, along with the money for her piece of cake. The Palestinian waiter took the button and handed Shapiro back her money.

"He kept saying, 'Thank you, thank you,' " said Shapiro. "Meanwhile, all these Israelis sitting around the cafeteria were watching this. There was this Orthodox man, a real black hat, who was just staring at me with this 'What-are-you-doing-with-that-filthy-Arab kind of look.' "

When the Palestinian waiter started to follow Shapiro out of the restaurant, she realized that this was not one of those cute little American-Jew-meets-Palestinian encounters, where a few words of Arabic are exchanged with the native and everyone goes home smiling.

"When we got outside, he asked me where I was from and I said America," said Shapiro. "And then—this was really strange—he said to me, 'Do you know what is happening?' It was as if we were in some spy movie and we were the only two people in the world who knew this secret of the *intifada*, and all the Israelis in the restaurant and the bus station were frozen. He just kept whispering, 'Do you know what is happening?' So I said, Yes, yes, I know what is happening. And we both just nodded our heads at each other. I shook his hand, and as he walked away he kept saying, 'Please, please come back again.' When he walked off, I was shaking so much I spilled half the coffee on my shirt."

Why were you so upset? I asked.

"Well, at first I had wanted to identify with him and say, Yes, yes, go on throwing stones, go on with your violence," Shapiro explained. "But then I started shaking because I realized that he didn't see me as I saw myself. He did not see me as a Jew but as an American, a non-Jewish American, as an ally. To put it crudely, he saw me as a pro-Arab American. I am a Jew and pro-Israeli, but I lived in an Arab village. I was angry with myself for not telling him that I was Jewish. Yet it was because he did not see me as I saw myself that we were able to talk at all. I could just see my mother watching this scene from high above me, shouting, 'These are not your people! What are you doing with that Arab?'

"The situation is so much more dangerous now for your identity," said Shapiro, in a voice riddled with anguish. "It is very easy to walk around with a button until the moment you have to make a choice. He thought I had already made a choice to come over to his side, but I hadn't. I was so angry with myself for not telling him, 'I am not who you think I am and that is very important for you to know.' The button said that I can identify with you and still feel strongly as a Jew, but the *intifada* said I couldn't. It said I had to make a choice. The P.S. to the story is that I have not gone into that cafeteria again. If I did, I would have to approach him as who I am, and I am not sure I want to do that."

*   *   *

It took Yasir Arafat several tries, but in December 1988, almost exactly one year after the *intifada* began, he finally publicly recognized Israel's right to exist. This process of getting Arafat to say the magic words began a month earlier, in November 1988, with a meeting of the Palestine National Council, the PLO's parliament-in-exile, in Algiers. During this PNC session, Arafat continued his traditional policy of trying to balance the interests of those West Bankers and Gazans who wanted the PLO to formally recognize Israel and create the conditions for real peace negotiations with those who still wanted to hold out for the dream of all of Palestine. What the PNC did, as a result, was to declare an independent Palestinian state, but without specifying its borders. At the same time, though, the PNC, in very convoluted language, conditionally accepted UN Resolutions 242 and 338 and the 1947 partition plan—thus implying a recognition of Israel within its pre-1967 boundaries. But when the PNC was over and Arafat was asked explicitly if he now recognized Israel, he ducked the question with his usual verbal fan dance.

The PNC meeting was then followed up by a series of statements by Arafat "clarifying" what the PNC resolutions "really" meant. Both moderate Arab leaders and West Bankers and Gazans urged the PLO chairman to be more specific about Israel. This clarification process culminated in Geneva. On December 13, 1988, Arafat addressed a special session of the UN General Assembly, gathered in Switzerland because the PLO chairman had been denied a visa to the United States by Secretary of State George Shultz on the grounds that he had not renounced terrorism. Arafat's UN speech fell an eyelash short of unconditional acceptance of Israel and renunciation of terrorism—which were Washington's preconditions for speaking with the PLO. Finally, the next day, in yet another clarification press conference, Arafat choked out his recognition of "the right of all parties concerned in the Middle East conflict to exist in peace and security, and, as I have mentioned, including the state of Palestine, Israel, and other neighbors." He added that the PLO "totally and absolutely renounced all forms of terrorism."

Secretary of State Shultz determined that Arafat's declaration finally satisfied American conditions for dealing with the PLO, and he immediately ordered U.S. diplomats in Tunis to open a dialogue with the organization. Most Israelis, however, and most Israeli politicians, did not rush to embrace Arafat.

Why?

The reasons vary from Israeli to Israeli, but they are important to understand because, unless they can be overcome, the prospects for Palestinian–Israeli peace will remain nil.

To begin with, many Israelis didn't even hear what Arafat said. Yes, they heard the word "Israel," but it in no way touched them. The words and language Arafat used in Geneva had one audience and one audience only in mind—the United States. Arafat wanted to end the PLO's diplomatic isolation from Washington, and in order to do so he had to speak words literally dictated by George Shultz. Shultz, in effect, told Arafat: "Read my lips," and after several tries Arafat finally read his lips. But for most Israelis, Arafat was speaking a dead language. He was speaking in the diplomatic Latin of international diplomacy, which involved such code words as: "242," "338," and "recognition." This was the language of 1947, and at best 1967, but not the language of 1988. It must be remembered that Israelis view any Arab peace overture in the context of Anwar Sadat's initiative. Israelis saw Sadat address their own parliament; they saw him salute the Israeli flag; they saw him kiss former Israeli Prime Minister Golda Meir on the cheek and visit the Israeli Holocaust memorial at Yad Vashem. What he did was so far-reaching, so clear-cut in its recognition of Israelis, that no one could challenge his sincerity. At the same time, Sadat, by going to Jerusalem, did something so courageous Israelis could not help but take notice. He put himself in a position where he could not afford to fail. There was little of this daring or sincerity in Arafat's recognition; there was little attempt to truly allay Israeli fears or suspicions about him.

A few days after Arafat's declaration, I called David Hartman to ask him his reaction to this event that had shaken the world. "That Arafat is prepared to recognize me as a fact is irrelevant," remarked David. "Israelis know they are a fact, they don't need Arafat to tell them. What they need to hear from Arafat and the Palestinians is that they see the Jews in Israel as having come home, because the deepest impulse that brought Jews back to Israel was their enormous sense of homelessness, of not having a real place in history. Arafat says I'm a fact, but then he calls my government a junta. He says I'm a fact, but an alien implant.

He says I'm a fact because I have power, not because I'm home. Until he speaks to Israelis in terms of how they see themselves, it will be as though he hasn't even spoken to them at all."

For some Israelis, though—like my grocer—nothing Arafat could have said in Geneva would have been taken as sincere. There was a supermarket on Jaffa Road where I used to shop almost every day. It was owned by an Iraqi Jewish family which had immigrated to Israel from Baghdad in 1943. The patriarch of the family, an elderly curmudgeon, manned the cash register. Sasson, as the old man was called, saw himself as an expert on three things—apples, oranges, and Arabs, and not necessarily in that order.

Everything Sasson had learned, smelled, and touched his whole life had led him to the conviction that the Arabs would never willingly accept a Jewish state in their midst and that any concessions to the Palestinians would eventually be used to destroy Israel, piece by piece. To emphasize this point, Sasson would hold up the index finger of his right hand and pretend that his left hand was a butcher knife. Balancing both hands on the top of his cash register, he would then pretend to chop off bits of his finger until he got down to the knuckle. When Sasson was all done chopping, and with the people standing in the checkout line behind me getting impatient, he would pronounce with great conviction and much head nodding, "That's what the Palestinians will do to us if we give them a chance."

Whenever Sasson heard Israeli or American Jewish doves saying that the Palestinians really wanted to live in peace with the Jews, it sounded as improbable to him as the notion that an apple was an orange. It simply ran counter to everything life in Iraq and Jerusalem had taught him, and neither the Camp David treaty with Egypt nor any declarations by Yasir Arafat could convince him otherwise.

As far as Sasson is concerned, the problem between himself and the Palestinians is not that they don't understand each other but that they do—all too well. Deep down, Sasson knows what he took from the Palestinians, and he knows that the Palestinians know what he took. He took their land—some of it he bought fair and square, some of it he expropriated and some of it he conquered in war. How he got it, though, doesn't matter. All he knows is that the Palestinians want it back—all of it—because they wanted it all in the beginning. So when Arafat comes forward one day and announces, in effect, that he has just had therapy, that he is a new man and is now ready to accept the 1947 partition plan, Sasson doesn't buy it. Instead, he just nods his head silently and says to Arafat, "Look, my friend, you stand up in front of the world and declare that you now want to implement the 1947 partition plan and that it was a great injustice that the Palestinian state in this plan was never born. But you never tell the world that you rejected this plan for forty years. I know you rejected it and you know you rejected it. If you can't be honest about where you've been, why should I believe you now when you say you're somewhere new? Yasir, you can trick the foreigner, but you can't trick me. We know each other; we've been fighting for one hundred years, so let's stop pretending to be new men."

Many other Israelis were not interested in what Arafat had to say because they didn't believe he can really deliver what they most want. Again, this argument can best be understood in light of the Sadat initiative. Sadat was able to offer the Israelis something total—an end to war with the largest Arab state, which, given the balance of power in the region, meant in effect an end to war between Israel and all Arab states, at least in the near term. When Israelis weigh making a deal with Arafat over the West Bank and Gaza Strip, they ask themselves, If I agree to give up these territories, will it be the end of the story between me and the Palestinians, even if Arafat has the best of intentions? The answer is no. They will still have to deal with Abu Nidal, Abu Musa, and all the other Palestinian refugees who refuse to live in the West Bank or Gaza and insist on returning to their homes in pre-1967 Israel. Therefore, they view the choice as between no peace with all the land and no peace with part of the land. Most of them would prefer no peace with all the land, at least for now.

This calculation is not entirely irrational. In the spring of 1988, I spent an evening in the Kalandia refugee camp interviewing a group of Palestinian teenagers about the *intifada*. As we sat around the sparsely furnished living room of one of the boys' homes, I asked them the following question: Let's assume that tomorrow the Israelis recognize you and give the Palestinians a West Bank–Gaza state, and the day after tomorrow hard-line Palestinian guerrilla leader George Habash comes and says he wants to launch a guerrilla raid against the Israeli city of Haifa, in an attempt to liberate it from the Jews. What would you say to him?

They all began talking at once: the curly-haired Palestinian youth to my right just kept nodding his head and repeating in Arabic, "From the river to the sea, from the river to the sea"— referring to the Palestinian claims to all of Palestine stretching from the Jordan River to the Mediterranean. The teenager next to him launched into a detailed explanation about Palestinian democracy and said that only a majority decision could approve such an attack and it never would, while the twenty-year-old next to him just waved his hand like a policeman directing traffic through an intersection, saying to Habash, "Please, please go right ahead."

Still, the truth is that the reluctance of Israelis to deal with Arafat exists not only because some cannot hear him and others do not trust him, but also because most of them don't want to hear him. All you have to do is ride the New York subway to understand why. Sometimes you get on the subway at Grand Central Station and take the last seat in the car. The train moves on to the next station and who should get on but a little old lady carrying two big grocery bags. What is the first thing you do? You take *The New York Times* you are reading and put it up in front of your face, covering your eyes, because if your eye meets her eye, you are going to have to give up your seat.

So it is with the Israelis and Arafat. The Jews have been standing on the subway of life for two thousand years. One day, in 1948, they finally got a seat. Ever since then, there has been this lady carrying two shopping bags standing over them, shouting, "Hey, Jew, you're in my seat. I've got that reservation. Get up." When the Jew refuses, she starts throwing cans and bottles, and everyone else in the car starts in: "Hey, Jew, get up. You're in the lady's seat." After forty years of this, though, the lady gets tired. She stops throwing cans and instead just pokes the Jew in the side with her umbrella, while mumbling under her breath that she would now be ready to share the seat with the Jew peacefully—if he would just move over a bit. But the Jew has gotten used to the whole seat. It is more comfortable and secure for him that way. After forty years of fighting with this woman, he prefers holding the whole seat over the psychological uncertainties in-

volved in sharing it—even with this lady poking him in the side
all the time. So he keeps *The New York Times* locked in front of
his face and mumbles back at the little old lady from behind his
newspaper, "Speak up, I can't hear you!" The lady eventually
starts shouting at the Jew: "I am ready to share. I am ready to
share," but the Jew just sits there with the newspaper in front of
his face, saying, "I can't hear you. I can't hear you."

The Jews' sense of finally getting a seat, after so many years
of standing, runs deep in the soul of Israel. Israel, in fact, is a
nation made up of people who have been evicted from their seats
on subways around the world. They have an almost metaphysical
attachment to the seat they are in, and they do not have much
sympathy for others who say they were evicted and must sit down
exactly where the Jew is. I am convinced that one day Yasir Arafat
is going to stand up and sing "Hatikva," the Israeli national anthem, in perfect Hebrew. When he does, some Israelis are going
to shake their heads and say, "Geez, we'd love to talk to you,
but you sang our national anthem in the wrong key. Come back
when you can sing it right."

This attitude is particularly strong among Israeli leaders who
know that deciding how much of the seat to give away could
embroil their nation in a civil war. Voluntarily relinquishing the
West Bank or Gaza to the Palestinians requires that Israelis definitively answer the question: Who are we as a nation? Are we
going to have biblical boundaries or pragmatic boundaries? Are
we here to pave the way for the Messiah or to build a Jewish
France? For reasons which I have already explained, most Israeli
leaders are not ready to answer this question. "What do I need
such headaches for?" they say. "Better to deal with the Palestinians as a technical security problem than tear ourselves apart in
order to give them a state." That is why Israelis are always ready
to talk to Egyptians, Jordanians, or even Syrians, even though
they have killed many more Israelis than the Palestinians ever
have, because talking to them does not force the Israelis to really
look in the mirror and answer the question: Who am I?

I was at a dinner party in Herzliya in the summer of 1988 and
was seated next to one of the most senior Labor Party Cabinet
ministers—a man deeply involved in security matters. We talked
about the usual things—America, the economy, the Arabs—before I asked him what kind of moral challenge the *intifada* was

posing to the Israeli army. The Labor Minister was eating some lamb at the time. He stopped chewing, turned to me with a piece of lamb on his fork, and said straightaway, "If you ask me, the sooner the Palestinians return to terrorism, the better it will be for us."

Then he went back to eating his lamb.

When might the Israelis be ready to hear Arafat's message?

Only when they have to. No nation-state in the history of the world has ever voluntarily given up a piece of territory that it wanted to hold, for either ideological or security reasons, and felt that it could hold. Israelis and Palestinians are no exception to this rule. In 1947, the Palestinians felt that all the land of Palestine belonged to them and that they had the power to hold on to it. When the United Nations suggested that Palestine be partitioned, the Palestinians rejected this proposal out of hand. It did not matter to the Palestinians that the Zionists had declared their willingness to share, and to recognize a Palestinian state next door. Unfortunately for them, the Palestinians did not appreciate the power realities at the time; the Zionists were much stronger than they appeared.

Now the tables are turned: the Israelis control all the land, and the Palestinians are seeking partition, and now it's the Israelis' turn to ignore the Palestinians for as long as they can. That may seem cruel and stupid, but that is how the game has always been played on this land. I am convinced that Israelis will be interested in hearing what Arafat and the Palestinians have to say as a nation only when the Israelis feel that they have no choice but to make a deal with the Palestinians as another nation on the land. A person is interested in the terms of a deal only when he feels he has to make a deal. The *intifada* has not, as of the writing of this book, exerted enough internal pressure on the Israelis, or offered them enough incentives, to convince a significant majority that they can and should share either power or sovereignty with the Palestinians in the West Bank and the Gaza Strip.

To be sure, the uprising has been serious enough to force the Israeli army to double from thirty days to sixty days the maximum amount of annual reserve duty required of Israeli males between the ages of twenty-one and fifty-five. Economically, as a result of

the *intifada*, Israel's Gross Domestic Product (GDP) grew between only 1 and 2 percent in 1988, compared with a growth of
5.2 percent in 1987. It did grow, however. In terms of casualties,
the eleven Israelis killed in the first year of the uprising amount
to roughly the number of people killed in traffic accidents on the
Israeli highways every two weeks. All of this adds up to a situation
which, while unpleasant, could hardly be described as leaving
Israelis with their backs to the wall.

I was having a drink one day in June 1988 at the Bonanza Bar
in Tel Aviv with Ze'ev Chafets. We sat in a corner booth at the
Bonanza and watched as the tables filled up with end-of-the-week
regulars—businessmen and poets, women on the make eyeing
men on the make, journalists, arms dealers, hucksters, and soldiers home for the weekend—a regular Israeli crowd. Even before
the band started playing, the room was reverberating with a symphony of voices: people arguing, laughing, and telling lies. A loud
voice from somewhere was talking about black panties. From the
Bonanza Bar, the *intifada*, the West Bank, the stone-throwers
were all a distant drum—something most Israelis read about in
the newspaper, something most Israelis thought about for a few
seconds on the way to work or sitting around with friends on
Friday evening. Like most Israelis, the folks at the Bonanza Bar
rarely visited the West Bank and Gaza even before the *intifada*,
so the fact that these areas had become even more dangerous
now was a purely academic matter for the army to deal with. In
Jerusalem, which is closer to the West Bank and where real Palestinian disturbances took place in the Arab half of the city, one
finds political graffiti in the men's toilets—things like STOP ISRAELI
BRUTALITY—but in the Bonanza Bar all there is on the wall is
SHIT YOU ASSHOLE. NO PARKING ALLOWED.

Shai, the bon vivant former boxer who owns the Bonanza,
explains the facts of life to me: "Nobody is really into the *intifada*
at the Bonanza. There isn't a single guy here who gets drunk
because of it. We are here to have fun, and we did it before the
intifada and we do it after. The simple Palestinian, he wants a
Palestinian country. I understand that. He doesn't like the Jews,
but here we are. My chef is from the Gaza Strip. There were a
couple of days he could not come to work, but it was not his fault.
He was loyal to me. He and the waiters realized that no money

is going to come from the *intifada*. I never talk politics with them, but I can tell you that a couple of months ago there was a feeling back there in the kitchen that they are going to have a Palestinian country. Now that's gone. Everything is back to normal with the Arab workers."

Shai moves on to greet some other customers, and the two-man band begins to play. Their medley begins with a popular Israeli folk song called "Eretz, Eretz, Eretz." Everyone in the bar sings along. Meanwhile, a friend of mine, Zvi el-Peleg, an Israeli Arabist and former governor of the Gaza Strip, spots me from across the bar, walks over, and pulls up a chair next to me. The band is playing very loud and the sing-along is getting rowdy. Peleg begins to ask me a question, but I cannot hear him over the noise.

"What?" I say, cupping a hand to my ear. "Speak up, I can't hear you."

Finally, practically shouting in my ear, Peleg says, "What did you think of the Abu Sharif statement?"

He was referring to an article published a day earlier by Bassam Abu Sharif, an aide to Yasir Arafat. The article called for direct peace talks between the PLO and Israel at an international conference. It was, at the time, the boldest overture to Israel ever to come out of the Arafat circle.

"I haven't seen it yet," I shouted back at Peleg.

He simply nodded his head.

We decided to wait until the music was finished before we continued. I turned my attention back to Chafets.

"What do the words to this song mean? Everyone seems to know it," I shouted across the table.

"The main verse," Chafets answered, "is Eretz [land], Eretz, Eretz, a land that we were born in, a land that we will live in, no matter what happens."

The symbol of the *intifada* has become a Palestinian throwing a stone. That is fine for the cover of *Newsweek*. But if the *intifada* is ever to achieve anything tangible for the Palestinians, it will never be through either stones or guns. The Israelis will always use their vastly superior force to smother both before they ever become truly threatening. The only way the Palestinians can really put meaningful pressure on the Israelis is by concentrating on their original tactic of civil disobedience.

There are two reasons why real civil disobedience is so threatening to Israel. The first is that, to be successful, it cannot be carried out by just one or a few people. It must be a communal act. "If only one Palestinian refuses to work in Israel, carry his identity card, or pay his taxes," explained Sari Nusseibeh, "that is not going to be meaningful; it only works if 100,000 people do it, and if 100,000 people do it, it would threaten the whole structure of the occupation, which is based on our voluntary cooperation." In fact, if 100,000 Palestinians refused to work in Israel, burned their identity cards, and failed to pay taxes, it would mean utter chaos for the Israeli military authorities. They would either have to arrest them all—and there would not be room enough in Israeli jails for so many people—or resign themselves to the fact that they could no longer tell these people what to do, because they won't play the game by the Israeli rules anymore. What this does is to turn the Palestinians' massive demographic weight, their sheer numbers, into real political weight. Ten Palestinians going out to get shot by Israeli troops is nothing for Israel. It doesn't threaten the occupation, it doesn't disturb most Israelis, because they view these people as troublemakers who deserve to be shot, and it doesn't force the Israelis to contend with the full demographic weight of the Palestinians. Even if 100 of them were shot, it wouldn't make a difference. But 100,000 Palestinians tearing up their identity cards, or refusing to work in Israel, is another matter. Israelis cannot shoot them and be done with it. They become a permanent problem. They become permanently indigestible for Israel, and there is nothing worse than permanent indigestion.

The second reason real civil disobedience is so threatening is that in order for Palestinians to be able to disengage socially, economically, and politically from the Israeli system and not starve to death, they would have to develop their own autonomous economic, educational, social, cultural, and political infrastructure. They would have to establish their own schools and their own mutual support systems. Civil disobedience, in other words, demands slow and painful communal power building. A successful effort of this sort would also translate the Palestinians' demographic weight into political weight. Palestinians rioting in the streets and shouting for an independent state will not impress Israelis. But Palestinians actually establishing the framework of an independent entity cannot be ignored; it proves to Israelis beyond any doubt that there is another national collective on the land yearning to be free. It becomes the tangible expression on the ground of the declaration of independence made by the PNC in Algiers.

The *intifada* began along this path of civil disobedience. There was a real attempt by Palestinians to set up their own schools and food-sharing and communal-support programs. In fact, the only time I really saw Israeli officials get truly worried during the uprising was when they felt the Palestinians might actually be disengaging from them. Israelis had faced one- and two-day commercial strikes from the Palestinians many times before, but never the kind of mass civil disobedience they witnessed in the early months of the *intifada*, when the underground Palestinian leadership ordered all shopkeepers to open only for a few hours each day; when hundreds of Palestinians who worked for the Israeli occupation administration, either as policemen or clerks, quit their jobs; when thousands of Palestinian laborers refused or were prevented from going to work in Israel; and when thousands of Palestinian merchants refused to pay their taxes or buy Israeli products.

This Palestinian civil disobedience and disengagement, however, bogged down after the first year of the uprising. The Israeli system was too powerful for the Palestinians to elude its grasp easily. Consider only one small example. In August 1987, four months before the *intifada*, the Israeli Ministry of Defense brought on line an $8.5 million computerized data bank for the occupied territories. The data bank was designed to keep track of every Palestinian's property, real estate, family ties, political attitude, involvement in illegal activities, licensing, occupation, and consumption pattern. As West Bank expert Meron Benvenisti put it, this computer "was the ultimate instrument of population control."

As soon as Palestinians tried to engage in civil disobedience, the Israelis put the computer to good use to break them—particularly in the Gaza Strip, whose inhabitants were almost entirely dependent on employment in Israel to earn their daily bread.

When some Palestinians in Gaza stopped paying taxes after the *intifada* erupted, Israel announced that it was issuing new identity cards. Any Palestinian who did not have a new card by a certain date would neither be allowed out of the Gaza Strip to work nor granted such crucial papers as a driver's license, travel document, water quota, or import-export permit. In order to obtain a new identity card, however, each Palestinian had to prove that he or she had paid up all back taxes and that no one in the family was wanted by the Israeli security forces. In other words, by simply pressing a few buttons on a computer, an Israeli officer could restore or revoke all the documents a Palestinian needed to survive under the Israeli occupation.

I went down to Gaza one day to see this carrot-and-stick operation firsthand. The Israeli army had set up rows and rows of benches in the courtyard of the Sheik Adjlin School in the beachfront neighborhood of Remal. The school was surrounded by coils of barbed wire, which in one spot were flattened to make an entryway. The idea that Palestinians had to step on barbed wire to get into this place struck me as the ultimate humiliation. The benches, which were packed with roughly 1,000 men at a time, were covered by mosquito netting to provide some protection from the blazing sun. Many people had been waiting two or three days to hear their name called. The place had all the trappings of a bingo game at the Minnesota State Fair, only in this case it was the audience which shelled out the prizes to those running the game. There was a loudspeaker at the front that would blare out a name; that person would then jump up, as though he had just scored a bingo, and disappear into a room at the front, where he would be rewarded by having all his records checked and being asked to pay his occupiers what he owed in back taxes. Then he would be presented with a new identity card. Anyone wanted by the Shin Bet would be arrested.

I walked to the middle of the benches, introduced myself as a reporter, and was immediately swarmed by angry Gazans desperate to tell someone, anyone, about their plight and discomfort. They kept saying to me, "If we talk to you, will it be in the newspaper in America tomorrow? You promise? Tomorrow?"

Why did you come here? I asked the men surrounding me. Why didn't you just tell the Israelis to shove it?

Riyad Feisal, a twenty-four-year-old Gazan refugee working as a waiter for $400 a month in a Jaffa fish restaurant, stepped forward to explain their predicament: "If we say no, we are going to suffer so much. Without the identity card, I can't travel, I can't work, and I am supporting six other people. The identity card is like my soul. If the Israelis take it away, it is like I am dead. Every Palestinian male when he wakes up in the morning to go to work always pats his back pocket to make sure that his identity card is in there. It is our new national custom."

The Israeli officer in charge of the operation put it to me in somewhat more brutal language. "Why are they here? Because we are basically stronger. Look, 60,000 people from the Gaza Strip go to work in Israel every day. Who is going to feed them if they stay home? The other day their leadership called a general strike. You know what happened? We had 4,000 people come here to get their identity cards. Usually we only get 2,800 a day. It means that they used their one-day strike not to protest but to get their identity cards from us. They all come like good children. The identity card is life. The Palestinian can't move without it. Why does a baby have an umbilical cord? To get food from the mother. The minute he has a bottle from someone else, he can get rid of the umbilical cord and live free of his mother. We are the mother, and the PLO was supposed to provide the bottle. But it never did."

The PLO tried to smuggle money in through various avenues, mostly Israeli Arabs. Some of it was intercepted by Israel, some was siphoned off by different hands along the way, and some got through—but nowhere near enough to support mass civil disobedience for a population of 1.7 million people. The Arab states did not send a dime.

"With proper organization and money we could have done wonders," said one West Bank Palestinian professor deeply involved in the uprising, "but we didn't have either. People were really ready to sacrifice, but our infrastructure never matched people's feelings. When some of the Palestinian policemen quit their jobs [in March 1988] with the Civil Administration, the whole community was watching to see what would happen to them. This wasn't just kids going into the streets; this was adults really ready to disengage from Israel. Many others were ready to follow. But the policemen who quit never got any support, so they had to go back to work. The whole community saw that, and that is why others were not ready to follow. The underground committees on health, finance, education, and welfare never really developed into an effective network. They could call strikes, but that is all."

What happened instead was that many Palestinians, but by no means all, went back to dealing with Israel or working in Israel—in some cases sporadically, in others on a reduced level—while young Palestinian children, often eleven- and twelve-year-olds, continued rioting, throwing stones, and getting shot. Their deaths seemed to become the warrant which allowed their parents to go on working in Israel and not engage in truly significant civil disobedience. Palestinians would point to the number of people being killed each day and say, "See, we are suffering. Now let us have our state."

This double bookkeeping explains some of the more unusual Israeli–Palestinian encounters which developed after the *intifada* was well under way.

Would you buy a used car from your occupier? For the first six months of the *intifada*, Ehud Gol was the official Israeli Foreign Ministry spokesman. Every day he had to go before the world's press and defend Israel's treatment of the Palestinians. But in the spring of 1988, Gol was made the Israeli Consul General in Rio de Janeiro and he had to sell his car before he left the country. Practically the first place he went was to a Palestinian car dealer in the West Bank town of Ramallah.

"*Intifada* or no *intifada*, this was business," Gol explained to me. "The car dealer even came down to the Foreign Ministry and we went over all the papers in my office. There I was, the Foreign Ministry spokesman, and this guy, whose son was probably out throwing stones, was ready to buy from me—and it was a used car!"

A Palestinian teacher I knew was driving from Ramallah to Jerusalem one afternoon when he saw a colleague of his from Bir Zeit University and offered to give him a lift. "This fellow came from a small village near Ramallah," said my teacher friend. "The whole way into Jersualem he was talking to me about the *intifada* and how it had changed his village, how everyone was involved, and how the local committees of the uprising were running the village and they were getting rid of all the collaborators. He was really enthusiastic, and I was really impressed. As we got close to Jerusalem, I asked him where he wanted to be dropped off and he said, 'The Hebrew University.' I was really surprised, so I said, 'What are you going there for?' and he said, 'I teach an Arabic class there.' It simply didn't occur to him that there was any contradiction between enthusiasm for the *intifada* and where he was going."

That was also true of the hundreds of people in Gaza who continued studying Hebrew. On August 4, 1988, the eighth month of the *intifada*, the *Ha'aretz* newspaper reported that the Israeli government's Hebrew adult-education course in Gaza was going as strong as ever, and that Hebrew language classes continued to be taught in Gaza's junior high schools throughout the uprising.

"A surrealistic scene," reported *Ha'aretz* from Gaza. "At the height of the *intifada*, Palestinian students were studying S. Y. Agnon's story 'From Foe to Friend,' Michal Snunit's book *Soulbird*, Hannah Senesh's prayer-poem 'God—may there be no end,' and the story of Rabbi Akiva's love for the daughter of Kalba Sabbua. Last month they had a final exam on this material."

An Israeli paratrooper in Gaza once told me that he was patrolling the Shati refugee camp when a Palestinian boy came walking down the street wearing a T-shirt from his high school in Petach Tiqvah, the Brenner School. When he asked the Palestinian where he got it, he said, "I don't know. I just found it."

The same paratrooper also was on duty at the gate of Shati one evening after Israel had clamped a curfew on the whole area, beginning at 6:00 p.m. "At around 8:00 p.m. this old Palestinian man shows up at the gate," said the Israeli soldier. "I asked him where he had been. He said he had come from Israel, so I said, 'What were you doing there?' and he started singing to me in Hebrew the song *'Mi Yivne Bayit.'* I just laughed and let him go."

The main verse to the song *"Mi Yivne Bayit"* is: "Who will build a house in Israel? We are the pioneers. We will build Israel, come along with us."

When I returned to America in the summer of 1988, I was struck at how Arab Americans were reacting to the Palestinian uprising. There was something familiar to me about the puffed-up pride with which they discussed the *intifada* on television and in the news media. Then I realized that it was the same way Jewish Americans had responded to Israel's victory in the 1967 war. The *intifada* was the Arab Americans' Six-Day War. They were living out all their fantasies of power and dignity through the Palestinian rock-throwers, the same way American Jews had lived vicariously through Israel's military achievements.

The problem was that not all the natives—neither the Jews nor the Arabs—wanted to cooperate in being material for the imagination of their compatriots in the viewing stands. They refused to be the tinder for the revolutionary fires raging in the minds of those who don't have to pay the price. While their supporters back in America treated them as flags to be waved, the Palestinians in the West Bank and Gaza were living human beings, with middle-class dreams and children to educate. The grand colors, those bright blues and reds and greens with which the *intifada* was painted on all the posters and pamphlets distributed in the West, always looked to be more shades of gray to the people actually living it. Those poor Palestinian villagers, camp dwellers, and shopkeepers were supposed to be so desperate that they had nothing to lose; that is very easy to say from the comfort of America. But in the real world, everyone has something to lose. To be sure, all Palestinians shared the *intifada*'s aspirations, but not all were ready to share its burdens. Life had taught them to have little faith in politics or history or uprisings.

In April 1988, I spent a morning at the American consulate in East Jerusalem interviewing Palestinians who were trying to go to America. The consulate had to be closed for the day thirty minutes after opening because it was besieged by so many Palestinians seeking visas to the United States or to put their American passports in order. According to American consul Howard Kavaler, during the first four months of the *intifada* Palestinian visa applications to the United States were up 30 percent over the same period the year before and 1,000 out of the 7,000 Palestinian Americans living in the West Bank returned to America.

"Just call me Abu Visa"—Howard smiled up at me as I entered his office and found him flipping through a stack of visa applications. "I don't know about the *intifada*; all I know is that I've got what they want. Palestinians who have the right to immigrant visas come here any way they can to pick them up. It doesn't matter if they are supposed to be on strike or whatever. They come. Our no-show rate for people granted visas is zero. Those who come and get turned down are really upset—especially males between the ages of eighteen and twenty-one. There is that moment when you tell them, 'No, I'm sorry,' and some of them get this anxiety reaction. It's very sad. Those who can get out are leaving. You don't have a sense when talking to them that they feel like they are on the verge of liberation. There is no euphoria. If we opened the gates and said any Palestinian who wants to come to America can come, well . . . Arafat and their love of this land notwithstanding, I don't think too many of them would be left here. That's true for plenty of Israelis, too. In our sitting room upstairs, Jews and Arabs wait together for their visas, and when it comes to that, they are all brothers. As soon as they each know they can go to America, all the anger between them disappears."

I spoke with several Palestinian visa applicants after Howard interviewed them. The first was a woman from Ramallah. She was a Palestinian whose husband was working in San Francisco and she had come to register her fourteen-year-old daughter for a passport.

"Why do you want to leave now?" I asked.

"My daughter has been out of school for four months," explained the stylishly dressed Palestinian woman, wearing spiked high heels and a white scarf around her neck. "I am concerned for her education. We don't know when school might open again. She could miss a whole year."

"But this is a crucial moment in Palestinian history," I said.

"It is very frightening," she responded, tying her fingers in knots. "No one knows what is going to happen. At night you hear all kinds of sounds and we are always worried that the Israelis are going to come."

"Are your neighbors upset with you for leaving?"

"Are you crazy?" she said, shaking her head no. "They say anyone who can get out should get out. They wish they were me."

Another businessman from Ramallah, a Christian town, was leaving. The elderly man with a broad white mustache had three of his six children already in the United States and wanted to visit them with one of his younger sons, who was standing by his side.

This is an important moment in your people's history, I said, don't you want your sons in America to be here now?

"No, no, no," he said emphatically. "They are all working in America. They have established themselves in America."

He was followed by Abdullah, a twenty-nine-year-old graduate of Bethlehem University, who said he had been accepted at an institute in New Jersey to study English literature.

What do you think of the *intifada?*

"Not good," he remarked, with a scowl. "Students cannot study."

But how can you leave now?

"It is painful—but I am going to study," he explained.

What will your neighbors say?

"The people will not be angry, because I am going to study, not to have a good time," he insisted.

The last in line was Najwa, a researcher at the West Bank's Bir Zeit University, who was going to her sister's graduation in Indiana.

What do you want out of the uprising? I asked.

"I would like to feel free," she answered without hesitation. "I cannot see a Palestinian state really coming about—but that is what I would like."

What do you think about all these people trying to get to America?

"I don't like the idea of people escaping from the situation," said Najwa. "Some don't like those who leave and some just don't care."

Such is the real world—ambiguous, unheroic, full of transient emotional highs and many more lows. Nevertheless, the *intifada* has done a great deal for the Palestinians. Most important, it got the Palestinian national movement to adopt the right methods— primarily non-lethal mass civil disobedience—and the right message—increasing recognition of Israel. In addition, it has given the Palestinians as a nation greater self-confidence, greater unity, a much improved international image, and a sense that their movement is really going somewhere. Who knows, one day soon it may even lead to direct negotiations between Israel and the PLO. For all these reasons the *intifada* must be considered a truly significant event in the history of the Palestinian–Israeli conflict.

But will it lead to a resolution of that conflict? The answer to this question is probably years away. In my opinion, the only way the *intifada* will produce *tangible* results for the Palestinians—not just pride, not just negotiations, not just another American peace plan, but a firm agreement by Israel to share with the Palestinians either real power or a real chunk of land—is if the Palestinians reenergize their uprising and continue much further with their original method of civil disobedience and their message of recognizing the Jews. The Palestinians will take nothing away from the bargaining table with Israel that they don't earn ahead of time through a combination of this method with this message. They will find no shortcuts through either Washington, Moscow, or the United Nations.

The Palestinians must make themselves so indigestible to Israelis that they want to disgorge them into their own state, while at the same time reassuring the Israelis that they can disgorge them without committing suicide. This is a very difficult trick which will be accomplished only with the stick of non-lethal civil disobedience and the carrot of explicit recognition. The Israelis have to be convinced from within, rather than by external American pressure, that the Palestinians are struggling not to destroy Israel but to build something for themselves alongside it. Only then will a *significant majority* of Israelis from the right and the left—without whom there will be no settlement—recognize and allow themselves to sympathize with what the Palestinians are doing. The Palestinians cannot permit their own self-discovery to turn into narcissism; in order to really meet themselves in the fullest sense, they have to meet the Israelis in the fullest sense.

This is not going to be easy for the Palestinians, because to make themselves indigestible through civil disobedience is going to require protracted economic and social hardship, and even after that, bringing away anything significant from the bargaining table will require additional political sacrifices. Given Israel's vastly superior power, the most Palestinians can hope for is some form of real autonomy under Israeli rule in the short run, and a ministate in parts of the West Bank and Gaza Strip—without Jerusalem—in the long run.

The more the West Bankers and Gazans suffer, the more they are going to want to get something for their efforts. This is bound to create tension between them and Arafat, because part of Arafat will always feel compelled to represent those refugees in Lebanon,

Jordan, and Syria, who nurtured the PLO. This means part of him will always try to keep some hope alive for the Arab and Palestinian hard-liners that one day Palestine in its entirety may be redeemed, as Arafat himself promised for so many years. Arafat can never totally turn his back on these peoples, because he was one of them, and he can never fully understand the needs and feelings of Palestinians under Israeli occupation, because he has never been one of them. Thus, it will be extremely difficult for him to make the kinds of concessions to the Israelis—and to speak the kinds of lines—which Palestinians in the West Bank and Gaza may inevitably demand when the cost of the uprising becomes too great for them to bear and they insist on making some type of deal with their occupiers. This is when the Palestinians whose problem is the Israeli in their house and the Palestinians whose problem is the Israeli on their roof are really going to have to face up to their differences. For now they have suspended these differences, as they each adhere to the official PLO position: Israeli evacuation from all of the West Bank, Gaza Strip, and East Jerusalem, the creation there of a Palestinian state, and then peace negotiations with Israel. But how long will those paying the price of the uprising chase this rainbow?

Possibly for as long as Yasir Arafat is alive. Yasir Arafat *is* the PLO, and the symbol of Palestinian nationalism. As a symbol, he unites the Palestinians on the land with those off the land. But he has no heirs, and when he is gone the unity of his organization is almost certain to fracture. Then there are likely to be many PLOs, and then, and only then, might West Bankers and Gazans have their own PLO, which will legitimize their own deal with Israel.

In the meantime, Israelis could make the Palestinians' lives much easier by giving Arafat some incentive to recognize them more and by taking the initiative to forge a territorial compromise that many Palestinians might accept. But this is not likely to happen. Israel has simply too much power and paranoia relative to the Palestinians to want to undergo the risks and the wrenching internal debates that would be required to really bring the Palestinians along and create the conditions for a territorial settlement. Israelis might respond to a Palestinian Anwar Sadat, but they won't go out and create one.

"Israelis are paralyzed," explained David Hartman. "The army is screaming at the Cabinet that it can't solve the uprising without a political solution, and the Cabinet is screaming at the army that it can't produce a political solution until the uprising is put down. There is no Israeli statesman ready to make the bold move that might get us out of this vicious cycle—to say to the Palestinians clearly, without ambiguity, that we now see that they are a nation as much as we are, that we now understand that our own declaration that they 'never had it so good under our occupation' was a vulgarity and one which Jews themselves suffered from for centuries, that we now recognize that the Palestinians' own dignity will never be fulfilled, any more than ours could have been, without political freedom."

No. For the time being it seems there will be no such far-reaching statements from the Israeli leadership, and none from the Palestinians either. Many Israelis still want to believe that the *intifada* is the storm before the lull, while many Palestinians want to believe that it is the storm that swept away everything in its path. It has been neither. If the Palestinians don't continue along the new road they have charted, and if the Israelis don't wake up to the fact that their superior power will never buy them the peace and quiet they so desperately seek, then the *intifada* will be remembered not for having changed reality but for having brought attention to a reality that never changes. The term *"intifada"* will continue, but only as a new name for the status quo— maybe a more violent, more painful, status quo, but a status quo with which both sides, nevertheless, will learn to live. The Israelis will remain on top, the Palestinians will make sure that they never enjoy it, and everything else will just be commentary.

In the quiet of their hearts, away from the glare of the television cameras and the euphoria of demonstrations, those Palestinians living on the land understand exactly how far they have come and how far they still have to go.

Fallah, a twenty-four-year-old candy seller I met in the Old City of Jerusalem, made this utterly clear when I paid him a visit a week after meeting a friend of his at the American consulate. A graduate of Bir Zeit University, the hotbed of Palestinian nationalism, Fallah took pride in the *intifada* when it began, but by the time it had dragged into its fifth month he had had enough.

Standing amid sacks of raisins and candies in his tiny shop in the
Arab market, Fallah answered my question about how his business was holding up—now that he was on strike for half the day—
with some basic English that got the point across: "It is not bad,
it is not too bad, it is too too bad.

"We cannot say yet whether the *intifada* is important or not,"
explained Fallah, "because we have not seen the results. Maybe
the situation will be worse. Maybe it will be fifty-fifty and maybe
it will be better. Now we, the sellers, are worse off."

As we talked, though, Fallah kept getting angrier and angrier
about the situation. There was no business. He was selling only
old stocks. Perishables he long ago had had to throw away.

"All of these people on the outside telling us, 'We want you
to do this, we want, we want, we want,' " he complained, voice
rising. "Well, I have not gotten one agora [Israeli penny] of help
from the people outside," he adds, pinching his thumb and fore-
finger together as if squeezing a dime. "Jordan, Egypt, Syria,
they say hoorah, hoorah. But did they take one extra Palestinian
into their universities?"

He paused for a moment to pop a raisin into his mouth. "You
know what this *intifada* is?" he said, spitting out the words. "It
is a drop of water in the sea."

15

Under the Spotlight

Israeli Major General Amram Mitzna had been in many battles before, but none stranger than this one.

Mitzna, the commander of Israel's central front, which includes the occupied West Bank, was driving up the highway from Jerusalem to Ramallah in January 1988. As his sand-colored Land Rover command car approached the Arab village of al-Ram, about five miles north of Jerusalem, Mitzna beheld through his front windshield a confrontation taking shape between some of his soldiers and a crowd of about fifty Palestinian teenagers. The Palestinian youths, their heads wrapped in checkered kaffiyehs, had erected a barricade of burning tires, broken car fenders, and boulders in the middle of the highway and were lobbing rocks and insults at ten Israeli soldiers standing in the road some 75 yards away.

But the combatants were not alone.

"When I arrived on the scene," Mitzna recalled, "I discovered that there were more journalists there than soldiers. I had some-

thing like fifteen soldiers in all, including those who came with
me, and there must have been at least twenty-five reporters, photographers, and video cameramen. At first, I ignored the journalists and told my soldiers to run with me to break up the
demonstrators. So I started running. As soon as I took one step,
though, I found myself surrounded by photographers on my right
and video cameramen on my left. They were running right along
with me! I could barely move. They were between me and my
men, and around us and inside us—cameras, still photographers,
everything. They were everywhere. So I stopped and I told the
journalists, 'Look, let me first make the news and I promise to
come back and talk to you about it after it's over. But for now,
please go back and stand on the other side of the road.' So one
of the journalists—he was an American—says to me, 'Show me
an official [military court order] declaring this a closed military
zone, otherwise I am not moving.' Can you imagine the chutzpah!
I said to him, 'You know me! You know who I am. Now move
away.' It was crazy. I am the supreme commander in the West
Bank and I had to argue my way past journalists to get to a battle."

This was hardly the first time journalists had outnumbered Israeli soldiers at a confrontation with Palestinians in the West
Bank, and it would not be the last. Consider just a few pieces of
data. Israel, in quiet times, plays host to one of the largest foreign
press contingents in the world, with some 350 permanently ac-
credited news organizations stationed in Jerusalem and Tel Aviv.
According to the Israel Government Press Office, an additional
700 journalists flocked to the country at the height of the 1987–
88 Palestinian uprisings. That influx amounted to 1 foreign correspondent for every 6,100 Israelis. That is the equivalent of
roughly 36,000 foreign correspondents suddenly descending on
Washington, D.C. A New York–based media analysis firm,
A.D.T. Research, compiles a monthly second-by-second record
of how much time the three major American networks, ABC,
CBS, and NBC, devote to individual news and feature stories
during their regular Monday through Friday thirty-minute evening
news broadcasts. According to A.D.T.'s tabulations, from December 1987, when the *intifada* erupted, through February 1988,
when it peaked, the story of the Palestinian demonstrations and
the Israeli responses occupied a total of 347 minutes of evening
news time on the three major American networks combined.

That, according to A.D.T., was almost 100 minutes more than the second most popular story during the same time period, the December 1987 Washington superpower summit between Ronald Reagan and Mikhail Gorbachev, which merited only 249 minutes, and it was almost 200 minutes more than the third most popular story, the 1988 New Hampshire presidential primary (139 minutes). Presidential candidate Michael Dukakis's entire campaign for August, September, and October 1988 totaled only 268 minutes on the three major American networks.

No wonder Jerusalem's mayor, Teddy Kollek, once remarked, "There is a hole in the floor of the nave of the church of the Holy Sepulchre in the Old City of Jerusalem. In ancient times, it was believed that Jerusalem was the center of the world and that this hole was the center of the center—the very navel of the universe. Sometimes I have the impression that the foreign correspondents who reside here, and the hundreds more who visit every year, still believe that. Why else would they so often focus the attention of millions of people upon this small city and this small country?"

Kollek is right. The Western media in general, and the American media in particular, clearly have a fascination with the story of Israel that is out of all proportion to the country's physical dimensions. It was obvious by the amount of coverage devoted to Israel's handling of the *intifada*, but it was apparent even before.

How can a tiny country with the population of greater Chicago and the size of the state of Delaware occupy as much news space as the Soviet Union, if not more?

There is no single or simple answer to this question. Israel's high profile in the Western news media is the result of a combination of factors—some of them historical, others cultural, others psychological, and still others political. Some have to do with the way Western man looks at the world, while others have to do with how Israel projects itself abroad.

Men have never taken the world just as it comes; our minds are not just blank pages upon which reality paints itself. Whether that reality is Israel or anything else, it is always filtered through certain cultural and historical lenses before being painted on our minds. Israeli political theorist Yaron Ezrahi calls these lenses "super stories." A super story, says Ezrahi, consists of a collection of myths, or ideological constructs, tied together by an overall narrative. This super story helps us to explain the world to ourselves, to determine what information we will treat as significant, and, most important, to record our experiences and shape our values. Like any colored lens, it lets certain rays of light in and blocks out others. Religions are the most popular super stories, but so, too, are universalist ideologies such as Marxism. As it happens, the oldest, most widely known super story of Western civilization is the Bible: its stories, its characters, and its values constitute the main lens through which Western man looks at himself and at the world. The Jews—the ancient Israelites—are the main characters in this biblical super story.

This fact alone accounts for a good deal of Israel's high visibility in the Western media. Put simply: news from modern Israel is more appealing and digestible for people in the West than from elsewhere, because the characters, the geography, and the themes involved are so familiar, so much a part of our cultural lenses. We are naturally predisposed to read about people and places we know, and these people, the Jews, and this holy land, Israel, we know, because we hear about them every weekend in churches and synagogues all across the Western world. We also read about them in general literature and contemplate them in art. Their Bible stories can be found from Milton to Rembrandt. As Lloyd George, the British Prime Minister when the 1917 Balfour Declaration promising the Jews a homeland was issued, once told the Zionist leader Chaim Weizmann, the names Judea, Samaria, and Jerusalem "are more familiar to me than the names of Welsh villages of my own childhood." Indeed, every American is familiar with a place like the Sea of Galilee—even though many states in the United States have lakes which are much bigger. But physical size is irrelevant in trying to understand why one country or people gets reported in the Western media and another doesn't. What matters is the size that country or people occupies in the super story, and when looked at that way, Israel becomes one of the largest of countries in the eyes of the West, while big countries such as China or Sudan become very small.

This process works in reverse as well. News about Israel in the Far East, where the biblical super story does not have wide currency, is generally treated as insignificant. American Jewish author Chaim Potok once told me that when the 1956 Sinai war broke out, he happened to be in Japan. "I was dying to find out what was happening," said Potok, an ordained rabbi, "but there was virtually no news about the war in the Japanese English-language newspapers. The Jews aren't part of their world view. Most Japanese don't really know what a Jew is, and Israel has no special significance for them. The only way I was able to really get caught up on what was happening in the Sinai war was by getting hold of *Stars & Stripes* [the American armed forces newspaper]."

News from modern Israel is not only intuitively familiar to the Western ear, it is also intuitively relevant. Modern Israel is not viewed by most Christians as a new country or a new story, but rather as the modern extension of a very old country and a very old drama involving God and man. Itzik Yaacoby, who heads the East Jerusalem Development Corporation, which is responsible for maintaining the Old City of Jerusalem and all its Christian, Muslim, and Jewish holy places, noticed that most Christian tourists he showed around the city felt as though they were walking through the pages of the Bible. The notion that Israel was just another twentieth-century nation-state created by the United Nations after World War II was totally alien to them.

When American astronaut Neil Armstrong, a devout Christian, visited Israel after his trip to the moon, he was taken on a tour of the Old City of Jerusalem by Israeli archaeologist Meir Ben-Dov. When they got to the Hulda Gate, which is at the top of the stairs leading to the Temple Mount, Armstrong asked Ben-Dov whether Jesus had stepped anywhere around there.

"I told him, 'Look, Jesus was a Jew,' " recalled Ben-Dov. "These are the steps that lead to the Temple, so he must have walked here many times."

Armstrong then asked if these were the original steps, and Ben-Dov confirmed that they were.

"So Jesus stepped right here?" asked Armstrong again.

"That's right," answered Ben-Dov.

"I have to tell you," Armstrong said to the Israeli archaeologist, "I am more excited stepping on these stones than I was stepping on the moon."

Because of this perception that modern Israel is really an extension of biblical Israel, the way the Jews living in modern Israel behave themselves is theologically relevant to the Christian world, and this is the second reason why news from Israel is treated with such extraordinary prominence in the West. The basic claim of Christianity was that revelation began with the Jews—that God originally revealed himself through them—but because they strayed from God's commandments, their Scriptures were ultimately superseded by the teachings of Jesus Christ. The destruction of the Second Jewish Commonwealth in A.D. 70, and the subsequent dispersion of the Jews for two thousand years, were often interpreted by Christianity as God's punishment of the Jews for their not having accepted Christ as the Messiah.

Therefore, the fact that the Jews have ended their dispersion, returned to their biblical homeland, and built there a modern, vital Jewish state—a Third Jewish Commonwealth—is extremely relevant to Christianity. While some evangelical Christians celebrate the Jews' return to Israel as the necessary first stage in the coming of the Messiah, others, particularly the Vatican, see it as a theological dilemma with implications for their own interpretation of Scripture. Because if for all these years it was thought that the Jews were wandering as their punishment for rejecting Jesus, if for all these years it was believed that the Jews were just a prelude to Christianity and then supposed to be reduced to a footnote, what in the world were they doing back in Israel flying F-15 fighter jets over the skies of Jerusalem? It is no accident that the Vatican has never recognized the state of Israel, and it was also no accident that when the Archbishop of New York, John Cardinal O'Connor, visited Israel in January 1987 the Vatican refused to allow him to meet Israeli President Chaim Herzog in his office. If Herzog is really at home in Jerusalem, then the Pope has a problem in Rome.

As the Christian theologian Paul van Buren once put it, "Modern Israel is both unsettling and exciting for the Christian world. It is unsettling because it was not supposed to happen this way—as we read the story. The very existence of Israel as a modern state is slightly mind-blowing. This was not in the script. You thought you had some understanding of the Jews and where they were, and now they are not there. If you reflect on it all, it becomes even more unsettling, because maybe you have to go back and rethink your own story a little bit. At the same time, it is exciting, because with Israel back on the scene again, the whole story suddenly becomes modern. For anyone with a biblical faith, the existence of this state, with Jerusalem as its capital, reawakens the whole possibility that this is not all in the past. Something about this is happening now. It is a problem we have to think about now. Maybe God is not as dead as we thought. I think this rings a note in the subconscious of even the most secular Christian."

The Austrian-born philosopher Ludwig Wittgenstein once re-marked that if you ask a man how much is 2 plus 2 and he tells you 5, that is a mistake. But if you ask a man how much is 2 plus 2 and he tells you 97, that is no longer a mistake. The man you are talking with is operating with a wholly different logic from your own.

Whenever I observed how Israel's treatment of the Palestinians during the *intifada* was handled by the Western news media, I was reminded of this story, because the extensive focus on Israeli soldiers beating, arresting, or shooting Palestinians was so ob-viously out of proportion to other similar and contemporaneous news stories—such as the Iraqi army's poison-gas attack on the Kurds, or the Algerian army's shooting to death of more than 200 student rioters in one week—that it could not be explained by Israel's familiarity and relevance alone.

That thought first occurred to me on the morning of March 22, 1988. I was eating breakfast in a London hotel and devouring the *International Herald Tribune* along with my eggs and toast. But there was something in the newspaper I could not quite digest. On the top of the front page—next to a story about Iran and Iraq attacking each other's cities with long-range missiles, killing scores of innocent civilians—was a four-column picture of an Israeli soldier grabbing a Palestinian youth. The caption read: "An Is-raeli soldier grabbed a Palestinian as he prepared to show his papers in Ramallah, on the West Bank, during a security check. The man was arrested and driven away. See World Briefs. Page 2."

In other words, the actual news story was so insignificant it merited only a two-paragraph brief inside the paper. Yet the lead picture in the *Herald Tribune* that day, at the very top of its front page, was of an Israeli soldier not beating, not killing, but grabbing a Palestinian. I couldn't help but say to myself, "Let's see, there are 155 countries in the world today. Say five people grabbed other people in each country; that makes 775 similar incidents worldwide. Why was it that this grab was the only one to be photographed and treated as front-page news?"

A similar lack of proportion could be found in some of the editorials which were written about Israel's handling of the Palestinian uprising. Take, for example, an editorial published February 18, 1988, by the *Boston Globe*, a serious newspaper, about an incident in which four Palestinian youths in the West Bank were buried alive under piles of sand by several Israeli reserve soldiers. (The four were quickly dug out by friends before suffering any serious injuries, although the Israelis who buried them apparently did so with the intent to kill; they received prison terms as a result.)

The *Globe*, in its editorial, declared that these four Palestinian "victims will be identified with an entire people. The dispossession of the Palestinians, their dispersal, the massacres they suffered, not only in their native land but also in Jordan and Lebanon, at the hands of Phalangists, Syrians and the Shi'ite Amal militia—all these horrors are evoked in the image of being buried alive. It is an image that calls up collective memories from the history of the Jewish people as well: the czarist pogroms, the centuries of homelessness and persecution, the mass grave at Babi Yar, the piled bodies found at Nazi death camps in 1945."

To be sure, Israel's handling of the Palestinian uprising was at times both brutal and stupid. But to compare it to the genocide at Babi Yar, where 33,000 Jews were massacred solely for being Jews? To the mass graves of 6 million Jews systematically liquidated by the Nazis? That is too much. Some other logic must be driving Israel onto the front pages.

I believe this logic has to do with the fact that because the Christian West views modern Israel as the continuation of a 3,000-year-old biblical drama, it also views modern Israel as the sovereign inheritor of the 3,000-year-old roles which the Jews played in Western civilization. What the West expected from the Jews of the past, it expects from Israel today.

That means two things in particular. First, the Jews historically were the ones to introduce the concept of a divine universal moral code of justice through the Ten Commandments. These divine laws, delivered at Mount Sinai, formed the very basis of what became known as Judeo-Christian morality and ethics. Modern Israel, therefore, is expected to reflect a certain level of justice and morality in its actions. But the Jews also played another role, which modern Israel is expected to live up to: as a symbol of optimism and hope. It was the Jews who proclaimed that history is not, as the Greeks taught, a cyclical process in which men get no better and no worse. No, said the Jews, history is a linear process of moral advancement, in which men can, if they follow the divine laws, steadily improve themselves in this world and one day bring about a messianic reign of absolute peace and harmony. Human history and politics, declared the Jews, can lead to something better: Slaves can be free; the Exodus from Egypt is possible; there is a Promised Land at the end of the desert.

Because Israel has inherited these two roles of the Jew in Western eyes—the yardstick of morality and the symbol of hope—the way Israel behaves has an impact on how men see themselves.

For instance, news from Israel can be psychologically liberating, unlike news from any other country. For the past two thousand years, the Jews were victims of other people's power, and as victims they could always stand up and preach about justice and ethics from a position of moral invincibility. After all these centuries of being lectured to by Jews, the West finally wants to see whether these same Jews, now that they have a state and power of their own, will live up to the standards they set for themselves and others.

As David Hartman put it, "Historically speaking, if the Jews behaved well, they made those around them feel deficient. If they misbehaved, those around them felt relieved of the moral demands the Jews represented in history. If Israel turns out to be the light unto the nations, which it initially proclaimed itself to be, then it will be a judgment, a moral critique, on the incompleteness and shortcomings of all other nations. Just as if Marxism had actually created a workers' paradise, it would have been a devastating living critique on capitalism. We feel guilty about ourselves if there really is an alternative option for building a more just social and political reality. On some level, I believe, the Western press wants to crush the messianic notion Jews gave to the West that human history and politics can lead to something better. The media take a perverse pleasure in labeling Israel South

Africa. It is the same pleasure you get when you catch your Sunday-school teacher misbehaving. If my Sunday-school teacher is misbehaving, then so can I. What the media are really telling the Jews through their saturation coverage of Israeli beatings and shootings in the West Bank is: 'Don't lecture me anymore that there is a Promised Land, that I could be better than I am, that there is a higher standard I could strive for. Look at yourself. If you are not, then I don't have to be. If Israel is just like South Africa, then we can all go play tennis.' "

I am sure very few reporters or editors are overtly conscious of these feelings. They are more subliminal; but they are very real. It was no accident that NBC subtitled its controversial 1987 documentary on twenty years of Israeli occupation of the West Bank "A Dream Is Dying." It was a perfect title, because at times the news reporting of Israeli behavior in the occupied territories was not just a story, it was a funeral wake—men toasting the end of the Jewish dream next to an open coffin. The television correspondents all might as well have been standing on hillsides with Israeli soldiers beating Palestinians in the background and announcing to their viewers, "It began here and it ended here. Here lies the Sunday sermon."

Can one imagine a documentary called *Hafez Assad's Syria*: "A Dream Is Dying"? No, because there has to be a dream which we all can relate to before its death is worth an hour on network television. When the Syrians kill thousands of their own people in Hama, it is not liberating or devastating for the West, because the West has no higher expectations of the Syrians and does not see any of its values emanating from Damascus.

"When the Syrians kill people it is a story about Syria," observed Yaron Ezrahi. "When the Jews kill, it somehow becomes a story about mankind. If Damascus is sinful, it is bad for the Syrians or the Arab world, but if Jerusalem is sinful, it means we are condemned to live in an unredeemable world."

The liberating quality of news from Israel has a particular appeal for Europeans who carry guilt over the Holocaust. Before 1967, if there was any unifying trend to European coverage of the Middle East, it was the tendency to overromanticize and oversentimentalize Israel in general and to highlight its military prowess in particular. This was particularly obvious in European documentaries about Israel during this period. It was as if by emphasizing Israel's strength the Europeans were telling themselves that the Jewish people had been resurrected and therefore the weight of what the Germans did to them during the Second World War could be lightened.

After Israel went from underdog to overdog, however, the mood of the European media shifted. There was a pronounced tendency in the German, French, and Italian media to focus on Israel as a triumphant and ruthless occupier, a new Prussia, in what seemed to be a not-so-subtle attempt by these countries to absolve themselves of some of their own guilt for how their own Jews were brutalized during World War II. Highlighting the Israeli involvement in the Sabra and Shatila massacre was a convenient way of saying, "Look, the Nazis were not unique; nations massacre other nations all the time. Moreover, we Europeans weren't so guilty when we said we didn't know what was going on inside the concentration camps. It happens to everybody— even the Jews."

Something of this European attitude seemed to be behind the remarks by the Norwegian ambassador to Israel, Torleiv Anda, who told Israeli reporters in February 1988 that the Nazi occupation was actually more enlightened than the Israeli one in the West Bank and Gaza. "What the Germans did," said Anda, "including beating and torturing prisoners and suspects, was very bad. But we do not remember [the Nazis] going out into the streets to break people's arms and legs or pulling children out of their homes at night. Norwegians did not expect such things from Israelis, and it has left a deep impression. One doesn't like people who behave like that."

Ambassador Anda later apologized for his selective memory of Nazi behavior. The point is that when Israel is the story, nobody comes empty-handed; everyone comes with an ax, some kind of an ax, to grind.

Yet, on another level, I think some of the very same reporters and readers who seem to relish news of Israel's misdeeds also hope that Israel will succeed—that it will one day fulfill its promise. Why? Because the identification with the dreams of biblical Israel and mythic Jerusalem runs so deep, particularly in American culture, that when Israel succeeds and lives up to its prophetic expectations many Americans feel part of it. Israel's success is their success. After all, the Puritans and other early American settlers actually saw themselves as inheritors of the Israelite dream and as fighters against the tyranny of the modern pharaoh in Great Britain. They spoke of building a "New Jerusalem" when they came to America. The Founding Fathers, Benjamin Franklin, Thomas Jefferson, and John Adams, even suggested to the Continental Congress that the seal of the United States picture the Israelites and Moses standing on the shore, while Pharaoh and his army drown in the Red Sea, surrounded by the motto "Rebellion to Tyrants Is Obedience to God." They settled instead for a bald eagle. Later, the black civil-rights movement led by Martin Luther King, Jr., adopted the story of Exodus from bondage as the underlying theme of its struggle for equality.

Former Israeli ambassador to Washington Simcha Dinitz once told me of a lecture he delivered in a black church in Washington, D.C., in the early sixties. "After my talk," said Dinitz, "a young girl came up to me and said, 'Where do you live?' I said, 'Jerusalem.' She thought about that for a minute and said, 'Jerusalem, is that a place on earth? I thought it was in heaven.' That's when I really understood that Jerusalem symbolizes every wish, every hope, every dream, every ideal. Everyone sees it how they want to see it. It may be the capital of Israel, but in every American's heart is a little bit of Jerusalem."

This is why I believe that people, and particularly Americans, can get an emotional high from news about Israel that they can't get from reading about Singapore. This helps to explain why Israel is overreported in America, not only when it behaves negatively, but when it performs positively as well—whether it is Israel "turning the desert green" (which many other countries have done without similar publicity) or rescuing hostages in Entebbe or vanquishing three Arab armies at once in the 1967 war.

On June 9, 1967, at the moment Americans first realized that Israel was not going to be destroyed in the Six-Day War, columnist Mary McGrory wrote in *The Washington Star* about a rally for Israel in Lafayette Park across from the White House: "Some of us never knew what a *simcha* [Hebrew for a real joy] was. We know now. It's what happens when the Arabs admit they've had it—again—and there are 30,000 Jews in Lafayette Park to celebrate. That's what a *simcha* is. We were all Jews in the park

yesterday. Instant Israelization was occurring all over. . . . Our
signs, many of them written in haste on the buses coming down,
showed a lot of chutzpah. 'God is not neutral,' 'Support Israel,
God's Little Acre' and 'Lyndon Johnson, Let's Be Jewish.' . . .
[When the cease-fire with Egypt was announced] we went wild
with joy. Then we wept, we embraced each other. We sang the
Israeli national anthem, 'Hatikva.' We observed a moment of
silence for all who had fallen, heard the melancholy summons of
the shofar.''

Finally, news from Israel is not only uniquely liberating and
uplifting, it is also uniquely compelling compared to news made
by other countries its size, because of all the historical and religious movements to which Israel is connected in Western eyes.
So many cultural and historical strands come together in Israel
that almost every story from there is two-dimensional; it is about
itself and something else.

In 1986, for instance, Spain established diplomatic relations
with Israel. On the one hand, it was a straightforward diplomatic
story. On the other, some people saw it as the final chapter in a
great historical saga that began in 1492, with the expulsion of the
Jews from Spain. The story of the Israeli Supreme Court accepting
as an Israeli citizen an American Gentile who was converted to
Judaism by a Reform rabbi is both an immigration story and a
fundamental statement about who is a Jew. Even a travel story
about kayaking down the Jordan River in Israel touches a certain
religious chord in some readers that kayaking down the Thames
does not. Since editors often find that in stories from Israel they
are getting two news items for the space of one, they are more
disposed to use them over those from other foreign countries
which don't pack as much punch per paragraph.

Whenever I think of this unique double dimension of news
from Israel, I am reminded of a story that Israeli poet Yehuda
Amichai told me about his daughter and Herod's tomb. Amichai
lives in the Yemin Moshe quarter of Jerusalem. Between his
home and the King David Hotel is a small garden, in the middle
of which is what looks like a stone well. In fact, it is the tomb of
Herod the Great, who ruled Judea from 37 to 4 B.C. and erected
some of Jerusalem's greatest buildings. One day, Amichai was
sitting in his Jerusalem home when his four-year-old daughter
rushed in and shouted, "Daddy, Daddy, my ball fell into Herod's

Tomb." For Amichai's daughter, that little pile of stones next to their house was just another playground with a name—Herod's Tomb—but it also happened to be Herod's tomb!—a landmark of historical significance.

Had the early Zionists taken up the British offer to establish their state in Uganda instead of in the holy land, news from Israel might have been a little less interesting. But the Jews chose to build a "normal" state in the one land that was totally abnormal, in the land that more than any other on earth was soaked with religious meaning and history and intimately tied to all the hopes and neuroses of Western civilization. Because the Jewish return to this particular land unleashes so many passions, touches so many memories, and is relevant for so many people in the West, Israel simply cannot avoid being extraordinarily newsworthy—not in Jerusalem, not now and not tomorrow.

But Israel's fascination for the West is only half the story, because Israel's high profile in the media is not only the result of the West looking in but also the result of Israel reaching out—sometimes frantically—to grab the world by the throat. From the day Israel was born as a nation, its leaders have invited, and even at times demanded, that the world take heed of its uniqueness and judge it with a different yardstick from other nation-states.

No one is more aware of this than Israeli statesman Abba Eban, who, in 1947, had the difficult task of presenting the Jewish people's claim for statehood before the United Nations, which was then considering the idea of partitioning Palestine.

"It was not easy to make our case," recalled Eban. "The entire region rejected us. We were forming a state for people who were not yet here. And we were not a majority in our country. We had to seize the ears of the world. We could not just rely on pure juridical arguments. We could not argue like Ghana. We had to make ourselves exceptional. So we based our claim on the exceptionality of Israel, in terms of the affliction suffered by its people, and in terms of our historical and spiritual lineage. We knew we were basically appealing to a Christian world for whom the biblical story was familiar and attractive, and we played it to the hilt. We are still the victims of our own rhapsodic rhetoric, and our own rhapsodic defense. [But] we chose the line. We chose to emphasize at the beginning of our statehood that Israel would represent the ancient Jewish morality. Some Israelis now complain about being judged by a different standard [from other countries in the Middle East]. But the world is only comparing us to the standard we set for ourselves. You can't go out and declare that we are the descendants of kings and prophets and then come and say, 'Why does the world demand that we behave differently from Syria?' "

Israel's quest for world attention was also related to its own insecurity. The trauma of two thousand years of Jews being rejected by the outside world and living on the margins of whatever society they happened to find themselves in lies deep in Israel's historical consciousness. This explains why Israelis have always felt a certain urgency about what the outside world thought of them. Israelis have a deep need to be visible, to be loved, to be admired, to be ushered out of their sense of loneliness and have the world take them by the elbow and say, "Yes, we see you. We recognize you are there and part of us." Israeli Foreign Ministry employees always like to tell the story about the time when an Italian Foreign Minister made his first visit to Israel. He stepped off his Alitalia flight onto the tarmac at Ben-Gurion Airport, walked directly into an airport press conference, and was immediately asked by an overeager Israeli reporter, "Sir, how do you like our country?"

When I was leaving Jerusalem after completing my reporting assignment last year, every person I dealt with, from the semiliterate moving men to the woman at the rental car agency, asked me, not in passing but with real concern, whether I had enjoyed my stay. When I answered yes, they would always look at me sideways and say in Hebrew, *"B'emet?"*—Really?

I found that nothing rankled Israelis more than to hear that a man of international prominence, such as John Cardinal O'Connor, had come to Israel and refused to meet "officially" with the Israeli President. After all, the very meaning of having a Jewish state was so that the Jews could project themselves into the larger drama of world politics and no longer be a marginal people. And nothing used to please Israelis more than to have world-renowned figures, particularly Gentiles like Jane Fonda or Frank Sinatra, visit their country and give it their stamp of approval. At tennis tournaments in Jerusalem, Israelis always got a special charge out of watching their home-grown tennis champion Amos Mansdorf being chummy with the likes of Jimmy Connors. You could almost hear people in the stands saying, "Look, we're one of the fellas!"

Take this congenital insecurity and couple it with Israel's near-total economic dependence on the United States and it becomes easy to understand why Israel is obsessed with how it is portrayed in the Western media in general and the American media in particular. In talking to Israelis, I have always felt that when they thought about news in America they imagined that every American had a television set with a voting box next to it, and after each broadcast of the evening news, Americans would vote on whether or not they still liked Israel. Or, as one senior Israeli official put it, "Israelis are certain that America is a country that spends all its time being either for or against Israel."

Being the *New York Times* correspondent in Jerusalem, I was both the beneficiary and the victim of this Israeli obsession with the American media. On the benefit side, it meant that every Israeli official returned my phone calls and that I could see everyone from the Prime Minister on down within forty-eight hours of a request. The negative side was that people read everything I wrote with the scrutiny of copy readers examining Torah scrolls for mistakes. My hate mail from readers who did not appreciate my reporting was often written in a tone reserved only for child molesters and convicted Nazi war criminals. In fact, one particularly obnoxious reader used to address all his letters to me "Dear Kapo"—the term used to describe those who manned the ovens in the Nazi death camps.

The speed with which Israelis would move to correct mistakes I made in *The New York Times* was measured not in days but in hours and minutes. After the Israeli government was formed following the July 1984 elections, my soft-spoken assistant, Moshe Brilliant, dictated by telephone to New York the list of new Cabinet ministers, which was released late at night and close to deadline. Moshe began with the Prime Minister and then read the names of the other new ministers over the telephone. When he got to the Minister of Religious Affairs, he said, "veteran National Religious Party leader Yosef Burg . . ." Well, the person taking dictation in New York heard "Bedouin" instead of "veteran." Sure enough, the Cabinet list was published and it read "Bedouin National Religious Party leader Yosef Burg." Considering that

Burg was an Orthodox Jew, a bigger mistake would be difficult to make. The first edition of *The New York Times* hits the streets about 11:00 p.m. At 11:01 p.m. someone called Burg in Israel, and at 11:02 p.m. he or one of his staff called the *Times*. By 11:03 p.m. the Cabinet list had been corrected for later editions.

Not surprisingly, Israel goes to extraordinary lengths to project and protect its image abroad. The Israeli Foreign Ministry commissions roughly one hundred freelance articles a year about different aspects of Israeli life, technology, and medicine and distributes them to roughly two thousand publications in the United States—from journals for dairy farmers to metropolitan newspapers. The Israel Broadcasting Service, a corporation set up by the Foreign Ministry, produces radio shows on various Israeli topics, sometimes tailor-made to interest specific Hispanic, black, or geographic audiences in America, and then issues them regularly to 550 radio stations around the United States, and to another 300 stations in Latin America, Europe, and the Far East. The Israeli government, working through a private distributor, also regularly sends local television stations across America special 90-second news videos about different developments in science or agriculture in Israel. These spots often get aired as straight news on local stations, without attribution as to the source. In addition, each year the Israeli Foreign Ministry brings to Israel at its own expense roughly 400–500 key opinion makers—journalists, priests, union leaders, student leaders, mayors, local politicians, and academics from communities all over the United States—to see the country and then return to their homes to talk or write about it. Israel's embassy and nine consulates in the United States closely monitor all the newspapers and television news shows in their regions, large and small, and when "hostile" articles or editorials appear, their staffs will meet with the editors of those news organizations and encourage local Jewish community activists to write letters to the editor or rebuttals, sometimes by the sackful.

In Jerusalem, the Government Press Office makes sure that foreign correspondents are kept abreast of all the news, both pro- and anti-government, by providing daily English translations of the main articles and editorials in all the Israeli newspapers. It even distributes them by computer directly to each correspondent's terminal. Moreover, the major foreign and local reporters in Israel are connected to a telephone system, nicknamed the "golem." (In Jewish folklore, the golem was an artificially created human being.) The golem allows the Government Press Office to call the entire foreign press corps simultaneously and inform them, at any hour, of everything from the Prime Minister's schedule to announcements by the army spokesman that someone has just hijacked a bus.

As an Israeli Foreign Ministry spokesman remarked one day after briefing foreign correspondents practically from dawn until dusk, "Let's face it, we are doing a striptease for the world every morning."

The intensity of the spotlight which has been focused on Israel has profoundly affected the way Israelis and Palestinians think of themselves and the way television viewers and readers in the West think of their conflict.

For the readers and television viewers, the spotlight on Israel has been so glaring at times that it has totally distorted people's ability to make sense of the Palestinian–Israeli conflict. Virtually every action, reaction, and declaration involving Israelis and Palestinians seems to get magnified out of all proportion to its actual impact on the ground. Because of this, the viewers in the West, who see the conflict only through the distorting lenses of television or the print media, expect all these actions and declarations to have a much bigger impact than they ever do.

This was obvious in the coverage of the *intifada*. The fact that news stories involving Palestinians in the West Bank and Gaza throwing stones and being beaten by Israeli soldiers were virtually all that many Westerners viewed from Israel and the occupied territories for several months left many people with the impression that this was all there was to life in this land. I am sure many viewers said to themselves, "My God, this is a war. How can the Israelis tolerate this uprising for another day?"

What the cameras usually did not show was that while Israeli troops were clashing with stone-throwers in one village, Palestinians in most other villages in the West Bank were going to work in Israel. What the cameras also did not show was that in the spring of 1988, while the *intifada* was raging on American television, thousands of Israelis were going to the Tel Aviv fairgrounds every evening to ride Ferris wheels, eat cotton candy, and visit all the booths at the exposition marking Israel's fortieth anniversary of independence. In the West, the *intifada* was viewed as an uprising that had left Israel ablaze, because that was virtually all that was shown. But Israelis and Palestinians always viewed the uprising in its real proportions: as a slice of life, not life itself. It involved sporadic "clashes," sometimes lethal, that disrupted the lives of some people and didn't even touch the lives of many others.

Whenever West Bank expert Meron Benvenisti comes to America and watches the way the American media overcover every twist and turn in the Palestinian–Israeli conflict, he always tells me after a few days that he must go back home. "What I am seeing on your television just doesn't correspond to the reality that I know," complains Benvenisti. "I feel as if I'm watching a tennis game being played on a vertical court."

For Palestinians, this spotlight has been both a blessing and a curse. The blessing for the Palestinians is that because their enemy happens to be the Jew, and their battlefield the holy land, both of which loom so large in Western eyes, the Palestinians have received more attention and visibility than any other refugee community or national liberation movement in the world. The Palestinians have had the great fortune to be cast as supporting actors in a large and long-running historical drama starring the Jew, who one season is playing a tortured Hamlet, the next season King Lear, and the next Goliath. This means that the Palestinians have always gotten a hearing, year after year, while other defeated nations, who didn't have the Jews for enemies, were ignored. Had the Palestinians had the bad luck of the Armenians, who got stuck with the Turks as their enemy, or of the Kurds (who were promised a state by the Allies after World War I), who ended up with the Iraqis, their cause would be as unknown in the West as Kurdish and Armenian nationalism.

Western news cameras do not flock to Israel to film Palestinian stones; they come to film Jewish billy clubs. Israel Television's Arab affairs reporter, Ehud Ya'ari, once witnessed an incident in the al-Amari refugee camp in the West Bank in which television cameramen literally stood around for hours outside the camp waiting, not to talk to Palestinians, but for that inevitable moment when Israeli soldiers would begin to beat some of them up.

"Israeli soldiers were standing off at a distance," said Ya'ari, "facing a big violent crowd of Palestinian demonstrators who were throwing rocks, bottles, Molotov cocktails. The following conversation took place between the [American] cameramen and the Israeli officer in charge. The officer said, 'We are not going to go in. We are not going to do it for you.' And the cameramen said, 'You will have to go in, so you might as well do it now.' Everyone understood his role very well. Eventually the soldiers went in, and as soon as they started breaking into homes to capture rioters who had fled, the cameras all started to roll."

When the Palestinians are not victims of the Jews, but of other Arabs, or when they themselves are victimizers, the West in general is simply not interested in their fate. That becomes clear from even the most cursory reading of newspapers during the past few years. When Israelis were indirectly involved in the massacre of Palestinians at the Sabra and Shatila refugee camps in Beirut in 1982, the story was front-page news for weeks. When Lebanese Shiites were directly involved in killing Palestinians in the very same camps from 1985 to 1988, it was almost always back-page news—if it was reported at all. This despite the fact that some 3,000 Palestinians were killed during the three years of fighting over the camps, including women who were shot by snipers while going out to buy bread and others who died of hunger after having run out of dogs to eat.

The abundance of reporters in Israel also clearly curtailed the amount of force Israel could use against Palestinians. An Israeli colonel in the West Bank was quite explicit when I asked him about the deterrent effect television has had on his treatment of West Bankers and Gazans.

"I used to be stationed in south Lebanon," said the colonel, "and in south Lebanon there is nothing between you and God Almighty. The only question you ask yourself when you are going to blow up someone's house is whether to use 50 kilos of dynamite or 25 kilos. Here in the West Bank you have to explain every little move you make to ten different people."

A senior Israeli commander in the West Bank said that he told his men specifically, "Do not beat anyone if you see a television camera. If you are already beating someone and you see a camera, stop. If you see someone else beating someone and you see a camera, stop him." The same officer told me, "Look, when my soldiers are involved in something not so kosher with Palestinians in a village, and television is not around, I can live with it. I may not like what they did, but I can live with it. But if television is there, I cannot live with it. Not at all."

But the attention the Palestinians received because their enemy was the Jew has also been a source of enormous frustration and confusion, because although the West seems to be talking about them, it doesn't seem to be really feeling for them. Instead, it only seems to truly feel for the Jew—sometimes it is feeling anger and other times compassion, but these emotions seem to be reserved largely for the Jew. It can be extremely frustrating to think that the world is talking about you but not feeling for you.

I once visited the Remal Health Center in the Gaza Strip, which is run by the United Nations Relief and Works Agency for Palestine Refugees (UNRWA), to talk to Palestinian women about their views on childbirth and fertility. As I was being shown around the maternity ward by Dr. Zuhni Yusef al-Wahidi, I stopped at several bedsides to interview Palestinian mothers who had just given birth. While I was in the middle of a conversation with one new mother, a middle-aged Palestinian nurse standing off to the side suddenly exploded with a question directed at me in a burst of staccato Arabic.

"Where are you from?" the nurse asked, with an arched eyebrow.

"I'm from America," I answered.

"Well, then can you tell me something?" she continued. "Why is it that when the Germans were killing the Jews everyone screamed, but when we are being killed by Israelis, the world calls us killers?"

The nurse's question was clearly spoken out of a deep psychic wound, a grievance that she herself had been nursing for a long time. Who could blame her? As I stood there, one hand on the new mother's bed railing and the other gripping my clipboard, I wanted to explain to her that the difference in treatment had nothing to do with the Israeli cause being somehow morally superior to that of the Palestinians and that it also had nothing to do with any conspiracy in the media. It had to do with the fact that the Palestinians simply are not part of the biblical super story through which the West looks at the world, and it is the super story that determines whose experiences get interpreted and whose don't, whose pain is felt and whose is ignored. That is why when it comes to winning the sympathies of the West the Palestinians can never quite compete with the Jews, no matter how hard they try and no matter how much they suffer.

Examples of this can be found in the newspaper every day. At the November 1988 meeting in Algiers of the Palestine National Council, Muhammad Abbas, the Palestinian guerrilla leader who planned the hijacking of the Italian cruise ship *Achille Lauro* in 1985, was being pressed by Western reporters as to whether he regretted the fact that his men murdered a wheelchair-bound passenger on the ship, Leon Klinghoffer, a sixty-nine-year-old New York Jew. Abbas eventually grew so exasperated with the reporters' questions, he blurted out at them, "I wish that the names of our victims and martyrs were as well known as the name of Klinghoffer. Can you name ten Palestinians who died from Israeli gas, or ten pregnant Palestinian women who were crushed and killed?"

Indeed, shortly after the Israeli army trapped the PLO in Beirut during the summer of '82, and the Palestinian issue became headline news around the globe, my colleague Bill Barrett, then the correspondent of the *Dallas Times Herald*, received a telex at the Commodore Hotel from his foreign editor back in Texas. The telex read: "Why can't the Palestinians go back to Palestine? Is there a problem with their papers or something?"

Bill's one-sentence reply was: "Because their mothers are not Jewish."

Bill remarked to me later that his answer seemed to confuse his editor even more. "I was a bit surprised," said Bill, "that a foreign editor would not know any of this, although I suppose his ignorance simply mirrored that of the American public. A few months later my editor quit the paper, left journalism, and became a real-estate agent."

In this same vein, Benjamin Netanyahu, Israel's former ambassador to the United Nations, once told me a story about being on Ted Koppel's *Nightline*, debating an Arab ambassador. A handsome, Western-looking figure with perfect English and an M.I.T. education, Netanyahu was in the same Washington studio with the Arab ambassador, but they were divided on air by a split screen. They had the usual debate about the Palestine question and each said the usual things. "After it was over," recalled Netanyahu, "I got up from my seat to leave the studio and one of the cameramen came up to me and said, 'You won.' I said, 'How do you know?' He said, 'You won even before you started.' I said, 'What do you mean?' He said, 'Look, you both have funny last names, but your first name is Benjamin and his is Abdullah. He didn't have a chance.' "

(The group of Americans who seemed to be most consistently and deeply disturbed about what Israel was doing to the Palestinians were American Jews, but that had little to do with concern for the Palestinians per se and more to do with concern for what Israel as a Jewish state was becoming.)

The spotlight on Israel has been a curse for Palestinians in another way as well. It has given them a grossly exaggerated sense of their real strength and convinced their leaders that time is somehow on their side. After all, if you are Yasir Arafat and senior editors of *Time* magazine are chasing after you for weeks to interview you on your private jet, how can you not feel important, how can you not feel powerful, how can you not feel that if you just tell your story enough times to the audience in the West it will force Israel to give you a state and spare you having to make either a real war or the real concessions for a settlement? To be a story is easy, and sometimes fun; to change reality is difficult, painful, and dangerous—especially in this theater called the Middle East, where no one uses fake ammunition and there are no stuntmen around to perform the difficult leaps.

Israeli policymakers have been no less affected by the spotlight focused on them than the Palestinians. On the one hand, the presence of the foreign media really forced Israelis to look at the true brutality of their occupation. Many times during the early months of the *intifada* Israel Television showed American television footage of Israelis clubbing or shooting Palestinians in the West Bank and Gaza Strip, because the four American networks had more crews—at least a dozen more—in the occupied territories than did Israel Television. Were it not for the presence of the American media, more than a few of the most disturbing scenes of the *intifada*, most notably the incident recorded by CBS News on February 26, 1988, in which four Israeli soldiers in

Nablus were involved in beating two Palestinian demonstrators with a stone for forty minutes, would have gone unrecorded.

On the other hand, because Israelis constantly felt that they were under a spotlight and were being judged by the whole world, their spokesmen and leaders spent more time and energy thinking up ways to explain why they were treating the Palestinians as they were than dealing with the underlying political causes of the uprising. The Israeli leadership were often more obsessed with the spotlight than with the reality upon which it was focused. There is a real danger in this: an actor who is always onstage reciting his lines can never really look at himself in a relaxed and critical manner and address his shortcomings in an honest and meaningful way.

Sometimes Israeli officials became so involved in reciting their lines that they no longer heard how phony they sounded. On February 28, 1988, at the height of the *intifada*, I was listening to the Voice of Israel Radio's 1:00 p.m. English news broadcast. The announcer read the following item—with no hint of irony in his voice:

"In the village of Burin, south of Nablus, a riot broke out today. An army patrol was sent into the village and came under a hail of stones. After firing in the air and rubber bullets failed to disperse the crowd, the army spokesman said the commander of the unit fired at the *legs* of the demonstrators. The result was that one demonstrator was shot in the *neck* and died" (emphasis mine).

When Israel was the darling of the West after the 1967 war, Israeli leaders and American Jews could not read enough stories in the newspapers about this "heroic little state"; no one in Israel then complained about the spotlight on their country. Twenty years later, though, after Israel's behavior in Lebanon and the West Bank has often cast it in a negative light, Israelis have become some of the loudest critics of the foreign press. Why us? they ask. Why all the excessive press attention? There are endless panel discussions and conferences held in Israel on why the foreign press is so biased against the Jewish state, as if it were all just a question of the foreign press and not anything Israel itself was doing.

Today, an increasing number of Israeli leaders find themselves unable to handle the intense judgmental spotlight any longer, but they are also unwilling to address the ugly reality of their occupation of the West Bank and the Gaza Strip. So they look for a curtain that will shield them from the piercing gaze of the West and allow them to maintain the status quo in the occupied territories. That curtain is called the Holocaust. From behind the curtain of the Holocaust, Israelis can scream out at the world, "You have no right to judge us. We are victims of Auschwitz! Go away! Go away!"

This was clearly the sentiment that motivated a statement by Prime Minister Yitzhak Shamir shortly after the *intifada* erupted and the networks began focusing on Israeli beatings. Shamir, who, like the Palestinians, also knows how to play only one role, King Lear, practically screamed at inquiring reporters one day when they asked about Israeli treatment of Palestinians: "We are not allowed to kill; we are not allowed to expel; we are not allowed to beat. You ask yourself, What are we allowed to do? Only to be killed, only to be wounded, only to be defeated." Shamir later added, "We have plenty of 'friends' in the world who would like to see us dead, wounded, trampled, and suppressed—and then it is possible to pity the wretched Jew. When Jews are killed in this country, does the United Nations discuss it? It has never yet happened. But we do not want to be deserving of pity, we want to fight for our lives."

When the Israelis join the Palestinians in wrapping themselves in the loincloth of the victim, all prospects of dealing with the underlying causes of their conflict get lost. In its place what you have is a theater in which Israelis and Palestinians are clubbing each other onstage, but instead of talking to each other straight, they are each looking out at the audience and declaring, "Did you see what he did to me? What did I tell you? I am the real victim. Don't judge me, judge him."

In recent years many Israelis could be heard wishing for the day when their country might be reported on like Norway, or even Syria. They cite the famous saying by the French philosopher Montesquieu: "Happy the people whose annals are blank in history books." A year after the *intifada* began, there were signs that their dreams were beginning to come true—that stories of Israeli troops shooting a three-year-old Palestinian boy, while dispersing a demonstration of ten- and eleven-year-old Palestinian children, were becoming boring to the West and worth only a small mention in the newspaper. The audience in the West seemed to be starting to lose interest in the misbehavior of Israeli Jews. If I were Israeli I would think twice before celebrating this new-found anonymity. When Israeli repression is no longer viewed as news, it means that the West no longer expects anything exceptional of Israel and Israel no longer expects anything exceptional of itself. That can only be a sign that something very essential in Israel's character and the character of the Jewish people has died.

The day when going from Beirut to Jerusalem means not going anywhere at all is a day Israel will rue forever.

16

Israel and American Jews: Who Is Dreaming about Whom?

Sir, I arrived in Israel five months ago and enrolled in the WUJS programme in Arad in an effort to learn Hebrew and to extend my embarrassingly limited knowledge of my people's history, tradition, culture and religion. The problems of maintaining a Jewish identity in the Diaspora seemed to me insurmountable and I felt it my duty to at least explore life in Israel. Imagine my sadness and bewilderment when, after talking to many [Israeli] high school students (ages 14 to 16), I discovered that all their dreams and aspirations centered on "making it in America. . . ."

> —William H. Finestone,
> Letter to the Editor in
> the JERUSALEM POST,
> December 24, 1986

Some people remember where they were the day President John F. Kennedy was shot. Others remember where they were when the space shuttle *Challenger* went down. I remember where I was the day I discovered Israel.

I don't mean discovered it on a map. I mean the day Israel really entered my consciousness and became something of an obsession. It was June 6, 1967. I was sitting in the family room of our home in Minneapolis watching the 5:30 p.m. CBS evening news. Walter Cronkite was broadcasting the first reports of Israel's dramatic victory in the Six-Day War, and to this day I can still see him sitting there reading the news with a map of Israel and the Sinai Desert projected behind him.

Although I had attended Hebrew school as a young boy, Israel had never really meant much to me before that day. But after June 6, 1967, I was never the same. Like so many American Jews of my generation, I was momentarily swept up by this heroic

Israel, which captured my imagination and made me feel different about myself as a Jew.

During high school, I spent all my summer vacations living on Kibbutz Hahotrim, south of Haifa. It was an exciting time to be in Israel; everything was in motion, the economy was booming, and, although there was a deadly war of attrition going on along the Suez Canal with the Egyptians, the flush of victory had not been erased from the cheeks of the Israeli boys. Everything and everyone in the country seemed larger than life. Every soldier was a hero, every politician a statesman, every girl a knockout. With the kibbutz teenagers my age, there were trips to the Sinai, hikes in the Golan, and long afternoons on the Mediterranean beach. I taught them how to play baseball and they taught me how to identify the different fighter planes in the Israeli air force (something which came in very handy when I later ended up in Beirut). The kibbutz was full of lost Jews, some from Europe, some from America, who had flocked to Israel in search of themselves. They made for a kind of Jewish foreign legion. Most of them stayed for a summer and never came back. But I was hooked. Whatever I was looking for, I had found.

During those post-1967 summers, I was constantly challenged by my Israeli hosts with the question: "Nu, when are you going to make *aliya?*"—When are you going to immigrate? "What is there for you in America? Here is where you belong."

Somehow I always managed to mumble my way out of these challenges, usually with something about how wonderful Minneapolis was with all its lakes. I liked the way Israel made me feel as an American Jew—the pride it instilled in me and the way it stiffened my spine—but I was never convinced that having an Israeli identity could be an end in itself for me.

Then a decade passed. There was college, graduate school, and eventually a career in journalism that by quirk of fate brought me back to Israel in 1984 as the correspondent for *The New York Times*. But when I drove into Jerusalem from Beirut that spring of '84, I found a very different country from the one I remembered as a youth.

Upon arrival, I braced myself for the seemingly inevitable question beginning "Nu, when are you going to immigrate?" But it never came. What came instead was "Nu, how do I get a Green

Card?" Or, "What's it like to live in New York City?" Or, "Can I really get a job in L.A.?"

After enough such conversations, it became clear to me that many Israelis had adopted a profoundly different view of America since those heady days after the 1967 war. After all, Israel had been founded on the thesis that the Diaspora was not a viable solution for Jewish national existence—that Jews could not survive there for long either culturally or physically and hence had to have a homeland of their own. Israel was going to be the center of the world, with its own original Hebrew culture, and all Jews were supposed to settle there. America, in the mind of Israel, was going to be little more than an afterthought. What I quickly discovered, however, was that America, with its bounty, its pluralism, and its burgeoning opportunities for Jews and other minorities was disproving the thesis of Israel's founding fathers. Not only was America attracting more Jews from the Soviet Union, Argentina, and South Africa than Israel, it was also attracting thousands of Israelis themselves. Just how much things had changed since I was in high school was driven home to me when my high-school history teacher from Minneapolis, Marjorie Bingham, visited Jerusalem in 1987 and told me, "When you were in high school, Tom, you and all your friends went to Israel. Now I have three Israeli immigrants in my class."

At the same time that I found Israelis looking differently at America, I also met many American Jews who were reassessing their views about the Jewish state. The Lebanon war, Israeli spying in Washington, the rising influence of the ultra-Orthodox in Israeli politics, and the Israeli response to the Palestinian uprising had combined to produce a profound rethinking on the part of many American Jews about their emotional ties to Israel, and its role in their own identity as Jews. Where all this rethinking will end is not easy to predict. But what is clear, undeniably clear, is that the relationship between Israeli Jews and American Jews is undergoing a radical transformation from that moment on June 6, 1967, when Walter Cronkite introduced me to my Jewish identity and introduced Israel to America.

Israel in the mind of American Jews always touched two emotional chords—one pride, the other fear. As such, Israel has traditionally played two roles for American Jews—one as a visible symbol which places the Jew in the world and integrates him with dignity, and the other as a haven that could protect the Jew from a world turned hostile.

Between 1948 and June 1967, the balance between these two roles was very much weighted in favor of Israel as a safe haven and not as a symbol of Jewish identity. Of course, American Jews took pride in Israel, but it was quiet and understated, the sort of pride you take in a good charity. Some people gave money to their synagogues, others gave to the local Jewish hospital, and others planted trees in Israel. Israel, to my mind then, was symbolized by the blue-and-white boxes I dropped coins in every week at Hebrew school to buy trees. True, Hebrew education became more popular after 1948, as did the Zionist element in Jewish summer camps. People played "Hava Nagila" and a few other Israeli songs at weddings, and they danced the hora along with the waltz, but for most American Jews that was the extent to which Israel touched their lives culturally.

The more important role played by Israel in the mind of most American Jews was as a bomb shelter, a haven against persecution, and a source of Jewish power and real estate that could protect Jews if another Hitler were to appear on the world scene. But even though they saw Israel as a haven, most American Jews thought of it as a haven for other Jews, refugee Jews, displaced Jews—not for themselves. That is why the reaction of most American Jews to Israel's victory in the 1948 war of independence was more relief than anything else—relief that the remnants of the Holocaust would have a place to go; very few American Jews moved there themselves. As one senior American Jewish official once confided to me, "Before 1967, Israel in the eyes of many American Jews was a nation of nebachs. In my family, Israel was where we sent our used clothing. Really. When I outgrew my shirts and pants we put them in a box and sent them to Israel. That is how I thought of the place—a place you send used clothes to."

After the 1967 war, the perception of Israel in the mind of many American Jews shifted radically, from Israel as a safe haven for other Jews to Israel as the symbol and carrier of Jewish communal identity. This radical transition, I believe, can be understood only in the context of the foreboding that preceded the Six-Day War, when many American Jews feared Israel was going to be erased: the people who came out of the death camps were going to be thrown back in.

Itzhak Galnoor, an Israeli political scientist who was studying in upstate New York in June 1967, attended a rally for Israel at a synagogue in Syracuse a few weeks before the war. "The meeting was devoted to what was developing in the Middle East," said Galnoor. "I can still see the rabbi standing up and saying, 'We in the congregation feel in total sympathy with our brave brothers and sisters in Israel, and we are sure that they will be able to take care of themselves and we will do everything we can to help.' But then he mentioned that the Jewish people had suffered disasters before. He mentioned the destruction of the Temple in Jerusalem and then added, 'If, God forbid, something should happen now to destroy Israel, we should not worry because, like our forefather Rabbi Yohanan ben Zakkai, who went and established a spiritual center in Yavne when the Romans besieged Jerusalem, we would establish a Jewish spiritual center in the United States.' You can imagine what I thought of all this. I said, 'Hey, wait a minute, we're gonna win!' "

And win they did—in a big way. When the smoke cleared and the extent of Israel's victory became apparent, American Jews pored over the headlines, watched all the television footage of Israeli soldiers swimming in the Suez Canal, and said to themselves, "My God, look who we are! We have power! We do not fit the Shylock image, we are ace pilots; we are not the cowering timid Jews who get sand kicked in their faces, we are tank commanders; we are not pale-faced wimps hiding in yeshivas, we are Hathaway Men, handsome charismatic generals with eye patches."

The whole image of the running, craven Jew was, at least momentarily, healed by the Six-Day War, and at the same time, a romance was born between American Jews and Israel. American Jews could not embrace Israel enough; they could not fuse their own identities with Israel enough. They visited Israel in droves, climbed on the captured Egyptian tanks, sat in the cockpits of Israeli Phantom jets, and posed arm in arm with literally any Israeli soldier who walked down the street. The impact of Israel on American Jews was so powerful that for many of them Israel actually replaced Torah, synagogue, and prayer as the carrier of their Jewish identity. Israel came along at a moment in American Jewish history when Judaism was ceasing to have a compelling religious hold on the vast majority of Jews. In this era of secularization and general loss of traditional values, Israel offered American Jews a new way to organize their own identity and remain connected to Jewish history—but without having to be observant, without having to go to synagogue every Saturday and "spoil" the weekend.

I know. I was the epitome of this transformation. It was Israel's victory in the 1967 war which prompted me to assert my own Jewishness—not five years of Hebrew school as a young boy, not five summers at Herzl Camp in Wisconsin, and not my bar mitzvah. Hebrew school only embarrassed me, because I had to get on the Hebrew bus in front of the Gentile kids at my elementary school, and my bar mitzvah bored me, except for opening the envelopes stuffed with money. But Israel as a badge of pride actually saved me as a Jew at a time when I easily could have drifted away, not only from religious practice, but from Jewish communal identification altogether.

But I was hardly unique. It is safe to say that thanks to the pride instilled in American Jews by Israel, the American Jewish community as a whole was transformed from a timid, sleepy, minority community focused largely on its own local needs and the war against anti-Semitism to a visible, nationally galvanized community of power focused around support for Israel and related issues such as freeing Soviet Jewry. In Minneapolis, as in every other Jewish community in America, virtually all Jewish philanthropy was funneled through the local United Jewish Appeal. Each year, there would be a kickoff dinner in which the wealthiest Jews in the community would have to stand up in front of each other and announce how much money they intended to give "for Israel" that year. The speaker would always have some connection with Israel, preferably a general with a heroic war record. He would breathe some fire, flex some muscles, tell some war stories, and the American Jews would puff out their chests and open their wallets. No one talked about the fact that some 50 percent of everything they gave "for Israel" actually remained in Minneapolis to pay for the local Jewish hospital, the home for the aged, and the Jewish community center. Israel enabled American Jewish communities to vastly increase their fund-raising and thereby build stronger, more self-sufficient, and more varied local Jewish institutions than ever before.

That wasn't all. The United Jewish Appeal fund-raising campaign replaced the synagogue as the source of Jewish leadership. Being on the synagogue board became passé; being on the UJA board reflected real power and status. The fund-raising campaign became the factory and testing ground for Jewish leaders. There was the UJA young leadership, old leadership, singles' leadership, women's leadership, lawyers' leadership, and doctors' leadership. Israel crowned a whole new generation of American Jews as "leaders," giving them status in America and status when they came to Israel. In fact, I discovered that plain old American Jews stopped visiting Israel after 1967. Instead, everyone who came seemed to be a "leader," and leaders had to meet with leaders, so when they came to Israel on fund-raising missions, they met with Peres, Rabin, and Shamir. I was always being asked to speak to visiting American Jewish groups in Jerusalem, but no one ever called me and said, "Come speak to a group of rich Jews from Chicago." I was always invited to speak to a group of "Jewish leaders" from Chicago.

Having become organized and energized around support for Israel, the American Jewish community began to really assert itself on the American political scene. The so-called Jewish lobby, the American Israel Public Affairs Committee (AIPAC), became one of the most powerful lobbying organizations in Washington, thanks to its ability to organize important constituencies of Jews all across America to vote in their local elections on the basis of which candidate was most supportive of aid to Israel and the cause of Soviet Jewry. In the old days, when American Jews were known to support an array of liberal issues, an American politician who received campaign contributions from Jews could not really know if that support was linked to his position on labor rights, civil rights, abortion, or school prayer. However, as key Jewish philanthropists formed political action committees focused exclusively on contributing money to those office seekers ready to support Israel, it became obvious to candidates that the most efficient way to raise funds was not by focusing on the five hundred issues which span the spectrum of liberal ideology, but rather by focusing exclusively on Israel and Soviet Jewry. The more that happened, the more American Jews realized that they could ride Israel and Soviet Jewish issues into the corridors of power. Jews did not get invited to the White House to discuss the Jewish aged or prayer in public schools. But a Jew who contributed large amounts of money to AIPAC, either at the local or the national level, might find himself being consulted by his congressman about a particular foreign aid bill, or, if he was really lucky, invited to the State Department for an audience with the Secretary of State himself. Tom Dine, the executive director of AIPAC, once remarked—not boastfully, but honestly—in a speech to a large gathering of American Jews, "Israel gave us our political pride and the opportunity to stand where we never stood before."

Ironically, as American Jews were spurred by Israel to become a more politically active and powerful community, they developed an even deeper sense of being at home in America. American Jewish leaders had real influence, they had real dignity, they felt part of their society, there was no occupation closed to them. There were Jewish senators and congressmen and a Conference of Presidents of Major American Jewish Organizations, whose members could see the American President virtually any time they requested. So with all of that going for them, many American Jews started to ask themselves, "Why move to Israel? I have everything I could ever want as a Jew right here in the U.S.A. If Scarsdale exists, who needs Tel Aviv?"

Just as American Jews fell in love with Israel after 1967, Israelis fell in love with America. It is easy to forget today that back in the early 1950s, when Israeli politics was dominated by the Labor Party, there was much talk about bipolarity and the importance of balancing Israel's relations between America and the Soviet Union—which was still referred to by many Zionist–Socialists as *"Ha'Moledet Hashniya"*—the second homeland. The Soviet Union was the first country to recognize the Jewish state and the social, cultural, and ideological links between the Eastern European Zionists and Moscow were far stronger than anything that existed between America and Israel. Ehud Gol, the former spokesman for the Israeli Foreign Ministry, liked to tell me, "I may be married to a nice Jewish girl from New York today, but when I am in the shower in the morning, I still sing all the Russian

Red Army songs I learned in my [Zionist] youth group in the fifties."

It was only after Stalin's anti-Semitic rampage and Israel's open support for America in the Korean War that the Soviet Union faded permanently as a potential Great Power patron of the Jewish state. But the instinct of Israeli leaders was still not to look toward Washington. Instead, Israel in the late 1950s and early 1960s began a love affair with Charles de Gaulle's France, which became the Jewish state's main arms supplier. French culture was all the rage in those days; the Israeli elite vacationed in Paris, and French singers like the Compagnons de la Chanson dominated the airwaves. Elvis was a distant echo. Few Israelis could afford to travel beyond Europe, and since television was not introduced in Israel until 1968, popular American culture was largely unfamiliar. What Israelis did know of American culture was often consciously rejected out of their then prevailing feeling of pioneer superiority.

"When I immigrated to Israel in the 1960s," observed Ze'ev Chafets, "I wouldn't say that people pitied me for being an American, but there was no great attraction. America was seen as being in eclipse then. There were race riots, drugs, Vietnam, hippies. Israelis laughed at Coca-Cola and women who shaved their legs and weird things like underarm deodorant."

But Israel's victory in 1967 injected a new spirit of grandiosity, of manifest destiny, into the Jewish state. It ushered out the pioneer era of simplicity in Israeli life and ushered in an era of consumerism, stock speculating, dollar accounts, credit cards, and living beyond one's means, which peaked in the 1970s, when Israel almost spent itself into bankruptcy. The material riches offered by America suddenly gained a new appeal for Israelis.

In the old days when you lived "American-style" in Israel, it meant you stood out like a sore thumb. After 1967, you stood out if you didn't. Israelis ate hamburgers at "MacDavid's" instead of "McDonald's," shopped at American-style supermarkets, counted their wealth in dollars not shekels, and were as likely to dress up as Rambo on the Halloween-like Purim festival as they were Haman or Esther. Americans who immigrated to Israel after 1967, attracted to the simple and primitive frontier ways of Israeli life, began to complain that Israel was turning into precisely what they were trying to escape.

I once heard an advertisement on Voice of Israel Radio for frozen food in which one actor said to another, "This is our frozen-food product." The second man responded, "Excuse me, are you from America?" The first man answered, "No, our system is, but thanks anyway for the compliment."

Yitzhak Rabin, the Israeli army's chief of staff during the Six-Day War, was sent as ambassador to Washington, and then came more generals and more heroes, and then the Israeli kids, and America wined and dined and spoiled them all. Israelis in America could do no wrong; everything they did was either "adorable" or "heroic." No wonder some of the Israeli envoys sent by the Jewish Agency to recruit American Jews to come to Israel ended up staying in America—including the one who came to Minneapolis and tried to convince me to emigrate.

The 1967 victory not only left individual Israelis "hooked" on America; it also, paradoxically, left Israel as a state hooked on America. De Gaulle's romance with Israel ended with the Six-Day War. On the eve of that conflict, the French President imposed an arms embargo on Israel. When Israel launched a preemptive strike against its Arab neighbors to break the stranglehold they were about to impose, de Gaulle was furious. He never forgave the Jewish state, or, it seems, the Jewish people, whom he described a few months later as "an elite people, self-assured and domineering." This forced Israel to look increasingly to Washington for the military support it needed in order to maintain a balance of power with Syria, Egypt, and Jordan, its three main opponents in the '67 conflict. Until 1963, the United States had not sold weapons systems to Israel and was leery about becoming her patron for fear that this would damage ties with the emerging Arab oil powers. However, after 1970, when the Soviets deepened their direct involvement with Egypt and backed a Syrian attempt to destabilize Jordan, the Nixon Administration felt compelled to supply Israel in order to maintain a regional balance of power as part of the global structure of détente which Nixon and Kissinger were trying to build with Moscow. Israel was not seen so much as an ally by Nixon as a local client, which, like Vietnam or Korea, needed to be kept strong enough to prevent its region from becoming a source of Soviet–American friction. It was only thanks to this perception that the real floodgates of economic and military aid from Washington to Jerusalem began to open. After the 1973 Middle East war, when Israel's defense costs soared astronomically due to its tank and aircraft losses, American aid became a matter of life and death for the Jewish state. Today, Israel receives $3 billion a year in American military and economic assistance, which is about 20 percent of the Israeli government's annual disposable budget.

No wonder Israelis like to repeat what their late Prime Minister, Levi Eshkol, once said when a group of farmers from the Negev came to visit him in his office to inform him that there was a drought.

"A drought!" exclaimed Mr. Eshkol. "Oh my God, where?"

The farmers answered, "In the Negev, where else?"

Mr. Eshkol looked relieved. "If it's in the Negev, okay," he said. "Just as long as there is no drought in America."

Although Israelis and American Jews began dating and fell in love after 1967, they never got married; they never made that total commitment to each other. Theirs was a romantic fling—an affair. As with any love affair, it was only skin deep; the two parties didn't really know that much about each other. In many ways, American Jews liked Israel for her body and Israelis liked American Jews for their money. Theirs was not a love based on true understanding, mutual respect, and mutual commitment. The relationship worked as long as the two parties dealt with each other in a facile, superficial manner—as long as not too many Israelis moved to America and saw how attractive life there really was compared to life in Israel, and as long as those American Jews who went to Israel never got off the tour bus or, if they did, met only heroes and dead people and then got right back on again.

But, as in any romance, there comes a moment when the starry-eyed couple discover who the other really is, and, just as important, who the other's relatives are hiding in the bedroom closet. Only if the relationship survives that process of mutual discovery can it really last. That mutual-discovery process began for American Jews and Israelis in the mid-1970s. American Jews suddenly found themselves exclaiming to Israelis, "Hey, I fell in love with Golda Meir. You mean to tell me that Rabbi Meir Kahane is in your family! I went out with Moshe Dayan—you mean to tell me that ultra-Orthodox are in your family! I loved someone who turns deserts green, not someone who breaks Palestinians' bones." Israelis eventually found themselves equally aghast and exclaiming, "Look, American Jew, just because we are dating doesn't mean you can tell me how to live my life. And anyway, American Jew, if we are in love, then you should move in with me. You can't just date me so that all your neighbors will ooh and aah, and then drop me off at the end of the evening. You also can't start taking aerobics classes and building up a physique of your own that my daughter finds so attractive she wants to move in with you! That's just not fair."

As the *New York Times* correspondent in Jerusalem, I was both an eyewitness to, and a catalyst for, this process of mutual discovery. At times it was funny, at times it was tragic; at times I saw it happen in synagogues and at times I saw it occur in places one would least imagine—like a tennis court.

It was a normal Saturday morning in Jerusalem, and Bob Slater, a correspondent for *Time*, and I were having our usual Saturday-morning tennis match at the Jerusalem Tennis Center. We happened to arrive at our assigned court two minutes before 10:00 a.m. and the Israeli players on the court were in the middle of a point. We walked onto the court but stayed over on the side so as not to disturb them. At that point, one of the Israeli players asked if we would please wait outside. We said no problem and stayed outside until the clock struck 10:00 a.m., at which point we returned to claim the court. They were still in the middle of a game and left reluctantly. As we passed each other, one of the Israelis began mumbling in Hebrew something about "arrogant Americans" pushing them off the courts. After a few seconds of this, I told the fellow that if he had something to say he should say it in English, at which point he erupted with a lava flow of vile invective: "Fucking Americans . . . arrogant Americans . . . go back to your own country where you belong."

When I calmly pointed out that without American money there would have been no Jerusalem Tennis Center, the man became positively apoplectic. The veins were bulging in his neck, and his playing partners had to literally drag him off the court, as he shook his fist at me and sputtered, "Go home, go back to America, arrogant Americans . . . arrogant . . ."

When the man was finally off the court, Bob and I just stared at each other across the net, dumbstruck. "What in the world was that about?" we asked each other.

It was clear to me that this Israeli was bothered by something more than just tennis etiquette. He must have been nursing a grudge against American Jews for a long time and our entering his court early simply lit his fuse. This contretemps occurred in 1987, just as the United States was putting heavy pressure on Israel to turn over for questioning several Israeli officials alleged to have been involved in the Israeli espionage caper in Washington. The key figure in the Israeli spying operation was a young American Jewish U.S. Navy intelligence analyst, Jonathan J. Pollard, who was arrested in November 1985 and two years later sentenced to life in prison for providing Israeli agents with a mountain of top-secret military data. At the time of Pollard's arrest, many American Jewish leaders were highly embarrassed by the fact that Israel had been spying in the United States, and they lectured Israeli ministers for weeks on how insolent this was—much to the annoyance of many Israelis, who felt that their country was as entitled to spy as any other and didn't have to put up with any lectures from American Jews.

It always seemed to me that this Israeli tennis player's anger was rooted somewhere in the resentment many Israelis had come to feel upon discovering, through the Pollard affair and other incidents, that they were not as superior to America and American Jewry as they might have thought. As my Jerusalem neighbor, Harvard-trained Israeli economist Yoram Ben-Porath, described it: "When I was much younger, Israel was at the takeoff of enormous achievement, growth, absorption of Jews, and turning the deserts green, with all the macho pioneer spirit that went with it. We had a certain supremacy complex toward American Jews. There was no doubt that we were in the right place for Jews. With our maturity we lost some of these elements. The society became more normal; it became clear after the 1973 war that the fight for survival was not a one-shot affair but a never-ending struggle. It wasn't so patently obvious that this was the safest or most exciting place for Jews. The sense of absolute moral superiority began to disappear."

Because Israeli leaders always had a romanticized notion of America—as a country that fawned all over them, adored them, and confirmed them as heroes—they never really took it seriously as a way of life for Jews, and hence they were very late in realizing the potential of a thriving America as a magnet for Jews, a magnet as powerful, if not more so, as Israel. One day, though, Israelis woke up, looked at the emigration-immigration statistics, and realized that America had become the greatest threat to the Zionist revolution.

By 1988, an estimated 300,000–400,000 of the roughly 4.2 million Israelis had moved to the United States on a permanent or semi-permanent basis—with an estimated 100,000 in California alone. These figures must be compared with the fact that only about 50,000 of the 6 million American Jews have moved to Israel since the Jewish state was founded in 1948—some of them having moved back since—and only 25 percent of American Jews are estimated by the Israeli Ministry of Tourism to have visited Israel even once in their lives. In the decade of the 1970s, 265,000 Jews left the Soviet Union. Of those, roughly 165,000 went to Israel and 100,000 to the United States and Canada, with the percentage of those going to North America rising so sharply in recent years— to 90 percent—that Israel has tried to force Soviet emigrants to take direct flights from Moscow to Tel Aviv, so that it would be impossible for them to "drop out" in European transit points and go to America as refugees instead.

It used to be a stigma for Israelis to immigrate to America. No Israeli ever left Israel for America for good, only for "visits"— or as one Israeli teacher remarked to me, "My sister went to New York for one year—fifteen years ago." No longer. In 1988, Bezek, the Israeli national telephone company, began running a television commercial during prime time featuring an elderly Israeli grandfather sitting in front of a shabby bare desk and dialing a number. Subtitled beneath the man were the words *Netanya, Israel, 6:30 a.m.* The screen was then given over to what appeared to be the Israeli grandfather's children living in Los Angeles. They were seated in a comfortable, affluent-looking living room, which included a color television and an Israeli boy playing with a football in the background. Their plush surroundings were subtitled: *Los Angeles, 8:30 p.m.* The family members then have a trans-Atlantic conversation in Hebrew.

This commercial occasioned the following letter to the editor in the *Jerusalem Post* from one Sarah M. Schachter of Jerusalem: "Sirs, I was appalled to see the new Bezek commercial. . . . The not-so-subliminal message: [Grandpa] is still in Netanya, but Los Angeles is the land of opportunity for the young and ambitious. Emigration is indeed a major problem for the state of Israel, but I think it is in poor taste for Bezek to legitimize and exploit this unfortunate fact, and I am surprised that the editors of Israel Television included this message on the air."

The letter was followed by an editor's note which read: "This public service announcement has been discontinued following complaints that it would encourage emigration."

It was bad enough for Israelis to find themselves in competition with America, but it was even more galling to find themselves dependent on an American Jewish community that Israel itself was largely responsible for emboldening, revitalizing, and transforming into an energetic community of power.

Although Israeli officials never admitted it aloud, they came to understand that Washington gave the extraordinary amounts of aid to Israel that it did in large part because of the electoral clout of the American Jewish community. It was not only American Jews' political lobbying of Congress that was important for Israel but also their lobbying of the American public at large—the way they kept Israel on the American agenda and reiterated its affinity with American values. Zvi Rafiah, who served as the congressional liaison for the Israeli embassy in Washington in the early 1980s, once conceded with unusual candor for an Israeli, "Pull the American Jews out of the [America-Israel] relationship and the whole thing will start to shake." In other words, Israelis discovered, their security and economic well-being had become partially dependent on assistance from America—assistance that would be forthcoming on a large scale only if there continued to be an energetic, wealthy, powerful American Jewish community that did not move to Israel.

That has not been an easy reality for Israelis to swallow, and they have responded in a variety of ways. One is to argue that America gives $3 billion a year to Israel not because of the electoral clout with Congress of American Jews but because Israel is such a "strategic asset." Or, as a well-known Israeli T-shirt emblazoned with an F-16 fighter jet says: *Don't worry, America, Israel is behind you.*

Another tendency has been to ignore American Jewish life. In 1987, the American Anti-Defamation League of B'nai B'rith brought an exhibit on the history of American Jewry to Israel. "When it was touring in America, it was called 'Jewish Life in America: Fulfilling the American Dream,' " said Harry Wall, the director of the ADL's Jerusalem office. "But when we brought it to Israel we decided that we had better change the name, so we took off the business about fulfilling a dream, because there is only supposed to be one dream and that is the Zionist dream. We just called the exhibit 'Jewish Life in America: From Pre-Revolutionary War to Today.' I invited the top people from the Ministry of Education to come to the opening, and when it was over I told them that they could have the exhibit. They said to me, 'Well, that would be just great, because we've never done anything about American Jews in our curriculum before.' I said to them, 'Huh? You've never taught about American Jewry?' They said no—a few little things here and there, but never anything comprehensive. I said, 'We're talking about the largest, most successful Jewish community in the world.'

"It turns out that every year they study about a different Jewish community," explained Harry. "They've done Russian Jews, European Jews, and Ethiopian Jews, but never American Jews. It seems that American Jews are too secure and too prosperous to be taught about here. It wasn't a stated policy not to teach Israeli kids about them. No one said, 'Don't teach about American Jews.' It was just understood that you didn't."

Still another Israeli response to the dependence on America has been to impugn American Jewish life, or hope for an outbreak of anti-Semitism there that will drive American Jews to Israel.

Yaron Ezrahi, the Hebrew University political theorist and a man deeply involved in the Israeli peace movement, encountered this latter trend in its baldest form when he was invited to debate a representative of the Gush Emunim settler movement before a visiting delegation of "Jewish leaders" from Florida.

"Before the debate began," recalled Ezrahi, "I prepared myself to try to explain to these Jews from Florida why the Gush Emunim settlement movement was destructive to our traditions and collective identity and not helpful to our security and dangerous for *aliya* [immigration]. The Gush man was the first to talk. He said that the West Bank belongs to the Jews, that it was part of Eretz Yisrael [the land of Israel] and that the Arabs don't count and that no one should dictate to the Jews what to do. This was a time when a lot of illegal settlements were being built. Then he gave this very impassioned speech about biblical and historical rights. So one guy from Florida stands up and says to him, 'You're counting on massive *aliya* from the West to realize your plan, aren't you?' And the man said yes. So the guy from Florida says, 'How can you possibly expect immigration from Western liberal democrats when what you project through the settlements is the kind of aggressive lack of consideration of minority rights and all kinds of other things which tarnish the image of Israel and can only encourage anti-Semitism abroad? Because the way you treat your minorities is how Jewish minorities will be treated. What right will we American Jews have to claim to be treated well as a minority?' So this Gush Emunim guy smiled from ear to ear. 'Sir,' he said, 'you don't understand what you're saying. Anti-Semitism is the means through which massive Jewish *aliya* will come, so if we can contribute by enabling you in the West to see all the anti-Semites around you, it will encourage you to emigrate—and especially to the West Bank. That is what we want.'

"Well," added Ezrahi, "these American Jews devoured him. There was so much anger directed at him from those people from Florida that I didn't have to say another thing. Israelis like this Gush Emunim guy believe only in *aliya* through Apocalypse Now. For him, the best news of the year was that Jesse Jackson was running for President. If he lived in Miami, he would have voted for Jackson. For him and his kind, the worst case scenario for American Jews is always the best possibility."

But such attitudes are by no means confined to the lunatic right. Many American Jews were shocked by an open "Letter to an American Friend" that the well-known Israeli political theorist Shlomo Avineri published on the back page of the *Jerusalem Post* on March 10, 1987, at the height of American Jewish criticism of Israel over its spying on America. Avineri, who, as I noted, was a leading Labor Party ideologue, once served as the Director-General of the Israeli Foreign Ministry.

Avineri began his open letter by saying that the Pollard case was bringing out "a degree of nervousness, insecurity, and even cringing on the part of the American Jewish community which runs counter to the conventional wisdom of American Jewry feeling free, secure, and unmolested in an open and pluralistic society. Let me not mince words: Some of the responses of American Jewish leaders after Pollard's sentencing remind me of the way in which Jewish leaders in Egypt under Nasser and in Iran under Khomeini ran for cover when members of their respective Jewish communities were caught spying for Israel. . . . You always told us Israelis that America was different. Of course, it is. . . . Of course no one will put you in jail or legislate against you: but you are afraid that Jews will not be able to get responsible positions in your bureaucracy, that Jewish employees in the defense and intelligence branches will be under some kind of handicap, that Jews will be denied access to sensitive positions. One Jewish spy— and look how deep you find yourself in *galut* [exile mentality]. . . . Don't misunderstand me: in no way am I condoning what Israel did in the Pollard affair. . . . But the truth of the matter is simple: You, in America, are no different from French, German, Polish, Soviet, and Egyptian Jews. Your Exile is different—comfortable, padded with success and renown. It is exile nonetheless."

What American Jews found so disturbing about this article was not only the fact that so intelligent a man as Avineri could make such a mistaken argument but that many Israelis endorsed it wholeheartedly. Avineri completely misread the American Jewish reaction to the Pollard case. To begin with, he equated the reaction of so-called American Jewish leaders with that of American Jews. Most American Jews I knew did not give the Pollard affair more than a passing shrug, which only showed how secure they really are. Those who did think about it, and articulated concerns, primarily leaders of Jewish organizations, were cringing—not out of fear for themselves, but in response to the monumental stupidity and breach of trust evinced by Israel by spying on its closest ally, thereby damaging its standing in Washington and the credibility of American Jews who had always argued that Israeli interests and American interests were synonymous. But American Jews were not cringing about their own future. They understood, rightly, that the Pollard affair would not undermine that.

American Jews have felt at home enough in America to lobby Congress for $3 billion in aid every year for the Jewish state. They have felt at home enough to stand up and defend Israel publicly in every embarrassing crisis it has been involved in—from Suez to the Lebanon war to the *intifada*—before and after the Pollard affair. To compare such American Jewish forthrightness with the behavior of Egyptian Jews or Iranian Jews is ludicrous.

Avineri's argument was rightly viewed by most American Jews as the panicked analysis of an ideologue fighting for his life. Secular Zionists, such as Avineri, have always argued that Jews can never really feel normal, safe, and rooted outside their own nation-state. That is why they all must come to live in Israel. Therefore, his ideology is threatened by the success of American Jews and the fact that they have "made it" in America, where they aren't just normal but truly comfortable. Avineri's ideology requires that American Jews not feel at home, hence his desperate attempt to equate them with Russian or Iranian Jews. Instead of selling Israel to American Jews as the most compelling adventure in Jewish cultural, political, and spiritual renaissance—and the most exciting and dynamic place for Jews to live—Avineri told them that they were doomed to live in Israel, so they might as well move now.

For American Jews, discovering the "real" Israel began in earnest in 1973, when Egyptian troops overran the Israeli army along the Suez Canal and American Jews realized that their Israeli heroes were not supermen after all. This was reinforced by the banking scandals and exposure of corruption under the Labor governments of the mid-1970s. But the real jolt for American Jews came in 1977, when Menachem Begin and his right-wing Likud Party took power for the first time, replacing the Labor Party pantheon—Abba Eban, Golda Meir, Shimon Peres, Yigal Allon, Yitzhak Rabin, Simcha Dinitz—with whom American Jews had been working since Israel was founded.

Begin brought to the government of Israel a whole new cast of characters, with an agenda that was alien to many liberal, non-Orthodox American Jews. Begin spoke of settling the whole West Bank, and was not ashamed to appear on American television wagging his finger and telling the United States that it had no right to lecture the Jews about what to do. Begin was ready to indulge messianic Jewish settlers and ultra-Orthodox rabbis who wanted to use the Israeli parliament to delegitimize the Reform and Conservative branches of Judaism. Begin was also ready to use Israel's military might, not only for defensive purposes, but for offensive ones as well.

Once American Jews were dragged off the tour bus and forced to look at Israel as a living reality, and not just as a symbol of Jewish identity, they found it quite different—both religiously and politically—from what they had imagined. Many of them still haven't gotten over the shock.

"Whores, whores, this is a whorehouse, a house of promiscuity, whores, whores," the black-coated rabbi bellowed with disgust at the predominantly American-born congregation of men and women dancing with Torah scrolls in the gymnasium-turned-synagogue.

"This is whoredom," the rabbi screamed at the congregants, while they danced even more vigorously with their scrolls. "Because of you there was a Holocaust."

It wasn't the usual synagogue sermon you would expect from the neighborhood rabbi, but then an American-style Reform service being conducted in Jerusalem was about as usual as a mosque operating in Great Neck. The day was Simchas Torah, the Jewish holiday commemorating the completion of the annual cycle of reading the Torah. The year was 1986. The scene was a new, makeshift Reform synagogue in the Baka neighborhood of Jerusalem. The story shows what happens when a group of Anglo-American immigrants to Israel try to open a Reform congregation in the Israeli capital.

The tale began in the early 1980s, when Levi Weiman-Kelman, an American-trained rabbi from the Conservative stream of Judaism, moved to Israel. After experimenting with several styles of life in the Jewish state—from the kibbutz to graduate school—Rabbi Kelman, then in his early thirties, decided he wanted to get back to the pulpit. But when he looked around Jerusalem for a non-Orthodox congregation with which to affiliate, he found none. While some 90 percent of synagogue-affiliated American Jews belong to either Reform or Conservative congregations, such synagogues are almost nonexistent in Israel. The Orthodox stream of Judaism is the only form of observance supported by Israel's national rabbinical council, known as the Chief Rabbinate. And since the Israeli government has officially sanctioned and funded the chief rabbinate to oversee all matters of religious practice involving the state—most notably marriages, divorces, and burials—it leaves little room for American Conservative or Reform rabbis to practice. A marriage performed by a Conservative or Reform rabbi in Israel is not recognized by the Chief Rabbinate, and hence the state of Israel, as legal and binding. (If the marriage is performed outside Israel by a Conservative or Reform rabbi, or by a justice of the peace, for that matter, it is recognized—but only because of reciprocal treaties between Israel and other countries to recognize marriages.) The Orthodox and ultra-Orthodox Israeli rabbinical establishment believes that Conservative and Reform rabbis do not operate in accordance with the totality of Jewish law, or *Halacha*, and therefore should not be allowed to marry or divorce Jews, let alone convert Gentiles to Judaism. More important, since the Orthodox have a monopoly on religious authority in Israel, they do not want to see their power and funding diluted by having to share it with the Reform and Conservative movements. After all, business is business.

Unable to find a synagogue to his liking, Rabbi Kelman did what Jews have been doing for centuries. He started his own. He first approached his Conservative movement for support, but they told him he was too avant-garde for Israel, so he turned to the American Reform movement's representatives in Israel, who were only too eager to help by arranging for Kelman to get access to a Labor Party–owned hall in the Baka neighborhood of Jerusalem. Baka is populated by a mélange of highly educated American, Australian, and South African–born Ashkenazi Jews and relatively poor Moroccan Oriental Jews. By simply spreading the word around the neighborhood, Kelman was able to attract some 150 people for his first Yom Kippur service, most of them immigrants from English-speaking countries who did not feel comfortable attending the rigidly Orthodox services—where men and women are not allowed to sit together and participate equally—that were held everywhere else in the neighborhood.

"I had a feeling that we were in the right place at the right time," Kelman recalled. "There was clearly a need for us that was not being met by the Israeli rabbinate. There is a tremendous thirst among immigrants to Israel, and among many nonobservant Israelis themselves, I think, for an alternative to the ultra-Orthodox Judaism that is practiced in Israel. The minute all these people from our service started spilling out into the street, people in the neighborhood noticed. Before long, the Orthodox Sephardi neighborhood rabbi, Eliyahu Aubergil, and the Ashkenazi rabbi, Avraham Auerbach, who had not been on speaking terms for many, many years, found an issue that they could agree on—attacking us. These guys are employees of the state. They get their salaries from the Ministry of Religious Affairs, which gets its money from me and other Israeli taxpayers. So these two Orthodox rabbis immediately began to put pressure on the Labor Party to have us evicted from the building. They just did not recognize Reform Judaism as being Jewish, and they saw us as a threat to their monopoly."

Within a week, the secular Labor Party caved in to the pressure of the local rabbis and the national ultra-Orthodox religious parties that stood behind them. Kelman and his congregants were told by the Labor Party to find another home, as though they were some strange sect practicing levitation and blood rituals instead of the same basic Jewish service observed in many synagogues throughout the Western world. Fortunately, the local neighborhood municipal council was not as craven as the Labor Party, and when its members heard about the eviction they directed the local community center to provide a room for the Reform group. Within one year, Kelman's congregation grew into the second largest in the neighborhood.

To mark the end of their first full year of reading the Torah together, Kelman planned a special evening for Simchas Torah, 1986. By then, his flock had outgrown their side room in the community center and overflowed into the gymnasium, where the ark containing the Torah scrolls was placed under the basketball hoop. Being a highly egalitarian congregation, Kelman's allowed women to read from the Torah and to dance with the scrolls on Simchas Torah. Such practices are forbidden by Orthodox Jews because of a Talmudic passage often interpreted as prohibiting women from reading from the Torah.

About 150 congregants gathered that evening for Simchas Torah, and as Kelman put it, "We were pretty high—not on drugs, but on the joy of the moment." Men, women, and children were dancing around in concentric circles, taking turns lifting the Torahs and singing a litany of table-stomping, toe-tapping Israeli religious songs.

Then all hell broke loose.

"All of a sudden," recalled Kelman, "I see Rabbi Aubergil coming into the corner of the gymnasium. He's a big guy and he came in with about thirty people of all shapes and ages and sizes that you could imagine—from little kids to old Haredim. Some of them were dressed in suits; some of them were dressed in army jackets and T-shirts. The look in Aubergil's eye was sort of confused for a moment, until he focused on the two women dancing with the Torahs. Then he was not confused. Then there was a rage and singleness of purpose that took over. What bugged him more than anything else, I think, was that there were men and women dancing together. Let me jump ahead for a minute. This is a guy, I found out later, who has never read a secular book in his life. I don't know if you can imagine that. He has never read *The Catcher in the Rye*. He has only read stuff from the Middle Ages, so what Reform meant to him, I have no idea. It meant Christian-like, I'm sure, and our service is as Jewish as anything else, except that men and women sit together.

"So he was standing there," continued Kelman, "and it was an incredibly visual scene. You have to imagine 150 people dancing in concentric circles to these hypnotic tunes, and people just really into it. Though people were getting tired, the minute Aubergil walked in, I had a sense of what was going to happen, so I went around the room and said to everyone, 'Get off your behinds and up there dancing. Under no circumstances are we to enter into a confrontation with these guys and under no circumstances are we going to stop our dancing. They are not going to tell us what to do.' So everyone got up and the dancing just took off again. It was then Aubergil started screaming, 'Whorehouse, whorehouse.' I went over to him and I said, 'Ah, excuse me, can I help you?' He said, 'I demand to speak before the congregation to say what a disgusting . . .' I said, 'Listen, this is not the time for talking. Now is the time for dancing. Why don't you join us in dancing?' So he just really started screaming. About that time, two guys from his entourage went into the middle of the circles and asked if they could dance with the Torahs. So I gave the order that they could get the Torahs, but under no circumstances should they be let out of the circles. They took the Torahs and immediately made a break for it, trying to get out of the circles. I got behind one of them and grabbed him by his belt and the back of his shirt,

and sort of danced him back into the middle of the circle, where
we started wrestling with this Torah. At one point, we were facing
each other and started wrestling with the Torah between us. You
have to imagine this scene. There are 150 people going around
in concentric circles and singing, really on the warpath, and there
are thirty people at the entrance screaming and cursing, shouting
at us, 'Because of you there was a Holocaust. You're evil . . .'
and I look at this guy I am wrestling with, and I wasn't thinking,
and I just started saying to him, 'I love you.' He screamed at me,
'I am going to kill you,' in Hebrew and English. It was clear that
I wasn't going to let go of him and it was then that he lifted his
knee and kicked me—right in the groin. At the same time, he let
go of the Torah and made a break for it."

Slowly, Kelman and his congregants widened their circles until
they pushed the local rabbi and his followers right out the door,
with the uninvited guests shouting on their way out, "We're never
going to let you pray. We'll keep bothering you until you close
this whorehouse."

The Baka synagogue incident became national news in Israel,
and gave Reform Judaism the biggest exposure it had ever had
in the Jewish state, shattering at the same time many of the
Orthodox-inspired myths about the supposedly Christian-like
quality of Reform services. Kelman filed criminal charges against
Aubergil, but he dropped them after the Orthodox rabbi reluctantly agreed to write a public letter of apology.

What happened to Kelman and his congregation—from the way
they were dumped by the Labor Party to being abused by the
Orthodox establishment—brought into stark relief the fundamental difference between the way in which many American and
other Western Jews relate to Judaism and the way in which Jews
in Israel relate to Judaism.

In America, Jewish life is organized around the synagogue, yet
most American Jews in this day and age join a synagogue not for
religious or ritual reasons but for communal solidarity. The synagogue is the island clung to by American Jews in order to avoid
assimilation in a sea of Gentiles. It is also the place to which they
come in order to rub shoulders with other Jews and to express
their own ethnic identity. The decision over whether to join a
Reform, Conservative, or Orthodox synagogue, for most Amer-

ican Jews, is a decision based on which one is most conveniently located, which one has the best nursery school, and whose rabbi gives the best sermon; the actual religious content of the synagogue's service is secondary for most people.

In Israel, by contrast, the vast majority are nonobservant Jews. They don't need to join a synagogue in order to avoid assimilation or feel part of a community, because there are other outlets for that which do not take synagogue or ritual forms. They avoid assimilation simply by paying taxes to a Jewish state, speaking Hebrew, and sending their children to state schools, which observe the Jewish holidays as national holidays. That is why a majority of Israelis neither belong to synagogues nor even know what to do once they get inside one.

I was once invited to speak to a group of Israeli army officers about how Americans perceive Israel. It was part of an educational seminar to prepare a group of Israeli colonels and majors for studying in the United States. Before I began my talk, the Israeli officer in charge of the seminar showed me the program of speakers. I was being followed by a lecture entitled "How to Behave in a Synagogue."

"What in the world is that for?" I asked the Israeli officer.

"Well," he explained, slightly embarrassed, "we have a lot of officers who have never been in a synagogue in their lives, so we have to prepare them for when they go to America. We show them what to do in case they get invited to a synagogue or are called on to read from the Torah or something. We had a little problem, though, getting a rabbi to come here and explain it to them, because all the army rabbis are Orthodox and they don't recognize Reform or Conservative, and they aren't willing to speak about how to behave in those kinds of synagogues. But we looked all around and we finally found this Orthodox rabbi, some guy who grew up in America, who said he would talk about Reform and Conservative as well as Orthodox."

Because nonobservant Israelis don't care about religious ritual, the only form of practicing Judaism that took root in Israel was that which was already there for centuries—the Orthodox and ultra-Orthodox streams, with small pockets of pro-Zionist modern Orthodoxy. Only in the last decade have the Reform and Conservative movements made a concerted effort to open congregations in Israel, such as Kelman's, in an attempt to offer nonobservant Israelis a spiritual alternative to rigid Orthodoxy.

Not only has the Israeli rabbinate tried to put obstacles in their way, but for the past fifteen years, the Israeli Orthodox parties have been trying to force the Israeli parliament to amend the Law of Return, which stipulates that any Jew in the world can come to Israel and automatically be granted citizenship. The so-called Who-is-a-Jew amendment—which Israel's Orthodox parties have been pushing—would, in effect, define as Jewish, and hence eligible for Israeli citizenship, only those persons born of a Jewish mother or converted to Judaism by an Orthodox rabbi according to Jewish law (*Halacha*). Any Gentile converted by Reform or Conservative rabbis would not be considered Jewish. Israel's Orthodox parties try to ram this amendment through anytime they feel that they can blackmail the Labor or Likud Party into supporting it. Following the November 1988 Israeli national elections, when both Labor and Likud were desperate to gain the support of religious parties in order to put together enough parliament seats to rule, Shimon Peres and Yitzhak Shamir each indicated a willingness to vote in favor of the amendment—Peres reluctantly, Shamir without any apology.

Although the amendment has yet to pass, the debate over it reveals how little American Jews and Israeli Jews understand about each other's relationship to Judaism and Israel. American Jewish leaders who rush to Israel to lobby against the Who-is-a-Jew amendment any time it appears close to passage could not believe how easily Shamir and his Likud Party gave in to the demands of the Orthodox and voted in favor of a bill that would essentially entail formal Israeli delegitimization of Reform and Conservative rabbis. What American Jews did not understand was that for Shamir, and most secular Israelis, either you observe or you don't observe, and if you observe, then you are either like Grandpa was in Europe—Orthodox—or you are not authentic. When a delegation of American Reform and Conservative rabbis once went to lobby Shamir against voting in favor of the Who-is-a-Jew amendment, Shamir began the meeting by asking the delegation, "Is it true that in America you can get a conversion to Judaism over the telephone?" (For years, the standard Israeli

junior-high-school textbook on modern Jewish history dealt with
the entire history of Reform Judaism in two pages. The section
heading read "Movement of Assimilation.") What is more,
Shamir would say to visiting American delegations, Why are you
so upset? The number of Gentiles who are actually converted by
Reform and Conservative rabbis and want to immigrate to Israel
are so few in number—maybe twenty-five a year—nobody will
really be affected.

What Shamir and many other secular Israelis didn't appreciate—because they didn't understand the role the synagogue and
Israel play in the life and identity of American Jews—was that
for the Israeli parliament to tell an American Reform Jew that
his rabbi was not legitimate was to tell him that his synagogue
was not legitimate. Since for most American Jews, support for
Israel and membership in a synagogue are the two links through
which they remain connected to Jewish history, this is a real
double blow. It is akin to having your life-long hero, the person
around whom you have modeled your whole identity, tell you
that you are a fraud—but don't take it personally. Not surprisingly, it has left many American Jews angry, confused, and wondering aloud, How can I support a Jewish homeland that makes
me feel less a Jew?

Most Israelis simply have no conception of how important they
and their state are for American Jews. Israelis are, understand-
ably, so involved with their own domestic issues of economics
and security that they have very little appreciation of how world
Jewry is actually constituted. They know Israel needs Diaspora
Jews, but they don't understand how Diaspora Jews need Israel—
how much they are enriched by Israel and how much Israel provides the glue that both connects them to Jewish history and holds
together their Jewish identities. Cut American Jews off from Israel
and many of them will have no reason to go to synagogue or
continue identifying as Jews; ritual will not sustain them. Then
they will really assimilate. If the Who-is-a-Jew bill ever passes,
Israel, instead of being a vehicle for saving Diaspora Jews, will
become a prime force for spiritually destroying them.

My father-in-law, Matthew Bucksbaum, got the bad news while
on a weekend visit to Aspen, Colorado, during the summer of

'82. It came via a business contact of his from New York City, who was also visiting the mountain resort. The message was short and not very sweet.

"Your son-in-law Tom Friedman," the man told Matthew gravely, "is the most hated man in New York City today."

What had I done to deserve this shame? My crime, it turned out, was that of the messenger. As the *Times* bureau chief in Beirut, I had helped to inform the Jews of New York City of the less-than-heroic behavior of the Israeli army in Lebanon, the Sabra and Shatila massacre, and other unsettling stories.

While some of the news reporting out of Beirut that summer left something to be desired, most of it was accurate and sober. I am convinced that the anger which the American Jewish community, from the leadership on down, directed at the news media, and reporters such as myself, was largely the result of the fact that they were deeply disturbed and confused by what Israel was doing in Lebanon. How could they not be? Israelis themselves were divided and confused over the invasion. But because most American Jews did not feel comfortable publicly criticizing Israel, they took out their anguish on Matthew Bucksbaum's son-in-law, among others.

As long as Israel was a story about David against Goliath, as long as it was a story about victims who showed courage and remarkable achievements, as long as it was a story about a pioneer frontier democracy, many American Jews were only too happy to have Israel be their visible body and face on the world stage. Naturally, they devoured every bit of press attention Israel received. In fact, they could not get enough of it. They never thought to criticize Israel, because it did not seem to warrant criticizing.

But the Lebanon invasion, the Pollard espionage affair, and the Palestinian *intifada* really forced American Jews to look at some of the more unpleasant, but very real, rhythms of political life in today's Israel—instead of just the episodic moments of celebration. Many American Jews seemed to say when they saw Israel bombing Beirut, or Israeli soldiers breaking Palestinians' bones on the evening news, "Wait a minute. If this is my visible body in history, then I don't recognize myself. Who am I?" Instead of Israel serving as a source of identity for American Jews, it became, for some, a source of confusion.

The confusion Israeli actions engendered was graphically displayed on the editorial pages of *The New York Times*, most notably in an Op Ed piece by Woody Allen published on January 28, 1988, when stories about Israeli brutality in the West Bank and Gaza were a daily affair. In his article, Allen echoed the sentiments of many American Jews when he said: "As a supporter of Israel, and as one who has always been outraged at the horrors inflicted on this little nation by hostile neighbors, vile terrorists and much of the world at large, I am appalled beyond measure by the treatment of the rioting Palestinians by Jews. I mean, fellas, are you kidding? . . . Breaking the hands of men and women so they can't throw stones? Dragging civilians out of their houses at random to smash them with sticks in an effort to terrorize a population into quiet? . . . Am I reading the newspapers correctly? . . . Are we talking about state-sanctioned brutality and even torture? My goodness! Are these the people whose money I used to steal from those little blue and white cans after collecting funds for a Jewish homeland? I can't believe it, and I don't know exactly what is to be done. . . ."

I happened to be vacationing in Minneapolis when the *intifada* was just beginning, and stopped in to see Herman Markowitz, the head of the Minneapolis Federation for Jewish Service, to get a sense of how my own hometown community was reacting to the *intifada*. A thoughtful man, committed both to Israel and to American Jewish life, Markowitz described the painful transition which American Jews were going through as they discovered Israel in the 1980s.

"Mr. Average American Jew," he explained, "looked at Israel as that wonderful country that prompted their Christian friends to say, 'Boy, your brothers and sisters in Israel—they are something else, a democracy, a friend of the United States, and they never ask for help from American boys. You guys are great.' And our chests swelled with pride, and we felt marvelous. But since Lebanon there have been all of these things. In the eyes of the unsophisticated American Jew, Israel for the first time is perceived as the aggressor. Then you see that television coverage and it shows the worst, and people don't understand it. People don't understand the nuances. They only see that Jews are doing something which is antithetical to the value system of Western Jews. Pollard wasn't helpful. American Jews are now feeling we are an aggressor, we are an occupier, we are taking away people's rights, we are killing eleven-year-olds, and we are shutting down universities. Now American Jews feel less good about Israel. They are concerned about being confronted by their Christian neighbors about Israel. They don't know how to respond. They don't have the tools to respond. At one time Israel enhanced Jews' self-image. We felt a lot better as Jews. We all felt three inches taller because of Israel, and now the Israelis are taking away those three inches."

Among the young generation of American Jews, and by that I mean those under forty, I have found some very different reactions to the widening awareness of the reality of Israeli life.

But first a joke.

Ya'akov Kirschen, the American-born Israeli cartoonist, who goes by the pen name Dry Bones, liked to tell this joke to visiting American Jewish groups just to see how many in the audience wouldn't laugh.

"There is this American Jew who immigrates to Israel," Kirschen would tell his audiences, "and he moves into a high-rise apartment in Tel Aviv and gets an office job. After a few days, he starts to feel that he is missing out on all the local color of being in the Middle East, so he goes out and buys a camel. Each day he rides the camel to work, while Israelis whiz past him on the highway in their cars. One day, his camel gets stolen, so he goes down to the police station and reports the theft to the police. The Israeli policeman takes out a Missing Camel form and starts to fill it in. 'This camel of yours,' the policeman says, 'what color was it?' 'Well,' says the American Jew, 'it was sort of brown and sort of gray, I don't really remember.' So the policeman writes down 'Color unknown.' Then the Israeli cop asks, 'This camel of yours, how many humps did it have? One or two?' 'Well,' says the American Jew, 'it's hard to say. You see I had a saddle on him and I couldn't tell if it was between two humps or on top of one.' So the policeman writes down 'Humps unknown.' Finally the cop asks him, 'This camel of yours, what sex was it?' So the American Jew says, 'It was a male.' So the cop says, 'Say, tell me something. You didn't know what color it was. You didn't know how many humps it had, so how come you know what sex it was?' The American Jew answered, 'Because every time I would ride him to work down the highway every Israeli who saw us go by would say, 'Look at the big shmuck on that camel.' "

In order to get the joke, explained Kirschen, "you have to know that 'shmuck' in Yiddish actually means penis, even though in modern English usage it has become a synonym for jerk. For the first ten years I was here every American whom I told that joke to laughed, but slowly the number of people who understood it, who understood enough Yiddish, began to dwindle. Now almost no one who comes from the new generation of American Jews understands it."

My parents' generation and the founding generation of Israel had a great deal in common: together they experienced anti-Semitism in the thirties, forties, and fifties, the horrors of the Holocaust, and the birth of the new Jewish state. They often shared common European roots and, most of all, a common language—Yiddish. When we first visited Israel in 1968, my dad got on better than I did, because with his Yiddish he could speak to more Israelis than I could with my pidgin Hebrew. But that is not true for the young generation—forty and under—of American Jews and their Israeli counterparts. About all that many of them have in common is Bruce Springsteen and the E Street Band.

"Our generation of American Jews," said Harry Wall, the ADL representative in Jerusalem, speaking for the under-forties, "came of age after the Holocaust and they grew up with little anti-Semitism. They felt as secure in America as an Israeli feels in Ashkelon. They also took for granted the existence and the durability of the state of Israel. Most of them have no common language and no real common experience with Israelis of their generation, who served in the army and speak Hebrew. They are also different culturally. Our parents and the founders of Israel both came from predominantly European backgrounds, while today you have American-born American Jews dealing with Israeli-born Sabras, a majority of whose parents come from Arabic-speaking Muslim countries. This has made emotional distancing between the two communities much easier in these difficult times. Of course, there is still a deep underlying sense of common peoplehood, and that will always remain. But to maintain a dynamic relationship and to keep the new generation of American Jews interested in and identifying with Israel is going to take a new approach. Fear of another Holocaust alone is not going to do it. There is a need to rekindle the old magic. We have to put some romance back in this relationship."

Most intelligent young American Jews cannot live with the idea that when South Africa does bad things to the blacks they should protest and when Israel does bad things to Palestinians they should remain silent. It is like the Jewish mother who is always telling her son, "Don't say anything that will upset your father, he'll have a heart attack." The average son's response after a while is "Look, Ma, I can't live with Dad that way. I am moving to the coast. I don't want him to die, but I can't live with him this way anymore." So the son drifts away, always loving Dad but unable to really have a relationship with him.

I find this emotional distancing particularly prominent among the Jewish boys I grew up with back in Minneapolis, who are all in their mid-thirties now. They rooted for the Israeli team when it was a winner and made them feel proud. But when the team started to lose some of the time, most of them stopped cheering, and some of them even stopped coming to the games. As one of my closest childhood friends said to me, "Look, Tommy, I signed up for the heroic Israel, not this crap." It is not surprising that during the *intifada*, the biggest drop in tourism to Israel was among American Jews. They simply cannot handle looking at an Israel in the throes of such a messy, unheroic dilemma.

To be sure, many young American Jews continue to be involved emotionally and institutionally with Israel. That was made clear when Prime Minister Shamir visited Washington in the spring of 1988, at a time when Israel's handling of the Palestinian uprising was being hotly debated in the American media. While Shamir was in Washington, he met with 3,000 members of the UJA Young Leadership, who had gathered together at the Washington Hilton from across America to listen to the Israeli Prime Minister on the eve of his meeting with President Reagan. The young American Jews greeted Shamir with a standing ovation, cheers, whistles, and repeated curtain calls.

"Twice Shamir sought to acknowledge the invigorating show of support by raising clenched hands in a gesture of victory," the *Jerusalem Post* reported. "And, indeed, a victory it was. His slight figure magnified on two large video screens, Shamir lambasted the distortions of the media [and] said he was 'astounded' that Israel was being asked to give back territories."

The *Jerusalem Post* correspondent Menachem Shalev was so stunned by the standing ovation given Shamir that he compared the behavior of the young American Jewish leaders to the behavior of teenagers at a "long-anticipated rock concert." An Israeli air force colonel I know was also in the audience at the time, and he told me later, "I felt so uncomfortable I wanted to go back to Jerusalem immediately. All I could think of was that these Americans were worshipping an Israel that doesn't exist anymore."

Shortly after Shalev's article appeared, the *Jerusalem Post* published the following letter to the editor:

> . . . I was one of the nearly 3,000 Jews at the three-day conference, and as one who is by no means a naïve observer of the Israeli scene, I must challenge Mr. Shalev to look deeper. Shamir did get a rousing welcome, but not because 100 percent of the audience sided with the Likud. Rather, it was because we wanted the world to see that we will not abandon Israel in times of crisis. Unlike some of our "co-religionists," we were not there to apologize for Israel, but to show a united front. I must also add that during the banquet I was seated with a number of prominent Israelis, not one of whom stood up, much less applauded, when their prime minister entered the room. I may not have voted for Ronald Reagan, but as an American, I stand out of respect for the office that he holds. Perhaps Mr. Shalev would have preferred us to greet Mr. Shamir (in front of all the network cameras) in the manner of many of the Israelis present. What message would that have sent to the enemies of Israel?
>
> —Gabrielle Rabin Tsabag,
> Los Angeles

The recognition among Israelis that their country no longer projects a heroic image in America has prompted a variety of reactions on their part as well.

One has been to say that if Israel can't be America's little David any longer, maybe it can be its Goliath. In the initial alliance between Israel and the United States, which lasted from 1948 to the late 1970s, Americans supposedly liked the Israelis for their "beautiful eyes," as Israeli philosopher Avishai Margalit liked to put it. "They liked Israelis for who they were and the values that they represented—democracy, pluralism, and a kind of pioneer spirit," said Margalit. Israel was always identified with the Democratic Party in America, with liberal causes and with the American labor movement, and was depicted as a country that wanted nothing more than peace with its neighbors and the American dream for its children.

However, after Begin and his Likud Party took power in Israel in 1977, they realized that they did not fit this image. The Likud "Young Republicans"—men such as Moshe Arens, Ehud Olmert, Dan Meridor, Uzi Landau, and Benjamin Netanyahu—wanted something more than the platitude of "peace with all our neighbors." They wanted the West Bank and Gaza Strip for ideological reasons. They realized that if Israel was going to continue holding these territories, and maintain an amicable relationship with the United States at the same time, it could not go on selling itself to Washington on the basis of beautiful eyes alone. Beautiful eyes did not go well with a Lebanon invasion or military occupations. So they took down the beautiful-eyes posters and replaced them with new ones: Israel as aircraft carrier, Israel as strategic asset, Israel as America's club against the Soviets and Soviet-backed regimes such as Syria and Libya, Israel as counterterrorist force. This approach happened to coincide with an administration in Washington—the Reagan Administration—which tended to look at the world as being divided between the pro-Western children of light and the pro-Communist children of darkness. Since the Reagan Administration put Israel into the category of the children of light, it did not particularly care if the Israeli moral light bulb had dimmed from 200 watts to 50 watts. Whether it was in the Lebanon war or in the West Bank, the Reagan Administration was ready to tolerate behavior by Israel that no other American administration would have countenanced, certainly not Reagan's predecessor Jimmy Carter. "The motto of the Labor Party era was strength through peace," said Netanyahu, Israel's former ambassador to the United Nations and one of the main proponents of the new basis of Israel–American ties. "Our motto was peace through strength. We tried to put the relationship with America into a larger context. Labor had no larger agenda. They were not animated by the threat of the Soviet Union or radical Soviet regimes in the Middle East. We were, and so was the Reagan Administration. So we put the relationship into a larger context, and when we did the West Bank and Gaza took on a much smaller perspective. The truth is that the ground was already moving in the United States in a more conservative trend, and people like Moshe Arens [who served as ambassador in Washington in 1982] and myself just helped give it some direction regarding the relationship with Israel. American Jews were also part of this shift. You walk into a room with ten American Jews and you will find that maybe two believe in strength through peace and the other eight all believe in peace through strength."

Instead of using the backing of the Reagan Administration as a source of strength that could be exploited to make Israel's bargaining position more flexible at the negotiating table with Jordan and the Palestinians, the Likud made the same mistake Amin Gemayel made in Lebanon. It said, When I am weak, how can I compromise? When I am strong, with the Americans behind me, why should I compromise? Therefore, the Reagan years must be remembered for Israel as the years the locust ate—the years in which Israel squandered every opportunity, and took virtually no initiative to reach out to the Palestinians and forge peace agreements with the help of an administration that would have provided Jerusalem with virtually any assurances and any inducements it wanted. Ironically, it was Reagan who, by accident of history more than by design, would be the one to open a dialogue between Washington and the PLO just as he was leaving office—thereby spoiling forever Israel's emotional monopoly in Washington and even bringing to life the Likud's ultimate nightmare: PLO–American cooperation in fighting terrorism.

The Likudniks were also ready to forge a relationship with the avowedly pro-Israel American Christian fundamentalists, who were particularly strong in shaping public opinion in the South. The fundamentalists saw a reborn Israel paving the way for the return of the Messiah and were not particularly concerned about the details of daily life in Israel or its Jewish and democratic values. The Messiah would straighten it all out when he arrived.

Many liberal Israelis and American Jews were deeply disturbed by Begin's friendship with the likes of Jerry Falwell and Pat Robertson and urged him to sever his relationship with such people. They explained to Begin that the fundamentalists were only supporting the Jewish state because they saw it as the necessary first stage in the return of Jesus Christ and the ultimate triumph of Christianity. To which Begin is said to have responded, "I tell you, if the Christian fundamentalists support us in Congress today, I will support them when the Messiah comes tomorrow."

But while some Israelis on the right of the political spectrum sought out new American allies who would not be disturbed by the direction in which the country was drifting, other Israelis, a significant but dwindling minority, appealed to the United States and American Jews to use their strength, influence, and resources to save Israel from its worst instincts. For example, on February 21, 1988, four distinguished Israeli writers, Yehuda Amichai, Amos Elon, Amos Oz, and A. B. Yehoshua, published a letter to the editor of *The New York Times* calling on American Jews to "speak up" about Israeli policies in the West Bank, because "the status quo will further corrupt Israeli society and inevitably lead to another major war." By their silence, said the Israeli authors, American Jews were "massively intervening in Israeli politics and silently but effectively supporting one side in the debate, the tragically wrong side. We implore them to speak up."

The letter was a cry from the heart of the Israel of beautiful eyes. But it was like a volcano appealing to a desert for help. American Jews were so stunned, so divided, and so confused about the Israel they woke up next to in the 1980s that they simply didn't know what to do with her.

The slogan with which the UJA raises money from American Jews for Israel is "We Are One." But it is clear today that American Jews and Israelis are not one; they are many. Whenever I think of Gabrielle Tsabag writing to Israelis, telling them to please be a good unified symbol, and Shlomo Avineri writing to American Jews, telling them that they are nothing more than the nervous Jews of Berlin in the 1930s, it becomes clear to me that the relationship between Israelis and American Jews may not survive another generation. Israel in the eyes of American Jews has gone in twenty years from a substitute religion to a source of religious delegitimization, and from a source of political identity to a source of political confusion; America in the eyes of Israelis has gone from a huge Disneyland to an essential lifeline, and from the world's largest pool of potential Jewish immigrants to Israel to the world's largest magnet for Jews, including Israelis. If Israel and American Jewry are ever to be one in any meaningful sense, then the foundations for real unity will have to be constructed anew from the bottom up, and that must begin with certain myths being set aside on both ends of the ocean.

Israelis were nurtured on the myth that the Diaspora does not count and that Jewish life there is not authentic, that American tolerance and pluralism won't last. But all indications are that life for Jews in America is viable. Most American Jews, except the ultra-Orthodox, are not going to immigrate to Israel, and if by some miracle they all did, it would be a disaster for Israel, since it would undermine the foundations of the United States–Israel government-to-government relationship. Instead of trying to compete for American Jews by offering them more fulfilling lives as Jews and as human beings, an increasing number of Israelis have opted for impugning American Jewish life and crying wolf about the coming pogrom in America. Israel would do itself, American Jewry, and their whole relationship a big favor by taking up the challenge posed by America. The more American Jews feel at home, the more they challenge Israel to be more than just a home against persecution. It is not enough anymore for Israel to proclaim its "centrality." With America out there, it now has to prove it.

What does that mean? As David Hartman taught me, it means that "Israel can't ask the Jewish people to give allegiance to it, to say that it is the central carrier of Jewish history, if the content of Israeli values and life is not something that a Jew living anywhere in the world could identify with and want to emulate. Israelis love to think that they are the center of Jewish history today, they love to be told that they are the center of Jewish history, but they don't always like the responsibility that comes with being the center."

If all Israel is about is developing into a nation that will be like all other nations, in the long run it will have nothing to offer American Jews.

But while Israelis are going to have to face up to the challenge
of America, American Jews are going to have to rethink some
of their basic attitudes toward Israel. Israel is not a Jewish summer
camp, where you come for a weekend and see that your kid is
eating okay and then go home; Israel also isn't a coffee-table book
with an introduction by Abba Eban that you keep out in the living
room and never read. Israel is the most difficult, outlandish experiment in Jewish history—an attempt to build a Jewish nation
out of Jews who have never lived together. Yes, they dreamed
about living together. Yes, they prayed about living together. But
in the real world radical Russian Jews and primitive Moroccan
Jews and wealthy South African Jews and hot-blooded Argenti-
nian Jews *never actually lived together* in the same space, let alone
in the harsh environment of the Middle East. Taking Jews from
so many diverse cultures and moral backgrounds and asking them
to form a society that will be the carrier of Jewish history in the
modern era is no easy task. When American Jews relate to Israel
as a heroic symbol, they are in effect saying that the task of
building this nation is over. The statue is complete. It is not. It
is an unfinished work. The country is still teeming with differences,
jealousies, unfulfilled dreams, not to mention people who have
to hustle their banker just to get to the end of the month and
who were not raised on the writings of Thomas Jefferson. It is
also filled with excitement, kinetic energy, and amazing achievements for so young a society.

That is why when people ask me, "So, Friedman, where do
you come out on Israel after this journey from Beirut to Jerusalem?" my answer is that I have learned to identify with and
feel affection toward an imperfect Israel. Mine is the story of a
young man who fell in love with the Jewish state back in the post-
1967 era, experienced a period of disillusionment in Lebanon,
and finally came out of Jerusalem saying, "Well, she ain't perfect.
I'll always want her to be the country I imagined in my youth.
But what the hell, she's mine, and for a forty-year-old, she ain't
too shabby."

Ya'akov Kirschen, the cartoonist, used to tell me that whenever
he heard American Jews complaining about the real Israel, he
would say to them, "You know what? You're right. Israel really
is an impossible place. If there were another Jewish state, I would
go live there instead. But there isn't. This Israel is all we've got."

Precisely because it's all they've got, the key question for many American Jews is how they can influence the still ongoing building process in Israel—to ensure that it develops as a modern, tolerant, democratic, pluralistic society—without actually living there.

I, and many others, are not particularly optimistic that American Jews will find the time, the understanding, or the commitment required to really deal with this challenge. One afternoon, before I left Jerusalem, I found myself in Rabbi Kelman's new Reform synagogue, listening while he poured his heart out in anguish over where the American Jewish–Israeli relationship was heading.

"American Jews can't understand our needs here, because the needs they have from Israel are different from what the real needs are," said Kelman. "They need a symbol, something black and white that they can rally around. That is why American Jews, who have a love of democracy and a love of individual freedom, instead of helping us to see reality, help us close our eyes. They helped us close our eyes by buying our myth of the benign occupation and not challenging it. Most of them never challenged it for a second. Never ever. And they ignored the voices in Israel who raised the issue from the beginning and stifled the voices of American Jewry that also tried to raise it. American Jews needed this lily-white symbol, so they never related to reality, never said, 'Hey, guys, let's look at our own history and see how people handled an occupation.' They could have been helpful; instead, it was see no evil, speak no evil, and hear no evil. You see, basically what it comes down to is this: I don't think American Jews really care about Israel. Because nobody really cares about a symbol. So few American Jews come to Israel. So, to begin with, if they don't know us in any real way, I don't know what we can talk about. When I talk about Israel with American Jews I have to discuss things in the most basic, simple, vulgar terms because they don't want to know from complexity."

The relationship between American Jews and Israeli Jews is "an infatuation," continued Kelman, his voice rich with emotion and anger. "Think of who you were in love with in high school. You didn't really know that person. A real love is knowing someone and knowing their faults and accepting their faults and learning how to help them, and learning how to listen. That's not an infatuation, that's a real relationship. I have to tell you one story that really moved me deeply. It happened just a couple of weeks ago. Richard Scheuer, who gave tons and tons of money to build the [Reform] World Union of Progressive Judaism complex [in Jerusalem], was being made an honorary fellow of Jerusalem. It was a beautiful ceremony. He's given some money to my synagogue, so I was invited. There were less than 150 people there. A quartet played some music and Abe Harman from the Hebrew University gave a beautiful erudite talk and Teddy Kollek gave a little talk and then it came time for Richard Scheuer to speak. And he gets up there and says, 'You know, I had a speech all prepared, but I'm not going to give you the speech. I want to just share with you'—and he is not a real speaker, you know— 'I just want to share with you how upset I am about what is going on in Jerusalem today and in Israel today. When I think about the Jerusalem that we imagined'—and he told all about meetings with the architect Moshe Safdie and Teddy Kollek and planning all sorts of Jewish–Arab things—and he said, 'I don't think they're going to happen.' And then he stood there and cried. He cried! The guy stood there and wept his eyes out. Well, needless to say, everyone in the room was devastated. Teddy got up there and put his arm around him. For about a minute no one was talking; they were just crying about the situation. So here is the exception—someone who comes to Israel every year and knows and cares. American Jews aren't crying about what is going on. American Jews aren't crying about the situation. They're embarrassed. They're embarrassed and angry. Well, fuck all their embarrassment and anger. They're not crying about what is going on. Because it is not them. You're angry, you're embarrassed, because the girl you're infatuated with embarrassed you in front of the goyim. Who cares! You're telling me what is going on now is bad because it is embarrassing? What is going on now is bad because the Jewish state might not make it! And all they can do is give Shamir a standing ovation.''

17

Conclusion:
From Beirut to Jerusalem
to Washington

As I reflect on what I've learned along this road from Beirut to
Jerusalem, I find myself drawn to a chapter in Mark Twain's *The
Innocents Abroad* in which he describes the moment during his
travels through the Middle East when he first beheld the River
Jordan:

> When I was a boy I somehow got the impression that the
> River Jordan was four thousand miles long and thirty-five
> miles wide. It is only ninety miles long, and so crooked that
> a man does not know which side of it he is on half the time.
> In going ninety miles it does not get over more than fifty
> miles of ground. It is not any wider than Broadway in New
> York. There is the Sea of Galilee and this Dead Sea—neither
> of them twenty miles long or thirteen wide. And yet when
> I was in Sunday school I thought they were sixty thousand
> miles in diameter.
> Travel and experience mar the grandest pictures and rob

us of the most cherished traditions of our boyhood. Well, let them go. I have already seen the Empire of King Solomon diminish to the size of Pennsylvania; I suppose I can bear the reduction of the seas and the river.

I too. After almost a decade of reporting on Arabs and Israelis, in late 1987 the *Times* asked me to move to Washington to become their diplomatic correspondent, covering the State Department and writing about the world at large. I jumped at the opportunity, maybe because, like Twain, the Middle East had first entered my consciousness in the wake of the Six-Day War as a grand tapestry, but the longer I stayed there, the more it seemed to become something very small.

A few weeks before we actually moved home from Jerusalem, my three-year-old daughter, Orly, asked me to take her out to lunch. Ann said she wanted to come, too, and bring along our two-month-old baby, Natalie, to make it a family outing. We decided to go to one of our favorite restaurants, the buffet at the Inter-Continental Hotel, which is located in East Jerusalem atop the Mount of Olives. Ann drove and the two girls sat in the back seat. As our little Daihatsu chugged slowly up Mount Scopus, a teenage Palestinian suddenly stepped out from behind a wall, stood in front of us, took careful aim, and threw a stone at Ann's face. It shattered the windshield into a spiderweb, but fortunately did not penetrate the glass. Orly saw the whole thing and began screaming hysterically from the back seat. Ann was paralyzed with fear. "Keep driving," I shouted at her, as the Palestinian youth loped away into the adjacent Arab village of el-Suwaneh.

None of us was hurt from the small shards of glass that dusted the interior of the car, just shaken. The only lasting scar from the incident seems to have been inflicted on Orly's psyche. She still asks about the "man with the stone," and I am afraid that as she grows older this incident will remain one of her earliest childhood memories. The Palestinian wasn't aiming at us specifically. He had simply seen the Israeli license plates on the car and that was enough for him to throw a stone and to inflict pain, no matter who was inside.

How ironic, I thought afterward. I had seen marching armies of many nations pass through Beirut and ultramodern fighter jets clash above its skies. I had seen the battleship *New Jersey* fire shells as big as Chevrolets, and I had seen my own apartment house reduced to dust by a pound of the most sophisticated high explosives known to man. I had seen massacres and car bombings and heard snipers until they had almost become routine. I had dodged them all for ten years, only to get hit by a stone.

It was a rather fitting punctuation mark for my journey. I had come to the Middle East just at the close of the 1970s, when the Arabs and Israelis were being painted by themselves and the world in bold colors and extra-large sizes. They fought big battles—in the 1973 war some of the biggest tank battles in the history of modern warfare were fought in the Sinai Desert and Golan Heights. They made big profits—thanks to the rise of OPEC in the mid-1970s there was a massive influx of oil wealth to the region that made men fantastically rich and gave them new pretensions, new temptations, new glitter, and new dreams of modernization. They even made peace in a big way—three months before I first left for Beirut, in March 1979, Egypt and Israel had signed their Peace Treaty. It was Pax Americana, packaged no less on American television, where Barbara Walters and Walter Cronkite played matchmakers to Menachem Begin and Anwar Sadat. Most of all, they thought in big ways—when I first came to Beirut, I listened to Lebanese tell me that they were the last frontier of Western civilization. A few years later I would even hear my own President, Ronald Reagan, proclaim that a premature withdrawal of the Marines from Beirut could "call into question the resolve of the West to carry out its responsibilities to help the free world defend itself." When I got to Israel I met Jews who were convinced that the prefab homes they were setting up on barren hills in the West Bank would pave the way for universal redemption. Yes, in the 1970s this was a big story with big claims.

"Men thought they were turning a corner," my friend Fouad Ajami remarked to me, "and guess what they met when they did? The past. In the 1970s men in this region were introduced to something new—to modernization on a very rapid scale, to large wealth and large machines, to Americanization and Westernization, to huge hotel chains and huge ideas, and, most of all, to a less tribal world. Palestinians were melting into Israelis, the Lebanese Muslims were becoming more and more like the Maronites—economically and socially—threatening their primacy. The Israelis after Camp David were becoming part of the Middle

East. But many people didn't like this new world, and were not ready to pay for it by what they would have to give up of themselves. This new world blurred identities. It threatened the boundaries between men and left them confused. So they drew back, and they changed this new world into something old. They went out with sticks and stones and drew sharp lines on the ground to distinguish themselves anew from each other. And so at the end of the 1980s the tribe returned with a vengeance; the region and its conflicts were rendered true to their original dimensions."

Indeed, the Lebanese, having dabbled with modern democracy and Western-style political parties, slipped back into tribal wars as bloody and unrestrained as those fought between Druse and Maronite peasants in 1860. The Israelis and Palestinians completed the same circle. Their conflict had begun sixty years earlier with Jews and Arabs fighting with pistols, knives, and rocks for control of Mandatory Palestine from the Mediterranean Sea to the Jordan River. After Israel was created, though, the Palestinian–Jewish conflict was subsumed in a wider war between the state of Israel and the surrounding Arab nations. But after the 1967 war, the Arab states gradually disengaged from the battle with Israel, leaving the Palestinians to fight alone. Since Israel had occupied the West Bank and the Gaza Strip and knit the original area of Palestine back together again, it was easy for Palestinians and Jews to start over from where they had begun— battling for control of this oft-Promised Land with the same clubs, pistols, rocks, and knives their forefathers had used a century ago.

And that is exactly how I left the Lebanese, Palestinians, and Israelis in late 1988—with swords drawn, standing sentry over their own primordial worlds. Faced with a choice between passion and modernity, they had chosen passion. Faced with a choice between expanding economies and the tribe, they had chosen the tribe. The marching armies had gone; the F-15s were grounded. The conflict was now reduced to men attacking each other according to identity cards and license plates, over olive trees and grazing rights. The war had come down to eye level: Israeli eyes against Palestinian eyes, Maronite eyes against Shiite eyes, looks meant to kill against looks meant to intimidate, darting glances versus blank stares, eyes begging for a little friendship meeting eyes hollow with fear. In Lebanese Arabic, when someone wants to say that he really vanquished someone else, he says, "I broke his eye." That is what the great Middle East that had swept me away in 1967 had come down to—men breaking each other's eyes.

Three weeks after the *intifada* began I went on patrol with a group of Israeli soldiers in Nablus. Their commander, Lieutenant Colonel Yisrael, a paratrooper, understood from the minute the Palestinian uprising began that he was in a whole new kind of war from anything he had been trained for. As we walked down a main street in the Balata refugee camp outside Nablus, he explained how personal it had all become. From one side of the road an elderly Palestinian with a lathered beard looked up from his barber chair to watch us pass. Across the street, a mother and four little children squeezed into a crack in a doorway and eyed the soldiers' every step. At the butcher shop, the vegetable stand, and the bakery, Palestinians peered out from behind a carcass of meat or a mountain of pita bread—and just stared.

"You know," said Colonel Yisrael, as he contemplated this scene, "a soldier wakes up in the morning here, and the sky is clear, and it is a fine day, and he just wants to smile. And we tell him, 'Fine, go ahead and smile.' And then he goes out onto the street, and he looks into people's eyes. It is all in the eyes. And what he sees usually does not want to make him smile anymore."

When I got back to the United States, I was surprised to discover how many of my new neighbors in Washington had come to share this perception that in the Middle East the past had buried the future, and possibly always will. America's missionary zeal for peacemaking in this part of the world had vanished in the decade I was gone. The excitement of watching Walter Cronkite and Barbara Walters bringing Anwar Sadat and Menachem Begin together on American television had been replaced by wrenching interviews with the families of Americans held hostage in Beirut and split-screen debates between Israelis and Palestinians arguing with each other with all the politesse of two alley cats. When I would mention the Middle East to American friends, they would either shake their heads silently, shudder with fear, or just wave me off with that get-away-from-me stare normally reserved for Hare Krishna devotees trying to hand you their literature in an airport terminal.

I think this attitude that the Middle East was something frightening and untamable began to take hold of the American psyche about 1979, when the United States became the target of a relentless series of attacks emanating from this region, beginning with the taking of American embassy personnel as hostages in Tehran. Then there was the suicide bombing of the Beirut American embassy in April 1983, then the Marine headquarters bombing, then another suicide attack on the American embassy in East Beirut in 1984, then the 1985 hijacking of a TWA jetliner to Beirut and the cold-blooded murder of an American seaman on board, whose body was dumped off the plane like so much garbage. This was soon followed by the hijacking of the *Achille Lauro* and another dumping—this time of wheelchair-bound Leon Klinghoffer—and then still another bombing of American servicemen, this time in a Berlin discotheque in 1986. As if all this were not enough, Americans were rudely awakened in December 1987 by another bad message: night after night of network news footage showing Israelis clubbing and shooting rock-throwing Palestinians in the West Bank and Gaza Strip. Those scenes from Israel, I am convinced, left many Americans exclaiming, "You too, Israelis? Even you Jews have this virus? And all these years we thought you were just like us."

America seemed to say to itself one day in 1988, Let's wash our hands of this part of the world. In an age of 99-cent-a-gallon gasoline, who needs it anyway?

Despite all I have witnessed, I still believe such a fatalistic attitude is both naïve and overly pessimistic. It is naïve because we simply have too many strategic, emotional, and religious interests at stake in this area of the world to turn our backs on it entirely. It is overly pessimistic because America still has much to offer the Middle East, much that would be welcomed. Maybe it is the Minnesota boy still in me, but I refuse to pronounce this region hopeless. It's not inviting, but it's not hopeless. Washington can still bring Arabs and Israelis the best of America's outlook, without being devoured by the feuds and passions that consume them.

The question is how. The answer, I believe, is by America learning to play several different diplomatic roles simultaneously.

She must learn to think like an obstetrician, behave like a friend, bargain like a grocer, and fight like a real son-of-a-bitch. Let me explain.

To begin with, America should think about Arabs and Israelis the same way an obstetrician would think about a couple who came to him claiming that they had been trying to get pregnant for forty years but just couldn't conceive most of the time. The first thing any obstetrician would do in such a case is to determine whether this couple was really trying to get pregnant, really ready to go all the way, or whether they weren't just talking about it while they were in the doctor's office and then going back home to sleep in separate bedrooms.

America cannot want peace either for the Lebanese or between Israelis and Arabs more than those parties want it for themselves. Arabs and Israelis each have to understand that we can only help to deliver a settlement that they produce out of their own desire and willingness to nurture something together. Otherwise, we should remain very cautious. We cannot create peace settlements for them; there is no artificial insemination in diplomacy. That is what the Marines learned in Lebanon. The Marines wanted to help the Lebanese rebuild their country, but the Lebanese had other fish to fry, other scores to settle, which came first. The same has been true for many Arabs and Israelis in recent years. Begin and Shamir wanted something more than peace with the Palestinians; they wanted Judea and Samaria, and many Israelis still do. Arafat for years wanted something more than a homeland for his people; he wanted his throne atop a united PLO, and although he has finally recognized Israel's existence in public in order to open a dialogue with Washington, it remains to be seen whether he can speak the kinds of words that would pave the way for a settlement with Jerusalem.

Henry Kissinger and Jimmy Carter were lucky to have been able to deal in the Middle East at historical junctures when key parties were obviously ready to get pregnant, and that, I believe, is why both of them were so effective in delivering a measure of peace. Kissinger came along after the 1973 war, when Egypt, Israel, and Syria each desperately needed some kind of agreement that would enable them to disengage from an unbearably costly conflict. President Carter came along after Anwar Sadat had already flown to Jerusalem and openly embraced Menachem Begin.

Secretary of State George P. Shultz, in contrast, tried to be a peacemaker at a time when no one was really ready. Shultz visited the Middle East three times in early 1988 to try to coax Israelis, Jordanians, and Palestinians to an international conference, only to be rebuffed each time. All the parties had beckoned Shultz to come, even welcomed him, but for the wrong reasons. Shamir wanted Shultz around so he could pretend to the Israeli public that he was really trying to find a political solution to the *intifada*; Peres wanted Shultz around to expose Shamir as an obstacle to peace on the eve of the Israeli elections; Arafat wanted Shultz around to use as leverage against the Israelis, in the hope that Washington would squeeze Israel on the PLO's behalf and spare him from having to make the concessions Israel would require for any kind of settlement, and King Hussein wanted Shultz around so he would have someone to blame for his inevitable decision to sit on the fence. When Shultz asked them each whether they wanted to get pregnant, they would all nod and say, "Yes, yes, of course we do." But they all wanted to get pregnant with America—not with each other.

I don't mean to suggest that America should set an impossibly high threshold for determining whether the parties are serious; it should be high enough that Washington is not chasing after every wink, nod, and declaration that the ball is now in its court, but not so high that we miss real calls for help, or unique historical opportunities that only last for a brief period. The way to measure how serious the parties are is the same way an obstetrician would do it—by observing what they say to each other, not what they say to us. Any party that makes a peace declaration that needs to be read eighteen times in order to be deciphered and that requires a Middle East expert to explain it is not serious enough; any party that is ready to talk only about the style of negotiations and insists on determining which of its enemies can attend— whether it should be an international conference or direct talks, whether the PLO can come or only Jordanians and West Bank-ers—is not serious enough. Only those parties who are ready to talk substance and peaceful intent in language a five-year-old can understand and with sincerity that can be felt in the gut are serious enough.

* * *

But even when the parties to the Middle East conflicts don't seem ready to get pregnant, America should not just sit on its hands. It should constantly be trying to nudge the parties together by behaving like a friend.

Israeli political theorist Yaron Ezrahi always liked to tell me that the most important thing an American friend can offer Arabs and Israelis is American optimism—exactly the kind of innocent can-do optimism that the Marines brought to Beirut. The Marines' almost childlike belief that every problem has a solution, that people will respond to reason, and that the future can triumph over the past is a wonderful thing, Yaron would remind me. It is a trait which Americans should never be ashamed of. Even though Arabs and Israelis sometimes make fun of our naïve optimism, the truth is, deep down they welcome it. They envy us our optimism, because theirs are deeply pessimistic societies, deeply scarred societies—societies hemmed in by ancient tribal and religious boundaries, where the most frequently heard political statement is "No, you can't."

Into this world weighed down by the past swaggers the naïve American with a brief announcement: "Yes, you can." History, he declares, is not a circular process of the past endlessly repeating itself; it is a linear process of steady improvements. "The future is open," he says. "The past is dead. Nothing is more sacred than the here and now." This message is crucial for Arabs and Israelis, who desperately need someone to free them from the paralyzing features of their past and to open their eyes to the opportunities of the present.

Another thing an American friend has to offer is the truth; only a real friend tells you the truth about yourself. Arabs and Israelis have a real tendency to get caught up in their private tribal worlds, in which all their fantasies and all their martyrs and all their dead ancestors begin to define the present. This is dangerous because in the world of fantasy each side believes that it can have it all and that the other side will disappear. In the Palestinian fantasy world, there are no Israelis; in the Israeli fantasy world, there are no Palestinians; in the Maronite fantasy, there are no Lebanese Muslims; in the Lebanese Muslim fantasy, there are no Maronites.

An American friend has to help jar these people out of their fantasies by constantly holding up before their eyes the mirror of reality. The Americans rarely did this with Amin Gemayel in Lebanon, and they have been weak in doing it with both Israelis and Palestinians. Now that the United States has opened a dialogue with the PLO, the Palestinians have to be told straight out to get rid of the notion that the Israelis are just modern-day Crusaders who will one day gather up their shields and swords and ride off into the sunset, or that the Americans are going to squeeze the Israelis on the Palestinians' behalf. The Israelis are not just passing through; they are home. But Israelis have to be told the same about the Palestinians; that they are inextricably tied to their land and at home in Palestine in the very deepest sense, too. Israeli fantasies about transferring Palestinians to Jordan or getting them to acquiesce in a permanent Israeli occupation of the West Bank and Gaza Strip, or getting them to drop the PLO as their representatives are just that—fantasies.

America, in effect, has to say to both Israelis and Palestinians, "You are two people with nothing in common—not language, not history, not culture, and not religion. I am not asking you to love each other. I don't expect you to love each other. The sooner you live apart, the better off you will both be. But the only way you can hope to live apart and at peace is by first coming together to produce a settlement that guarantees Israelis their security and Palestinians their right to self-determination in the West Bank and Gaza Strip. Nothing short of that will ever bring peace."

But a real friend not only tells you the truth, he helps you deal with it; he walks you to school on that first day, and maybe even all year. He lets you know that there is a world out there independent of blood ties and tribal ties that can be trusted. In playing this kind of friend for both Israelis and Arabs, America can show them that facing the truth does not necessarily lead to a terrifying abyss. By being a good friend, by being patient, by being understanding, by not constantly threatening, by offering aid, America can do a great deal to coax the parties to the negotiating table and beyond.

Here again the behavior of George Shultz as Secretary of State is instructive. Shultz knew how to play the friend, at least vis-à-vis the Israelis. He understood better than any diplomat I have ever watched that when dealing with the Israelis the most effective way to pressure them is never through a head-on confrontation *in public*. This only gives their most recalcitrant leaders an opportunity to dig in their heels and exploit the open confrontation with Washington to look strong before their own people. In the Middle East, some politicians have made whole careers by defying Great Powers—Nasser, Khomeini, Begin, and Assad have all played this game at one time or another. They all knew that anyone who could say no to a superpower is himself a superpower.

In Israel's case, an open confrontation only plays into the deepest fears of the Israeli public that they are alone in the world and must man the barricades. Of course, economic or diplomatic pressure should still be used at times, but it should be done subtly, indirectly, and should always be accompanied by expressions of great regret, pointing out that the "policy reassessment" or the "unfortunate delay in an arms shipment" is being done in sorrow not anger, out of affection not alienation. The audience will get the message.

Nothing would unite Israelis more than an American diplomat who came in and declared that if Jerusalem did not do X or Y tomorrow America would cut off all its aid. "For American optimism to work in the Middle East it has to be based on relationships of trust, especially with Israel," said Ezrahi. "America is Israel's last hope. De Gaulle betrayed us. England betrayed us. If America does the same it would be the end of Middle East diplomacy and the ultimate victory for Israeli isolationism."

When Shultz came to Israel, played the good friend from the American Middle West, and invited Shamir for blueberry pancakes, what he was really doing was reducing Shamir to his real size—which is not very big—and preventing him from puffing himself up in a way that would make him unmanageable. At the same time, Shultz's soothing approach also built up enormous trust in himself and in America in the eyes of the Israeli public. Unfortunately, Shultz never cashed in on that trust; he never led it anywhere, because he didn't understand how to play the third role of an American diplomat—the grocer.

If the day should come when America is convinced that the parties are serious about peacemaking, or that conditions in the region are so hot that they have to be serious about it, then America should don the messy apron of a corner grocer in order to help the parties forge an agreement.

Why a grocer? Because the prevailing political culture in the Arab world and Israel is a merchant culture, where men have traditionally lived by trading, bargaining, and negotiating with their wits. Fouad Ajami always likes to say that there are basically two political types in Middle East history: the messiah and the merchant. The messiahs, or *mahdis*, as they are known in Arabic, come and go with the political seasons. One season it is Gamal Abdel Nasser selling Arab nationalism, another season it is Ayatollah Khomeini selling Islamic fundamentalism. But after a while, the messiahs always pass on, like hurricanes which, after stirring up the landscape, sooner or later move out to sea, leaving behind what was always there: the grocer, whose ancient and familiar culture does not come and go with the seasons but is rooted in the earth.

What this means is that any statesman dealing in the Middle East has to learn to look beyond the banners and the ideology and see the merchant in every man there. And when he does, he must remember that there are two things that every good Middle Eastern merchant understands. One is that you should never take no for an answer. There is always some way to make a sale if you have confidence in your merchandise. Just because a customer says no doesn't mean he isn't buying. You just have to sift your way through all the rhetoric and get to the heart of the deal.

The best example I ever heard of this sort of cut-the-crap-let's-get-down-to-business approach was when Robert S. Strauss, the Texas lawyer and Democratic Party boss, who was appointed by President Carter in May 1979 to be the special Middle East envoy with responsibility for getting the stalled Camp David autonomy talks moving, came to the region. (Unfortunately, he did not stay in his job long enough to see it through.) On his first official visit to Jerusalem, Strauss—who had never had any previous diplomatic experience in the Middle East—took a helicopter tour of the entire West Bank accompanied by a group of American reporters. After the tour was over, Strauss and the reporters retired to the King David Hotel in Jerusalem. Naturally, the reporters were anxious to hear Strauss's reaction to what he had seen—the settlements, the terraced hillsides, the winding furrowed valleys. As they pressed Strauss for a reaction to this ancient piece of turf, contested by Arabs and Jews, he kept parrying them with his Texas good ol' boy drawl, saying, "Awh, I couldn't tell you."

But the reporters were insistent: What did he think of the West Bank? "Awh, I couldn't tell you," Strauss repeated. Finally, though, the American envoy relented.

"Well, it's like this," one of the reporters quoted Strauss as saying of the West Bank. "I don't know why one of them would want it, and why the other would even give a damn."

The other thing every good grocer knows is that everything must have a price tag on it, otherwise you can't do business. Therefore, any American statesman dealing with Israelis, Palestinians, or Lebanese has to attach a price tag to everything he is selling. There has to be a price for saying no—and sticking to that no—and there has to be a windfall for saying yes.

The Reagan Administration, however, consistently dealt with Israel and the Arabs without any sense of pricing or Middle Eastern–style bargaining. Despite coming to Israel three times in early 1988 to try to convince Shamir to attend an international peace conference, Secretary of State Shultz never established with Shamir a price for his saying no. So, naturally, Shamir said no. Before each Shultz trip Shamir and his aides nervously waited for the American Secretary of State to set the price, to lower the boom, but he never did.

George Shultz was a thoroughly decent, dignified, well-meaning American diplomat—and that was his problem. His straightforward behavior always reminded me of the American tourist who goes into the Arab market in Jerusalem to buy a carpet. He walks into the shop, sees a Persian carpet on the wall that he wants, and asks the shopkeeper, "How much is that carpet?" The shopkeeper just shakes his head back and forth and then says wistfully, "Oh, Mr. Shultz. Wouldn't you know it? You picked the most expensive carpet in the store. That carpet has been in the family for two hundred years. I'm not even sure I want to sell that carpet. But for you and you only . . . $5,000." Instead of running his fingers over the carpet and telling the shopkeeper that it's a piece of junk made in Pakistan and not worth $10—which is what the merchant expects to hear—Shultz takes out his traveler's checks and hands over the $5,000. The shopkeeper laughs all the way to the bank. To this day, Shamir is always ready to talk about what a nice guy George Shultz was. Whenever I heard Shamir praising Shultz, I was always reminded of a shopkeeper in the souk who, after separating a tourist from all his money, says, "Come back here for coffee anytime you're in the neighborhood." I never heard Shamir say that to Jimmy Carter or Henry Kissinger, but then neither of them paid retail.

The effective American statesman must not only know how to establish a price like a grocer but how to impose it as well. Shultz was wonderful at playing the good friend from America when dealing with the Israelis in public. When he got behind closed doors, however, when the television lights were turned off and it was just he and Shamir sitting on the couch together, that was the time for Shultz to switch from the Middle Western friend to the Middle Eastern grocer, but he never did. Shultz, I am told, was as avuncular with Shamir in private as he was in public, and that simply won't work. In the Middle East, and particularly in Israel, there is a basic contentiousness to social and political discourse that is foreign, and perhaps distasteful, to most Americans. A friendly discussion between two Israelis sounds like four Americans having an argument.

While public confrontations in such an environment can be counterproductive, private confrontations at a very high-decibel level can be fruitful. Think for a moment about Yitzhak Shamir's day as Prime Minister. Before someone like Shultz arrived for his meeting, Shamir had probably already taken three phone calls from Rabbi Yitzhak Peretz of the ultra-Orthodox Shas Party, during which Peretz threatened to bring down the whole government and end Shamir's political life unless the Prime Minister installed a kosher kitchen in the Ministry of Interior building by 6:00 p.m. An hour later, Shamir's fellow Likud Party member Ariel Sharon might have stopped by just to say that he wouldn't be voting for Shamir at the next party meeting because he wanted his job; before leaving, Sharon probably took out a tape measure and started measuring the carpet in Shamir's office. Into this snake pit walked George Shultz, talking in his polite, restrained American manner. Shamir probably looked at Shultz as a *relief* from the people he had to deal with, and that is deadly for any American diplomat. In the political culture of the Middle East, people simply won't take you seriously unless you show them that you are ready to break a little of their furniture for your ideas.

The shouting, of course, has to be credible. Henry Kissinger was famous for telling Israelis that he was breaking their furniture in the name of President Richard Nixon—probably far more often than Nixon ever realized. But Kissinger understood that a bark with no bite was just so much noise, and if there is anything Arabs and Israelis are used to, it's noise.

Finally, if an American statesman is successful at brokering some type of Arab–Arab or Arab–Israeli settlement, then he must understand how to play one more role in order to preserve that settlement, and America's other interests in the region, from those who would undermine them. He must also be a real son-of-a-bitch. He must understand that he is dealing with grocers who often play by their own rules, and their own rules are Hama Rules.

Consider the various attacks on American citizens and soldiers in Lebanon. Between July 19, 1982, when David Dodge, then acting president of the American University of Beirut, was kidnapped, and February 17, 1988, when Lieutenant Colonel William Higgins, who was on assignment with the United Nations, was kidnapped, seventeen American citizens were abducted in Lebanon. According to Western intelligence sources, some of the kidnappings were carried out by private families trying to secure the release of relatives in Kuwaiti jails, and others by gangs just out for lucre. The connections between these families and gangs and various Middle Eastern governments is murky at best.

However, the lion's share of these abductions were carried out by the pro-Iranian Lebanese Shiite militia Hizbullah. Hizbullah, which calls for the formation of an Islamic republic in Lebanon, was founded in 1982 in Baalbek, in Lebanon's Bekaa Valley, by Sayyid Abbas al-Mussawi, Sheik Subhi al-Tufayli, and other Shiite clergymen educated in Iran. It quickly became an effective fighting force thanks to training and weaponry provided by Iranian Revolutionary Guards (*Pasdaran*), who were dispatched to Baalbek ostensibly to fight Israel. The Revolutionary Guards, in turn, received their orders, finances, and logistical support from Tehran via the Iranian embassy in Damascus.

American and Lebanese intelligence officials have determined that the Iranian Revolutionary Guards not only have enormous influence over the Hizbullah kidnappers but have also ordered specific abductions for their own foreign policy purposes. In this division of labor, Hizbullah was responsible for getting access to the personnel files of institutions such as the American University of Beirut, in order to ascertain which faculty were American citizens, then abducting the targets and holding them for months or years. The Iranian Revolutionary Guards back in Tehran provided some funding for "hostage maintenance" and salaries for the hostage guards, while also helping to set the overall policy as to which hostages should be released or traded and for what price—most of which was dependent on Iranian interests. David Dodge was actually transferred from Beirut to Tehran and held captive there.

The Lebanese clergymen who were supposed to have been the spiritual guides of Hizbullah, such as Sheik Sayyid Muhammad Hussein Fadlallah, whose pamphlets and sermons are often dissected by Middle East experts for explanations of the kidnappers' ideological motives, were little more than a façade. "Fadlallah is just a cover," said one Shiite militia source privy to the inner workings of the Beirut Shiite underground. "He knows little about operations. The people organizing the kidnappings are totally isolated from ideology. Ideology means nothing to them. They are professionals. It is like a play. There are the actors who recite the lines and there is the director who coordinates everything. Never confuse the actors for the director. This is business."

The business was the business that was always there—the business of state, the business of regional influence, and the business of staying in power instead of the next guy. Beginning in 1982, as I noted earlier, the United States had thrown its weight behind one coalition in the Middle East—Egypt, Israel, and Saudi Arabia—and against another—Syria, Libya, and Iran. For this latter group, kidnapping and suicide bombings were not acts of religious fanaticism but diplomacy by other means—a cheap and effective way to push the Americans out, undermine their local allies, and gain some bargaining chips to trade for future financial and political concessions—without risking an open conventional war in which they would be at a disadvantage. America hurt them in its way, and they hurt America back in theirs.

The Iran–Contra arms-for-hostage bartering demonstrated as well as anything could have just how cynical this grocery shopping was. Colonel Oliver North thought he was dealing with Iranian "moderates" when he was really dealing with Iranian grocers; he had no idea how to bargain with the original rug merchants. He should have taken business lessons from Libyan leader Muammar Qaddafi. After the United States bombed Tripoli, Libya, on April

15, 1986, in retaliation for a series of Libyan-sponsored terrorist attacks, the Libyan leader got in touch with the Lebanese Shiites holding American hostage Peter Kilburn, a librarian at the American University of Beirut who was abducted on December 3, 1984. Qaddafi literally bought Kilburn from his captors, right off the shelf, so to speak, for a reported $1 million. Then, according to American intelligence sources, on April 17, 1986, Qaddafi had the sixty-one-year-old Kilburn murdered as his retaliation for the American air raid. It was a nice arm's-length deal, which enabled Qaddafi to exact his revenge—without the obvious fingerprints which might have prompted another visit from the American Lone Ranger. Colonel North could also have learned something about bargaining from the French, who in May 1988 secured the release of three of their hostages in Beirut after agreeing to pay Tehran $330 million, plus interest, which France owed Iran from a $1 billion loan it had secured from the Shah but never fully repaid.

While ideologies such as Islamic fundamentalism and Arab nationalism may no longer play the seemingly all-pervasive roles they once did in guiding the actions of certain political elites in the Middle East, they still have an important hold on some of the young urban poor in countries such as Iran or Lebanon. These ideologies are the cheap currency, in fact, with which Middle Eastern regimes purchase the lives of the young men who actually carry out the suicide car bombings or guard the hostages or walk through the minefields. These young, urban poor are economically, socially, and psychologically vulnerable to promises of the millennium, to the intoxication of sacred religious texts or to the illusion of a quick fix. But they are nothing more than carry-out boys at the grocery store. One must always look beyond them to the real retailers of violence—the intelligence professionals of Iran, Syria, and Libya—and their subcontractors, such as the infamous Palestinian terrorist-for-hire Abu Nidal. They are the ones with whom America has real business. They are the ones who unleash the kidnappers and suicide bombers and who can call them back. We in the West who relate to these "revolutionary" countries only by reading the political banners they hold aloft are imputing to them higher ideological motives than they could ever meet. Don't read their lips, just watch their moves. They may talk like fanatics, but they behave like grocers; they may preach martyrdom, but always for the other guy's son.

It is in order to deal with this dimension of Middle East politics that an effective American statesman must know how to play hardball. This means being ready, if necessary, to engage in operations that directly threaten either the life or the domestic stability of the leaders of those countries which threaten America's interests. Here the Reagan Administration deserves credit. When Reagan ordered the 2:00 a.m. bombing of Qaddafi's tent—nearly killing the Libyan leader in his own bed—Qaddafi got the message and has barely been heard from since. Reagan's dispatching of American warships to the Persian Gulf, ostensibly to protect the oil shipping lanes, forced Iran to divert men, attention, and resources from the Iraqi front and thereby contributed significantly to the general exhaustion of the Iranians, which ultimately led Khomeini to accept Iraq's cease-fire offer.

You can't come to a hockey game and expect to play by the rules of touch football; Middle East diplomacy is a contact sport.

Of course, no American statesman can be, or should be, an obstetrician, a friend, a grocer, and a son-of-a-bitch all the time. The effective statesman will be the one who knows *when* to play each role—when to be an obstetrician and when to be a son-of-a-bitch, how not to be such an inveterate grocer that he drives the customer away and how not to be such a good friend that his customer forgets that there is a price to be paid. That is a matter of timing and instinct—the stuff of great diplomacy that can never be taught.

I am well aware that there are enormous constraints on any American statesman who would want to play all these roles. Some of those constraints are cultural, others institutional. Nevertheless, I believe that there is a basic American consensus for both the policy approach I have outlined and for the tools. Jimmy Carter and Henry Kissinger demonstrated that an American statesman ready to articulate a clear, sober, and fair policy on the Middle East, and ready to devote the resources and energy needed to push it along—when the people in the region are serious—will enjoy broad support from Americans in general and Jewish Americans in particular.

After all, there has to be something more to Middle East politics than the endless feud—at least God intended there to be. Surely that is the meaning of that critical portion in the Book of Exodus when God commands Moses to liberate his people from bondage in Egypt. After receiving his assignment from the Lord, Moses asks God a simple question: What's your name? How should I identify you to my people? God gives Moses an intriguing answer. On the one hand, He tells Moses to tell the Children of Israel that He, the Lord, is the God of their fathers, "the God of Abraham, the God of Isaac and the God of Jacob." Some modern rabbis have interpreted this as God telling Moses, "I am the God of your past, of your memories, of your historical roots, of your ancestors, all of which I know are important to you; I was with you in your suffering and in your joy wherever you were."

On the other hand, though, God tells Moses to tell the Children of Israel that He, the Lord, is also someone else. God says, tell the people "I will be who I will be." The rabbis interpreted this as God saying, "Although I was with you in your past, I am also a God who invites new possibilities for the future. Your past, while essential to your identity, does not exhaust all that you can become—either as individuals or as a community. When I tell you that there is a Promised Land out there, I am telling you that the future can be different from the past, that you and your community can become something new."

It may be that America just doesn't have the energy anymore for liberating Arabs and Israelis from the chains of their past. If so, that is unfortunate, not only for us, but for the peoples of the Middle East as well. I have met my share of scoundrels in that part of the world, but I have met even more—many more—Arabs, Israelis, Palestinians, and Lebanese, who are desperate for what America has to offer their region. They are men and women who are starved for alternatives and who cry out for sources of optimism. America can be the bridge builder between them. Even when America doesn't have all the answers, it can keep asking the right questions. It can keep hope alive; it can keep the discussion alive; it can keep reminding people what the Good Lord tried to tell Moses: how exciting it is to know that tomorrow can be different from yesterday.

Epilogue

And there was a strife between the herdmen of Abram's cattle and the herdmen of Lot's cattle . . . And Abram said unto Lot: Let there be no strife, I pray thee . . . between my herdmen and thy herdmen; for we be brethren. Is not the whole land before thee? Separate thyself, I pray thee, from me; if thou wilt take the left hand, then I will go to the right; or if thou depart to the right hand, then I will go to the left.

—Genesis 13:7–9

I personally don't like Arabs and Arabs don't like me. Forty years in the same bed. There hasn't been love; there hasn't been sex. I want a divorce.

—Israeli Major General (Res.)
Avigdor Ben-Gal, former commander
of Israel's northern front, 1988

After this book was first published in the United States, many readers wrote me to say that while they appreciated the way I had diagnosed the Israeli–Palestinian conflict, they regretted that I had not provided prescriptions for a solution. This was intentional. First of all, I wanted readers to focus on my journey from Beirut to Jerusalem and not debate any proposals I might have. Equally important, as I made clear in my concluding chapter, I believe that until the parties themselves are "ready to get pregnant"—ready, that is, to make the fundamental compromises and sacrifices for a settlement—there is very little of use that any outsider can suggest.

History teaches us that in the Middle East, only overwhelming pain or pleasure—only war or a Sadat-like overture—will really make the parties ready to get pregnant. Neither appears to be on the horizon. As I write this epilogue in the autumn of 1989, Israelis and Palestinians are arguing about how to organize a dialogue that would discuss how to elect Palestinians to negotiate with Israel on its offer of autonomy for the Arab inhabitants of the West Bank and Gaza Strip. In other words, they are negotiating for a negotiation about organizing negotiations for an interim solution. Even if one or two of these hurdles were surmounted, a settlement would be a long way off.

So what to do? Most likely, Israelis and Palestinians will do nothing, other than learn to live with the status quo, with all of the unpleasantness this will entail. I myself think the status quo is very destructive for both communities. Hence, I have put all of my energies into trying to imagine ways in which one party or the other might take some bold, unilateral initiative to unlock the present deadlock—without the stimulus of either overwhelming pain or pleasure.

What follows, I am the first to admit, is something of a fantasy. It is, however, the way an Israeli leader could break the impasse. Let me emphasize, I don't see any Israeli leader on the horizon who would adopt my approach. For all the reasons given in the previous chapters, Israelis will respond only to overwhelming pain or pleasure, and the Palestinians at this time cannot produce either. Nevertheless, with that caveat in mind, this is how I would proceed.

I base my approach on several assumptions. First, Israel holds virtually all the cards. By that I mean it controls all of the West Bank and Gaza Strip, which are the bargaining chips for any agreement. So, the only relevant question is, What might induce Israelis to trade part or all of those territories for a secure and stable relationship with the Palestinians? Palestinians can demand or claim all they want, but the fact is only the Israelis are in a position to unilaterally initiate a settlement.

Second, there are many aspects of my approach that Palestinians might find offensive, even cruel. I mean no cruelty or offense to anyone. But Palestinians will have to learn to distinguish between what they want and how they get it. A Palestinian state is not going to come to them wrapped in a dainty bow. It is not going to come to them accompanied by the soothing tones of a Mozart concerto. I believe that the only way it is going to come to them is if Israelis, for their own reasons of self-interest, brutal self-interest, convince themselves that they are better off allowing such a state to come into being than opposing it.

Third, such a momentous step for Israel as withdrawing from the territories in exchange for a new relationship with the Palestinians cannot be based on a narrow majority. Like the peace treaty with Egypt, it must be based on the approval of at least a two-thirds majority of the Israeli public. Otherwise, it would not be stable and there could be serious civil strife.

Therefore, in my opinion, the most important question for the peace process today is what it will take to patch together such an Israeli majority for territorial compromise, because only such a majority can change the history of the region in the immediate sense.

Before I offer an answer, let me first remind the reader of my grocer in Jerusalem. As I noted in Chapter 14, "The Earthquake," there was a supermarket in Jerusalem where I shopped for fruits and vegetables almost every day. It was owned by an Iraqi Jewish family who had immigrated to Israel from Baghdad in the early 1940s. The patriarch of the family, Sasson, was an elderly curmudgeon in his sixties. Sasson's whole life had left him with the conviction that the Arabs would never willingly accept a Jewish state in their midst and that any concessions to the Palestinians would eventually be used to liquidate the Jewish state. Whenever Sasson heard Israeli doves saying that the Palestinians really wanted to live in peace with the Jews, but that they just couldn't always come out and declare it, it sounded ludicrous to him. It simply ran counter to everything life in Iraq and Jerusalem had taught him, and neither the Camp David treaty with Egypt nor declarations by Yasir Arafat—nor the Palestinian uprising itself—had convinced him otherwise. As I said, as far as Sasson was concerned, the problem between himself and the Palestinians was not that they didn't understand each other, but that they did—all too well. Sasson, I should add, did not appear to be ideologically committed to Israel's holding the West Bank and Gaza Strip. He was a grocer, and ideology did not trip easily off his tongue. I am sure he rarely, if ever, went to the occupied territories. Like a majority of Israelis, he viewed the Israeli presence in the West Bank and Gaza Strip primarily in terms of security.

I believe that Sasson is the key to a Palestinian–Israeli peace settlement—not him personally, but his world view. He is the Israeli silent majority. He is the Israeli two-thirds. You don't hear much from the Sassons of Israel. They don't talk much. They are not as interesting to interview as wild-eyed messianic West Bank settlers, or as articulate as Peace Now professors who speak with an American accent. But they are the foundation of Israel, the gravity that holds the country in place. And, more important, years of reporting from Israel have taught me that there is a little bit of Sasson's almost primitive earthiness in every Israeli—not only all those in the Likud Party on the right side of the political spectrum, but a majority of those in the Labor Party as well; not only those Israelis born in Arab countries, but those born in Israel as well.

Indeed, the Israeli public is not divided fifty-fifty on the question of peace with the Palestinians. The truth is, the Israeli public is divided in three. One segment, on the far left—maybe 5 percent of the population—is ready to allow a Palestinian state in the West Bank and Gaza tomorrow, and sincerely believes the Palestinians are ready to live in peace with the Jews. Another segment, on the far right—maybe 20 percent of the population— will never be prepared, for ideological reasons, to allow a Palestinian state in the West Bank and Gaza. They are committed to holding forever all the Land of Israel, out of either nationalist or messianic sentiments. In between these two extremes you have the Sassons, who make up probably 75 percent of the population. The more liberal Sassons side with the Labor Party, the more hard-line Sassons side with the Likud, but they all share a gut feeling that they are locked in an all-or-nothing communal struggle with the Palestinians.

Today the Sassons of Israel, and many of their American Jewish friends, are confused. The Palestinian *intifada* has made it clear that the price in physical and moral terms of maintaining the status quo is going to get higher every year, yet none of the alternatives seem very appealing. Arafat's hints about finally accepting a two-state solution based on the 1967 boundaries, with a Palestinian state in all of the West Bank, the Gaza Strip, and East Jerusalem, do not really attract them—because they have no confidence in what Arafat says and no desire to return to the pre-1967 lines. The Labor Party's talk about withdrawing from densely populated portions of the Gaza Strip and West

Bank may be appealing, but Labor has no Arab or Palestinian partner for this concept. Labor Party leaders would still like to negotiate with Jordan over the future of the West Bank, but King Hussein has declared that he will have no more to do with the future of the West Bank. The Likud and other right-wing parties talk about holding on to the West Bank and Gaza Strip forever and offering the Palestinians living there autonomy according to the Camp David accords, but there are no Palestinians who will accept such an arrangement. So the situation remains deadlocked.

I think this deadlock can be broken with the right kind of Israeli leader and the right kind of plan. The kind of leader it will take will be what Leon Wieseltier has described in another context as a "bastard for peace"; only a son-of-a-bitch for a solution will be able to gain Sasson's confidence, and show him at the same time that Israel has an alternative to remaining in the West Bank and Gaza forever. Sasson is the key. You can talk about what is just and you can talk about what should be, you can talk about UN resolutions and Palestinian rights and you can talk about fancy peace plans and declarations by Yasir Arafat, but unless you talk about what will move Sasson, you'll be talking to yourself. The problem with the Israeli peace movement is that for so many years now they have been talking to themselves. Instead of validating Sasson's fears and emotions, they dismiss them as "fascist." But Sasson is no fascist and his fears are for real. The only way to begin building a stable majority for peace is by letting Sasson know that you and he share the same gut emotions. Once you have established that, he will listen—and he may even move.

I have two suggestions as to what might move the Sassons of Israel—one I call a tribal solution to a communal war, and the other a diplomatic solution to a communal war. Both approaches, I must emphasize, are based on unilateral Israeli initiatives. This is because I believe that Israel not only holds all the cards but has the power, and the incentive, to shape its own future without waiting for international conferences or outside mediators or even for a Palestinian partner. An Israeli leader, an Israeli "bastard for peace," interested in using my first approach—the tribal solution—might present it to the Israeli public with the following speech from the podium of the Knesset:

"My friends, we live in a wilderness of tigers. We are in a struggle for our survival. The Palestinians and the Arabs have never wanted us here and will never want us here. Any chance they get to drive us off the land, any weakness we expose, they will exploit. That is who they are. But the real question is, Who do we want to be? We live in a unique moment in Jewish history—the moment when the third Jewish commonwealth has been created, and when the Jewish people in Israel have an enormous power to determine their own future. Do we want to be the kind of people, or see the kind of Israel, that is sure to develop from us having to hold under occupation 1.7 million Palestinians in the West Bank and Gaza Strip for the rest of our lives, our sons' lives, and our sons' sons' lives? According to our own Central Bureau of Statistics, as of 1985 there were more Arab children under the age of four in Israel, the West Bank, and Gaza Strip than there were Jewish children. By the early twenty-first century, if present demographic trends continue, Arabs in Israel, the West Bank, and Gaza put together will outnumber Jews in the same area. In other words, a continuation of the status quo promises an Israel that is not going to be Jewish, democratic, or secure. Is that what you want? If your answer is no—that is not the kind of Israeli you want to be or the kind of Israel you want to see—then we have the same starting point. We both agree that in their heart of hearts the Arabs want to erase the Jewish state, and yet we both agree that, if it were possible, we would prefer not to spend the rest of our lives, and our children's lives, sitting on top of them in the West Bank and Gaza Strip. So what can we do about it?

"Frankly, when you have an Anwar Sadat to negotiate with on the other side, then you can think about peace treaties like that negotiated at Camp David. But the Palestinians have no Anwar Sadat—not in King Hussein and not in Yasir Arafat. If you don't have an Anwar Sadat, then I believe your only option is south Lebanon. What I mean by that is that we reached a situation in Lebanon in 1984 in which the status quo was untenable for us. Our army was sinking in the Lebanese mud and being transformed from a conventional fighting machine into a police force. Back home our nation was deeply and bitterly divided over Lebanon policy. Worse, there was no Lebanese government or militia whom we trusted to implement a peace arrangement to cover our withdrawal. The idea of leaving looked bad, staying looked even worse. After much debate we decided to choose bad over worse. We decided that peace simply was not an option for Israel in Lebanon, but that some degree of security could still be salvaged. So, what did we do? We re-arranged our security. In the language of the American Wild West, we circled our wagons in a different formation. We unilaterally withdrew from almost all of south Lebanon, save for a small zone that our army said was necessary to ensure a reasonable degree of security for our northern border. You will recall that when we prepared to do this many people said, 'How can you just withdraw like that? Are you crazy? The minute we go, the Palestinians and Iranian-backed Shiites will rain Katyusha rockets down on the Galilee, the sky will fall.' To which the army general staff responded, 'Better we should deal with these threats as a conventional army, where our real strength lies— that is, with artillery, the air force, and helicopters—than a policeman sitting in every Lebanese village trying to control every family.'

"When we withdrew from Lebanon, then Defense Minister Yitzhak Rabin warned the various Lebanese and Palestinian communities living in south Lebanon not to interpret this as a sign of Israeli weakness. He told the Lebanese point-blank that if they threatened Israel's security, the Israeli army would make sure that 'life for them will not be worth living.' So far, that deterrent has worked—not perfectly by any means, but as I said, peace was not an option for us in Lebanon. Our only option was more efficient security arrangements consistent with the values of the kind of society we want to build and the kind of people we want to be.

"I think we should adopt the same approach in the West Bank and Gaza—unilateral withdrawal, in phases, from those areas and settlements not essential to our security. Many Israeli generals believe that Israel can withdraw from significant portions of the West Bank and Gaza Strip without endangering itself, provided the army is allowed to retain whatever areas and security arrangements it deems necessary. These would include positions along the Jordan River and along the strategic mountain ridge running through the middle of the West Bank, as well as buffer zones around Tel Aviv and Jerusalem. Since 85 percent of the West Bank Jewish settlers reside in ten urban areas clustered around Tel Aviv and Jerusalem, most of them would be able to remain in their homes; others falling outside the security plan would have to be relocated. As in south Lebanon, we would act unilaterally. We would not ask anyone's consent— not the world's, not Jordan's, and not the Palestinians'—for the security arrangements we would leave behind. These security arrangements would be determined by us and maintained by us alone. Once we pulled out, the rules of the game would be, as they were in south Lebanon, Chicago Rules: You pull a knife, we'll pull a gun; you put one of ours in the hospital, we'll put 200 of yours in the morgue; you start in with Katyusha rockets, we'll come back with artillery; you start in with artillery, we'll come back with the air force; you create problems along the border, we will not allow any of you to work in Israel.

"My fellow citizens, will this approach bring peace? The answer is no. There will be incidents along the border, just as there are in south Lebanon—hopefully, as few as there are in south Lebanon. What I am offering you is a way to rearrange our security in a manner that will be more consistent with the Jewish and democratic society we are trying to preserve, and in a manner that will get our army out of police work—which is sapping its strength and morale every day—and back to being the conventional fighting machine it was trained to be. This will make us stronger as a nation, more unified as a nation—a nation that Jews around the world would not only remain proud of but want to live in. I believe we should undertake this unilaterally because to wait for the day when Yasir Arafat, George Habash, Hafez Assad, and King Hussein all agree on a formula for negotiating with Israel is to wait forever. And even if by some miracle they did agree among themselves, we wouldn't trust them anyway. So what are we waiting for?"

My Prime Minister would then conclude his remarks with an address to the Palestinians, saying, "My neighbor, my enemy, we would prefer to live in the Land of Israel, all of the Land of Israel, without you. That is who we are. The question before you is, Who do you want to be? Do you want to be stone throwers and victims all your life, or do you want to try to build a little dignity and a national home of your own? I am giving you that opportunity. You can establish whatever state you want in the areas we evacuate. You want a Maoist state, have a Maoist state. You want a Jeffersonian democracy, have a Jeffersonian democracy. You want an Islamic republic, have an Islamic republic. Whatever it is, it won't be as big as you would like or as militarily powerful as you would like. But that is the price you are going to have to pay for forty years of rejectionism. This is the best opportunity you are ever going to get within the current power realities. I urge you to exploit it. But understand one thing. Our withdrawal from these areas is not a sign of weakness. We are doing what we do out of a clear sense of our own strength, and out of a clear desire to preserve our own identity. We are ready to enter into normal relations with whatever state you build, and we are also ready to obliterate whatever state you build if you use it to threaten us in any way. If I have to send my army back, it is not going to be to sit on you again. I'm tired of that. It is going to be to throw you over the Jordan River. Have no doubt about it.''

That is a tribal solution for a tribal war. It is a solution that Sasson can intuitively understand, because it grows right out of his gut. It is a solution that assumes the worst about both sides— which is exactly what most Palestinians and Israelis assume about each other—and then attempts to draw from that assumption a workable formula that would break the status quo. As solutions go, it is not pretty. As my mother would say, "It's not nice." But you can't always build a settlement on what is nice. The "nice" Israelis, the "dovish" Israelis, the Israelis who like to do the right thing for the right reasons, they'll always be there for any settlement that calls for withdrawing from the West Bank and Gaza Strip. They're not the ones who need to be reached, because they are not the majority. Those who need to be reached are the Israelis who will only do the right thing for the "wrong" reasons, for the harsh reasons, for Sasson's reasons, because without them there will never be a stable majority for a territorial compromise.

Now someone might legitimately ask, Why must there be a tribal solution? Why can't there be a diplomatic solution? After all, before Sadat came to Jerusalem in November 1977 many Israelis looked at the Egyptians with the same visceral mistrust and gut fear as they do the Palestinians. That is true, which is why I have a second alternative for those who impute slightly better motives to the two sides.

Let us begin by examining the key features that made the Sadat initiative work—how it managed to galvanize a majority of Israelis behind a withdrawal from the Sinai—and then try to see what it would take to apply those same features to the Palestinian–Israeli conflict in a way that might be acceptable to the Sassons of Israel and produce what I call a diplomatic solution to a communal war.

I believe the Sadat initiative succeeded because it was able to overcome the three major obstacles to any Arab–Israeli peace. The first obstacle it overcame was the traditional obsession of both Arabs and Israelis with their "legitimate rights," as opposed to their legitimate interests. As long as any party to the Arab–Israeli conflict is focused entirely on obtaining his historical or God-given "rights," as he sees them, he is not going to be able to make decisions exclusively on the basis of interests. This always creates problems because rights are derived from the past, from gods or ancestors, and are therefore immutable and do not allow for compromise, while interests derive from today, from the ephemeral and from immediate needs and limitations. Therefore they invite compromise.

The genius of the Sadat initiative was its ability to transform the debate within Israel about relations with Egypt from a debate about rights to a debate about interests. How? Sadat, by recognizing Israel's right to exist, by going to Jerusalem and guaranteeing Israelis psychological space for their own dignity and independence, removed the question of sacred rights from the table and allowed Israelis to debate the question of peace with Egypt almost exclusively on the basis of their interests. The security and economic advantages of holding the Sinai buffer and its oil wells could be rationally weighed against the benefits of peace with the largest Arab nation. To put it another way, by assuring the Israelis a seat on the subway, Sadat got them to stop worrying about whether or not their reservation would be honored and to concentrate instead on how much of a seat they really needed in order to be comfortable. What the Israelis discovered under these new conditions was that they would actually feel more comfortable and secure vis-à-vis Egypt with a smaller seat.

It is true that the Israeli state had never claimed a "right" to the Sinai as part of its historic claim to Palestine. Nevertheless, the Israelis' occupation of the Sinai had become an extension of their claim to the right of statehood in Palestine. Israeli took the Sinai from Egypt in 1967 when Egypt challenged Israel's right to exist. Had Sadat not been willing to recognize the right of Israelis to statehood within their pre-1967 borders, Israelis would have continued to hold on to the Sinai at virtually any price.

The second traditional obstacle the Sadat initiative overcame was the deep-rooted Israeli obsession with stated Arab intentions, as opposed to actual Arab capabilities. The Israelis, like all Jews, are a text-oriented people and they read the Arabic press and speeches with great scrutiny. Because an Arab country like Egypt is made up of many political streams—from Islamic fundamentalist to Arab nationalist to liberal democratic—there was, and always will be, some politician making a speech or some poet writing a verse calling for the elimination of the Jewish state. These words always provided ammunition for the Sassons of Israel, who would stand up, wave the offending article, and exclaim, "How can you make peace with such people? Look what they are saying about us!" This behavior is not surprising. Many Israeli Jews are still haunted by the fact that Hitler clearly laid out all of his plans for the Jews in *Mein Kampf* and other publications long before he came to power, but no one paid attention.

In order to overcome the Israeli obsession with Arab intentions, Sadat agreed to demilitarize the Sinai Desert. He consented not only to limit the number of Egyptian troops that could be stationed there and the weapons they could carry, but also to accept the presence of an American-dominated multinational peacekeeping force to monitor the demilitarization. Only after the Israelis were able to limit the capabilities of Egypt's soldiers were they ready to ignore the intentions of her poets.

The third obstacle the Sadat initiative overcame was the deep mistrust Israelis had in any kind of land-for-peace agreement with a country that had been seeking their destruction for forty years. Even Sadat's kissing of former Israeli Prime Minister Golda Meir on the cheek could not undo the trauma many Israelis felt toward their neighbor to the west, with whom they had fought four wars. Too many things had been said for too many years. Too many people had died. Words alone were not sufficient to undo that. There had to be a new living reality. Only behavioral therapy, not Freudian analysis, could produce an accumulation of experiences that might heal each side's suspicion. Therefore the Camp David agreement was implemented gradually, in phases, over a three-year period. Each phase of Israel's withdrawal from the Sinai was conditioned on Egypt's fulfillment of certain obligations for demilitarization and normalization of relations. Both sides not only got to hear the other's words, but got to feel them, before the agreement was culminated.

All three of these obstacles exist between Israelis and Palestinians. The only difference is that they are ten times as high. Take, for instance, the question of rights. Egypt and Israel were two distinctly different countries, with different boundaries and different capitals. There was a natural dividing line between them, which made mutual recognition of each other's rights to statehood relatively easy. That is not the case between Palestinians and Israelis. There is no natural dotted line separating them. The Israelis claim Jerusalem as their capital and the Palestinians claim Jerusalem as their capital; the Israelis claim Haifa and the Palestinians claim Haifa. Many Israelis claim the West Bank not, like Sinai, as an extension of their right to statehood in Palestine, but as an integral part of that right. Many Palestinians claim Jaffa not as an extension of their right to a state in the West Bank, but as an essential part of it.

Because of these overlapping historical claims, it is much more difficult for Israelis and Palestinians to recognize each other's basic rights in Palestine without feeling that they are undermining their own historical positions. Imagine how difficult it would have been to solve the problems of Europe if there had been no Berlin and no Paris, but just Germans and Frenchmen each claiming Paris as their rightful capital.

What about intentions and capabilities? Here, too, the problems between Palestinians and Israelis are enormous. Egypt was an authoritarian state, which could exert some control over its

press and public officials. But the PLO is an umbrella organization encompassing eight different Palestinian factions spread out
all over the Middle East. Some of those factions take their
orders not from Yasir Arafat, but from Arab governments. There
are also Palestinian organizations, such as the Muslim fundamentalists in Gaza, who are very strong on the ground and
answer to no one but themselves. The result is that the Israelis
can always find some egregious Palestinian statement or poem
calling for their destruction, which is then used to discredit any
Israeli or Palestinian moderate who dares to claim that the
Palestinians are ready to live in peace with a Jewish state.

As for mistrust, what the Egyptians and Israelis had to overcome seems like a minor tiff compared with the tribal-like feud
between Jews and Palestinians. The Palestinian–Jewish conflict
doesn't date back just to 1948, but goes back a hundred years.
Moreover, it is not a conflict between strangers separated by 200
miles of desert, but rather a conflict between neighbors, between
cousins, who have looked each other in the eye before shooting
each other in the gut. This Cain-versus-Abel–style conflict has
bred so much mistrust and so much hatred that there is nothing
Yasir Arafat could say to Israelis that would have the same
instantly reassuring impact as did Sadat's recognition. Moreover, the Palestinians, unlike the Egyptians, don't have a state.
The PLO is a movement with a leadership that lives on airplanes
and with institutions scattered in a dozen Arab countries; it has
no fixed address. Israel could make peace with a state like
Egypt—with its capital, flag, and army—because a state can
make promises and be held accountable, but a movement spread
out all over the Middle East cannot. Therefore the Palestinians,
in their current dispersed state, cannot, by definition, recognize
the Israelis in a way that would be truly meaningful and reassuring to them. If the PLO, formally and unequivocally, recognized
Israel tomorrow, many Israelis would say, So what?

I have always felt that a good deal of the Israeli interest in
making a deal for the West Bank with Jordan, rather than with
the PLO, was generated not solely because negotiating with
Jordan was a way to avoid recognizing the Palestinians but,
equally important, because Jordan was a concrete state, a fixed
address, which could be held accountable and which had a long,
credible record of keeping its border with Israel quiet.

* * *

Despite the lofty heights of all these obstacles, I don't believe they are insurmountable. You just need the right pole to vault over them. I think there can be a diplomatic solution to a tribal war that might just satisfy the Sasson in every Israeli, and I also believe it can be initiated through a unilateral Israeli gesture. A Prime Minister of Israel could present it with the following speech:

"My friends, if there is one lesson that we can learn from the past hundred years of conflict with the Palestinians, it is this: As long as your neighbor is your enemy, your house will never be a home. It will be a fortress, and in a fortress you can never really take your shoes off and relax. What this means is that we will never really be able to feel at home here in Palestine, we will never really be able to end our exile, unless the Palestinians, our neighbors, feel at home as well. I wish this were not the case. But the truth is we cannot save ourselves unless we save them too. And they cannot save themselves unless they save us too. But can we save them without committing suicide, which my friend Sasson here is not going to do? And can they save us without totally surrendering, which they are not going to do?

"In order to make a settlement with the Palestinians both possible and meaningful, I believe we Israelis, for our own self-interest, must begin by doing for the Palestinians what Anwar Sadat did for us: give them at least part of a seat on the subway, or at least recognize the validity of their reservation. Specifically, we should declare our readiness to accept the establishment of a Palestinian state in parts of the West Bank and Gaza Strip. Just as it was Sadat, the one who had the seat on the subway, who had the strength and self-confidence to move over a bit for his own good and make room for the ones who had no seat, so we Israelis, who have a seat, should use our strength and security in order to move over and make some psychological and physical space for the Palestinians so they can stop focusing exclusively on their rights and start thinking more about their interests. The Palestinians will have a real incentive to curtail their demands and control their most extreme elements only when they have some real interests to lose. Today the price for Palestinians of attacking Israel is bad headlines and a few casualties. If they had their own state, the price of attacking

Israel could be the loss of everything they had managed to build.

"But we are not in the charity business. We would make our offer to the Palestinians only if their representatives—whoever they might be—accepted the following three conditions.

"First, the Palestinian representatives would have to agree to explicitly recognize our right to exist as a Jewish state in the Middle East.

"Second, the Palestinian representatives would have to agree that their state would be permanently demilitarized, and that Israel would be allowed to maintain all the early-warning and security systems which its army deemed necessary to ensure that this Palestinian state could never—ever—threaten Israel's existence, even if it wanted to. Israel and Israel alone would monitor the demilitarization of the Palestinian state through such measures as advanced observation posts and checkpoints at the Jordan bridges and all other potential entry points to ensure that no heavy weapons whatsoever could be brought in. There would be no UN troops and no multinational forces. We will not entrust our vital security to third parties. Only by totally controlling Palestinian capabilities will it be possible to get a majority of our people to overlook Palestinian intentions, poetry, and PLO charters. Neither we nor the Palestinians can be expected to dispense with our dreams about Palestine; they are fundamental aspects of our identities. But we cannot allow each other's fantasies to prevent a settlement in reality.

"Third, the Palestinians must agree that implementation of this plan would occur in stages over a period of five years. It would begin with free Palestinian elections in the West Bank and Gaza Strip (in which outside Palestinians could vote by absentee ballot) to form a government. Only when the Palestinian movement is transformed into a concrete state-like autonomous government based in the West Bank will it have the attributes, incentives, and credibility to recognize the Israelis in a way that will be as meaningful and reassuring as the recognition from Egypt. That Palestinian government will be granted autonomy over all those areas that will eventually be relinquished to it by Israel at the culmination of the transition period. Only such a lengthy transition period, which puts the declarations of each side to the test, can produce the kind of healing and trust that will make an agreement workable and lasting.

"Now you will ask, What if the Palestinians, when presented with such a state by us, don't behave according to their rational interests, but instead on the basis of their rights, as they see them? What if they use such a state not to heal their dreams about recovering all of Palestine, but instead to feed them? The answer is that their state will only come to them in stages of autonomy, after they have proven their willingness at each stage to be responsible neighbors. If at any time in that process they physically endanger us in any way, the entire process will be scrapped. But we will be as much a loser from that as the Palestinians.

"Let me add a few remarks to our Palestinian neighbors. My neighbor, my enemy, I know many of you will look at this plan and consider it insufficient. You are only going to get a ministate in part of the West Bank and Gaza Strip—less even than what you were promised in the 1947 UN partition plan. And even that is not going to be a fully sovereign state, because you will be in effect surrounded by Israeli troops, subject to Israeli security measures, and only be allowed to maintain a police force with light weapons. But to these complaints I can only say two things. First, what you could have had in 1947, you cannot have now; and what you can get today, you won't be able to get tomorrow. I urge you to stop focusing only on what you think is right and just and to think instead only about what is possible. This is the most that is possible today. As for not being able to have an army of your own, you have to make a choice. Do you want a state or do you want an army? If it's an army you want, then you already have one in the PLO. If it is a state you want, then it is a state I am offering—but these are the terms.

"As for my Israeli critics, I can only say that while this plan may seem to you to be a noble offer—too noble, too moralizing, too naïve—I consider it quite Machiavellian. I am trying to turn my enemy who never allows me to feel at home in my own house into a neighbor with whom I can live comfortably side by side. I have a healthy respect for the ability of all parties to this conflict, both the Palestinians and ourselves, to behave in totally irrational ways. I am in no way suggesting that this approach is risk-free. It is not. But the status quo is not risk-free either. Real Israeli security can never come from the club, but only from having a neighbor who is a dignified, responsible, and self-determining human being. Maybe the Palestinians are not willing to be such a neighbor and maybe the Arabs are not willing to allow the Palestinians to be such a neighbor. But better for us to take the very limited risk of putting the Palestinians to the test and possibly create a new relationship than to continue with an equally risky status quo that promises only an endless war between neighbors and a future filled with yesterdays."

Acknowledgments

This book is the product of a journey, the journey the product of a lifetime. Along the way, I racked up many IOU's to friends, family, and colleagues, which I can only begin to acknowledge here.

There are several men who were responsible for launching my career as a journalist: Gilbert Cranberg, the editorial page editor of the *Des Moines Register*, and Harold Chucker, the editorial page editor of the *Minneapolis Star*, who gave me my first break by publishing my op-ed articles about Middle East politics when I was in college. Leon Daniel, a fine and dedicated newsman, gave me my start by hiring me as a cub reporter for UPI in London; I will forever be indebted to him for that opportunity. A. M. Rosenthal hired me from UPI for *The New York Times*. Without him this book simply would not have been. He broke every mold at *The New York Times* by sending me first to Beirut as bureau chief and then to Jerusalem. I am equally indebted to the *Times* publisher Arthur Ochs Sulzberger, Executive Editor

Max Frankel, and Foreign Editor Joseph Lelyveld for granting me a one-year sabbatical to write this book. They each understood my obsession with this project and accommodated me in every way to make it possible.

While I was stationed in Beirut, there were two people without whom I simply could not have survived—my assistant Mohammed Kasrawi and the *Times* local reporter, Ihsan Hijazi. Mohammed, who figures prominently in the first chapter of this book, was the most loyal and loving comrade-in-arms a foreign correspondent could ever hope for. We met in Beirut, coming from two ends of the world—I a Jew from Minnesota, he a Palestinian refugee from Jerusalem. During our years together, though, we became family. Some of our bonding moments were times of great tragedy, but there were many happy memories as well. Though we each have since retreated to the different worlds from whence we came, the bond between us will never be broken. This is no less true for myself and Ihsan, who, in my opinion, is the finest Arab journalist working today. His wisdom informed my reporting; his friendship sustained me during some of Beirut's darkest hours.

Four friends in particular played major roles in helping me conceptualize this book and to better understand the events I witnessed in Beirut and Jerusalem. They are Fouad Ajami, Meron Benvenisti, Yaron Ezrahi, and David Hartman. Fouad, who teaches at the School for Advanced International Studies, Johns Hopkins University, is in a class by himself when it comes to thinking originally about the Middle East. His help was indispensable in enabling me to fully comprehend Beirut and its constituent communities. His intellectual courage was also an inspiration. It was through endless conversations with Meron, a genius much misunderstood by his own people, that I came to truly understand the dynamics of the Jewish–Palestinian conflict. Yaron, with his incisive grasp of political theory, always helped me to appreciate the universal in some of my particulars. His insights into why Israel is in the news and how America relates to the Middle East opened up new avenues of inquiry for me. Sidra, his wife, taught me much about the impact of the Holocaust on Israelis. One of the things I miss most about Jerusalem are the raucous debates we held around their dinner table. No one is quoted in this book more than David Hartman, for the simple reason that no one taught me more about Israel and the Jewish people than he did. His ideas contributed enormously to my reporting from Israel, and they infuse almost every chapter of this book as well. My debt to him as a teacher and a friend is incalculable.

The manuscript was read in advance by Fouad, Yaron, and David, as well as by a wise historian, Professor J. C. Hurewitz of Columbia University. A part was read with perspicacity by the Israeli expert on the Bedouin, Clinton Bailey. My friends Michael Sandel and his wife, Kiku Adatto, both of Harvard University, also sat patiently through a reading of an early draft, which they helped me to sharpen.

Those who have read my articles in the *Times* during my tenures in Beirut and Jerusalem will note that in a few chapters I have occasionally drawn on previously reported material and quotations, although I have tried to keep this to a minimum. Wherever I have quoted people by only a first name, it was done at their request for reasons of personal safety.

I am also indebted to two institutions for their support in my research and writing. The John Simon Guggenheim Memorial Foundation provided me with a generous grant. The Woodrow Wilson International Center for Scholars extended me funding, office space, and a researcher. In particular, I would like to thank Sam Wells and Robert Litwak from the Wilson Center for making my stay there both possible and congenial. It goes without saying that the statements and views expressed in this book are mine alone and are not necessarily those of the Wilson Center or the Guggenheim Foundation.

Laura Blumenfeld served as my researcher and translator in Israel; she brought real insight and enthusiasm to everything she prepared for me. John Wilner did the same in his capacity as my assistant at the Wilson Center. Julie Somech and Debra Retyk, my assistants at the *Times* bureau in Jerusalem, were always there to help.

My Aunt Bev and Uncle Hy and friends Morrie and Jake came through for me after my father died in ways that will never be forgotten. My in-laws, Matthew and Carolyn Bucksbaum, allowed me to make a mess of their Aspen house during the six weeks I worked in their basement, which is only typical of the way they have supported me at every turn in my career.

My editor, Jonathan Galassi, and the whole team at Farrar,

Straus and Giroux treated this project with tender loving care from beginning to end. They were an author's dream. My agent, Esther Newberg, handled all my business affairs with her usual blend of professionalism and class.

This book is dedicated to my father, Harold Friedman, of blessed memory, and my mother, Margaret. It would never have been written, though, without the encouragement and loving support of my wife, Ann, who accompanied me from the beginning of this journey to its end. Lord knows, what she put up with could also fill a book. Without her friendship and strength (and editing) I never would have made it. My daughters, Orly and Natalie, had to get by with an absent father for too long as this book was in progress. I only hope when they grow old enough to read it, they will appreciate why.

Thomas L. Friedman
Washington, D.C.
March 1989

Index

534

Index